Reading Women's Lives

WS: 200: Introduction to Women's Studies

Department of Gender and Race Studies
University of Alabama

Compiled by The Department of Gender and Race Studies and Brittney Cooper, Ph.D.

Learning Solutions

New York Boston San Francisco
London Toronto Sydney Tokyo Singapore Madrid
Mexico City Munich Paris Cape Town Hong Kong Montreal

Senior Vice President, Editorial and Marketing: Patrick F. Boles
Senior Sponsoring Editor: Natalie Danner
Development Editor: Mary Kate Paris
Assistant Editor: Jill Johnson
Operations Manager: Eric M. Kenney
Production Manager: Jennifer Berry
Rights Manager: Jillian Santos
Art Director and Cover Designer: Renée Sartell

Special thanks to the contributors: The Faculty of the Department of Women's Studies at the Ohio State University.

Cover Art: Art Collage, Copyright © Joanne Stichweh, *Four Faces* courtesy of Kaadaa/Veer Incorporated.

Printed in the United States of America.

Please visit our website at *www.pearsoncustom.com.*

Attention bookstores: For permission to return any unsold stock, contact us at *pe-uscustomreturns@pearson.com.*

Pearson Learning Solutions, 501 Boylston Street, Suite 900, Boston, MA 02116
A Pearson Education Company
www.pearsoned.com

ISBN 10: 0-558-90452-1
ISBN 13: 978-0-558-90452-4

Contents

Introduction

Bodies, Politics, and Power

Uses of the Erotic: The Erotic as Power (1978)
Audre Lorde 3

Abortion, Vacuum Cleaners, and the Power Within
Inga Muscio 11

And So I Choose
Allison Crews 19

The Body Politic (1995)
Abra Fortune Chernik 27

Beyond Pro-Choice versus Pro-Life: Women of Color and Reproductive Justice
Andrea Smith 37

Outcast Mothers and Surrogates: Racism and Reproductive Politics in the Nineties (1993)
Angela Davis 59

Living Incubators, Fetal Container or Womb with Legs
Melanie J. DeMaeyer 75

It's a Big Fat Revolution
Nomy Lamm . . . 93

"Arroz con Pollo" vs. Slim Fast (1992)
Linda Delgado . . . 103

Maid to Order: The Politics of Other Women's Work
Barbara Ehrenreich . . . 107

The Globetrotting Sneaker (1995)
Cynthia Enloe . . . 117

The Politics of Housework (1970)
Pat Mainardi . . . 129

Women in Culture

Teen Mags: How to Get a Guy, Drop 10 Pounds, and Lose Your Self Esteem
Anastasia Higginbotham . . . 137

Excerpt from "The Beauty Myth" (1991)
Naomi Wolf . . . 145

Black Beauty Myth
Sirena Riley . . . 159

A Way Outa No Way: Eating Problems Among African American, Latina and White Women (1996)
Becky W. Thompson . . . 169

I See the Same Ho: Video Vixens, Beauty Culture, and Diasporic Sex Tourism
T. Denean Sharpley-Whiting . . . 191

Ladies is Pimps, Too
Jami Harris . . . 211

Your Life as a Girl (1995)
Curtis Sittenfeld . . . 227

Straightening Our Hair (1989)
bell hooks . . . 237

Dyes and Dolls: Multicultural Barbie and the Merchandising of Difference (1994)
Ann duCille . . . 247

The Managed Hand: The Commercialization of Bodies and Emotions in Korean Immigrant Owned Nail Salons
Miliann Kang 273

Feminism Amplified (1996)
Kim France 299

Herstory of Women's Liberation and Feminism

Declaration of Sentiments and Resolutions (1848)
The Seneca Falls Women's Rights Convention of 1848 313

Ain't I a Woman? (1851)
Sojourner Truth 319

National Organization for Women Statement of Purpose (1966) and Bill of Rights (1968)
National Organization for Women 321

A Day without Feminism & Third Wave Manifesta: A Thirteen-Point Agenda (2000)
Jennifer Baumgardner and Amy Richards 331

Becoming the Third Wave (1992)
Rebecca Walker 341

A Black Feminist Statement (1974)
Combahee River Collective 345

"Womanist" (1983)
Alice Walker 357

In Pursuit of Latina Liberation (1995)
Elizabeth Martinez 359

La Concienca de la Meztiza: Towards a New Consciousness
Gloria Anzaldua 373

Theorizing Difference from Multiracial Feminism (1996)
Maxine Baca Zinn and Bonnie Thornton Dill 389

Theories of Socialization & Hierarchies of Identity

White Privilege: Unpacking the Invisible Backpack (1989)
Peggy McIntosh 403

"Night to His Day": The Social Construction of Gender (1994)
Judith Lorber 411

Owning My Advantage, Uncovering My Collusion (1997)
Judith H. Katz 427

The Other Body: Reflections on Difference, Disability, and Identity Politics (1993)
Ynestra King 431

The Social Construction of Disability
Susan Wendell 439

A Question of Class (1994)
Dorothy Allison 455

Confessions of a Recovering Misogynist (2000)
Kevin Powell 477

Gender and Sexualities

We Are All Works in Progress
Leslie Feinberg 487

Oppression (1983)
Marilyn Frye 497

It's Your Gender, Stupid!
Riki Anne Wilchins 513

Homophobia: A Weapon of Sexism (1988)
Suzanne Pharr 525

ReScripting the Closet
Jami Harris 547

Excerpt from White Weddings (1999)
Chrys Ingraham 567

I'm Not Fat, I'm Latina
Christy Haubegger 579

Learning from Drag Queens
Verta Taylor and Leila Rupp 583

Transgender Feminism
Susan Stryker 593

X: A Fabulous Child's Story
Lois Gould 605

Department of Gender and Race Studies

University of Alabama

Mission Statement:

The Department of Gender and Race Studies is committed to examining and producing knowledge that promotes social justice approaches to gender and race inequities by recognizing the intersections of categories of difference and the operations of social hierarchies, and by providing a forum for interdisciplinary research, teaching, and service that facilitates the critical investigation of the status and roles of women, African Americans and other people of color locally, nationally and globally.

Degrees and Programs of Study

The Department of Gender and Race Studies offers an undergraduate major and minor in African American Studies, an undergraduate minor in Women's Studies, and an Master's of Arts and graduate certificate in Women's Studies.

Core Faculty

Derrick Bryan, Ph.D., Assistant Professor
Brittney C. Cooper, Ph.D., Assistant Professor
DoVeanna Fulton Minor, Ph.D., Associate Professor and Chair
Maha Marouan, Ph.D., Assistant Professor
Jennifer Purvis, Ph.D., Associate Professor
Jennifer Shoaff, Ph.D., Assistant Professor

Bodies, Politics, and Power

Uses of the Erotic: The Erotic as Power (1978)

Audre Lorde

This classic 1978 essay by African-American poet, writer and activist Audre Lorde redefines the concept of "the erotic" as not only a sexual force but also a creative and spiritual source of power in women's lives. Lorde combats what she sees to be limiting and male-centered understandings of the erotic and celebrates it as an "assertion of the life power of women" that gives meaning to our lives, our work and our connections with others. Lorde's work is a call for women to explore their sense of personal power for satisfaction and for social justice. Lorde is the author of numerous essays, poems and autobiographical works including Undersong: Chosen Poems, Old and New, Sister Outsider *and* Zami: A New Spelling of My Name. *She died from breast cancer in 1992.*

There are many kinds of power, used and unused, acknowledged or otherwise. The erotic is a resource within each of us that lies in a deeply female and spiritual plane, firmly rooted in the power of our unexpressed or unrecognized feeling. In order to perpetuate itself, every oppression must corrupt or distort those various sources of power within the culture of the oppressed that can provide energy for change. For women, this has meant a suppression of the erotic as a considered source of power and information within our lives.

We have been taught to suspect this resource, vilified, abused, and devalued within western society. On one hand the superficially erotic has been encouraged as a sign of female inferiority—on the other hand women have been made to suffer and to feel both contemptible and suspect by virtue of its existence.

It is a short step from there to the false belief that only by the suppression of the erotic within our lives and consciousness can women be truly strong. But that strength is illusory, for it is fashioned within the context of male models of power.

As women, we have come to distrust that power which rises from our deepest and non-rational knowledge. We have been warned against it all our lives by the male world, which values this depth of feeling enough to keep women around in order to exercise it in the service of men, but which fears this same depth too much to examine the possibilities of it within themselves. So women are maintained at a distant/inferior position to be psychically milked, much the same way ants maintain colonies of aphids to provide a life-giving substance for their masters.

But the erotic offers a well of replenishing and provocative force to the woman who does not fear its revelation, nor succumb to the belief that sensation is enough.

The erotic has often been misnamed by men and used against women. It has been made into the confused, the trivial, the psychotic, the plasticized sensation. For this reason, we have often turned away from the exploration and consideration of the erotic as a source of power and information, confusing it with its opposite, the pornographic. But pornography is a direct denial of the power of the erotic, for it represents the suppression of true feeling. Pornography emphasizes sensation without feeling.

The erotic is a measure between the beginnings of our sense of self, and the chaos of our strongest feelings. It is an internal sense

---

"Uses of the Erotic: The Erotic as Power," by Audre Lorde. A paper originally delivered at the Fourth Berkshire Conference on the History of Women, Mt. Holyoke College, August 25, 1978. An *Out and Out Pamphlet*, distributed by the Crossing Press.

of satisfaction to which, once we have experienced it, we know we can aspire. For once having experienced the fullness of this depth of feeling and recognizing its power, in honor and self-respect we can require no less of ourselves.

It is never easy to demand the most from our selves, and from our lives, and from our work. To go beyond the encouraged mediocrity of our society is to encourage excellence. But giving in to the fear of feeling and working to capacity is a luxury only the unintentional can afford, and the unintentional are those who do not wish to guide their own destinies.

This internal requirement toward excellence which we learn from the erotic must not be misconstrued as demanding the impossible from ourselves nor from others. Such a demand incapacitates everyone in the process, for the erotic is not a question only of what we do. It is a question of how acutely and fully we can feel in the doing. For once we know the extent to which we are capable of feeling that sense of satisfaction and fullness and completion, we can then observe which of our various life endeavors bring us closest to that fullness.

The aim of each thing which we do is to make our lives and the lives of our children more possible and more rich. Within the celebration of the erotic in all our endeavors, my work becomes a conscious decision—a longed-for bed which I enter gratefully and from which I rise up empowered.

Of course, women so empowered are dangerous. So we are taught to separate the erotic demand from most vital areas of our lives other than sex. And the lack of concern for the erotic root and satisfactions of our work is felt in our disaffection from so much of what we do. For instance, how often do we truly love our work?

The principal horror of any system which defines the good in terms of profit rather than in terms of human need, or which defines human need to the exclusion of the psychic and emotional components of that need—the principal horror of such a system is that it robs our work of its erotic value, its erotic power and life appeal and fulfillment. Such a system reduces work to a travesty of necessities, a duty by which we earn bread or oblivion for ourselves and those we love. But this is tantamount to blinding a painter and then telling her to improve her work, and to enjoy the act of painting. It is not only next to impossible, it is also profoundly cruel.

As women, we need to examine the ways in which our world can be truly different. I am speaking here of the necessity for reassessing the very quality of all the aspects of our lives and of our work.

The very word 'erotic' comes from the Greek word *eros,* the personification of love in all its aspects—born of Chaos, and personifying creative power and harmony. When I speak of the erotic, then, I speak of it as an assertion of the life-force of women, of that creative energy empowered, the knowledge and use of which we are now reclaiming in our language, our history, our dancing, our loving, our work, our lives.

There are frequent attempts to equate pornography and eroticism, two diametrically opposed uses of the sexual. Because of these attempts, it has become fashionable to separate the spiritual (psychic and emotional) away from the political, to see them as contradictory or antithetical. "What do you mean, a poetic revolutionary, a meditating gun-runner?" In the same way, we have attempted to separate the spiritual and the erotic, reducing the spiritual thereby to a world of flattened affect—a world of ascetic who aspires to feel nothing. But nothing is farther from the truth. For the ascetic position is one of the highest fear, the gravest immobility. The severe abstinence of the ascetic becomes the ruling obsession. And it is one, not of self-discipline, but of self-abnegation.

The dichotomy between the spiritual and the political is also false, resulting from an incomplete attention to our erotic knowledge. For the bridge which connects them is formed by the erotic—the sensual—those physical, emotional, and psychic expressions of what is deepest and strongest and richest within each of us, being shared: the passions of love, in its deepest meanings.

The considered phrase, "It feels right to me," acknowledges the strength of the erotic into a true knowledge, for what that means and feels is the first and most powerful guiding light towards any understanding. And understanding is a handmaiden which can only wait upon, or clarify, that knowledge, deeply born. The erotic is the nurturer or nursemaid of all our deepest knowledge.

The erotic functions for me in several ways, and the first is in the power which comes from sharing deeply any pursuit with another person. The sharing of joy, whether physical, emotional, psychic or intellectual, forms a bridge between the sharers which can be the basis for understanding much of what is not shared between them, and lessens the threat of their difference.

Another important way in which the erotic connection functions is the open and fearless underlining of my capacity for joy. In the way my body stretches to music and opens into response, hearkening to its deepest rhythms, so every level upon which I sense also opens to the erotically satisfying experience, whether it is dancing, building a bookcase, writing a poem, examining an idea.

That self-connection shared is a measure of the joy which I know myself to be capable of feeling, a reminder of my capacity for feeling. And that deep and irreplaceable knowledge of my capacity for joy comes to demand from all of my life that it be lived within the knowledge that such satisfaction is possible, and does not have to be called marriage, nor god, nor an afterlife.

This is one reason why the erotic is so feared, and so often relegated to the bedroom alone, when it is recognized at all. For once we begin to feel deeply all the aspects of our lives, we begin to demand from ourselves and from our lives' pursuits that they feel in accordance with that joy which we know ourselves to be capable of. Our erotic knowledge empowers us, becomes a lens through which we scrutinize all aspects of our existence, forcing ourselves to evaluate those aspects honestly in terms of their relative meaning within our lives. And this is a grave responsibility, projected from within each of us, not to settle for the convenient, the shoddy, the conventionally expected, nor the merely safe.

During World War II, we bought sealed plastic packets of white, uncolored margarine, with a tiny, intense pellet of yellow coloring perched like a topaz just inside the clear skin of the bag. We would leave the margarine out for a while to soften, and then we would pinch the little pellet to break it inside the bag, releasing the rich yellowness into the soft pale mass of margarine. Then taking it carefully between our fingers, we would knead it gently back and forth, over and over, until the color had spread throughout the whole pound bag of margarine, leaving it thoroughly colored.

I find the erotic such a kernel within myself. When released from its intense and constrained pellet, it flows through and colors my life with a kind of energy that heightens and sensitizes and strengthens all my experience.

We have been raised to fear the yes within ourselves, our deepest cravings. For the demands of our released expectations lead us inevitably into actions which will help bring our lives into accordance with our needs, our knowledge, our desires. And the fear of our deepest cravings keeps them suspect, keeps us docile and loyal and obedient, and leads us to settle for or accept many facets of our oppression as women.

When we live outside ourselves, and by that I mean on external directives only, rather than from our internal knowledge and needs, when we live away from those erotic guides from within our selves, then our lives are limited by external and alien forms, and we conform to the needs of a structure that is not based on human need, let alone an individual's. But when we begin to live from within outward, in touch with the power of the erotic within ourselves, and allowing that power to inform and illuminate our actions upon the world around us, then we begin to be responsible to ourselves in the deepest sense. For as we begin to recognize our deepest feelings, we begin to give up, of necessity, being satisfied with suffering, and self-negation, and with the numbness which so often seems like their only alternative in our society. Our acts against oppression become integral with self, motivated and empowered from within.

In touch with the erotic, I become less willing to accept powerlessness, or those other supplied states of being which are not native to me, such as resignation, despair, self-effacement, depression, self-denial.

And yes, there is a hierarchy. There is a difference between painting a back fence and writing a poem, but only one of quantity. And there is, for me, no difference between writing a good poem and moving into sunlight against the body of a woman I love.

This brings me to the last consideration of the erotic. To share the power of each other's feelings is different from using another's feelings as we would use a kleenex. And when we look the other way from our experience, erotic or otherwise, we use rather than share the feelings of those others who participate in the experience with us. And use without consent of the used is abuse.

In order to be utilized, our erotic feelings must be recognized. The need for sharing deep feeling is a human need. But within the european-american tradition, this need is satisfied by certain proscribed erotic comings together, and these occasions are almost always characterized by a simultaneous looking away, a pretense of calling them something else, whether a religion, a fit, mob violence, or even playing doctor. And this misnaming of the need and the deed give rise to that distortion which results in pornography and obscenity—the abuse of feeling.

When we look away from the importance of the erotic in the development and sustenance of our power, or when we look away from ourselves as we satisfy our erotic needs in concert with others, we use each other as objects of satisfaction rather than share our joy in the satisfying, rather than make connection with our similarities and our differences. To refuse to be conscious of what we are feeling at any time, however comfortable that might seem, is to deny a large part of the experience, and to allow ourselves to be reduced to the pornographic, the abused, and the absurd.

The erotic cannot be felt secondhand. As a Black Lesbian Feminist, I have a particular feeling, knowledge, and understanding for those sisters with whom I have danced hard, played, or even fought. This deep participation has often been the forerunner for joint concerted actions not possible before.

But this erotic charge is not easily shared by women who continue to operate under an exclusively european-american, male tradition. I know it was not available to me when I was trying to adapt my consciousness to this mode of living and sensation.

Only now, I find more and more woman-identified women brave enough to risk sharing the erotic's electrical charge without having to look away, and without distorting the enormously powerful and creative nature of that exchange. Recognizing the power of the erotic within our lives can give us the energy to pursue genuine change within our world, rather than merely settling for a shift of characters in the same weary drama.

For not only do we touch our most profoundly creative source, but we do that which is female and self-affirming in the face of a racist, patriarchal, and anti-erotic society.

Questions

1. What does Lorde mean by "the erotic"? How is the erotic usually understood? Why is this a limiting understanding? What is the difference to Lorde between the pornographic and the erotic?
2. How does the erotic function personally for Lorde? Why is it feared? Why does she believe that women usually distrust their deepest fears, desires and knowledge? Why are empowered women dangerous?
3. What does Lorde mean when she says we live in an "anti-erotic" society? Why is eroticism in Lorde's definition not usually available to women in a European male tradition? What does she mean when she says, "the principle horror of any system which defines the good in terms of profit rather than in terms of human need robs our work of erotic values"?

Abortion, Vacuum Cleaners and the Power Within

Inga Muscio

> *"The fight for human rights does not take place on some bureaucratic battleground. The real fight for human rights is inside each and every individual on this earth."*

One of my mottoes, a little saying I hope to see made into bumper stickers motoring down the nation's byways, is ABORTION SUCKS. That's right, I, a young lady, being of sound feminist mind and undeniably womanly body, am adamantly against clinical abortions.

"Abortion Sucks" is a literal statement, made in reference to the machine employed in ridding a woman of her unwanted pregnancy. This machine is a vacuum cleaner. In theory, if not design, it's quite like the Hoover upright, the Dustbuster or the Shop-Vac in your closet at home.

Vacuum cleaners are useful for cleaning up messes, and in our society, a pile of kitty litter on the floor is treated much the same as an undesired embryo. The main difference, though hardly recognizable to Western science, is that kitty litter is sucked from cold linoleum and an embryo is sucked from a warm-blooded living being's womb.

Women and linoleum floors, sure is hard to tell us apart, ain't it? Maybe I sound bitter, and maybe I feel that I have every right to, for

---

Reprinted from *Listen Up: Voices From the Next Feminist Generation*, Seal Press.

I've been on somewhat intimate terms with that appliance. That's right, 'cause good ol' childless me has been knocked up not once, not twice, but three times in my dear life. While this may be a testimony to my previous irresponsibility and ignorance regarding available methods of birth control, that is another fly in the ointment of women's health care and fertile ground for another essay altogether.

The first time I got pregnant, I was nineteen. I lived in California and was within weeks of moving away from home for the first time in my life, to Seattle. The idea of making such a major move with a tiny human growing inside me seemed a pretty contradictory way of setting off on my own, so I went to Planned Parenthood.

In the waiting room were fifteen to twenty other women. Each had a horror-stricken look on her face. It was one of those situations where you can assume that you have the same expression as everyone else without having to look in the mirror. I sat there for an hour and a half, nervously leafing through *People* magazines in a desperate attempt to give a rat's ass about the lives of Daryl Hannah and Princess Di.

When they called my name, I probably would have shit my pants if there had been any digestion going on in my intestines, which there wasn't. It's hard to eat when you're pregnant with a child you do not want.

My boyfriend accompanied me into the exam room. I was told to strip and lie on the table, feet in the stirrups. I still remember the ugly swirl designs and water marks on the ceiling. After a while, the nurse came in and explained what would be happening. She said, "Are you sure this is what you want?" I think she asked because I was crying uncontrollably. What other goddamn choice did I have? I'm sure. What an idiot. I wasn't crying from indecision, I was crying from fear. I muttered, "Just do it, please."

With the ugliest needle I had ever seen, she shot something into my cervix. I don't think my cervix was residing under the belief that it would someday have a large needle plunged into it, so it protested accordingly. The pain was overwhelming; my head swam into the netherworld between intense clarity and murky subconscious.

Then I heard a quiet motor whirring.

The lady told me to recite my ABCs.

"A, B, C, D, E . . ." Something entered my vagina, deeper, deeper, deeper than I imagined anything could go.

"F, G, H, I, O, W . . ." The walls of my uterus were being sucked, felt like they were gonna cave in. I screamed "O, P, X, X, D, VOWELS, WHAT ARE THE VOWELS? R? K? A! A's A VOWEL!" And then my organs were surely being mowed down by a tiny battalion of Lawn-Boys.

"S, did I say S?" My boyfriend was crying too and didn't tell me whether I had said S or not.

There was a two-inch-thick pad between my legs, and blood gushing out of me. The motor had stopped whirring. I was delirious. I asked, "What do you do with all the fetuses? Where do they go? Do you bury them?" The lady ignored me, which was fine; I had to puke. She led me into a bathroom, and I vomited bilious green foam. Then I went to a recovery room, lay down and cried. There was another nurse in there. She patted my hand and said, "I know just how you feel." I said, "You've had an abortion before too?" She said, "No, but I know how you feel." I told her to get the fuck away from me.

For two weeks, there was a gaping wound in my body. I could hardly walk for five days.

And then, stupid me, a couple of years later, I got pregnant again. I still lived in Seattle but was just about to move to Olympia, Washington, to begin school at the Evergreen State College. Since I thought this was no way to begin a college education, I had to face the reality of going to that machine once again. This time I was even more petrified, 'cause I knew what that rectangular box and its quiet motor had planned for my reproductive system. Have you any idea how it feels to willingly and voluntarily submit to excruciating torture because you dumbly forgot to insert your diaphragm, which gives you ugly yeast infections and hurts you to fuck unless you lie flat on your back? I had to withstand this torture because I was a bad girl. I didn't do good, I fucked up. So I had the same choice as before, that glowing, outstanding choice we ladies fight tooth and nail for: the choice to get my insides ruthlessly sucked by some inhuman shit pile, invented not by my foremothers, but by someone who would never, ever in a million years have that tube jammed up his dickhole and turned on full blast, slurping everything in its path.

On one of Olympia's main thoroughfares is an abortion clinic. I passed it every day on my way to and from school. Almost always, there were old women, young girls and duck hunters standing on the corner outside the clinic, holding signs that showed pictures of dead fetuses. The signs often had words to the effect that this aborted fetus may have been the next president of the United States of America.

Whenever I saw those people out there, especially the young girls, I'd see myself yanking the bus cord (in all probability snapping it in two), vaulting off the bus, crossing the street and turning into a walking killing machine, kicking in faces, stomping on hands. There were times when I gripped my wrist so I wouldn't yank that cord.

Upon examining my desire to physically mutilate individuals whose convictions were in direct opposition to mine, I realized I had to get hold of myself. I had studied different kinds of medicines and healing methods in the past, and I decided that now would be a perfect time to immerse myself in histories and applications of medicines far and wide. Maybe if I better understood the situation, I'd feel less of an inclination to beat up duck hunters.

I found one thing that was a constant: Healing starts from within. It appeared to be some kind of law, no, more than a law. Is breathing a law? Is waking up every day a law? If so, maybe the notion of healing coming from within is a law as well. At any rate, this concept is completely alien, even deviant, in our culture. In this society, we look to the outside for just about everything: love, entertainment, well-being, self-worth and health. We stare into the TV set instead of speaking of our own dreams, wait for a vacation instead of appreciating each day, watch the clock rather than listen to our hearts. Every livelong day we are bombarded with realities from the outside world, seemingly nonstop. Phones, car alarms, pills, coffee, beepers, ads, radios, elevator music, fax machines, gunshots, bright lights, fast cars, airplanes overhead, computer screens, sirens, alcohol, newspapers. One hardly has the opportunity to look inside for peace and love and other nice things like that.

Western medicine, that smelly dog who farts across the house and we just don't have the heart to put out of its misery, is based on a law opposite the one the rest of the universe goes by, namely, Healing Has Nothing To Do With You; It's Something Only Your Doctor Can Control.

In the U.S., we don't (and we're also not encouraged to) look inside ourselves for healing or for finding truths or answers. If you want to know something, you find out what the Person In Charge Of This Area says. The weather is not to be discerned by looking at the sky or the mountains in the distance or by listening to the song of the wind. You will find it in the Report of the Meteorologist. Likewise, if you are pregnant and don't want to be, you don't look to yourself and the resources in your immediate world, you pay a visit to the Abortionist, who will subsequently predict the climate in your body for nine days to two weeks, guaranteed. And so, la dee dah, once, twice, three times a lady . . . I got pregnant again.

It was the same boyfriend as the other two times, only now we were breaking up. It was the stupidest one of all because I didn't want to be with this man and I shouldn't have fucked him, but it was his birthday and he was fun to romp with and blah dee blah blah blah. No force on earth could make me feel that I wanted this child, and furthermore, I promptly decided there was to be no grotesque waltzing with that abhorrent machine.

So I started talking to my girlfriends. Looking to my immediate community for help led me to Judy, the masseuse, who rubbed me in places you aren't supposed to touch pregnant ladies. She also did some reflexology in the same vein. Panacea told me where to find detailed recipes for herbal abortifacients and emmenagogues. Esther supported me and stayed with me every day. Bridget brought me flowers. Possibly most important was the fact that I possessed not one single filament of self-doubt. With that core of supportive women surrounding me and with my mind made up, I was pretty much invincible.

So, one morning, after a week of nonstop praying, massaging, tea drinking, talking and thinking, I was brushing my teeth at the sink and felt a very peculiar mmmmbloommmp-like feeling. I looked at the bathroom floor, and there, between my feet, was some blood and a little round thing. It was clear but felt like one of them unshiny Super Balls. It was the neatest thing I ever did see. An orb of life and energy, in my hand.

So strange.

So real.

And Jesus H., wasn't I the happiest clam? It hardly hurt at all, just some mild contractions. I bled very little, felt fine in two days. I wore black for a week and had a little funeral in my head. This was definitely one of the top ten learning experiences in my life thus far. You know, it's like when Germany invaded Poland. I once read how in the ghettos of Warsaw, the people fighting the

Nazis were amazed at first that a Nazi soldier would die if you shot him. They suspected that Nazis could die, but felt like they were somehow superhuman.

That's how I felt after I aborted a fetus without paying a visit to that sickening vacuum cleaner. I felt like I imagine any oppressed individual feels when they see that they have power, and nobody—not even men and their machines, nobody—can take that away.

I learned that the fight for human rights does not take place on some bureaucratic battleground with a bevy of lawyers running from congressional suite to congressional suite, sapping resources into laws. The war for peace and love and other nice things like that is not waged in protests on the street. These forms of fighting acknowledge the oppressor outside of yourself, giving that entity yet more life. The real fight for human rights is inside each and every individual on this earth.

While traversing along this line of thought, I realize that I just might sound like a young woman who has never experienced the unspeakable horror of back-alley abortions, and I am. I also realize that it might seem as if I'm ungrateful to all the women and men who have fought their hearts raw for equal rights and legal abortions, but I am not. I think of it like this: The fact that there now exists a generation of women who can actually consider clinical abortions to be an oppressive diversion to one's own power is based wholly upon the foundation that our mothers and sisters have built for us. I sincerely thank the individuals who have fought so hard for themselves and their daughters. I thank the people who bent over backwards so that I can have the luxury of experiencing the beliefs I now hold. Evolutionarily speaking, however, it is quite natural for this fight to progress into a new arena, since by no stretch of the imagination is this fight over. The squabble between pro-lifers and pro-choicers serves only to keep our eyes off the target: patriarchal society.

Concentrating on the power within our own circle of women was once a major focus of the women's health movement. I think we would benefit from once again creating informal health collectives where we discuss things like our bodies and our selves. If we believed in our own power and the power of our immediate communities, then abortion clinics, in their present incarnation, would be completely unnecessary. Let the fundamentalist dickheads burn all those vacuum cleaners to the ground. If alternative organic abortions were explored and taken more seriously, there wouldn't be much of an abortion debate. Abortion would be a personal, intimate thing among friends.

Can you say Amen.

AND SO I CHOSE

Allison Crews

"After much prayer and divination, many tears and several horrible poems, I made a choice to bear a child."

As the editor of a small website designed by and for empowered, feminist teen mothers, I am forced to be creative in order to attract the amount of traffic that the site needs. In a desperate attempt to gather a few more hits for our counter, I decided to leave fliers in the waiting room of a "crisis pregnancy center." As soon as I put them down, my fliers were promptly picked up and handed back to me. I was not allowed to advertise there, I was curtly told, by a woman who identified herself as the center's director. I asked this Bible-carrying woman, Why not? This website was, after all, designed for the very girls who frequented her facility. We could offer them support, encouragement and friendship, I told her.

"Is your website *pro-life?"* the woman demanded.

"Well, no. We really don't have an official opinion on abortion. We just intend to support young mothers," I quickly replied.

It was then suggested to me that I put up some testimonials about abortion, perhaps some information about fetal development and post-abortion syndrome. The center, I was told, had a purpose. When I asked what that purpose was, the director answered, "To end abortion." I left soon after, but was reminded, as I walked to the door, that the center would be more likely to promote my site if I added more FAQs about abortion.

Reprinted from *Listen Up: Voices From the Next Feminist Generation*, Seal Press.

The next day, I received two emails. One was from an anti-abortion mother who was angry at our site's silence regarding abortion issues: We needed to *do* something to "stop the horrors," she wrote. The second email came from the mother of a three-year-old who had recently had an abortion, and she, too, wished we had more information about abortion on our site—in the form of a support forum for mothers who have elected to have abortions as well as raise children.

They both made an important point in requesting more information: Young mothers need to be supported in their choices, whatever they may be. Whether they elect to abort a pregnancy, to place a child for adoption or to raise their children, resources to help young women make and cope with their choices need to be readily available. Women must speak boldly and proudly of their choices, so that other women feel safe in making their own.

I doubt that many of us—feminists born to women of the Second Wave—remember a time when our freedom of reproductive choice was virtually nonexistent. I doubt that many of us, conceived after *Roe v. Wade* became law, remember a time when birth control pills had yet to be invented and diaphragms and condoms were not readily available to unmarried women. A time when a woman faced with an unplanned pregnancy could either give birth, or risk mutilation of her body and possibly death. Of those who gave birth, most young, unwed women were made to give their children away to anonymous strangers, or face a life of forced domesticity, with little chance to educate themselves or begin a career. Even if a woman was raped, even when she thought she was protected, even if she had a medical condition that prevented her from safely carrying a pregnancy to term, even when revealing her pregnancy meant facing violence and abuse, she had no legal option other than to give birth to the child. All teenage mothers, like myself, have faced making a choice between abortion and motherhood. Even those mothers who are staunchly anti-abortion know what it is like to make this vital choice, whether they choose to acknowledge it or not.

I was raised in a pro-life home, and lost many of my mother's weekends to Operation Rescue events and "Life Chains." I had model fetuses as toys. *Model fetuses.* A succession of pregnant teenagers stayed in my home—girls my mother met through the crisis pregnancy center where she worked and brought home to feed and clothe. I fought with pro-choice women in front of abortion clinics before I was ten years old, arguing the anti-abortion points that had been burned into my mind.

One fall morning, when I was twelve, I stood with my mother and her fellow activists in front of our local Planned Parenthood. I held a sign high in the chilly air above my head, a sign with a picture of a man's fingers pinching two tiny feet that supposedly belonged to a ten-week-old aborted fetus. That morning, I watched a girl—probably only a few years older than myself—drive up to the clinic with her mother. A crowd of women escorted her from her car to the clinic doors we blocked, singing Christian hymns. They all wore blue T-shirts, and were locked arm-in-arm while they huddled around the girl, a living, protective force field. Several hours later, after the clinic escorts had all gone home, after the girl's procedure was over, she re-emerged from the clinic doors. Her mother held her as she shook—the same way I would shake about three and a half years later, after my son's birth. Her face was pale and her eyes downcast. A man behind me began to shout, "Ask for forgiveness, the blood is on your hands! You know what you did; only God can wash the blood away!"

The girl looked up, and her gaze met mine. I smiled at her, because I didn't know what else to do. I saw no blood on her hands, but the pain I saw on her face was unmistakable. She looked at the large, laminated sign that I held in my hands and she began to cry. The shouting stopped. A woman called out, "I will pray for you!" The girl's mother gathered her into her arms, and they walked away. I watched as they pulled themselves into their small white car. I watched as they sat for a moment, their lips still, hung their heads together, touched foreheads and sobbed. They drove past me, once again, the girl staring intently at me. Heavy tears hung in her eyes, threatening to fall down her scarlet cheeks, and her lips quivered. I never forgot her face.

I never protested with my mother again. I knew that whatever pain that girl felt—walking away from the choice she made—our presence, our shouting and our signs only intensified it. I wished for her sake that the escorts who had helped her inside the building had been there to help her out; I wished that I had been able to help them protect her. She had a right to feel protected, a right to feel safe. She had the right to make a choice for herself and her future without being harassed and intimidated.

And her rights were ignored because she was young, she was female, and she was pregnant. Three afflictions that, to the protesters outside of the clinic, meant that she had no rights at all.

Three years later, I was a sophomore in high school. I was now pregnant, and I was scared. I had become one of those girls who once filled my home with their empty sadness; the girls whom I had heard, when I listened through the crack of my bedroom door, crying on my mother's shoulder. I scheduled three consecutive abortion appointments and systematically canceled each one. With each new appointment, my due date grew closer, the price of the abortion grew higher, and the distance that I would have had to travel for the procedure grew longer.

Yet, I never carried through with any of those appointments. Something kept me from promptly "taking care" of it, and to this day I cannot pinpoint what it was. Several possible reasons come to mind: lack of transportation, as I did not drive and the clinic would not allow you to leave without a ride; lack of money, and the seemingly endless hoops I had to jump through to sign up for Medicare, as well as to ensure my confidentiality. Maybe it was because when I called the same clinic I had once protested in front of to schedule my own abortion, I remembered that girl. I was now about the age she was when I watched her, walking to and from those doors. I prayed to a god that I wasn't sure existed anymore that I would not encounter any of my mother's friends as I walked inside. I prayed that when I went to the appointment, the women who had helped that girl walk through the clinic doors would be there to walk with me. I prayed that someone would be there to listen to me sob; I prayed for a place to be able to cry and a place to feel safe.

Whatever the reasons, whether they were beyond my control or self-created, I did not abort my pregnancy. Perhaps because I was not sure of the choice to abort, I delayed my appointments at Planned Parenthood. Perhaps because I was scared I was making the wrong choice, I purposely showed up late to appointments at the social services office, knowing that I would then need to reschedule. After much prayer and divination, many tears and several horrible poems, I made a choice to bear a child.

I tried to find solace in parts of the feminist, pro-choice online community. Surely, these women would understand my choice. These women had fought, in various ways, for my right to make this choice. They would not condemn me for having wanted an abortion, or even for being a pregnant teenager. Instead, I was sure, they would support my right to choose, support my right to become a mother; surely, they would support me. But, in many of these chatrooms and message boards, I encountered a response similar to the one pregnant girls considering abortion receive from the anti-abortion camp: I was questioned and I was made fun of. I was told that girls like me were almost completely responsible for the "backsliding of the feminist movement." I opened my email each morning to find messages proclaiming me an "irresponsible teenager" and a "hopeless breeder." I was told that it wasn't too late to abort and that I should save myself before it was too late. Judgment and antimother rhetoric spewed from my computer screen, leaving me feeling hopelessly alone and disconnected. I cut all ties with this community. I was not safe there, as I had hoped to be. While many of these women professed to be "pro-choice," I quickly learned that for them the only choice that is acceptable is the choice they consider "right."

To add to the confusion, the pressure to give my forming child up for adoption soon became immeasurable and emotionally crushing. Counselors, family members, strangers, nurses: It seemed as if everyone I encountered felt that they had a right to force their opinion on me regarding the best choice for my child's future—and this choice was almost exclusively to give him up for adoption. I was told that I did not deserve my child, that there was no way I could ever be an adequate mother, by both the anti- and pro-abortion communities. Some days I woke up and felt as if my body were imploding: I struggled for breath, my son's feet digging into my rib cage, his body crowding my organs. Tears and snot dried onto my face like makeup. My soul felt as confined as my tiny son's body must have been, trapped inside my womb. My spirit was being crushed. Slowly, methodically, effectively, they picked at me. It felt as if those closest to me—those I trusted with my medical care, those who were paid to counsel me—were all trying to knock the very ground I stood on out from under me, attempting to take away my choices by dissolving the last shreds of hope and confidence that I clung to like a life raft.

A couple was approved to adopt my child, before I was even allowed to utter a word of permission. A nursery was decorated for him, clothes were chosen and a baby shower was thrown for the woman while I was at home alone, crying. She called me several days later to tell me about *her* shower for *her* baby—clearly there was no reason for *me* to celebrate. I was a passive bystander, watching the story unfold before me. I was alone, unable to make the choices that I wanted to, unable to express my grief, denied the right to speak my mind and control my own life. All because I was "too young to know any better." I was told, over and over again, that teenage girls are immature, they are selfish, they can't possibly decide what is best, and so others must step in and make these choices for them. This broken record replayed itself in my mind until it became my unintended, living mantra. A mantra that nourished the self-doubt and fear that grew within me, like my son's shadow twin.

I cried to my mother, and she counseled me, as she had been trained to do years before. I felt disconnected from her, though, wary of and scared by her alliance with the woman who wished to adopt my son. What she had in common with this other woman was far greater than what I thought she shared with me. With my younger sister having been adopted, my mother knew all the ropes. She joked with the "other mother"; she shared advice and information. I couldn't see what she, a pro-life activist and adoptive mother, could have had in common with me, a pro-choice and pregnant teenager. This disconnection intensified my feelings of loneliness. She felt distant, even when I talked with her. She seemed to be coming from a faraway place, with no concept of the turmoil that boiled inside of me. But, I realized later, she had been there for me all along. And as testament to her spirit, one rich with compassion and love, she did support me wholly, no matter what choices I made.

When it came time for me to give birth, not one person believed I was capable of birthing on my own. When I asked my doctor about the possibility of birthing in my home, he laughed at me. There was no way I could handle the pain and horror of childbirth alone, in my bedroom and sanctuary, as I wished to do. I needed a man, trained to care for women, to see me through my labor. I needed to be monitored, strapped to a bed, cleaned from the inside, shaven smooth and knocked out cold. I was a little girl, and delivering babies is a man's job.

As my labor approached, I reached my outer emotional limits. I could not physically or psychologically handle any more pressure, any more shame, any more negative expectations. I was tired of people—who seemed to come at me from every angle and direction—trying to deny me my right to reproductive freedom. I was tired of being treated poorly because of my age, tired of being pushed around, tired of feebly (and ineffectually) defending my rights. There were only two things that I could do now: I could finally break under the pressure of the past nine months, give up all hope, and lose my child to another woman. Or I could spit truth into the faces that scorned me, deflect the lies that they hurled at me and turn and run in the other direction, strong, with my child in my arms.

I labored for five hours and birthed naturally, with little intervention from the doctors who had doubted me. I roared like a lioness and pushed my son out in a matter of minutes. He slid from my body, slimy and new, screaming the kitten-cries that only a fresh infant can make. And as he emerged, I was reborn. I birthed like a goddess, and regained the power and freedom that I felt had been stolen away from me. I felt that power radiate from within me, touching my son, and bringing me joy. Through giving birth, I loudly and publicly proclaimed my freedom of choice.

I latched my tired son onto my swollen breast, and I ordered everyone to leave my room as I held him. He was my choice, and, finally, this was my life. I felt at peace with myself, after feeling torn and alone for so long. I had grown in a way that I had not thought possible, and found a happiness that I had once only hoped existed. My choices allowed me this. And I refused to let another person deny me this joy ever again. No one would again deny me the right to choose, I promised myself, while I sat on lochia-stained sheets, cradling my sleeping child.

Being pro-woman, being pro-choice, means being supportive of any reproductive choice a woman makes for herself. Women, of any age, in any social situation, have the right to bear children. We have the right to choose when, where, with whom and how we bear children. We have the right to abort a pregnancy, for whatever reason we may have. If we have no money, if we have no support, if we wish to continue our education or career uninterrupted, if we are being abused, if we were raped, it is our right to not bear a child. If we become pregnant, through any circumstance, we have the right to give birth the way we want to. We have the right to elect to have our child removed by cesarean section on a convenient date. We have the right to choose to deliver alone in our home, catching our babies with our own hands. We have the right to be respected as mothers, to be seen as the responsible, hardworking parents that we are. We have the right to remain child-free forever, to find fulfillment through our careers and personal adventures. We have the right to bear as many children as our body will allow, and to be fulfilled through the nurturing of our children. We have the right to nourish and nurture our children at our breasts, for as many years as they may need to and we allow. We have the right to keep our body to ourselves once we give birth, if we cannot handle the physical or emotional aspects of breastfeeding, and feed our children artificial breastmilk. We have the right to choose to become parents and the right to delay parenting. We have the right to share a bed with our children, and we have the right to put them to sleep in beds of their own. We have the right to mother the way we want to, to ignore the "well-meaning" advice and criticism of others. We have the right to an education, no matter how old we are and what grade we are in when we give birth. We have the right to a career, to daycare, to financial aid. We have the right to stay home and postpone a career until our children are grown. Our bodies are our own, our futures ours to mold. No one should be allowed to interfere with them. Whatever our reproductive choices, nobody can ever deny us our right to them. And this is what being pro-choice means to me.

THE BODY POLITIC (1995)

Abra Fortune Chernik

Body hatred is something many women share in what Abra Chernik terms a "diet culture," but the life-threatening aspects of anorexia and bulimia are sometimes dismissed. In the following narrative from Listen Up! Voices From the Next Feminist Generation, *screenwriter and activist Abra Chernik describes her hospitalization for anorexia and her struggle to overcome the illusion of power and control that she felt in her anorexic world.*

My body possesses solidness and curve, like the ocean. My weight mingles with Earth's pull, drawing me onto the sand. I have not always sent waves into the world. I flew off once, for five years, and swirled madly like a cracking brown leaf in the salty autumn wind. I wafted, dried out, apathetic.

I had no weight in the world during my years of anorexia. Curled up inside my thinness, a refugee in a cocoon of hunger, I lost the capacity to care about myself or others. I starved my body

---

and twitched in place as those around me danced in the energy of shared existence and progressed in their lives. When I graduated from college crowned with academic honors, professors praised my potential. I wanted only to vanish.

It took three months of hospitalization and two years of outpatient psychotherapy for me to learn to nourish myself and to live in a body that expresses strength and honesty in its shape. I accepted my right and my obligation to take up room with my figure, voice and spirit. I remembered how to tumble forward and touch the world that holds me. I chose the ocean as my guide.

Who disputes the ocean's fullness?

Growing up in New York City, I did not care about the feminist movement. Although I attended an all-girls high school, we read mostly male authors and studied the history of men. Embracing mainstream culture without question, I learned about womanhood from fashion magazines, Madison Avenue and Hollywood. I dismissed feminist alternatives as foreign and offensive, swathed as they were in stereotypes that threatened my adolescent need for conformity.

Puberty hit late; I did not complain. I enjoyed living in the lanky body of a tall child and insisted on the title of "girl." If anyone referred to me as a "young woman," I would cry out, horrified, "Do not call me the W word!" But at sixteen years old, I could no longer deny my fate. My stomach and breasts rounded. Curly black hair sprouted in the most embarrassing places. Hips swelled from a once-flat plane. Interpreting maturation as an unacceptable lapse into fleshiness, I resolved to eradicate the physical symptoms of my impending womanhood.

Magazine articles, television commercials, lunchroom conversation, gymnastics coaches and write-ups on models had saturated me with diet savvy. Once I decided to lose weight, I quickly turned expert. I dropped hot chocolate from my regular breakfast order at the Skyline Diner. I replaced lunches of peanut butter and Marshmallow Fluff sandwiches with small platters of cottage cheese and cantaloupe. I eliminated dinner altogether and blunted my appetite with Tab, Camel Lights, and Carefree bubble gum. When furious craving overwhelmed my resolve and I swallowed an extra something, I would flee to the nearest bathroom to purge my mistake.

Within three months, I had returned my body to its preadolescent proportions and had manipulated my monthly period into drying up. Over the next five years, I devoted my life to losing my weight. I came to resent the body in which I lived, the body that threatened to develop, the body whose hunger I despised but could not extinguish. If I neglected a workout or added a pound or ate a bite too many, I would stare in the mirror and drown myself in a tidal wave of criticism. Hatred of my body generalized to hatred of myself as a person, and self-referential labels such as "pig," "failure" and "glutton" allowed me to believe that I deserved punishment. My self-hatred became fuel for the self-mutilating behaviors of the eating disorder.

As my body shrank, so did my world. I starved away my power and vision, my energy and inclinations. Obsessed with dieting, I allowed relationships, passions and identity to wither. I pulled back from the world, off of the beach, out of the sand. The waves of my existence ceased to roll beyond the inside of my skin.

And society applauded my shrinking. Pound after pound the applause continued, like the pounding ocean outside the door of my beach house.

The word "anorexia" literally means "loss of appetite." But as an anorexic, I felt hunger thrashing inside my body. I denied my appetite, ignored it, but never lost it. Sometimes the pangs twisted so sharply, I feared they would consume the meat of my heart. On desperate nights I rose in a flannel nightgown and allowed myself to eat an unplanned something.

No matter how much I ate, I could not soothe the pangs. Standing in the kitchen at midnight, spotlighted by the blue-white light of the open refrigerator, I would frantically feed my neglected appetite: the Chinese food I had not touched at dinner; ice cream and whipped cream; microwaved bread; cereal and chocolate milk; doughnuts and bananas. Then, solid sadness inside my gut, swelling agitation, a too-big meal I would not digest. In the bathroom I would rip off my shirt, tie up my hair, and prepare to execute the desperate ritual, again. I would ram the back of my throat with a toothbrush handle, crying, impatient, until the food rushed up. I would vomit until the toilet filled and I emptied, until I forgave myself, until I felt ready to try my life again. Standing up from my position over the toilet, wiping my mouth, I would believe that I was safe. Looking in the mirror through puffy eyes in a tumescent face, I would promise to take care of myself. Kept awake by the fast, confused beating of my heart and the ache in my chest, I would swear I did not miss the world outside. Lost within myself, I almost died.

By the time I entered the hospital, a mess of protruding bones defined my body, and the bones of my emaciated life rattled me crazy. I carried a pillow around because it hurt to sit down, and I shivered with cold in sultry July. Clumps of brittle hair clogged the drain when I showered, and blackened eyes appeared to sink into my head. My vision of reality wrinkled and my disposition turned mercurial as I slipped into starvation psychosis, a condition associated with severe malnutrition. People told me that I resembled a concentration camp prisoner, a chemotherapy patient, a famine victim or a fashion model.

In the hospital, I examined my eating disorder under the lenses of various therapies. I dissected my childhood, my family structure, my intimate relationships, my belief systems. I participated in experiential therapies of movement, art and psychodrama. I learned to use words instead of eating patterns to communicate my feelings. And still I refused to gain more than a minimal amount of weight.

I felt powerful as an anorexic. Controlling my body yielded an illusion of control over my life; I received incessant praise for my figure despite my sickly mien, and my frailty manipulated family and friends into protecting me from conflict. I had reduced my world to a plate of steamed carrots, and over this tiny kingdom I proudly crowned myself queen.

I sat cross-legged on my hospital bed for nearly two months before I earned an afternoon pass to go to the mall with my mother. The privilege came just in time; I felt unbearably large and desperately wanted a new outfit under which to hide gained weight. At the mall, I searched for two hours before finally discovering, in the maternity section at Macy's, a shirt large enough to cover what I perceived as my enormous body.

With an hour left on my pass, I spotted a sign on a shop window: "Body Fat Testing, $3.00." I suggested to my mother that we split up for ten minutes; she headed to Barnes & Noble, and I snuck into the fitness store.

I sat down in front of a machine hooked up to a computer, and a burly young body builder fired questions at me:

"Age?"

"Twenty-one."

"Height?"
"Five nine."
"Weight?"
"Ninety-nine."

The young man punched my statistics into his keyboard and pinched my arm with clippers wired to the testing machine. In a moment, the computer spit out my results. "Only ten percent body fat! Unbelievably healthy. The average for a woman your age is twenty-five percent. Fantastic! You're this week's blue ribbon winner."

I stared at him in disbelief. *Winner? Healthy? Fantastic?* I glanced around at the other customers in the store, some of whom had congregated to watch my testing, and I felt embarrassed by his praise. And then I felt furious. Furious at this man and at the society that programmed him for their ignorant approbation of my illness and my suffering.

"I am dying of anorexia," I whispered. "Don't congratulate me."

I spent my remaining month in the hospital supplementing psychotherapy with an independent examination of eating disorders from a social and political point of view. I needed to understand why society would reward my starvation and encourage my vanishing. In the bathroom, a mirror on the open door behind me reflected my backside in a mirror over the sink. Vertebrae poked at my skin, ribs hung like wings over chiseled hip bones, the two sides of my buttocks did not touch. I had not seen this view of myself before.

In writing, I recorded instances in which my eating disorder had tangled the progress of my life and thwarted my relationships. I filled three and a half Mead marble notebooks. Five years' worth of: *I wouldn't sit with Daddy when he was alone in the hospital because I needed to go jogging; I told Derek not to visit me because I couldn't throw up when he was there; I almost failed my comprehensive exams because I was so hungry; I spent my year at Oxford with my head in the toilet bowl; I wouldn't eat the dinner my friends cooked me for my nineteenth birthday because I knew they had used oil in the recipe; I told my family not to come to my college graduation because I didn't want to miss a day at the gym or have to eat a restaurant meal.* And on and on for hundreds of pages.

This honest account of my life dissolved the illusion of

anorexic power. I saw myself naked in the truth of my pain, my loneliness, my obsessions, my craziness, my selfishness, my defeat. I also recognized the social and political implications of consuming myself with the trivialities of calories and weight. At college, I had watched as classmates involved themselves in extracurricular clubs, volunteer work, politics and applications for jobs and graduate schools. Obsessed with exercising and exhausted by starvation, I did not even consider joining in such pursuits. Despite my love of writing and painting and literature, despite ranking at the top of my class, I wanted only to teach aerobics. Despite my adolescent days as a loud-mouthed, rambunctious class leader, I had grown into a silent, hungry young woman.

And society preferred me this way: hungry, fragile, crazy. *Winner! Healthy! Fantastic!* I began reading feminist literature to further understand the disempowerment of women in our culture. I digested the connection between a nation of starving, self-obsessed women and the continued success of the patriarchy. I also cultivated an awareness of alternative models of womanhood. In the stillness of the hospital library, new voices in my life rose from printed pages to echo my rage and provide the conception of my feminist consciousness.

I had been willing to accept self-sabotage, but now I refused to sacrifice myself to a society that profited from my pain. I finally understood that my eating disorder symbolized more than "personal psychodynamic trauma." Gazing in the mirror at my emaciated body, I observed a woman held up by her culture as the physical ideal because she was starving, self-obsessed and powerless, a woman called beautiful because she threatened no one except herself. Despite my intelligence, my education, and my supposed Manhattan sophistication, I had believed all the lies; I had almost given my life in order to achieve the sickly impotence that this culture aggressively links with female happiness, love and success. And everything I had to offer to the world, every tumbling wave, every thought and every passion, nearly died inside me.

As long as society resists female power, fashion will call healthy women physically flawed. As long as society accepts the physical, sexual and economic abuse of women, popular culture will prefer women who resemble little girls. Sitting in the hospital the summer after my college graduation, I grasped the absurdity of a nation of adult women dying to grow small.

Armed with this insight, I loosened the grip of the starvation disease on my body. I determined to recreate myself based on an image of a woman warrior. I remembered my ocean, and I took my first bite.

Gaining weight and getting my head out of the toilet bowl was the most political act I have ever committed.

I left the hospital and returned home to Fire Island. Living at the shore in those wintry days of my new life, I wrapped myself in feminism as I hunted sea shells and role models. I wanted to feel proud of my womanhood. I longed to accept and honor my body's fullness.

During the process of my healing, I had hoped that I would be able to skip the memory of anorexia like a cold pebble into the dark winter sea. I had dreamed that in relinquishing my obsessive chase after a smaller body, I would be able to come home to rejoin those whom I had left in order to starve, rejoin them to live together as healthy, powerful women. But as my body has grown full, I have sensed a hollowness in the lives of women all around me that I had not noticed when I myself stood hollow. I have made it home only to find myself alone.

Out in the world again, I hear the furious thumping dance of body hatred echoing every place I go. Friends who once appeared wonderfully carefree in ordering late-night french fries turn out not to eat breakfast or lunch. Smart, talented, creative women talk about dieting and overeating and hating the beach because they look terrible in bathing suits. Famous women give interviews insulting their bodies and bragging about bicycling twenty-four miles the day they gave birth.

I had looked forward to rejoining society after my years of anorexic exile. Ironically, in order to preserve my health, my recovery has included the development of a consciousness that actively challenges the images and ideas that define this culture. Walking down Madison Avenue and passing emaciated women, I say to myself, *those women are sick.* When smacked with a diet commercial, I remind myself, *I don't do that anymore.* I decline invitations to movies that feature anorexic actors, I will not participate in discussions about dieting, and I refuse to shop in stores that cater to women with eating-disordered figures.

Though I am critical of diet culture, I find it nearly impossible to escape. Eating disorders have woven their way into the fabric of my society. On television, in print, on food packaging, in casual conversation and in windows of clothing stores populated by ridiculously gaunt mannequins, messages to lose my weight and control my appetite challenge my recovered fullness. Finally at home in my body, I recognize myself as an island in a sea of eating disorders, a sea populated predominantly by young women.

A perversion of nature by society has resulted in a phenomenon whereby women feel safer when starving than when eating. Losing our weight boosts self-esteem, while nourishing our bodies evokes feelings of self-doubt and self-loathing.

When our bodies take up more space than a size eight (as most of our bodies do), we say, *too big*. When our appetites demand more than a Lean Cuisine, we say, *too much*. When we want a piece of a friend's birthday cake, we say, *too bad*. Don't eat too much, don't talk too loudly, don't take up too much space, don't take from the world. Be pleasant or crazy, but don't seem hungry. Remember, a new study shows that men prefer women who eat salad for dinner over women who eat burgers and fries.

So we keep on shrinking, starving away our wildness, our power, our truth.

Hiding our curves under long T-shirts at the beach, sitting silently and fidgeting while others eat dessert, sneaking back into the kitchen late at night to binge and hating ourselves the next day, skipping breakfast, existing on diet soda and cigarettes, adding up calories and subtracting everything else. We accept what is horribly wrong in our lives and fight what is beautiful and right.

Over the past three years, feminism has taught me to honor the fullness of my womanhood and the solidness of the body that hosts my life. In feminist circles I have found mentors, strong women who live with power, passion and purpose. And yet, even in groups of feminists, my love and acceptance of my body remains unusual.

Eating disorders affect us all on both a personal and a political level. The majority of my peers—including my feminist peers—still measure their beauty against anorexic ideals. Even among feminists, body hatred and chronic dieting continue to consume lives. Friends of anorexics beg them to please start eating; then these friends go home and continue their own diets. Who can deny that the millions of young women caught in the net of disordered eating will frustrate the potential of the next wave of feminism?

Sometimes my empathy dissolves into frustration and rage at our situation. For the first time in history, young women have the opportunity to create a world in our image. But many of us concentrate instead on recreating the shape of our thighs.

As young feminists, we must place unconditional acceptance of our bodies at the top of our political agenda. We must claim our bodies as our own to love and honor in their infinite shapes and sizes. Fat, thin, soft, hard, puckered, smooth, our bodies are our homes. By nourishing our bodies, we care for and love ourselves on the most basic level. When we deny ourselves physical food, we go hungry emotionally, psychologically, spiritually and politically. We must challenge ourselves to eat and digest, and allow society to call us too big. We will understand their message to mean too powerful.

Time goes by quickly. One day we will blink and open our eyes as old women. If we spend all our energy keeping our bodies small, what will we have to show for our lives when we reach the end? I hope we have more than a group of fashionably skinny figures.

Questions

1. How can individual eating problems actually be considered political problems? What factors contribute to the existence of eating problems?
2. What is the meaning and significance of "body hatred"? What are the effects of body hatred for both the individual and society?
3. How does Chernik change through the course of her narrative? What issues does Chernik face in her struggle for personal growth as a woman? How does she feel about her experiences?

Beyond Pro-Choice Versus Pro-Life: Women of Color and Reproductive Justice

Andrea Smith

Once, while taking an informal survey of Native women in Chicago about their position on abortion—were they "pro-life" or "pro-choice"—I quickly found that their responses did not neatly match up with these media-mandated categories.

Example 1:
ME: Are you pro-choice or pro-life?
RESPONDENT 1: Oh I am definitely pro-life.
ME: So you think abortion should be illegal?
RESPONDENT 1: No, definitely not. People should be able to have an abortion if they want.
ME: Do you think then that there should not be federal funding for abortion services?
RESPONDENT 1: No, there should be funding available so that anyone can afford to have one.

Example 2:
ME: Would you say you are pro-choice or pro-life?
RESPONDENT 2: Well, I would say that I am pro-choice, but the most important thing to me is promoting life in Native communities.

Reprinted from *NWSA Journal* 17, no. 1 (2005), by permission of Johns Hopkins University Press.

These responses make it difficult to categorize the Native women queried neatly into "pro-life" or "pro-choice" camps. Is Respondent #1 pro-life because she says she is pro-life? Or is she pro-choice because she supports the decriminalization of and public funding for abortion? I would argue that, rather than attempt to situate these respondents in pro-life or pro-choice camps, it is more useful to recognize the limitations of the pro-life/pro-choice dichotomy for understanding the politics around reproductive justice. Unlike pro-life versus pro-choice advocates who make their overall political goal either the criminalization or decriminalization of abortion, the reproductive frameworks these Native women are implicitly articulating are based on fighting for life and self-determination of their communities. The criminalization of abortion may or may not be a strategy for pursuing that goal.

In previous works, I have focused more specifically on Native women and reproductive justice (Smith 2001). Here, I am using these Native women's responses to questions about abortion to argue that the pro-life versus pro-choice paradigm is a model that marginalizes women of color, poor women, and women with disabilities. The pro-life versus pro-choice paradigm reifies and masks the structures of white supremacy and capitalism that undergird the reproductive choices that women make, and it also narrows the focus of our political goals to the question of criminalization of abortion. Ironically, I will contend, while the pro-choice and pro-life camps on the abortion debate are often articulated as polar opposites, both depend on similar operating assumptions that do nothing to support either life or real choice for women of color. In developing this analysis, I seek to build on previous scholarship that centers women of color as well as reflect on my fifteen years as an activist in the reproductive justice movement through such organizations as Illinois National Abortion and Reproductive Rights Action League (NARAL), the Chicago Abortion Fund, Women of All Red Nations, Incite! Women of Color Against Violence, and Committee on Women, Population and the Environment. I begin by examining the limitations of the pro-life position. I then explore the problems with the pro-choice position. The paper concludes with suggestions for moving beyond this binary stalemate between "pro-life" and "pro-choice."

Pro-life Politics, Criminalization of Abortion, and the Prison Industrial Complex

The fetus is a life—but sometimes that life must be ended.

—*Jeanette Bushnell, Seattle-based Native health activist* (2004)

The pro-life position maintains that the fetus is a life; hence abortion should be criminalized. Consequently, the pro-life camp situates its position around moral claims regarding the sanctity of life. In a published debate on pro-life versus pro-choice positions on the issue of abortion, Gray Crum (former vice-president of South Carolina Citizens for Life) argues that the pro-life position is "ethically pure" (Crum and McCormack 1992, 54). Because of the moral weight he grants to the protection of the life of the fetus, Crum contends that abortion must be criminalized. Any immoral actions that impact others should be a "serious crime under the law" (1992, 28). The pro-choice position counters this argument by asserting that the fetus is not a life, and hence policy must be directed toward protecting a woman's ability to control her own body. To quote sociologist Thelma McCormack's response to Crum: "Life truly begins in the . . . hospital room, not in the womb" (Crum and McCormack 1992, 121). Gloria Feldt, president of Planned Parenthood, similarly asserts that if the fetus is established as a life, the principles of *Roe v. Wade* must necessarily be discarded (Feldt 2004, 90).

Jeanette Bushnell's statement that "*The fetus is a life—but sometimes that life must be ended*" suggests, however, a critical intervention in the pro-life argument. That is, the major flaw in the pro-life position is NOT the claim that the fetus is a life, but the conclusion it draws from this assertion: that because the fetus is a life, abortion should be criminalized. In this regard, reproductive rights activists and scholars could benefit from the analysis of the anti-prison movement which questions criminalization as an appropriate response to social issues. As I shall demonstrate, assuming a criminal justice regime fails to address social problems or to adjudicate reproductive issues and results in further marginalization of poor women and women of color. To make this connection,

I must first provide a critical history of the failures of the prison system to deal effectively with social problems.

The anti-prison industrial complex movement has highlighted the complete failure of the prison system to address social concerns. In fact, not only do prisons not solve social problems, such as "crime," they are more likely to increase rather than decrease crime rates (Currie 1998; Donziger 1996; Walker 1998). Most people in prison are there for drug or poverty-related crimes. Prisons do not provide treatment for drug addiction, and it is often easier to access drugs in prison than on the outside. For people who are in prison because of poverty-related crimes, a prison record ensures that it will be much more difficult for them to secure employment once they are released. Consistently, study after study indicates that prisons do not have an impact on decreasing crime rates. . . . In fact, changes in crime rates often have more to do with fluctuations in employment rates than with increased police surveillance or increased incarceration rates (Box and Hale 1982; Jankovic 1977). In addition, as documented by prison activist groups such as the Prison Activist Resource Center, government monies are siphoned away from education and social services into prisons, thus destabilizing communities of color and increasing their vulnerability to incarceration (Prison Activist Resource Center 2004).

The failure of prisons is well known to policymakers. . . . Given that this failure is well known, it then becomes apparent that the purpose of prisons has never been to stop crime. Rather, as a variety of scholars and activists have argued, the purpose has been in large part to control the population of communities of color. . . . In 1994, for instance, one out of every three African American men between the ages of 20 and 29 was under some form of criminal justice supervision (Mauer 1999). Two-thirds of men of color in California between the ages of 18 and 30 have been arrested (Donziger 1996, 102–4). Six of every ten juveniles in federal custody are American Indian and two-thirds of women in prison are women of color (Prison Activist Resource Center 2004).

In a statement that also applies to the criminalization of abortion, Davis further argues that it is critical to disarticulate the equation between crime and punishment because the primary purpose is not to solve the problem of crime. . . . Prisons simply are not only ineffective institutions for addressing social concerns, they drain resources from institutions that could be more effective. They also mark certain peoples, particularly people of color, as inherently "criminal," undeserving of civil and political rights—thus increasing their vulnerability to poverty and further criminalization.

Davis's principle of disarticulation is critical in reassessing the pro-life position. That is, whether or not one perceives abortion to be a crime, it does not therefore follow that punishment in the form of imprisonment is a necessary response. Criminalization individualizes solutions to problems that are the result of larger economic, social, and political conditions. Consequently, it is inherently incapable of solving social problems or addressing crime. . . . Thus, even if we hold that a top social priority is to reduce the number of abortions, there is no evidence to suggest that involving the criminal justice system will accomplish that goal, given that it has not been effective in reducing crime rates or addressing social problems. In addition, increased criminalization disproportionately affects people of color—and in the case of abortion, women of color and poor women. An interrogation of the assumptions behind the pro-life movement suggests that what distinguishes the pro-life position is not so much a commitment to life (since criminalization promotes death rather than life, particularly in communities of color and poor communities), but rather a commitment to criminal justice interventions in reproductive justice issues. . . .

. . . The pro-life position implicitly supports the prison industrial complex by unquestioningly supporting a criminal justice approach that legitimizes rather than challenges the prison system. As Davis (2003) argues, it is not sufficient to challenge the criminal justice system; we must build alternatives to it. Just as the women of color anti-violence movement is currently developing strategies for ending violence (Smith 2005/in press), a consistent pro-life position would require activists to develop responses to abortion that do not rely on the prison industrial complex. Otherwise, these pro-life activists will continue to support policies that are brutally oppressive, particularly to communities of color and poor communities.

Interestingly, this critique of the prison system is prevalent even within conservative evangelical circles. For example, Charles Colson, a prominent Christian Right activist, founder of Prison Fellowship, and former attorney with the Nixon administration, served time in prison for his role in the Watergate break-in.

Following his imprisonment, Colson began to work on prison reform, organizing the Prison Fellowship and its associated lobbying arm, Justice Fellowship. . . . In fact, Colson argues that 50 percent of people in prison today should be released immediately (Fager 1982, 23). To quote Colson:

> The whole system of punishment today is geared toward taking away people's dignity, putting them in an institution, and locking them up in a cage. Prisons are overcrowded, understaffed, dirty places. Eighty percent of American prisons are barbaric— not just brutal, but barbaric. . . . Prison as a punishment is a failure. Mandatory sentences and longer sentences are counterproductive. . . the tougher the laws, I'm convinced, the more lawless and violent we will become. As for public safety, it can hardly be said that prisons contribute to public safety. . . . Prisons obviously are not deterring criminal conduct. The evidence is overwhelming that the more people we put in prison, the more crime we have. All prisons do is warehouse human beings and at exorbitant cost. (Colson 1983, 15; Fager 1982, 23; Forbes 1982,34)

Yet, despite his sustained critique of the failure of the prison system, Colson never critiques the wisdom of criminalization as the appropriate response to abortion. In the name of promoting life, the pro-life movement supports one of the biggest institutions of violence and death in this society. But given that this critique of criminalization is not inaccessible to large sectors of the pro-life movement, there should be opportunities to make anti-criminalization interventions into pro-life discourse. Thus, the major flaw in the pro-life position is not so much its claim that the fetus is a life, but its assumption that because the fetus is a life, abortion should be criminalized. A commitment to criminalization of social issues necessarily contributes to the growth of the prison system because it reinforces the notion that prisons are appropriate institutions for addressing social problems rather than causes of the problems. Given the disproportionate impact of criminalization on communities of color, support for criminalization as public policy also implicitly supports racism.

In addition, I am suggesting that those committed to pro-choice positions will be more effective and politically consistent if they contest the pro-life position from an anti-prison perspective. For instance, increasingly, poor women and women of color are finding their pregnancies criminalized. As Dorothy Roberts (1997) and others have noted, women of color are more likely to be arrested and imprisoned for drug use because, as a result of greater rates of poverty in communities of color, they are more likely to be in contact with government agencies where their drug use can be detected. While white pregnant women are slightly *more* likely to engage in substance abuse than black women, public health facilities and private doctors are more likely to report black women than white women to criminal justice authorities (Maher 1990; Roberts 1997, 175). Meanwhile, pregnant women who would like treatment for their addiction can seldom get it because treatment centers do not meet the needs of pregnant women. One study found that two-thirds of drug treatment centers would not treat pregnant women (Roberts 1997, 189). Furthermore, the criminalization approach is more likely to drive pregnant women who are substance abusers from seeking prenatal or other forms of health care for fear of being reported to the authorities (Roberts 1997, 190). Roberts critiques communities of color for often supporting the criminalization of women of color who have addictions and for failing to understand this criminalization as another strategy of white supremacy that blames women for the effects of poverty and racism. Lisa Maher (1990) and Rickie Solinger (2001, 148) note that a simple choice perspective is not effective for addressing this problem because certain women become marked as women who make "bad choices" and hence deserve imprisonment.

Similarly, Elizabeth Cook-Lynn (1998) argues in "The Big Pipe Case" that at the same time Native peoples were rallying around Leonard Peltier, no one stood beside Marie Big Pipe when she was incarcerated on a felony charge of "assault with intent to commit serious bodily harm" because she breast-fed her child while under the influence of alcohol. She was denied services to treat her substance abuse problem and access to abortion services when she became pregnant. But not only did her community not support her, it supported her incarceration. Cook-Lynn argues that in doing so, the community supported the encroachment of U.S. federal jurisdiction on tribal lands for an issue that would normally be under tribal jurisdiction (1998, 110–25). Cook-Lynn recounts how this demonization of Native women was assisted by the publication of Michael Dorris's (1989) *The Broken Cord*, which narrates his adoption of a Native child who suffered from fetal alcohol syndrome. While this book has been crucial in sensitizing many communities to the realities of fetal alcohol syndrome, it also portrays the mother of the child unsympathetically and advocates repressive legislative solutions targeted against women substance abusers. Thus, within Native communities, the growing demonization of Native women substance abusers has prompted tribes to collude with the federal government in whittling away their own sovereignty.

In the larger society, Barbara Harris started an organization called CRACK (Children Requiring a Caring Kommunity) in Anaheim, California, which gives women $200 to have sterilizations. Their mission is to "'save our welfare system' and the world from the exorbitant cost to the taxpayer for each 'drug addicted birth' by offering 'effective preventive measures to reduce the tragedy of numerous drug-affected pregnancies'" (Kigvamasud'Vashi 2001). Some of CRACK's initial billboards read, "Don't let a pregnancy ruin your drug habit" (Kigvamasud'Vashi 2001). The organization has since opened chapters in several cities around the country, and has changed its name to Positive Prevention to present a less inflammatory image. Nonetheless, its basic message is the same—that poor women who are substance abusers are the cause of social ills and that the conditions that give rise to poor women becoming substance abusers do not need to be addressed.

Unfortunately, as both Roberts (1997) and Cook-Lynn (1998) point out, even communities of color, including those who identify as both pro-life and pro-choice, have supported the criminalization of women of color who have addiction issues. The reason they support this strategy is because they focus on what they perceive to be the moral culpability of women of color for not protecting the life of their children. If we adopt an anti-prison perspective, however, it becomes clear that even on the terms of moral culpability (which I am not defending) it does not follow that the criminal justice approach is the appropriate way to address this social concern. In fact, criminal justice responses to unwanted pregnancies and/or pregnant women who have addiction issues demonstrate an inherent contradiction in the pro-life position. Many pro-life organizations have been ardent opponents of population control programs and policies—advocating against the promotion of dangerous contraceptives or the promotion of sterilization in third-world countries. Yet, their position depends on the prison industrial complex that is an institution of population control for communities of color in the United States.

Meanwhile, many pro-choice organizations, such as Planned Parenthood, have supported financial incentives for poor and criminalized women to be sterilized or to take long-acting hormonal contraceptives (Sale-tan 2003). As I will discuss later, part of this political inconsistency is inherent in the articulation of the pro-choice position. But another reason is that many in the pro-choice camp have also not questioned criminalization as the appropriate response for addressing reproductive health concerns. The pro-choice camp may differ from pro-life groups regarding which acts should be criminalized, but it does not necessarily question the criminalization regime itself.

The Pro-choice Position and Capitalism

The pro-choice camp claims a position that offers more choices for women making decisions about their reproductive lives. A variety of scholars and activists have critiqued the choice paradigm because it rests on essentially individualist, consumerist notions of "free" choice that do not take into consideration all the social, economic, and political conditions that frame the so-called choices that women are forced to make (Patchesky 1990; Smith 1999; Solinger 2001). Solinger further contends that in the 1960s and 1970s, abortion rights advocates initially used the term "rights" rather than choice; rights are understood as those benefits owed to all those who are human regardless of access to special resources. By contrast, argues Solinger, the concept of choice is connected to possession of resources, thus creating a hierarchy among women based on who is capable of making legitimate choices (2001, 6). Consequently, since under a capitalist system, those with resources are granted more choices, it is not inconsistent to withdraw reproductive rights choices from poor women through legislation such as the Hyde Amendment (which restricts federal funding for abortion) or family caps for TANF (Temporary Assistance for Needy Families) recipients. Solinger's argument can be demonstrated in the writings of Planned Parenthood. In 1960, Planned Parenthood commissioned a study which concluded that poor and working-class families lacked the rationality to do family planning, and that this lack of "rationality and early family planning as middle-class couples" was "embodied in the particular personalities, world views, and ways of life" of the poor themselves (Rainwater 1960, 5, 167). As Solinger states:

> "Choice" also became a symbol of middle-class women's arrival as independent consumers. Middle-class women could afford to choose. They had earned the right to choose motherhood, if they liked. According to many Americans, however, when choice was associated with poor women, it became a symbol of illegitimacy. Poor women had not earned the right to choose. (2001, 199–200)

What Solinger's analysis suggests is that, ironically, while the pro-choice camp contends that the pro-life position diminishes the rights of women in favor of "fetal" rights; the pro-choice position actually does not ascribe inherent rights to women either. Rather, women are viewed as having reproductive choices if they can afford them or if they are deemed legitimate choice-makers.

William Saletan's (1998) history of the evolution of the pro-choice paradigm illustrates the extent to which this paradigm is a conservative one. Saletan contends that pro-choice strategists, generally affiliated with National Abortion and Reproductive Rights Action League (NARAL), intentionally rejected a rights-based framework in favor of one that focused on privacy from *big government*. That is, government should not intervene in the woman's right to decide if she wants to have children. This approach appealed to those with libertarian sensibilities who otherwise might have had no sympathy with feminist causes. The impact of this strategy was that it enabled the pro-choice side to keep *Roe v. Wade* intact—but only in the most narrow sense. This strategy undermined any attempt to achieve a broader pro-choice agenda because the strategy could be used against a broader agenda. For instance, the argument that government should not be involved in reproductive rights decisions could also be used by pro-life advocates against federal funding for abortions (Saletan 2003). Consequently, Saletan argues, "Liberals have not won the struggle for abortion rights. Conservatives have" (1998, 114).

Furthermore, this narrow approach has contributed to some pro-choice organizations, such as Planned Parenthood and

NARAL, often developing strategies that marginalize women of color. Both supported the Freedom of Choice Act in the early 1990s that retained the Hyde Amendment (Saletan 2003). The Hyde Amendment, besides discriminating against poor women by denying federal funding for abortion services, discriminates against American Indian women who largely obtain healthcare through Indian Health Services, a federal agency. One of NARAL's petitions stated: "The Freedom of Choice Act (FOCA) will secure the original vision of *Roe v. Wade*, giving *all* women reproductive freedom and securing that right for future generations [emphasis mine]." Apparently, poor women and indigenous women do not qualify as "women."[6]

Building on this analysis, I would argue that while there is certainly a sustained critique of the choice paradigm, particularly among women of color reproductive rights groups, the choice paradigm continues to govern much of the policies of mainstream groups in a manner that sustains the marginalization of women of color, poor women, and women with disabilities. One example is the extent to which pro-choice advocates narrow their advocacy around legislation that affects the one choice of whether or not to have an abortion without addressing all the conditions that gave rise to a woman having to make this decision in the first place. Consequently, politicians, such as former President Bill Clinton, will be heralded as "pro-choice" as long as they do not support legislative restrictions on abortion regardless of their stance on other issues that may equally impact the reproductive choices women make. Clinton's approval of federal welfare reform that places poor women in the position of possibly being forced to have an abortion because of cuts in social services, while often critiqued, is not viewed as an "anti-choice" position. On Planned Parenthood's and NARAL's websites (www.plannedparenthood.org; www.naral.org) there is generally no mention of welfare policies in these organizations' pro-choice legislation alerts.

A consequence of the choice paradigm is that its advocates frequently take positions that are oppressive to women from marginalized communities. For instance, this paradigm often makes it difficult to develop nuanced positions on the use of abortion when the fetus is determined to have abnormalities. Focusing solely on the woman's choice to have or not have the child does not address the larger context of a society that sees children with disabilities as having worthless lives and that provides inadequate resources to women who may otherwise want to have them. As Martha Saxton notes: "Our society profoundly limits the 'choice' to love and care for a baby with a disability" (1998, 375). If our response to disability is to simply facilitate the process by which women can abort fetuses that may have disabilities, we never actually focus on changing economic policies that make raising children with disabilities difficult. Rashmi Luthra (1993) notes, by contrast, that reproductive advocates from other countries such as India, who do not operate from this same choice paradigm, are often able to develop more complicated political positions on issues such as this one.

Another example is the difficulty pro-choice groups have in maintaining a critical perspective on dangerous or potentially dangerous contraceptives, arguing that women should have the "choice" of contraceptives. Many scholars and activists have documented the dubious safety record of Norplant and Depo-Provera, two long-acting hormonal contraceptives (Krust and Assetoyer 1993; Masterson and Guthrie 1986; Roberts 1997; Smith 2001). In fact, lawsuits against Norplant have forced an end to its distribution (although Norplant that remains on the shelves can be sold to women). In 1978, the FDA denied approval for Depo-Provera on the grounds that: (1) dog studies confirmed an elevated rate of breast cancer; (2) there appeared to be an increased risk of birth defects in human fetuses exposed to the drug; and (3) there was no pressing need shown for use of the drug as a contraceptive (Masterson and Guthrie 1986). In 1987, the FDA changed its regulations and began to require cancer testing in rats and mice instead of dogs and monkeys; Depo-Provera did not cause cancer in these animals, but major concerns regarding its safety persist (Feminist Women's Health Centers 1997). Also problematic is the manner in which these contraceptives are frequently promoted in communities of color and often without informed consent (Krust and Assetoyer 1993; Masterson and Guthrie 1986; Smith 2001). Yet none of the mainstream pro-choice organizations have ever seriously taken a position on the issue of informed consent as part of their agenda. Indeed, Gloria Feldt, president of Planned Parenthood, equates opposition to Norplant and Depo-Provera as opposition to "choice" in her book *The War on Choice* (Feldt 2004, 34, 37). Planned Parenthood and NARAL opposed restrictions against sterilization abuse, despite the thousands of women of color who were being sterilized without their consent, because they saw such policies as interfering with a woman's "right to choose" (Nelson 2003, 144; Patchesky 1990, 8).

Particularly disturbing has been some of the support given by these organizations to the Center for Research on Population and Security, headed by Stephen Mumford and Elton Kessel, which distributes globally a form of sterilization, Quinacrine. Quinacrine is a drug that is used to treat malaria. It is inserted into the uterus where it dissolves, causing the fallopian tubes to scar, rendering the woman irreversibly sterile. Family Health International conducted four *in vitro* studies and found Quinacrine to be mutagenic in three of them (Controversy over Sterilization Pellet 1994; Norsigian 1996). It, as well as the World Health Organization, recommended against further trials for female sterilization, and no regulatory body supports Quinacrine. However, the North Carolina-based Center for Research on Population and Security has circumvented these bodies through private funding from such organizations as the Turner Foundation and Leland Fykes organization (which incidentally funds pro-choice *and* anti-immigrant groups). The Center for Research on Population and Security has been distributing Quinacrine for free to researchers and government health agencies. There are field trials in eleven countries, with more than 70,000 women sterilized. In Vietnam, a hundred female rubber plant workers were given routine pelvic exams during which the doctor inserted the Quinacrine without their consent. Thus far, the side effects linked to Quinacrine include ectopic pregnancy, puncturing of the uterus during insertion, pelvic inflammatory disease, and severe abdominal pains. Other possible concerns include heart and liver damage and exacerbation of pre-existing viral conditions. In one of the trials in Vietnam, a large number of cases that had serious side effects were excluded from the data (Controversy over Sterilization Pellet 1994; Norsigian 1996).

Despite the threat to reproductive justice that this group represents, Feminist Majority Foundation featured the Center for Research on Population and Security at its 1996 Feminist Expo because, I was informed by the organizers, they promoted choice for women. Then in 1999, Planned Parenthood almost agreed to sponsor a Quinacrine trial in the United States until outside pressure forced it to change its position (Committee on Women, Population and the Environment 1999). A prevalent ideology within the mainstream pro-choice movement is that women should have the choice to use whatever contraception they want. This position does not consider: (1) that a choice among dangerous contraceptives is not much of a choice (2) the millions of dollars pharmaceutical companies and the medical industry have to promote certain contraceptives, compared to the few women's advocacy groups have to provide alternative information on these same contraceptives; and (3) the social, political, and economic conditions in which women may find themselves are such that using dangerous contraceptives may be the best of even worse options.

One reason that such groups have not taken a position on informed consent in the case of potentially dangerous contraceptives is due to their investment in population control. As Betsy Hartmann (1995) has argued, while contraceptives are often articulated as an issue of choice for white women in the first world, they are articulated as an instrument of population control for women of color and women in the third world (Hartmann 1995). The historical origins of Planned Parenthood are inextricably tied to the eugenics movement. Its founder, Margaret Sanger, increasingly collaborated with eugenics organizations during her career and framed the need for birth control in terms of the need to reduce the number of those in the "lower classes" (Roberts 1997, 73). In a study commissioned in 1960, Planned Parenthood concluded that poor people "have too many children" (Rainwater 1960, 2); yet something must be done to stop this trend in order to "disarm the population bomb" (Rainwater 1960, 178). Today, Planned Parenthood is particularly implicated in this movement as can be seen clearly by the groups it lists as allies on its website (www.plannedparenthood.org): Population Action International, the Population Institute, Zero Population Growth, and the Population Council. A central campaign of Planned Parenthood is to restore U.S. funding to the United Nations Population Fund. In addition it asserts its commitment to addressing *rapid population growth* on this same website. I will not repeat the problematic analysis, critiqued elsewhere, of this population paradigm that essentially blames third-world women for poverty, war, environmental damage, and social unrest, without looking at the root causes of all these phenomena (including population growth)—colonialism, corporate policies, militarism, and economic disparities between poor and rich countries (Bandarage 1997; Hartmann 1995; Silliman and King 1999).

As Hartmann (1995) documents, the United Nations Population Fund has long been involved in coercive contraceptive policies throughout the world. The Population Council produced Norplant and assisted in Norplant trials in Bangladesh and other countries without the informed consent of the trial participants (Hartmann 1995). In fact, trial administrators often refused to remove Norplant when requested (Cadbury 1995). All of these population organizations intersect to promote generally long-acting hormonal contraceptives of dubious safety around the world (Hartmann 1995). Of course, Planned Parenthood provides valuable family planning resources to women around the world as well, but it does so through a population framework that inevitably shifts the focus from family planning as a right in and of itself to family planning as an instrument of population control. While population control advocates, such as Planned Parenthood, are increasingly more sophisticated in their rhetoric and often talk about ensuring social, political, and economic opportunity, the *population* focus of this model still results in its advocates working to reduce population rather than to provide social, political and economic opportunity.

Another unfortunate consequence of uncritically adopting the choice paradigm is the tendency of reproductive rights advocates to make simplistic analyses of who our political friends and enemies are in the area of reproductive rights. That is, all those who call themselves pro-choice are our political allies while all those who call themselves pro-life are our political enemies. An example of this rhetoric is Gloria Feldt's description of anyone who is pro-life as a "right-wing extremist" (Feldt 2004, 5). As I have argued elsewhere, this simplistic analysis of who is politically progressive versus conservative does not actually do justice to the complex political positions people inhabit (Smith 2002). As a result, we often engage uncritically in coalitions with groups that, as anti-violence activist Beth Richie states, "do not pay us back" (2000, 31). Meanwhile, we often lose opportunities to work with people with whom we may have sharp disagreements, but who may, with different political framings and organizing strategies, shift their positions.

To illustrate: Planned Parenthood is often championed as an organization that supports women's rights to choose with whom women of color should ally. Yet, as discussed previously, its roots are in the eugenics movement and today it is heavily invested in the population establishment. It continues to support population control policies in the third world, it almost supported the development of Quinacrine in the United States, and it opposed strengthening sterilization regulations that would protect women of color. Meanwhile, the North Baton Rouge Women's Help Center in Louisiana is a crisis pregnancy center that articulates its pro-life position from an anti-racist perspective. It argues that Planned Parenthood has advocated population control, particularly in communities of color. It critiques the Black Church Initiative for the Religious Coalition for Reproductive Choice for contending that charges of racism against Sanger are *scare tactics* (Blunt 2003, 22). It also attempts to provide its services from a holistic perspective—it provides educational and vocational training, GED classes, literary programs, primary health care and pregnancy services, and child placement services. Its position: "We cannot encourage women to have babies and then continue their dependency on the system. We can't leave them without the resources to care for their children and then say, 'Praise the Lord, we saved a baby'" (Blunt 2003, 23).

It would seem that while the two organizations support some positions that are beneficial to women of color, they both equally support positions that are detrimental to them. If we are truly committed to reproductive justice, why should we presume that we should necessarily work with Planned Parenthood and reject the Women's Help Center? Why would we not instead position ourselves independently from both of these approaches and work to shift their positions to a stance that is truly liberatory for all women?

Beyond Pro-life Versus Pro-choice

To develop an independent position, it is necessary to reject the pro-life versus pro-choice model for understanding reproductive justice. Many reproductive advocates have attempted to expand the definitions of either pro-life or pro-choice depending on which side of this divide they may rest. Unfortunately, they are trying to expand concepts that are inherently designed to exclude the experiences of most women, especially poor women, women of color, indigenous women, and women with disabilities.

If we critically assess the assumptions behind both positions, it is clear that these camps are more similar than they are different. As I have argued, they both assume a criminal justice regime for adjudicating reproductive issues (although they may differ as to which women should be subjected to this regime). Neither position endows women with inherent rights to their body—the pro-life position pits fetal rights against women's rights whereas the pro-choice position argues that women should have freedom to make choices rather than possess inherent rights to their bodies regardless of their class standing. They both support positions that reinforce racial and gender hierarchies that marginalize women of color. The pro-life position supports a criminalization approach that depends on a racist political system that will necessarily impact poor women and women of color who are less likely to have alternative strategies for addressing unwanted pregnancies. Meanwhile, the pro-choice position often supports population control policies and the development of dangerous contraceptives that are generally targeted toward communities of color. And both positions do not question the capitalist system—they focus solely on the decision of whether or not a woman should have an abortion without addressing the economic, political, and social conditions that put women in this position in the first place.

Consequently, it is critical that reproductive advocates develop a framework that does not rest on the pro-choice versus pro-life framework. Such a strategy would enable us to fight for reproductive justice as a part of a larger social justice strategy. It would also free us to think more creatively about who we could work in coalition with while simultaneously allowing us to hold those who claim to be our allies more accountable for the positions they take. To be successful in this venture, however, it is not sufficient to simply articulate a women of color reproductive justice agenda—we must focus on developing a nationally coordinated women of color movement. While there are many women of color reproductive organizations, relatively few actually focus on bringing new women of color into the movement and training them to organize on their own behalf. And to the extent that these groups do exist, they are not generally coordinated as national mobilization efforts. Rather, national work is generally done on an advocacy level with heads of women of color organizations advocating for policy changes, but often working without a solid base to back their demands (Silliman et al. 2005/in press).

Consequently, women of color organizations are not always in a strong position to negotiate with power brokers and mainstream pro-choice organizations or to hold them accountable. As an example, many women of color groups mobilized to attend the 2004 March for Women's Lives in Washington, D.C., in order to expand the focus of the march from a narrow pro-choice abortion rights agenda to a broad-based reproductive rights agenda. While this broader agenda was reflected in the march, it became co-opted by the pro-choice paradigm in the media coverage of the event. My survey of the major newspaper coverage of the march indicates that virtually no newspaper described it as anything other than a pro-choice or abortion rights march. To quote New Orleans health activist Barbara Major, "When you go to power without a base, your demand becomes a request" (2003). Base-building work, on which many women of color organizations are beginning to focus, is very slow work that may not show results for a long time. After all, the base-building of the Christian Right did not become publicly visible for 50 years (Diamond 1989). Perhaps one day, we will have a march for women's lives in which the main issues addressed and reported will include: (1) repealing the Hyde Amendment; (2) stopping the promotion of dangerous contraceptives; (3) decriminalizing women who are pregnant and who have addictions; and (4) ending welfare policies that punish women, in addition to other issues that speak to the intersections of gender, race, and class in reproductive rights policies.

At a meeting of the United Council of Tribes in Chicago, representatives from the Chicago Pro-Choice Alliance informed us that we should join the struggle to keep abortion legal or else we would lose our reproductive rights. A woman in the audience responded, "Who cares about reproductive rights; we don't have any rights, period." What her response suggests is that a reproductive justice agenda must make the dismantling of capitalism, white supremacy, and colonialism *central* to its agenda, and not just as principles added to organizations' promotional material designed to appeal to women of color, with no budget to support making these principles a reality. We must reject single-issue, pro-choice politics of the mainstream reproductive rights movement as an agenda that not only does not serve women of color, but actually promotes the structures of oppression which keep women of color from having real choices or healthy lives.

References

"Abortion-Rights Marchers Crowd D.C." 2004. *Connecticut Post,* April 26.

Bandarage, Asoka. 1997. *Women, Population and Global Crisis*. London: Zed.

Belser, Ann. 2004. "Local Marchers Have Many Issues." *Pittsburgh Post-Gazette,* April 26, A4.

Black, Joe. 2004. "Marchers Rally for Abortion Rights." *Houston Chronicle,* April 26, A1.

Blunt, Sheryl. 2003. "Saving Black Babies." *Christianity Today* 47 (February): 21–23.

Box, Steve, and Chris Hale. 1982. "Economic Crisis and the Rising Prisoner Population in England and Wales." *Crime and Social Justice* 17:20–35.

Bushnell, Jeanette. 2004. Interview with author, 21 May.

Committee on Women, Population and the Environment. 1999. Internal correspondence.

Controversy over Sterilization Pellet. 1994. *Political Environments* 1 (Spring):9.

Cook-Lynn, Elizabeth. 1998. *Why I Can't Read Wallace Stegner and Other Essays*. Madison: University of Wisconsin Press.

Crum, Gary, and Thelma McCormack. 1992. *Abortion: Pro-Choice or Pro-Life*? Washington, DC: American University Press.

Currie, Elliott. 1998. *Crime and Punishment in America*. New York: Metropolitan Books.

Dart, Bob. 2004. "Abortion-Rights Backers March." *Dayton Daily News,* April 26, A1.

Dart, Bob, and Mary Lou Pickel. 2004. "Abortion Rights Supporters March." *Atlanta Journal-Constitution,* April 26, 1A.

Davis, Angela. 2003. *Are Prisons Obsolete*? New York: Seven Stories Press.

Diamond, Sara. 1989. *Spiritual Warfare*. Boston: South End Press.

Diemer, Tom. 2004. "Thousands Rally for Choice: 500,000 to 800,000 March in D.C. in Support of Abortion Rights." *Cleveland Plains Dealer,* April 26, A1.

Donziger, Steven. 1996. *The Real War on Crime*. New York: HarperCollins.

Dorris, Michael. 1989. *The Broken Cord*. New York: Harper & Row.

Feldt, Gloria. 2004. *The War on Choice*. New York: Bantam Books.

Feminist Women's Health Centers. 1997. "Depo-Provera (The Shot)," http://www.fwhc.org/bcdepo.html.

Gadoua, Renee. 2004. "A Woman Should Decide." *Post-Standard*, April 26, B1.

Gibson, Gail. 2004. "Thousands Rally for Abortion Rights." *Baltimore Sun*, April 26, 1A.

Hartmann, Betsy. 1995. *Reproductive Rights and Wrongs: The Global Politics of Population Control*. Boston: South End Press.

Jankovic, Ivan. 1977. "Labour Market and Imprisonment." *Crime and Social Justice* 8:17–31.

Kigvamasud'Vashi, Theryn. 2001. "Fact Sheet on Positive Prevention/CRACK (Children Requiring a Caring Kommunity)." Seattle: Communities Against Rape and Abuse.

Krust, Lin, and Charon Assetoyer. 1993. "A Study of the Use of Depo-Provera and Norplant by the Indian Health Services." Lake Andes: South Dakota: Native American Women's Health Education Resource Center.

Luthra, Rashmi. 1993. "Toward a Reconceptualization of 'Choice': Challenges at the Margins." *Feminist Issues* 13 (Spring):41–54.

Madigan, Erin. 2004. "Hundreds of Thousands March for Abortion Rights." *Milwaukee Journal Sentinel*, April 26, 3A.

Maher, Lisa. 1990. "Criminalizing Pregnancy—The Downside of a Kinder, Gentler Nation?" *Social Justice* 17 (Fall): 111–35.

Major, Barbara. 2003. Keynote Address, National Women's Studies Association National Conference. New Orleans, June.

"Marchers Say Bush Policies Harm Women." 2004. *Marin Independent Journal*, April 26, Nation/World.

Marinucci, Carla. 2004. "Hundreds of Thousands in D.C. Pledge to Take Fight to Polls." *San Francisco Chronicle*, April 26, A1.

Masterson, Mike, and Patricia Guthrie. 1986. "Taking the Shot." *Arizona Republic*, n.p.

Mauer, Marc. 1999. *Race to Incarcerate*. New York: New Press/W.W. Norton.

Mink, Gendolyn, ed. 1999. *Whose Welfare?* Ithaca: Cornell University Press.

Nelson, Jennifer. 2003. *Women of Color and the Reproductive Rights Movement*. New York: New York University Press.

Norsigian, Judy. 1996. "Quinacrine Update." *Political Environments* 3 (Spring):26–27.

O'Rourke, Lawrence. 2004. "Thousands Rally for Abortion Rights." *Star Tribune*, April 26, 1A.

Patchesky, Rosalind. 1990. *Abortion and Woman's Choice*. Boston: Northeastern University Press.

Phelps, Timothy. 2004. "Demonstration in D.C." *New York Newsday*, April 26, A05.

Prison Activist Resource Center. 2004. http://www.prisonactivist.org.

Rainwater, Lee. 1960. *And the Poor Get Children*. Chicago: Quadrangle Books.

Richie, Beth. 2000. "Plenary Presentation." In *The Color of Violence: Violence Against Women of Color*, ed. Incite! Women of Color Against Violence, 124. University of California, Santa Cruz: Incite! Women of Color Against Violence.

Riskind, Jonathan. 2004. "Supporters of Abortion Rights Seek Forefront." *The Columbus Dispatch*, April 25, 1A.

Roberts, Dorothy. 1997. *Killing the Black Body*. New York: Pantheon Books.

Ryan, Joseph. 2004. "Abortion Rights Supporters Jump in to Rejuvenate Cause." *Chicago Daily Herald*, April 26, 15.

Saletan, William. 2003. *Bearing Right*. Berkeley: University of California Press.

——. 1998. "Electoral Politics and Abortion." In *The Abortion Wars*, ed. Rickie Solinger, 111–23. Berkeley: University of California Press.

Saxton, Martha. 1998. "Disability Rights." In *The Abortion Wars*, ed. Rickie Solinger, 374–93. Berkeley: University of California Press.

Segars, Melissa. 2004. "Rally For Women's Rights." *The Capital Times*, April 26, 1A.

Silliman, Jael, Loretta Ross, Marlene Gerber Fried, and Elena Gutierrez. 2005/in press. *Undivided Rights*. Boston: South End Press.

Silliman, Jael, and Ynestra King, eds. 1999. *Dangerous Intersections: Feminist Perspectives on Population, Environment and Development*. Boston: South End Press.

Smith, Andrea. 2005/in press. "Domestic Violence, the State, and Social Change." In *Domestic Violence at the Margins: A Reader at the Intersections of Race, Class, and Gender*, ed. Natalie Sokoloff. New Brunswick: Rutgers University Press.

——. 2002. "Bible, Gender and Nationalism in American Indian and Christian Right Activism." Sanata Cruz: University of California.

——. 2001. "'Better Dead Than Pregnant' The Colonization of Native Women's Health." In *Policing the National Body*, ed. Anannya Bhattacharjee and Jael Silliman, 123–46. Boston: South End Press.

Smith, Justine. 1999. "Native Sovereignty and Social Justice: Moving Toward an Inclusive Social Justice Framework." In *Dangerous Intersections: Feminist Perspectives on Population, Environment and Development*, ed. Jael Silliman and Ynestra King, 202–13. Boston: South End Press.

Smith, Tammie. 2004. "Marchers Call for 'A Choice' About Reproductive Rights." *Richmond Times Dispatch*, April 26, A1.

Solinger, Rickie. 2001. *Beggers and Choosers*. New York: Hill and Wang.

Stephenson, Kathy. 2004. "Utahns Take Part in D.C. and at Home." *Salt Lake Tribune*, April 26, A6.

Sweeney, Annie. 2004. "Chicagoans Head to D.C. for Pro-Choice March." *Chicago Sun-Times*, April 26, 18.

Toner, Robin. 2004. "Abortion Rights Marches Vow to Fight Another Bush Term." *The New York Times*, April 26, A1.

Varoqua, Eman. 2004. "N.J. Supporters Form Large Column for Rights." *The Record*, April 26, A01.

Walker, Samuel. 1998. *Sense and Nonsense About Crime*. Belmont: Wadsworth.

Wolfe, Elizabeth. 2004. "Rights March Packs Mall." *The Commercial Appeal*, April 26, A4.

Wynn, Kelli. 2004. "Hundreds Go to D.C. for March Today." *Dayton Daily News*, April 25, B1.

Outcast Mothers and Surrogates: Racism and Reproductive Politics in the Nineties (1993)

Angela Davis

Angela Davis is a professor in the History of Consciousness program at the University of California at Santa Cruz. A long time activist and scholar, Davis is the author of a number of books: Women, Race and Class *(1981),* Women, Culture and Politics *(1989) and the forthcoming* Blues Legacies and Black Feminism *(1998).*

Davis' concern in this essay stems from the way modern reproductive technologies, such as surrogacy and in-vitro fertilization, can be used to perpetuate sexist and racist notions of motherhood. Drawing connections between nineteenth century slave moth-

erhood and a variety of twentieth century forms, Davis contends that reproduction is far more than an individually-defined experience—it is a political site where women are praised or condemned depending on their race and class.

The historical construction of women's reproductive role, which is largely synonymous with the historical failure to acknowledge the possibility of reproductive self-determination, has been informed by a peculiar constellation of racist and misogynist assumptions. These assumptions have undergone mutations even as they remain tethered to their historical origins. To explore the politics of reproduction in a contemporary context is to recognize the growing intervention of technology into the most intimate spaces of human life: from computerized bombings in the Persian Gulf, that have taken life from thousands of children and adults as if they were nothing more than the abstract statistics of a video game, to the complex technologies awaiting women who wish to transcend biological, or socially induced infertility. I do not mean to suggest that technology is inherently oppressive. Rather, the socioeconomic conditions within which reproductive technologies are being developed, applied, and rendered accessible or inaccessible maneuver them in directions that most often maintain or deepen misogynist, anti-working class, and racist marginalization.

To the extent that fatherhood is denied as a socially significant moment in the process of biological reproduction, the politics of reproduction hinge on the social construction of motherhood. The new developments in reproductive technology have encouraged the contemporary emergence of popular attitudes—at least among the middle classes—that bear a remarkable resemblance to the nineteenth-century cult of motherhood, including the moral, legal, and political taboos it developed against abortion. While the rise of industrial capitalism led to the historical obsolescence of the domestic economy and the ideological imprisonment of (white and middle-class) women within a privatized home sphere, the late twentieth-century breakthroughs in reproductive technology are resuscitating that ideology in bizarre and contradictory ways. Women who can afford to take advantage of the new technology—who are often career women for whom motherhood is no longer a primary or exclusive vocation—now encounter a mystification of maternity emanating from the possibility of transcending biological (and socially defined) reproductive incapacity. It is as if the recognition of infertility is now a catalyst—among some groups of women—for a motherhood quest that has become more compulsive and more openly ideological than during the nineteenth century. Considering the anti-abortion campaign, it is not difficult to envision this contemporary ideological mystification of motherhood as central to the efforts to deny all women the legal rights that would help shift the politics of reproduction toward a recognition of our autonomy with respect to the biological functions of our bodies.

In the United States, the nineteenth-century cult of motherhood was complicated by a number of class- and race-based contradictions. Women who had recently immigrated from Europe were cast, like their male counterparts, into the industrial proletariat, and were therefore compelled to play economic roles that contradicted the increasing representation of women as wives/mothers. Moreover, in conflating slave motherhood and the reproduction of its labor force, the moribund slave economy effectively denied motherhood to vast numbers of African women. My female ancestors were not led to believe that, as women, their primary vocation was motherhood. Yet slave women were imprisoned within their reproductive role as well. The same sociohistorical reasons for the ideological location of European women in an increasingly obsolete domestic economy as the producers, nurturers, and rearers of children caused slave women to be valuated in accordance with their role as breeders. Of course, both motherhood, as it was ideologically constructed , and breederhood, as it historically unfolded, were contingent upon the biological birth process. However, the one presumed to capture the moral essence of womaness, while the other denied, on the basis of racist presumptions and economic necessity, the very possibility of morality and thus also participation in this motherhood cult.

During the first half of the nineteenth century, when the industrial demand for cotton led to the obsessive expansion of slavery at a time when the importation of Africans was no longer legal, the "slaveocracy" demanded of African women that they bear as many children as they were biologically capable of bearing. Thus, many women had 14, 15, 16, 17, 18, 19, 20 children. My own grandmother, whose parents were slaves, was one of 13 children.

At the same time, therefore, that nineteenth-century white women were being ideologically incarcerated within their biological reproductive role, essentialized as mothers, African women were forced to bear children, not as evidence of their role as mothers, but for the purpose of expanding the human property held by slave owners. The reproductive role imposed upon African slave women bore no relationship to a subjective project of motherhood. In fact, as Toni Morrison's novel, *Beloved,* indicates—inspired as it is by an actual historical case of a woman killing her daughter—some slave women committed infanticide as a means of resisting the enslavement of their progeny.

Slave women were *birth mothers* or *genetic mothers* —to employ terms rendered possible by the new reproductive technologies—but they possessed no legal rights as mothers of any kind. Considering the commodification of their children—and indeed, of their own persons—their status was similar to that of the contemporary *surrogate mother.* I am suggesting that the term *surrogate mother* might be invoked as a retroactive description of their status because the economic appropriation of their reproductive capacity reflected the inability of the slave economy to produce and reproduce its own laborers—a limitation with respect to the forces of economic production that is being transformed in this era of advanced capitalism by the increasing computerization and robotization of the economy.

The children of slave mothers could be sold away by their owners for business reasons or as a result of a strategy of repression. They could also be forced to give birth to children fathered by their masters, knowing full well that the white fathers would never recognize their Black children as offspring. As a consequence of the socially constructed invisibility of the white father—a pretended invisibility strangely respected by the white and Black community alike—Black children would grow up in an intimate relation to their white half-brothers and sisters, except that their biological kinship, often revealed by a visible physical resemblance, would remain shrouded in silence. That feature of slave motherhood was something about which no one could speak. Slave women who had been compelled—or had, for their own reasons, agreed—to engage in sexual intercourse with their masters would be committing the equivalent of a crime if they publicly revealed the fathers of their children.[1] These women knew that it was quite likely that their children might also be sold or brutalized or beaten by their own fathers, brothers, uncles, or nephews.

If I have lingered over what I see as some of the salient reproductive issues in African-American women's history, it is because they seem to shed light on the ideological context of contemporary technological intervention in the realm of reproduction. Within the contemporary feminist discourse about the new reproductive technologies—in vitro fertilization, surrogacy, embryo transfer, etc.—concern has been expressed about what is sometimes described as the "deconstruction of motherhood"[2] as a unified biological process. While the new technological developments have rendered the fragmentation of maternity more obvious, the economic system of slavery fundamentally relied upon alienated and fragmented maternities, as women were forced to bear children, whom masters claimed as potentially profitable labor machines. Birth mothers could not therefore expect to be mothers in the legal sense. Legally these children were chattel and therefore motherless. Slave states passed laws to the effect that children of slave women no more belonged to their biological mothers than the young of animals belonged to the females that birthed them.[3]

At the same time, slave women and particularly those who were house slaves were expected to nurture and rear and mother the children of their owners. It was not uncommon for white children of the slave-owning class to have relationships of a far greater emotional intensity with the slave women who were their "mammies" than with their own white biological mothers. We might even question the meaning of this conception of "biological motherhood" in light of the fact that the Black nurturers of these white children were frequently "wet nurses" as well. They nourished the babies in their care with the milk produced by their own hormones. It seems, therefore, that Black women were not only treated as surrogates with respect to the reproduction of slave labor, they also served as surrogate mothers for the white children of the slave-owners.

A well-known lullaby that probably originated during slavery has been recorded in some versions that powerfully reflect the consciousness of slave women who were compelled to neglect their own children, while lavishing their affection on the children of their masters. "Hushaby,/Don't you cry/Go to sleep, little baby./And when you wake,/You shall have a cake/And all the pretty little ponies."[4]

In all likelihood, this version—or verse—was directed to the white babies, while the following one evoked the forced isolation of their own children: "Go to sleep, little baby,/When you wake/ You shall have/All the mulies in the stable./Buzzards and flies/ Picking out its eyes,/Pore little baby crying,/Mamma, mamma!"[5]

A similar verse was sung to a lullaby entitled "Ole Cow": "Ole cow, ole cow,/Where is your calf?/Way down yonder in the meadow/The buzzards and the flies/A-pickin' out its eyes,/The po' little thing cried, Mammy."[6]

The economic history of African-American women—from slavery to the present—like the economic history of immigrant women, both from Europe and colonized or formerly colonized nations, reveals the persisting theme of work as household servants. Mexican women and Irish women, West Indian women and Chinese women have been compelled, by virtue of their economic standing, to function as servants for the wealthy. They have cleaned their houses and—our present concern—they have nurtured and reared their employers' babies. They have functioned as surrogate mothers. Considering this previous history, is it not possible to imagine the possibility that poor women—especially poor women of color—might be transformed into a special caste of hired pregnancy carriers? Certainly such fears are not simply the product of an itinerant imagination. In any event, whether or not such a caste of women baby-bearers eventually makes its way into history, these historical experiences constitute a socio-historical backdrop for the present debate around the new reproductive technologies. The very fact that the discussion over surrogacy tends to coincide, by virtue of corporate involvement and intervention in the new technologies, with the debate over surrogacy for profit, makes it necessary to acknowledge historical economic precedents for surrogate motherhood. Those patterns are more or less likely to persist under the impact of the technology in its market context. The commodification of reproductive technologies, and, in particular, the labor services of pregnant surrogate mothers, means that money is being made and that, therefore, someone is being exploited.

Once upon a time—and this is still the case outside the technologically advanced capitalist societies—a woman who discovered that she was infertile would have to reconcile herself to the impossibility of giving birth to her own biological offspring. She would therefore either try to create a life for herself that did not absolutely require the presence of children, or she chose to enter into a mothering relationship in other ways. There was the possibility of foster motherhood, adoptive motherhood, or play motherhood.[7] This last possibility is deeply rooted in the Black community tradition of extended families and relationships based both on biological kinship—though not necessarily biological motherhood—and on personal history, which is often as binding as biological kinship. But even within the biological network itself, relationships between, for example, an aunt and niece or nephew, in the African-American and other family traditions, might be as strong or stronger than those between a mother and daughter or son.

My own mother grew up in a family of foster parents with no siblings. Her best friend had no sisters and brothers either, so they invented a sister relation between them. Though many years passed before I became aware that they were not "really" sisters, this knowledge had no significant impact on me: I considered my Aunt Elizabeth no less my aunt later than during the earlier years of my childhood. Because she herself had no children, her relation to me, my sister, and two brothers was one of a second mother.

If she were alive and in her childbearing years today, I wonder whether she would bemoan the fact that she lacked the financial resources to employ all the various technological means available to women who wish to reverse their infertility. I wonder if she would feel a greater compulsion to fulfill a female vocation of motherhood. While working-class women are not often in the position to explore the new technology, infertile women—or the wives/partners of infertile men—who are finally able to do so are increasingly expected to try everything. They are expected to try in vitro fertilization, embryo transplants, surrogacy. The availability of the technology further mythologizes motherhood as the true vocation of women. In fact, the new reproductive medicine sends out a message to those who are capable of receiving it: motherhood lies just beyond the next technology. The consequence is an ideological compulsion toward a palpable goal: a child one creates either via one's own reproductive activity or via someone else's.

Those who opt to employ a surrogate mother will participate in the economic as well as ideological exploitation of her services. And the woman who becomes a surrogate mother earns relatively low wages. A few years ago, the going rate was twenty thousand dollars. Considering the fact that pregnancy is a 24-hour-a-day job, what might seem like a substantial sum of money is actually not even a minimum wage. This commodification of motherhood is quite frightening in the sense that it comes forth as permission to allow women and their partners to participate in a program that is generative of life. However, it seems that what is really generated is sexism and profits.

The economic model evoked by the relationship between the surrogate mother and the woman [or man] who makes use of her services is the feudalistic bond between servant and her employer. Because domestic work has been primarily performed in the United States by women of color, native-born as well as recent immigrants (and immigrant women of European descent), elements of racism and class bias adhere to the concept of surrogate motherhood as potential historical features, even in the contemporary absence of large numbers of surrogate mothers of color.

If the emerging debate around the new reproductive technologies is presently anchored to the socioeconomic conditions of relatively affluent families, the reproductive issues most frequently associated with poor and working-class women of color revolve around the apparent proliferation of young single parents, especially in the African-American community. For the last decade or so, teenage pregnancy has been ideologically represented as one of the greatest obstacles to social progress in the most impoverished sectors of the Black community. In actuality, the *rate* of teenage pregnancy in the Black community—like that among white teenagers—has been waning for quite a number of years. According to a National Research Council study, fertility rates in 1960 were 156 births per 1,000 Black women aged 15 to 19, and 97 in 1985.[8] What distinguishes teenage pregnancy in the Black community today from its historical counterpart is the decreasing likelihood of teenage marriage. There is a constellation of reasons for the failure of young teenagers to consolidate traditional two-parent families. The most obvious one is that it rarely makes economic sense for an unemployed young woman to marry an unemployed young man. As a consequence of shop closures in industries previously accessible to young Black male workers—and the overarching deindustrialization of the economy—young men capable of contributing to the support of their children are becoming increasingly scarce. For a young woman whose pregnancy results from a relationship with an unemployed youth, it makes little sense to enter into a marriage that will probably bring in an extra adult as well as a child to be supported by her own mother/father/grandmother, etc.

The rise of single motherhood cannot be construed, however, as synonymous with the "fall" of the nuclear family within the Black community—if only because it is an extremely questionable proposition that there was such an uncontested structure as the nuclear family to begin with. Historically, family relationships within the Black community have rarely coincided with the traditional nuclear model. The nuclear family, in fact, is a relatively recent configuration, integrally connected with the development of industrial capitalism. It is a family configuration that is rapidly losing its previous, if limited, historical viability: presently, the majority of U.S. families, regardless of membership in a particular cultural or ethnic group, cannot be characterized as "nuclear" in the traditional sense. Considering the gender-based division of labor at the core of the nuclear model, even those families that consist of the mother-father-children nucleus—often popularly referred to as "nuclear families"—do not, rigorously speaking, conform to the nuclear model. The increasingly widespread phenomenon of the "working mother," as opposed to the wife/mother whose economic responsibilities are confined to the household and the children, thoroughly contradicts and renders anachronistic the nuclear family model. Not too many mothers stay at home by choice anymore; not too many mothers can afford to stay at home, unless, of course, they benefit from the class privileges that accrue to the wealthy. In other words, even for those whose historical realities were the basis of the emergence of this nuclear family model, the model is rapidly losing its ability to contain and be responsive to contemporary social/economic/psychic realities.

It angers me that such a simplistic interpretation of the material and spiritual impoverishment of the African-American community as being largely rooted in teenage pregnancy is so widely accepted. This is not to imply that teenage pregnancy is unproblematic. It is extremely problematic, but I cannot assent to the representation of teenage pregnancy as "the problem." There are reasons why young Black women become pregnant and/or desire pregnancy. I do not think I am far off-target when I point out that few young women who choose pregnancy are offered an alternative range of opportunities for self-expression and development. Are those Black teenage girls with the potential for higher education offered scholarships permitting them to study at colleges and universities like Le Moyne? Are teenagers who choose pregnancy offered even a vision of well-paying and creative jobs?

Is it really so hard to grasp why so many young women would choose motherhood? Isn't this path toward adulthood still thrust upon them by the old but persisting ideological constructions of femaleness? Doesn't motherhood still equal adult womanhood in the popular imagination? Don't the new reproductive technologies further develop this equation of womanhood and motherhood? I would venture to say that many young women make conscious decisions to bear children in order to convince themselves that they are alive and creative human beings. As a consequence of this choice, they are also characterized as immoral for not marrying the fathers of their children.

I have chosen to evoke the reproductive issue of single motherhood among teenagers in order to highlight the absurdity of locating motherhood in a transcendent space—as the anti-abortion theorists and activists do—in which involuntary motherhood is as sacred as voluntary motherhood. In this context, there is a glaring exception: motherhood among Black and Latina teens is constructed as a moral and social evil—but even so, they are denied accessible and affordable abortions. Moreover, teen mothers are ideologically assaulted because of their premature and impoverished entrance into the realm of motherhood while older, whiter, and wealthier women are coaxed to buy the technology to assist them in achieving an utterly commodified motherhood.

Further contradictions in the contemporary social compulsion toward motherhood—contradictions rooted in race and class—can be found in the persisting problem of sterilization abuse. While poor women in many states have effectively lost access to abortion, they may be sterilized with the full financial support of the government. While the "right" to opt for surgical sterilization is an important feature of women's control over the reproductive functions of their bodies, the imbalance between the difficulty of access to abortions and the ease of access to sterilization reveals the continued and tenacious insinuation of racism into the politics of reproduction. The astoundingly high—and continually mounting—statistics regarding the sterilization of Puerto Rican women expose one of the most dramatic ways in which women's bodies bear the evidence of colonization. Likewise, the bodies of vast numbers of sterilized indigenous women within the presumed borders of the U.S. bear the traces of a 500-year-old tradition of genocide. While there is as yet no evidence of large-scale sterilization of African-American and Latina teenage girls, there is documented evidence of the federal government's promotion and funding of sterilization operations for young Black girls during the 1960s and 70s. This historical precedent convinces me that it is not inappropriate to speculate about such a future possibility of preventing teenage pregnancy. Or—to engage in further speculation—of recruiting healthy young poor women, a disproportionate number of whom would probably be Black, Latina, Native American, Asian, or from the Pacific Islands, to serve as pregnancy carriers for women who can afford to purchase their services.

A majority of all women in jails and prisons are mothers and 7 to 10 percent are pregnant.[9] On the other hand, women's correctional institutions still incorporate and dramatically reveal their ideological links to the cult of motherhood. Even today, imprisoned women are labeled "deviant," not so much because of the crimes they may have committed, but rather because their attitudes and their behavior are seen as blatant contradictions of prevailing expectations—especially in the judicial and law enforcement systems—of women's place. They are mothers who have failed to find themselves in motherhood.

Since the onset of industrial capitalism, women's "deviance" has been constructed in psychological terms; the site of female incarceration has been less the prison and more the mental institution. For this reason, the population of jails and prisons is majority male and a minority female, while the reverse is the case in the mental institutions. The strategic role of domesticity in the structure and correctional goals of women's prisons revolves around the notion that to rehabilitate women, you must teach them how to be good wives and good mothers. Federal prisons such as Alderson Federal Reformatory for women in West Virginia and state institutions like the California Institute for Women and Bedford Hills in the state of New York attempt to architecturally—albeit mechanistically—evoke family life. Instead of cells there are cottages; here women have historically "learned" how to keep house, wash and iron clothes, do the dishes, etc. What bearing does this have on the politics of reproduction? I would suggest that there is something to be learned from the egregious contradiction of this emphasis on training for motherhood within a prison system that intransigently refuses to allow incarcerated women to pursue any meaningful relationship with their own children.

In the San Francisco Bay area, there are only three alternative institutions where women serving jail sentences may live with their children—the Elizabeth Fry Center, Mandela House, and Keller House. In all three places combined, there is space for about 20 to 25 women. In the meantime, thousands of women in the area suffer the threat—or reality—of having their children taken away from them and made wards of the court. Imprisoned women who admit that they have drug problems and seek to rehabilitate themselves often discover that their admissions are used as evidence of their incapacity to be good mothers. In the jails and prisons where they are incarcerated, they are presumably being taught to be good mothers, even as they are powerless to prevent the state from seizing their own children. Excepting a small minority of alternative "correctional" institutions, where social stereotypes are being questioned (although in some instances, the structure of incarceration itself is left unchallenged), the underlying agenda of this motherhood training is to turn aggressive women into submissive and dependent "mothers," whose children are destined to remain motherless.

The process through which a significant portion of the population of young Black, Latina, Native American, Asian, and Pacific women are criminalized, along with the poor European women, who, by their association with women of color are deemed criminal, hinges on a manipulation of a certain ideological representation of motherhood. A poor teenage Black or Latina girl who is a single mother is suspected of criminality simply by virtue of the fact that she is poor and has had a child "out of wedlock." This process of criminalization affects the young men in a different way—not as fathers, but rather by virtue of a more all-embracing racialization. Any young Black man can be potentially labeled as criminal: a shabby appearance is equated with drug addiction, yet an elegant and expensive self-presentation is interpreted as drug dealing. While it may appear that this process of criminalization is unrelated to the construction of the politics of reproduction, there are significant implications here for the expansion of single motherhood in Black and Latino communities. The 25 percent of African-American men in jails and prisons,[10] for example, naturally find it difficult, even in a vicarious sense, to engage in any significant parenting projects.

In pursuing a few of the ways in which racism—and class bias—inform the contemporary politics of reproduction, I am suggesting that there are numerous unexplored vantage points from which we can reconceptualize reproductive issues. It is no longer acceptable to ground an analysis of the politics of reproduction in a conceptual construction of "woman" as a sex. It is not enough to assume that female beings whose bodies are distinguished by vaginas, ovarian tubes, uteri, and other biological features related to reproduction should be able to claim such "rights" to exercise control over the processes of these organs, as the right to abortion. The social/economic/political circumstances that oppress and marginalize women of various racial, ethnic, and class backgrounds, and thus alter the impact of ideological conceptions of motherhood, cannot be ignored without affirming the same structures of domination that have led to such different—but related—politics of reproduction in the first place.

In conclusion, I will point to some of the strategic constellations that should be taken into consideration in reconceiving an agenda of reproductive rights. I do not present the following points as an exhaustive list of such goals, but rather I am trying to allude to a few of the contemporary issues requiring further theoretical examination and practical/political action. While the multiple arenas in which women's legal abortion rights are presently being assaulted and eroded can account for the foregrounding of this struggle, the failure to regard economic accessibility of birth control and abortion has equally important results in the inevitable marginalization of poor women's reproductive rights. With respect to a related issue, the "right" and access to sterilization is important, but again, it is equally important to look at those economic and ideological conditions that track some women toward sterilization, thus denying them the possibility of bearing and rearing children in numbers they themselves choose.

Although the new reproductive technologies cannot be construed as inherently affirmative or violative of women's reproductive rights, the anchoring of the technologies to the profit schemes of their producers and distributors result in a commodification of motherhood that complicates and deepens power relationships based on class and race. Yet, beneath this marriage of technology, profit, and the assertion of a historically obsolete bourgeois individualism lies the critical issue of the right to determine the character of one's family. The assault on this "right"—a term I have used throughout, which is not, however, unproblematic—is implicated in the ideological offensive against single motherhood as well as in the homophobic refusal to recognize lesbian and gay family configurations—and especially in the persisting denial of custody (even though some changes have occurred) to lesbians with children from previous heterosexual marriages. This is one of the many ways in which the present-day ideological compulsion toward motherhood that I have attempted to weave into all of my arguments further resonates. Moreover, this ideology of motherhood is wedded to an obdurate denial of the very social services women require in order to make meaningful choices to bear or not to bear children. Such services include health care—from the prenatal period to old age—child care, housing, education, jobs, and all the basic services human beings require to lead decent lives. The privatization of family responsibilities—particularly during an era when so many new family configurations are being invented that the definition of family stretches beyond its own borders—takes on increasingly reactionary implications. This is why I want to close with a point of departure: the reconceptualization of family and of reproductive rights in terms that move from the private to the public, from the individual to the social.

NOTES

1. See Harriet A. Jacobs. *Incidents in the Life of a Slave Girl*. Edited and Introduction by Jean Fagan Yellin. Cambridge, Mass.: Harvard University Press, p. 1087.
2. See Michelle Stanworth, ed. *Reproductive Technologies: Gender, Motherhood and Medicine*. Minneapolis: University of Minnesota Press, 1987.
3. See Paula Giddings. *When and Where I Enter: The Impact of Black Women on Race and Sex in America*. New York: William Morrow, 1984.
4. Dorothy Scarborough, *On the Trail of Negro Folksongs*, Hatboro, Pennsylvania: Folklore Associates, Inc., 1963. (original edition published by Harvard University Press, 1925), p. 145.

5. *Ibid.*, p. 148.
6. *Ibid.*
7. The tradition of Black women acting as "play mothers" is still a vital means of inventing kinship relations unrelated to biological origin.
8. Gerald David Jaynes and Robin M. Williams, Jr., ed. *A Common Destiny: Blacks and American Society*, Washington, D.C.: National Academy Press, 1989, p. 515.
9. See Ellen M. Barry. "Pregnant Prisoners," *Harvard Women's Law Journal*, vol. 12, 1989.
10. See Marc Mauer, "Young Black Men and the Criminal Justice System: A Growing National Problem." A Report by the Sentencing Project, 918 F Street, N.W., Suite 501, Washington, D.C. 20004, February 1990.

Questions

1. What are the parallels Davis draws between contemporary surrogate motherhood and slave motherhood? What are Davis' concerns about surrogacy in the 20th century? How can the use of reproductive technologies perpetuate racism and sexism? What relationships between economics and reproduction are evident in this essay?
2. What differences exist among the varied types of motherhood Davis discusses? How does Davis define "motherhood"? What factors influence what form motherhood takes? What factors influence how it is perceived?
3. Why is so much attention paid to the "crisis of black pregnancy"? Why does Davis feel it is problematic? What is contradictory about the situation of mothers who are in prison?

Living Incubator, Fetal Container, or a "Womb with Legs"?

Considering Fetal Personhood and Maternal Subjectivity in Reproductive Images and Technologies

Melanie DeMaeyer

"The library card catalogue contains dozens of entries under the heading 'pregnancy': clinical treatises detailing signs of morbidity; volumes cataloguing studies of foetal development, with elaborate drawings; or popular manuals in which physicians and others give advice on diet and exercise for the pregnant woman . . . No card appears listing a work which is concerned with the subject, the mother as the site of her proceedings."

Iris Marion Young, *Throwing Like a Girl and Other Essays in Feminist Philosophy and Social Theory*

"The moment when all eyes turn away from my belly, and toward the monitor, even I become a passive observer of an 'Other,' an 'Other' which cannot be seen with the eye. For the fetus to be seen as an independent entity, the woman must drop out of the image."

Sharon Lehner, "My Womb, the Mosh Pit"

****

Reprinted by permission of the author.

Simone de Beauvoir writes in *The Second Sex*, "All agree in recognizing the fact that females exist in the human species; today as always they make up about one half of humanity. And yet we are told that femininity is in danger; we are exhorted to be women, remain women, become women," (xiii). But what does it mean to *be* woman, to *remain* woman, *become* woman? What must one do to be seen and interpreted as woman? "Woman? Very simple, say the fanciers of simple formulas: she is a womb, an ovary; she is a female—this word is sufficient to define her," writes Beauvoir (3). In her assessment, society declares that in order for a person to be a woman, she must first and always be a womb, anything less and she is inconsequential, endangering femininity.

But what happens when, as we see today, a pregnant woman has little autonomy and her sole purpose for existence is to be a womb, an existence in which she is reduced to and remains a vessel for the fetus? Contemporary theorist, Lauren Berlant writes, "At this time in America the reproducing woman is no longer cast as a potentially productive citizen, except insofar as she procreates: her capacity for other kinds of creative agency has become an obstacle to national reproduction" (153). As a woman's pregnancy begins to become public, that is, as she shares the information willingly or because her body with its morning sickness or protruding abdomen tells others for her, she becomes a site of concern, often not for herself, but for that of her unborn fetus.

In her essay, "America, 'Fat' the Fetus," Berlant discusses a video her sister gives to her of her nephew's first two years of life. The "document of family-making," as Berlant describes it, begins with a sonogram. Recounting the opening scenes of the video, Berlant observes:

> [It begins] in the sonogram room, where my sister (Valerie), my mother, the technician, and my brother-in-law (Richard) are commenting on the sonogram screen. Valerie and my mother are briefly visible in this scene; otherwise the commentary is *disembodied* and the sonogram *dominates* the frame. Richard's voice carries a great deal of authority—he's a doctor and he knows how to interpret the images Valerie generates. (192, *emphasis mine*)

Valerie, the person who is "generating" images is not seen, her voice while present is not associated visually with a person, and the focus is instead the fetal image on the sonogram screen.

In many ways this is a parallel for the way we see, or rather fail to see, pregnant women. They are not their own subject, or their own being, but instead play "other" to the fetus, the "subject", they are carrying.

Where does this fixation on the fetus originate? One might begin with the technology that allows us to see pregnancy publicly, that is, not just among those we know or the strangers we pass on the street, but the people on our television screens and on magazine covers. Berlant discusses the real-life pregnancy of Lucille Ball on the long running, popular, 1950s sitcom, *I Love Lucy*. Ball's pregnancy was one of the first real-time celebrity pregnancies that American's could watch, and it broke boundaries, as it brought a formerly taboo, private subject into the homes of Americans. Berlant writes of Lucy's comedic attempts to inform her husband, and thus the audience, of her pregnancy:

> This surplus of failed performances reveals the frantic improvisation around the new, often unpredicted knowledge that pregnancy heralds: how do you tell, what do you tell, who do you tell, what are you telling, when should you tell? The technological reconfiguration of privacy through the sign of Lucy's pregnancy does not eliminate the difficulty of these questions but intensifies it, (188).

As Ball's pregnancy progressed so did the comfort level of American's in seeing a real-time public pregnancy; a phenomenon made possible through the technology of cameras and television screens.

What does it mean to be publicly pregnant? Robyn Longhurst found, while doing research for her essay, "Breaking Corporeal Boundaries: Pregnant Bodies in Public Places," that the 31 pregnant women she interviewed "experienced a shrinking of their lifeworlds" (82). Her findings stand in stark contrast to the images of pregnant celebrities we see photographed in great detail on the covers of magazines in our local grocery store checkout. Their bodies it seems are not held to the same standards of the pregnant bodies that Longhurst writes about. She notes, "Pregnant bodies are not to be trusted, rather, they are to be dreaded, when occupying a public space" (82). By contrast, this dread of "everyday" pregnant bodies is caused by the fear that they will not appropriately maintain borders, positions, and rules in the manner of the contained corporeality of the "rational man" in a public space

(Longhurst 84). In a paragraph which links Kristeva's concept of the abject and Grosz's thoughts on women's bodies as "modes of seepage" Longhurst writes:

> Their bodies are often considered to constantly threaten to expel matter from inside—they may vomit, cry, need to urinate more frequently, produce colostrum which may leak from their breasts, have a "show" appear, have their waters break . . . even more than these leakages, they constantly "threaten" to split their one self into two or more. (84)

Posing a challenge to the fear of seeing "ordinary" pregnant women in public spaces, Sandra Matthews and Laura Wexler wrote *Pregnant Pictures* (2000) a compilation of theoretical writing and photographs of pregnant women. Wexler and Matthews sought to address popular notions of the pregnant body as "carnal," "sentimental," and "grotesque" as well as to photograph "the pregnant woman as an individual" (1). Of the joining of their artistic medium and the pregnant woman, they write, "The physical productions of the pregnant body are indiscreet—a subject for the doctor's office, the bedroom, and the private talk of women. Camera work, on the other hand, is tasteful, an appropriate topic for the dinner table conversation, the museum symposium, the chic magazine" (1). They catalog a wide range of images of pregnant women, most interestingly, women whose bodies which might be considered a form of the abject, therefore improper for public viewing.

Additionally, Wexler and Matthews dedicate an entire chapter to the phenomenon of public celebrity pregnancy. They discuss in great detail the now iconic image of actress Demi Moore, on the front cover of *Vanity Fair* and attribute its publication to the beginning of a public pregnant icon (201). The image of Moore, who posed nude for the photograph, is far removed from what most women in the late stages of pregnancy probably feel is accessible, that is the image is not widely representative of the many women who struggle to attain a proper body for the public sphere during pregnancy. In this image taken by famed photographer, Annie Leibowitz, Moore is perfectly coiffed, glamorous, and even a bit incandescent. She shows no signs of the stretch marks, swollen ankles, or fatigue from sleepless nights or the strain of carrying additional weight. All signs of "ordinary" and "everyday" pregnancy are vanished from view through skillful use of airbrushing.

Wexler and Matthews assert that Moore represents a consumable, albeit scandalous version of a pregnant woman, achieving pregnant icon status through the mere glamour she exudes.

Even Moore, whose image spawned numerous copycat photographs, was not allowed to be entirely visible; the issue of *Vanity Fair* was sold with a plastic wrapper and a white sheet of paper covering much of her nude form (Wexler and Matthews 201). Pregnant icons, while still censored to some degree are certainly growing in number since the 1991 photograph of Moore first appeared, but the women in these images still do not represent the women Longhurst spoke to who felt their "lifeworlds" becoming smaller. Carol Stabile attempts to explain this lack of representation in her essay, "Shooting the Mother: Fetal Photography and the Politics of Disappearance":

> In a culture which places such a premium on thinness, the pregnant body is anathema. Not only is it perhaps the most visible and physical mark of sexual difference, it is also the sign for deeply embedded fears about femininity and the female reproductive system. (191)

Therefore, a woman's body which bares the physical markings of pregnancy cannot achieve the status of an icon. Her body will never be interpreted as glamorous, her stretching skin and leaky orifices so threatening to propriety are not safe for public viewing or discourse.

This fear of pregnant women in public spaces is incongruous, as in order to be considered a subject women must first be a womb and when they are wombs women no longer occupy proper bodies for public spaces. If women cannot occupy public spaces, then they cannot be seen as full citizens with the rights and privileges that designation entails. In their article, "Citizen Bodies: Embodying Citizens—A Feminist Analysis," Chris Beasley and Carol Bacchi note that traditionally, "[The] notion of citizenship as active *public* participation privileges 'hegemonic masculinity' as well as marginalizing women, amongst others, given their association with the private sphere. To the extent that citizenship is equated with the public sphere, women are not and cannot be 'full citizens'" (340). Not having access to full citizenship and as a result, lacking full autonomy and bodily integrity leaves women with little power in public discourse and decisions.

The Supreme Court based their ruling, legalizing abortion, in *Roe v. Wade* on the right to privacy, yet in their decision they left room for state intervention into the private lives of women. They argue:

> The pregnant woman cannot be isolated in her privacy. She carries an embryo and, later, a fetus, if one accepts the medical definitions of the developing young in the human uterus . . . it is reasonable and appropriate for the state to decide that at some point in time another interest, that of the health of the mother or that of the potential for human life, becomes significantly involved. The woman's right is no longer sole and any right of privacy she possesses must be measured accordingly. (*Roe v. Wade* 1973 410 U.S. at 158)

Their decision, while granting bodily integrity to women in one breath, takes it away in another. The stipulation in the ruling is not congruent with other Supreme Court rulings dealing with bodily integrity and privacy, particularly when the rulings involve the bodies of men. Modern feminist philosopher, Susan Bordo discusses another Supreme Court ruling, *McFall v. Shimp*, which hinged on the right to privacy and bodily integrity. Bordo writes, "Shimp's bodily integrity was legally protected to the extent that he was permitted to refuse a procedure (a bone-marrow extraction and donation) that could have prevented his cousin's otherwise certain death from aplastic anemia" (73). She notes that similar cases in which a Seattle woman sought to have the father of her child with leukemia donate his bone marrow and one in which a father sued the mother of his son's half-siblings to have tests done for bone marrow matches for his son maintained the precedent (73).

The legal precedent confirmed in these cases and in the case of Shimp, does not extend to the bodies of pregnant women; not in the *Roe* decision and not in the actions which have followed it have women's total bodily integrity or subjectivity been protected or respected. Bordo writes:

> The doctrine of informed consent is a protection of the *subjectivity* of the person involved—that is, it is an acknowledgement that the body can never be regarded merely as a site of quantitative processes that can be assessed objectively, but must be treated as invested with personal meaning, history, and value that are determinable only by the subject who lives "within" it. (74)

If informed consent is not protected for pregnant women then in the eyes of the law they are neither full citizens nor subjects. In one egregious example of disregard for the informed consent of a pregnant woman, George Washington University Hospital won a court order to perform a caesarean section on a terminally ill woman; an order which went against the decisions made by the woman, her husband, and her doctors. The woman and her baby died after the forced operation. Bordo writes, "A woman who *no court in the country would force to undergo a blood transfusion for a dying relative* had come to be legally regarded, when pregnant, as a mere life-support system for a fetus" (77). Other women have been placed in similar positions by the courts and by the Catholic church, namely in situations where families and hospitals have been ordered to keep pregnant women who are brain-dead on life support until the fetus is viable (Bordo 81). In a country where there has been forced sterilization, caesareans, and a whole host of other court-ordered obstetrical interventions/invasions, we see that women's bodies are often considered property of the state as objects for manipulation or experimentation and are subject to its whims and rulings.

Pregnant women's bodies are regarded not only as state property but also as the property of the men who are the fathers of their future children. When interviewed for the television series *Nightline* about "father's rights" during pregnancy one man responded:

> . . . I feel like by her having the right to abort that child is her having the right to destroy a part of me without me having any say-so. And—she—you know, she wants control of her body. *But what about me? Am I not allowed to have control of my body?* That baby is a part of my body also. (Bordo 91, *emphasis mine*)

One must wonder what this would-be father is really interested in: "protecting" the fetus from the woman carrying it, or ensuring, as Susan Bordo so aptly assesses, "that his desires not merely *equal* but *supersede* those of the mother" (89). It seems apparent that he is more interested in the property of his body, the baby which is a part himself he claims to be intrinsically linked to and in addition, clearly what this man wants and others with similar arguments want, is not to have control over their bodies but the bodies of pregnant women. Moreover, by appropriating the language of bodily control this man and other men, who, like him, are members of the National Right to Life Committee, twist feminist rhetoric which argues for the bodily rights of pregnant women and use it to reaffirm their own power. Bordo writes, "[The description] of himself as so intertwined and interconnected with the fetus that not only is *he* 'part of that child'—which is true—but *the child* is a 'part of [his body] as well—which is not true" (92). While this man is not physically linked to the fetus while in utero, as the pregnant woman is, the actions he takes before and during the woman's pregnancy have been shown to impact the fetus, implications of which I will discuss later in this paper.

Women's bodies, in contrast to those of men's, are inherently linked to the fetus they are carrying. Feminist theorist, Luce Irigaray, interviewed Helene Rouch about the relationship between the mother and child in utero, focusing their discussion on placental economy. Rouch describes the placenta as:

> A tissue, formed by the embryo, which while being closely imbricated with the uterine mucosa remains separate from it. There is a commonly held [misconception] that the placenta is a mixed formation, half maternal, half fetal. However, although the placenta is a formation of the embryo, it behaves like an organ that is practically independent of it. It plays a mediating role . . . as the mediating space between the mother and the fetus . . . and a system regulating exchanges between the two organisms. (38)

The placenta is therefore a mutually beneficial organ, which facilitates the life of the pregnant woman and the growth of her fetus. Rouch states that the pregnant body immediately recognizes the embryo as a foreign body and tries to reject it in the manner it would with a transplanted organ, but because of the mediating role of the placenta, her body, and therefore she, does not reject the embryo. Rouch tells Irigaray:

> There has to be a recognition of the other, of the non-self, in order for placental factors to be produced. It's as if the mother always knew that the embryo (and thus the placenta) was other, and that she lets the placenta know this, which then produces the factors enabling the maternal organism to accept it as other. (Irigaray 41)

In this way, it becomes the choice of the pregnant woman's body whether or not she will accept the other, the placenta and thus, the embryo. In a placental economy the pregnant woman has subjectivity, a right she does not have in the public sector where she has been forced from view.

Irigaray writes about the placental economy and the implications for its absence in science and technology:

> The placental economy is an organized economy, one *not in a state of fusion*, which respects the one and the other. Unfortunately our cultures, split off from the natural order—and the scientific methods used to get back to it more often than not accentuate that distance—neglect or fail to recognize the almost ethical character of the fetal relation. (41, *emphasis mine*)

The neglect and failure to recognize which Irigaray writes about can be seen in the ways we are able to view the fetus through photography and other view enhancing technologies. In 1965, ten years after Lucille Ball appeared pregnant on *I Love Lucy, Life* magazine ran Lennart Nilsson's famous series of fetal photographs in an article entitled, "Drama of Life Before Birth" (Berlant 166). This was the first time that American's were able to see a fetus separate from a woman's womb, a feat which relied upon technology to reach the desired effect. "Through back lighting and the deployment and removal of the woman's body, such as the womb, the placenta and the embryonic sac, the effect is created of a live discrete being" (Tyler 80). The series featured one image of a living fetus, while the others photographed had been miscarried or aborted. In order to capture the image of the fetus, in color and in utero, Nilsson had to use a specially developed wide angle lens and a flash attached to a surgical scope (Berlant 166). Imogen Tyler writes in her 2001 essay, "Skin Tight: Celebrity, Pregnancy, and Subjectivity" about the stages of gestational pictures we begin to see following Nilsson's pictorial:

> Early gestational pictures often show the fetus floating within the embryonic sac: a spherical container that stands in for the skin and marks the fetus as separate and self-contained. Later photographs, more clearly depict it as a being with skin; with carefully lit close-ups often of the face, hands, and feet. What is disavowed within these images is not only the *pia mater*, the mother's skin, but also, and as a consequence the pregnant woman who is the structuring absence of these photographs. (80)

Nilsson's pictorial contributed to a discourse which began to separate the body of the pregnant woman from the fetus; depicting the fetus as an entity apart from and not a part of the pregnant woman's body. Separation of the maternal body from that of the fetus gives the still developing fetus personhood, and is an opportunity which allows fetal activists to argue for the protection of fetus from the potentially harmful pregnant woman. So then, who is the subject of pregnancy? Who are we watching, is it the pregnant woman or the fetus? Can women ever be their own subject, or must they always exist in relation to someone, whether it is to man or fetus, or both? If one must be a womb in order to be a woman, a participant in society and reproduction, what happens once this is accomplished? Must her bodily integrity be relinquished; was it ever really hers to begin with? Beauvoir writes, "The close bond between mother and child will be for her a source or dignity or indignity according to the value placed upon the child—which is highly variable—and this very bond, as we have seen will be recognized or not according to the presumptions of the society concerned" (36). We see this very value in who we choose to see as a full subject, whether it be to the mother or to the fetus.

In her 1981 essay, "Pregnant Embodiment: Subjectivity and Alienation," Iris Marion Young discusses the pregnant woman's relationship to the fetus, "She feels the movements of the fetus, the contractions of her uterus, with an immediacy and certainty that no one can share" (59). At the time of the essay's original publication, sonograms, fetal heart monitors, and the fetal monitor during labor were just beginning to be used to monitor the bodies of pregnant women. Young states:

> Recently invented machines tend to devalue [the knowledge of the mother]. The fetal-heart sensor projects the heartbeat of a six-week-old fetus into the room so that all can hear it in the same way. The fetal monitor attached during labor records the duration and intensity of each contraction; the woman's reports are no longer necessary. (59)

First, Nilsson's photographs let us see the separation of the fetus from the body of the pregnant woman in print and now, it is here, at this time in the world of reproductive medicine, that we can see the beginning of a separation of the pregnant body from the fetus, even during labor. If a woman is no longer needed to tell the story of her pregnancy or her labor or to describe what she feels happening within and to her body, then she is reduced to a holding cell, or as Anne Balsamo phrases it, "a womb with legs" (87).

The meaning of the ultrasound imaging of fetuses functions on three levels, the level of "evidence (diagnosis)," the level of "surveillance (intervention)," and also the level of "fantasy or myth" (Pollack Petchesky 70). Feminist political theorist, Rosalind Pollack Petchesky writes:

> Evidence shades into fantasy when the fetus is visualized as though removed from the pregnant woman's body. This is a form of fetishization, and it occurs repeatedly whenever ultrasound images construct the fetus through indications which sever its functions and parts from their organic connection to pregnant women. (70)

Removing the woman's body and her voice, denying her the experience of her corporeal and phenomenological experiences, privileges the male gaze. The gaze of technology, the one that eliminates a woman's full subjecthood, is not of the woman. Pollack Petchesky writes, "Visualization and objectification as privileged ways of knowing are *specifically masculine*" (68).

Women who do seek medical intervention and reproductive technology in attempts to become pregnant open their bodies to a technological gaze, ". . . literally penetrating the female body to scrutinize the biological functioning of its reproductive organs. In the process the female 'potentially maternal' body is objectified as a medium to look through" (Balsamo 93). The "potentially maternal" body becomes nothing more than a shell which holds the pieces— the eggs and the uterus—necessary in order to create and sustain a fetus. Women, who conceive through reproductive technology using in vitro fertilization, artificial insemination, or similar techniques, are rarely outside of the technological gaze during their pregnancy. They are scheduled for a myriad of tests on themselves and on the fetus, closely monitored office visits, and they are screened throughout their pregnancy for complications such as diabetes. Balsamo writes:

> Some experts unabashedly agree that part of the new concern for the fetus is due to advances in visualization technologies and the promise of fetal medicine as a new medical specialty . . .The same technological advances that foster objectification of the female body through the visualization of internal functioning also encourages the "personification" of the fetus. (93)

Personification, in medical reproductive technologies, has extended so far as to include frozen, fertilized embryos. There are laws which protect frozen embryos and if a couple decides to break up or get a divorce they must go through court proceedings to determine who will get custody of the embryos. Frozen embryos cannot be donated to medical science due to a national ban which prohibits them being used for stem cell research (Gettelman 45). Balsamo asserts:

> New reproductive technologies do not, in a singularly deterministic sense, construct these new social tensions. But they are implicated in the production of a new set of possibilities, wherein the rights of the pregnant woman are set against the 'rights' of other people to intervene in her pregnancy or to act on behalf of the unborn fetus. (98)

Of course, reproductive technology is not all bad. In many ways it allows for women and men to conceive outside of the bounds of heterosexual relationships. Women can choose, if they have the financial resources available, to use a surrogate mother, in vitro fertilization, or artificial insemination, based on the specifics of their circumstances. Reproductive technology also gives hope to the many women who were once thought to be infertile because of difficulty conceiving outside of the laboratory. Although, in these technologically influenced discourses a woman is rendered separate from the fetus, and the fetus is thus granted personhood, she is still responsible for the well-being of the fetus and can be held accountable for it.

In granting the fetus personhood, anti-abortion activists find support in their argument that the fetus must be protected as an entity separate and as important as the pregnant woman. If a pregnant woman chooses to abort a fetus, she is met with laws and restrictions which impede her right to do so and which hinge on the personhood of the fetus. In addition, women who do not abort are still held accountable for their actions in regard to the fetus they are carrying. In particular, women with limited or no access to prenatal care or women who have a history of substance abuse are implicated in their responsibility to the fetus.

Anne Balsamo discusses some of the surrounding debates about what appear to be benign public health services. She questions:

> Medical research that establishes a broader list of substances and behaviors that endanger a fetus, an expanded argument about the relationship between maternal behavior and fetal

> development, new public health programs that seek to increase minority patient/client participation and institutional/clinic surveillance, and the criminalization of certain forms of drug consumption. (103)

Fetal advocates use medical surveillance in public health as way of protecting the fetus and regulating the behaviors of pregnant or potentially pregnant women. In one instance fetal advocates proposed that state officials use a monitoring system to enforce laws on pregnant women. In this case, and in others similar to it, "Women would be forced to attend their prenatal visits and obey doctor's orders; and women could be prosecuted and punished for smoking or using drugs during pregnancy" (Balsamo 109). These are issues which directly impede women's access to public health services and punish women who do not abide by regulations put in place to control their bodies. Additionally, women who do not have to seek public health resources for prenatal care are not subjected to these regulations as closely as those who do.

These regulations and laws are heavily embedded in race and class issues. Take for example the campaign to raise awareness about "crack babies" which was targeted primarily at poor women of color. The campaign was based on studies which argued for the connection between crack use and birth defects, but failed to take into account the serious implications of alcohol use, poor nutrition, and inadequate prenatal care, all of which have been implicated in causal relationships with birth defects (Shivas and Charles 186).

Whether or not they were seeking public services there have been many women who have been prosecuted for endangering the life of their unborn fetus. For example in the last decade pregnant women have been charged with manslaughter because the vehicle they were driving was involved in an accident and the fetus died, as well as with providing alcohol to a minor when drinking while pregnant (Daniels 83).

But what about fathers, are they prosecuted in the same way? They are not, and for all the posturing of The National Right to Life Committee and its male members about "babies" in utero being a part of their bodies if they were subject to the discrimination, invasion, and intervention that pregnant women are, I do not think they would be as apt to align themselves with the fetus. Many feminists are hesitant to point to the connections of male exterior behavior and the health of the fetus for fear that establishing connectivity will only give power to the patriarchal regime (Daniels 85). I believe, however, that it is important to point to the (exterior) connections the father has to the fetus in order to begin to alleviate the persecution of pregnant women for fetal harm.

Scientists have documented, and continue to research, the connections between the toxins that are passed through the father's sperm to the gamete, and which later develop as, or contribute to birth defects (Daniels 88). While this is important research, it is not what I wish to focus on here. Of utmost importance to me, is how the social behaviors of the father are attributed to fetal harm. For instance men who are addicted to drugs or are physically abusive may create environments where maternal body is subjected to undue stress (Daniels 89). These men are not prosecuted or for that matter persecuted in the same ways that pregnant women are. In fact, in the case of abuse, it is often the woman who is blamed for any harm to the fetus because she has "chosen" to stay in an abusive relationship.

The balance here is a tricky one, and I will not pretend to have a formula or even a discourse which would protect or ensure the pregnant woman's rights and autonomy. Cynthia Daniels, in her essay, "Fathers, Mothers, and Fetal Harm: Rethinking Gender Difference and Reproductive Responsibility" writes of a need to incorporate the dialog of paternal responsibility while maintaining the pregnant woman's right to corporeality. As a beginning to a discourse of collective responsibility she states:

> First, [we must] include men in thinking about prevention of and culpability for fetal harm. Second, while we recognize the contributions both men and collective institutions make to fetal harm, the nature of both biology and social structure requires that we address what is unique about women's particular relation to reproductive responsibilities. Third, any talk about reproductive responsibility must begin and end with talk about corporate and social responsibility for fetal harm. Lastly, as a collectivity, we have failed to address basic requirements of health care and reproductive choice, we must do this in order to move forward. (96)

This is not a simple agenda, nor should it be, but in beginning to address what Daniels has articulated and by continuing the work of further articulation we might find ourselves with a more nuanced approach to reproduction.

We must begin this work through seeing the intersections of women, fetality, the public/private spilt, and technology. Sharon Lehner writes in her essay, "My Womb, the Mosh Pit," of the connection of technology to her own experiences of pregnancy and abortion:

> The relationship between technology and biology becomes the relationship between mother and child. I bonded with an image, I aborted an image, and I deeply mourn an image. The image does not supersede the material presence of a pregnancy, it *mediates, interprets, and supports* the physical presence of an unborn child. (Lehner 548, *emphasis mine*)

Lehner's words are reminiscent of the role of the placenta in a placental economy, that of a mediator and support system providing both separation and connection to woman and fetus.

Today we see the ways technology intersects with pregnancy in many venues. In science we see how cloning is eliminating the need for an embodied pregnancy. Take for example, yet another issue of *Life* magazine, which printed a photograph of a researcher in Japan, described in the article as a proud father, ". . . in his lab with a plastic box serving the function of a uterus in which a goat is gestating," (Wexler and Matthews 216). This researcher and the subsequent picture raises the possibility of a completely disembodied reproductive process.

In the mass media we see pregnancy and debates around reproduction becoming increasingly prevalent. There are celebrity "bump watches" and women who like Nadya "Octomom" Suleman, become celebrities because of the sheer amount of children they are able to bare. As Michelle Duggar does, there are women who advocate publicly against birth control, as part of the Quiver Full movement, who believe that each new child is a "gift" and choose not to control reproduction with medical or technological intervention. There are women who seek medical and technological interventions in order to conceive and women who use different technologies in order not to conceive. Is it still true as one theorist wrote in 1997 that, "We are in danger of losing sight of the fact that pregnancies when they occur, occur in women's bodies?" (Hartouni 67) Or are we so fixated on fetal health and well-being that we have begun to obsess over these bodies, not as their own entities, but as the parcel in which the fetus will be brought to us, and thus only see them in a fragmented state? Perhaps it is as Berlant so eloquently states, that "The pregnant woman and the fetus register changes in the social meanings of gender and maternity; as they meet up in national culture, they also raise questions about intimacies, identities, politics, pictures, and public spheres" (150). We can measure women's subjectivity by the status of fetal personhood, a measurement which acts as a barometer for what and whom our culture, our society, is willing to tolerate, support and protect. As Rosalind Pollack Petchesky wrote in 1987, just as the rise of fetal ultrasounds began to occur, "We must create new images that recontextualize the fetus: that place it back into the uterus, and the uterus back into the woman's body and her body back into social space" (78). We are still working on her vision, and whether we have made progress is often difficult to tell. However, feminist interventions, in the form of intersectional analysis and their concomitant activist approaches are much needed and represent positive future directions for maternal subjectivities in an age of advancing reproductive pregnancies and ever-more-public pregnancies.

Works Cited

Balsamo, Anne. "Public Pregnancies and Cultural Narratives of Surveillance." *Technologies of the Gendered Body: Reading Cyborg Women*: Durham: Duke University Press, 1996. 80–115.

Beasley, Chris and Carol Bacchi. "Citizen Bodies: Embodying Citizens—A Feminist Analysis" *International Feminist Journal of Politics* 2.3 (2000): 337–358.

Berlant, Lauren. "America, 'Fat,' the Fetus." *boundary* 2 21.3 (1994): 145–95.

Bordo, Susan. "Are Mothers Persons?: Reproductive Rights and the Politics of Subject-ivity." *Unbearable Weight: Feminism, Western Culture, and the Body*: Berkeley: University of California Press, 1993. 71–97.

Daniels, Cynthia. "Fathers, Mothers, and Fetal Harm: Rethinking Gender Difference and Reproductive Responsibility." *Fetal Subjects, Feminist Positions*. Lynn M. Morgan and Meredith W. Michaels (Eds.). Philadelphia: University of Pennsylvania Press, 1999.

De Beauvoir, Simone. *The Second Sex*. 2nd ed. Trans. H.M. Parshley. New York: Alfred A. Knopf, 1968.

Gettelman, Elizabeth. "Splitting the Baby." *Mother Jones* July-August 2006: 45.

Hartouni, Valerie. *Cultural Conceptions: On Reproductive Technologies and the Remaking of Life*. Minneapolis: University of Minnesota Press, 1997.

Irigaray, Luce. *Je, Tu, Nous: Toward a Culture of Difference*. Trans. Alison Martin. New York: Routledge, 1993.

Lehner, Sharon. "My Womb, the Mosh Pit." *The Feminism and Visual Culture Reader*. Amelia Jones (Ed.). London: Routledge, 2003. 545–548.

Longhurst, Robyn. "Breaking Corporeal Boundaries: Pregnant Bodies in Public Spaces." *Contested Bodies*. Eds. Ruth Holliday and John Hassard. New York: Routledge, 2001. 81–94.

Matthews, Sandra, and Laura Wexler. *Pregnant Pictures*. New York: Routledge, 2000.

Petchesky, Rosalind Pollack. "Foetal Images: The Power of Visual Culture in the Politics of Reproduction." *Reproductive Technologies: Gender, Motherhood, and Medicine*. Michelle Stanworth (Ed.). Minneapolis: University of Minnesota Press, 1987.

Roe v. Wade. No. 410 Supreme Court of the US. 22 January 1973.

Shivas, Tricha and Sonya Charles. "Behind Bars or Up on a Pedestal: Motherhood and Fetal Harm." *Women and Children First: Feminism, Rhetoric, and Public Policy*. Sharon Meagher and Patrice Diquinzio (Eds.). New York: SUNY Press, 2005. 283–201.

Stabile, Carol. "Shooting the Mother: Fetal Photography and the Politics of Disappearance." *Camera Obscura: A Journal of Feminism and Film Theory* 28 (1992), 191–192.

Tyler, Imogen. "Skin Tight: Celebrity, Pregnancy and Subjectivity." *Thinking Through the Skin*. Eds. Sara Ahmed and Jackie Stacey. London: Routledge, 2001. 69–83.

Young, Iris Marion. "Pregnant Embodiment: Subjectivity and Alienation." *On Female Body Experience: 'Throwing Like a Girl' and Other Essays*. New York: Oxford UP, 2005. 46–61.

It's a Big Fat Revolution

Nomy Lamm

"My body is fucking beautiful, and every time I look in the mirror and acknowledge that, I am contributing to the revolution."

I am going to write an essay describing my experiences with fat oppression and the ways in which feminism and punk have affected my work. It will be clear, concise and well though-out, and will be laid out in the basic thesis paper, college essay format. I will deal with these issues in a mature and intellectual manner. I will cash in on as many fifty-cent words as possible.

I lied. (You probably already picked up on that, huh?) I can't do that. This is my life, and my words are the most effective tool I have for challenging Whiteboyworld (that's my punk-rock cutesy but oh-so-revolutionary way of saying "patriarchy"). If there's one thing that feminism has taught me, it's that the revolution is gonna be on my terms. The revolution will be incited through my voice, my words, not the words of the universe of male intellect that already exists. And I know that a hell of a lot of what I say is totally contradictory. My contradictions can coexist, cuz they exist inside of me, and I'm not gonna simplify them so that they fit into the linear, analytical pattern that I know they're supposed to. I think it's important to recognize that all this stuff does contribute to the revolution, for real. The fact that I write like this cuz it's the way I want to write makes this world just that much safer for me.

Reprinted from *Listen Up: Voices From the Next Feminist Generation*, Seal Press.

I wanna explain what I mean when I say "the revolution," but I'm not sure whether I'll be able to. Cuz at the same time that I'm being totally serious, I also see my use of the term as a mockery of itself. Part of the reason for this is that I'm fully aware that I still fit into dominant culture in many ways. The revolution could very well be enacted against me, instead of for me. I don't want to make myself sound like I think I'm the most oppressed, most punk-rock, most revolutionary person in the world. But at the same time I do think that revolution is a word I should use as often as I can, because it's a concept that we need to be aware of. And I don't just mean it in an abstract, intellectualized way, either. I really do think that the revolution has begun. Maybe that's not apparent to mainstream culture yet, but I see that as a good sign. As soon as mainstream culture picks up on it, they'll try to co-opt it.

For now the revolution takes place when I stay up all night talking with my best friends about feminism and marginalization and privilege and oppression and power and sex and money and real-life rebellion. For now the revolution takes place when I watch a girl stand up in front of a crowd of people and talk about her sexual abuse. For now the revolution takes place when I get a letter from a girl I've never met who says that the zine I wrote changed her life. For now the revolution takes place when the homeless people in my town camp out for a week in the middle of downtown. For now the revolution takes place when I am confronted by a friend about something racist that I have said. For now the revolution takes place in my head when I know how fucking brilliant my girlfriends and I are.

And I'm living the revolution through my memories and through my pain and through my triumphs. When I think about all the marks I have against me in this society, I am amazed that I haven't turned into some worthless lump of shit. Fatkikecripplecuntqueer. In a nutshell. But then I have to take into account the fact that I'm an articulate, white, middle-class college kid, and that provides me with a hell of a lot of privilege and opportunity for dealing with my oppression that may not be available to other oppressed people. And since my personality/being isn't divided up into a privileged part and an oppressed part, I have to deal with the ways that these things interact, counterbalance and sometimes even overshadow each other. For example, I was born with one leg. I guess it's a big deal, but it's never worked into my body image in the same way that being fat has. And what does it mean to be a white woman as opposed to a woman of color? A middle-class fat girl as opposed to a poor fat girl? What does it mean to be fat, physically disabled and bisexual? (Or fat, disabled and *sexual at all*?)

See, of course, I'm still a real person, and I don't always feel up to playing the role of the revolutionary. Sometimes it's hard enough for me to just get out of bed in the morning. Sometimes it's hard enough to just talk to people at all, without having to deal with the political nuances of everything that comes out of their mouths. Despite the fact that I do tons of work that deals with fat oppression, and that I've been working so so hard on my own body image, there are times when I really hate my body and don't want to deal with being strong all the time. Because I am strong and have thought all of this through in so many different ways, and I do have naturally high self-esteem, I've come to a place where I can honestly say that I love my body and I'm happy with being fat. But occasionally, when I look in the mirror and I see this body that is so different from my friends', so different from what I'm told it should be, I just want to hide away and not deal with it anymore. At these times it doesn't seem fair to me that I have to always be fighting to be happy. Would it be easier for me to just give in and go on another diet so that I can stop this perpetual struggle? Then I could still support the fat grrl revolution without having it affect me personally in every way. And I know I know I know that's not the answer and I could never do that to myself, but I can't say that the thought never crosses my mind.

And it doesn't help much when my friends and family, who all know how I feel about this, continue to make anti-fat statements and bitch about how fat they feel and mention new diets they've heard about and are just dying to try. "I'm shaped like a watermelon." "Wow, I'm so happy, I now wear a size seven instead of a size nine." "I like this mirror because it makes me look thinner."

I can't understand how they could still think these things when I'm constantly talking about these issues, and I can't believe that they would think that these are okay things to talk about in front of me. And it's not like I want them to censor their conversation around me. . . . I just want them to not think it. I know that most of this is just a reflection of how they feel about themselves and isn't intended as an attack on me or an invalidation of my work, but it makes it that much harder for me. It puts all those thoughts inside me. Today I was standing outside of work and I caught a glimpse of myself in the window and thought, "Hey, I don't look that fat!" And I immediately realized how fucked up that was, but that didn't stop me from feeling more attractive because of it.

I want this out of me. This is not a part of me, and theoretically I can separate it all out and throw away the shit, but it's never really gone. When will this finally be over? When can I move on to other issues? It will never be over, and that's really fucking hard to accept.

I am living out this system of oppression through my memories, and even when I'm not thinking about them they are there, affecting everything I do. Five years old, my first diet. Seven years old, being declared officially "overweight" because I weigh ten pounds over what a "normal" seven-year-old should weigh. Ten years old, learning to starve myself and be happy feeling constantly dizzy. Thirteen years old, crossing the border from being bigger than my friends to actually being "fat." Fifteen years old, hearing the boys in the next room talk about how fat (and hence unattractive) I am. Whenever I perform, I remember the time when my dad said he didn't like the dance I choreographed because I looked fat while I was doing it. Every time I dye my hair I remember when my mom wouldn't let me dye my hair in seventh grade because seeing fat people with dyed hair made her think they were just trying to cover up the fact that they're fat, trying to look attractive despite it (when of course it's obvious what they should really do if they want to look attractive, right?). And these are big memorable occurrences that I can put my finger on and say, "This hurt me." But what about the lifetime of media I've been exposed to that tells me that only thin people are lovable, healthy, beautiful, talented, fun? I know that those messages are all packed in there with the rest of my memories, but I just can't label them and their effects on my psyche. They are elusive and don't necessarily feel painful at the time. They are well disguised and often even appear alluring and romantic. (I will never fall in love because I cannot be picked up and swung around in circles. . . .)

All my life the media and everyone around me have told me that fat is ugly. Which of course is just a cultural standard that has many, many medical lies to fall back upon. Studies have shown that fat people are unhealthy and have short life expectancies. Studies have also shown that starving people have these same peculiarities. These health risks to fat people have been proven to be a result of continuous starvation—dieting—and not of fat itself. I am not fat due to lack of willpower. I've been a vegetarian since I was ten years old. Controlling what I eat is easy for me. Starving myself is not (though for most of my life I wished it was). My body is supposed to be like this, and I've been on plenty of diets where I've kept off some weight for a period of several months and then gained it all back. Two years ago I finally ended the cycle. I am not dieting anymore because I know that this is how my body is supposed to be, and this is how I want it to be. Being fat does not make me less healthy or less active. Being fat does not make me less attractive.

On TV I see a thin woman dancing with a fabulously handsome man, and over that I hear, "I was never happy until I went on [fill in the blank] diet program, but now I'm getting attention from men, and I feel so good! I don't have to worry about what people are saying about me behind my back, because I know I look good. You owe it to yourself to give yourself the life you deserve. Call [fill in the blank] diet program today, and start taking off the pounds right away!" TV shows me a close-up of a teary-eyed fat girl who says, "I've tried everything, but nothing works. I lose twenty pounds, and I gain back twenty-five. I feel so ashamed. What can I do?" The first time I saw that commercial I started crying and memorized the number on the screen. I know that feeling of shame. I know that feeling of having nowhere left to turn, of feeling like I'm useless because I can't lose all that "unwanted fat." But I know that the unhappiness is not a result of my fat. It's a result of a society that tells me I'm bad.

Where's the revolution? My body is fucking beautiful, and every time I look in the mirror and acknowledge that, I am contributing to the revolution.

I feel like at this point I'm expected to try to prove to you that fat can be beautiful by going into descriptions of "rippling thighs and full smooth buttocks." I won't. It's not up to me to convince you that fat can be attractive. I refuse to be the self-appointed full-figured porno queen. Figure it out on your own.

It's not good enough for you to tell me that you "don't judge by appearances"—so fat doesn't bother you. Ignoring our bodies and "judging only by what's on the inside" is not the answer. This seems to be along the same line of thinking as that brilliant school of thought called "humanism": "We are all just people, so let's ignore trivialities such as race, class, gender, sexual preference, body type and so on." Bullshit! The more we ignore these aspects of ourselves, the more shameful they become and the more we are expected to be what is generally implied when these qualifiers are not given—white, straight, thin, rich, male. It's unrealistic to try to overlook these exterior (and hence meaningless, right?) differences, because we're still being brainwashed with the same shit as everyone else. This way we're just not talking about it. And I don't want to be told, "Yes you're fat, but you're beautiful on the inside." That's just another way of telling me that I'm ugly, that there's no way that I'm beautiful on the outside. Fat does not equal ugly, don't give me that. My body *is* me. I want you to see my body, acknowledge my body. True revolution comes not when we learn to ignore our fat and pretend we're no different, but when we learn to use it to our advantage, when we learn to deconstruct all the myths that propagate fat-hate.

My thin friends are constantly being validated by mainstream feminism, while I am ignored. The most widespread mentality regarding body image at this point is something along these lines: Women look in the mirror and think, "I'm fat," but really they're not. Really they're thin.

Really they're thin. But really I'm fat. According to mainstream feminist theory, I don't even exist. I know that women do often look in the mirror and think that they are fatter than they are. And yes, this is a problem. But the analysis can't stop there. There are women who *are* fat, and that needs to be dealt with. Rather than just reassuring people, "No, you're not fat, you're just curvy," maybe we should be demystifying fat and dealing with fat politics as a whole. And I don't mean maybe, I mean it's a necessity. Once we realize that fat is not "inherently bad" (and I can't even believe I'm writing that—"inherently bad"—it sounds so ridiculous), then we can work out the problem as a whole instead of dealing only with this very minute part of it. All forms of oppression work together, and so they have to be fought together.

I think that a lot of the mainstream feminist authors who claim to be dealing with this issue are doing it in a very wrong way. Susie Orbach, for example, with *Fat Is a Feminist Issue*. She tells us: Don't diet, don't try to lose weight, don't feed the diet industry. But she then goes on to say: But if you eat right and exercise, you will lose weight! And I feel like, great, nice, it's so very wonderful that that worked for her, but she's totally missing the point. She is trying to help women, but really she is hurting us. She is hurting us because she's saying that there's still only one body that's okay for us (and she's the one to help us get it!). It's almost like that *Stop the Insanity* woman, Susan Powter. One of my friends read her book and said that the first half of it is all about fat oppression and talks about how hard it is to be fat in our society, but then it says: So use my great new diet plan! This kind of thing totally plays on our emotions so that we think, Wow, this person really understands me. They know where I'm coming from, so they must know what's best for me.

And there are so many "liberal" reasons for perpetuating fat-hate. Yes, we're finally figuring out that dieting never works. How, then, shall we explain this horrible monstrosity? And how can we get rid of it? The new "liberal" view on fat is that it is caused by deep psychological disturbances. Her childhood was bad, she was sexually abused, so she eats and gets fat in order to hide herself away. She uses her fat as a security blanket. Or maybe when she was young her parents caused her to associate food with comfort and love, so she eats to console herself. Or maybe, like with me, her parents were always on diets and always nagging her about what she was eating, so food became something shameful that must be hoarded and kept secret. And for a long, long time I really believed that if my parents hadn't instilled in me all these fucked-up attitudes about food, I wouldn't be fat. But then I realized that my brother and sister both grew up in exactly the same environment, and they are both thin. Obviously this is not the reason that I am fat. Therapy won't help, because there's nothing to cure. When will we stop grasping for reasons to hate fat people and start realizing that fat is a totally normal and natural thing that cannot and should not be gotten rid of?

Despite what I said earlier about my friends saying things that are really hurtful to me, I realize that they are actually pretty exceptional. I don't want to make them seem like uncaring, ignorant people. I'm constantly talking about these issues, and I feel like I'm usually able to confront my friends when they're being insensitive, and they'll understand or at least try to. Sometimes when I leave my insular circle of friends I'm shocked at what the "real world" is like. Hearing boys on the bus refer to their girlfriends as their "bitches," seeing fat women being targeted for harassment on the street, watching TV and seeing how every fat person is depicted as a food-obsessed slob, seeing women treated as property by men who see masculinity as a right to power. . . . I leave these situations feeling like the punk scene, within which most of my interactions take place, is so sheltered. I cannot imagine living in a community where I had nowhere to go for support. I cannot imagine living in the "real world."

But then I have to remember that it's still there in my community—these same fucked-up attitudes are perpetuated within the punk scene as well; they just take on more subtle forms. I feel like these issues are finally starting to be recognized and dealt with, but fat hating is still pretty standard. Of course everyone agrees that we shouldn't diet and that eating disorders are a result of our oppressive society, but it's not usually taken much further than that. It seems like people have this idea that punk is disconnected from the media. That because we are this cool underground subculture, we are immune to systems of oppression. But the punkest, coolest kids are still the skinny kids. And the same cool kids who are so into defying mainstream capitalist "Amerika" are the ones who say that fat is a symbol of capitalist wealth and greed. Yeah, that's a really new and different way of thinking: Blame the victim. Perpetuate institutionalized oppression. Fat people are not the ones who are oppressing these poor, skinny emo boys.

This essay is supposed to be about fat oppression. I feel like that's all I ever talk about. Sometimes I feel my whole identity is wrapped up in my fat. When I am fully conscious of my fat, it can't be used against me. Outside my secluded group of friends, in hostile situations, I am constantly aware that at any moment I could be harassed. Any slight altercation with another person could lead to a barrage of insults thrown at my body. I am always ready for it. I've found it doesn't happen nearly as often as I expect it, but still I always remain aware of the possibility. I am "The Fat Girl." I am "The Girl Who Talks About Fat Oppression." Within the punk scene, that's my security blanket. People know about me and know about my work, so I assume that they're not gonna be laughing behind my back about my fat. And if they are, then I know I have support from other people around me. The punk scene gives me tons of support that I know I wouldn't get elsewhere. Within the punk scene, I am able to put out zines, play music, do spoken-word performances that are intensely personal to me. I feel really strongly about keeping nothing secret. I can go back to the old cliché about the personal being political, and no matter how trite it may sound, it's true. I went for so long never talking about being fat, never talking about how that affects my self-esteem, never talking about the ways that I'm oppressed by this society. Now I'm talking. Now I'm talking, I'm talking all the time, and people listen to me. I have support.

And at the same time I know that I have to be wary of the support that I receive. Because I think to some people this is just seen as the cool thing, that by supporting me they're somehow receiving a certain amount of validation from the punk scene. Even though I am totally open and don't keep secrets, I have to protect myself.

This is the revolution. I don't understand the revolution. I can't lay it all out in black and white and tell you what is revolutionary and what is not. The punk scene is a revolution, but not in and of itself. Feminism is a revolution; it is solidarity as well as critique and confrontation. This is the fat grrl revolution. It's mine, but it doesn't belong to me. Fuckin' yeah.

Arroz Con Pollo vs. Slim Fast (1992)

Linda Delgado

Female body norms and the meanings of food differ according to culture. This can be confusing for young women who must negotiate the gender ideals of several different cultures. In this brief essay, Linda Delgado explains the conflicting messages she encountered about beauty and body size as a Latina woman in the United States.

To many white American women, thinness and tallness are essential parts of beauty. Yet in Spanish, the words *delgada* and *flaca* have a different connotation. Both words mean thin. *Delgada* connotes thin and weak, while *flaca* connotes thin as in skinny. Neither is very flattering. In fact, the question that usually follows after someone notices you are looking rather *delgada* is whether you have been ill.

Weight problems, aside from their health implications, are not seen as important in Latino culture as they are in mainstream American culture. There is a ceremonial importance to food and many rituals assigned to the sharing of food with others. Recently

"Arroz con Pollo vs. Slim Fast," by Linda Delgado, from *Women: Images and Realities—A Multicultural Anthology*, ed. Amy Kesselman, Lily D. McNair and Nancy Schneidewind, Mayfield Publishing Company, 1995. Reprinted by permission of the author.

during a warm-up exercise in a new class, students were asked to introduce themselves by identifying with a particular food. A young Dominican woman said she was like *arroz con pollo* (rice with chicken). Her reason for picking this dish was that rice with chicken symbolized warmth, love, and acceptance. It is a dish made for new neighbors, new in-laws, and new friends to celebrate important events. It means welcome and good luck.

The breaking of bread with family, friends, and strangers is part of Latino hospitality. "*Mi casa, su casa*" is an unaltered tradition. When you visit my aunt's house, for example, go there hungry! The variety and amounts of food are quite extraordinary. I get full just looking at the table! Not only must you partake of everything there, you must also keep in mind that there are at least three or four desserts to follow. On special occasions, such as Easter, Christmas, and Mother's Day, everyone has a signature dish, and part of the celebration is sharing these delicacies. Failure to eat the right amount will cause personal distress to the hostess. What did she do wrong? At my aunt's house, usually my grandmother will ask if you have been sick or if your children have been giving you a hard time. There must be some explanation why you have not eaten your share of food. By "your share of food" they mean enough to feed a small army! The word "diet" or "calories" is never mentioned. For the current generations, these messages can be confusing.

Putting weight on your bones, as my grandmother explains it, is necessary for many reasons. First of all, how else can you carry the burdens of being a woman? You have to eat in order to have the strength to deal with a husband and/or children (regardless of the fact that, at present, you may be 11 years old). You have to eat to have the strength to deal with *lo que Dios te mande,* whatever God sends you because *uno nunca sabe lo de mañana, so uno tierne que aprobechar lo de hoy*, we never know what tomorrow may bring, so we have to enjoy what we have today. Living in New York, you also have to eat in order to deal with the cold, wintry weather. There is always a good reason for a second or third helping of food. In the film *Acting Our Age*, an African-American woman about the age of 65 expresses her concern for the next generation of young women. She says, "Now that black women are being used as models and thought of as beautiful, they will pick up the same false notions about beauty as white women." I think this is also true for Latinas in the United States.

One of my childhood memories was an episode involving my grandmother when I was in the fifth grade. She picked me up at school and told my mother we were going shopping. Well, we did, but first she had someplace to take me. For as long as I could remember, I was a tall and very skinny child. That day, my grandmother and I took a bus ride into Manhattan to a nutrition clinic. She swore I was undernourished and that something was wrong. The doctor said I was healthy and of a good weight. My grandmother was quite surprised and, in fact, didn't believe him.

Having a "good set of hips" means not only that you can carry a child well but also that you can manage whatever your husband has in store for you. "You have to eat in order to have strength." So, from the time you are an infant, chubbiness is applauded as healthy. As you grow older, mental and physical well-being are assessed by your outer appearance. Thin is not sexy. It is unhealthy, unappealing, and sad. My grandmother told me that I didn't look strong enough to carry my bookbag and asked how was I going to carry whatever God sent my way. I learned early in life to expect to bear something! That was part of the gender-role experience.

Interestingly, flabbiness is not acceptable, either. Flabbiness is a sign of laziness and overindulgence. Formal exercise is not part of the Latino culture for women, while men often play softball, handball, or paddle ball. It is generally accepted that women who are flabby and out of shape must not be taking care of their homes, themselves, or their children. They must be watching *novelas*. Women's exercise happens in the course of cleaning, cooking, and caring for children.

In the dating game, life gets really confusing for young Latinas. If women look too much like the models, they will be considered the kind of women men play with but don't necessarily marry. A man brings a woman who is a size 10 or 12 home to mother and a family dinner, but a woman who is size 5 or 6, you have to keep away from your brother! A 16-year-old Puerto Rican student recently told me that her boyfriend wanted her to put on some weight before the summer. She said that he was not pleased at the fact that other men were watching her on the beach last summer. The other side of the problem was that her mother had taught her that if she gained weight, she would not have any boyfriends. When I heard this story, it reminded me of the African-American woman in the film and her description of "false notions about beauty."

Some of my fondest memories are wrapped in the warmth of mealtimes. Special foods are part of special holidays. Watching generations of women cook and exchange recipes, taking in all the wonderful aromas and feeling their sense of pride and accomplishment as they fulfilled their understood role, was positive for me. Although their place of power was in the kitchen, I learned how that power worked. Being in the kitchen did not mean being passive or subservient. It meant doing your share of the business of parenting and partnering, since the kitchen is the center of family activity. It is a place of importance in the Latino household. Feeding those whom you care about is nurturing the entire unit, and eating all of your *arroz con pollo* means you are loved for your efforts in return.

There are many mixed messages to negotiate in a cross-cultural environment. Immigrants, like everyone else, want to belong. They find themselves trapped somewhere between the cultural values of their home and their host country. Although some can negotiate the conflict better than others, it nevertheless distorts views of the self. Reconciliation of different cultural repertoires is quite a challenge, especially for young Latinas who are trying to "fit in."

QUESTIONS

1. What is the ideal body size for women within Latino culture? How is this ideal different from the dominant U.S. cultural definition of beauty?
2. How "natural" and universal are beauty norms? Why are they so powerful? What effect do these powerful standards have on women who are exposed to multiple and differing cultural messages?
3. What meanings are attached to food in different communities? What experiences did Delgado have with food in her childhood?

Maid to Order: The Politics of Other Women's Work

Barbara Ehrenreich

In line with growing class polarization, the classic posture of submission is making a stealthy comeback. "We scrub your floors the old-fashioned way," boasts the brochure from Merry Maids, the largest of the residential-cleaning services that have sprung up in the last two decades, "on our hands and knees." This is not a posture that independent "cleaning ladies" willingly assume—preferring, like most people who clean their own homes, the sponge mop wielded from a standing position. In her comprehensive 1999 guide to homemaking, *Home Comforts,* Cheryl Mendelson warns: "Never ask hired housecleaners to clean your floors on their hands and knees; the request is likely to be regarded as degrading." But in a society in which 40 percent of the wealth is owned by 1 percent of households while the bottom 20 percent reports negative assets, the degradation of others is readily purchased. Kneepads entered American political discourse as a tool of the sexually subservient, but employees of Merry Maids, The Maids International, and other corporate cleaning services spend hours every day on these kinky devices, wiping up the drippings of the affluent.

I spent three weeks in September 1999 as an employee of The Maids International in Portland, Maine, cleaning, along with my fellow team members, approximately sixty houses containing a total of about 250 scrubbable floors—bathrooms, kitchens, and entryways requiring the hands-and-knees treatment. It's a different

Reprinted from *Women's Voices, Feminist Visions: Classic and Contemporary Readings,* International Creative Management.

world down there below knee level, one that few adults voluntarily enter. Here you find elaborate dust structures held together by a scaffolding of dog hair; dried bits of pasta glued to the floor by their sauce; the congealed remains of gravies, jellies, contraceptive creams, vomit, and urine. Sometimes, too, you encounter some fragment of a human being: a child's legs, stamping by in disgust because the maids are still present when he gets home from school; more commonly the Joan & David–clad feet and electrolyzed calves of the female homeowner. Look up and you may find this person staring at you, arms folded, in anticipation of an overlooked stain. In rare instances she may try to help in some vague, symbolic way, by moving the cockatoo's cage, for example, or apologizing for the leaves shed by a miniature indoor tree. Mostly, though, she will not see you at all and may even sit down with her mail at a table in the very room you are cleaning, where she would remain completely unaware of your existence unless you were to crawl under that table and start gnawing away at her ankles.

Housework, as you may recall from the feminist theories of the Sixties and Seventies, was supposed to be the great equalizer of women. Whatever else women did—jobs, school, child care—we also did housework, and if there were some women who hired others to do it for them, they seemed too privileged and rare to include in the theoretical calculus. All women were workers, and the home was their workplace—unpaid and unsupervised, to be sure, but a workplace no less than the offices and factories men repaired to every morning. If men thought of the home as a site of leisure and recreation—a "haven in a heartless world"—this was to ignore the invisible female proletariat that kept it cozy and humming. We were on the march now, or so we imagined, united against a society that devalued our labor even as it waxed mawkish over "the family" and "the home." Shoulder to shoulder and arm in arm, women were finally getting up off the floor.

In the most eye-catching elaboration of the home-as-workplace theme, Marxist feminists Maria Rosa Dallacosta and Selma James proposed in 1972 that the home was in fact an economically productive and significant workplace, an extension of the actual factory, since housework served to "reproduce the labor power" of others, particularly men. The male worker would hardly be in shape to punch in for his shift, after all, if some woman had not fed him, laundered his clothes, and cared for the children who were his contribution to the next generation of workers. If the home was a quasi-industrial workplace staffed by women for the ultimate benefit of the capitalists, then it followed that "wages for housework" was the obvious demand.

But when most American feminists, Marxist or otherwise, asked the Marxist question *cui bono*? they tended to come up with a far simpler answer—men. If women were the domestic proletariat, then men made up the class of domestic exploiters, free to lounge while their mates scrubbed. In consciousness-raising groups, we railed against husbands and boyfriends who refused to pick up after themselves, who were unaware of housework at all, unless of course it hadn't been done. The "dropped socks," left by a man for a woman to gather up and launder, joined lipstick and spike heels as emblems of gender oppression. And if, somewhere, a man had actually dropped a sock in the calm expectation that his wife would retrieve it, it was a sock heard round the world. Wherever second-wave feminism took root, battles broke out between lovers and spouses over sticky countertops, piled-up laundry, and whose turn it was to do the dishes.

The radical new idea was that housework was not only a relationship between a woman and a dust bunny or an unmade bed; it also defined a relationship between human beings, typically husbands and wives. This represented a marked departure from the more conservative Betty Friedan, who, in *The Feminine Mystique*, had never thought to enter the male sex into the equation, as either part of the housework problem or part of an eventual solution. She raged against a society that consigned its educated women to what she saw as essentially janitorial chores, beneath "the abilities of a woman of average or normal human intelligence," and, according to unidentified studies she cited, "peculiarly suited to the capacities of feeble-minded girls." But men are virtually exempt from housework in *The Feminine Mystique*—why drag them down too? At one point she even disparages a "Mrs. G.," who "somehow couldn't get her housework done before her husband came home at night and was so tired then that he had to do it." Educated women would just have to become more efficient so that housework could no longer "expand to fill the time available."

Or they could hire other women to do it—an option approved by Friedan in *The Feminine Mystique* as well as by the National Organization for Women [NOW], which she had helped launch. At the 1973 congressional hearings on whether to extend the Fair

Labor Standards Act to household workers, NOW testified on the affirmative side, arguing that improved wages and working conditions would attract more women to the field, and offering the seemingly self-contradictory prediction that "the demand for household help inside the home will continue to increase as more women seek occupations outside the home." One NOW member added, on a personal note: "Like many young women today, I am in school in order to develop a rewarding career for myself. I also have a home to run and can fully conceive of the need for household help as my free time at home becomes more and more restricted. Women know [that] housework is dirty, tedious work, and they are willing to pay to have it done. . . ." On the aspirations of the women paid to do it, assuming that at least some of them were bright enough to entertain a few, neither Friedan nor these members of NOW had, at the time, a word to say.

So the insight that distinguished the more radical, post-Friedan cohort of feminists was that when we talk about housework, we are really talking, yet again, about power. Housework was not degrading because it was manual labor, as Friedan thought, but because it was embedded in degrading relationships and inevitably served to reinforce them. To make a mess that another person will have to deal with—the dropped socks, the toothpaste sprayed on the bathroom mirror, the dirty dishes left from a late-night snack—is to exert domination in one of its more silent and intimate forms. One person's arrogance—or indifference, or hurry—becomes another person's occasion for toil. And when the person who is cleaned up after is consistently male, while the person who cleans up is consistently female, you have a formula for reproducing male domination from one generation to the next.

Hence the feminist perception of housework as one more way by which men exploit women or, more neutrally stated, as "a symbolic enactment of gender relations." An early German women's liberation cartoon depicted a woman scrubbing on her hands and knees while her husband, apparently excited by this pose, approaches from behind, unzipping his fly. Hence, too, the second-wave feminists, revulsion at the hiring of maids, especially when they were women of color: At a feminist conference I attended in 1980, poet Audre Lorde chose to insult the all-too-white audience by accusing them of being present only because they had black housekeepers to look after their children at home. She had the wrong crowd; most of the assembled radical feminists would no sooner have employed a black maid than they would have attached Confederate flag stickers to the rear windows of their cars. But accusations like hers, repeated in countless conferences and meetings, reinforced our rejection of the servant option. There already were at least two able-bodied adults in the average home—a man and a woman—and the hope was that, after a few initial skirmishes, they would learn to share the housework graciously.

A couple of decades later, however, the average household still falls far short of that goal. True, women do less housework than they did before the feminist revolution and the rise of the two-income family: down from an average of 30 hours per week in 1965 to 17.5 hours in 1995, according to a July 1999 study by the University of Maryland. Some of that decline reflects a relaxation of standards rather than a redistribution of chores; women still do two thirds of whatever housework—including bill paying, pet care, tidying, and lawn care—gets done. The inequity is sharpest for the most despised of household chores, cleaning: in the thirty years between 1965 and 1995, men increased the time they spent scrubbing, vacuuming, and sweeping by 240 percent—all the way up to 1.7 hours per week—while women decreased their cleaning time by only 7 percent to 6.7 hours per week. The averages conceal a variety of arrangements, of course, from minutely negotiated sharing to the most clichéd division of labor, as described by one woman to the *Washington Post:* "I take care of the inside, he takes care of the outside." But perhaps the most disturbing finding is that almost the entire increase in male participation took place between the 1970s and the mid-1980s. Fifteen years after the apparent cessation of hostilities, it is probably not too soon to announce the score: in the "chore wars" of the Seventies and Eighties, women gained a little ground, but overall, and after a few strategic concessions, men won.

Enter then, the cleaning lady as *dea ex machina*, restoring tranquility as well as order to the home. Marriage counselors recommend her as an alternative to squabbling, as do many within the cleaning industry itself. A Chicago cleaning woman quotes one of her clients as saying that if she gives up the service, "my husband and I will be divorced in six months." When the trend toward hiring out was just beginning to take off, in 1988, the owner of a Merry Maids franchise in Arlington, Massachusetts, told the

Christian Science Monitor, "I kid some women. I say, 'We even save marriages. In this new eighties period you expect more from the male partner, but very often you don't get the cooperation you would like to have. The alternative is to pay somebody to come in. . . ." Another Merry Maids franchise owner has learned to capitalize more directly on housework-related spats; he closes between 30 and 35 percent of his sales by making follow-up calls Saturday mornings, which is "prime time for arguing over the fact that the house is a mess." The micro-defeat of feminism in the household opened a new door for women, only this time it was the servants' entrance.

In 1999, somewhere between 14 and 18 percent of households employed an outsider to do the cleaning, and the numbers have been rising dramatically. Mediamark Research reports a 53 percent increase, between 1995 and 1999, in the number of households using a hired cleaner or service once a month or more, and Maritz Marketing finds that 30 percent of the people who hired help in 1999 did so for the first time that year. Among my middle-class, professional women friends and acquaintances, including some who made important contributions to the early feminist analysis of housework, the employment of a maid is now nearly universal. This sudden emergence of a servant class is consistent with what some economists have called the "Brazilianization" of the American economy: We are dividing along the lines of traditional Latin American societies—into a tiny overclass and a huge underclass, with the latter available to perform intimate household services for the former. Or, to put it another way, the home, or at least the affluent home, is finally becoming what radical feminists in the Seventies only imagined it was—a true "workplace" for women and a tiny, though increasingly visible, part of the capitalist economy. And the question is: As the home becomes a workplace for someone else, is it still a place where you would want to live?

. . .

The trend toward outsourcing the work of the home seems, at the moment, unstoppable. Two hundred years ago women often manufactured soap, candles, cloth, and clothing in their own homes, and the complaints of some women at the turn of the twentieth century that they had been "robbed by the removal of creative work" from the home sound pointlessly reactionary today. Not only have the skilled crafts, like sewing and cooking from scratch, left the home but many of the "white collar" tasks are on their way out, too. For a fee, new firms such as the San Francisco-based Les Concierges and Cross It Off Your List in Manhattan will pick up dry cleaning, baby-sit pets, buy groceries, deliver dinner, even do the Christmas shopping. With other firms and individuals offering to buy your clothes, organize your financial files, straighten out your closets, and wait around in your home for the plumber to show up, why would anyone want to hold on to the toilet cleaning?

Absent a major souring of the economy, there is every reason to think that Americans will become increasingly reliant on paid housekeepers and that this reliance will extend ever further down into the middle class. For one thing, the "time bind" on working parents shows no sign of loosening; people are willing to work longer hours at the office to pay for the people—house-cleaners and baby-sitters—who are filling in for them at home. Children, once a handy source of household help, are now off at soccer practice or SAT prep classes; grandmother has relocated to a warmer climate or taken up a second career. Furthermore, despite the fact that people spend less time at home than ever, the square footage of new homes swelled by 33 percent between 1975 and 1998, to include "family rooms," home entertainment rooms, home offices, bedrooms, and often bathrooms for each family member. By the third quarter of 1999, 17 percent of new homes were larger than 3,000 square feet, which is usually considered the size threshold for household help, or the point at which a house becomes unmanageable to the people who live in it.

One more trend impels people to hire outside help, according to cleaning experts such as Aslett and Mendelson: fewer Americans know how to clean or even to "straighten up." I hear this from professional women defending their decision to hire a maid: "I'm just not very good at it myself" or "I wouldn't really know where to begin." Since most of us learn to clean from our parents (usually our mothers), any diminution of cleaning skills is transmitted from one generation to another, like a gene that can, in the appropriate environment, turn out to be disabling or lethal. Upper-middle-class children raised in the servant economy of the Nineties are bound to grow up as domestically incompetent as their parents and no less dependent on people to clean up after them. Mendelson sees this as a metaphysical loss, a "matter of no longer being physically centered in your environment." Having cleaned the rooms of many overly privileged teenagers in my stint with The Maids, I think the problem is a little more urgent than that. The American overclass is raising a generation of young people who will, without constant assistance, suffocate in their own detritus.

If there are moral losses, too, as Americans increasingly rely on paid household help, no one has been tactless enough to raise them. Almost everything we buy, after all, is the product of some other person's suffering and miserably underpaid labor. I clean my own house (though—full disclosure—I recently hired someone else to ready it for a short-term tenant), but I can hardly claim purity in any other area of consumption. I buy my jeans at The Gap, which is reputed to subcontract to sweatshops. I tend to favor decorative objects no doubt ripped off, by their purveyors, from scantily paid Third World craftspersons. Like everyone else, I eat salad greens just picked by migrant farm workers, some of them possibly children. And so on. We can try to minimize the pain that goes into feeding, clothing, and otherwise provisioning ourselves—by observing boycotts, checking for a union label, etc.—but there is no way to avoid it altogether without living in the wilderness on berries. Why should housework, among all the goods and services we consume, arouse any special angst?

And it does, as I have found in conversations with liberal-minded employers of maids, perhaps because we all sense that there are ways in which housework is different from other products and services. First, in its inevitable proximity to the activities that compose "private" life. The home that becomes a workplace for other people remains a home, even when that workplace has been minutely regulated by the corporate cleaning chains. Someone who has no qualms about purchasing rugs woven by child slaves in India or coffee picked by impoverished peasants in Guatemala might still hesitate to tell dinner guests that, surprisingly enough, his or her lovely home doubles as a sweatshop during the day. You can eschew the chain cleaning services of course hire an independent cleaner at a generous hourly wage, and even encourage, at least in spirit, the unionization of the housecleaning industry. But this does not change the fact that someone is working in your home at a job she would almost certainly never have chosen for herself—if she'd had a college education, for example, or a little better luck along the way—and the place where she works, however enthusiastically or resentfully, is the same as the place where you sleep.

It is also the place where your children are raised, and what they learn pretty quickly is that some people are less worthy than others. Even better wages and working conditions won't erase the hierarchy between an employer and his or her domestic help, because the help is usually there only because the employer has "something better" to do with her time, as one report on the growth of cleaning services puts it, not noticing the obvious implication that the cleaning person herself has nothing better to do with her time. In a merely middle-class home, the message may be reinforced by a warning to the children that that's what they'll end up doing if they don't try harder in school. Housework, as radical feminists once proposed, defines a human relationship and, when unequally divided among social groups, reinforces preexisting inequalities. Dirt, in other words, tends to attach to the people who remove it—"garbagemen" and "cleaning ladies." Or, as cleaning entrepreneur Don Aslett told me with some bitterness—and this is a successful man, chairman of the board of an industrial cleaning service and frequent television guest—"The whole mentality out there is that if you clean, you're a scumball."

One of the "better" things employers of maids often want to do with their time is, of course, spend it with their children. But an underlying problem with post-nineteenth-century child-raising, as Deirdre English and I argued in our book *For Her Own Good* years ago, is precisely that it is unmoored in any kind of purposeful pursuit. Once "parenting" meant instructing the children in necessary chores; today it's more likely to center on one-sided conversations beginning with "So how was school today?" No one wants to put the kids to work again weeding and stitching; but in the void that is the modern home, relationships with children are often strained. A little "low-quality time" spent washing dishes or folding clothes together can provide a comfortable space for confidences—and give a child the dignity of knowing that he or she is a participant in, and not just the product of, the work of the home.

There is another lesson the servant economy teaches its beneficiaries and, most troubling, the children among them. To be cleaned up after is to achieve a certain magical weightlessness and immateriality. Almost everyone complains about violent video games, but paid housecleaning has the same consequence-abolishing effect: you blast the villain into a mist of blood droplets and move right along; you drop the socks knowing they will eventually levitate, laundered and folded, back to their normal dwelling place. The result is a kind of virtual existence, in which the trail of litter that follows you seems to evaporate all by itself. Spill syrup on the floor and the cleaning person will scrub it off when she comes on Wednesday. Leave *The Wall Street Journal* scattered around your airplane seat and the flight attendants will deal with it after you've deplaned. Spray toxins into the atmosphere from your factory's smokestacks and they will be filtered out eventually by the lungs of the breathing public. A servant economy breeds callousness and solipsism in the served, and it does so all the more effectively when the service is performed close up and routinely in the place where they live and reproduce.

Individual situations vary, of course, in ways that elude blanket judgment. Some people—the elderly and disabled, parents of new babies, asthmatics who require an allergen-free environment—may well need help performing what nursing-home staff call the "ADLs," or activities of daily living, and no shame should be attached to their dependency. In a more generous social order, housekeeping services would be subsidized for those who have health-related reasons to need them—a measure that would generate a surfeit of new jobs for the low-skilled people who now clean the homes of the affluent. And in a less gender-divided social order, husbands and boy-friends would more readily do their share of the chores.

However we resolve the issue in our individual homes, the moral challenge is, put simply, to make work visible again: not only the scrubbing and vacuuming but all the hoeing, stacking, hammering, drilling, bending, and lifting that goes into creating and maintaining a livable habitat. In an ever more economically unequal culture, where so many of the affluent devote their lives to such ghostly pursuits as stock-trading, image-making, and opinion-polling, real work—in the old-fashioned sense of labor that engages hand as well as eye, that tires the body and directly alters the physical world—tends to vanish from sight. The feminists of my generation tried to bring some of it into the light of day, but, like busy professional women fleeing the house in the morning, they left the project unfinished, the debate broken off in midsentence, the noble intentions unfulfilled. Sooner or later, someone else will have to finish the job.

THE GLOBETROTTING SNEAKER (1995)

Cynthia Enloe

Cynthia Enloe, professor of government at Clark University and author of The Morning After: Sexual Politics at the End of the Cold War, *discusses the production and marketing of the American athletic shoe and what it means for women workers in Asia. Companies like Nike and Reebok borrow the empowerment rhetoric of the U.S. women's movement to sell their product to women at home. At the same time, they abandon corporate responsibility for fair wages and safe working conditions for women workers abroad.*

Four years after the fall of the Berlin Wall marked the end of the Cold War, Reebok, one of the fastest growing companies in United States history, decided that the time had come to make its mark in Russia. Thus it was with considerable fanfare that Reebok's executives opened their first store in downtown Moscow in July 1993. A week after the grand opening, store managers described sales as well above expectations.

"The Globetrotting Sneaker," by Cynthia Enloe, from *Ms.* magazine, Vol. 5, No. 5, March/April 1995. Reprinted by permission of *Ms.* magazine, copyright © 1995.

Reebok's opening in Moscow was the perfect post-Cold War scenario: commercial rivalry replacing military posturing; consumerist tastes homogenizing heretofore hostile peoples; capital and managerial expertise flowing freely across newly porous state borders. Russians suddenly had the "freedom" to spend money on U.S. cultural icons like athletic footwear, items priced above and beyond daily subsistence: at the end of 1993, the average Russian earned the equivalent of $40 a month. Shoes on display were in the $100 range. Almost 60 percent of single parents, most of whom were women, were living in poverty. Yet in Moscow and Kiev, shoe promoters had begun targeting children, persuading them to pressure their mothers to spend money on stylish, Western sneakers. And as far as strategy goes, athletic shoe giants have, you might say, a good track record. In the U.S. many inner-city boys who see basketball as a "ticket out of the ghetto" have become convinced that certain brand-name shoes will give them an edge.

But no matter where sneakers are bought or sold, the potency of their advertising imagery has made it easy to ignore this mundane fact: Shaquille O'Neal's Reeboks are stitched by someone; Michael Jordan's Nikes are stitched by someone; so are your roommate's, so are your grandmother's. Those someones are women, mostly Asian women who are supposed to believe that their "opportunity" to make sneakers for U.S. companies is a sign of their country's progress—just as a Russian woman's chance to spend two months' salary on a pair of shoes for her child allegedly symbolizes the new Russia.

As the global economy expands, sneaker executives are looking to pay women workers less and less, even though the shoes that they produce are capturing an ever-growing share of the footwear market. By the end of 1993, sales in the U.S. alone had reached $11.6 billion. Nike, the largest supplier of athletic footwear in the world, posted a record $298 million profit for 1993—earnings that had nearly tripled in five years. And sneaker companies continue to refine their strategies for "global competitiveness"—hiring supposedly docile women to make their shoes, changing designs as quickly as we fickle customers change our tastes, and shifting factories from country to country as trade barriers rise and fall.

The logic of it all is really quite simple; yet trade agreements such as the North American Free Trade Agreement (NAFTA) and the General Agreement on Tariffs and Trade (GATT) are, of

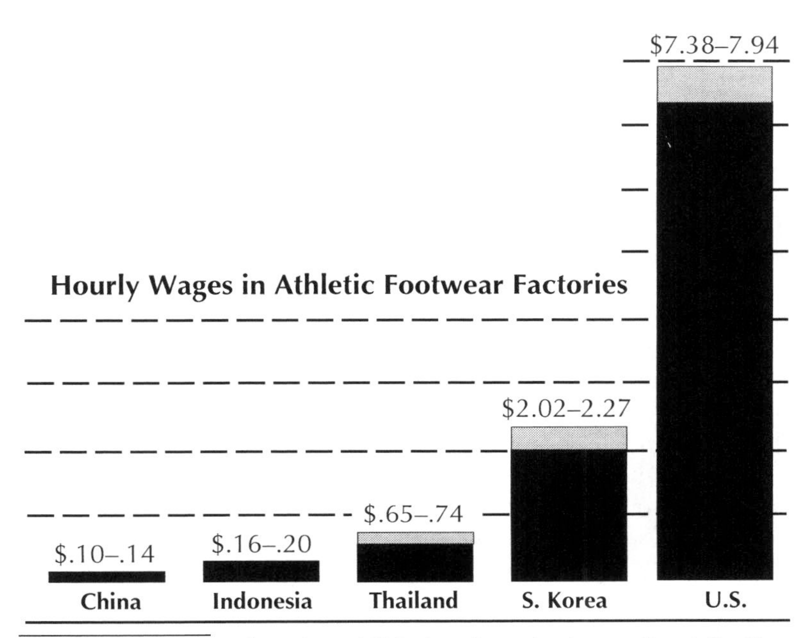

Figures are estimates based on 1993 data from the International Textile, Garment, and Leather Workers foundation; International Labor Organization; and the U.S. Bureau of Labor Statistics.

course, talked about in a jargon that alienates us, as if they were technical matters fit only for economists and diplomats. The bottom line is that all companies operating overseas depend on trade agreements made between their own governments and the regimes ruling the countries in which they want to make or sell their products. Korean, Indonesian, and other women workers around the world know this better than anyone. They are tackling trade politics because they have learned from hard experience that the trade deals their governments sign do little to improve the lives of workers. Guarantees of fair, healthy labor practices, of the rights to speak freely and to organize independently, will usually be left out of trade pacts—and women will suffer. The recent passage of both NAFTA and GATT ensures that a growing number of private companies will now be competing across borders without restriction. The result? Big business will step up efforts to pit working women in industrialized countries against much lower-paid working women in "developing" countries, perpetuating the misleading notion that they are inevitable rivals in the global job market.

All the "New World Order" really means to corporate giants like athletic shoemakers is that they now have the green light to accelerate long-standing industry practices. In the early 1980s, the field marshals commanding Reebok and Nike, which are both U.S.-based, decided to manufacture most of their sneakers in South Korea and Taiwan, hiring local women. L.A. Gear, Adidas, Fila, and Asics quickly followed their lead. In short time, the coastal city of Pusan, South Korea, became the "sneaker capital of the world." Between 1982 and 1989 the U.S. lost 58,500 footwear jobs to cities like Pusan, which attracted sneaker executives because its location facilitated international transport. More to the point, South Korea's military government had an interest in suppressing labor organizing, and it had a comfortable military alliance with the U.S. Korean women also seemed accepting of Confucian philosophy, which measured a woman's morality by her willingness to work hard for her family's well-being and to acquiesce to her father's and husband's dictates. With their sense of patriotic duty, Korean women seemed the ideal labor force for export-oriented factories.

U.S. and European sneaker company executives were also attracted by the ready supply of eager Korean male entrepreneurs with whom they could make profitable arrangements. This fact was central to Nike's strategy in particular. When they moved their production sites to Asia to lower labor costs, the executives of the Oregon-based company decided to reduce their corporate responsibilities further. Instead of owning factories outright, a more efficient strategy would be to subcontract the manufacturing to wholly foreign-owned—in this case, South Korean—companies. Let them be responsible for workers' health and safety. Let them negotiate with newly emergent unions. Nike would retain control over those parts of sneaker production that gave its officials the greatest professional satisfaction and the ultimate word on the product: design and marketing. Although Nike was following in the footsteps of garment and textile manufacturers, it set the trend for the rest of the athletic footwear industry.

But at the same time, women workers were developing their own strategies. As the South Korean pro-democracy movement grew throughout the 1980s, increasing numbers of women rejected traditional notions of feminine duty. Women began organizing in response to the dangerous working conditions, daily humiliations, and low pay built into their work. Such resistance was profoundly threatening to the government, given the fact that South Korea's emergence as an industrialized "tiger" had depended on women accepting their "role" in growing industries like sneaker manufacture. If women re-imagined their lives as daughters, as wives, as workers, as citizens, it wouldn't just rattle their employers; it would shake the very foundations of the whole political system.

At the first sign of trouble, factory managers called in government riot police to break up employees' meetings. Troops sexually assaulted women workers, stripping, fondling, and raping them "as a control mechanism for suppressing women's engagement in the labor movement," reported Jeong-Lim Nam of Hyosung Women's University in Taegu. It didn't work. It didn't work because the feminist activists in groups like the Korean Women Workers Association (KWWA) helped women understand and deal with the assaults. The KWWA held consciousness-raising sessions in which notions of feminine duty and respectability were tackled along with wages and benefits. They organized independently of the male-led labor unions to ensure that their issues would be taken seriously, in labor negotiations and in the pro-democracy movement as a whole.

The result was that women were at meetings with management, making sure that in addition to issues like long hours and low pay, sexual assault at the hands of managers and health care were on the table. Their activism paid off: in addition to winning the right to organize women's unions, their earnings grew. In 1980, South Korean women in manufacturing jobs earned 45 percent of the wages of their male counterparts; by 1990, they were earning more than 50 percent. Modest though it was, the pay increase was concrete progress, given that the gap between women's and men's manufacturing wages in Japan, Singapore, and Sri Lanka actually *widened* during the 1980s. Last but certainly not least, women's organizing was credited with playing a major role in toppling the country's military regime and forcing open elections in 1987.

Without that special kind of workplace control that only an authoritarian government could offer, sneaker executives knew that it was time to move. In Nike's case, its famous advertising slogan—"Just Do It"—proved truer to its corporate philosophy than its women's "empowerment" ad campaign, designed to rally women's athletic (and consumer) spirit. In response to South

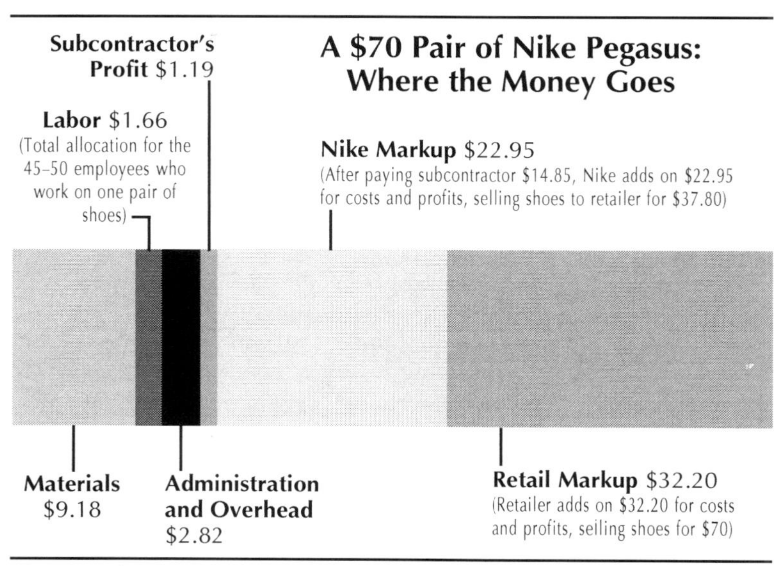

Source: Nike, Inc.

Korean women workers' newfound activist self-confidence, the sneaker company and its subcontractors began shutting down a number of their South Korean factories in the late 1980s and early 1990s. After bargaining with government officials in nearby China and Indonesia, many Nike subcontractors set up shop in those countries, while some went to Thailand. China's government remains nominally Communist; Indonesia's ruling generals are staunchly anti-Communist. But both are governed by authoritarian regimes who share the belief that if women can be kept hard at work, low paid, and unorganized, they can serve as a magnet for foreign investors.

Where does all this leave South Korean women—or any woman who is threatened with a factory closure if she demands decent working conditions and a fair wage? They face the dilemma confronted by thousands of women from dozens of countries. The risk of job loss is especially acute in relatively mobile industries; it's easier for a sneaker, garment, or electronics manufacturer to pick up and move than it is for an automaker or a steel producer. In the case of South Korea, poor women had moved from rural villages into the cities searching for jobs to support not only themselves, but parents and siblings. The exodus of manufacturing jobs has forced more women into the growing "entertainment" industry. The kinds of bars and massage parlors offering sexual services that had mushroomed around U.S. military bases during the Cold War have been opening up across the country.

But the reality is that women throughout Asia are organizing, knowing full well the risks involved. Theirs is a long-term view; they are taking direct aim at companies' nomadic advantage, by building links among workers in countries targeted for "development" by multinational corporations. Through sustained grassroots efforts, women are developing the skills and confidence that will make it increasingly difficult to keep their labor cheap. Many looked to the United Nations conference on women in Beijing, China as a rare opportunity to expand their cross-border strategizing.

The Beijing conference will also provide an important opportunity to call world attention to the hypocrisy of the governments and corporations doing business in China. Numerous athletic shoe companies followed Nike in setting up manufacturing sites throughout the country. This included Reebok—a company claiming its share of responsibility for ridding the world of "injustice, poverty, and other ills that gnaw away at the social fabric," according to a statement of corporate principles.

Since 1988, Reebok has been giving out annual human rights awards to dissidents from around the world. But it wasn't until 1992 that the company adopted its own "human rights production standards"—after labor advocates made it known that the quality of life in factories run by its subcontractors was just as dismal as that at most other athletic shoe suppliers in Asia. Reebok's code of conduct, for example, includes a pledge to "seek" those subcontractors who respect workers' rights to organize. The only problem is that independent trade unions are banned in China. Reebok has chosen to ignore that fact, even though Chinese dissidents have been the recipients of the company's own human rights award. As for working conditions, Reebok now says it sends its own inspectors to production sites a couple of times a year. But they have easily "missed" what subcontractors are trying to hide—like 400 young women workers locked at night into an overcrowded dormitory near a Reebok-contracted factory in the town of Zhuhai, as reported last August in the *Asian Wall Street Journal Weekly*.

Nike's co-founder and CEO Philip Knight has said that he would like the world to think of Nike as "a company with a soul that recognizes the value of human beings." Nike, like Reebok, says it sends in inspectors from time to time to check up on work conditions at its factories; in Indonesia, those factories are run largely by South Korean subcontractors. But according to Donald Katz in a recent book on the company, Nike spokesman Dave Taylor told an in-house newsletter that the factories are "[the subcontractors'] business to run." For the most part, the company relies on regular reports from subcontractors regarding its "Memorandum of Understanding," which managers must sign, promising to impose "local government standards" for wages, working conditions, treatment of workers, and benefits.

The minimum wage in the Indonesian capital of Jakarta is $1.89 *a day*—among the highest in a country where the minimum wage varies by region. And managers are required to pay only 75 percent of the wage directly; the remainder can be withheld for "benefits." By now, Nike has a well-honed response to growing criticism of its low-cost labor strategy. Such wages should not be seen as exploitative, says Nike, but rather as the first rung on the ladder of economic opportunity that Nike has extended to workers with few options. Otherwise, they'd be out "harvesting coconut meat in the tropical sun," wrote Nike spokesman Dusty Kidd, in a letter to the *Utne Reader*. The all-is-relative response craftily shifts attention away from reality: Nike didn't move to Indonesia to help Indonesians; it moved to ensure that its profit margin continues to grow. And that is pretty much guaranteed in a country where "local standards" for wages rarely take a worker over the poverty line. A 1991 survey by the International Labor Organization (ILO) found that 88 percent of women working at the Jakarta minimum wage at the time—slightly less than a dollar a day—were malnourished.

A woman named Riyanti might have been among the workers surveyed by the ILO. Interviewed by *The Boston Globe* in 1991, she told the reporter who had asked about her long hours and low pay: "I'm happy working here. . . . I can make money and I can make friends." But in fact, the reporter discovered that Riyanti had already joined her coworkers in two strikes, the first to force one of Nike's Korean subcontractors to accept a new women's union and the second to compel managers to pay at least the minimum wage. That Riyanti appeared less than forthcoming about her activities isn't surprising. Many Indonesian factories have military men posted in their front offices who find no fault with managers who tape women's mouths shut to keep them from talking among themselves. They and their superiors have a political reach that extends far beyond the barracks. Indonesia has all the makings for a political explosion, especially since the gap between rich and poor is widening into a chasm. It is in this setting that the government has tried to crack down on any independent labor organizing—a policy that Nike has helped to implement. Referring to a recent strike in a Nike-contracted factory, Tony Nava, Nike representative in Indonesia, told *The Chicago Tribune* in November 1994 that the "troublemakers" had been fired. When asked about Nike policy on the issue, spokesman Keith Peters struck a conciliatory note: "If the government were to allow and encourage independent labor organizing, we would be happy to support it."

Indonesian workers' efforts to create unions independent of governmental control were a surprise to shoe companies. Although their moves from South Korea have been immensely profitable [see chart, previous page], they do not have the sort of immunity from activism that they had expected. In May 1993, the murder of a female labor activist outside Surabaya set off a storm of local and international protest. Even the U.S. State Department was forced to take note in its 1993 worldwide human rights report, describing a system similar to that which generated South Korea's boom 20 years earlier: severely restricted union organizing, security forces used to break up strikes, low wages for men, lower wages for women—complete with government rhetoric celebrating women's contribution to national development.

Yet when President Clinton visited Indonesia, he made only a token effort to address the country's human rights problem. Instead, he touted the benefits of free trade, sounding indeed more enlightened, more in tune with the spirit of the post-Cold War era than do those defenders of protectionist trading policies who coat their rhetoric with "America first" chauvinism. But "free trade" as actually being practiced today is hardly *free* for any workers—in the U.S. or abroad—who have to accept the Indonesian, Chinese, or Korean workplace model as the price of keeping their jobs.

The not-so-new plot of the international trade story has been "divide and rule." If women workers and their government in one country can see that a sneaker company will pick up and leave if their labor demands prove more costly than those in a neighbor country, then women workers will tend to see their neighbors not as regional sisters, but as competitors who can steal their precarious livelihoods. Playing women off against each other is, of course, old hat. Yet it is as essential to international trade politics as is the fine print in GATT.

But women workers allied through networks like the Hong Kong-based Committee for Asian Women are developing their own post-Cold War foreign policy, which means addressing women's needs: how to convince fathers and husbands that a woman going out to organizing meetings at night is not sexually promiscuous; how to develop workplace agendas that respond to family needs; how to work with male unionists who push women's demands to the bottom of their lists; how to build a global movement.

These women refused to stand in awe of the corporate power of the Nike or Reebok or Adidas executive. Growing numbers of Asian women today have concluded that trade politics have to be understood by women on their own terms. They came to Beijing in September 1996, ready to engage with women from other regions to link the politics of consumerism with the politics of manufacturing. If women in Russia and eastern Europe can challenge Americanized consumerism, if Asian activists can solidify their alliances, and if U.S. women can join with them by taking on trade politics—the post-Cold War sneaker may be a less comfortable fit in the 1990s.

Questions

1. According to Enloe, why do trade deals between countries do little to improve the lives of workers? How are women pitted against each other in the global competition for expanding markets and cheap labor? What factors keep women's labor cheap?

2. Describe the working conditions for those who produce the shoes. How are women and human rights advocates organizing to end harmful labor practices? What are the risks and benefits for working women? How are the companies responding?

3. Why are consumers at home and abroad willing to pay so much for shoes? Where does the money go? What are some of the contradictions involved in Nike's support for women's athletics?

THE POLITICS OF HOUSEWORK (1970)

Pat Mainardi

Pat Mainardi is an art historian, critic and to some a radical feminist—a distinction she earned because of her membership in Redstockings (founded in 1969; it was an offshoot of one of the oldest women's liberation organizations—New York Radical Women). Mainardi has lectured and written on art and gender extensively, including a number of works that explore the dynamics of sexism in art: Art and Politics of the Second Empire *(1987);* The End of the Salon: Art and the State in the Early Third Republic, *(1993); and the* Persistence of Classicism *(1995).*

The "Politics of Housework" was written in 1970 when the gender roles of men and women were being reexamined in light of how they reflected and reinforced the power dynamics of patriarchy. Here Mainardi takes a satirical look at housework—a seemingly trivial matter—to demonstrate that power dynamics are present in every aspect of male/female relations.

"The Politics of Housework" by Pat Mainardi, Reprinted from *Sisterhood is Powerful* Ed. Robin Morgan. New York: Random House, 1970.

> Though women do not complain of the power of husbands, each complains of her own husband, or of the husbands of her friends. It is the same in all other cases of servitude; at least in the commencement of the emancipatory movement. The serfs did not at first complain of the power of the lords, but only of their tyranny.
>
> (John Stuart Mill, *On the Subjection of Women*)

Liberated women—very different from women's liberation! The first signals all kinds of goodies, to warm the hearts (not to mention other parts) of the most radical men. The other signals—*housework.* The first brings sex without marriage, sex before marriage, cozy housekeeping arrangements ("You see, I'm living with this chick") and the self-content of knowing that you're not the kind of man who wants a doormat instead of a woman. That will come later. After all, who wants that old commodity anymore, the Standard American Housewife, all husband, home and kids. The New Commodity, the Liberated Woman, has sex a lot and has a Career, preferably something that can be fitted in with the household chores—like dancing, pottery, or painting.

On the other hand is women's liberation—and housework. What? You say this is all trivial? Wonderful! That's what I thought. It seemed perfectly reasonable. We both had careers, both had to work a couple of days a week to earn enough to live on, so why shouldn't we share the housework? So I suggested it to my mate and he agreed—most men are too hip to turn you down flat. "You're right," he said, "It's only fair."

Then an interesting thing happened. I can only explain it by stating that we women have been brainwashed more than even we can imagine. Probably too many years of seeing television women in ecstasy over their shiny waxed floors or breaking down over their dirty shirt collars. Men have no such conditioning. They recognize the essential fact of housework right from the very beginning. Which is that it stinks. Here's my list of dirty chores: buying groceries, carting them home and putting them away; cooking meals and washing dishes and pots; doing the laundry, digging out the place when things get out of control; washing floors. The list could go on but the sheer necessities are bad enough. All of us have to do these things, or get some one else to do them for us. The longer my husband contemplated these chores, the more repulsed he became, and so proceeded the change from normally sweet considerate Dr. Jekyll into the crafty Mr. Hyde who would stop at nothing to avoid the horrors of—*housework.* As he felt himself backed into a corner laden with dirty dishes, brooms, mops, and reeking garbage, his front teeth grew longer and pointier, his fingernails haggled and his eyes grew wild. Housework trivial? Not on your life! Just try to share the burden.

So ensued a dialogue that's been going on for several years. Here are some of the high points:

"I don't mind sharing the housework, but I don't do it very well. We should each do the things we're best at."

Meaning: Unfortunately I'm no good at things like washing dishes or cooking. What I do best is a little light carpentry, changing light bulbs, moving furniture (*how often do you move furniture?*).

Also Meaning: Historically the lower classes (black men and us) have had hundreds of years experience doing menial jobs. It would be a waste of manpower to train someone else to do them now.

Also Meaning: I don't like the dull stupid boring jobs, so you should do them.

"I don't mind sharing the work, but you'll have to show me how to do it."

Meaning: I ask a lot of questions and you'll have to show me everything everytime I do it because I don't remember so good. Also don't try to sit down and read while I'm doing my jobs because I'm going to annoy the hell out of you until it's easier to do them yourself.

"We used to be so happy!" (Said whenever it was his turn to do something.)

Meaning: I used to be so happy.

Meaning: Life without housework is bliss. (*No quarrel here. Perfect agreement.*)

"We have different standards, and why should I have to work to your standards. That's unfair."

Meaning: If I begin to get bugged by the dirt and crap I will say "This place sure is a sty" or "How can anyone live like this?" and wait for your reaction. I know that all women have a sore called "Guilt over a messy house" or "Household work is ultimately my responsibility." I know that men have caused that sore—if anyone visits and the place *is* a sty, they're not going to leave and say, "He sure is a lousy housekeeper." You'll take the rap in any case. I can outwait you.

Also Meaning: I can provoke innumerable scenes over the housework issue. Eventually doing all the housework yourself will be less painful to you than trying to get me to do half. Or I'll suggest we get a maid. She will do my share of the work. You will do yours. It's women's work.

"I've got nothing against sharing the housework, but you can't make me do it on your schedule."

Meaning: Passive resistance. I'll do it when I damned well please, if at all. If my job is doing dishes, it's easier to do them once a week. If taking out laundry, once a month. If washing the floors, once a year. If you don't like it, do it yourself oftener, and then I won't do it at all.

"I *hate* it more than you. You don't mind it so much."

Meaning: Housework is garbage work. It's the worst crap I've ever done. It's degrading and humiliating for someone of *my* intelligence to do it. But for someone of *your* intelligence . . .

"Housework is too trivial to even talk about."

Meaning: It's even more trivial to do. Housework is beneath my status. My purpose in life is to deal with matters of significance. Yours is to deal with matters of insignificance. You should do the housework.

"This problem of housework is not a man-woman problem! In any relationship between two people one is going to have a stronger personality and dominate."

Meaning: That stronger personality had better be *me*.

"In animal societies, wolves, for example, the top animal is usually a male even where he is not chosen for brute strength but on the basis of cunning and intelligence. Isn't that interesting?"

Meaning: I have historical, psychological, anthropological, and biological justification for keeping you down. How can you ask the top wolf to be equal?

"Women's liberation isn't really a political movement."

Meaning: The Revolution is coming too close to home.

Also Meaning: I am only interested in how *I* am oppressed, not how I oppress others. Therefore the war, the draft, and the university are political. Women's liberation is not.

"Man's accomplishments have always depended on getting help from other people, mostly women. What great man would have accomplished what he did if he had to do his own housework?

Meaning: Oppression is built into the System and I, as the white American male, receive the benefits of this System. I don't want to give them up.

Postscript

Participatory democracy begins at home. If you are planning to implement our politics, there are certain things to remember.

1. He *is* feeling it more than you. He's losing some leisure and you're gaining it. The measure of your oppression is his resistance.

2. A great many American men are not accustomed to doing monotonous repetitive work which never ushers in any lasting let alone important achievement. This is why they would rather repair a cabinet than wash dishes. If human endeavors are like a pyramid with man's highest achievements at the top, then keeping oneself alive is at the bottom. Men have always had servants (us) to take care of this bottom strata of life while they have confined their efforts to the rarefied upper regions. It is thus ironic when they ask of women—where are your great painters, statesmen, etc.? Mme. Matisse ran a millinery shop so he could paint. Mrs. Martin Luther King kept his house and raised his babies.

3. It is a traumatizing experience for someone who has always thought of himself as being against any oppression or exploitation of one human being by another to realize that in his daily life he has been accepting and implementing (and benefiting from) this exploitation; that his rationaliza-

tion is little different from that of the racist who says "Black people don't feel pain" (women don't mind doing the shitwork); and that the oldest form of oppression in history has been the oppression of 50 percent of the population by the other 50 percent.

4. Arm yourself with some knowledge of the psychology of oppressed peoples everywhere and a few facts about the animal kingdom. I admit playing top wolf or who runs the gorillas is silly but as a last resort men bring it up all the time. Talk about bees. If you feel really hostile bring up the sex life of spiders. They have sex. She bites off his head.

   The psychology of oppressed people is not silly. Jews, immigrants, black men, and all women have employed the same psychological mechanisms to survive: admiring the oppressor, glorifying the oppressor, wanting to be like the oppressor, wanting the oppressor to like them, mostly because the oppressor held all the power.

5. In a sense, all men everywhere are slightly schizoid—divorced from the reality of maintaining life. This makes it easier for them to play games with it. It is almost a cliché that women feel greater grief at sending a son off to war or losing him to that war because they bore him, suckled him, and raised him. The men who foment those wars did none of these things and have a more superficial estimate of the worth of human life. One hour a day is a low estimate of the amount of time one has to spend "keeping" oneself. By foisting this off on others, man gains seven hours a week—one working day more to play with his mind and not his human needs. Over the course of generations it is easy to see whence evolved the horrifying abstractions of modern life.

6. With the death of each form of oppression, life changes and new forms evolve. English aristocrats at the turn of the century were horrified at the idea of enfranchising working men—were sure that it signaled the death of civilization and a return to barbarism. Some working men were even deceived by this line. Similarly with the minimum wage, abolition of slavery, and female suffrage. Life changes but it goes on. Don't fall for any line about the death of

everything if men take a turn at the dishes. They will imply that you are holding back the Revolution (their Revolution). But you are advancing it (your Revolution).

7. Keep checking up. Periodically consider who's actually *doing* the jobs. These things have a way of backsliding so that a year later once again the woman is doing everything. After a year make a list of jobs the man has rarely if ever done. You will find cleaning pots, toilets, refrigerators and ovens high on the list. Use time sheets if necessary. He will accuse you of being petty. He is above that sort of thing—(housework). Bear in mind what the worst jobs are, namely the ones that have to be done every day or several times a day. Also the ones that are dirty—it's more pleasant to pick up books, newspapers, etc. than to wash dishes. Alternate the bad jobs. It's the daily grind that gets you down. Also make sure that you don't have the responsibility for the housework with occasional help from him. "I'll cook dinner for you tonight" implies it's really your job and isn't he a nice guy to do some of it for you.

8. Most men had a rich and rewarding bachelor life during which they did not starve or become encrusted with crud or buried under the litter. There is a taboo that says that women mustn't strain themselves in the presence of men: we haul around 50 pounds of groceries if we have to but aren't allowed to open a jar if there is someone around to do it for us. The reverse side of the coin is that men aren't supposed to be able to take care of themselves without a woman. Both are excuses for making women do the housework.

9. Beware of the double whammy. He won't do the little things he always did because you're now a "Liberated Woman," right? Of course he won't do anything else either . . .

I was just finishing this when my husband came in and asked what I was doing. Writing a paper on housework. Housework? he said, *Housework?* Oh my god how trivial can you get. A paper on housework. . . .

Questions

1. Why does Mainardi preface her article with the excerpt from John Stuart Mill's *On the Subjection of Women?* What distinction does Mainardi suggest between a liberated woman and "women's liberation"?
2. What is the tone of Mainardi's essay? What do you think her goals might be in writing it?
3. Are women more concerned about housework than men in heterosexual relationships today? Why or why not? What do the traditional assumptions concerning housework signify for Mainardi? What are the politics of housework?

Women in Culture

Teen Mags: How to Get a Guy, Drop 20 Pounds, and Lose Your Self-Esteem

Anastasia Higginbotham

I used to be the teen magazine market's ideal consumer: vain, terribly insecure, white, and middle class. I craved affection and approval from boys (often at the expense of meaningful relationships with girls), spent far too much time staring at myself in the mirror, and trusted the magazines' advice on all sorts of really, really important issues, like lip gloss and *luv*.

I plastered my family's refrigerator with pictures of models I'd torn out of *YM, Seventeen, Sassy*, and *'Teen*, and also *Vogue, Cosmopolitan*, and *Mademoiselle*—a strategy I used to remind me not to eat. I hoped they would inspire me to do great things, like be in a David Lee Roth video. I wish I were kidding.

Though this characterization might lead you to believe I was kind of a doorknob, I assure you I was merely acting like most girls my age at whom these magazines are directed, aspiring to an ideal that I knew would bring me much success in the social world. In my first 14 years, I learned that the pretty girl who knows how to play the game wins the prize. The "prize" being older, cooler, all-star boyfriends, multiple mentions and pictures throughout the school yearbook, and seasonal dubbings as makeshift teen royalty (Homecoming Queen, May Queen, blow-job queen, and so on). And so I absorbed the rules of the game, with teen magazines serving as a reliable source of that information.

Reprinted by permission of *Ms. Magazine*.

Ten years later, I pore over these magazines to see what they're telling girls today. As I flip through the pages of *YM, Seventeen, Sassy*, and *'Teen*, my blood begins to boil and my eyes cloud with anger; teen magazines make millions off of girls by assuming that girls need improving, and then telling girls how to make themselves prettier, cooler, and better. Has anything changed?

As horrified as I am by these magazines, I cannot deny their raging success. *Seventeen* and *YM* (which used to stand for *Young Miss* and now stands for *Young and Modern*) rake in nearly two million subscriptions each from their teen-to-early-twenties market. *'Teen* and *Sassy*, with readerships of 1.3 million and 800,000 respectively, cater to the younger end of the spectrum.

In each of the magazines, cover lines offer the girls "Model hair: how to get it," "Boy-magnet beauty," "Your looks: what they say about you," and "Mega makeovers: go from so-so to supersexy." Their image of the ideal girl is evidenced by the cover models: white, usually blond, and invariably skinny.

When I asked why this is, Caroline Miller, editor in chief of *Seventeen*, explained, "There's a traditional expectation that African Americans don't sell magazines." *Seventeen* has recently tested this proposition (which, by the way, fails to address the invisibility of Asian and Native American models) by featuring pop star Brandy on its April cover and another African American model on October's cover (both months are normally hot sellers). October sold just as well as the typical white-model cover, while the Brandy cover was possibly *Seventeen*'s best-selling April issue ever. Despite *Seventeen*'s success, rather than jeopardize newsstand sales and advertising dollars, well-intentioned editors at other magazines like *'Teen* and *Sassy* compromise by featuring some white-looking black model in a month that typically has the worst sales. Meanwhile, *YM* would probably be satisfied with a different shot of Drew Barrymore each month.

In the wake of *Sassy*'s transmogrification from bold, feminist teen mag into dumbed-down, superficial teen rag (*Sassy* was sold to Peterson Publishing, the same company that owns *'Teen*, in December 1994 after years of controversy with advertisers and parents over its content), *Seventeen*, under Miller, has taken up the *Sassy* mantle with smart stories about interracial dating, student activists, and African American girls' body image. *YM*, on the other hand, offers nothing more than bullshit and bad advice, and *'Teen* is not much better. The new *Sassy* lacks much of the brains, courage, and wit of the old *Sassy;* something that its editors, tragically, see as a good thing.

Just what are the messages in the teen magazines? A series of catch-22s—ugliness is next to nothingness and a girl with insufficient interest in boys is referred to as a "deserted island," yet one who is too sexy is also in trouble. For instance, April 1995 *Sassy* warns girls to watch who they flirt with because men cannot distinguish between harmless flirting and a full-on pass. According to *Sassy*, while a girl is flirting, "there's always a chance [men are] wondering what you look like without your clothes on." This mentality is used to justify the behavior of grown men who "get a little carried away sometimes" and harass, insult, and assault young women. A girl bears the responsibility of attracting every "hottie" (hot guy) on the beach, but if one of them jumps her, well then, it sucks to be her. Using *Sassy*'s logic, that girl should have known she was dealing with a potential psychopath.

YM echoes this sentiment in the July 1995 episode of "Love Crisis," a column in which Editor in Chief Sally Lee solves "agonizing love problems." A girl reveals that she was invited by her boyfriend to a party that turned out to be just him and his two male friends. They got her really drunk and she "ended up . . . having sex with all of them!" She writes, "I feel so dirty. . . . How could I have been so stupid?" The letter is signed "Mortified." *YM* apparently wonders the same thing: a caption on the page with her letter reads "Wake up and face the facts: you made a pretty big mistake." Lee then chastises the girl for underage drinking and not asserting herself.

Even if the girl has not actually been gang-raped, Lee's complete disregard for a girl who was tricked and humiliated by her boyfriend and his friends is unforgivable. *YM* shamelessly promotes boy-catching tactics with articles like "the ultimate get-a-guy guide," then acts surprised, even judgmental, when the tricks actually work. Girls are bombarded with messages about the thrill of catching boys, so why is it shocking when a girl's pursuit includes a little creative compromise, like forgiving her boyfriend for lying about the party, drinking when he tells her to drink, and being too drunk to care (or too drunk to resist) when he and his friends fuck her? *YM* shows girls 100 asinine ways to be supersexy and then provides them with no follow-up skills, self-defense, or self-esteem—as if ignorance will keep them from going all the way. If *YM* ever changes its name again, I suggest *Dicktease*.

Likewise, when it comes to body image, teen magazines send a convoluted message. Girls are encouraged to love their bodies, no matter what they look like, by magazines with fashion spreads featuring only stick-thin, flawless-faced white models in expensive outfits. Granted, there is that one light-skinned black girl in every fashion layout. But she's just as thin as the white girl standing next to her, and that white girl is *always* there—like a chaperone. Like it's the white girl's responsibility to keep the black girl in line, make sure she doesn't mingle with other black folks, start a riot or something. The black model doesn't have any black girlfriends; she's lucky if she gets a similarly nonthreatening black boyfriend for the prom. Maybe they think if they surround her with enough white people no one will even notice she's black.

The thin factor is equally dismaying. While the old *Sassy* strictly enforced a no-diet policy, forbidding publication of any and all diet advice (including the kind masquerading as a fitness article), the new *Sassy* eats it up. Catherine Ettlinger, until recently the editorial director of the new *Sassy*, rejects the connection between articles offering diet tips and girls' obsession with thinness: "We present them with options. 'If you want to eat more low-fat stuff, here's some information; if you don't, fine.'"

If it were that simple, girls would not be getting sick. In a culture that all but demands that a women weigh no more than 120 pounds, girls do not want for diet advice. Girls do not need more low-fat options, nor do they need to learn how to shed or hide "excess fat." Similarly, when *'Teen*, *YM*, and *Seventeen* take a turn on the self-love/body-pride trip, they tend to fall flat on their faces. Photos that accompany the stories typically depict a model—who isn't the least bit fat. Readers are supposed to empathize with girls who weigh 125 pounds but who are afraid to put on a bathing suit, exposing what they perceive to be huge thighs and bulging stomachs. Girls are reminded that because of their "low self-esteem" (certainly not because of patriarchy), they imagine their bodies to be much larger than they actually are. So, if they can get over that self-esteem thing and realize that they're not fat, they have nothing to worry about.

While body hatred of this type is epidemic, presenting body image as being about thin girls who think they're fat does nothing to undermine the essential prejudice against fatness, especially fat women. Is a fat girl beautiful? Should she worry? If she relies on these magazines for affirmation of her self-worth, yes, she should. And so should we.

Teen magazines' glorification of boy-focused, looks-based, prom-obsessed idiocy reinforces every negative stereotype that has ever been used to justify—and ensure—women's second-class status. But as a woman with very clear memories of high school, I understand the trauma associated with fitting in and finding love. I was not prepared for a feminist revolution at 16; I could barely deal with what the humidity did to my hair.

I wanted to find out what girls think about teen magazines nowadays, so I staged an informal survey with a group of teenagers and showed them issues of *'Teen, Sassy, Seventeen,* and *YM*. Some girls criticized the magazines for being too white, too into skinny, and too superficial, but readily admitted to delighting in them anyway.

Kate Stroup from Philadelphia subscribes to *Seventeen*, as well as to various "adult" fashion magazines. "I like the ads," she says. Stroup and her friends can spend hours looking at the pictures, talking about the articles, "even talking about how bad it is." She explains, "It gives us something to bond over."

Girls looking for something easy and entertaining are sure to find it within the pages of teen magazines. Just as I lapped up celebrity gossip while researching this story, the girls I spoke with see no harm in learning a stupid hair trick.

Some girls read them for tips on navigating the social scene and dealing with relationships. "Sometimes I like to read about what guys say, not saying that I would actually follow their advice," says Kenya Hooks of Memphis.

But Roshanda Betts from Dallas no longer reads teen magazines. "I can't relate to them and I don't really think that they're made for me," she says, referring to the unrealistic size requirements for girls, racist definitions of beauty, and what she sees as the magazines' self-contradictions. "They have articles talking about, 'You should love yourself for who you are,' and then they have the seven-day diet."

The girls all like *Seventeen*'s "School Zone," which each month features six pages of photos and quotes from a different high school and which, according to Betts, "shows the spectrum of what's really happening." It's the only place in any of the magazines where kids from various racial and ethnic backgrounds, with "imperfect" shapes and "flawed" complexions, are portrayed in all their splendor. "School Zone" puts the rest of the images in the magazine to shame merely by providing a glimpse of truth.

In the articles, reality often comes in the form of "real-life stories" injected into each magazine, it seems, to scare the hell out of the girl reading it. We can choose from "one girl's battle with depression," another's physically abusive relationship, the story of a woman who sank to 55 pounds, a girl who was "raped, shot, and left for dead," and many more. Without some analysis or a context in which to place these stories (Why did she starve herself? How can we avert these tragedies?), they are nothing more than tales of tabloid horror.

Several months' worth of *'Teen, Seventeen, YM* and *Sassy* left me with a blur of contradictory messages about how to navigate life as an adolescent girl. The sum of it is this: be pretty, but not so pretty that you intimidate boys, threaten other girls, or attract inappropriate suitors, such as teachers, bosses, fathers, and rapists; be smart, but not so smart that you intimidate boys or that, god forbid, you miss the prom to study for finals; be athletic, but not so athletic that you intimidate boys or lead people to believe that you are aggressive, asexual, or (gasp!) a lesbian or bisexual; be happy with yourself, but not if you're fat, ugly, poor, gay, disabled, antisocial, or can't at least pass as white.

The creators of teen magazines claim to reflect the reality of girls' lives; they say that they're giving girls what the girls say they want and, I'm sure that sometimes what girls want is, in fact, a new hairstyle and a prom date. But filling girls full of fluff and garbage—under the pretense that this is their reality—is patronizing, cowardly, and just plain lazy. Magazines that pride themselves on teaching girls beauty tips to "hide what they hate" ought to stop reflecting a reality marred by heterosexist double standards and racist ignorance and start changing it.

I understand the tremendous pressures that editors deal with from parents and advertisers who hold pristine ideas about teendom and girlhood and impose those ideas backed by the mighty dollar. But it's very clear where these editors and advertisers draw their lines. If they really wanted girls to love their bodies, they'd give them a few more shapes and colors to choose from, they'd provide articles exploring some of the real reasons why a girl might plow through a box of Oreos one moment, yak her guts out the next, and then zone in front of the television for sixteen hours a day. If they can be so brazen about teaching a girl how to kiss the boy of her dreams, they can teach her how to kiss a girl. They just won't. [1996]

THE BEAUTY MYTH (1991)

Naomi Wolf

Feminist writer and theorist Naomi Wolf, whose 1991 book The Beauty Myth *is excerpted below, was born in San Francisco in 1962. A graduate of Yale University and a Rhodes Scholar, Wolf has lectured extensively on women's issues and authored several books including* Fire with Fire *(1993) and* Promiscuities *(1996). In this selection, Wolf explores Western beauty ideology by examining both its historical roots and its contemporary effects. She argues that modern beauty ideology is based on a mythical perception of "beauty"—a socially constructed set of ideas about how female bodies should appear and behave—that has become more rigid and restrictive even as women have gained political and economic ground.*

At last, after a long silence, women took to the streets. In the two decades of radical action that followed the rebirth of feminism in the early 1970s, Western women gained legal and reproductive rights, pursued higher education, entered the trades and the professions, and overturned ancient and revered beliefs about their social role. A generation on, do women feel free?

The affluent, educated, liberated women of the First World, who can enjoy freedoms unavailable to any women ever before, do not feel as free as they want to. And they can no longer restrict to the subconscious their sense that this lack of freedom has something to do with—with apparently frivolous issues, things that really should not matter. Many are ashamed to admit that such trivial concerns—to do with physical appearance, bodies, faces, hair, clothes—matter so much. But in spite of shame, guilt, and denial, more and more women are wondering if it isn't that they are entirely neurotic and alone but rather that something important is indeed at stake that has to do with the relationship between female liberation and female beauty.

The more legal and material hindrances women have broken through, the more strictly and heavily and cruelly images of female beauty have come to weigh upon us. Many women sense that women's collective progress has stalled; compared with the heady momentum of earlier days, there is a dispiriting climate of confusion, division, cynicism, and above all, exhaustion. After years of much struggle and little recognition, many older women feel burned out; after years of taking its light for granted, many younger women show little interest in touching new fire to the torch.

During the past decade, women breached the power structure; meanwhile, eating disorders rose exponentially and cosmetic surgery became the fastest-growing medical specialty. During the past five years, consumer spending doubled, pornography became the main media category, ahead of legitimate films and records combined, and thirty-three thousand American women told researchers that they would rather lose ten to fifteen pounds than achieve any other goal. More women have more money and power and scope and legal recognition than we have ever had before; but in terms of how we feel about ourselves *physically*, we may actually be worse off than our unliberated grandmothers. Recent research consistently shows that inside the majority of the West's controlled, attractive, successful working women, there is a secret "underlife" poisoning our freedom; infused with notions of beauty, it is a dark vein of self-hatred, physical obsessions, terror of aging, and dread of lost control.

It is no accident that so many potentially powerful women feel this way. We are in the midst of a violent backlash against feminism that uses images of female beauty as a political weapon against women's advancement: the beauty myth. It is the modern version of a social reflex that has been in force since the Industrial Revolution. As women released themselves from the feminine mystique of domesticity, the beauty myth took over its lost ground, expanding as it waned to carry on its work of social control.

The contemporary backlash is so violent because the ideology of beauty is the last one remaining of the old feminine ideologies that still has the power to control those women whom second wave feminism would have otherwise made relatively uncontrollable: It has grown stronger to take over the work of social coercion that myths about motherhood, domesticity, chastity, and passivity no longer can manage. It is seeking right now to undo psychologically and covertly all the good things that feminism did for women materially and overtly.

This counterforce is operating to checkmate the inheritance of feminism on every level in the lives of Western women. Feminism gave us laws against job discrimination based on gender; immediately case law evolved in Britain and the United States that institutionalized job discrimination based on women's appearances. Patriarchal religion declined; new religious dogma, using some of the mind-altering techniques of older cults and sects, arose around age and weight to functionally supplant traditional ritual. Feminists, inspired by Friedan, broke the strangle hold on the women's popular press of advertisers for household products, who were promoting the feminine mystique; at once, the diet and skin care industries became the new cultural censors of women's intellectual space, and because of their pressure, the gaunt, youthful model supplanted the happy housewife as the arbiter of successful womanhood. The sexual revolution promoted the discovery of female sexuality; "beauty pornography"—which for the first time in women's history artificially links a commodified "beauty" directly and explicitly to sexuality—invaded the mainstream to undermine women's new and vulnerable sense of sexual self-worth. Reproductive rights gave Western women control over our own bodies; the weight of fashion models plummeted to 23 percent below that of ordinary women, eating disorders rose exponentially, and a mass neurosis was promoted that used food and weight to strip women of that sense of control. Women insisted on politicizing health; new technologies of invasive, potentially deadly "cosmetic" surgeries developed apace to re-exert old forms of medical control of women.

Every generation since about 1830 has had to fight its version of the beauty myth. "It is very little to me," said the suffragist Lucy Stone in 1855, "to have the right to vote, to own property, etcetera, if I may not keep my body, and its uses, in my absolute right." Eighty years later, after women had won the vote, and the first wave of the organized women's movement had subsided, Virginia Woolf wrote that it would still be decades before women could tell the truth about their bodies. In 1962, Betty Friedan quoted a young woman trapped in the Feminine Mystique: "Lately, I look in the mirror, and I'm so afraid I'm going to look like my mother." Eight years after that, heralding the cataclysmic second wave of feminism, Germaine Greer described "the Stereotype": "To her belongs all that is beautiful, even the very word beauty itself . . . she is a doll . . . I'm sick of the masquerade." In spite of the great revolution of the second wave, we are not exempt. Now we can look out over ruined barricades: A revolution has come upon us and changed everything in its path, enough time has passed since then for babies to have grown into women, but there still remains a final right not fully claimed.

The beauty myth tells a story: The quality called "beauty" objectively and universally exists. Women must want to embody it and men must want to possess women who embody it. This embodiment is an imperative for women and not for men, which situation is necessary and natural because it is biological, sexual, and evolutionary: Strong men battle for beautiful women, and beautiful women are more reproductively successful. Women's beauty must correlate to their fertility, and since this system is based on sexual selection, it is inevitable and changeless.

None of this is true. "Beauty" is a currency system like the gold standard. Like any economy, it is determined by politics, and in the modern age in the West it is the last, best belief system that keeps male dominance intact. In assigning value to women in a vertical hierarchy according to a culturally imposed physical standard, it is an expression of power relations in which women must unnaturally compete for resources that men have appropriated for themselves.

"Beauty" is not universal or changeless, though the West pretends that all ideals of female beauty stem from one Platonic

Ideal Woman; the Maori admire a fat vulva, and the Padung, droopy breasts. Nor is "beauty" a function of evolution: Its ideals change at a pace far more rapid than that of the evolution of species, and Charles Darwin was himself unconvinced by his own explanation that "beauty" resulted from a "sexual selection" that deviated from the rule of natural selection; for women to compete with women through "beauty" is a reversal of the way in which natural selection affects all other mammals. Anthropology has overturned the notion that females must be "beautiful" to be selected to mate: Evelyn Reed, Elaine Morgan, and others have dismissed sociobiological assertions of innate male polygamy and female monogamy. Female higher primates are the sexual initiators: not only do they seek out and enjoy sex with many partners, but "every nonpregnant female takes her turn at being the most desirable of all her troop. And that cycle keeps turning as long as she lives." The inflamed pink sexual organs of primates are often cited by male sociobiologists as analogous to human arrangements relating to female "beauty," when in fact that is a universal, nonhierarchical female primate characteristic.

Nor has the beauty myth always been this way. Though the pairing of the older rich men with young, "beautiful" women is taken to be somehow inevitable, in the matriarchal Goddess religions that dominated the Mediterranean from about 25,000 B.C.E. to about 700 B.C.E., the situation was reversed: "In every culture, the Goddess has many lovers. . . . The clear pattern is of an older woman with a beautiful but expendable youth—Ishtar and Tammuz, Venus and Adonis, Cybele and Attis, Isis and Osiris . . . their only function the service of the divine 'womb.'" Nor is it something only women do and only men watch: Among the Nigerian Wodaabes, the women hold economic power and the tribe is obsessed with male beauty; Wodaabe men spend hours together in elaborate makeup sessions, and compete—provocatively painted and dressed, with swaying hips and seductive expressions—in beauty contests judged by women. There is no legitimate historical or biological justification for the beauty myth; what it is doing to women today is a result of nothing more exalted than the need of today's power structure, economy, and culture to mount a counteroffensive against women.

If the beauty myth is not based on evolution, sex, gender, aesthetics, or God, on what is it based? It claims to be about intimacy and sex and life, a celebration of women. It is actually composed of emotional distance, politics, finance, and sexual repression. The beauty myth is not about women at all. It is about men's institutions and institutional power.

The qualities that a given period calls beautiful in women are merely symbols of the female behavior that that period considers desirable: *The beauty myth is always actually prescribing behavior and not appearance.* Competition between women has been made part of the myth so that women will be divided from one another. Youth and (until recently) virginity have been "beautiful" in women since they stand for experiential and sexual ignorance. Aging in women is "unbeautiful" since women grow more powerful with time, and since the links between generations of women must always be newly broken: Older women fear young ones, young women fear old, and the beauty myth truncates for all the female life span. Most urgently, women's identity must be premised upon our "beauty" so that we will remain vulnerable to outside approval, carrying the vital sensitive organ of self-esteem exposed to the air.

Though there has, of course, been a beauty myth in some form for as long as there has been patriarchy, the beauty myth in its modern form is a fairly recent invention. The myth flourishes when material constraints on women are dangerously loosened. Before the Industrial Revolution, the average woman could not have had the same feelings about "beauty" that modern women do who experience the myth as continual comparison to a mass-disseminated physical ideal. Before the development of technologies of mass production—daguerreotypes, photographs, etc.—an ordinary woman was exposed to few such images outside the Church. Since the family was a productive unit and women's work complemented men's, the value of women who were not aristocrats or prostitutes lay in their work skills, economic shrewdness, physical strength, and fertility. Physical attraction, obviously, played its part; but "beauty" as we understand it was not, for ordinary women, a serious issue in the marriage marketplace. The beauty myth in its modern form gained ground after the upheavals of industrialization, as the work unit of the family was destroyed, and urbanization and the emerging factory system demanded what social engineers of the time termed the "separate sphere" of domesticity, which supported the new labor category of the "breadwinner" who left home for the workplace during the day. The middle class expanded, the standards of living and of literacy rose, the size of families shrank; a new class of literate, idle women developed, on whose submission to enforced domesticity the evolving system of industrial capitalism depended. Most of our assumptions about the way women have always thought about "beauty" date from no earlier than the 1830s, when the cult of domesticity was first consolidated and the beauty index invented.

For the first time new technologies could reproduce—in fashion plates, daguerreotypes, tintypes, and rotogravures—images of how women should look. In the 1840s the first nude photographs of prostitutes were taken; advertisements using images of "beautiful" women first appeared in mid-century. Copies of classical artworks, postcards of society beauties and royal mistresses, Currier and Ives prints, and porcelain figurines flooded the separate sphere to which middle-class women were confined.

Since the Industrial Revolution, middle-class Western women have been controlled by ideals and stereotypes as much as by material constraints. This situation, unique to this group, means that analyses that trace "cultural conspiracies" are uniquely plausible in relation to them. The rise of the beauty myth was just one of several emerging social fictions that masqueraded as natural components of the feminine sphere, the better to enclose those women inside it. Other such fictions arose contemporaneously: a version of childhood that required continual maternal supervision; a concept of female biology that required middle-class women to act out the roles of hysterics and hypochondriacs; a conviction that respectable women were sexually anesthetic; and a definition of women's work that occupied them with repetitive, time-consuming, and painstaking tasks such as needlepoint and lacemaking. All such Victorian inventions as these served a double function—that is, though they were encouraged as a means to expend female energy and intelligence in harmless ways, women often used them to express genuine creativity and passion.

But in spite of middle-class women's creativity with fashion and embroidery and child rearing, and, a century later, with the role of the suburban housewife that devolved from these social fictions, the fictions' main purpose was served: During a century and a half of unprecedented feminist agitation, they effectively counteracted middle-class women's dangerous new leisure, literacy, and relative freedom from material constraints.

Though these time- and mind-consuming fictions about women's natural role adapted themselves to resurface in the postwar Feminine Mystique, when the second wave of the women's movement took apart what women's magazines had portrayed as the "romance," "science," and "adventure" of homemaking and suburban family life, they temporarily failed. The cloying domestic fiction of "togetherness" lost its meaning and middle-class women walked out of their front doors in masses.

So the fictions simply transformed themselves once more: Since the women's movement had successfully taken apart most other necessary fictions of femininity, all the work of social control once spread out over the whole network of these fictions had to be reassigned to the only strand left intact, which action consequently strengthened it a hundredfold. This reimposed onto liberated women's faces and bodies all the limitations, taboos, and punishments of the repressive laws, religious injunctions and reproductive enslavement that no longer carried sufficient force. Inexhaustible but ephemeral beauty work took over from inexhaustible but ephemeral housework. As the economy, law, religion, sexual mores, education, and culture were forcibly opened up to include women more fairly, a private reality colonized female consciousness. By using ideas about "beauty," it reconstructed an alternative female world with its own laws, economy, religion, sexuality, education, and culture, each element as repressive as any that had gone before.

Since middle-class Western women can best be weakened psychologically now that we are stronger materially, the beauty myth, as it has resurfaced in the last generation, has had to draw on more technological sophistication and reactionary fervor than ever before. The modern arsenal of the myth is a dissemination of millions of images of the current ideal; although this barrage is generally seen as a collective sexual fantasy, there is in fact little that is sexual about it. It is summoned out of political fear on the part of male-dominated institutions threatened by women's freedom, and it exploits female guilt and apprehension about our own liberation—latent fears that we might be going too far. This frantic aggregation of imagery is a collective reactionary hallucination willed into being by both men and women stunned and disoriented by the rapidity with which gender relations have been transformed: a bulwark of reassurance against the flood of change. The mass depiction of the modern woman as a "beauty" is a contradiction: Where modern women are growing, moving, and expressing their individuality, as the myth has it, "beauty" is by definition inert, timeless, and generic. That this hallucination is necessary and deliberate is evident in the way "beauty" so directly contradicts women's real situation.

And the unconscious hallucination grows ever more influential and pervasive because of what is now conscious market manipulation: powerful industries—the $33-billion-a-year diet industry, the $20-billion cosmetics industry, the $300-million cosmetic surgery industry, and the $7-billion pornography industry—have arisen from the capital made out of unconscious anxieties, and are in turn able, through their influence on mass culture, to use, stimulate, and reinforce the hallucination in a rising economic spiral.

This is not a conspiracy theory; it doesn't have to be. Societies tell themselves necessary fictions in the same way that individuals and families do. Henrik Ibsen called them "vital lies," and psychologist Daniel Goleman describes them working the same way on the social level that they do within families: "The collusion is maintained by directing attention away from the fearsome fact, or by repackaging its meaning in an acceptable format." The costs of these social blind spots, he writes, are destructive communal illusions. Possibilities for women have become so open-ended that they threaten to destabilize the institutions on which a male-dominated culture has depended, and a collective panic reaction on the part of both sexes has forced a demand for counterimages.

The resulting hallucination materializes, for women, as something all too real. No longer just an idea, it becomes three-dimensional, incorporating within itself how women live and how they do not live: It becomes the Iron Maiden. The original Iron Maiden was a medieval German instrument of torture, a body-shaped casket painted with the limbs and features of a lovely, smiling young woman. The unlucky victim was slowly enclosed inside her; the lid fell shut to immobilize the victim, who died either of starvation or, less cruelly, of the metal spikes embedded in her interior. The modern hallucination in which women are trapped or trap themselves is similarly rigid, cruel, and euphemistically painted. Contemporary culture directs attention to imagery of the Iron Maiden, while censoring real women's faces and bodies.

Why does the social order feel the need to defend itself by evading the fact of real women, our faces and voices and bodies, and reducing the meaning of women to these formulaic and endlessly reproduced "beautiful" images? Though unconscious personal anxieties can be a powerful force in the creation of a vital lie, economic necessity practically guarantees it. An economy that depends on slavery needs to promote images of slaves that "justify" the institution of slavery. Western economies are absolutely dependent now on the continued underpayment of women. An ideology that makes women feel "worth less" was urgently needed to counteract the way feminism had begun to make us feel worth more. This does not require a conspiracy; merely an atmosphere. The contemporary economy depends right now on the representation of women within the beauty myth. Economist John Kenneth Galbraith offers an economic explanation for "the persistence of the view of homemaking as a 'higher calling'": the concept of women as naturally trapped within the Feminine Mystique, he feels, "has been forced on us by popular sociology, by magazines, and by fiction to disguise the fact that woman in her role of consumer has been essential to the development of our industrial society. . . . Behavior that is essential for economic reasons is transformed into a social virtue." As soon as a woman's primary social value could no longer be defined as the attainment of virtuous domesticity, the beauty myth redefined it as the attainment of virtuous beauty. It did so to substitute both a new consumer imperative and a new justification for economic unfairness in the workplace where the old ones had lost their hold over newly liberated women.

Another hallucination arose to accompany that of the Iron Maiden: The caricature of the Ugly Feminist was resurrected to dog the steps of the women's movement. The caricature is unoriginal; it was coined to ridicule the feminists of the nineteenth century. Lucy Stone herself, whom supporters saw as "a prototype of womanly grace . . . fresh and fair as the morning," was derided by detractors with "the usual report" about Victorian feminists: "a big masculine woman, wearing boots, smoking a cigar, swearing like a trooper." As Betty Friedan put it presciently in 1960, even before the savage revamping of that old caricature: "The unpleasant image of feminists today resembles less the feminists themselves than the image fostered by the interests who so bitterly opposed the vote for women in state after state." Thirty years on, her conclusion is more true than ever: That resurrected caricature, which sought to punish women for their public acts by going after their private sense of self, became the paradigm for new limits placed on aspiring women everywhere. After the success of the women's movement's second wave, the beauty myth was perfected to checkmate power at every level in individual women's lives. The modern neuroses of life in the female body spread to woman after woman at epidemic rates. The myth is undermining—slowly, imperceptibly, without our being aware of the real forces or erosion—the ground women have gained through long, hard, honorable struggle.

The beauty myth of the present is more insidious than any mystique of femininity yet: A century ago, Nora slammed the door of the doll's house; a generation ago, women turned their backs on the consumer heaven of the isolated multiapplianced home; but where women are trapped today, there is no door to slam. The contemporary ravages of the beauty backlash are destroying women physically and depleting us psychologically. If we are to free ourselves from the dead weight that has once again been made out of femaleness, it is not ballots or lobbyists or placards that women will need first; it is a new way to see.

NOTES

Cosmetic surgery: *Standard and Poor's Industry Surveys* (New York: Standard and Poor's Corp., 1988).

Pornography main media category: See "Crackdown on Pornography: A No-Win Battle," *U.S. News & World Report*, June 4, 1984. The Association of Fashion and Image Consultants tripled its membership between 1984 and 1989 alone (Annetta Miller and Dody Tsiantar, *Newsweek*, May 22, 1989). During the five or six years prior to 1986, consumer spending rose from $300 billion to $600 billion.

Thirty-three thousand American women, University of Cincinnati College of Medicine, 1984: Wooley, S. C., and O. W. Wooley, "Obesity and Women: A Closer Look at the Facts," *Women's Studies International Quarterly*, vol. 2 (1979), pp. 69–79. Data reprinted in "33,000 Women Tell How They Really Feel About Their Bodies," *Glamour*, February 1984.

Recent research shows: See Dr. Thomas Cash, Diane Cash, and Jonathan Butters, "Mirror-Mirror on the Wall: Contrast Effects and Self-Evaluation of Physical Attractiveness," *Personality and Social Psychology Bulletin*, September 1983, vol. 9, no. 3. Dr. Cash's research shows very little connection between "how attractive women are" and "how attractive they feel themselves to be." All the women he treated were, in his terms, "extremely attractive," but his patients compare themselves only to models, not to other women.

Very little to me: Lucy Stone, 1855, quoted in Andrea Dworkin, *Pornography: Men Possessing Women* (New York: Putnam, 1981), p. 11.

A doll: Germaine Greer, *The Female Eunuch* (London: Paladin Grafton Books, 1970), pp. 55, 60.

Myth: See also Roland Barthes's definition: "It [myth] transforms history into nature. . . . Myth has the task of giving an historical intention a natural justification, and making contingency appear eternal." Roland Barthes, "Myth Today," *Mythologies* (New York: Hill and Wang, 1972), p. 129.

Anthropologist Bronislaw Malinowski's definition of "a myth of origin" is relevant to the beauty myth: A myth of origin, writes Ann Oakley, "tends to be worked hardest in times of social strain, when the state of affairs portrayed in the myth are called into question." Ann Oakley, *Housewife: High Value/Low Cost* (London: Penguin Books, 1987), p. 163.

Platonic: See Plato's discussion of Beauty in *Symposium*. For varying standards of beauty, see Ted Polhemus, *BodyStyles* (Luton, England: Lennard Publishing, 1988).

Sexual selection; Darwin . . . was unconvinced: See Cynthia Eagle Russett, "Hairy Men and Beautiful Women," *Sexual Science: The Victorian Construction of Womanhood* (Cambridge, Mass.: Harvard University Press, 1989), pp. 78–103.

On page 84 Russett quotes Darwin: "Man is more powerful in body and mind than woman, and in the savage state he keeps her in a much more abject state of bondage, than does the male of any other animal; therefore it is not surprising that he should have gained the power of selection. . . . As women have long been selected for beauty, it is not surprising that some of their successive variations should have been transmitted exclusively to the same sex; consequently that they should have transmitted beauty in a somewhat higher degree to their female than to their male offspring, and thus have become more beautiful, according to general opinion, than men." Darwin himself noticed the evolutionary inconsistency of this idea that, as Russett puts it, "a funny thing happened on the way up the ladder: among humans, the female no longer chose but was chosen." This theory "implied an awkward break in evolutionary continuity," she observes: "In Darwin's own terms it marked a rather startling reversal in the trend of evolution."

See also Natalie Angier, "Hard-to-Please Females May Be Neglected Evolutionary Force," *The New York Times*, May 8, 1990, and Natalie Angier, "Mating for Life? It's Not for the Birds or the Bees," *The New York Times*, August 21, 1990.

Evolution: See Evelyn Reed, *Woman's Evolution: From Matriarchal Clan to Patriarchal Family* (New York: Pathfinder Press, 1986); and Elaine Morgan, *The Descent of Woman* (New York: Bantam Books, 1979). See especially "the upper primate," p. 91.

Goddess: Rosalind Miles, *The Women's History of the World* (London: Paladin Grafton Books, 1988), p. 43. See also Merlin Stone, *When God Was a Woman* (San Diego: Harvest Books, 1976).

Wodaabe tribe: Leslie Woodhead, "Desert Dandies," *The Guardian*, July 1988.

In the West African Fulani tribe young women choose their husbands on the basis of their beauty: "The contestants . . . take part in the yaake, a line-up in which they sing and dance, stand on tip-toe and make faces, rolling and crossing their eyes and grimacing to show off their teeth to the judges. They keep this up for hours, aided by the consumption of stimulating drugs beforehand. Throughout all this, old ladies in the crowd hurl criticisms at those who do not live up to the Fulani idea of beauty." [Polhemus, op. cit., p. 21]

See also Carol Beckwith and Marion van Offelen, *Nomads of Niger* (London: William Collins Sons & Co. Ltd., 1984), cited in Carol Beckwith, "Niger's Wodaabe: People of the Taboo," *National Geographic*, vol. 164, no. 4, October 1983, pp. 483–509.

Paleolithic excavations suggest that it has been human males rather than females to whom adornment was assigned in prehistoric societies; in modern tribal communities men generally adorn at least as much as women, and often hold "a virtual monopoly" over adornment. The Sudanese Nuba, the Australian Waligigi, and the Mount Hagen men of New Guinea also spend hours painting themselves and perfecting their hairstyles to attract the women, whose toilette takes only minutes. See Polhemus, op. cit., pp. 54–55.

Technologies: See, for example, Beaumont Newhall, *The History of Photography from 1839 to the Present* (London: Secker & Warburg, 1986), p. 31. Photograph *Academie*, c. 1845, photographer unknown.

Powerful industries: Diet items are a $74-billion-a-year industry in the United States, totaling one-third the nation's annual food bill. See David Brand, "A Nation of Healthy Worrywarts?," *Time*, July 25, 1988.

$33-billion-a-year diet industry: Molly O'Neill, "Congress Looking into the Diet Business," *The New York Times*, March 28, 1990.

$300-million-a-year cosmetic surgery industry: *Standard and Poor's Industry Surveys*, op. cit. 1988.

$7 billion pornography industry, "Crackdown on Pornography," op. cit.

Vital lies: Daniel Goleman, *Vital Lies, Simple Truths: The Psychology of Self-Deception* (New York: Simon and Schuster, 1983), pp. 16–17, quoting Henrik Ibsen's phrase: "The vital lie continues unrevealed, sheltered by the family's silence, alibis, stark denial."

A higher calling: John Kenneth Galbraith, quoted in Michael H. Minton with Jean Libman Block, *What Is a Wife Worth?* (New York: McGraw-Hill, 1984), pp. 134–135.

Ugly Feminist: Marcia Cohen, *The Sisterhood: The Inside Story of the Women's Movement and the Leaders Who Made It Happen* (New York: Ballantine Books, 1988), pp. 205, 206, 287, 290, 322, 332.

Swearing like a trooper: Betty Friedan, *The Feminine Mystique* (London: Penguin Books, 1982), p. 79, quoting Elinor Rice Hays, *Morning Star: A Biography of Lucy Stone* (New York: Harcourt, 1961), p. 83.

Unpleasant image: Friedan, op. cit., p. 87.

Questions

1. Why does Wolf contend that understanding the beauty myth is critical to an understanding of women's status in contemporary society?
2. What is the "beauty myth"? What are the myth's interrelated components? Why does Wolf call it a "myth"? How does the myth affect women's lives today? Why doesn't it affect men's lives in the same way?
3. How is the beauty myth an ideology? To what does the term *beauty ideology* refer? What are its historical origins? What is a social fiction? How does Wolf employ the images of the Ugly Feminist and the Iron Maiden?
4. What does Wolf mean when she refers to "the colonization of female consciousness"? How is this "colonization" part of a dangerous "private reality" women face? Why does Wolf assert that the beauty myth actually prescribes *behavior* rather than *appearance*?

THE BLACK BEAUTY MYTH

Sirena J. Riley

For those of you well versed in the study of body image, I don't need to tell you that negative body image is an all too common phenomenon. The issue of young women's and girls' dissatisfaction with their bodies in the United States has slowly garnered national attention and has made its way into the public discourse. Unfortunately, the most visible discussions surrounding body image have focused on white women. As a result, we presume that women of color don't have any issues when it comes to weight and move on. As a black woman, I would love to believe that as a whole we are completely secure with our bodies. But that would completely miss the racism, sexism and classism that affect the specific ways in which black women's beauty ideals and experiences of body dissatisfaction are often different from those of white women.

To our credit, black women have often been praised for our positive relationships with our bodies. As a teenager, I remember watching a newsmagazine piece on a survey comparing black and white women's body satisfaction. When asked to describe the "perfect woman," white women said she'd be about five foot ten, less than 120 pounds, blond and so on. Black women described this ideal woman as intelligent, independent and self-confident, never mentioning her looks. After the survey results were revealed to the group of both black and white twentysomethings, the white women stood, embarrassed and humiliated that they could be so petty and shallow. They told stories of starving

Reprinted from *Colonize This: Young Women of Color on Today's Feminism*, Seal Press.

themselves before dates and even before sex. The black women were aghast! What the hell were these white women talking about?!

I was so proud. I went around telling everyone about the survey results. I couldn't believe it. Black women being praised on national television! There they were telling the whole country that their black men loved the "extra meat on their bones." Unfortunately, my pride also had a twinge of envy. In my own experience, I couldn't quite identify with either the black women or the white women.

In my black middle-class suburban family, we were definitely expected to be smart. My family didn't work so hard so that we could be cute and dumb. I'd expressed interest in medical school and I got nothing but support in my academics. Raised by a single mother, independence was basically in my blood. But in a neighborhood of successful, often bourgeois black families, it was obvious that the "perfect woman" was smart, pretty and certainly not overweight. As a child, no one loved the "extra meat" on my bones. I was eight years old when I first started exercising to Jane Fonda and the cadre of other leotard-clad fitness gurus. I knew how to grapevine and box step as well as I knew my multiplication tables. I now have a sister around that age, and when I look at her and realize how young that is, it breaks my heart that I was so concerned about weight back then.

Still, I consider myself lucky. I had an even temper. That made me no fun to tease, since I wouldn't give the perpetrator any satisfaction by reacting. Plus, I had good friends who would be there to have my back. But despite this support, I was a very self-conscious middle-school girl. And that's where I gained the most weight, sixty pounds in the course of three years. Because hindsight is twenty-twenty, it is easy to understand why I put on so much weight then. My mom got married when I was ten years old. The next year she had my first little sister, and then another sister was added when I turned fourteen. I love them, but that's a lot of stress for a little kid. My single-parent, only-child home had turned into a pseudo-nuclear family almost overnight. My grades started slipping and the scale started climbing.

Enter my first year of high school. Being an overweight teenager, I don't need to describe the hell that was gym class. To my relief, I only had to take one year of gym and then never had to do it again. Plus, in high school I had options. In addition to regular gym, there was an aerobic dance class and something called "physical training." Now, considering that Jane Fonda and I were well acquainted, I wanted to take the aerobics class. But when I went to register, the class was full. I guess I wasn't the only one who'd had it with the kickball scene. I was left with either regular gym or this physical training class. I decided that I'd played my last game of flag football and opted for the latter.

Physical training turned out to be running and lifting weights. And when I say weights, I mean *real* weights. None of those wimpy three-pound dumbbells. We were lifting heavy weights and learning professional weight-lifting moves. Well, it worked. By sophomore year I'd lost over forty pounds. The thing is, I didn't even know it. Remember, I had only enrolled in the class to get out of regular gym. I'd thought it might have been nice to lose some weight, but that wasn't what I was concentrating on. After all, I'd been doing exercise videos since I was a kid and I'd only managed to gain weight.

How did I not notice that I'd lost weight? Well, I was completely out of touch with my body. I didn't want to live there. I don't even think I really considered it a part of *me*. No one ever said anything good about it, so I just pretended it didn't exist. I basically swept my body under the rug. All I was wearing back then were big baggy jeans and sweatshirts, so most of my clothes still fit despite the weight loss. People had been asking me for several months if I'd lost weight before I noticed. They were also asking me how I did it, as if I knew. While back-to-school shopping before my sophomore year, I decided to just see if I could fit into size 10 jeans. Not only did those fit me, I could even squeeze into a size 8.

Ironically, it wasn't being overweight that really screwed up my body image and self-esteem, it was *losing* weight. All of a sudden I was pretty. No one had ever really told me that I was pretty before. So if I was pretty now, then I must have been ugly then. My perception of myself before my weight loss was forever warped. I ripped up pictures of myself from middle school. I never wanted to be fat again! Boys had never really been interested in me before, but now guys were coming out of the woodwork. Family I hadn't seen in years just couldn't believe it was *me*. Some even told me that they always knew I'd grow out of my "baby fat" to become a beautiful woman. At fifteen, this was my introduction to womanhood. I had dates now. I could go shopping and actually fit into cool clothes. I was planning for college and looking forward to my new life as a pretty, smart, successful, independent black superwoman.

For a few years I actually did eat and exercise at what I'd consider a comfortable rate. But after that year of intense exercising, it was impossible to completely maintain my significant weight loss. I just didn't have the time, since it wasn't built into my schedule anymore. I settled in at around a size 12, although at the time I still wanted to be a "perfect" size 8. This actually was the most confusing time for me. I kept telling everyone that I still wanted to lose twenty pounds. Even my family was divided on this one. My grandmother told me that I was fine the way I was now, that I shouldn't gain any weight, but I didn't need to lose any more. She didn't want me to be fat but thought it was good that I was curvy. Meanwhile, my grandfather told me that if I lost twenty more pounds, he'd give me one thousand dollars to go shopping for new clothes. And my mom thought that my skirts were too short and my tops too low cut, even though as a child she prompted me to lose weight by saying that if I stayed fat, I wouldn't be able to wear pretty clothes when I grew up. What the hell did these people want from me?

I wasn't overeating and my self-esteem had improved but for all of the wrong reasons. I thought I was happier because I was thinner. In reality, I still hadn't made peace with myself or my body. Over the years I gained the weight back, but not before dabbling in some well-known eating disorders. I had a stint with bulimia during my second semester of my first year away at college. But I never got to the clinical stage. I pretty much only did it when something bad happened, not on a daily basis. I didn't binge on huge amounts of food. I'd eat two bowls of Lucky Charms and the next thing you know, I'd be sticking the spoon down my throat. This was not at all like the bulimics I saw on those after-school specials. They were eating sheets of cake, loaves of bread, sticks of butter, anything and everything they could get their hands on. That wasn't me.

Then I started compulsively exercising. I mean I couldn't think straight if I hadn't been to the gym that morning. And even after I went to the gym, all I could think about was how great it was going to be to work out tomorrow. I was also planning my whole day around my food. It wasn't necessarily that I was dieting, but I was always aware of when I was going to eat, how much and how long it would be until I ate again. I was completely obsessed.

Around my junior year in college, I finally realized that something was wrong. I just couldn't take it anymore, so I started seeing a counselor on campus. At first I didn't tell her about my encounters with bulimia, but any trained therapist could see right through me. One day she asked me point blank if I'd ever had an eating disorder, so I told her everything. I realized then that what I had been doing was considered disordered eating. I also realized that inherently I knew it wasn't right, since this was the first time I had breathed a word about it to anyone. I had never even tried to articulate it. I decided not to exercise or worry about what I ate until I got through therapy.

Throughout my course of therapy, I was in three body image and eating disorder therapy groups with other young women on my campus. I was always the only black woman. The memory of that television news survey I had seen as a teen comparing body image issues for black and white women stayed with me over the years. Looking at the other women in my therapy groups, I had to wonder if I was an anomaly. I had read one or two stories in black women's magazines about black women with eating disorders, but it was still treated like a phenomenon that was only newsworthy because of its rarity.

As a women's studies major in college, body image was something we discussed almost ad nauseam. It was really cathartic because we embraced the personal as political and felt safe telling our stories to our sister feminists. Whenever body image was researched and discussed as a project, however, black women were barely a footnote. Again, many white feminists had failed to step out of their reality and see beyond their own experiences to understand the different ways in which women of color experience sexism and the unattainable beauty ideals that society sets for women.

Discussions of body image that bother to include black women recognize that there are different cultural aesthetics for black and white women. Black women scholars and activists have attacked the dominance of whiteness in the media and illuminated black women's tumultuous history with hair and skin color. The ascension of black folks into the middle class has positioned them in a unique and often difficult position, trying to hold onto cultural ties while also trying to be a part of what the white bourgeois has created as the American Dream. This not only permeates into capitalist material goals, but body image as well, creating a distinctive increase in black women's body dissatisfaction.

White women may dominate pop culture images of women, but black women aren't completely absent. While self-deprecating racism is still a factor in the way black women view themselves, white women give themselves too much credit when they assume that black women still want to look like them. Unfortunately, black women have their own beauty ideals to perpetually fall short of. The representation of black women in Hollywood is sparse, but among the most famous loom such beauties as Halle Berry, Jada Pinkett Smith, Nia Long, Iman and Angela Bassett. In the music scene there are the young women of Destiny's Child, Lauryn Hill and Janet Jackson. Then, of course, there is model Naomi Campbell and everyone's favorite cover girl, Tyra Banks. Granted, these women don't necessarily represent the waif look or heroin chic that plagues the pages of predominately white fashion and entertainment magazines, but come on. They are still a hard act to follow.

In addition to the pressure of unrealistic body images in the media, another force on women's body image can be men's perspectives. In this category black men's affinity for big butts always comes up. Now, I'm not saying that this is a completely false idea—just about every black guy I know has a thing for the ass. I've heard both black guys and white guys say, "Damn, she's got a big ass"—the former with gleeful anticipation and the latter with loathsome disgust. Of course, dwelling on what men find attractive begs the question, why the hell do we care so much what they think anyway, especially when not all women are romantically involved with men?

Indeed, many songs have been written paying homage, however objectifying, to the black behind. "Baby Got Back," "Da Butt" and "Rumpshaker" are by now old standards. There's a whole new crop of ass songs like "Shake Ya Ass," "Wobble Wobble" and everyone's favorite, "The Thong Song." But did anyone actually notice what the girls in the accompanying videos look like? Most of those women are models, dancers and aspiring actresses whose full-time job it is to make sure they look unattainably beautiful. So what if they're slightly curvier?

Now that rap music is all over MTV, the rock videos of the eighties and early nineties featuring white women in leather and lace have been replaced with black and Latino models in haute couture and designer thongs. Rappers of the "ghetto-fabulous" genre are selling platinum several times over. Everyday, their videos are requested on MTV's teen-driven Total Request Live (TRL) by mostly white, suburban kids—the largest group of consumers of hip-hop culture. It is the latest mainstream forum for objectifying women of color, because almost all of the ghetto-fabulous black male rappers have the obligatory video girls parading around everywhere from luxury liner cruise ships to mansions in the Hamptons. If this doesn't speak to the distinctive race/class twist that these images add to the body image discussion, I don't know what does.

The old mantra "You can never be too rich, or too thin" may have been associated with the excessive eighties, but some of that ideal still holds true today. Obesity is associated with poverty and in our society, poverty is not pretty. Being ghetto-fabulous is all about going from rags to riches. It includes having the money, house(s), car(s), clothes and throngs of high-maintenance women at your disposal. An ironic twist to the American Dream, considering many of these rappers claim to have attained their wealth not with a Puritan work ethic but through illegal activity.

Overweight women of color aren't included in these videos because they aren't seen as ghetto-fabulous, just ghetto (Not that I'm waiting for the day when *all* women can wash rappers' cars in cutoffs with twelve of their girlfriends, but you get the picture). Talented comedienne Mo'nique, star of UPN's *The Parkers*, is representative of this idea. She is a full-figured woman whose character, Nikki, has a crush on a black, upwardly mobile college professor who lives in her apartment building. Through his eyes she's seen as uncouth and out of control. For the audience her sexual advances are funny because she's loud, overweight and can't take a hint. He squirms away from her at every turn and into the arms of some slim model-type.

The professor in *The Parkers* views Nikki the same way that many middle-class people view overweight people, greedy and out of control. Instead, we get to see it through a black lens—ghetto women with no class, talking loud, wearing bright colors and tight clothes. I'm sure in true sitcom fashion, the professor and Nikki will eventually get together, but well after we've had our fun at Nikki's expense.

For the past few years a popular black R&B radio station in Washington, D.C., has a contest where they give away free plastic surgery every summer. You know, to get ready for thong season. Needless to say, the average contestant is a woman. At first it was just breast implants and reductions, but now they've expanded to liposuction and even pectoral implants for the men. That hasn't had much impact on the demographics of the participants. Despite the expanded offerings, the contestant pool remains overwhelmingly female. In order to win the "prize" you have to send in a letter, basically pouring out all of your insecurities to get the DJs to see why you need the surgery more than the other contestants do. Sick, isn't it? Anyone who thinks that black women are oblivious to body insecurities needs to listen to some of these letters, which by the way pour in by the thousands. The one thing they have in common is that all the women really want to "feel better about themselves." Even in this black middle-class metropolis, somewhere these women got the idea that plastic surgery is the way to go. Clearly, it is not just white America telling them this.

Sexism has played a starring role in every facet of popular culture, with men by and large determining what shows up on TV and in the movies, and the fact is that they've fallen for it, too. I have male friends and relatives who buy into these unrealistic beauty ideals and feel no shame in letting me know where they think I stack up, so to speak. Just yesterday, for example, my grandfather decided to make it his business to know how much weight I had gained in the past few months. Now I'm old enough and secure enough to know that his and other men's comments have nothing to do with me, with who I am. But growing up, these comments shaped the way I saw myself.

I've consciously decided to treat my body better by not being obsessed with diet and exercise and not comparing myself to anyone (including my former self). When I'm eating well and exercising regularly, I'm usually in the size 12 to 14 range. This is OK with me, but I know for a fact that this is another place where many white women and I don't connect. As much as we get praised for loving our full bodies, many young white women would rather be dead than wear a size 14. They nod their heads and say how great it is that we black women can embrace our curves, but they don't want to look like us. They don't adopt our presumably more generous beauty ideals. White women have even told me how lucky black women are that our men love and accept our bodies the way they are. I've never heard a white woman say that she's going to take her cue from black women and gain a few pounds, however. In a way it is patronizing, because they're basically saying, "It's OK for you to be fat, but not me. You're black. You're different."

In this society we have completely demonized fat. How many times have you had to tell a friend of yours that she isn't fat? How many times has she had to tell you the same thing? Obviously, when people have unrealistic perceptions of themselves it should not go unnoticed, but in this act, while we are reassuring our friends, we put down every woman who is overweight. The demonization of fat and the ease of associating black women with fat exposes yet another opportunity for racism.

If we really want to start talking more honestly about all women's relationships with our bodies, we need to start asking the right questions. Just because women of color aren't expressing their body dissatisfaction in the same way as heterosexual, middle-class white women, it doesn't mean that everything is hunky-dory and we should just move on. If we are so sure that images of rail-thin fashion models, actresses and video chicks have contributed to white girls' poor body image, why aren't we addressing the half-naked black female bodies that have replaced the half-naked white female bodies on MTV? Even though young black women slip through the cracks from time to time, I still believe that feminism is about understanding the intersections of all forms of oppression. It only works when we all speak up and make sure that our voices are heard. I don't plan to wait any longer to include young women of color in a larger discussion of body image.

"A Way Outa No Way": Eating Problems Among African American, Latina, and White Women (1996)

Becky W. Thompson

Although researchers have long recognized that women experience eating problems more often than men, studies have mainly been directed at only one female demographic—those who are white and middle-class. In the following selection, social researcher Becky Thompson, author of a book-length study entitled A Hunger So Wide and So Deep, *presents interviews with women of color and working-class women who have experienced eating problems to understand how race, ethnicity, class and sexuality shape their experiences. Moving beyond the "culture of thinness" model to explain eating problems, Thompson suggests other factors that may contribute to their development.*

"'A Way Outa No Way': Eating Problems Among African American, Latina, and White Women," by Becky W. Thompson, reprinted from *Race, Class, and Gender*, edited by Esther Ngan-ling Chow, Doris Wilkinson, and Maxine Baca Zinn, 1996, by permission of Sage Publications, Inc.

Bulimia, anorexia nervosa, binging, and extensive dieting are among the many health issues women have been confronting in the last twenty years. Until recently, however, there has been almost no research about eating problems among African American, Latina, Asian American, or Native American women, working-class women, or lesbians.[1] In fact, according to the normative epidemiological portrait, eating problems are largely a white, middle-, and upper-class heterosexual phenomenon. Further, while feminist research has documented how eating problems are fueled by sexism, there has been almost no attention paid to how other systems of oppression may also be implicated in the development of eating problems.

In this chapter, I reevaluate the portrayal of eating problems as issues of appearance based on the "culture of thinness." I propose that eating problems begin as ways women cope with various traumas including sexual abuse, racism, classism, sexism, heterosexism, and poverty. Showing the interface between these traumas and the onset of eating problems explains why women may use eating to numb pain and cope with violations to their bodies. This theoretical shift also permits an understanding of the economic, political, social, educational, and cultural resources that women need to change their relationship to food and their bodies.

Existing Research on Eating Problems

There are three theoretical models used to explain the epidemiology, etiology, and treatment of eating problems. The biomedical model offers important scientific research about possible physiological causes of eating problems and the physiological dangers of purging and starvation (Copeland 1985; Spack 1985). However, this model adopts medical treatment strategies that may disempower and traumatize women (Garner 1985; Orbach 1985). In addition, this model ignores many social, historical, and cultural factors that influence women's eating patterns. The psychological model identifies eating problems as "multidimensional disorders" that are influenced by biological, psychological, and cultural factors (Garfinkel and Garner 1982). While useful in its exploration of effective therapeutic treatments, this model, like the biomedical one, tends to neglect women of color, lesbians, and working-class women.

The third model, offered by feminists, asserts that eating problems are gendered. This model explains why the vast majority of people with eating problems are women, how gender socialization and sexism may relate to eating problems, and how masculine models of psychological development have shaped theoretical interpretations. Feminists offer the *culture of thinness model* as a key reason why eating problems predominate among women. According to this model, thinness is a culturally, socially, and economically enforced requirement for female beauty. This imperative makes women vulnerable to cycles of dieting, weight loss, and subsequent weight gain, which may lead to anorexia nervosa and bulimia (Chernin 1981; Orbach 1978, 1985; Smead 1984).

Feminists have rescued eating problems from the realm of individual psychopathology by showing how the difficulties are rooted in systematic and pervasive attempts to control women's body sizes and appetites. However, researchers have yet to give significant attention to how race, class, and sexuality influence women's understanding of their bodies and appetites. The handful of epidemiological studies that include African American women and Latinas casts doubt on the accuracy of the normative epidemiological portrait. The studies suggest that this portrait reflects which particular populations of women have been studied rather than actual prevalence (Andersen and Hay 1985; Gray, Ford, and Kelly 1987; Hsu 1987; Nevo 1985; Silber 1986).

More important, this research shows that bias in research has consequences for women of color. Tomas Silber (1986) asserts that many well-trained professionals have either misdiagnosed or delayed their diagnoses of eating problems among African American and Latina women due to stereotypical thinking that these problems are restricted to white women. As a consequence, when African American women or Latinas are diagnosed, their eating problems tend to be more severe due to extended processes of starvation prior to intervention. In her autobiographical account of her eating problems, Retha Powers (1989), an African American woman, describes being told not to worry about her eating problems since "fat is more acceptable in the Black community" (p. 78). Stereotypical perceptions held by her peers and teachers of the "maternal Black woman" and the "persistent mammy-brickhouse Black woman image" (p. 134) made it difficult for Powers to find people who took her problems with food seriously.

Recent work by African American women reveals that eating problems often relate to women's struggles against a "simultaneity of oppressions" (Clarke 1982; Naylor 1985; White 1991). Byllye Avery (1990), the founder of the National Black Women's Health Project, links the origins of eating problems among African American women to the daily stress of being undervalued and overburdened at home and at work. In Evelyn C. White's (1990) anthology, *The Black Women's Health Book: Speaking for Ourselves,* Georgiana Arnold (1990) links her eating problems partly to racism and racial isolation during childhood.

Recent feminist research also identifies factors that are related to eating problems among lesbians (Brown 1987; Dworkin 1989; Iazzetto 1989; Schoenfielder and Wieser 1983). In her clinical work, Brown (1987) found that lesbians who have internalized a high degree of homophobia are more likely to accept negative attitudes about fat than are lesbians who have examined their internalized homophobia. Autobiographical accounts by lesbians have also indicated that secrecy about eating problems among lesbians partly reflects their fear of being associated with a stigmatized illness ("What's Important" 1988).

Attention to African American women, Latinas, and lesbians paves the way for further research that explores the possible interface between facing multiple oppressions and the development of eating problems. In this way, this study is part of a larger feminist and sociological research agenda that seeks to understand how race, class, gender, nationality, and sexuality inform women's experiences and influence theory production.

Methodology

I conducted eighteen life history interviews and administered lengthy questionnaires to explore eating problems among African American, Latina, and white women. I employed a snowball sample, a method in which potential respondents often first learn about the study from people who have already participated. This method was well suited for the study since it enabled women to get information about me and the interview process from people they already knew. Typically, I had much contact with the respondents prior to the interview. This was particularly important given the secrecy associated with this topic (Russell 1986;

Silberstein, Striegel-Moore, and Rodin 1987), the necessity of women of color and lesbians to be discriminating about how their lives are studied, and the fact that I was conducting across-race research.

To create analytical notes and conceptual categories from the data, I adopted Glaser and Strauss's (1967) technique of theoretical sampling, which directs the researcher to collect, analyze, and test hypotheses during the sampling process (rather than imposing theoretical categories onto the data). After completing each interview transcription, I gave a copy to each woman who wanted one. After reading their interviews, some of the women clarified or made additions to the interview text.

Demographics of the Women in the Study

The 18 women I interviewed included 5 African American women, 5 Latinas, and 8 white women. Of these women, 12 are lesbian and 6 are heterosexual. Five women are Jewish, 8 are Catholic, and 5 are Protestant. Three women grew up outside of the United States. The women represented a range of class backgrounds (both in terms of origin and current class status) and ranged in age from 19 to 46 years old (with a median age of 33.5 years).

The majority of the women reported having had a combination of eating problems (at least two of the following: bulimia, compulsive eating, anorexia nervosa, and/or extensive dieting). In addition, the particular types of eating problems often changed during a woman's life span. (For example, a woman might have been bulimic during adolescence and anorexic as an adult.) Among the women, 28 percent had been bulimic, 17 percent had been bulimic and anorexic, and 5 percent had been anorexic. All of the women who had been anorexic or bulimic also had a history of compulsive eating and extensive dieting. Of the women, 50 percent were either compulsive eaters and dieters (39 percent) or compulsive eaters (11 percent) but had not been bulimic or anorexic.

Two-thirds of the women have had eating problems for more than half of their lives, a finding that contradicts the stereotype of eating problems as transitory. The weight fluctuation among the women varied from 16 to 160 pounds, with an average fluctuation of 74 pounds. This drastic weight change illustrates the degree to which the women adjusted to major changes in body size at least once during their lives as they lost, gained, and lost weight again.

The average age of onset was 11 years old, meaning that most of the women developed eating problems prior to puberty. Almost all of the women (88 percent) considered themselves as still having a problem with eating, although the majority believed they were well on the way to recovery.

The Interface of Trauma and Eating Problems

One of the most striking findings in this study was the range of traumas the women associated with the origins of their eating problems, including racism, sexual abuse, poverty, sexism, emotional or physical abuse, heterosexism, class injuries, and acculturation.[2] The particular constellation of eating problems among the women did not vary with race, class, sexuality, or nationality. Women from various race and class backgrounds attributed the origins of their eating problems to sexual abuse, sexism, and emotional and/or physical abuse. Among some of the African American and Latina women, eating problems were also associated with poverty, racism, and class injuries. Heterosexism was a key factor in the onset of bulimia, compulsive eating, and extensive dieting among some of the lesbians. These oppressions are not the same nor are the injuries caused by them. And certainly, there are a variety of potentially harmful ways that women respond to oppression (such as using drugs, becoming a workaholic, or committing suicide). However, for all these women, eating was a way of coping with trauma.

Sexual Abuse

Sexual abuse was the most common trauma that the women related to the origins of their eating problems. Until recently, there has been virtually no research exploring the possible relationship between these two phenomena. Since the mid-1980s, however, researchers have begun identifying connections between the two, a task that is part of a larger feminist critique of traditional psychoanalytic symptomatology (DeSalvo 1989; Herman 1981; Masson 1984). Results of a number of incidence studies indicate that between one-third and two-thirds of women who have eating problems have been abused (Oppenheimer et al. 1985; Root and Fallon 1988). In addition, a growing number of therapists and researchers have offered interpretations of the meaning and impact of eating problems for survivors of sexual abuse (Bass and Davis 1988; Goldfarb 1987; Iazzetto 1989; Swink and Leveille 1986). Kearney-Cooke (1988) identifies dieting and binging as common ways in which women cope with frequent psychological consequences of sexual abuse (such as body image disturbances, distrust of people and one's own experiences, and confusion about one's feelings). Root and Fallon (1989) specify ways that victimized women cope with assaults by binging and purging: bulimia serves many functions, including anesthetizing the negative feelings associated with victimization. Iazzetto's innovative study (1989), based on in-depth interviews and art therapy sessions, examines how a woman's relationship to her body changes as a consequence of sexual abuse. Iazzetto discovered that the process of leaving the body (through progressive phases of numbing, dissociating, and denying) that often occurs during sexual abuse parallels the process of leaving the body made possible through binging.

Among the women I interviewed, 61 percent were survivors of sexual abuse (11 of the 18 women), most of whom made connections between sexual abuse and the beginning of their eating problems. Binging was the most common method of coping identified by the survivors. Binging helped women "numb out" or anesthetize their feelings. Eating sedated, alleviated anxiety, and combated loneliness. Food was something that they could trust and was accessible whenever they needed it. Antonia (a pseudonym) is an Italian American woman who was first sexually abused by a male relative when she was four years old. Retrospectively, she knows that binging was a way she coped with the abuse. When the abuse began, and for many years subsequently, Antonia often woke up during the middle of the night with anxiety attacks or nightmares and would go straight to the kitchen cupboards to get food. Binging helped her block painful feelings because it put her back to sleep.

Like other women in the study who began binging when they were very young, Antonia was not always fully conscious as she binged. She described eating during the night as "sleep walking. It was mostly desperate—like I had to have it." Describing why she ate after waking up with nightmares, Antonia said, "What else do you do? If you don't have any coping mechanisms, you eat." She said that binging made her "disappear," which made her feel protected. Like Antonia, most of the women were sexually abused before puberty; four of them before they were five years old. Given their youth, food was the most accessible and socially acceptable drug available to them. Because all of the women endured the psychological consequences alone, it is logical that they coped with tactics they could use alone as well.

One reason Antonia binged (rather than dieted) to cope with sexual abuse is that she saw little reason to try to be the small size girls were supposed to be. Growing up as one of the only Italian Americans in what she described as a "very WASP town," Antonia felt that everything from her weight and size to having dark hair on her upper lip were physical characteristics she was supposed to hide. From a young age she knew she "never embodied the essence of the good girl. I don't like her. I have never acted like her. I can't be her. I sort of gave up." For Antonia, her body was the physical entity that signified her outsider status. When the sexual abuse occurred, Antonia felt she had lost her body. In her mind, the body she lived in after the abuse was not really hers. By the time Antonia was 11, her mother put her on diet pills. Antonia began to eat behind closed doors as she continued to cope with the psychological consequences of sexual abuse and feeling like a cultural outsider.

Extensive dieting and bulimia were also ways in which women responded to sexual abuse. Some women thought that the men had abused them because of their weight. They believed that if they were smaller, they might not have been abused. For example, when Elsa, an Argentine woman, was sexually abused at the age of 11, she thought her chubby size was the reason the man was abusing her. Elsa said, "I had this notion that these old perverts liked these plump girls. You heard adults say this too. Sex and flesh being associated." Looking back on her childhood, Elsa believes she made fat the enemy partly due to the shame and guilt she felt about the incest. Her belief that fat was the source of her problems was also supported by her socialization. Raised by strict German governesses in an upper-class family, Elsa was taught that a woman's weight was a primary criterion for judging her worth. Her mother "was socially conscious of walking into places with a fat daughter and maybe people staring at her." Her father often referred to Elsa's body as "shot to hell." When asked to describe how she felt about her body when growing up, Elsa described being completely alienated from her body. She explained,

> Remember in school when they talk about the difference between body and soul? I always felt like my soul was skinny. My soul was free. My soul sort of flew. I was tied down by this big bag of rocks that was my body. I had to drag it around. It did pretty much what it wanted and I had a lot of trouble controlling it. It kept me from doing all the things that I dreamed of.

As is true for many women who have been abused, the split that Elsa described between her body and soul was an attempt to protect herself from the pain she believed her body caused her. In her mind, her fat body was what had "bashed in her dreams." Dieting became her solution but, as is true for many women in the study, this strategy soon led to cycles of binging and weight fluctuation.

Ruthie, a Puerto Rican woman who was sexually abused from 12 until 16 years of age, described bulimia as a way she responded to sexual abuse. As a child, Ruthie liked her body. Like many Puerto Rican women of her mother's generation, Ruthie's mother did not want skinny children, interpreting that as a sign that they were sick or being fed improperly. Despite her mother's attempts to make her gain weight, Ruthie remained thin through puberty. When a male relative began sexually abusing her, Ruthie's sense of her body changed dramatically. Although she weighed only 100 pounds, she began to feel fat and thought her size was causing the abuse. She had seen a movie on television about Romans who made themselves throw up and so she began doing it, in hopes that she could look like the "little kid" she was before the abuse began. Her symbolic attempt to protect herself by purging stands in stark contrast to the psychoanalytic explanation of eating problems as an "abnormal" repudiation of sexuality. In fact, her actions and those of many other survivors indicate a girl's logical attempt to protect herself (including her sexuality) by being a size and shape that does not seem as vulnerable to sexual assault.

These women's experiences suggest many reasons why women develop eating problems as a consequence of sexual abuse. Most of the survivors "forgot" the sexual abuse after its onset and were unable to retrieve the abuse memories until many years later. With these gaps in memory, frequently they did not know why they felt ashamed, fearful, or depressed. When sexual abuse memories resurfaced in dreams, they often woke feeling upset but could not remember what they had dreamed. These free-floating, unexplained feelings left the women feeling out of control and confused. Binging or focusing on maintaining a new diet were ways women distracted or appeased themselves, in turn, helping them regain a sense of control. As they grew older, they became more conscious of the consequences of these actions. Becoming angry at themselves for binging or promising themselves they would not purge again was a way to direct feelings of shame and self-hate that often accompanied the trauma.

Integral to this occurrence was a transference process in which the women displaced onto their bodies painful feelings and memories that actually derived from or were directed toward the persons who caused the abuse. Dieting became a method of trying to change the parts of their bodies they hated, a strategy that at least initially brought success as they lost weight. Purging was a way women tried to reject the body size they thought was responsible for the abuse. Throwing up in order to lose the weight they thought was making them vulnerable to the abuse was a way to try to find the body they had lost when the abuse began.

Poverty

Like sexual abuse, poverty is another injury that may make women vulnerable to eating problems. One woman I interviewed attributed her eating problems directly to the stress caused by poverty. Yolanda is a Black Cape Verdean mother who began eating compulsively when she was twenty-seven years old. After leaving an abusive husband in her early twenties, Yolanda was forced to go on welfare. As a single mother with small children and few financial resources, she tried to support herself and her children on $539 a month. Yolanda began binging in the evenings after putting her children to bed. Eating was something she could do alone. It would calm her, help her deal with loneliness, and make her feel safe. Food was an accessible commodity that was cheap. She ate three boxes of macaroni and cheese when nothing else was available. As a single mother with little money, Yolanda felt as if her body was the only thing she had left. As she described it,

> I am here [in my body] 'cause there is nowhere else for me to go. Where am I going to go? This is all I got . . . that probably contributes to putting on so much weight 'cause staying in your body, in your home, in yourself, you don't go out. You aren't around other people. . . . You hide and

> as long as you hide you don't have to face . . . nobody can see you eat. You are safe.

When she was eating, Yolanda felt a momentary reprieve from her worries. Binging not only became a logical solution because it was cheap and easy but also because she had grown up amid positive messages about eating. In her family, eating was a celebrated and joyful act. However, in adulthood, eating became a double-edged sword. While comforting her, binging also led to weight gain. During the three years Yolanda was on welfare, she gained seventy pounds.

Yolanda's story captures how poverty can be a precipitating factor in eating problems and highlights the value of understanding how class inequalities may shape women's eating problems. As a single mother, her financial constraints mirrored those of most female heads of households. The dual hazards of a race- and sex-stratified labor market further limited her options (Higginbotham 1986). In an article about Black women's health, Byllye Avery (1990) quotes a Black woman's explanation about why she eats compulsively. The woman told Avery,

> I work for General Electric making batteries, and, I know it's killing me. My old man is an alcoholic. My kids got babies. Things are not well with me. And one thing I know I can do when I come home is cook me a pot of food and sit down in front of the TV and eat it. And you can't take that away from me until you're ready to give me something in its place. (p. 7)

Like Yolanda, this woman identifies eating compulsively as a quick, accessible, and immediately satisfying way of coping with the daily stress caused by conditions she could not control. Connections between poverty and eating problems also show the limits of portraying eating problems as maladies of upper-class adolescent women.

The fact that many women use food to anesthetize themselves, rather than other drugs (even when they gained access to alcohol, marijuana, and other illegal drugs), is partly a function of gender socialization and the competing demands that women face. One of the physiological consequences of binge eating is a numbed state similar to that experienced by drinking. Troubles and tensions are covered over as a consequence of the body's defensive response to massive food intake. When food is eaten in that way, it effectively works like a drug with immediate and predictable effects. Yolanda said she binged late at night rather than getting drunk because she could still get up in the morning, get her children ready for school, and be clearheaded for the college classes she attended. By binging, she avoided the hangover or sickness that results from alcohol or illegal drugs. In this way, food was her drug of choice since it was possible for her to eat while she continued to care for her children, drive, cook, and study. Binging is also less expensive than drinking, a factor that is especially significant for poor women. Another woman I interviewed said that when her compulsive eating was at its height, she ate breakfast after rising in the morning, stopped for a snack on her way to work, ate lunch at three different cafeterias, and snacked at her desk throughout the afternoon. Yet even when her eating had become constant, she was still able to remain employed. While her patterns of eating no doubt slowed her productivity, being drunk may have slowed her to a dead stop.

Heterosexism

The life history interviews also uncovered new connections between heterosexism and eating problems. One of the most important recent feminist contributions has been identifying compulsory heterosexuality as an institution which truncates opportunities for heterosexual and lesbian women (Rich 1986). All of the women interviewed for this study, both lesbian and heterosexual, were taught that heterosexuality was compulsory, although the versions of this enforcement were shaped by race and class. Expectations about heterosexuality were partly taught through messages that girls learned about eating and their bodies. In some homes, boys were given more food than girls, especially as teenagers, based on the rationale that girls need to be thin to attract boys. As the girls approached puberty, many were told to stop being athletic, begin wearing dresses, and watch their weight. For the women who weighed more than was considered acceptable, threats about their need to diet were laced with admonitions that being fat would ensure becoming an "old maid."

While compulsory heterosexuality influenced all of the women's emerging sense of their bodies and eating patterns, the women who linked heterosexism directly to the beginning of their eating problems were those who knew they were lesbians when very young and actively resisted heterosexual norms. One working-class Jewish woman, Martha, began compulsively eating when she was 11 years old, the same year she started getting clues of her lesbian identity. In junior high school, as many of her female peers began dating boys, Martha began fantasizing about girls, which made her feel utterly alone. Confused and ashamed about her fantasies, Martha came home every day from school and binged. Binging was a way she drugged herself so that being alone was tolerable. Describing binging, she said, "It was the only thing I knew. I was looking for a comfort." Like many women, Martha binged because it softened painful feelings. Binging sedated her, lessened her anxiety, and induced sleep.

Martha's story also reveals ways that trauma can influence women's experience of their bodies. Like many other women, Martha had no sense of herself as connected to her body. When I asked Martha whether she saw herself as fat when she was growing up, she said, "I didn't see myself as fat. I didn't see myself. I wasn't there. I get so sad about that because I missed so much." In the literature on eating problems, *body image* is the term that is typically used to describe a woman's experience of her body. This term connotes the act of imagining one's physical appearance. Typically, women with eating problems are assumed to have difficulties with their body image. However, the term *body image* does not adequately capture the complexity and range of bodily responses to trauma experienced by the women. Exposure to trauma did much more than distort the women's visual image of themselves. These traumas often jeopardized their capacity to consider themselves as having bodies at all.

Given the limited connotations of the term body image, I use the term *body consciousness* as a more useful way to understand the range of bodily responses to trauma.[3] By body consciousness I mean the ability to reside comfortably in one's body (to see oneself as embodied) and to consider one's body as connected to oneself. The disruptions to their body consciousness that the women described included leaving their bodies, making a split between their body and mind, experiencing being "in" their bodies as painful, feeling unable to control what went in and out of their bodies, hiding in one part of their bodies, or simply not seeing themselves as having bodies. Binging, dieting, or purging were common ways women responded to disruptions to their body consciousness.

Racism and Class Injuries

For some of the Latinas and African American women, racism coupled with the stress resulting from class mobility related to the onset of their eating problems. Joselyn, an African American woman, remembered her white grandmother telling her she would never be as pretty as her cousins because they were lighter skinned. Her grandmother often humiliated Joselyn in front of others, as she made fun of Joselyn's body while she was naked and told her she was fat. As a young child, Joselyn began to think that although she could not change her skin color, she could at least try to be thin. When Joselyn was young, her grandmother was the only family member who objected to Joselyn's weight. However, her father also began encouraging his wife and daughter to be thin as the family's class standing began to change. When the family was working class, serving big meals, having chubby children, and keeping plenty of food in the house was a sign the family was doing well. But, as the family became mobile, Joselyn's father began insisting that Joselyn be thin. She remembered, "When my father's business began to bloom and my father was interacting more with white businessmen and seeing how they did business, suddenly thin became important. If you were a truly well-to-do family, then your family was slim and elegant."

As Joselyn's grandmother used Joselyn's body as territory for enforcing her own racism and prejudice about size, Joselyn's father used her body as the territory through which he channeled the demands he faced in the white-dominated business world. However, as Joselyn was pressured to diet, her father still served her large portions and bought treats for her and the neighborhood children. These contradictory messages made her feel confused about her body. As was true for many women in this study, Joselyn was told she was fat beginning when she was very young even though she was not overweight. And, like most of the women, Joselyn was put on diet pills and diets before even reaching puberty, beginning the cycles of dieting, compulsive eating, and bulimia.

The confusion about body size expectations that Joselyn associated with changes in class paralleled one Puerto Rican woman's association between her eating problems and the stress of assimilation as her family's class standing moved from poverty to working class. When Vera was very young, she was so thin that her mother took her to a doctor who prescribed appetite stimulants.

However, by the time Vera was eight years old, her mother began trying to shame Vera into dieting. Looking back on it, Vera attributed her mother's change of heart to competition among extended family members that centered on "being white, being successful, being middle class, . . . and it was always, 'Ay Bendito. She is so fat. What happened?'"

The fact that some of the African American and Latina women associated the ambivalent messages about food and eating to their family's class mobility and/or the demands of assimilation while none of the eight white women expressed this (including those whose class was stable and changing) suggests that the added dimension of racism was connected to the imperative to be thin. In fact, the class expectations that their parents experienced exacerbated standards about weight that they inflicted on their daughters.

Eating Problems as Survival Strategies

Feminist Theoretical Shifts

My research permits a reevaluation of many assumptions about eating problems. First, this work challenges the theoretical reliance on the culture-of-thinness model. Although all of the women I interviewed were manipulated and hurt by this imperative at some point in their lives, it is not the primary source of their problems. Even in the instances in which a culture of thinness was a precipitating factor in anorexia, bulimia, or binging, this influence occurred in concert with other oppressions.

Attributing the etiology of eating problems primarily to a woman's striving to attain a certain beauty ideal is also problematic because it labels a common way that women cope with pain as essentially appearance-based disorders. One blatant example of sexism is the notion that women's foremost worry is about their appearance. By focusing on the emphasis on slenderness, the eating problems literature falls into the same trap of assuming that the problems reflect women's "obsession" with appearance. Some women were raised in families and communities in which thinness was not considered a criterion for beauty. Yet they still developed eating problems. Other women were taught that women should be thin but their eating problems were not primarily in reaction to this imperative. Their eating strategies began as logical solutions to problems rather than problems themselves as they tried to cope with a variety of traumas.

Establishing links between eating problems and a range of oppressions invites a rethinking of both the groups of women who have been excluded from research and those whose lives have been the basis of theory formation. The construction of bulimia and anorexia nervosa as appearance-based disorders is rooted in a notion of femininity in which white middle- and upper-class women are portrayed as frivolous, obsessed with their bodies, and overly accepting of narrow gender roles. This portrayal fuels women's tremendous shame and guilt about eating problems—as signs of self-centered vanity. This construction of white middle- and upper-class women is intimately linked to the portrayal of working-class white women and women of color as their opposite: as somehow exempt from accepting the dominant standards of beauty or as one step away from being hungry and therefore not susceptible to eating problems. Identifying that women may binge to cope with poverty contrasts the notion that eating problems are class bound. Attending to the intricacies of race, class, sexuality, and gender pushes us to rethink the demeaning construction of middle-class femininity and establishes bulimia and anorexia nervosa as serious responses to injustices.

Understanding the link between eating problems and trauma also suggests much about treatment and prevention. Ultimately, their prevention depends not simply on individual healing but also on changing the social conditions that underlie their etiology. As Bernice Johnson Reagon sings in Sweet Honey in the Rock's song "Oughta Be a Woman," "A way outa no way is too much to ask/too much of a task for any one woman" (Reagon 1980).[4] Making it possible for women to have healthy relationships with their bodies and eating is a comprehensive task. Beginning steps in this direction include ensuring that (1) girls can grow up without being sexually abused, (2) parents have adequate resources to raise their children, (3) children of color grow up free of racism, and (4) young lesbians have the chance to see their reflection in their teachers and community leaders. Ultimately, the prevention of eating problems depends on women's access to economic, cultural, racial, political, social, and sexual justice.

NOTES

1. I use the term *eating problems* as an umbrella term for one or more of the following: anorexia nervosa, bulimia, extensive dieting, or binging. I avoid using the term *eating disorder* because it categorizes the problems as individual pathologies, which deflects attention away from the social inequalities underlying them (Brown 1985). However, by using the term *problem* I do not wish to imply blame. In fact, throughout, I argue that the eating strategies that women develop begin as logical solutions to problems, not problems themselves.

2. By trauma I mean a violating experience that has long-term emotional, physical, and/or spiritual consequences that may have immediate or delayed effects. One reason the term *trauma* is useful conceptually is its association with the diagnostic label Post Traumatic Stress Disorder (PTSD) (American Psychological Association 1987). PTSD is one of the few clinical diagnostic categories that recognizes social problems (such as war or the Holocaust) as responsible for the symptoms identified (Trimble 1985). This concept adapts well to the feminist assertion that a woman's symptoms cannot be understood as solely individual, considered outside of her social context, or prevented without significant changes in social conditions.

3. One reason the term *consciousness* is applicable is its intellectual history as an entity that is shaped by social context and social structures (Delphy 1984; Marx 1964). This link aptly applies to how the women described their bodies because their perceptions of themselves as embodied (or not embodied) directly relate to their material conditions (living situations, financial resources, and access to social and political power).

4. Copyright © 1980. Used by permission of Songtalk Publishing.

REFERENCES

American Psychological Association. 1987. *Diagnostic and statistical manual of mental disorders*. 3rd ed. rev. Washington, DC: American Psychological Association.

Andersen, Arnold, and Andy Hay. 1985. Racial and socioeconomic influences in anorexia nervosa and bulimia. *International Journal of Eating Disorders* 4:479–87.

Arnold, Georgiana. 1990. Coming home: One Black woman's journey to health and fitness. In *The Black women's health book: Speaking for ourselves*, edited by Evelyn C. White. Seattle, WA: Seal.

Avery, Byllye Y. 1990. Breathing life into ourselves: The evolution of the National Black Women's Health Project. In *The Black women's health book: Speaking for ourselves*, edited by Evelyn C. White. Seattle, WA: Seal.

Bass, Ellen, and Laura Davis. 1988. *The courage to heal: A guide for women survivors of child sexual abuse*. New York: Harper & Row.

Brown, Laura S. 1985. Women, weight and power: Feminist theoretical and therapeutic issues. *Women and Therapy* 4:61–71.

_____. 1987. Lesbians, weight and eating: New analyses and perspectives. In *Lesbian psychologies*, edited by the Boston Lesbian Psychologies Collective. Champaign: University of Illinois Press.

Chernin, Kim. 1981. *The obsession: Reflections on the tyranny of slenderness*. New York: Harper & Row.

Clarke, Cheryl. 1982. *Narratives*. New Brunswick, NJ: Sister Books.

Copeland, Paul M. 1985. Neuroendocrine aspects of eating disorders. In *Theory and treatment of anorexia nervosa and bulimia: Biomedical sociocultural and psychological perspectives*, edited by Steven Wiley Emmett. New York: Brunner/Mazel.

Delphy, Christine. 1984. *Close to home: A materialist analysis of women's oppression*. Amherst: University of Massachusetts Press.

DeSalvo, Louise. 1989. *Virginia Woolf: The impact of childhood sexual abuse on her life and work.* Boston: Beacon.

Dworkin, Sari H. 1989. Not in man's image: Lesbians and the cultural oppression of body image. In *Loving boldly: Issues facing lesbians*, edited by Ester D. Rothblum and Ellen Cole. New York: Harrington Park.

Garfinkel, Paul E., and David M. Garner. 1982. *Anorexia nervosa: A multidimensional perspective*. New York: Brunner/Mazel.

Garner, David. 1985. Iatrogenesis in anorexia nervosa and bulimia nervosa. *International Journal of Eating Disorders* 4:701–26.

Glaser, Barney G., and Anselm L. Strauss. 1967. *The discovery of grounded theory: Strategies for qualitative research*. New York: Aldine DeGruyter.

Goldfarb, Lori. 1987. Sexual abuse antecedent to anorexia nervosa, bulimia and compulsive overeating: Three case reports. *International Journal of Eating Disorders* 6:675–80.

Gray, James, Kathryn Ford, and Lily M. Kelly. 1987. The prevalence of bulimia in a Black college population. *International Journal of Eating Disorders* 6:733–40.

Herman, Judith. 1981. *Father-daughter incest*. Cambridge, MA: Harvard University Press.

Higginbotham, Elizabeth. 1986. We were never on a pedestal: Women of color continue to struggle with poverty, racism and sexism. In *For crying out loud*, edited by Rochelle Lefkowitz and Ann Withorn. Boston: Pilgrim.

Hsu, George. 1987. Are eating disorders becoming more common in Blacks? *International Journal of Eating Disorders* 6:113–24.

Iazzetto, Demetria. 1989. When the body is not an easy place to be: Women's sexual abuse and eating problems. Ph.D. diss., Union for Experimenting Colleges and Universities, Cincinnati, OH.

Kearney-Cooke, Ann. 1988. Group treatment of sexual abuse among women with eating disorders. *Women and Therapy* 7:5–21.

Marx, Karl. 1964. *The economic and philosophic manuscripts of 1844*. New York: International.

Masson, Jeffrey. 1984. *The assault on the truth: Freud's suppression of the seduction theory*. New York: Farrar, Strauss & Giroux.

Naylor, Gloria. 1985. *Linden Hills*. New York: Ticknor & Fields.

Nevo, Shoshana. 1985. Bulimic symptoms: Prevalence and ethnic differences among college women. *International Journal of Eating Disorders* 4:151–68.

Oppenheimer, R., K. Howells, R. L. Palmer, and D. A. Chaloner. 1985. Adverse sexual experience in childhood and clinical eating disorders: A preliminary description. *Journal of Psychiatric Research* 19:357–61.

Orbach, Susie. 1978. *Fat is a feminist issue*. New York: Paddington.

_____. 1985. Accepting the symptom: A feminist psychoanalytic treatment of anorexia nervosa. In *Handbook of psychotherapy for anorexia nervosa and bulimia*, edited by David M. Garner and Paul E. Garfinkel. New York: Guilford.

Powers, Retha. 1989. Fat is a Black women's issue. *Essence*, Oct., 75, 78, 134, 136.

Reagon, Bernice Johnson. 1980. Oughta be a woman. On Sweet Honey in the Rock's album, *Good News*. Music by Bernice Johnson Reagon; lyrics by June Jordan. Washington, DC: Songtalk.

Rich, Adrienne. 1986. Compulsory heterosexuality and lesbian existence. In *Blood, bread and poetry*. New York: Norton.

Root, Maria P. P., and Patricia Fallon. 1988. The incidence of victimization experiences in a bulimic sample. *Journal of Interpersonal Violence* 3:161–73.

_____. 1989. Treating the victimized bulimic: The functions of binge-purge behavior. *Journal of Interpersonal Violence* 4:90–100.

Russell, Diana E. 1986. *The secret trauma: Incest in the lives of girls and women*. New York: Basic Books.

Schoenfielder, Lisa, and Barbara Wieser, eds. 1983. *Shadow on a tightrope: Writings by women about fat liberation*. Iowa City, IA: Aunt Lute Book Co.

Silber, Tomas. 1986. Anorexia nervosa in Blacks and Hispanics. *International Journal of Eating Disorders* 5:121–28.

Silberstein, Lisa, Ruth Striegel-Moore, and Judith Rodin. 1987. Feeling fat: A woman's shame. In *The role of shame in symptom formation*, edited by Helen Block Lewis. Hillsdale, NJ: Lawrence Erlbaum.

Smead, Valerie. 1984. Eating behaviors which may lead to and perpetuate anorexia nervosa, bulimarexia, and bulimia. *Women and Therapy* 3:3 7–49.

Spack, Norman. 1985. Medical complications of anorexia nervosa and bulimia. In *Theory and treatment of anorexia nervosa and bulimia: Biomedical sociocultural and psychological perspectives*, edited by Steven Wiley Emmett. New York: Brunner/Mazel.

Swink, Kathy, and Antoinette E. Leveille. 1986. From victim to survivor: A new look at the issues and recovery process for adult incest survivors. *Women and Therapy* 5:119–43.

Trimble, Michael. 1985. Post-traumatic stress disorder: History of a concept. In *Trauma and its wake: The study and treatment of post-traumatic stress disorder*, edited by C. R. Figley. New York: Brunner/Mazel.

What's important is what you look like. 1988. *Gay Community News*, July, 24–30.

White, Evelyn C., ed. 1990. *The Black women's health book: Speaking for ourselves*. Seattle, WA: Seal Press.

_____. 1991. Unhealthy appetites. *Essence*, Sept., 28, 30.

Questions

1. What is the "culture of thinness" model for eating problems? In what ways is this a "feminist" model?
2. How does Thompson challenge the "culture of thinness" model for explaining eating problems? Why is this model inappropriate for all women? What other models does she advance?
3. According to Thompson, what other factors lead to eating problems? On what evidence does she base her argument? What steps did the author find might prevent the development of eating problems?
4. What meanings are attached to food in different communities? How can a woman grow up in a family that does not equate beauty with thinness, yet still develop an eating problem?

"I See the Same Ho" Video Vixens, Beauty Culture, and Diasporic Sex Tourism

T. Denean
Sharpley-Whiting

Every other video . . .
I see the same ho

—Tupac (featuring Nate Dogg, YGD Tha Top Dawg), "All About U"

Watching the videos, you see the long curly hair [and] think, "Man that would be nice to have some long, curly hair."

—Sela, eighteen-year-old undergraduate

Brazilian women are usually desirable, as often women of mixed ethnicities are. . . . Our leaders should make a law demanding intercultural breeding to fill our planet . . . thus ending all the world's problems.

—AskMen.Com, Top 99 Most Desirable Women 2005

When Michelle "Micki" Burks decided to take on the role of eye candy in the now-defunct rap-reggae group Ruff Neck Sound System's music videos "Stick by Me" and "Luv Bump," little did she know that her decision would land her years later in the category of "video ho." Her performances in the music videos did not involve provocative backside acrobatics, but her video persona in "Luv Bump" is interestingly transmogrified into a "hoochie" by the video's end due to fast-living and hustling men. Shot in New York, the video aired in 1995 on the Rachel-hosted Black Entertainment Television format *Caribbean Rhythms*. At 5'8" with long brown highlighted hair and honey-toned skin, Micki attended the prestigious Berklee School of Music in Boston from 1986 to 1990. A soprano with a superb vocal range, she toured Europe and Japan, releasing an album called *Inca*, and then took up modeling with Models, Inc. in Boston as a side gig until her music career took off. She met the Ruff Neck crew in the Boston music scene. Her then-boyfriend, Chris, was a well-known producer who had teamed with such venerable acts as the late Donnie Hathaway's daughter Lahla.

When asked about the moniker "video ho," she emphatically rejects any description of her experiences as degrading. She does nonetheless lament the portrayals of women in hip hop videos of late, stating that, "It is unnecessary. They don't have to treat the women like that." When asked if she would work in the emerging lucrative music video industry today if the opportunity presented itself again, the still-lithe thirty-six-year-old says with a laugh, "Yeah, if I were thinner [and] as a model not a 'video ho.'"

While sales in the music industry continue a downward spiral that even the gestalt of rapper 50 Cent's *The Massacre* (which moved over one million units in just under four days) cannot break, the music video DVD has emerged as a boon to the recording industry. In an April 7, 2004, press release, Jay Berman, Chairman of IFPI (International Federation of the Phonographic Industry), an affiliate of the Recording Industry Association of America (RIAA), the organization responsible for the world's largest music market, noted that music video sales are rapidly becoming an important revenue stream for the industry. The music video, popularized by the launch of cable television stations such as Black Entertainment Television (BET), Music Television (MTV), and Video Hits I (VHI), represents the lion's share of formatting for these stations. Launched in 1980, 1981, and 1985 respectively, the first popular music video to debut on MTV was The Buggles's "Video Killed the Radio Star," a video that predicted rather prematurely that the music video genre would supplant the radio. Music videos have exploded, with budgets as large as some indie film projects, more developed narratives and sets, and digital technology, which has also allowed for a clearer picture and a larger than life celluloid image. The hip hop music video in particular also provides brand product placement with a bumping beat. Like a four-to six-minute advertisement, the music video DVD sells music and the fabulous lifestyle signified by whatever material acquisitions are worn (or not), driven, or drank within its frames—all at a general sticker price between thirteen and eighteen dollars. Borrowing from cultural critic Greg Tate's observations on hip hop culture in "Nigs R Us, or How Blackfolk Became Fetish Objects," the hip hop video has "collapsed art, commerce, and interactive technology into one mutant animal." Similar to the film industry, which ties its potential box office take to A-list stars as well as well-known directors, the directors of music videos have become a highly sought after group, particularly veterans such as Hype Williams, Paul Hunter, Little X, and Chris Robinson. Recording artists recognize that the music video can make or break a career, and heavy rotation on MTV, BET, and VH1 all but guarantees break-out success. Indeed, 70 percent of BET's programming, the go-to station for urban hip hop generationers, is music videos and infomercials. And the cable station reaches some eighty million homes.

In "All about U," a Tupac Shakur, Nate Dogg, and YDG Tha Top Dawg collaboration, the rap artists bond over their disdain for "video ho's" and "groupies" who they encounter in every city they tour and video they see. Like Micki, many of these women are singers, professional models, dancers, and aspiring actresses, earning their rent, tuition monies, or commercial exposure for a day's work on a shoot. And some dance and shake for free for their five minutes of fame, jumping in front of the camera when Young Buck or any one of the St. Lunatics roll up on a North Nashville or North St. Louis block with a film crew in tow. As Atlanta hip hop industry insider and videographer Tiona McClodden suggests, "Many of the background video models use their bodies as demos because they know that much of what is shot will be left on the floor of the editing room. They have one opportunity. If they do something provocative enough to stand out, they anticipate that the shot just may remain in the final video." That the impact of these sexually suggestive videos is undeniably regressive in terms of gender politics and young girls and women's self-identity is revealed in a 2003 year-long study conducted by the Center for AIDS Research (CFAR) at Emory University. Tracking 522 Alabama girls' hip hop video consumption and behaviors, the study revealed that a higher consumption of hip hop videos corresponded negatively with higher frequency of sexually transmitted diseases, alcohol and drug abuse (60 percent), and multiple sex partners (twice as likely).

But just as important as the complex motivations behind young women's suggestive performances in hop-hop videos—rumps moving with the alacrity of a jackhammer, hips gyrating like a belly dancer on amphetamines, limbs akimbo, mouths agape in a perpetual state of the orgasmic "oh"—is the repetition of particular ideals of femininity. Hip hop is now as much about images as it is skills and beats. That the vast majority of the young women in these videos are either fairer-skinned, ethnically mixed, or of indeterminate ethnic/racial origins, with long, straight, or curly hair would suggest that along with the stereotype of hypersexuality and sexual accessibility, a particular type of beauty is offered up as ideal. In some respects, the majority of these women represent what historian Tiffany Patterson calls "ascriptive mulattas," that is, those whose physical beauty transcends characteristics such as darker hues, full lips, and the like, historically prefigured as less than ideal (non-European). The "mulatta" figure, a pejorative term if ever there was one, is typically depicted as tragic because of her "in-between" racial status. Yet the "mulatta" has also been deemed in literary and film annals as the most ideal in the arena of feminine beauty, and the secretly longed for in the heterosexual marketplace of desire. This status comes about precisely because of her mixed-race heritage involving some configuration of "black" and "white," which in the European and American male imagination signals the perfect blending of skillfulness in matters of sex (read: black) and physical beauty (read: white).

The physical appeal to both white and black men of Gabrielle Union, Ciara, Beyoncé, and Tyra Banks falls into ascriptive mulatta territory, as did that of Lena Horne and Dorothy Dandridge—just ask the men at askmen.com where Union, Ciara, Banks, and Beyoncé are ranked among the 2006 edition of the top ninety-nine most desirable women. On any given segment of MTV's *Top Twenty*, or BET's *Rap City* and *106 & Park*, roughly 70 percent of the videos feature superbly toned, nubile, hybrid flesh. One could certainly argue that practically all seemingly black flesh in the "New World" is a hybrid given the history of transracial contact. But it is precisely because of the enormous *range* of blackness (as a result of consensual and non-consensual) sex that the incredibly narrow prototype of beauty is even more troubling.

As writer Kevin Powell argues in *Who's Gonna Take the Weight*, hip hop generationers still do not fully appreciate the range of black women's beauty. Even the fallout in the hip hop community from the 2002 Grammy Awards ceremony over Alicia Key's multiple Grammy wins over India Arie hinged unfortunately (and mistakenly I would add) for some on the issue of color. Another example is the ruckus over the fall 2004 season of *America's Next Top Model (ANTM)*, a reality show that attempts to demystify high-fashion modeling by demonstrating that models, while born with certain assets like height, are primarily talent-development projects and that "can-do" attitudes go the distance. The show is undeniably in the service of beauty culture, which in general has been less accepting, if not hostile, to black women. However, in the 2004 season *ANTM* was UPN's highest-rated program among women ages eighteen to forty-nine as well as teens. As the network's newest cash cow, it was also one of the top ten programs among African American adults, and the highest-rated reality show among African Americans. Its host, übermodel Tyra Banks, consistently emphasizes personality over a particular "look." Nonetheless, the conclusion of the fall 2004 season caused viewer squabbles regarding the hair and skin color of the final two contestants, Yaya DaCosta Johnson and Eva Pigford. In an interview with *TV Guide*'s Daniel Coleridge, the runner-up, Yaya, a Brown University graduate, responded to the interviewer's perception of her "look" as "Afrocentric," a perception that may have contributed to her loss:

> I'm not Afrocentric, I'm just natural. But in this country, black women who don't straighten their hair with chemical processing are stereotyped and labeled. Not *all* black women with straight hair need chemical processing, but I would have to to achieve that look. Just because we don't straighten our hair doesn't mean we're trying to be anything else—we're being ourselves. If anything hurts me about that, it's that I wasn't allowed the luxury of being myself like the other girls were. Nobody asks Cassie, Ann or Amanda to be "less white." I'm used to having to defend my very being. That makes me a little sensitive.

DaCosta Johnson's browner skin and unprocessed hair moved her into an Afrocentric space when compared to Eva Pigford's African American girl-next-door look with chemically straightened hair, light eyes, and lighter hue.

DaCosta Johnson's predicament on *Top Model* raises old questions in this new era on assimilation, identity, and beauty. And yet, the mixing bowl with a wee bit of nutmeg and cinnamon standard of beauty endorsed ostensibly by American culture (more specifically on Madison Avenue) parallels the shifting ideas of beauty in hip hop videos that are, some would argue, necessarily still derivative of a white ideal.

In "Generation E.A.: Ethnically Ambiguous," a feature in the Fashion & Style section of *The New York Times*, advertising executives and fashion magazine editors offered running commentaries that ranged from disquieting to just plain dim on marketing trends to "tweens," teens, and hip hop generationers in both the mainstream and high-end market-place: "Today what's ethnically neutral, diverse, or ambiguous has tremendous appeal"; "What is perceived as good, desirable, successful is often a face whose heritage is hard to pin down"; "We're seeing more of a desire for the exotic, left-of-center beauty . . . [It] represents the new reality of America, which includes considerable mixing . . . It's the changing face of American beauty." That racial categories are social constructs rather than biological realities—though this does not alter the lived experiences of those who occupy those categories—that "considerable" "race" mixing is not "a new reality" but has been historically widespread in the United States, and that America is not as "white" as it believes itself to be has been duly noted since at least the nineteenth century by writers and activists such as Frances Ellen Harper Watkins in her novel *Iola Leroy*. Even in *The Birth of a Nation*, a racist film posing as an American cinematic masterpiece, racial amalgamation is a core preoccupation because of its prevalence. The contemporary scholarly writing of philosophers of race Kwame Anthony Appiah and Naomi Zack are only a few examples of our awareness of the power of social constructs. Both Appiah and Zack have argued that "race" and therefore categories of race are biologically non-existent, dishonest, and in bad faith. That we as a culture cling to them relates more to our desires to enact and maintain social, political, and economic powers and privileges.

In effect, racial categories are themselves racist. In her 1993 book *Race and Mixed Race*, Zack argues presciently for the category of *gray*, an almost uncanny predecessor to "ethically ambiguous." Therefore, the excited tone of discovery evoked in the "Generation E.A." article seems more than a bit out of touch. The rhetoric that still situates whiteness at the center of American beauty culture and darker hues on this schematic shifting to the left (one wonders what right of center beauty looks like) quite simply reinforces a hierarchy of beauty, as well as the notion of fixed racial categories. Indeed, ethnic ambiguity does not guarantee racial ambiguity, particularly in relationship to those possessing "African" ethnicities and origins. One may be ethnically mixed (ambiguous) but racially marked as black.

Despite the hubbub about Generation E.A., editors and ad executives admit that whiteness continues to dominate the beauty and fashion industries. Where does, pray tell, such a hierarchy leave Generation Non-E.A. (non–ethnically ambiguous) black women? In her widely read book *Beauty Myth*, Naomi Wolf relates how the beauty industry essentially creates angst in women regarding their choices—Yaya DeCosta Johnson, for example. While not a treatise against the beauty industry and practices of adornment (though some critics have reductively read the book as Wolf's feminist cri de coeur against lipstick wearing), *The Beauty Myth* in fact argues for something very basic: a women's right to choose. Wolf makes the radical assertion that women should choose how they want to look, without fear of employment discrimination, or of being castigated as unfeminine, or of being subjected to the litany of other charges leveled at those whose beauty practices (or lack thereof) run counter to dominant ideas about what it means to be a woman.

Women who choose not to indulge in beauty practices are often disadvantaged and made to feel guilty for their lack of conformity in a culture that overemphasizes physical appearance. Simultaneously women who embrace beauty products and their images still "second guess" themselves and are subject to descriptions such as "high maintenance" and "not natural." And those women who embrace beauty culture and also fall outside the current rage over Generation E.A. or Ascriptive Mulattas are left to endlessly negotiate a maze of images and ideas that are not especially affirming and seem, at each turn, to lead to a dead end.

As with the behavioral implications for hip hop video consumption, the collision between hip hop culture and beauty culture, the marketing and packaging of the "same" video girl who resembles the high-fashion model who resembles the latest Hollywood "It" girl, also has a clear and deleterious impact on what young black female consumers come to identify as desirable. And the desire to be desirable seems especially costly and laborious for young black women, as the product-hawking, image-projecting hip hop video pumps cash into the mainstream and hip hop's multibillion-dollar fashion and beauty industries. In effect, what young black women cannot be, they now buy.

Who can forget the purchased artifices of Lil' Kim? Her "so unpretty" motivations for doffing and donning colored contact lens, purported skin-lightening procedures, nose contourings, platinum hair, breast augmentation, and liposuction. The visceral pain she articulated watching her Svengali-lover-father figure and public and very private abuser, the Notorious B.I.G., marry the lighter-skinned, fairer-maned hip hop/R&B singer Faith Evans nine days after meeting her. Or the cracks of insecurity seeping from her admission: "Halle Berry, Sally Richardson, Stacy Dash, Jada Pinkett? I used to wish I looked like them motherfuckers!"? On the question of breast augmentation, she says, "I laughed at first. But then I went home and really thought about it. I went to the best, most expensive doctor available, but that was the most pain I ever felt in my life."

As with Lil' Kim, the overwhelming majority of us black and Latina women offer our labor in a marketplace—one that still does not pay us equally—in order to purchase some happiness through beauty. (The median weekly earnings of black women who worked full time in 2001 was $451 compared with $521 for white women, $518 for black men, and $694 for white men; these figures are for non-college-educated black women; in 2004, college-educated black women, roughly two million, outearned both the white women and Latinas.) Using data from over three thousand households surveyed by the Department of Commerce, marketers and corporations have determined that black women, with their increasing income, have the most influence on the growth in African American spending. Between 2001 and 2002, our spending on personal care products increased (by 18 percent), as did our expenditures on women's apparel and footwear

(2 percent and13 percent, respectively). Our generosity with ourselves was rivaled only by our generosity with others, as gift spending spiked by 155 percent.

The July 2004 report released by *The U.S. Multicultural Women Market* suggests that the buying power of multicultural women (defined as African American, Asian American, and Hispanic American) will exceed $1 trillion by 2008 and African American women over eighteen years of age will keep the dominant share of the market. African American women's educational attainment is high; we are more confident and secure with ourselves, and one in four of us occupy professional or managerial positions. Yet, we are simultaneously least likely to be married (as our race loyalties tend to constrain our options) or even in fulfilling relationships with a female partner; dieting and exercise appear less of a concern while health risks are high. We are also very brand conscious, loyal, and receptive—or vulnerable, depending on your interpretation of the data—to media, and particularly to television.

Savvy marketers will continue to pitch products that seem to tap into our greatest strengths and deepest insecurities about beauty and desirability. Hair-care products accounted for $174 million of our disposable income in 2002. Plastic surgery, once the strict domain of white women and a taboo subject, is now democratized and featured prominently in the same headline as the words "black or African American" in magazines and online portals such as *Essence*, *News-week*, and *AOL Black Voices* (though most African American women seek surgeries for breast reduction and tummy tucks). These spending trends on beauty and fashion have been chalked up to "African-American women hav[ing] finally just decided that it's time to love ourselves" by *Essence* beauty editor Miki Taylor. While Asian American women also spend a great deal, more even, on fashion and beauty products and are just as brand conscious, they are also the leading consumers among women of financial services. One wonders if our "loving ourselves" reflects our "security and confidence," or, given our marked receptivity to *all* media, our insecurity and self-doubt bred by the confluence of media, beauty, and hip hop culture? Shouldn't the slicing away, camouflage, and enhancement offered by plastic surgery and beauty products considered part of this new phenomenon of "loving ourselves" include a concomitant up-tick in financial investments as well as diet- and exercise-related spending given our health risks? Purchased beauty is undeniably a depreciating asset, while health and financial solvency guarantees some degree of longevity. And yet, I am clearly aware that there are those hip hop generation women who would argue that if beauty enhancement lands you a "baller," it was money well spent.

In the end, despite all the hype about diversity and Generation E.A., hegemony prevails. Blondes, the stand-in for unadulterated whiteness, still have more fun. Generation E.A. comes in at quite a distant second, and Generation A.M (Ascriptive Mulattas)—those left-of-center beauties—clinch third. Those of us who remain—the *un*aesthetically pleasing, racially marked plebeians, or Generation B (read: black)—anchor the bottom or the far left of the beauty schema, particularly with respect to mainstream culture.

Hip hop culture as represented through the "video vixens" and Madison Avenue collide on the beauty hierarchy in the ambiguous space between generations E.A. and A.M. And who determines the contours of this space? More often than not, it is black men. Besides sports—which has generated a cottage industry of books on the black male athlete—hip hop culture represents another cultural terrain dominated and shaped by black men. Certainly Erica Kennedy's hilarious debut novel *Bling!*, a tale of the hip hop industry, offers interesting commentary on black men as cultural brokers of desire who resemble modern-day Svengalis as they develop, control, and project what is desirable and equally cultivate the public's desire for E.A. and A.M. artists who nonetheless read "black." In Kennedy's make-believe world that seamlessly channels the contradictions of hip hop culture, darker skin among women is a handicap to be overcome; dreaded, braided, or "happy to be nappy" hair are "no-no's"; and "big," as in body type, is definitely not beautiful.

Lest one get the impression that those women who self-identify as black and fall into the E.A. and A.M. categories of desirability do not also contend with demons not of their own making, they do. Idealization is often accompanied by alienation, "trophied" status, and petty jealousies. Anita Lewis, former Communications/Public Relations Liaison for Pennsylvania State Senator Vincent Hughes and one of *Philadelphia Business Journal*'s "40 Under 40," admits that being a lighter-skinned black woman has its own challenges:

> The fighting began in middle school with other girls pulling my hair, trying to put glue in it, and taking swipes, with their fingernails, at my face. As a professional, there are those who think I have landed certain positions because of my looks. Undoubtedly, there are those who may perceive me as less threatening, more acceptable. I cut my hair extremely short at one point in my career so that people, especially men, would take me seriously, stop fixating on my hair and listen to what I was saying. My looks may have allowed my foot in the door, but my talents and skills keep me there.

Singer Beyoncé Knowles, part of a roundtable discussion with other professional black women featured in *Newsweek*, also spoke to these very issues of color and beauty and her experiences as a lighter-skinned black woman. Knowles, who is incidentally identified as part of "Generation E.A." in *The New York Times* article, ranked number eight on 2005's askmen.com's top ninety-nine, and somersaulted Jennifer Lopez off the "booty pedestal" with her "Bootylicious" anthem and appearance on Q magazine's cover with the headline, "The Ass that Shook the World," offered: "Well, I could complain about being light-skinned. But that's life. People judge you by the way you look, unfortunately. . . ."

So while black men may have questionable standards of beauty for black women, they are not, unlike Madison Avenue, necessarily worshipping at the altar of white beauty. They linger rather, as I have suggested, somewhere between Generation E.A. and Generation A.M. That heterosexual black youth culture leans toward "left-of-center beauty" is a direct result of the political landscape, ideology, and social gains offered by both the civil rights and black power movements. While integration offered by the civil rights movement presented access to corridors, classrooms, and bedrooms heretofore inaccessible, the 1970s' slogan "Black Is Beautiful" carried over into the 1980s and helped shape the worldview of the hip hop generation. It is not so much that black is no longer beautiful but too familiar. The forbidden-fruit aura once enveloping white women has also been thoroughly demystified as they too avail themselves of the most hedonistic offerings of hip hop culture, ergo the pornographic videos *Girls Gone Wild* with Snoop Dogg and *Groupie Love* with G-Unit. Moreover, beauty culture's stoking of white women's obsession with thinness, the aim for 103 lbs. whether one is 5'1" or 5'10", disinvites the development of "junk in the trunk," those protuberant charms essentialized in hip hop culture. Most white women are left "assed out."

Besides breeding misogyny and sexism, a surprising ancillary effect of such black male privilege and familiarity has been the desire for the unknown, the "exotic" feminine ideal. The ideal woman is indeed black-derived, curvy, and "thick," but she is "paprika'd" and salted with difference, as with the October 2004 Black-Irish-Cherokee-Asian "Eye Candy" centerfold in the hip hop magazine *XXL*, or December 2004's African-American-Egyptian-Brazilian "Eye Candy" spread. Beginning at opposite ends of the great chain of beauty's color spectrum, hip hop culture and mainstream beauty culture meet somewhere in the middle in their fetishization of ethnic brewing.

The desire for the unknown, the exotic and highly ethnically seasoned black woman of late has been satiated beyond U.S. borders—namely among the black diaspora in countries like Brazil. The mirror of Brazil is being reflected back on U.S. women. This latest "desire for the exotic," as the Generation E.A. article put it, then transcends not only "rigid social categories of race, class," but U.S. borders as well. Raquel Rivera has skillfully argued in *New York Ricans in the Hip-Hop Zone* that Latinas as the *buttapecans*, the *mamis*, have often served as the exotic detour in the predominantly black male world of hip hop. The interesting reality is that they too have now become part of "The Known World" (borrowing Edward P. Jones's Pulitzer prize-winning novel's title). The search for the beautiful is now in the *favelas* (the ghettos) of Brazil. Hence it is no small surprise to see advertisements by Game, Inc., a company based out of Las Vegas, Nevada, for the porn collection *Hip-Hop Honeys: Brazil Boom Boom*, "with the bootylicious bodies that make Brazil a fantasy favorite for the hip hop generation" in "hip hop on a higher level" magazines like *XXL*.

In some respects, hip hop generation African American men's latest fetish parallels Brazil's own fetishizing of racial admixture as embodied by the mulatta figure. In a country where a cliché on the order of "white woman to wed, mulatta to bed, black woman to work" is befitting, Alma Guillermoprieto, author of *Samba*, notes:

> *Mulatas* are glorified sex fetishes, sanitized representations of what whites view as the savage African sex urge, but they are also, of course, tribute and proof of the white male's power: his sexual power, and his economic power, which allowed him to

> wrest the *mulata*'s black mother away from her black partner. At the same time the *mulata* serves to perpetuate one of the myths that Brazilians hold most dear, that there is no racism in Brazil, that miscegenation has been natural and pleasant for both parties, that white people really, sincerely, do like black people. In fact, the aesthetic superiority accorded to light-skinned black women—*mulatas*—underlines the perceived ugliness of blacks before they have been "improved" with white blood. The white skin also serves to lighten a sexual force that in undiluted state is not only threatening but vaguely repulsive, and at the same time, the myth goes, irresistible.

The fleshy hips, thighs, ample posterior, and thrust-forward breasts of the mulatta figure is offered as a sign of all things Brazilian, specifically Rio de Janeiro, as is Sugar Loaf, Corcovado (the Jesus Christ statue reigning majestically high above the city of Rio de Janeiro), the historic district of Lapa, Capoeira, and the *favelas*. As if taking cues from its northerly American neighborhoods, racial and ethnic brewing is celebrated but whiteness dominates the high-end billboards of Ipanema and the beauty industry. In interviewing a model talent scout for a May 2005 article on Brazil entitled "Beauty and the Beach," *Condé Nast Traveler* writer Julia Chapin uncovered that "right now what's hot are girls who have a European face but the body movements and attitude of a Latin." The talent scout admits that "dark-skinned girls from northern Brazil have a harder time getting work."

The summer of 2003 brought the upbeat, radio-ready "Beautiful" collaboration between Snoop Dogg, Pharrell, and Uncle Charlie Wilson, formerly of the Gap Band. We all sang along in Pharrell's Marvin Gaye-esque falsetto, ignoring the first refrain offered by Snoop about "Long hair, wit'cha big fat booty." By the time Snoop arrived at, "Black and beautiful, you the one I'm choosin' / Hair long and black and curly like you're Cuban," some black women were singing, "No, No, No, No!" instead of "Yeah, Yeah, Yeah!"—mocking the Pharrell and Charlie Wilson refrain. The heavily rotated Chris Robinson-directed video was shot on location in Brazil. Stunning because of the locale and the women, "Beautiful" the video provides a visual representation of the new black feminine ideal in hip hop culture with the charge to "Look far Southward!" to find it. Surrounded by a bevy of Brazilian beauties, Snoop and Pharrell move through this postcard-like sonata, showcasing the history of New World race mixing of imported African captives, indigenous Indians, and conquering Europeans. While some have argued that the video vixens were not *Brasilieras*, the fact of the matter is that the video provides the illusion of an authentic Brazilian experience. The video has become perhaps the best advertisement the Brazilian travel and tourism industry could hope for in its recent attempts to tap into a specifically African American market.

Snoop is not the first hip hop artist to use Brazil and its women as backdrops, nor will he be the last. Indeed, southern rapper T.I. finds himself in Rio among frolicking women on Copacabana Beach in his 2006 "Why You Wanna" video. The Neptunes, the Pharrell Williams-Chad Hugo hit-making duo, acted in *Dude: We're Going to Rio*, the 2003 hip hop musical comedy directed by C. B. Harding. In this campy tale of love at first sight, Pharrell sees a travel poster for Brazil featuring a Brazilian woman with whom he falls in love, and he travels to Rio de Janeiro to find her. Ja Rule's video "Holla, Holla," directed by Hype Williams and from the 1999 CD *Venni Vetti Vicci*, broke ranks at the time of its release by featuring Brazilian women and shooting on location in Brazil. In an interview with AllHipHop.com, Ja Rule relates that

> At that point in Hip-Hop, it was still about your n*ggas in the videos with you. We flew out to Brazil, and it was magic instantly. We set up cameras, scouting ladies. There were mad beautiful chicks coming to the camera, and on the beach topless. All types of shit, man! I was extra amped! We turned the cameras on, and girls started flocking. We only brought one professional girl (Gloria Velez), and the rest were just girls from Brazil that wanted to get down.

While "Holla, Holla" is an anthem to the rough-and-tumble life of thugdom, playin' bitches and poppin' snitches, "Beautiful" is purposely G-rated commercial fare, untarnished by bleeps; it is an ode to beauty by one of hip hop culture's legendary gangsta pimps, Snoop Dogg, a purveyor of style, a barometer for "what" and "who" is the "in" thing to do and screw.

When revolutionary writer Frantz Fanon wrote in his 1963 "handbook of the Black Revolution," *The Wretched of the Earth*, of "the pitfalls of national consciousness" and globalization with respect to developing nations and tourism, who would have imagined how prophetic his pronouncements were? And who would have thought that hip hop generation black men would join the Western bourgeois tourist "avid for the exotic . . . the beaches of Rio, the little Brazilian . . . girls . . . , [t]he banking magnates, the technocrats, and the big businessmen of the United States [who] have only to step onto a plane and they are wafted into subtropical climes, there for a space of a week or ten days to luxuriate in . . . delicious depravities"? Despite harrowing statistics about poverty, unemployment, incarceration, HIV/AIDS, and drug use, hip hop generation black men have been able to access, generate, and benefit from the unprecedented wealth that has made the United States the most powerful capitalist nation in the world.

The Selig Center for Economic Growth's survey *The Multicultural Economy 2004* reports that African Americans have enjoyed a steady rise in income, resulting in $723 billion in buying power as of September 2004, an increase of 3.9 percent over the $631 billion earned in 2002 as reported in the 2003 Target Market News' analysis *The Buying Power of Black America*. This extraordinary wealth generation has allowed them the means and opportunity to act in many respects with the same arrogance and license as their white American and European male contemporaries and the imperialist tourists of Fanon's era.

Latin America, Fanon wrote, is "Europe's brothel," and Brazil, in particular, has become to the heterosexual black American male what Tahiti was to the nineteenth-century painter Paul Gauguin—an idyllic place where one could "fuck, tan, and eat," or "*baiser, bronzer et bouffer*," as the French Club Med experience was once described. According to a BBC report on sex tourism and prostitution in Brazil, sex work in Brazil is on the upswing, as Brazilian women and girls look for a way out of dire poverty. Brazil has been pressed into the role of purveyor of sex tourism as a result of the void left by Asia—specifically Thailand—and the tsunami crisis. A casualty of its savvy and relentless marketing, particularly with respect to women and sex, Brazil is identified as the land of samba, sensuality, the bikini wax, and the Brazilian *bunda*, a string/thong bikini. Such are the obsessions with Brazilian sexuality that plastic surgeons offer a procedure called the Brazilian butt lift. For a few Brazilian *reais*, which amount to nominal amounts in American dollars (and sometimes the promise of a better life for Brazilians in the United States), one can experience the fantasy that is Brazil—and generally from women from the *favelas*.

In Brazil, the reputedly large parties thrown by moguls such as Damon Dash and Sean "Puffy" Combs during Carnivale and the Brazilian fascination with all things Americana, especially mass-produced and globally exported black commodities such as music and music videos, provide cultural currency for hip hop generation black men that gives them a Brazilian ghetto tour pass that includes discounts on women. For those poor and working-class black men unable to procure the fantasy on the ground, their imaginations, like those writers of beguiling eighteenth- and nineteenth-century travel narratives of exotic places and eager-to-be-had women, will travel for them. For a mere $72 including shipping and handling—a far cry from a $1,000 plane ticket to Rio—they can be transported to Brazil via pornographic visual aids like *Hip Hop Honeys: Brazil Boom Boom's* three-volume set and a poster.

In 2004, African Americans spent $4.6 billion on travel, lodging, and transportation. While the Caribbean and Africa have long been heavily marketed to African Americans by the travel and tourism industry, partnerships between the Brazilian government and African American media moguls like *Essence* magazine founder Clarence Smith have resulted in deal-brokering between Varig Airlines and Avocet Travel and Entertainment that now includes direct flights from New York to Salvador, Bahia. Brazil represents an untapped market for African American businesses, and vice versa. As *Brazzil Online Magazine* suggests,

> This place (Brazil) has so much to offer African-Americans. Much more than any place on the continent of Africa. The environment here is stable; there is no civil war here. There are no famines on the scale of what a visitor would encounter in Africa. Brazil offers access to state of the art telecommunications, reliable banking systems, good roads and health facilities.

Furthermore, the emergence of interest groups on the Web such as "African American Men & Brazilian Women" signals the global inclinations and democratization of wanderlust and leisure afforded by the U.S. economic boom. Replete with visuals, The African American Men & Brazilian Women message board also provides insight into some of the kinds of leisure activities sought. There is a "do's and don'ts" list offered by one aficionado of Brazilian women. A sort of "Mr. Manners" for African American men traveling to Brazil, *ChgoBachelor31_4u* took his counsels from postings at Rioexposed.com and Brazilmensclub.com, sites that promote sex tourism. Among other things, *ChgoBachelor31_4u* advises African American men not to "flirt with females unless your [*sic*] serious" or "go in the *favelas* unless your [*sic*] with someone you know & trust," but do "wear a condom," and "if your [*sic*] there (1) week you should average 10 females, if your [*sic*] there (2) weeks you should average 20 females," and finally, "Even if you dont [*sic*] need it fellas, 'blue devils' aka viagra. dont [*sic*] be ashamed to use it."

For those interested in making "honest women" out the *Brasilieras, bgcaliber1* offers some handy tips as well:

1. Though it may be tough . . . try to see her a few times in Brazil b4 bringing her back. Learn some Portuguese (or bring someone who knows the language) and try to ask around her neighborhood what type of girl she is from the local guys (last thing you want to do is bring back a full fledged hoe). See how her family is (full of nice spiritual people or a group of thieves). Remember, the apple doesn't fall far from the tree.
2. If you do eventually get her here, do not trust her to visit other girlfriends living here by herself. KEEP HER AWAY FROM OTHER BRAZILIAN GIRLS HERE IN THE STATES (unless you're absolutely sure the girl is living a clean simple life). If she has to visit, go with her. Unless you're independently wealthy and can afford to give her money to send back to Brazil, she'll want to start working. With limited English and no papers yet, where is the 1st place she'll think about going. You got it . . . THE STRIP CLUB! Once some of these girls find out how much other girls make in the sex trade . . . you're screwed!
3. Many of these girls really do just want the papers. Once they get them, many times it's . . . ADIOS! Unless you . . . (refer to #4 & #6)
4. If your libido isn't up to par, you better get those blue pills. The majority of Brasilieras I know love sex and if you're not doing the job. . . .
5. Keep tabs and don't give too much freedom (at least in the beginning) to go off by herself (or not calling in to check up on her). Once again, refer to #2 & #4.
6. LEARN THE LANGUAGE! You will meet SO MANY MORE Brazilian women if you can even basically commuicate [*sic*]

> with them and you will tend to keep them longer (never mind the fact that you will be able to understand what she's talking about on the phone). . . .
> Good luck in finding your ideal woman brothers!

While many of my colleagues in second language acquisition studies cringe at such utilitarian approaches to language learning, as a professor of French studies, I can in principle appreciate *bgcaliberI*'s emphatic suggestion to learn the Portuguese language, despite the suggestion's questionable context. But that context necessarily feeds into the myth that these ethereal beauties, these "ideal wom[e]n," are sex goddesses to boot. They require constant monitoring for fear of cuckolding, are predisposed to work in the sex entertainment industry, and require flaccid-penised paramours to come with a prescription of Viagra. In the Brazilian woman, the African American male has met his sexual match—at least in these scripts of sexual insatiability penned by African American men. Better still, with all this talk of Viagra, the African American male, that quintessential cocksman, "the keeper of the impalpable gate," in Fanon speak, "that opens into the realm of orgies, of bacchanals, of delirious sexual sensations," has been bested by *Brasilieras*.

That the mania over Brazil has reached an interesting pitch is bizarrely revealed by a certain John Nicholson who claims to be an associate of pioneering filmmaker Warrington Hudlin, whose box office draws *Boomerang* and *House Party* helped to establish hip hop film as a subgenre of American cinema. Nicholson wants African American men on the African American Men & Brazilian Women message board to provide him and Hudlin insight into their Brazil connections as they are purportedly making a documentary on Brazil, much to the chagrin of many of the men who frequent the site:

> This is John Nicholson, and i [*sic*] would like to address what appears to be some growing concerns expressed by some of the men about the motives and results of the documentary Warrington Hudlin and I are working on about african american men who love/enjoy the women in brasil. First, my 100% goal is to present a very fair and unbiased look at the entire situation on Rio. I have zero interest in making a T&A (tits and ass) documentary, this will be a serious and fair look at Rio.
> Now some have expressed concerns that i am interested in doing this documentary at all. I and Warrington feel that its a compelling and interesting story to be told. Some have said that

> they prefer if we did not complete the documentary at [all], for fear that too many people will find out and ruin a "good thing." I think its fair to say that after Snoops [*sic*] music video, if it was a secret before, it certainly is not one now.
>
> Men need to keep in mind, that the talk about Brasil is spreading in the african american community, and while my goal is to do a fair look at this issue, there may be others who might simply want to make a one sided and sensational type piece, that would not be fair and balanced. Maybe some show like Oprah will eventually send down a production team with hidden camera's and mics and blow brothers out the water with the video.
>
> Which is why its important to me that i complete this project and get it out there as soon as i can. I will gladly answers any concerns, issues or questions any of you may have, please feel free to email me at JNicholson30339@yahoo.com.

What is most telling about Nicholson's posting is the exclusive reference to Rio de Janeiro, his use of "or," signaled by the slash between "love/enjoy," rather than "and" in reference to loving "or" enjoying Brazilian women, and the "good thing" his documentary will ruin—sexual paradise spoiled by a sea of competing African American males. African American men have choices. They can "love" Brazilian women, as many of them genuinely do, but *Brasilieras* can also be merely enjoyed, sampled like exotic victuals as *ChgoBachelor31_4U* suggests, depending on "if your [*sic*] there (1) week . . . (10 females) . . . (2) (20 females)." Indeed, the sheer number of Brazilian female dishes available depending on one's travel schedule rather resembles a colonial Indonesian rice table in which the wealthy colonists selected the finest and most succulent dishes from the isles of Asia.

The exclusive mention of Rio tells yet another story. The Avocet T&E-Varig deal to Bahia is targeted to African American females between the ages of twenty-five and fifty-five, seeking a more spiritual vacation. The first imported enslaved Africans arrived in Salvador, Bahia in the sixteenth century. Bahia and northern Brazil represent the stronghold of African culture with the ever-present martial-art school teaching the Angolan-inspired Capoeira and Yoruban-derived spiritual practices such as Candomblé. Though sex tourism is a persistent problem in Salvador da Bahia and the North, and the Bahian Carnival is also ballyhooed on sex tourist sites like Brazilmensclub.com as such a celebration that "every man owes it to himself to go once in his life," Rio becomes the exclusive playground for African American male sexual prerogatives. And the arrest of twenty-nine African American men on charges of sexual tourism with forty Brazilian sex workers (*garota de programa*, also known as GDP) on the schooner *Shangrilá*, leaving the Marina da Glòria in Rio on June 11, 2005, demonstrates the exercising of those prerogatives. It is then not particularly surprising that Rio, the *favelas*, and the women are varyingly put to use in hip hop culture.

With "Beautiful," "Why You Wanna," *Dude: We're Going to Rio*, and "Holla, Holla" videos, Snoop, T.I., Pharrell, and Ja Rule not only represented the mobility, influence, and access to affluence available to African American hip hop generation men as part of our new global condition, but also offered up the latest fetishized commodity of beauty in the heterosexual African American male realm of desire. That the "Eye Candy" section of hip hop magazines like *XXL* and the Dirty South's *Ozone* feature video vixens remarkably similar to the women in "Beautiful" is no coincidence. That we seem to see the "same ho[s]," using Tupac's rancid poetic maneuver, in Brazil, in *XXL*, and in hip hop videos in general is unfortunately a conundrum of the new black gender politics that uses art, technological innovation, and globalization in the service of color chauvinism, sexist exploitation, and hair neurosis. It is a new black gender politics completely in the service of a jack-legged black masculinity. And that black masculinity has been cobbled together from the stultifying remains of white supremacy, media, and the undeserved privileges accrued globally by American manhood.

That young black women continue to negotiate these impossible ideals that literally gyrate around them in videos, assail them from above in Madison Avenue billboards, and stare back at them in mainstream and hip hop magazines in myriad ways is nothing new. We have always attempted to carve spaces for ourselves in an American culture that has resolutely tried to deny our very humanity and womanhood. But the spaces that have emerged in commercial hip hop are categorically one-dimensional. Beauty is nothing short of the helpmate to sex; and we have become reducible to our sexuality as the predominate arbiter of our reality. Into this rotten strew of hypersexuality and insatiability, one can add the distressing outcome of sexual abuse—of which young black women and girls are 10 percent more likely to be survivors.

"Ladies is Pimps Too": Examining Black Female Masculinities within Hip Hop Culture

Jami Harris

> *Music has long permeated the daily life of most African-Americans; it has played a central role in the normal socialization process; and during moments characterized by intense movements for social changes, it has helped to shape the necessary political consciousness. Any attempt, therefore, to understand in depth the evolution of women's consciousness within the Black community requires a serious examination of the music which has influenced them—particularly that they themselves have created.*
>
> —Angela Davis, *Black Women and Music: A Historical Legacy of Struggle*

The title of this project derives from Jay-Z's chart topping single from *The Black Album*, released in 2003, titled "Dirt off your shoulder," and featuring the lyrics, "If you feelin' like a pimp nigga, go and brush your shoulders off/Ladies is pimps too, go and brush your shoulders off." This simple phrase asked participants of

Reprinted by permission of the author.

mainstream Hip Hop culture to question whether or not "Pimpin," an inherently masculine space denoting the commodification of female bodies, was a space that could be occupied by women themselves. Therefore this project investigates attempts by Black women Hip Hop artists/performers to re-appropriate masculinity as a way to subvert the dominant spaces available to women within Hip Hop culture: that of "Video Ho," "Bitch," "Wifey," "Baby Momma," etc. This paper illustrates how Black female masculinities attempt to challenge the dominant tropes of sexuality and identity but seem to fall short by simply occupying the historical space of the "Strong Black Woman" narrative. I focus on the artistic work of women such as Lil Kim and Khia, among others, and demonstrate how Black female masculinity joins together both mimicry (of the worst of male behavior) and conformity (to the stereotypes of female sexuality), while masquerading as women's liberation. Additionally, this project will examine the potentiality of queer Black female Hip Hop performers, such as Kin 4 Life, to possibly re-script these tropes of masculinity onto subversive female bodies.

As seen throughout Hip Hop culture, Black female Hip Hop performers (when visible) have occupied a space of interpretation and articulation. They have utilized their voices to express the fears, disappointment, pleasures and dreams of young Black women whose voices have historically been relegated to the margins of public discourse. "They are the integral and resistant voices in rap music and in popular music in general who sustain an ongoing dialogue with their audiences and with male rappers about sexual promiscuity, emotional commitment, infidelity, the drug trade, racial politics, and black cultural history" (Rose, *Black Noise* 146). In other words, Hip Hop women occupy a complex space that by their very presence seems to challenge the masculine dominance of the Hip Hop's varied cultural expressions. Within this space, Black women artists counter Black men's primary social criticisms of dominant culture's policing of their bodies and denial of their manhood, to discuss Black female sexual politics. As Tricia Rose points out, "female rappers have been uniformly touted as sexually progressive, antisexist voices in rap music. . . accompanied by an understanding of male rappers as uniformly sexist" (147). However, it is important to acknowledge that gender politics have shifted since Rose published this text in 1994.

This analysis of Hip Hop gender politics creates a dichotomous relationship between male and female Hip Hop performers as sexist/antisexist. "A dichotomy or dichotomous thinking is a process of dividing or categorizing people, things, or ideas into supposedly mutually exclusive groups" (Gines 98). Some examples of such thinking are conceptions of Black versus white, male versus female, reason versus emotion, and especially, in these cases the virgin versus the whore. "Challenging these dichotomies require acknowledging and confronting the objectification of women and moving towards empowering women as subjects or agents of their own sexuality" (Gines 99). However, a repositioning of female artists as attempting to occupy a similar space of working within and against dominant sexual and racial narratives in American culture should be considered. For example, "works by black women rappers that place black women's bodies in the spotlight have a contradictory effect; they affirm black female beauty and yet often preserve the logic of female sexual objectification" (Rose, *Black Noise* 147). Are these female artists responding to male artists' sexist constructions of Black female bodies? Or, are they responding to the larger dominant social discourses surrounding Black sexuality? Are these artists appropriating some aspects of Black hegemonic masculinity to succeed in the world of Hip Hop? Or, are they carving out their own space of sexual freedom and expression? Can these "Black female masculinities" simply be reinscribing the characteristics of the historical Strong Black Woman trope?

The Strong Black Woman (SWB) trope is a historical reflection of "Black women's extensive work and family demands, as well as their accomplishments under far from favorable social conditions" (Beauboef-Lafontant 2). This trope has been used in dominant culture to defend and maintain a stratified social order by obscuring Black women's experiences of suffering, acts of desperation, and anger. They are required to be, as Zora Neal Hurston famously described, "de mule[s] of the world" (Hurston 14). As Michele Wallace explains in *Black Macho and the Myth of the Superwoman:*

> Through the intricate web of mythology, which surrounds the black woman, a fundamental image emerges. It is of a woman of inordinate strength, with an ability for tolerating an unusual amount of misery and heavy, distasteful work. This woman does not have the same fears, weaknesses, and insecurities as

> other women, but believes herself to be and is, in fact, stronger emotionally than most men. Less of a woman in that she is less "feminine" and helpless, she is really more of a woman in that she is the embodiment of Mother Earth, the quintessential mother with infinite sexual, life-giving, and nurturing reserves. In other words, she is a superwoman. (107)

Similar to the plethora of "controlling images" outlined by Patricia Hill Collins, the SBW is used as a representation of this subordinated group to guide behavior and constrain what is seen and believed about Black women, and when internalized, profoundly influence their self-perceptions. The concept of controlling images does go a bit further than simple stereotypes: "these generalizations do not simply emerge from erroneous thinking but are created by an oppressive order to police marginalized groups and naturalize their disempowerment" (Beauboef-Lafontant 22). Because controlling images are deployed to bring thought and behavior in accordance with the matrix of domination,[1] to cause people to become "docile bodies[2]" rather than transformative subjects, they provide a "disguise, or mystification, of objective social relations" (Carby 22). Rendering social injustices into "natural, normal, and inevitable parts from everyday life," controlling images are the ideological glue that secures the matrix of domination and its goal of reproducing "rich, white, Christian, male, heterosexual power" (Collins, *Black Feminist* 69).

The personification of the SBW typically means enduring abuse, whether physical, emotional or sexual, constructed as normative Black femininity. Normative Black femininity is constructed as an abused positionality. Additionally, for many Black women, the institution of motherhood has become a primary site

[1] According to Patricia Hill Collins' *Black Feminist Thought*, "the term matrix of domination describes this overall social organization within which intersecting oppressions originate, develop and are contained. In the United States, such domination has occurred through schools, housing, employment, government, and other social institutions that regulate the actual patterns of intersecting oppressions that Black women encounter" (228).

[2] "Docile Bodies" comes from the work of *Discipline and Punish*, in which Michel Foucault argues that individuals are under constant surveillance and regulation in ways that are often subtle and thereby seemingly invisible, leading to normalization and acceptance of such systems.

where the SBW representation holds sway. Through motherhood, Black women exercise strength, demonstrate power and as a result suffer the consequences (Collins, *Black Sexual* 208). As Joan Morgan states; "I'd internalized the SBW credo: No matter how bad shit gets, handle it alone, quietly, and with dignity" (Morgan 90). Referencing Wallace's explanation of the myths of the superwoman, the mammy, the jezebel, and the sapphire, Morgan contends that these myths have metamorphosed into the contem porary figures of, among others, the "Ghetto Bitch. . .Hoochie Mama. . .Skeezer. . .Too independent. . .Don't need no man. . . [and] Waiting to Exhale" women (100). She believes that the older myths justifying slave-owners brutality against Black women, transformed into contemporary conservative welfare myths. As racist and sexist as the SBW trope may be, many have posed her as the authentic or "real" Black woman. The authentic Black femininity consists of a traditional gender ideology of the "ornamental, passive female whose sexuality should be placed in service to men of her racial, ethnic, and/or social class group" (Collins, *Black Sexual* 209). However, "Black hip-hop feminists' challenges to the Strong Black Woman persona reject traditional Black gender ideology and encourage us to think differently about Black women's bodies as an important step in reclaiming Black women's sexuality as a site of agency and pleasure" (209). Yet on the other side of this freedom from the "traditional" is a gender ideology that discredits free, powerful, strong women.

In Gwendoyln Pough's text *Check it While I Wreck it*, she examines the public space of Hip Hop created by a very masculinized culture to examine the roles available to women, and their uses of this public space to tell their stories, represent "their people" and "bring wreck" to the world of Hip-Hop. "Bringing wreck, for Black participants in the public sphere historically, has meant reshaping the public gaze in such a way as to be recognized as human beings—as functioning and worthwhile members of society—and not to be shut out or pushed away from the public sphere" (Pough 17). Black women throughout Hip-Hop culture bring wreck by showing up in public spaces and demanding a voice, while simultaneously challenging the dominant scripts that have excluded them in the first place. Some Black women have used public space of Hip Hop to reclaim their sexuality through self-expression. This, of course, is in direct contrast to the "politics of silence,"[3] developed by the Black middle-class. These women display their sexuality seemingly in their own terms. However, artists such as Khia and Lil' Kim display their sexuality openly, as pleasure; they are in possession of their own bodies. On the other hand, they are commonly viewed throughout dominant culture as simply upholding the historical image of the Jezebel,[4] or loose woman. Subsequently, they occupy a controversial border between empowerment and objectification. Echoing Kimberly Springer, is the embodiment of the Strong Black Woman as sexually raunchy, always hot, and ready for sex empowering? Or, as Carol Vance asks: "Can women be sexual actors? Can we act on our own behalf? Or are we purely victims?"

One way to respond to the Strong Black Woman-Jezebel paradigm has been to embrace one extreme or a combination of both, and redefine it in a more positive or empowering way. "Heterosexuality itself is constructed via binary thinking that juxtaposes male and female sexuality, with male and female gender roles pivoting on perceptions of appropriate male and female sexual expression. Men are active, and women should be passive" (Collins, *Black Feminist* 83). These female artists' sexual empowerment seems to come directly from their re-appropriation of dominant masculine constructions of sexuality. "Lil' Kim utilizes this strategy in her rap lyrics and music videos in which she comfortably asserts her sexuality. She is arguably the most successful female rappers taking up and popularizing the image of the *ho* and the *bitch* unapologetically" (Gines 99). Therefore, when Lil' Kim displays an active or even aggressive sexuality, or sexual appetite, she is performing a sort of masculinity. "Lil' Kim represents a type of power. She is the queen of the streets, the Queen Bitch, the Queen Bee, the Black Madonna of rap music" (Richardson 190).

[3] The "politics of silence" as described by Evelyn Brooks Higginbotham, emerged as a political strategy by Black women reformers who hoped by their silence and by the promotion of the "cult of true womanhood" and Victorian morality to "expose" the image of the sexually immoral Black woman as a fallacy (262).

[4] "Black jezebel is the bad female who is promiscuous, the embodiment of lust. She uses her sexually alluring nature and lewdness to entrap men and she can never be sexually exhausted, chaste or truthful" (Richardson 188).

Lil' Kim's violation of sexual mores is threatening to some. The primary source of her sexual power is her irreverence towards the morally based sexual constrictions placed on her as a woman. Her defiance of the moral, sexual restrictions on women come from her display of a sexual spectacle of gratification similar to that of men. Lil' Kim, whose alias is Queen Bee (standing for Queen Bitch), made space for herself in a male-dominated world of Hip Hop misogyny. Her name is an example of her first re-appropriation, where she took a derogatory term, Bitch, and made it an empowering symbol for her independent sexuality. "Her lyrics graphically expose the double standards of sexuality for men and women. When men sleep around they are players and pimps, but when women do it they are bitches and hos" (Gines 99). Consider her lyrics from "Suck My D**k: "Imagine if I was a dude and hittin cats from the back. . ./Yeah nigga, picture that!/I treat y'all niggas like y'all treat us." Then when asked "Why you actin' like a bitch?" Queen Bee replies" "Cause y'all niggas ain't shit/and if I was a dude/I'd tell y'all to suck my dick." Lil Kim re-appropriates phrases that have been used to belittle women or put them "in their place" and she is throwing them back into men's faces. "Lil' Kim also 'flips the script' on men in the bedroom by demanding oral sex, something it was thought only men could demand" (Gines 99). For example, in her hit single "How Many Licks," she expresses a kind of sexuality typically forbidden to women:

> Dan my nigga from Down South
> Used to like me to spank him and cum in his mouth. . .
> He ate my pussy from dark till the mornin'
> Called his girl up and told her we was bonin'
> Puerto Rican papi', used to be a Deacon
> But now he be sucking me off on the weekend
> And this black dude I called King Kong
> He had a big ass dick and a hurricane tongue

Lil' Kim's possession of these men for sexual pleasure, as well as her objectification of them is reminiscent of the kind of sexism we as feminists protest within mainstream commercial Hip Hop. She also discusses an act of sexual deviance that is rarely discussed in popular culture, due to the lack of direct male gratification. However, her sexually explicit language is used to tease and attract the male viewer who could misinterpret her sexual freedom as an open invitation (Rose, *Hip Hop Wars* 167). Lil' Kim's pleasure comes directly from her assertion of power over these men, an attitude of supply and demand; she has it and they need it. She seemingly flips the script on dominant culture by stepping into the masculine role of strength and dominance.

Similarly, the artist Khia has created a persona of being sexually perverse as well as powerful. In her single "My Neck, My Back," she also discusses the sexually deviant act of demanding oral sex:

> My neck, my back
> Lick my pussy and my crack
> First you gotta put your neck into it
> Don't stop, just do, do it
> Then you roll your tongue, from the crack back to the front
> then suck it off til I shake and cum nigga
> make sure I keep bustin nuts nigga
> all over your face and stuff

Khia, within these lyrics, creates a space of deviance and subversion by occupying this space of power. Her lyrics seem to be in dialogue with male-centered Hip Hop hits such as Three 6 Mafia's "Slob on My Knob," in which member Juicy J is straight-forward in his demands, telling his partner firmly "Lay on the bed, and give me head/Don't have to ask, don't have to beg." Khia re-appropriates hegemonic masculinity by possessing subjectivity and agency through the subjugation of the opposite sex, apparently flipping the binary of gendered oppression. She seemingly reclaims actions, sexualities, and body parts that were previously used in a way disparaging towards women.

Additionally, with their sexually explicit lyrics, both Lil' Kim and Khia's music and videos create an inversion of the aesthetic hierarchy that typically renders Black women's bodies as inadequate and sexually unattractive. According to bell hooks, contemporary popular music is one of the primary cultural locations for discussions of Black sexuality. In their song lyrics, the Black female body "is talked about in ways that attempt to challenge racist assumptions that suggest it is an ugly sign of inferiority, even as it remains a sexualized sign" (hooks 115). In other words, they bring to the center the Black female body and her subsequent sexuality, to be in conversation with the demonization of their bodies by dominant culture as well as the commodification of their bodies by Black male rap artists, aka Pimps.

The pimp is not just a man that provides sex on demand by soliciting clients for his prostitutes. Being a pimp is a way of dressing and carrying oneself, and having the general attitude that women are sexual objects to be used and manipulated for one's own pleasure or gain (Gines 102). As Jay-Z put it in "Big Pimpin": "You know I—thug em, fuck em, love em, leave em/Cause I don't fucking' need em." These female artists are "merely seeking to move men from the subject to the object position where she can manipulate them as sexual objects" (Gines 100). According Kathryn Gines, "This attempted reversal of sexual status strengthens rather than undermines the prevailing distorted image of Black sexuality. In the end, Black women are still hos and bitches while Black men are players and pimps, and these images reinforce one another" (Gines 100). However, as stated above, "Ladies is Pimps Too," in that Lil' Kim, and Khia both possess and portray the attributes allocated to the "pimp" lifestyle and persona. They might be pimpin' themselves, or maybe flippin the script and pimpin' men. What they are not doing is becoming the passive victims of Hip Hop misogyny by being used up and tossed aside by men.

The image these women are co-opting, that of the "Pimp," is inherently problematic. "Buttressing both the image of the rapist and the more contemporary image of the 'pimp' is the idea that Black men have an insatiable, even animalistic appetite for sex or sexual perversion" (Gines 102). These women are empowering themselves by first making a spectacle of themselves, not allowing themselves to be made spectacle of through objectification by male artists or viewers. The gender ideology exhibited here is based on a conception of racialized sexuality that continues to couple strength with sexual dominance. The empowerment would come from this uncoupling, along with Black women challenging this gender ideology and "developing new understandings of Black sexuality that rejects perceptions of Black promiscuity" (Collin, *Black Sexual* 209). Some Black female Hip Hop artists' public displays of physical and sexual freedom seem to challenge these dominant notions of female sexuality and pleasure. They are carving out a space for themselves outside of the dominant controlling image of the Strong Black woman as the domineering mother, but instead, in control of her own body and sexuality. These women are trading one set of problematic images for another, one seemingly less vulnerable. However, what these women seem to not understand is the power of redefinition, as opposed to re-appropriation.

This redefinition could come through the recognition that the space created by Hip Hop offers for these female artists a racialized context for the performance of gender and sexuality. As theorist Judith Butler argues, sex and gender (and race) have been constructed and figuratively inscribed on our bodies. Participants within the Hip Hop culture (as well as all people) are all habitually performing socially constructed gender roles, or enacting gender performativity. By performativity, she means that gender roles are constantly acted out and acquire meaning when they are "properly" and repeatedly performed (Butler, *Gender Trouble* xxi). On the other hand, in the case of these Black female masculine performances, Butler states "it is not possible to oppose the 'normative' forms of gender without at the same time subscribing to a certain normative view of how the gendered world ought to be" (xxii). This view of gender as performative is used to show that what dominant culture takes to be essential or given is in fact manufactured through a "sustained set of acts, posited through the gendered stylization of the body" (xv). The masculinity attributed to these Black women's performances is a sort of satiric mimicry, a sort of drag that is inherently queer.

Through Hip Hop, participants can create radically different conceptions of gender and sexuality that do not at all conform to preexisting stereotypes. Once conscious of this fact, artists have the opportunity to choose whether to be authentic or inauthentic in their performance. As Sartre explains: "Authenticity. . . consists in having a true and lucid consciousness of the situation in assuming the responsibilities and risks that it involves" (Sartre 90). In other words, authenticity requires these Black female Hip Hop artists to possess authentic empowerment, rather than simply re-appropriating a problematic hegemonic masculinity. One possibility here can be a "counter-appropriation" of masculinity, performed by queer Hip Hop groups such as Kin 4 Life or the "Aggressive" queer community of New York. It is important to note the difference being made here between re-appropriation and counter-appropriation. The major difference is that counter-appropriation is, in part, defined by its effects, rather than by the initial action of occupying a forbidden space.

Artists like Kin 4 Life work to put pressure on racialized categories and identities of sex and gender by creating new spaces.

Similar to the oppressive bind surrounding female participants within Hip Hop, queer women of color have an unarguably contentious relationship to Hip Hop. "These artists do not fit easily into the commonly accepted mold of womanhood in hip-hop, which assumes women are heterosexual or the objects of straight desire. Yet they continue to participate in a musical realm long male-dominated" (Pritchard 20). These growing numbers of "out" queer women of color are carrying the torch in the form of Hip Hop activism that provides a voice to those who have been silenced by rampant marginalization and erasure. "This contentious relationship is a result of the continuum of blatant homophobia and heterosexism that exists in the larger society overall and hip hop as well" (21). In other words, this issue is not concentrated within the Hip Hop community. However, Hip Hop seems to have a much more complex and complicated relationship to gender, sexuality, and bodies, because the producers (primarily people of color) have very complex relationships to those structures.

The gendered performance of Kin 4 Life makes visible their lesbian identities, and by their very presence brings wreck by attacking the problems of homophobia and misogyny through their music. KIN is comprised of 2 members: IQ and Nor, who produce their own music out of their independent record label Noriq. They cite on their MySpace page that their biggest influences as the "self-proclaimed Pimps," Notorious B.I.G and Jay-Z, as well as, Missy Elliot, P. Diddy and "every female MC before them." They do not present themselves as a radical answer to homophobia within Hip Hop, they simply present themselves as Hip Hop's answer to the question "what happened to the female rap game." However, they do present themselves as queer women who redefine hegemonic masculinity by resisting it on multiple levels, i.e. counter-appropriation. This differs from the work of Lil' Kim and Khia's re-appropriation of hegemonic masculinity, as re-appropriation is an attempt to transfer a certain kind of performance onto a body which shares a certain kind of privilege (read: straight). Whereas counter-appropriation seems to be an attempt to resist or subvert, since by contrast the bodies doing the transfer share no dominant forms of privilege (i.e. gender or sexuality) with the hegemonic group.

This masculine performance can be seen in Kin 4 Life's first major music video for their single "Make Up Girl." Throughout the video, both Nor and IQ, play the part of cheating lovers pleading for redemption from their same-sex partners. This performance harkens back to classic R&B music videos where a man in a heterosexual relationship typically occupies this space. The women of Kin 4 Life, though overly feminized in the music video (i.e. wearing make-up) appear to take up the space when and where a man is missing. This possession or counter-appropriation of hegemonic masculinity is evident in the choice of their female partners to date men following their break-ups. Also, throughout the video, the only other relationships that are shown are those of strictly heterosexual couples, where the male partner is pleading for redemption for a wrongdoing. This is important to note because instead of creating a strictly queer space within the video, Nor and IQ seem to simply super-impose themselves into a heteronormative space. These images can be read as either subversive, as queer identities and personifications occupying the same space with heteronormativity, or as simply hegemonic themselves.

On the other hand, during their live stage performances, Kin 4 Life displays a very aggressive and "thuggish" performance. They can be seen grabbing their crotches, poppin' their finger like they're shooting a gun, and towering over the audience in a dominating manner. They also have songs with lyrics that differ greatly from the "soft" R&B style of "Make Up Girl." In their song "Gettinsome," the lyrics confess how both women "know" that they will be "gettin' some ass/I'm getting' some ass tomorrow." Through this song the tell a story of meeting a very "forward" woman in a coffee shop, who invites IQ or Nor to her hotel room for sex. They use typically heteronormative language of "rounding the bases" to discuss sexual acts: "but tomorrow girl I promise we can get it down/and I'm just hopin' she ain't playin' cuz I'm ready babe/we can go from second to third base/a home-runner have you screaming my name." However similar, this incarnation of Black gender non-conforming masculine subjectivity always means something different than when that act is performed by any privileged male subject, of any racial identity.

Another act of masculine counter-appropriation attempting to achieve the goal of resistance is seen in the "Aggressive" or Ag culture of lesbians of color in NYC. At its most basic definition an "aggressive" or "stud" is a lesbian who is generally displays more masculine attributes than the feminine ones. There are degrees to this, of course, and many different ways in which an Ag or stud might express her masculine side. Although, some would say that being a stud does not have anything to do with masculinity but with a dominant personality or dominant role in relationships. Studs also may dress in more masculine way to achieve their "masculine" performance, and this can really run the gamut. This culture has been "exposed" by the documentary, The Aggressives, which explores the lives of six New York City "women" who assume the category of "aggressive" through masculine roles, behavior, and dress. Each woman defines their gender roles in unique and profound ways through footage that includes intimate interviews and clips from talk shows and drag balls. Identified as "queer" women of color, they stand "in direct contrast to normalizing tendencies of hegemonic sexuality rooted in ideas of static, stable sexual identities and behaviors" (Cohen 241). However, these women's self-defining attribute of being "aggressive" are all the characteristics and performances of dominant hegemonic masculinity; aggressive, dominant, "in control," "wears the pants," etc. This is reminiscent of feminist criticisms of the butch-femme relationships, as a supposed "poor imitation" of hetero norms. Even their "thuggish" appearance plays a role in creating this performance. The queer space created by the Ag culture still engages in harmful acts towards one another through the objectification of women. In a scene where one Ag woman competes in a drag performance, we see a girl being bent over to the front and being told to touch her toes and having her do so in high heels and a thong, which is in no way liberating.

Although the masculinities displayed by mainstream Black female Hip Hop artists differ from that of Queer women of color in the Hip Hop community, both exhibit an application of problematic traits that re-inscribe dominant paradigms. Both groups take the idea of "sampling" to another level and restage the sexual politics of Hip Hop and the active components of Black masculinity by channeling them through a sort of "drag" act. Judith Halberstam's article "F2M: the Making of Female Masculinity," is useful in illustrating the notion of masculinity as "dress." "Dress" is a costume that becomes equivalent to the self: the masculinity she both wears and owns. "We all pass or we don't, we all wear our drag, and we all derive a different degree of pleasure–sexual or otherwise–from our costumes" (212). This act of appropriation is exhibited by individuals and impersonators such as "Drag Kings/Queens." However, Butler contends that there is no "proper" gender, "a gender proper to one sex rather than another" (Butler, "Imitation" 127). Therefore all gender, as well as sexuality, is drag. "Drag constitutes the mundane way in which genders are appropriated, theatricalized, worn, and done; it implies that all gendering is a kind of impersonation and approximation" (127). Whether these women are dressing as "hard" as the men in the rap videos or utilizing the sexual power allotted to masculine subjects, Black masculinity is changed in that these women are exploring their masculinity as women. However, it is apparent that the same objectification and violence towards women can happen regardless of the gender of the protagonist. The queer communities and Hip Hop communities both reflect and resist dominant and popular culture. The gender ideology that couples strength with dominance, which women seem to have also internalized, suggests that a re-appropriation or counter-appropriation of hegemonic masculinity will always be problematic and therefore disempowering. However, counter-appropriation does in some way disrupt hegemonic masculinity by forcing us to view masculine performance on other bodies, all the while making queer sexuality and performance visible in a way that cannot easily be co-opted for the male pornographic imagination or pleasure. In this way, counter-appropriation of hegemonic masculinities in Hip Hop culture does expand the options available to non-normative subjects.

Works Cited

Beauboeuf-Lafontant, Tamara. *Behind the Mask of the Strong Black Woman: Voice and the Embodiment of a Costly Performance.* Pennsylvania: Temple University Press, 2009.

Butler, Judith. "Imitation and Gender Insubordination." *The Judith Butler Reader.* Ed. Sara Salih. Massachusetts:Blackwell Publishing, 2004. 119–37.

—. *Gender Trouble: Feminism and the Subversion of Identity.* New York: Routledge Classics, 1999.

Carby, Hazel V. *Reconstructing Womanhood: the Emergence of the Afro American Woman Novelist.* New York: Oxford University Press, 1987.

Cohen, Cathy J. "Punks, Bulldaggers, and Welfare Queens: The radical Potential of Queer Politics." *Still Brave: The Evolution of Black Women's Studies.* Ed. Beverly Guy-Sheftall. New York: The Feminist Press at the City University of New York, 2009.

Collins, Patricia Hill. *Black Feminist Thought: Knowledge, Consciousness, and the Politics of Empowerment.* 2nd ed. New York: Routlege, 2000.

—. *Black Sexual Politics: African Americans, Gender, and The New Racism.* New York: Routlege, 2005.

Davis, Angela. "Black Women and Music: A Historical Legacy of Struggle." *Black Feminist Cultural Criticism.* Ed. Jacqueline Bobo. Massachusetts: Blackwell Publishing, 2001. Pgs 217–232.

Foucault, Michel and Alan Sheridan. *Discipline and Punish: The Birth of the Prison; Translated from the French by Alan Sheridan.* Harmondsworth: Penguin, 1979

Gines, Kathryn. "Queen Bees and Big Pimps: Sex and Sexuality in Hip Hop." *Hip Hop and Philosophy: Rhyme to Reason.* Ed. Derrick Darby. Chicago: Open Court Publishing Company, 2005.

Halberstam, Judith. "F2M: the Making of Female Masculinity." *The Lesbian Postmodern.* Ed. Laura Doan. New York: Columbia University Publishing, 1994. 210–228.

Hammonds, Evelynn M. "Black (W)holes and the Geometry of Black Female Sexuality." *Skin Deep, Spirit Strong: The Black Female Body in American Culture,* ed. Kimberly Wallace-Sanders. Ann Arbor: The University of Michigan Press, 2002. 301–20.

Higginbotham, Evelyn Brooks. "African-American Women's History and the Metalanguage of Race." *Signs* Vol. 17, No. 2 (1992): 251–74

hooks, bell. "Selling Hot Pussy: Representations of Black Female Sexuality in the Cultural Marketplace." *Writing on the Body: Female Embodiment and Feminist Theory*. Ed. Katie Conboy et al. New York: Columbia University Press, 1997. 113–28.

Morgan, Joan. *When Chickenheads Come Home to Roost: A Hip-Hop Feminist Breaks it Down*. New York: Touchstone, 1999.

Neale Hurston, Zora. *Their Eyes are Watching God*. Connecticut: Fawcett, 1937.

Pritchard, Eric Darnell and Maria L. Bibbs. "Sista' Outsider: Queer Women of Color and Hip Hop." *Home Girls Make Some Noise: Hip Hop Feminism Anthology*. Ed. Gwendolyn D. Pough. Mira Loma: Parker Publishing, 2007.

Richardson, Elaine. "Lil' Kim, Hip-Hop Womanhood, and the Naked Truuf." *Home Girls Make Some Noise: Hip Hop Feminism Anthology*. Ed. Gwendolyn D. Pough. Mira Loma: Parker Publishing, 2007.

Rose, Tricia. *Black Noise: Rap Music and Black Culture in Contemporary America*. Connecticut: Wesleyan University Press, 1994.

—. *Hip Hop Wars: What We Talk About When We Talk About Hip Hop—and Why it Matters*. New York: Basic Books, 2008

Sartre, Jean-Paul. *Anti-Semite and Jew*. Paris: Schocken Books, 1948

Wallace, Michele. *Black Macho and the Myth of the Super-Woman*. New York: Warner Books, 1978.

YOUR LIFE AS A GIRL (1995)

Curtis Sittenfeld

What does it mean to be a girl? Why do athletic, assertive little girls sometimes grow to be anxious, self-conscious teens, less interested in school than in appearance? What behavior is considered "appropriate" for girls and how are these rules communicated and absorbed? The scenarios Curtis Sittenfield presents in "Your Life As a Girl"—scenarios that may seem familiar—illustrate the process of gender socialization and the impact some gender messages can have on girls' development. Curtis Sittenfield, born in 1975, is a writer and student. She has published articles in Ms. *and* Seventeen *magazines, and* Listen Up! Voices From the Next Feminist Generation *(1995), from which the following selection was taken. She has also published two coming-of-age novels,* Prep *(2005) and* The Man of My Dreams *(2006).*

In fifth grade, you can run faster than any other girl in your class. One day in the spring, the gym teacher has all of you do a timed mile, and by the third lap, half the girls are walking. You come in seventh, and the boys who are already finished stick up their hands, and you high-five them. When you play kickball you're the first girl to be picked, and when you play capture the flag you're the one who races across the other team's side to free the prisoners. At recess, you're the foursquare queen. You slam the red rubber ball onto your three opponents' patches of pavement, and you gloat when they get disqualified. Sometimes your teacher supervises, standing in a raincoat by the door to the school building. Once, after she's rung the bell to call you inside, you pass her, your body still tense and excited, your face flushed. She says in a low voice, a voice that sounds more like the one she uses with adults and not with the other children in your class, "Anna, aren't you being just a bit vicious?" The next time you're playing, you fumble and let the ball slide beyond the thin white lines that serve as boundaries.

By sixth grade, your friends no longer like foursquare. Neither, really, do you, though you teach the game to your younger sister and sometimes play it with her in your driveway, in the evenings. At school, you sit with the other girls on top of the jungle gym by the swing set, and you argue about how often you're supposed to shave your legs. Your friend Nell says every two days. You probably talk about other things, but later, you can't remember what they are.

When Nell spends a Saturday night at your house, her boyfriend Steve calls seven times. At eleven o'clock, you grab the phone from Nell and say: "Steve, we have to go. My parents will be home soon, and they'll be mad if we're still talking to you." He protests but then relents and asks to say good-bye to Nell. You pass her the phone. After she's hung up, she says that he told her to tell you that you're a bitch.

You can't learn how to play football. Early in the winter of seventh grade, you stand with your junior high gym class on the field behind the cafeteria. The gym teacher, whose name is Ted and who has a mustache, goes over various kinds of passes. They all seem alike to you though, and mid-game, when someone tosses you the ball, you just stand there with no idea what to do. "Throw it," bellow the boys on your team, so you do, but you don't want to watch where it lands or who catches it. After that, for the remaining weeks of football and even on into basketball and volleyball season, you're careful to station yourself in the back, or at the edges, wherever you're least likely to be accountable.

In the spring, you get moved from the higher to the lower math class, because you have a C-plus average. At first, you don't mind because in lower math you have the best grade in your class. Your teacher, Mr. Willet, asks for the answers to problems he's working out on the chalkboard, and he's pleased when you respond. But sometimes he doesn't call on you, even when you're the only one raising your hand, and he says in a humorless voice: "Well, we all know Anna has the answer. Let's see if anyone else does." On the comments sent home to your parents, Mr. Willet writes that though he appreciates your hard work, he wishes you'd give other students a chance to speak. He says that you're intimidating them.

At the Halloween dance in eighth grade, when you and Nell are standing by the buffet table, Jimmy Wrightson appears from nowhere and says, "Hey, Anna, can I suck your tits?" At first you don't understand what he's said, but he's coming closer, and Nell is giggling, and then Jimmy is pawing you. You press your fists into his stomach, pushing him away. He smirks at you before he saunters back to where his friends are waiting. You still don't know what he's said, and you have to ask Nell.

You don't tell any teachers, of course. You're not a snitch, and besides, you can take care of yourself. In social studies class the following Monday, you're sitting next to Nate, one of Jimmy's friends. You ask why Jimmy tried to feel you up, and Nate shrugs and says, "Probably someone dared him to." You say, "Yeah, well it was kind of obnoxious." Nate gives you a scornful expression. "It was a joke," he says. "Take it easy."

You hear that Jimmy got ten dollars.

In the summers, you swim for the team at the country club near your house. Before your races you wander around in a huge T-shirt, and you never eat. You and your friends go on a thousand diets, and you don't say anything else as often as you say that you're fat. In June, your father keeps the air-conditioning blasting through your house. You always wear sweat pants, even though it's ninety degrees outside. You spend the mornings making elaborate desserts: lemon tarts, puddings, pies. You allow yourself to eat the batter but not the finished product. You jog in place, or you do jumping jacks, leaping around your kitchen like a crazy lady. Two or three years later, you find photographs of yourself from that summer when you were fourteen. The girl you see looks grim, pale and so thin her collarbone sticks out like a rod.

In ninth grade, you go away to boarding school, where you begin to practice making ashamed facial expressions in the mirror. You embarrass yourself on a daily basis, so you want to make sure you're acting appropriately. Everything about you is horrifying: your voice, body, hair, inability to be witty and panicky desires for approval and companionship. In classes you speak as infrequently as possible and walk around with your head lowered. You play on the soccer team, but if boys ever watch, you make only halfhearted attempts to kick the ball.

To your mother's dismay, you begin reading romance novels. The covers show chesty, lusty heroines in torn clothing and men with long hair and fierce stares. The premises of the stories are identical, though the specifics change: The man and woman are attracted to each other, they quarrel, they end up alone together, they have wild sex. The women always say they don't want it, but they really do. The characters live in eighteenth-century France or on the Scottish moors or in Hawaii. You start to think that you were born at the wrong time. You would have done better a hundred years ago, when a girl knew that she'd be protected, that she wouldn't have to find a man because one would come to claim her.

When you're in tenth grade the students who write for your high school yearbook compile a list of people's nicknames and what they're known for. You hear that for your roommate they're going to write "doesn't like cherries." This is supposed to be a subtly amusing reference to the fact that at a party in the fall, she had sex with a guy she barely knew. You go to the yearbook editor and say, looking at the floor, that you think your roommate would be very upset if that particular line were printed. Afterward you blush, which is something you've just begun to do. You're glad that you got the hang of it because there certainly is a lot for you to be ashamed of. When you walk away from the editor, you hear him murmur, "What a weirdo."

On your grandmother's bed, she has a small pillow that says in needlepoint, "Women are such expensive things." When you and your sister go to your grandmother's house for brunch, your grandmother gives the two of you advice about men. First off, she says, learn to dance. And be a good conversationalist. Read book reviews, and even read the newspaper from time to time, in case he's an intellectual. Never turn down a date, because he might have a handsome brother. Once when your mother cannot open a jam jar, she passes it to your father, and your grandmother says chirpily, "The women admit their natural inferiority." "I think I'm going to throw up," says your sister. You laugh as if you agree, but for a minute you're not even sure what she's referring to.

Every day during the summer after your junior year in high school, you run two miles to the country club, then you climb 250 flights on the StairMaster. You wear elasticized running shorts that make you feel like your legs are pieces of sausage, and you pant the whole time. Men stick their heads out the windows of their cars and hoot at you as you run past. At first you take their yells as compliments, but you realize how hideous you look, and then you realize that they aren't seeing you, not as a person. They are seeing you as long hair and bare legs, and you are frightened. Recently, you have found yourself wishing that you'd get raped now, and then it would be done with. It will happen sooner or later; you've read the news reports, and you'd rather just get it out of the way.

Senior year, you develop a schedule: Sunday mornings you burn your skin. Not in glory, though, not you: What you do is rub hot wax onto your calves, and then for half a day, your legs are as smooth as pebbles. Or you use rotating silver coils that rip out hair from the root, or you use bleaching cream. You stand in front of the mirror, bleeding and stinging and knowing full well that the boys in your class will never think you're beautiful anyway.

Sometimes the boys are just so rich and handsome and indifferent. They get drunk on Saturday nights, and after they've seen a movie with an attractive woman in it, they say, "Hell yeah, I'd do her." It is hard to explain how your insides collapse when they say those words, how far apart from them you start to feel. Maybe they don't know that you want terribly to like them, or maybe they know that you'll like them anyway, however they act. When you protest, even mildly, the boys have words for you: cunt, ho, bitch. They say feminist like it's a nasty insult.

You've changed a little. You've read magazine articles that discuss other teenage girls who get eating disorders and flunk math, and now you know that you're a statistic, not a freak. Somewhere inside, you start to feel a little pissed off. You think of the fairy tales your mother read to you when you were small: Cinderella and Snow White and Rapunzel and the rest of their dippy, flaxen-haired sisters. You think of the songs you chanted with the neighborhood kids, tapping each other to see who had to be "it" when you were playing tag or hide-and-seek: "Inka-binkabottle-of-ink/The cork falls off and you stink/Not because you're dirty/Not because you're clean/Just because you kissed the boy behind the magazine." Or, "My mother and your mother were hanging up clothes/My mother punched your mother in the nose/What color blood came out?" The world has given you two options: You can be a slut or a matron.

Late at night a kind of sadness descends and grips the girls in your dorm. You watch television shows about men and women who go to work in the morning, who experience amusing mishaps like getting stuck in elevators with their bosses or having their mother's parakeet die, and then they go on, to sleep or home or to more places where equally witty encounters are had by the handful. The characters' lives unfold in front of you, brisk and brightly colored, and you are sitting on the common room floor or on lumpy, worn couches, you're eating pork-flavored noodles and raw cookie dough, and you have four papers to write before Tuesday. You're waiting for your life to start.

And maybe the boys can save you. Maybe if you do sit-ups before you go to bed at night your stomach will be flat, and they'll love you well. Not that you actually believe that, not that you haven't been told a million times about just waiting until college where dozens of guys will treat you nicely. But you want love now, you want to have a boy standing there after you've failed a French test or fought with your roommate. The boy can hold you up with his strong arms and his common sense. You'll start to cry, and he'll get embarrassed and shuffle around and say, "Come on, Anna, don't worry like this." You'll worship his incoherence. You'll wish that you could stay up all night like he does. At two in the morning, guys watch the Home Shopping Network with the younger kids in the dorm, or they set up hockey games with bottles of ketchup, or they play complex tricks involving vacuum cleaners on each other, and the next morning they snore through math class.

Friday night the boy next to you is feeling playful. No one has more than three classes the following morning, so you stay at dinner an hour and a half. The boy keeps saying he's in love with you. He rubs your shoulders and says, "Your hair is magnificently soft," and everyone at the table cracks up. You say, "I forgot to wish you Happy Birthday yesterday," so he says, "Do it now," and he sticks out his cheek for you to kiss. You say, "No way!" You're grinning ferociously, you're practically hyper from the attention, and you think that if he offers you the option of kissing him, you couldn't be that gross after all. And then on Saturday morning, when you pass in the hall, he looks at you exhaustedly and says not a word.

Girls like you are well-fed and well-clothed and are loved by parents who send checks and say that you don't call home enough. Alumni return to tell you that when God was creating the world, He smiled just a little longer on your campus. On sunny days you believe this. But in the middle of the term, when the sky is gray and your notebooks are shabby and your skin is dry, it gets harder. The weather grows so cold it reminds you of cruelty.

You and your friends get sick with fevers, and you are hungry for something immense. You say, "Let's buy hamburgers, let's order pizza," and you walk to town blowing your noses on your parkas. At the grocery store you are so overwhelmed by the variety of food that you don't buy anything but Pepsi.

In the morning, after the heater has roared all night, your skin is so dehydrated you tell your roommate you're starting the Roasted Nostrils Club, only boarding school students need apply. You find yourself deliciously witty over toothpaste and Ivory soap, and then at breakfast you start slipping. It's the boys' tiredness. They kill you with their tiredness. You just wish they were more interested. You wish you knew the thing to say to make them stop shoveling oatmeal in their mouths. You want to shout, "Look at me! Dammit!" But you murmur, "I'm worried about the physics quiz/I heard it's supposed to rain tomorrow."

Once when it snows, you and your friends go to the lower fields and make angels. Other eighteen-year-olds are enlisting in the army or getting married, but at boarding school, you still open Advent calendars. When a group of boys in your class comes over the hill and down toward where you are standing, you pack the snow into balls and throw them. The boys fly forward, retaliating, smothering you. The air is filled with powdery flakes and everyone is yelling and laughing. One of the boys grabs you around the waist and knocks you down, and he's on top of you, stuffing snow in your mouth. At first you are giggling, and then you are choking and spitting, and you say, "Stop, come on." Your hat has fallen off, and the boy is pressing his arm on your hair so that your head is pulled backward. "Please," you gasp. "Come on." For an instant, your eyes meet his. Your faces are only about three inches apart, and his stare is like a robot's. You think he is breaking your neck, you're going to die or be paralyzed. But then the other boys are wanting to leave, and the boy pulls away and towers over you.

"What the hell is wrong with you?" you ask. You're still lying on the ground shaking, but you're furious, which is something you haven't been for a long time. Your fury gives you power. "Why did you just do that?"

The boy grins sickeningly and says, "Suck it up, Anna." Then he turns and walks away.

You never tell your friends because you yourself can hardly believe it happened. Later, it seems like a nightmare—rapid, violent, vague. When you were a first-year student, there was a beautiful senior girl in your dorm, and her boyfriend was president of the student council. You heard that they'd go for walks off campus and get in fights. He'd beat her and leave her there, and later, bearing roses or pieces of jewelry, he'd apologize tearfully. It sounded glamorous to you, at the time.

When the sun is out, the boys tease you again. From across the quadrangle, they shout your name in an enthusiastic voice, then they walk over, thrilled to see you, and the golden sky shines down, lighting their hair from behind, and they are wonderfully good-looking and clever, and you think how absolutely happy they sometimes make you.

After class, you are feeling so good that you boldly announce they'd better do their parts of the lab that's due on Monday, and they give you a phony smile and turn away. They are walking with a boy you know less well than the other boys, and they gesture toward you and mutter something to him. You cannot hear everything they say, but you make out your name and the word "nagging." You have overstepped your boundaries, and they have put you in your place.

You've had trouble sleeping lately. You can fall asleep easily enough, but you awaken during the night as many as nine times. Often, your heart is pounding, and you have the sensation that you've narrowly missed something disastrous, but you never can identify what it was. The dark hours pass slowly, and when it's finally light outside, you start to relax. Your bones loosen, your head feels large and soft. You fall asleep again around dawn, and dreams from a long time ago come to you: across all the distance of your life so far, you go back to elementary school, to the afternoon when you ran a timed mile. The air was warm and green, your lungs were burning, and clear, pure lines of sweat fell down the sides of your face. You crossed the finish line, and your eyes met the eyes of the six boys who were already cooling down. For a minute, in the sunlight, they smiled at you, and you smiled back as if you all had something in common.

QUESTIONS

1. What transformations occur in the behavior and feelings of the girls Sittenfeld presents? Why do they act differently? Why might Sittenfeld have chosen "you" as the subject of her essay?
2. What messages do girls receive about appropriate behavior in our culture? Where do these messages come from? What might be the culminating effect of years of receiving such messages? What damage might be caused by girls' extensive self-scrutiny of their own appearance and behavior?
3. What messages might encourage girls to behave actively and assertively? Which of Sittenfeld's descriptions are consistent with your own experiences or those of women that you know?

STRAIGHTENING OUR HAIR (1989)

bell hooks

bell hooks is a well-known African-American scholar and Distinguished Professor of English at City College of New York. She has been a long time activist in the feminist movement and has written extensively on feminist and racial issues, including Black Looks: Race and Representation *(1992),* Teaching to Transgress: Education as the Practice of Freedom *(1994) and* Bone Black: Memories of Girlhood *(1996). In this selection, hooks describes the cultural politics embedded in what at surface glance seems to be a relatively innocent cosmetic practice—hair straightening.*

On Saturday mornings we would gather in the kitchen to get our hair fixed, that is straightened. Smells of burning grease and hair, mingled with the scent of our freshly washed bodies, with collard greens cooking on the stove, with fried fish. We did not go to the hairdresser. Mama fixed our hair. Six daughters—there was no way we could have afforded hairdressers. In those days, this process of straightening black women's hair with a hot comb (invented by Madame C. J. Walker) was not connected in my mind with the effort to look white, to live out standards of beauty set by white supremacy. It was connected solely with rites of initiation into womanhood. To arrive at that point where one's hair could be straightened was to move from being perceived as child (whose hair could be neatly combed and braided) to being almost a woman. It was this moment of transition my sisters and I longed for.

Hair pressing was a ritual of black women's culture—of intimacy. It was an exclusive moment when black women (even those who did not know one another well) might meet at home or in the beauty parlor to talk with one another, to listen to the talk. It was as important a world as that of the male barber shop—mysterious, secret. It was a world where the images constructed as barriers between one's self and the world were briefly let go, before they were made again. It was a moment of creativity, a moment of change.

I wanted this change even though I had been told all my life that I was one of the "lucky" ones because I had been born with "good hair"—hair that was fine, almost straight—not good enough but still good. Hair that had no nappy edges, no "kitchen," that area close to the neck that the hot comb could not reach. This "good hair" meant nothing to me when it stood as a barrier to my entering this secret black woman world. I was overjoyed when mama finally agreed that I could join the Saturday ritual, no longer looking on but patiently waiting my turn. I have written of this ritual: "For each of us getting our hair pressed is an important ritual. It is not a sign of our longing to be white. There are no white people in our intimate world. It is a sign of our desire to be women. It is a gesture that says we are approaching womanhood. . . Before we reach the appropriate age we wear braids, plaits that are symbols of our innocence, our youth, our childhood. Then, we are comforted by the parting hands that comb and braid, comforted by the intimacy and bliss. There is a deeper intimacy in the kitchen on Saturdays when hair is pressed, when fish is fried, when sodas are passed around, when soul music drifts over the talk. It is a time without men. It is a time when we work as women to meet each other's needs, to make each other feel good inside, a time of laughter and outrageous talk."

Since the world we lived in was racially segregated, it was easy to overlook the relationship between white supremacy and our obsession with hair. Even though black women with straight hair were perceived to be more beautiful than those with thick, frizzy hair, it was not overtly related to a notion that white women were a more appealing female group or that their straight hair set a beauty standard black women were struggling to live out. While this was probably the ideological framework from which the process of straightening black women's hair emerged, it was expanded so that it became a real space of black woman bonding through ritualized, shared experience. The beauty parlor was a space of consciousness raising, a space where black women shared life stories—hardship, trials, gossip; a place where one could be comforted and one's spirit renewed. It was for some women a place of rest where one did not need to meet the demands of children or men. It was the one hour some folk would spend "off their feet," a soothing, restful time of meditation and silence. These positive empowering implications of the ritual of hair pressing mediate but do not change negative implications. They exist alongside all that is negative.

Within white supremacist capitalist patriarchy, the social and political context in which the custom of black folks straightening our hair emerges, it represents an imitation of the dominant white group's appearance and often indicates internalized racism, self-hatred, and/or low self-esteem. During the 1960s black people who actively worked to critique, challenge, and change white racism pointed to the way in which black people's obsession with straight hair reflected a colonized mentality. It was at this time that the natural hairdo, the "afro," became fashionable as a sign of cultural resistance to racist oppression and as a celebration of blackness. Naturals were equated with political militancy. Many young black folks found just how much political value was placed on straightened hair as a sign of respectability and conformity to societal expectations when they ceased to straighten their hair. When black liberation struggles did not lead to revolutionary change in society the focus on the political relationship between appearance and complicity with white racism ceased and folks who had once sported afros began to straighten their hair.

In keeping with the move to suppress black consciousness and efforts to be self-defining, white corporations began to acknowledge black people and most especially black women as potential consumers of products they could provide, including hair-care products. Permanents specially designed for black women eliminated the need for hair pressing and the hot comb. They not only cost more but they also took much of the economy and profit out of black communities, out of the pockets of black women who had previously reaped the material benefits (see Manning Marable's *How Capitalism Underdeveloped Black America,* South End Press). Gone was the context of ritual, of black woman bonding. Seated under noisy hair dryers black women lost a space for dialogue, for creative talk.

Stripped of the positive binding rituals that traditionally surrounded the experience, black women straightening our hair seemed more and more to be exclusively a signifier of white supremacist oppression and exploitation. It was clearly a process that was about black women changing their appearance to imitate white people's looks. This need to look as much like white people as possible, to look safe, is related to a desire to succeed in the white world. Before desegregation black people could worry less about what white folks thought about their hair. In a discussion with black women about beauty at Spelman College, students talked about the importance of wearing straight hair when seeking jobs. They were convinced and probably rightly so that their chances of finding good jobs would be enhanced if they had straight hair. When asked to elaborate they focused on the connection between radical politics and natural hairdos, whether natural or braided. One woman wearing a short natural told of purchasing a straight wig for her job search. No one in the discussion felt black women were free to wear our hair in natural styles without reflecting on the possible negative consequences. Often older black adults, especially parents, respond quite negatively to natural hairdos. I shared with the group that when I arrived home with my hair in braids shortly after accepting my job at Yale my parents told me I looked disgusting.

Despite many changes in racial politics, black women continue to obsess about their hair, and straightening hair continues to be serious business. It continues to tap into the insecurity black women feel about our value in this white supremacist society. Talking with groups of women at various college campuses and with black women in our communities there seems to be general consensus that our obsession with hair in general reflects continued struggles with self-esteem and self-actualization. We talk about the extent to which black women perceive our hair as the enemy, as a problem we must solve, a territory we must conquer. Above all it is a part of our black female body that must be controlled. Most of us were not raised in environments where we learned to regard our hair as sensual or beautiful in an unprocessed state. Many of us talk about situations where white people ask to touch our hair when it is unprocessed then show surprise that the texture is soft or feels good. In the eyes of many white folks and other non-black folks, the natural afro looks like steel wool or a helmet. Responses to natural hairstyles worn by black women usually reveal the extent to which our natural hair is perceived in white supremacist culture as not only ugly but frightening. We also internalize that fear. The extent to which we are comfortable with our hair usually reflects on our overall feelings about our bodies. In our black women's support group, *Sisters of the Yam,* we talk about the ways we don't like our bodies, especially our hair. I suggested to the group that we regard our hair as though it is not part of our body but something quite separate—again a territory to be controlled. To me it was important for us to link this need to control with sexuality, with sexual repression. Curious about what black women who had hot-combed or had permanents felt about the relationship between straightened hair and sexual practice I asked whether people worried about their hairdo, whether they feared partners touching their hair. Straightened hair has always seemed to me to call attention to the desire for hair to stay in place. Not surprisingly many black women responded that they felt uncomfortable if too much attention was focused on their hair, if it seemed to be too messy. Those of us who have liberated our hair and let it go in whatever direction it seems fit often receive negative comments.

Looking at photographs of myself and my sisters when we had straightened hair in high school I noticed how much older we looked than when our hair was not processed. It is ironic that we live in a culture that places so much emphasis on women looking young, yet black women are encouraged to change our hair in ways that make us appear older. This past semester we read Toni Morrison's *The Bluest Eye* in a black women's fiction class. I ask students to write autobiographical statements which reflect their thoughts about the connection between race and physical beauty. A vast majority of black women wrote about their hair. When I asked individual women outside class why they continued to straighten their hair, many asserted that naturals don't look good on them, or that they required too much work. Emily, a favorite student with very short hair, always straightened it and I would tease and challenge her. She explained to me convincingly that a natural hairdo would look horrible with her face, that she did not have the appropriate forehead or bone structure. Later she shared that during spring break she had gone to the beauty parlor to have her perm and as she sat there waiting, thinking about class reading and discussion, it came to her that she was really frightened that no one else would think she was attractive if she did not straighten her hair. She acknowledged that this fear was rooted in feelings of low self-esteem. She decided to make a change. Her new look surprised her because it was so appealing. We talked afterwards about her earlier denial and justification for wearing straightened hair. We talked about the way it hurts to realize connection between racist oppression and the arguments we use to convince ourselves and others that we are not beautiful or acceptable as we are.

In numerous discussions with black women about hair one of the strongest factors that prevent black women from wearing unprocessed hairstyles is the fear of losing other people's approval and regard. Heterosexual black women talked about the extent to which black men respond more favorably to women with straight or straightened hair. Lesbian women point to the fact that many of them do not straighten their hair, raising the question of whether or not this gesture is fundamentally linked to heterosexism and a longing for male approval. I recall visiting a woman friend and her black male companion in New York years ago and having an intense discussion about hair. He took it upon himself to share with me that I could be a fine sister if I would do something about my hair (secretly I thought mama must have hired him). What I remember is his shock when I calmly and happily asserted that I like the touch and feel of unprocessed hair.

When students read about race and physical beauty, several black women describe periods of childhood when they were overcome with longing for straight hair as it was so associated with desirability, with being loved. Few women had received affirmation from family, friends, or lovers when choosing not to straighten their hair and we have many stories to tell about advice we receive from everyone, including total strangers, urging to understand how much more attractive we would be if we would fix (straighten) our hair. When I interviewed for my job at Yale, white female advisers who had never before commented on my hair encouraged me not to wear braids or a large natural to the interview. Although they did not say straighten your hair, they were suggesting that I change my hairstyle so that it would most resemble theirs, so that it would indicate a certain conformity. I wore braids and no one seemed to notice. When I was offered the job I did not ask if it mattered whether or not I wore braids. I tell this story to my students so that they will know by this one experience that we do not always need to surrender our power to be self-defining to succeed in an endeavor. Yet I have found the issue of hairstyle comes up again and again with students when I give lectures. At one conference on black women and leadership I walked into a packed auditorium, my hair unprocessed wild and all over the place. The vast majority of black women seated there had straightened hair. Many of them looked at me with hostile contemptuous stares. I felt as though I was being judged on the spot as someone out on the fringe, an undesirable. Such judgments are made particularly about black women in the United States who choose to wear dreadlocks. They are seen and rightly so as the total antithesis of straightening one's hair, as a political statement. Often black women express contempt for those of us who choose this look.

Ironically, just as the natural unprocessed hair of black women is the subject of disregard and disdain we are witnessing return of the long dyed, blonde look. In their writing my black women students described wearing yellow mops on their heads as children to pretend they had long blonde hair. Recently black women singers who are working to appeal to white audiences, to be seen as crossovers, use hair implanting and hair weaving to have long straight hair. There seems to be a definite connection between a black female entertainer's popularity with white audiences and the degree to which she works to appear white, or to embody aspects of white style. Tina Turner and Aretha Franklin were trend setters; both dyed their hair blonde. In everyday life we see more and more black women using chemicals to be blonde. At one of my talks focusing on the social construction of black female identity within a sexist and racist society, a black woman came to me at the end of the discussion and shared that her seven-year-old daughter was obsessed with blonde hair, so much so that she had made a wig to imitate long blonde curls. This mother wanted to know what she was doing wrong in her parenting. She asserted that their home was a place where blackness was affirmed and celebrated. Yet she had not considered that her processed straightened hair was a message to her daughter that black women are not acceptable unless we alter our appearance or hair texture. Recently I talked with one of my younger sisters about her hair. She uses bright colored dyes, various shades of red. Her skin is very dark. She has a broad nose and short hair. For her these choices of straightened dyed hair were directly related to feelings of low self-esteem. She does not like her features and feels that the hairstyle transforms her. My perception was that her choice of red straightened hair actually called attention to the features she was trying to mask. When she commented that this look receives more attention and compliments, I suggested that the positive feedback might be a direct response to her own projection of a higher level of self-satisfaction. Folk may be responding to that and not her altered looks. We talked about the messages she is sending her dark-skinned daughters—that they will be most attractive if they straighten their hair.

A number of black women have argued that straightened hair is not necessarily a signifier of low self-esteem. They argue that it is a survival strategy; it is easier to function in this society with straightened hair. There are fewer hassles. Or as some folk stated, straightened hair is easier to manage, takes less time. When I responded to this argument in our discussion at Spelman by suggesting that perhaps the unwillingness to spend time on ourselves, caring for our bodies, is also a reflection of a sense that this is not important or that we do not deserve such care. In this group and others, black women talked about being raised in households where spending too much time on appearance was ridiculed or considered vanity. Irrespective of the way individual black women choose to do their hair, it is evident that the extent to which we suffer from racist and sexist oppression and exploitation affects the degree to which we feel capable of both selflove and asserting an autonomous presence that is acceptable and pleasing to ourselves. Individual preferences (whether rooted in self-hate or not) cannot negate the reality that our collective obsession with straightening black hair reflects the psychology of oppression and the impact of racist colonization. Together racism and sexism daily reinforce to all black females via the media, advertising, etc. that we will not be considered beautiful or desirable if we do not change ourselves, especially our hair. We cannot resist this socialization if we deny that white supremacy informs our efforts to construct self and identity.

Without organized struggles like the ones that happened in the 1960s and early 1970s, individual black women must struggle alone to acquire the critical consciousness that would enable us to examine issues of race and beauty, our personal choices, from a political standpoint. There are times when I think of straightening my hair just to change my style, just for fun. Then I remind myself that even though such a gesture could be simply playful on my part, an individual expression of desire, I know that such a gesture would carry other implications beyond my control. The reality is: straightened hair is linked historically and currently to a system of racial domination that impresses upon black people, and especially black women, that we are not acceptable as we are, that we are not beautiful. To make such a gesture as an expression of individual freedom and choice would make me complicit with a politic of domination that hurts us. It is easy to surrender this freedom. It is more important that black women resist racism and sexism in every way; that every aspect of our self-representation be a fierce resistance, a radical celebration of our care and respect for ourselves.

Even though I have not had straightened hair for a long time, this did not mean that I am able to really enjoy or appreciate my hair in its natural state. For years I still considered it a problem. (It wasn't naturally nappy enough to make a decent interesting afro. It was too thin.) These complaints expressed my continued dissatisfaction. True liberation of my hair came when I stopped trying to control it in any state and just accepted it as it is. It has been only in recent years that I have ceased to worry about what other people would say about my hair. It has been only in recent years that I could feel consistent pleasure washing, combing, and caring for my hair. These feelings remind me of the pleasure and comfort I felt as a child sitting between my mother's legs feeling the warmth of her body and being as she combed and braided my hair. In a culture of domination, one that is essentially anti-intimacy, we must struggle daily to remain in touch with ourselves and our bodies, with one another. Especially black women and men, as it is our bodies that have been so often devalued, burdened, wounded in alienated labor. Celebrating our bodies, we participate in a liberatory struggle that frees mind and heart.

QUESTIONS

1. What did the ritual of hair straightening mean to hooks and the other females in her family when she was a child? What tone does she use to describe her memories of this time? Refer to specific words or phrases in the text. What did having "good" hair mean?
2. How did cultural politics change the meaning of hair straightening? How does hooks see hair straightening and lightening linked to racist oppression, low self-esteem and fear? How can it reflect internalized racism? How is it tied to issues of control?
3. Why does hooks believe that men and white women are uncomfortable when African-American women wear their hair naturally? What are the possible negative economic and personal consequences of going "natural"? What are the possible benefits?
4. What political statement does your hair make? What cultural or political meanings do weaves, extensions and dreadlocks have among African-Americans today? Do hip-hop hairstyles have any particular meanings? What might it mean for a white person to wear dreadlocks? Or for a man to wear long hair? Can a hairstyle ever be just a hairstyle?

Dyes and Dolls: Multicultural Barbie and the Merchandising of Difference (1994)

Ann duCille

Ann duCille, professor of literature at the University of California San Diego, analyzes Barbie's power as a symbol of femininity in U.S. culture—one that defines "femininity" as white. Tracing the history of multicultural Barbies, duCille suggests that even though these dolls are marketed as diverse and "authentic" "role models" for girls, they actually serve to maintain a white standard of beauty at the same time that they increase profit for Mattel. She asks us to consider the possibility that images of beauty as white cost the consumer more than just money.

The white missionaries who came to Saint Aug's from New England were darling to us. They gave Bessie and me these beautiful china dolls that probably were very expensive.

"Dyes and Dolls: Multicultural Barbie and the Merchandising of Difference," by Ann duCille, reprinted by permission from *differences: A Journal of Feminist Cultural Studies*, Vol. 6, No. 1, Spring 1994.

> Those dolls were white, of course. You couldn't get a colored doll like that in those days. Well, I loved mine, just the way it was, but do you know what Bessie did? She took an artist's palette they had also given us and sat down and mixed the paints until she came up with a shade of brown that matched her skin. Then she painted that white doll's face! None of the white missionaries ever said a word about it. Mama and Papa just smiled. (Sarah Delaney)
>
> This is my doll story (because every black journalist who writes about race gets around to it sometime). Back when I started playing with Barbie, there were no Christies (Barbie's black friend, born in 1968) or black Barbies (born in 1980, brown plastic pored into blond Barbie's mold). I had two blonds, which I bought with Christmas money from girls at school.
>
> I cut off their hair and dressed them in African-print fabric. They lived together (polygamy, I guess) with a black G. I. Joe bartered from the Shepp boys, my downstairs neighbors. After an "incident" at school (where all of the girls looked like Barbie and none of them looked like me). I galloped down our stairs with one Barbie, her blond head hitting each spoke of the banister, thud, thud, thud. And galloped up the stairs, thud, thud, thud, until her head popped off, lost to the graveyard behind the stairwell. Then I tore off each limb, and sat on the stairs for a long time twirling the torso like a baton. (Lisa Jones)

Growing up in the 1950s, in the shadow of the second world war, it was natural for children—including little black children like my two brothers and me—to want to play war, to mimic what we heard on the radio, what we watched in black and white on our brand new floor model Motorola. In these war games, everyone wanted to be the Allied troops—the fearless, conquering white male heroes who had made the world safe for democracy, yet again, and saved us all from yellow peril. No one, of course, wanted to play the enemy—who most often was not the Germans or the Italians but the Japanese. So the enemy became or, more rightly, remained invisible, lurking in bushes we shot at with sticks we pretended were rifles and stabbed at with make-believe bayonets. "Take that," we shouted, liberally peppering our verbal assaults with racial epithets. "And that! And that!" It was all in fun—our venom and vigor. All's fair in wars of words. We understood little of what we said and nothing of how much our child's play reflected the sentiments of a nation that even in its finer, prewar moments had not embraced as citizens its Asian immigrants or claimed as countrymen and women their American-born offspring.

However naively imitative, our diatribe was interrupted forever one summer afternoon by the angry voice of our mother, chastising us through the open window. "Stop that," she said. "Stop that this minute. It's not nice. You're talking about the Japanese. *Japanese*, do you understand? And don't let me ever hear you call them anything else." In the lecture that accompanied dinner that evening, we were made to understand not the history of Japanese-Americans, the injustice of internment, or the horror of Hiroshima, but simply that there were real people behind the names we called; that name-calling always hurts somebody, always undermines someone's humanity. Our young minds were led on the short journey from "Jap" to "nigger"; and if we were too young then to understand the origins and fine points of all such pejoratives, we were old enough to know firsthand the pain of one of them.

I cannot claim that this early experience left me free of prejudice, but it did assist me in growing up at once aware of my own status as "different" and conscious of the exclusion of others so labeled. It is important to note, however, that my sense of my own difference was affirmed and confirmed not simply by parental intervention but also by the unrelenting sameness of the tiny, almost exclusively white town in which I was raised. There in the country confines of East Bridgewater, Massachusetts, the adults who surrounded me (except for my parents) were all white, as were the teachers who taught me, the authors who thrilled me (and instilled in me a love of literature), and the neighborhood children who called me nigger one moment and friend the next. And when my brothers and I went our separate ways into properly gendered spheres, the dolls I played with—like almost everything else about my environment—were also white: Betsy Wetsy, Tiny Tears, and Patty Play Pal.

It seems remarkable to me now, as I remember these childish things long since put away, that, for all the daily reminders of my blackness, I did not take note of its absence among the rubber-skin pinkness of Betsy Wetsy, the bald-headed whiteness of Tiny Tears, and the blue-eyed blondness of Patty Play Pal. I was never tempted like Elizabeth Delany to paint the dolls I played with brown like me or to dress them in African-print fabric like Lisa Jones. (Indeed, I had no notion of such fabrics and little knowledge of the "dark continent" from which they came.) Caught up in fantasy, completely given over to the realm of make-believe, for most of my childhood I neither noticed nor cared that the dolls I played with did not look like me. The make-believe world to which I willingly surrendered more than just my disbelief was thoroughly and profoundly white. That is to say, the "me" I invented, the "I" I imagined, the Self I daydreamed in technicolor fantasies was no more black like me than the dolls I played with. In the fifties and well into the sixties of my childhood the black Other who was my Self, much like the enemy Other who was the foreign body of our war games, could only be imagined as faceless, far away, and utterly unfamiliar.

As suggested by my title, I am going to use the figure of multicultural Barbie to talk about the commodification of race and gender difference. I wanted to back into the present topic, however, into what I have to say about Barbie as a gendered, racialized icon of contemporary commodity culture, by reaching into the past—into the admittedly contested terrain of the personal—to evoke the ideological work of child's play. More than simple instruments of pleasure and amusement, toys and games play crucial roles in helping children determine what is valuable in and around them. Dolls in particular invite children to replicate them, to imagine themselves in their dolls' images. What does it mean, then, when little girls are given dolls to play with that in no way resemble them? What did it mean for me that I was nowhere in the toys I played with?

If the Japan and the Africa of my youth were beyond the grasp (if not the reach) of my imagination, children today are granted instant global gratification in their play—immediate, hands-on access to both Self and Other. Or so we are told by many of the leading fantasy manufacturers—Disney, Hasbro, and Mattel, in particular—whose contributions to multicultural education include such play things as Aladdin (movie, video, and dolls), G.I. Joe (male "action figures" in black and white), and Barbie (now available in a variety of colors and ethnicities). Disneyland's river ride through different nations, like Mattel's Dolls of the World Collection, instructs us that "It's a Small World After All." Those once distant lands of Africa, Asia, Australia, and even the Arctic regions of the North Pole (yes, Virginia, there is an Eskimo Barbie) are now as close to home as the local Toys R Us and F.A.O. Schwartz. And lo and behold, the inhabitants of these foreign lands—from Disney's Princess Jasmine to Mattel's Jamaican Barbie—are just like us, dye-dipped versions of archetypal white American beauty. It is not only a small world after all, but, as the Grammy award-winning theme from *Aladdin* informs us, "it's a whole new world."

Many of the major toy manufacturers have taken on a global perspective, a kind of nearsightedness that constructs this whole new world as small and cultural difference as consumable. Perhaps nowhere is this universalizing myopia more conspicuous than in the production, marketing, and consumption of Barbie dolls. By Mattel's reckoning, Barbie enjoys 100 percent brand name recognition among girls ages three to ten, ninety-six percent of whom own at least one doll, with most owning an average of eight. Five years ago, as Barbie turned thirty, *Newsweek* noted that nearly 500 million Barbies had been sold, along with 200 million G.I. Joes—"enough for every man, woman, and child in the United States and Europe" (Kantrowitz 59–60). Those figures have increased dramatically in the past five years, bringing the current world-wide Barbie population to 800 million. In 1992 alone, $1 billion worth of Barbies and accessories were sold. Last year, Barbie dolls sold at an average of one million per week, with overall sales exceeding the $1 billion all-time high set the year before. As the *Boston Globe* reported on the occasion of Barbie's thirty-fifth birthday on March 9, 1994, nearly two Barbie dolls are sold every second somewhere in the world; about fifty percent of the dolls sold are purchased here in the United States (Dembner 16).

The current Barbie boom may be in part the result of new, multiculturally oriented developments both in the dolls and in their marketing. In the fall of 1990, Mattel, Inc. announced a new marketing strategy to boost its sales; the corporation would "go ethnic" in its advertising by launching an ad campaign for the black and Hispanic versions of the already popular doll. Despite the existence of black, Asian, and Latina Barbies, prior to the fall of 1990 Mattel's print and TV ads featured only white dolls. In what *Newsweek* described as an attempt to capitalize on ethnic spending power, Mattel began placing ads for Multicultural Barbies in such Afrocentric publications as *Essence* magazine and on such Latin-oriented shows as "Pepe Plata" after market research revealed that most black and Hispanic consumers were unaware of the company's ethnic dolls. This targeted advertising was a smart move, according to the industry analysis cited by *Newsweek*, because "Hispanics buy about $170 billion worth of goods each year, [and] blacks spend even more." Indeed, sales of black Barbie dolls reportedly doubled in the year following this new ethnically-oriented ad campaign.[1] But determined to present itself as politically correct as well as financially savvy, Mattel was quick to point out that ethnic audiences, who are now able to purchase dolls who look like them, also have profited from the corporation's new marketing priorities. Barbie is a role model for all of her owners, according to product manager Deborah Mitchell, herself an African American. "Barbie allows little girls to dream," she asserted—to which the *Newsweek* reporter, added (seemingly without irony): "now, ethnic Barbie lovers will be able to dream in their own image" (Berkwitz 48).

Dream in their own image? The *Newsweek* columnist inadvertently put his finger on precisely what is so troubling to many parents, feminist scholars, and cultural critics about Barbie and dolls like her. Such toys invite, inspire, and even demand a potentially damaging process not simply of imagining but of interpellation. When little girls fantasize themselves into the conspicuous consumption, glamour, perfection, and, some have argued, anorexia of Barbie's world, it is rarely, if ever, "in their own image that they dream."[2] Regardless of what color dyes the dolls are dipped in or what costumes they are adorned with, the image they present is of the same mythically thin, long-legged, luxuriously-haired, buxom beauty. And while Mattel and other toy manufacturers may claim to have the best interests of ethnic audiences in mind in peddling their integrated wares, one does not have to be a cynic to suggest that profit remains the motivating factor behind this merchandising of difference.[3]

Far from simply playing with the sixty or so dolls I have acquired in the past year, then, I take them very seriously. In fact, I regard Barbie and similar dolls as Louis Althusser might have regarded them: as objects that do the dirty work of patriarchy and capitalism in the most insidious way—in the guise of child's play. But, as feminists have protested almost from the moment she hit the market, Barbie is not simply a child's toy or just a teenage fashion doll; she is an icon—perhaps *the* icon—of true white womanhood and femininity, a symbol of the far from innocent ideological stuff of which the (Miss) American dream and other mystiques of race and gender are made.

Invented by Ruth Handler, one of the founders of Mattel, and named after her daughter, Barbie dolls have been a very real force in the toy market since Mattel first introduced them at the American Toy Fair in 1959. In fact, despite the skepticism of toy store buyers—who at the time were primarily men—the first shipment of a half million dolls and a million costumes sold out immediately (Larcen A7). The first Barbies, which were modeled after a sexy German doll and comic strip character named Lilli, were all white, but in 1967 Mattel premiered a black version of the doll called "Colored Francie." "Colored Francie," like white "Francie Fairchild" introduced the year before, was supposed to be Barbie's "MOD'ern" younger cousin. As a white doll modeled and marketed in the image of Hollywood's Gidget, white Francie had been an international sensation, but Colored Francie was not destined to duplicate her prototype's success. Although the "black is beautiful" theme of both the civil rights and black power movements may have suggested a ready market for a beautiful black doll, Colored Francie in fact did not sell well.

Evelyn Burkhalter, owner, operator, and curator of the Barbie Hall of Fame in Palo Alto, California—home to 16,000 Barbie dolls—attributes Colored Francie's commercial failure to the racial climate of the times. Doll purchasing patterns, it seems, reflected the same resistance to integration that was felt elsewhere in the nation. In her implied family ties to white Barbie, Colored Francie suggested more than simple integration. She implied miscegenation: a make-believe mixing of races that may have jeopardized the doll's real market value. Cynthia Roberts, author of *Barbie: Thirty Years of America's Doll* (1989), maintains that Colored Francie flopped because of her straight hair and Caucasian features (44), which seemingly were less acceptable then than now. No doubt Mattel's decision to call its first black Barbie "Colored Francie" also contributed to the doll's demise. The use of the outmoded, even racist term "colored" in the midst of civil rights and black power activism suggested that while Francie might be "MOD'ern," Mattel was still in the dark(y) ages. In any case, neither black nor white audiences bought the idea of Barbie's colored relations, and Mattel promptly took the doll off the market, replacing her with a black doll called Christie in 1968.

While a number of other black dolls appeared throughout the late sixties and seventies—including the Julia doll, modeled after the TV character played by black singer and actress Diahann Carroll—it was not until 1980 that Mattel introduced black dolls that were called Barbie like their white counterparts. Today, Barbie dolls come in a virtual rainbow coalition of colors, races, ethnicities, and nationalities—most of which look remarkably like the prototypical white Barbie, modified only by a dash of color and a change of costume. It is these would-be multicultural "dolls of the world"—Jamaican Barbie, Nigerian and Kenyan Barbie, Malaysian Barbie, Chinese Barbie, Mexican, Spanish, and Brazilian Barbie, et cetera, et cetera, et cetera—that interest me. For me these dolls are at once a symbol and a symptom of what multiculturalism has become at the hands of the contemporary commodity culture: an easy and immensely profitable way off the hook of Eurocentrism that gives us the face of cultural diversity without the particulars of racial difference.

If I could line up across the page the ninety "different" colors, cultures, and other incarnations in which Barbie currently exists, the fact of her unrelenting sameness (or at least similarity) would become immediately apparent. Even two dolls might do the trick: "My First Barbie" in white and "My First Barbie" in black, for example, or white "Western Fun Barbie" and black "Western Fun Barbie." Except for their dye jobs, the dolls are identical: the same body, size shape, and apparel. Or perhaps I should say *nearly* identical because in some instances—with black and Asian dolls in particular—coloring and other subtle changes (stereotypically slanted eyes in the Asian dolls, thicker lips in the black dolls) suggest differently coded facial features.

In other instances, when Barbie moves across cultural as opposed to racial lines, it is costume rather than color that distinguishes one ethnic group or nation from another. Nigeria and Jamaica, for instance, are represented by the same basic brown body, dolled-up in different native garbs—or Mattel's interpretation thereof.[4] With other costume changes, this generic black body becomes Western Fun Barbie or Marine Barbie or Desert Storm Barbie, and even Presidential Candidate Barbie, who, by the way, comes with a Nancy Reagan-red taking-care-of-business suit as well as a red, white, and blue inaugural ball gown. Much the same is true of the generic Asian doll—sometimes called Kira—who reappears in a variety of different dress-defined ethnicities. In other words, where Barbie is concerned, clothes not only make the woman, they mark the racial and/or cultural difference.

Such difference is marked as well by the cultural history and language lessons that accompany each doll in Mattel's international collection. The back of Jamaican Barbie's box tells us, for example, "*How-you-du* (Hello) from the land of Jamaica, a tropical paradise known for its exotic fruit, sugar cane, breathtaking beaches, and reggae beat!" The box goes on to explain that most Jamaicans have ancestors from Africa. Therefore, "even though our official language is English, we speak patois, a kind of '*Jamaica Talk*,' filled with English and African words." The lesson ends with a brief glossary (eight words) and a few more examples of this "Jamaica Talk," complete with translations: "*A hope yu wi come-a Jamaica!* (I hope you will come to Jamaica!)" and "*Teck care a yusself, mi fren!* (Take care of yourself, my friend!)" A nice idea, I suppose, but for me these quick-and-dirty ethnographies only enhance the extent to which these would-be multicultural dolls treat race and ethnic difference like collectibles, contributing more to commodity culture than to the intercultural awareness they claim to inspire.

Is the current fascination with the black or colored body—especially the female body—a contemporary version of the primitivism of the 1920s? Is multiculturalism to postmodernism what primitivism was to modernism? It was while on my way to a round table discussion on precisely this question that I bought my first black Barbie dolls in March of 1993. As carbon copies of an already problematic original, these colorized Mattel toys seemed to me the perfect tools with which to illustrate the point I wanted to make about the collapse of multiculturalism into an easy pluralism that simply adds what it constructs as the Other without upsetting the fundamental precepts and paradigms of Western culture or, in the case of Mattel, without changing the mold.

Not entirely immune to such critiques, Mattel sought expert advice from black parents and early childhood specialists in the development and marketing of its newest line of black Barbie dolls. Chief among the expert witnesses was clinical psychologist Darlene Powell Hopson, who co-authored with her husband Derek S. Hopson a study of racism and child development entitled *Different and Wonderful: Raising Black Children in a Race-Conscious Society* (1990). As part of their research for the book, the Hopsons repeated a ground-breaking study conducted by black psychologists Kenneth and Mamie Clark in the 1940s.

The Clarks used black and white dolls to demonstrate the negative effects of racism and segregation on black children. When given a choice between a white doll and a black doll, nearly 70 percent of the black children in the study chose the white doll. The Clarks' findings became an important factor in *Brown v. the Board of Education* in 1954. More recently, some scholars have called into question not necessarily the Clarks' findings but their interpretation: the assumption that, in the realm of make-believe, a black child's choosing a white doll necessarily reflects a negative self concept.[5] For the Hopsons, however, the Clarks' research remains compelling. In 1985 they repeated the Clarks' doll test and found that an alarming 65 percent of the black children in their sample chose a white doll over a black one. Moreover, 76 percent of the children interviewed said that the black dolls "looked bad" to them (Hopson xix).

In addition to the clinical uses they make of dolls in their experiments, the Hopsons also give considerable attention to what they call "doll play" in their book, specifically mentioning Barbie. "If your daughter likes 'Barbie' dolls, by all means get her Barbie," they advise black parents. "But also choose Black characters from the Barbie world. *You do not want your child to grow up thinking that only White dolls, and by extension White people, are attractive and nice*" (Hopsons 127, emphasis original). (Note that "Barbie," unmodified in the preceding passage, seems to mean *white* Barbie dolls.) The Hopsons suggest that parents should not only provide their children with black and other ethnic dolls but that they should get involved in their children's doll play. "Help them dress and groom the dolls while you compliment them both," they advise, offering the following suggested routine: "'This is a beautiful doll. It looks just like you. Look at her hair. It's just like yours. Did you know your nose is as pretty as your doll's?'" (119) They also suggest that parents use "complimentary words such as *lovely, pretty, or nice* so that [the] child will learn to associate them with his or her own image" (124).

Certainly it is important to help children feel good about themselves. One might argue, however, that the "just like you" simile and the beautiful doll imagery so central to these suggestions for what the Hopsons call positive play run the risk of transmitting to the child a colorized version of the same old beauty myth. Like Barbie dolls themselves, they make beauty—and by implication worth—a matter of physical characteristics.

In spite of their own good intentions, the Hopsons, in linking play with "beautiful" dolls to positive self-imagining, echoed Mattel's own marketing campaign. It is not surprising, then, that the Hopsons' findings and the interventional strategies they designed for using dolls to instill ethnic pride caught the attention of Mattel. In 1990 Darlene Hopson was asked to consult with the corporation's product manager Deborah Mitchell and designer Kitty Black-Perkins—both African Americans—in the development of a new line of "realistically sculpted" black fashion dolls. Hopson agreed and about a year later Shani and her friends Asha and Nichelle became the newest members of Barbie's ever-expanding family.

Shani means "marvelous" in Swahili, according to the dolls' press kit. But as *Village Voice* columnist Lisa Jones has noted, the name has other meanings as well: "startling, a wonder, a novelty" (36). My own research indicates that while Shani is a Swahili female name meaning marvelous, the Kiswahili word "shani" translates as "an adventure, something unusual" (Stewart 120). So it seems that Mattel's new play thing is not just marvelous, too marvelous for words, but, as her name also suggests, she is difference incarnate—a novelty, a new enterprise or, perhaps, as the black female Other so often is, an exotic. Mattel, it seems to me, both plays up and plays on what it presents as the doll's exotic black-is-beautiful difference. As the back of her package reads:

> Shani means marvelous in the Swahili language . . . and marvelous she is! With her friends Asha and Nichelle, Shani brings to life the special style and beauty of the African American woman.
>
> Each one is beautiful in her own way, with her own lovely skin shade and unique facial features. Each has a different hair color and texture, perfect for braiding, twisting and creating fabulous hair styles! Their clothes, too, reflect the vivid colors and ethnic accents that showcase their *exotic looks* and fashion flair!
>
> Shani, Asha and Nichelle invite you into their glamorous world to share the fun and excitement of being a top model. Imagine appearing on magazine covers, starring in fashion shows, and going to Hollywood parties as you, Shani, Asha and Nichelle live your dreams of beauty and success, loving every marvelous minute! (emphasis added)

While these words attempt to convey a message of black pride—after the fashion of the Hopsons' recommendations for positive play—that message is clearly tied to bountiful hair, lavish and exotic clothes, and other outward and visible signs not of brains but of beauty, wealth, and success. Shani may be a top fashion model, but don't look for her (or, if Mattel's own oft-articulated theory of Barbie as role model holds, yourself or your child) at M.I.T.

Like any other proud, well-to-do parents of a debutante, Mattel gave Shani her own coming out party at the International Toy Fair in February of 1991. This gala event included a tribute to black designers and an appearance by En Vogue singing, the Negro National Anthem, "Lift Every Voice and Sing"—evidently the song of choice of the doll Mattel describes as "tomorrow's African American woman." Also making their debuts were Shani's friends Asha and Nichelle, notable for the different hues in which their black plastic skin comes—an innovation due in part to Darlene Hopson's influence. Shani, the signature doll of the line, is what we call in the culture "brown-skinned"; Asha is honey-colored (some would say "high-yella"); and Nichelle is deep mahogany. Their male friend Jamal, added in 1992, completes the collection.

For the un(make-)believing, the three-to-one ratio of the Shani quartet—three black females to one black male—may be the most realistic thing about these dolls. In the eyes and the advertising of Mattel, however, Shani and her friends are the most authentic black female thing the mainstream toy market has yet produced. "Tomorrow's African American woman" (an appellation which, as Lisa Jones has noted, both riffs and one-ups *Essence*'s "Today's Black Woman") has broader hips, fuller lips, and a broader nose, according to product manager Deborah Mitchell. Principal designer Kitty Black-Perkins, who has dressed black Barbies since their birth in 1980, adds that the Shani dolls are also distinguished by their unique, culturally-specific clothes in "spice tones, [and] ethnic fabrics," rather than "fantasy colors like pink or lavender" (qtd. in Jones 36)—evidently the colors of the faint of skin.

The notion that fuller lips, broader noses, wider hips, and higher derrières somehow make the Shani dolls more realistically African American raises many difficult questions about authenticity, truth, and the ever-problematic categories of the real and the symbolic, the typical and the stereotypical. Just what are we saying when we claim that a doll does or does not "look black"? How does black look? What would it take to make a doll look authentically African American? What preconceived, prescriptive ideals of legitimate blackness are inscribed in such claims of authenticity? How can doll manufacturers or any other image makers—the film industry, for example—attend to cultural, racial, and phenotypical differences without merely engaging the same simplistic big-lips/broad-hips stereotypes that make so many of us—blacks in particular—grit our (pearly white) teeth? What would it take to produce a line of dolls that more fully reflects the wide variety of sizes, shapes, colors, hair styles, occupations, abilities, and disabilities that African Americans—like all people—come in? In other words: what price difference?

If such specificity—such ethnic "authenticity"—were possible to achieve in a doll, its purchase price, I suspect, would be much higher than a profit-driven corporation like Mattel would be willing to pay. Let me again invoke Shani to prove my point. On the one hand, Mattel was concerned enough about producing an ethnically correct black doll to seek the advice of black image specialists such as Darlene Hopson in the development and marketing of the Shani line. Ultimately, however, the company was not willing to follow the advice of such experts where doing so would cost the corporation more than the price of additional dyes and ethnic fabrics.

For example, Hopson reportedly argued not just for gradations in skin tones in the Shani dolls but also for variations in body type and lengths and styles of hair—for an Afro here or an asymmetrical cut there. But, while Mattel acknowledged both the legitimacy and the ubiquity of such arguments, profit motive mediated against the very realism the corporation set out to achieve in these dolls. "To be truly realistic, one [Shani doll] should have shorter hair," Deborah Mitchell confessed to Lisa Jones. "But little girls of all races love hair play. We added more texture. But we can't change the fact that long, combable hair is still a key seller" (Jones 36).

Mitchell, of course, has a point. It is after all the taste of consumers that is inscribed in Barbie's long, combable hair. In the process of my own archival research—poking around in the dusty aisles of Toys R Us—I encountered a black teenage girl in search, like me, of the latest black Barbie. During the impromptu interview that ensued, my subject confessed to me in gory, graphic details the many Barbie murders and mutilations she had committed over the years. "It's the hair," she said emphatically several times. "The hair, that hair; I want it. I want it." Her words recalled my own torturous childhood struggles with the straightening combs, curling irons, and relaxers that bi-weekly transformed my wooly, "just like a sponge" kinks into what the white kids at school marveled at as my "Cleopatra [read straight] hair." During one of those bi-weekly sessions with my mother and the straightening comb, I was foolish enough to say out loud what I had wished for a long time: that I had straight hair, like the white girls at school. I still remember my mother's hurt, her sense of her daughter's racial heresy. Mitchell and Mattel indeed have a point. The difficult truth may just be that part of Shani's and black Barbie's attraction for little black girls in particular is the escape from their own often shorter, harder-to-comb hair that these dolls' lengthy straight locks represent.

Barbie's svelte figure, like her long combable hair, became Shani's body type as well. And here too marketability seems to have overruled professed attempts to capture the "unique facial features" and the "special style and beauty of the African American people." Even the reported subtle changes that are supposed to signify Shani's black difference—her much-remarked broader hips and elevated buttocks, for example—are little more than optical illusions, according to anthropologists Jacqueline Urla and Alan Swedlund of the University of Massachusetts at Amherst. Urla and Swedlund, who have been studying the anthropometry—the body measurements—of Barbie for some time, argue that, while Shani's hips may appear to be wider, they are actually smaller in both circumference and breadth than those of other Barbie dolls. It is essential, after all, that all the dolls be able to share the same clothes, thus making any dramatic alterations in body type unlikely. The effect of a higher buttocks is achieved, Urla and Swedlund maintain, by changing the angle of the doll's back. In other words, The Shani doll's buttocks may appear stereotypically higher, but she is not really dimensionally different from all the other eleven-and-a-half inch fashion dolls.

Lisa Jones concludes her *Village Voice* article on Barbie by noting that the women behind Shani—black women like Hopson and Mitchell—want the doll to be more than just a Barbie in blackface. While Hopson, in particular, certainly hoped for—shall I say—*different* difference she nevertheless maintains that the

Shani dolls demonstrate "social consciousness on Mattel's part" (Jones 36). British fashion designer and Barbie aficionado extraordinaire BillyBoy made a similar point in praising Mattel for integrating Barbie's family with first Colored Francie and then Christie in the late 1960s (BillyBoy 82). After nearly thirty years, I think we can forgive Mattel its Colored Francie faux pas and perhaps even applaud the attempt. But if Shani (who came out in a new scantily clad Soul Train edition in 1993) stands as Mattel's best effort to "go ethnic," as it were—to corner the contemporary mainstream market in "realistically sculpted" black dolls that "bring to life" the "special style and beauty of the African-American people"—she stands on shaky ground.

And yet it may not be fair to single out Mattel as an example of what seems to be a national if not international phenomenon. Racial difference, like ethnic Barbie, is a hot commodity, and it isn't only Mattel who is making money. In the words of David Rieff, a contributing editor of *Harper's Magazine*:

> Everything is commodifiable, even Afrocentrism (there is money being made on all Kinte [sic] cloth and Kwanza [sic] paraphernalia that are the rage among certain segments of the black community, and not only the black community), bilingualism (currently the hottest growth market in publishing is Spanish language children's books), and the other "multicultural" tendencies in American society that conservatives fear so desperately.

Rieff goes so far as to call this newly globalized consumer economy multiculturalism's silent partner. I want to be careful in expressing my own concerns about the relationship between multiculturalism and the conspicuous consumption of difference, however, lest my critique appear complicit with that of the conservatives to whom Rieff refers, who fear the possibilities of a truly transformative social, cultural, and economic order, which I in fact would welcome.

All cultural commodities are not created equal. It seems to me that however profitable their production may be for the publishing industry, Spanish-language children's books serve a useful, educational function for their target audiences. On the other hand, even taking into account the argument that black girls need black dolls to play with, I have a difficult time locating the redeeming social value in Mattel's little plastic women, even—or perhaps especially—when they are tinted brown and decorated in Kente cloth and Kufi hats, as the new Soul Train Shani dolls are. And while I am certain that hordes of black consumers are grateful for the black haircare products and cosmetics marketed by mainstream corporations such as Clairol, Revlon, and Mary Kay, I am less convinced that J.C. Penney's target audience will really find much cultural enlightenment in the Kente cloth potholders, napkin rings, and dish towels that the store is currently marketing as "expressions of cultural pride."

In *Fashion Influences*, a catalog clearly intended to cater to what it takes to be the tastes of black audiences, J.C. Penney advertises an assortment of housewares, ethnic artifacts, and exclusive designer fashions with "Afrocentric flair." Such specialty items as triple-woven cotton throws, which sell for $50 each, are available in four culturally edifying patterns: 01 Kwanzaa; 02 Kente; 03 Martin Luther King; and 04 Malcolm X. For another $40, customers can complement their Kwanzaa-patterned throw with a Kwanzaa needlepoint pillow. (For the not quite multiculturally literate shopper, Penney's provides a cultural history lesson: "Kwanzaa means 'first fruits of the harvest' in Swahili," the catalog informs. "Created in 1966, Kwanzaa is a seven-day celebration synthesizing elements from many African harvest festivals.") And just so consumers know precisely how politically correct their Penney's purchases are, many of the catalog descriptions inform shoppers that these Afrocentric items are made in the U.S.A. The Ivory Coast Table Linens, for example, are billed as an "exuberantly colored interpretation of authentic African woven cloth. . . . Made in the U.S.A." The Kente-cloth pillows are made in the U.S.A. of fabric imported from Africa, but the MLK and Malcolm X throws are just plain made in the U.S.A. In other words, for not-so-modest prices, culturally and socially-conscious American consumers can look for the union label as they shop for these and other interpretations-of-authentic-African-inspired-made-in-America goods.

Thus it is that from custom-designed bedroom coordinates inspired by mud cloth from Mali in West Africa to an embroidered metallic caftan or "Uwe (pronounced yoo-way, meaning dress)" inspired by "garments worn by the royal court on special occasions," what J.C. Penney is trading in and trading on in this blaxploitation catalog is cultural difference and, if you will, misspent racial pride. Although I doubt that Penney's cares who buys its Kufi hats, black-on-black dishware, and "In Search of Identity" games, it is also clear that the company does not waste such catalogs on just any body. I, for example, have been a loyal Penney's catalog shopper for years; I receive the annual seasonal catalogs, as well as special fliers advertising queen-size fashions. I only happened upon Penney's blax-ploitation catalog recently, however, when it was mailed not to me—faithful shopper—not to my home but to the Center for African American Studies at Wesleyan University. While my shopping history identified me as larger-sized, there was evidently nothing about my purchasing pattern that identified me as black. Penney's marketing division seems to have assumed—quite cleverly, I think—that a Center for African American Studies would be a likely place to find middle-class, culturally-conscious black consumers who might actually be able to afford the high-prized items in its Afrocentric catalog. (What a miscalculation in that last regard.)

I suspect that such catalogs are mailed not only to black studies departments but also to black beauty parlors (indeed I found a similar catalog from Spiegel at the shop where I get my hair cut) and black churches, where there is sure to be a ready-made market for the Sunday-go-to-meetin' hats, high-heel shoes, and church-lady suits "with an Afrocentric flair" that fill their pages. Just to bring this discussion full circle, let me note that six Black Barbie dolls are available through this special catalog—Black Desert Storm Barbie and Ken and Soul Train Shani and her three friends Asha, Nichelle, and Jamal. Army Barbie and Ken are dressed in "authentic desert fatigues with authentic insignias for enlisted personnel," and the Shani dolls are decked out in "cool hip-hop fashions inspired by the hot T.V. dance show." But don't let these patriotic, all-American girls and boys fool you; they are all imported from Malaysia.

The Body Politic(s) of Barbie

> Barbie's body is a consumer object itself, a vehicle for the display of clothing and the spectacular trappings of a wealthy teenage fantasy life. Her extraordinary body exists not simply as an example of the fetishized female form typical of those offered up to the male gaze, but as a commodity vehicle itself whose form seduces the beholder

> and sells accessories, the real source of corporate profit. Like Lay's chips, no one can buy just one outfit for the doll. Barbie is the late capitalist girl incarnate. (McCombie)

In focusing thus far on the merchandising of racial, perhaps more so than gender difference, I do not mean to imply that racial and gender identities are divisible, even in dolls. Nor, in observing that most if not all of Mattel's "dolls of the world" look remarkably like what the company calls the "traditional, blond, blue-eyed Barbie," do I mean to suggest that the seemingly endless recapitulation of the white prototype is the only way in which these dolls are problematic. In fact, the most alarming thing about Barbie may well be the extent to which she functions as what M.G. Lord calls a teaching tool for femininity, whatever her race or ethnicity. Lord, the author of *Forever Barbie: The Unauthorized Biography of a Real Doll*, due out later this year, describes Barbie as a "space-age fertility icon. She looks like a modern woman, but she's a very primitive totem of female power" (qtd. in Dembner 1).

Barbie has long had the eye and ire of feminists, who, for the most part, have reviled her as another manifestation of the damaging myths of female beauty and the feminine body that patriarchy perpetuates through such vehicles as popular and commodity culture. A counter narrative also exists, however, one in which Barbie is not an empty-headed, material girl bimbo, for whom math class is tough, but a feminist heroine, who has been first in war (a soldier who served in the Gulf, she has worn the colors of her country as well as the United Colors of Benetton), first in peace (she held her own summit in 1990 and she's a long-time friend of UNICEF, who "loves all the children of the world"), and always first in the hearts of her country (Americans buy her at the rate of one doll every second). While time does not allow me to reiterate or to assess here all the known critiques and defenses of Barbie, I do want to discuss briefly some of the gender ideals that I think are encoded in and transmitted by this larger-than-life little woman and what Barbie's escalating popularity says about contemporary American culture.

In *Touching Liberty: Abolition, Feminism, and the Politics of the Body* (1993), Karen Sanchez-Eppler argues that all dolls are intended to teach little girls about domesticity (133). If such tutelage is Barbie's not so secret mission, methodology is far more complex and contradictory than that of the Betsy Wetsy and Tiny Tears baby dolls I played with thirty-five years ago. Those dolls invoked and evoked the maternal, as they and the baby bottles and diapers with which they were packaged invited us to nestle, nurse, and nurture. Barbie's curvaceous, big-busted, almost fully female body, on the other hand, summons not the maternal but the sexual, not the nurturant mother but the sensuous woman. As Mel McCombie has argued, rather than rehearsing parenting, as a baby doll does, Barbie's adult body encourages children to dress and redress a fashion doll that yields lessons about sexuality, consumption, and teenage life (3). Put another way, we might say that Barbie is literally and figuratively a titillating toy.

Bodacious as they may be, however, Barbie's firm plastic breasts have no nipples—nothing that might offend, nothing that might suggest her own pleasure. And if her protruding plastic mounds signify a simmering sensuality, what are we to make of her missing genitalia? McCombie suggests that Barbie's genital ambiguity can be read as an "homage to 'good taste'" and as a "reflection of the regnant mores for teenage girls—to be both sexy and adult yet remain virginal" (4). I agree that her body invites such readings, but it also seems to me that there is nothing ambiguous about Barbie's crotch. It's missing in inaction. While male dolls like Ken and Jamal have bumps "down there" and in some instances simulated underwear etched into the plastic, most Barbies come neither with drawers nor with even a hint of anything that needs covering, even as "it" is already covered or erased. As an icon of idealized femininity, then, Barbie is locked into a never-never land in which she must be always already sexual without the possibility of sex. Conspicuously sensual on top but definitively nonsexual below, her plastic body indeed has inscribed within it the very contradictory, whore/madonna messages with which patriarchy taunts and even traumatizes young women in particular.

This kind of speculation about Barbie's breasts has led the doll's creator, Ruth Handler, to chide adults for their nasty minds. "In my opinion people make too much of breasts," Handler has complained. "They are just part of the body" (qtd. in BillyBoy 26). Mrs. Handler has a point (or maybe two). I feel more than just a little ridiculous myself as I sit here contemplating the body parts and sex life of a piece of plastic. What is fascinating, however, what I think is worth studying, what both invites and resists theorizing, is not the lump of molded plastic that is Barbie, but the imaginary life that is not—that is *our* invention. Barbie as a cultural artifact may be able to tell us more about ourselves and our society—more about society's attitudes toward *its* women—than anything we might say about the doll her- or, rather, *it-self*.

In the nineteenth century, Alexis de Tocqueville and others argued that you could judge the character, quality, and degree of advancement of a civilization by the status and treatment of its women. What is the status of women in soon to be twenty-first-century America, and can Barbie serve as a barometer for measuring that status? Barbie, it seems to me, is a key player in the process of socialization—of engendering and racialization—that begins in infancy and is furthered by almost everything about our society, including the books children read, the toys they play with, and the cartoons they watch on television.

While changing channels one Saturday morning, I happened upon a cartoon, just a glimpse of which impelled me to watch on. At the point that I tuned in, a big, gray, menacingly male bulldog was barking furiously at a pretty, petite, light-colored cat, who simply batted her long lashes, meowed coquettishly, and rubbed her tiny feline body against his huge canine leg in response. The more the dog barked and growled, the softer the cat meowed, using her slinky feline body and her feminine wiles to win the dog over. Her strategy worked; before my eyes—and, I imagine, the eyes of millions of children, the ferocious beast was transformed into a lovesick puppy dog, who followed the cat everywhere, repeatedly saving her from all manner of evil and danger. Time and time again, the bulldog rescued the helpless, accident-prone pussy from falling girders, on-coming traffic, and other hazards to which she, in her innocent frailty, was entirely oblivious. By the end, the once ferocious bulldog was completely domesticated, as his no longer menacing body became a kind of bed for the cat to nestle in.

There are, of course, a number of ways to read the gender and racial politics of this cartoon. I suppose that the same thought process that theorizes Barbie as a feminist heroine for whom men are mere accessories might claim the kitty cat, too, as a kind of feminist feline, who uses her feminine wiles to get her way. What resonates for me in the cartoon, however, are its beauty and the beast, light/dark, good/evil, female/male, race and gender codes: light, bright, cat-like femininity tames menacing black male bestiality. Make no mistake, however; it is not wit that wins out over barbarism but a mindless, can't-take-care-of-herself femininity.

Interestingly enough, these are the kinds of messages of which fairy tales and children's stories are often made. White knights rescue fair damsels in distress from dark, forbidding evils of one kind or another. As Darlene and Derek Hopson argue: "Some of the most blatant and simplistic representations of white is good and black is evil are found in children's literature," where evil black witches and good white fairies—heroes in white and villains in black—abound (121).

What Barbie dolls, cartoons like the one outlined above, and even the seemingly innocent fairy tales we read to our children seem to me to have in common are the mythologies of race and gender that are encoded in them. Jacqueline Urla and Alan Swedlund maintain that Barbie's body type constructs the bodies of other women as deviant and perpetuates an impossible standard of beauty. Attempting to live up to the Barbie ideal, others argue, fosters eating and shopping disorders in teenage girls—nightmares instead of dreams. BillyBoy, one of Barbie's most ardent supporters, defends his heroine against such charges by insisting that there is nothing abnormal about the proportions of Barbie's body. Rather, he asserts, "she has the ideal that Western culture has insisted upon since the 1920s: long legs, long arms, small waist, high round bosom, and long neck" (22). The irony is that BillyBoy may be right. "Unrealistic" or not, Barbie's weight and measurements (which if proportionate to those of a woman 5'6" tall would be something like 110 pounds and a top-heavy 39-18-33) are not much different from those of the beauty queens to whom Bert Parks used to sing "Here she is, Miss America. Here she is, our ideal."[6] If Barbie is a monster, she is our monster, our ideal.

"But is Barbie bad?" Someone asked me the other day if a black doll that looks like a white doll isn't better than no black doll at all. I must admit that I have no ready answer for this and a number of other questions posed by my own critique. Although, as I acknowledged in the beginning, the dolls I played with as a child were white, I still remember the first time I saw a black doll. To me, she was the most beautiful thing I had ever seen; I wanted her desperately, and I was never again satisfied with white Betsy Wetsy and blond, blue-eyed Patty Play Pal. She was something else, something *Other*, like me, and that, I imagine, was the source of her charm and my desire.

If I did not consciously note my own absence in the toys I played with, that absence, I suspect, had a profound effect on me nevertheless. We have only to read Toni Morrison's chilling tale *The Bluest Eye* to see the effect of the white beauty myth on the black child. And while they were by no means as dire for me as for Morrison's character Pecola Breedlove, I was not exempt from the consequences of growing up black in a white world that barely acknowledged my existence. I grew up believing I was ugly: my kinky hair, my big hips, the gap between my teeth. I have spent half my life smiling with my hand over my mouth to hide that gap, a habit I only began to get over in graduate school when a couple of Nigerian men told me that in their culture, where my body type is prized much more than Barbie's, such gaps are a sign of great beauty. I wonder what it would have meant for me as a child to see a black doll—or any doll—with big hips and a gap between her two front teeth.

Today, for $24.99, Mattel reaches halfway around the world and gives little girls—black like me—Nigerian Barbies to play with. Through the wonders of plastic, dyes, and mass production, the company brings into the homes of African American children a Nigeria that I as a young child did not even know existed. The problem is that Mattel's Nigeria does not exist either. The would-be ethnic dolls of the world Mattel sells, like their "traditional, blond, blue-eyed" all-American girl prototype, have no gaps, no big ears, no chubby thighs or other "imperfections." For a modest price I can dream myself into Barbie's perfect world, so long as I dream myself in her image. It may be a small world, a whole new world, but there is still no place for me as *me* in it.

This, then, is my final doll story. Groucho Marx said that he wouldn't want to belong to a club that would have him as a member. In that same vein, I am not so sure that most of us would want to buy a doll that "looked like us." Indeed, efforts to produce and market such truer-to-life dolls have not met with much commercial success. Cultural critics like me can throw theoretical stones at her all we want, but part of Barbie's infinite appeal is her very perfection, the extent to which she is both product and purveyor of the dominant white Western ideal of beauty.

And what of black beauty? If Colored Francie failed thirty years ago in part because of her Caucasian features, what are we to make of the current popularity and commercial success of Black Barbie and Shani, straight hair and all? Have we progressed to a point where "difference" makes no difference? Or have we regressed to such a degree that "difference" is only conceivable as similarity—as a mediated text that no matter what its dye job ultimately must be readable as white. Listen to our language: we "*tolerate* difference"; we practice "racial tolerance." Through the compound fractures of interpellation and universalization, the Other is reproduced not in her own image but in ours. If we have gotten away from "Us" and "Them," it may be only because Them R Us.

Is Barbie bad? Barbie is just a piece of plastic, but what she says about the economic base of our society—what she suggests about gender and race in our world—ain't good.

I am particularly pleased to be publishing this essay in differences, *since its genesis was at a roundtable discussion on multiculturalism and postmodernism, sponsored by the Pembroke Center for Teaching and Research on Women at Brown University, in March of 1993. I wish to thank the many friends and colleagues who have encouraged this project, especially Indira Karamcheti and her four-year-old daughter Gita, who introduced me to the miniature Barbies that come with McDonald's "Happy Meals," and Erness Brody, who, with her daughter Jennifer Brody, is a veteran collector of vintage dolls. I owe a special debt to fellow "Barbiologists" M. G. Lord, Mel McCombie, Jacqueline Urla, and Eric Swedlund, who have so generously shared their research, and to Darlene Powell Hopson for talking with me about her work with Mattel. I wish to acknowledge as well the work of Erica Rand, an art historian at Bates College, who is also working on Barbie.*

NOTES

1. Mattel introduced the Shani doll—a black, Barbie-like doll—in 1991, which also may have contributed to the rise in sales, particularly since the company engaged the services of a PR firm that specializes in targeting ethnic audiences.

2. Of course, the notion of "dreaming in one's own image" is always problematic since dreams, by definition, engage something other than the "real."

3. Olmec Toys, a black-owned company headed by an African American woman named Yla Eason, markets a line of black and Latina Barbie-like dolls called the Imani Collection. Billed on their boxes as "African

American Princess" and "Latin American Fantasy," these dolls are also presented as having been designed with the self images of black children in mind. "We've got one thing in mind with all our products," the blurbs on the Imani boxes read: "let's build self-esteem. Our children gain a sense of self importance through toys. So we make them look like them." Given their obvious resemblance to Barbie dolls—their long, straight hair and pencil-thin plastic bodies—Imani dolls look no more "like them," like "real" black children, than their prototype. Eason, who we are told was devastated by her son's announcement that he couldn't be a super-hero because he wasn't white, may indeed want to give black children toys to play with that 'look like them.' Yet, in order to compete in a market long dominated by Mattel and Hasbro, her company, it seems, has little choice but to conform to the Barbie mold.

4. After many calls to the Jamaican Embassy in Washington, D.C. and to various cultural organizations in Jamaica, I have determined that Jamaican Barbie's costume—a floor-length granny-style dress with apron and headrag—bears some resemblance to what is considered the island's traditional folk costume. I am still left wondering about the decision-making process, however: why the doll representing Jamaica is figured as a maid, while the doll representing Great Britain, for example, is presented as a lady—a blond, blue-eyed Barbie doll dressed in a fancy riding habit with boots and hat.

5. See among others Morris Rosenburg's books *Conceiving the Self* (1979) and *Society and the Adolescent Self-Image* (1989) and William E. Cross's *Shades of Black: Diversity in African American Identity* (1991), all of which challenge the Clarks' findings. Cross argues, for example, that the Clarks confounded or conflated two different issues: attitude toward race in general and attitude toward the self in particular. How one feels about race is not necessarily an index of one's self-esteem.

6. In response to criticism from feminists in particular, the Miss America Pageant has attempted to transform itself from a beauty contest to a talent competition, whose real aim is to give college scholarships to smart, talented women (who just happen to look good in bathing suits and evening gowns). As part of its effort to appear more concerned with a woman's IQ than with her bra size, the pageant did away with its long-standing practice of broadcasting the chest, waist, and hip measurements, as well as the height and weight, of each contestant.

Works Cited

Berkwitz, David N. "Finally, Barbie Doll Ads Go Ethnic." *Newsweek*, Aug. 13, 1990: 48.

BillyBoy. *Barbie: Her Life and Times*. New York: Crown, 1987.

Cross, William E., Jr. *Shades of Black: Diversity in African American Identity*. Philadelphia: Temple UP, 1991.

Delany, Sarah, and Delany, A. Elizabeth. *Having Our Say: The Delany Sisters' First 100 Years*. New York: Kodansha, 1993.

Dembner, Alice. "Thirty-five and Still a Doll." *Boston Globe*, March 9, 1994: 1+.

Jones, Lisa. "A Doll Is Born." *Village Voice*, March 26, 1991: 36.

Kantrowitz, Barbara. "Hot Date: Barbie and G.I. Joe." *Newsweek*, February 20, 1989: 59–60.

Hopson, Darlene Powell and Derek S. *Different and Wonderful: Raising Black Children in a Race-Conscious Society*. New York: Simon, 1990.

Larcen, Donna. "Barbie Bond Doesn't Diminish with Age." *Hartford Currant*, Aug. 17, 1993: A6–7.

Lord, M. G. *Forever Barbie: The Unauthorized Biography of a Real Doll*. New York: Morrow, 1994.

McCombie, Mel. "Barbie: Toys Are Us." Unpublished essay.

Morrison, Toni. *The Bluest Eye*. New York: Washington Square, 1970.

Rieff, David. "Multiculturalism's Silent Partner." *Harper's* Aug. 1993: 62–72.

Roberts, Cynthia. *Barbie: Thirty Years of America's Doll*. Chicago: Contemporary, 1989.

Rosenberg, Morris. *Conceiving the Self*. New York: Basic, 1979.

_____. *Society and the Adolescent Self-Image*. Middletown: Wesleyan UP, 1989.

Sanchez-Eppler, Karen. *Touching Liberty: Abolition, Feminism, and the Politics of the Body*. Berkeley: U. of California P., 1993.

Stewart, Julia. *African Names*. New York: Carol, 1993.

Urla, Jacqueline and Alan Swedlund. "The Anthropometry of Barbie: Unsettling Ideals of the Feminine in Popular Culture." *Deviant Bodies*.

Ed. Jennifer Terry and Jacqueline Urla. Bloomington: Indiana UP, forth-coming.

QUESTIONS

1. What is the commodification of difference? How does Barbie serve as a "teaching tool for femininity"? According to duCille, what messages do the bodily constructions of multicultural Barbies send to young girls?
2. Discuss duCille's unanswered question about whether a Black Barbie is better than no Black doll at all. To what other types of popular culture might we direct this question?
3. What "narratives" about Barbie are presented in this essay? How do these narratives complicate the discussion of Barbie's meaning? What conclusions does duCille draw about Barbie?

The Managed Hand: The Commercialization of Bodies and Emotions in Korean Immigrant—Owned Nail Salons

Miliann Kang

The title of [Arlie] Hochschild's (1983) groundbreaking study of emotional labor, *The Managed Heart*, provides a rich metaphor for the control and commercialization of human feeling in service interactions. The title of this article, "The Managed Hand," plays on Hochschild's to capture the commercialization of both human feelings and bodies and to introduce the concept of body labor, the provision of body-related services and the management of feelings that accompanies it. By focusing on the case study of Korean immigrant manicurists and their relations with racially and socioeconomically diverse female customers in New York City nail salons, I broaden the study of emotional labor to illuminate its neglected embodied dimensions and to examine the intersections of gender, race, and class in its performance.

The past decade has witnessed a turn toward "Bringing Bodies Back In" (Frank 1990) to theory and research in sociology and feminist scholarship. What can be gained by "bringing the body back in" to the study of emotional labor and, more broadly, of gendered work? What are the dimensions of body labor, and what

Reprinted from *Feminist Frontiers*, McGraw-Hill Companies.

factors explain the variation in the quality and quantity of its performance? An embodied perspective on gendered work highlights the feminization of the body-related service sector and the proliferation of intricate practices of enhancing the appearance of the female body. A race, gender, and class perspective highlights the increasing role of working-class immigrant women in filling body-related service jobs and the racialized meanings that shape the processes of emotional management among service workers.

This study compares nail salons in three racially and socioeconomically diverse settings, employing participant observation and in-depth interviews ($N = 62$) in the tradition of feminist ethnography and the extended case method. After providing a brief overview of the case study of Korean-owned nail salons in New York City, the data presentation maps out the physical and emotional dimensions of body labor in three different nail salons and explains patterns of variation according to the race and class of the clientele and neighborhood.

In addition to contributing original empirical research on Korean immigrant women's work in the new and expanding niches of body service work, this article broadens the scholarship on emotional labor by addressing its performance by racial-ethnic and immigrant women in the global service economy. It demonstrates how the gendered processes of physical and emotional labor in nail salon work are steeped with race and class meanings that reinforce broader structures of inequality and ideologies of difference between women.

Theoretical Framework

Emotional Labor in Body Service Work: Race, Gender, and Class Intersections

Work on the body requires not only physical labor but extensive emotional management, or what Hochschild's (1983) seminal work describes as emotional labor. The concept of body labor makes two important contributions to the study of emotional labor: (1) It explores the embodied dimensions of emotional labor and (2) it investigates the intersections of race, gender, and class in shaping its performance. By bringing together an embodied analysis of emotional labor with an integrative race, gender, and class perspective, I show how this case study of nail salon work retheorizes emotional labor to have greater applicability to gendered occupations dominated by racialized immigrant women.

Building on Hochschild's (1983) work, studies of emotional labor have illuminated the increasing prevalence of emotional management in specific occupations and industries, the gendered composition of the emotional labor force, wage discrimination, burnout, and other occupational health issues (Hall 1993; Leidner 1999; Lively 2000; Wharton 1999). Steinberg and Figart (1999) provide a comprehensive overview of the field that examines both qualitative case studies of the contours of emotional labor in specific work sites and quantitative investigations of its prevalence and its impact on job satisfaction and compensation. Despite the many dimensions of emotional labor that have been addressed by feminist scholars, the body-related contours of emotional labor as it is manifested in low-wage service work dominated by racial-ethnic women, particularly in the beauty industry, have yet to be examined in depth.

While the study of beauty and the beauty industry presents a rich opportunity to explore the emotional work involved in servicing female bodies, this literature has focused attention almost exclusively on the experiences of middle-class white women consumers and their physical and psychological exploitation by the male-dominated beauty industry (Banner 1983; Bordo 1993; Chapkis 1986; Wolf 1991), neglecting the substandard working conditions, unequal power relations, and complex emotional lives of the women who provide these services. Several excellent ethnographies of beauty salons (Gimlan 1996; Kerner Furman 1997) have explored the dimensions of class and age in beauty shop culture, but they have not addressed the experiences of women of color as either customers or body service workers. Studies of the bodies of women of color, while illuminating cultural representations of racialized bodies as inferior and exotic (hooks 1990) and studying the politics of body alteration, particularly regarding hair (Banks 2000; Rooks 1996), have also neglected the actual interactions between consumers and providers of body-related services and the hierarchies that govern these exchanges.

In addition to neglecting emotional work in body service jobs, the literature on emotional labor has framed the processes of interactive service work primarily through a gender lens and paid less attention to the crosscutting influences of gender, race and class. Russell Hochschild's original case study of flight attendants and subsequent applications to other female-dominated occupations have emphasized the gendered employment experiences of native-born white women as paralegals (Pierce 1995), nannies and au pairs (Macdonald 1996), fast food and insurance sales workers (Leidner 1993), and police officers (Schmitt and Yancey Martin 1999). My research expands this work not only in its empirical focus on immigrant women of color doing gendered, emotional labor but through the theoretical framework of race, gender, and class as "interactivesystems" and "interlocking categories of experience" (Anderson and Hill Collins 2001, xii). This framework critiques additive models that append race and class to the experiences of white middle-class women and instead highlights the simultaneity and reciprocity of race, gender, and class in patterns of social relations and in the lives of individuals (Baca Zinn 1989; Hill Collins 1991; hooks 1981; Hurtado 1989; Nakano Glenn 1992; Ngan-Ling Chow 1994). Thus, I demonstrate that different expectations or "feeling rules" (Hochschild 1983, x) shape the performance of emotional labor by women according to the racial and class context.

Drawing from Hochschild's (1983) definition of emotional labor, I incorporate this intersectional analysis to define important parallels and distinctions between the concepts of body labor and emotional labor. First, Hochschild's definition of emotional labor focuses on a particular form that "requires one to induce or suppress feeling in order to sustain the outward countenance that produces the proper state of mind in others—in this case, the sense of being cared for in a convivial and safe place" (1983, 7). While Hochschild develops this definition in reference to the specific case of flight attendants and the feeling rules that govern their work, this kind of caring, attentive service has become a widely generalized definition, rather than being regarded as one particular form of emotional labor performed by mostly white, middle-class women largely for the benefit of white, middle- and upper-class men. Korean-owned nail salons thus serve as a contrasting site to explore other forms of emotional labor that emerge in work sites that are differently gendered, differently racialized, and differently classed. The patterns of emotional labor described in this study can illuminate similar sites in which emotional labor involves women serving women (as opposed to mainly women serving men), and is not necessarily governed by the social feeling rules of white, middle-class America.

Furthermore, while Hochschild and other scholars of emotional labor have examined certain embodied aspects of emotional labor concerned with gendered bodily display, ranging from control of weight to smiles, this study highlights emotional management regarding bodily contact in service interactions. The dynamics of extended physical contact between women of different racial and class positions complicate and intensify the gendered performance of emotional labor. Body labor not only demands that the service worker present and comport her body in an appropriate fashion but also that she induces customers' positive feelings about their own bodies. This is a highly complicated enterprise in a culture that sets unattainable standards for female beauty and pathologizes intimate, nurturing physical contact between women, while it normalizes unequal relations in the exchange of body services.

By investigating the understudied area of body-related service occupations through an intersectional race, gender, and class analysis, this study of body labor reformulates the concept of emotional labor to dramatize how the feeling rules governing its exchange are shaped by interlocking oppressions that operate at the macro level (Hill Collins 1991) and then emerge as different styles of emotional service at the micro level.

Background for the Study

In this section, I provide context for my study by describing nail salons as a niche for Korean immigrant women's work and discussing the dynamics of race and ethnicity in its development. As one of the few arenas in which immigrant and native-born women encounter each other in regular, sustained, physical contact, Korean immigrant women-owned nail salons in New York City illuminate the complex performance and production of race, gender, and class as they are constructed in feminized work sites in the global service economy. Since the early 1980s, Korean women in New York City have pioneered this new ethnic niche with more than 2,000 Korean-owned nail salons throughout the metropolitan area, or approximately 70 percent of the total, as estimated by the Korean American Nail Association of New York. Each salon employs an average of five workers, suggesting an occupational niche of roughly 10,000 women. While the New York State licensing bureau does not keep track of nail salon licenses by ethnic group, their figures reveal an overall 41-percent growth in the nail industry (from 7,562 licensed nail technicians in 1996 to 10,684 in 2000) in New York City, Westchester County, and Nassau County. These numbers undercount a sizable number of women who do not possess licenses or legal working status.

While concentrating on Korean immigrant women, this study examines both race and ethnicity as salient categories of analysis. I designate the salon owners and workers according to ethnicity, but I recognize shared racial positions that push not only Korean but also other Asian immigrant women into this niche. For example, in New York, there is a significant presence of Chinese- and Vietnamese- as well as Korean-owned nail salons, and on the West Coast, the niche is almost solely dominated by Vietnamese women (www.nailsmag.com). Common factors such as limited English-language ability, unrecognized professional credentials from their countries of origin, undocumented immigration status, and coethnic resources in the form of labor, start-up capital, and social networks explain why Asian immigrant women of various ethnic groups cluster in the nail salon industry. Similarities across Asian ethnic groups include not only the human capital of the women themselves but also the conditions of the labor market and the U.S. racial hierarchy that they encounter. Through their shared race, gender, and class locations, Asian women have been coveted as productive and docile workers, whose "nimble fingers" (Ong 1987) make them desirable and exploitable in an increasingly feminized, impoverished, and unprotected labor force (Cheng and Bonacich 1984; Hu-DeHart 1999). Racialized perceptions of Asian women as skilled in detailed handiwork and massage further contribute to customers' preference for their manicuring services, as evidenced by the fact that many customers racially identify the salons as owned by Asians or "Orientals," as opposed to by specific ethnic group.

In sum, because it would be methodologically unsound to generalize findings based on a limited sample of Korean women to include all Asian immigrant women in the nail industry, this study maintains ethnicity as the significant category for describing the workers and owners but frames differences between the customers and variation in service interactions according to race. Thus, I discuss the different dimensions of Korean-immigrant women's performance of body labor through the integrative lens of race, gender, and class rather than a more specific focus on Korean ethnicity.

Research Design and Method

This study situates itself within feminist methodology and epistemology by beginning from the standpoint of women to investigate the "relations of ruling" in contemporary capitalist society (Smith 1987). At the same time, it does not privilege gender as the only or the most important framework for defining and investigating differences and aims instead for an understanding of race, gender, and class as crosscutting forces. By examining contrasting patterns of body labor between women of different racial and class backgrounds, this study reconstructs theories of emotional labor by addressing its embodied dimensions and the simultaneous influence of gender, race, and class on its performance. In doing so, it follows the extended case method of making critical interventions in existing theory by explaining anomalies between similar phenomena, rather than seeking generalizations toward the discovery of new theory, as in the contrasting approach of grounded theory. According to Burawoy (1991, 281), the primary architect of the extended case method, "The importance of the single case lies in what it tells us about society as a whole rather than about the population of similar cases." Thus, my study examines cases of specific nail salons, not to formulate generalizations about all similar nail salons but instead to explain how social forces influence variation in the service interactions at these sites.

The data collection for this project involved 14 months of fieldwork in New York City nail salons. The research design included in-depth interviews ($N = 62$) and participant observation at three sites: (1) "Uptown Nails," located in a predominantly white, middle- and upper-class commercial area; (2) "Downtown Nails," located in a predominantly Black (African American and

Caribbean) working-and lower-middle-class commercial neighborhood; and (3) "Crosstown Nails," located in a racially mixed lower-middle and middle-class residential and commercial area. I spent at least 50 hours at each salon over the course of several months. In the case of Crosstown Nails, which was located near my home, visits were shorter (2 to 3 hours) and more frequent (several times a week). The other two salons required long commutes, so I usually visited once a week for 6 to 7 hours.

In addition to hundreds of unstructured conversational interviews conducted as a participant-observer, the research included in-depth structured interviews with 10 Korean nail salon owners, 10 Korean nail salon workers, 15 Black customers, and 15 white customers. The customers interviewed at each salon are as follows. Uptown Nails included a lawyer, professor, pharmacist, flight attendant, secretary, personal trainer, accessories importer, homemaker (formerly a computer programmer), fashion designer, and real estate broker. Customers interviewed at Downtown Nails included a package clerk, student/waitress, student/mother, grocery cashier, ambulatory service driver, county government administrative assistant, laboratory technician, nanny, therapist, and elementary school principal. At Crosstown Nails, I interviewed 10 customers (five white, five Black). The white customers included a bartender, high school teacher, hairdresser, homemaker, and retired insurance bookkeeper. The Black customers included a clinical researcher, theater technician/musician, management consultant, homemaker, and student.

In-depth interviews averaged 45 minutes for customers and two hours for owners and workers. Customers were interviewed in English at the salon while they were having their manicures, and when necessary, a follow-up meeting or telephone interview was arranged. Owners and workers were interviewed in both Korean and English, depending on their preference and level of fluency. Bilingual research assistants helped with translation, transcription, and follow-up interviews. I tape-recorded interviews in which consent was given, but in cases in which respondents refused, I took extensive handwritten notes that I typed immediately afterward. Both customers and service providers are referred to by pseudonyms that approximate the names they use in the salons. This convention captures the naturalistic setting where even coworkers commonly refer to each other by the "American name" that they employ at work. I have added a surname to citations and descriptions of owners and workers to differentiate customers from service providers.

Finally, I conducted key respondent interviews with two officials of the Korean Nail Salon Association of New York, two Korean ethnic press journalists, one New York State licensing official, and a representative of a Korean-operated nail school. I interviewed two Vietnamese nail salon owners and one Chinese and one Russian manicurist to provide preliminary comparisons to other ethnically owned nail salons. To provide comparisons to other Korean-owned small businesses, I engaged in limited participant observation in a Korean-owned grocery store and interviewed the owner and manager.

Findings

The Contours of Body Labor

Body labor involves the exchange of body-related services for a wage and the performance of physical and emotional labor in this exchange. My study's findings illustrate three dimensions of body labor: (1) the physical labor of attending to the bodily appearance and pleasure of customers, (2) the emotional labor of managing feelings to display certain feeling states and to create and respond to customers' feelings regarding the servicing of their bodies, and (3) variation in the performance of body labor as explained through the intersection of gender with race and class. These dimensions vary across the different research sites and emerge as three distinct patterns of body labor provision: (1) high-service body labor involving physical pampering and emotional attentiveness serving mostly middle- and upper-class white female customers, (2) expressive body labor involving artistry in technical skills and communication of respect and fairness when serving mostly working- and lower-middle-class African American and Caribbean female customers, and (3) routinized body labor involving efficient, competent physical labor and courteous but minimal emotional labor when serving mostly lower-middle and middle-class racially mixed female customers. The data presentation admittedly flattens some of the variation within each site to clarify distinctions between them, but this typology highlights the dominant physical and emotional style of service at each salon.

Uptown Nails: High-Service Body Labor

A seasoned Korean manicurist who has worked at Uptown Nails for nearly 10 years, Esther Lee is in high demand for her relaxing and invigorating hand massages. She energetically kneads, strokes, and pushes pressure points, finishing off the massage by holding each of the customer's hands between her own and alternately rubbing, slapping, and gently pounding them with the flare that has wooed many a customer into a regular nail salon habit. Margie, a white single woman in her mid-30s who works for an accounting firm, smiles appreciatively and squeezes Esther's hand: "I swear, I couldn't stay in my job without this!" Esther reciprocates a warm, somewhat shy smile.

Uptown Nails boasts leafy green plants, glossy framed pictures of white fashion models showing off well-manicured hands, recent fashion magazine subscriptions stacked neatly on a coffee table, and classical CDs on the stereo system. The salon has been in operation for 13 years, and three of the six employees have worked there for more than 10 years. The customers sit quietly sipping their cappuccinos, updating their appointment books, or at times politely conversing with each other about the weather or the color of the nail polish they are wearing. Located in a prosperous business district of Manhattan, an Uptown Nails manicuring experience involves not only the filing and polishing of nails but attention to the customer's physical and emotional comfort. From the gentle removal of undernail dirt, to the careful trimming of cuticles and buffing of calluses, to the massaging of hands and feet, Korean manicurists literally rub up against their customers, who are mostly white middle- and upper-class women. The owner, one of the earliest pioneers in the nail salon industry, currently operates six very profitable salons in prime Manhattan locations and visits this salon only once a week to take care of paperwork. The owner, manager, and employees are all middle-aged Korean women with fluent English-language ability, reflecting the greater expectations for communications with customers. The physical dimensions of body labor in Uptown Nails, including hot cotton towels, bowls of warm soaking solution, sanitized utensils, and calming background music, all indicate considerable attention to creating a pleasurable sensory experience for the customer. Particular attention is given to avoiding nicks and cuts and sterilizing and apologizing profusely when they occur.

In addition to this extensive physical pampering, Uptown Nails prioritizes the emotional needs of customers regarding the servicing of their bodies. The mostly white middle-class customers at this salon place great importance on emotional attentiveness as a crucial component of the service interaction. Kathy, a personal trainer, elaborated,

> Having them done is a pleasure, a luxury. Doing them myself is tedious, having them done is a treat. It's the whole idea of going and having something nice done for myself. If I do them myself, it's just routine upkeep of my body—like washing your hair or keeping your clothes clean. . . . Of course it makes it more enjoyable if they are friendly and can talk to you. If they can't remember my name that's okay, but I think they should recognize me.

The proper performance of body labor thus transforms a hygienic process, otherwise equated with washing hair or clothes, into a richly rewarding physical and emotional experience. The satisfaction Kathy experiences from the manicure derives not only from the appearance of the nails but the feeling of being special that accompanies attentive body servicing. To generate this feeling, customers expect the manicurist to display a caring demeanor and engage in pleasant one-on-one conversation with them.

Service providers recognize customers' high expectations with regard to both the physical and emotional dimensions of body labor, and they respond accordingly. Judy Cha, a 34-year-old who immigrated in 1993, describes the emotional and physical stressors that accompany high-service body labor, particularly giving massages to earn tips and engaging in conversation.

> Three years ago we didn't give a lot of massages but now customers ask more and more. It makes me weak and really tired. . . . I guess because I don't have the right training to do it in a way that doesn't tire my body. Some manicurists give massage all the time to get tips, but sometimes I don't even ask them, if I'm tired. Owners keep asking you to ask them, but on

> days I'm not feeling well, I don't ask. . . . One of my biggest fears working in the salon is, what if I don't understand what the customer is saying? They don't really talk in detail, just say, "how is the weather." But in order to have a deeper relationship, I need to get past that and to improve my English. It makes it very stressful.

Thus, manicurists work hard to conform to the high service expectations of middle-class white women, but while the performance of caring, attentive emotional labor is noticeably higher than that afforded in the other research sites, it often does not meet customers' expectations. In particular, many Uptown Nails customers disapprove of the use of Korean language by the manicursits as a violation of proper attentiveness in beauty service transactions and suspect that they are being talked about (Kang 1997).

Cathy Hong, a 32-year-old manicurist who immigrated in 1999, sums up the assumptions many of the Uptown Nails customers have regarding access to a regular manicure delivered with high-service body labor: "These women get their nails done regularly because it has become a habit to them, they take it for granted. Just as we wash our face daily, American women get their nails done."

Downtown Nails: Expressive Body Labor

Entering another borough, the scene inside Downtown Nails differs as radically as the neighborhoods in which these two salons are located. Squeezed between a Caribbean bakery and a discount clothing store, a worn-out signboard displays the single word "NAILS" and a painting of a graceful, well-manicured hand holding a long-stemmed rose and pointing to a staircase leading to the second-story entrance. Upon being buzzed in through the locked door, the customer is greeted with a display of hundreds of brightly colored airbrushed nail tips lining an entire wall. The noise level in the salon is high, as various electronic nail-sculpting tools create a constant buzz to match the flow of the lively conversations among the mostly Black customers. On a weekend afternoon, Downtown Nails is filled to capacity, and the wait for a preferred "nail artist" can be more than an hour. Mostly Caribbean and African American women, the customers engage in animated conversations while sharing coco buns and currant rolls from the downstairs bakery. The banter ranges from vivid accounts of a recent mugging near the salon to news about the pay freeze in the nearby hospital where many of the women work as nurses or technicians.

A far cry from the spa-like pampering experience of Uptown Nails, a nail job at Downtown Nails is closer to a stint on a factory assembly line: highly mechanized and potentially toxic. Absent are the elaborate sanitizing machines and solutions, let alone the soft pampering touches. Despite these appearances, body labor at Downtown Nails involves a complex mix of physical and emotional labor that accommodates customers' desires to express a unique sense of self through their nail designs and their expectations that service providers demonstrate both individual respect and appreciation to the community.

The manicurists, or nail artists, provide less of the traditional, attentive style of emotional labor but focus their emotional management on communicating a sense of respect and fairness. These women tend to be more recent immigrants from more working-class backgrounds with less English-language fluency and are more likely to be working without legal immigration status or licenses. The owners, Mr. and Mrs. Lee, are a married couple, both formerly school teachers, who immigrated in 1981 to pursue better educational opportunities for their children. Two years after their arrival, they opened a salon in this location because the rent was affordable, the customer base was strong, and they reside in a nearby neighborhood. The customers at Downtown Nails span a broad range in socioeconomic status but most are working to lower-middle class.

The importance of the physical appearance of the nails themselves as opposed to the pampering experience of receiving these services is dramatized by customers' concern with the design of the nails versus the massage and other services that customers at Uptown Nails regard as integral and Downtown Nails customers view as extraneous. Jamilla, a 26-year-old African American part-time student and waitress, proudly displays her inch-and-a-half-long nails, each one adorned with the skyline of New York City in bold black, framed by an orange and yellow sunset. A regular patron of Downtown Nails for six years, she explains why she is willing to spend "$50–$60 every two weeks" for elaborate hand-painted designs:

> Because I don't like looking like anyone else. My nails say "me." They're the first thing people notice about me. I have big hands for a female. I never had those long, thin ladylike fingers. My father used to say my hands were bigger than his. I want long nails because they make my hands look more feminine.

Indicating a preference for nails that reflect very different norms of femininity than the demure, pastel tones prevalent at Uptown Nails, Jamilla elaborates further on her nail aesthetics. "It all depends on my mood. Like this design makes me feel like I'm on top of the city, like it can't bring me down [laughing]. . . . No one's gonna mess with you when you got nails like these." Jamilla's pride in having originally designed nails that no one else can reproduce suggests the importance of her nails as an expression of her individuality that also communicate a sense of self-efficacy and protection, as indicated in her comments that no one would "mess" with a women with nails like hers. To meet the expectations of customers such as Jamilla, body labor at Downtown Nails calls for development of expertise in sculpting and painting original nail designs rather than in the soothing, pampering services offered at Uptown Nails. Thus, the physical demands of body labor are not less but simply of a different type.

Similarly, the emotional dimensions of body labor at Downtown Nails are not different in degree so much as kind. The customer's race and class location intersect to produce much lower expectations among working-class Black customers for emotional attentiveness than the white middle-class women at Uptown Nails. While it is clearly less attentive, Serena, an African American grocery store cashier, assesses the emotional labor at Downtown Nails positively.

> It's very good, I'm satisfied with it. They really just do the nails, no massages. That's fine with me. I just go in with my Walkman and listen to some good music and maybe just have a little basic conversation.

Customers at Downtown Nails rarely are on a first-name basis with the service providers, and their preference for a particular manicurist is based much more on her technical skills than her emotional attentiveness. Serena elaborated,

> There are a few people I like and I go to whoever's open, but I'll stay away from certain people. I know they're not good

> cause I hear other people complain—I see someone come back and say that their nail cracked the next day, or I see someone get nicked with a filer. . . . No, it's not because they're rude or anything, it's because I know they don't do a good job. . . . Just like some people just can't do hair, some people just can't do nails.
>
> [Regarding relations with her current manicurist] I feel comfortable with her, but it's more that she does an excellent job. If a wrap cracks or looks funny or I lose a nail, I'm not going back to her no matter how nice she is.

While many working-class Black customers like Serena give little importance to a caring, attentive emotional display, they demand another style of emotional labor.

Emotional labor at Downtown Nails calls less for sensitivity to pampering of individual customers and more for demonstration of values of respect and fairness that recognize the complex dynamics of Korean businesses operating in Black neighborhoods. This includes efforts such as sponsoring a Christmas party to thank customers for their patronage, participating in community events, displaying Afro-centric designs, and playing R&B and rap music. Mrs. Lee, the co-owner of the salon, allows regulars to run an informal tab when they are short of money and keeps a change jar that customers dip into for bus fare, telephone calls, or other incidentals. It is not uncommon for customers to drop by even when they are not getting their nails done to use the bathroom or leave shopping bags behind the front desk while they complete errands. These efforts at "giving back to the community" entail a distinct form of emotional labor that conforms not to white middle-class women's feeling rules of privilege and pampering but to Black working-class women's concerns about being treated with respect and fairness.

Jamilla described the importance of a sense of fairness and respect to Black customers and how this demands a particular form of emotional labor from Korean manicurists.

> It's kind of a Catch-22. Some customers feel like they're getting disrespected if you don't refer back to them or if you're having a side conversation. Then the Koreans get upset and think African Americans have an attitude, which then makes them talk more about us. You see, in the African American community, you can't outright say anything you want to say because we always have our guard up. We get it all the time, from the cops or whoever. I've seen it in the Hispanic community too—

> this thing about honor and respect. "Don't disrespect me just because I'm Black or Hispanic. What I say does count."

Thus, while the caring, pampering style of service is virtually absent at Downtown Nails, another form of emotional labor is necessary to negotiate and avoid conflicts with customers that can quickly become racialized into heated confrontations (Lee 2002). Serena described a scene at another salon that illustrates how the failure to perform appropriately respectful emotional labor can quickly erupt into shouting matches that take on racialized and anti-immigrant overtones: "I've seen some customers really go off on them, 'You're not in your country, speak English.'" Her comments underscore how the race and class of the neighborhood complicate the processes of emotional management inside the salons.

Although disagreements between Downtown Nails' customers and workers do arise, at times resulting in heated exchanges, the relations in the salon are congenial overall, as the expressive style of emotional labor enables customers and service providers to voice and, for the most part, "work out" their differences. Mrs. Lee explained that she prefers serving Black customers for this reason and actually moved back to working in a low-income Black neighborhood after working for a period in Long Island.

> Working in the white neighborhood didn't match my personality. I don't deal well with picky customers. . . . In the Black neighborhood, it's more relaxed. They don't leave tips but they don't expect so much service either. . . . [In Long Island] they want you to go slow and spend time with them. Here I just concentrate on doing a good job and working quickly.

Service providers invest less energy in displaying and creating convivial feeling states, which in some cases allows for a genuine affinity with Black customers and less of a sense of burnout from the effort involved in the manufacture of falsely convivial feelings.

Expressive body labor thus priortizes both the meanings of the nails as a form of self-expression to working-class Black customers and the expression of symbolic but tangible efforts to respond to the feeling rules of respect and fairness governing Korean immigrant service providers in predominantly Black working-class neighborhoods.

Crosstown Nails: Routinized Body Labor

Located on the second floor above a fashionable boutique, Crosstown Nails is clean but sparse and utilitarian. In many ways, this salon is representative of the most prevalent style of service offered in Korean-owned nail salons: fast, cheap, basic manicures and pedicures with no frills. The McDonald's of the nail salon industry, Crosstown Nails offers a manicure that is standardized and predictable in both its physical and emotional aspects.

This salon often has customers waiting, but even when it is busy, the line moves quickly as each customer is whisked in and out of the manicuring seat with crisp efficiency. The customer chooses her nail color, presents it to the manicurist who asks her to specify the desired shape of the nail, and then soaks her nails briefly in a softening solution. Depending on her preference, her nails are either trimmed or pushed back. The manicurist offers to give a massage, but it is perfunctory and lasts usually not more than a minute. After carefully layering on two coats of polish and a quick-drying topcoat, the customer moves to a heated hand dryer where she converses with other customers or more often "zones out."

Many customers come from the neighboring hospital during lunch hour or after work. Situated on the edge of a fashionable, high-rent, racially diverse residential district and a lower-income but also racially mixed neighborhood, Crosstown Nails captures the broad range of customer interactions that many Korean service providers negotiate in a given day. In large, high-immigrant-receiving cities such as New York, service interactions often involve multiracial rather than binary interactions between Korean and Blacks or Koreans and whites.

Susan Lee, age 39, founded Crosstown Nails in 1989 and is the sole owner. Divorced with one son, age 10, she emigrated in 1982 from Seoul with her husband, a graduate student. She graduated college with a degree in tourism and worked as a travel agent in Korea. In New York City, she first worked in a retail store in Manhattan, then began to work in a nail salon in Brooklyn to support her husband while he studied. After their marriage ended, she brought her mother from Korea in 1988 and with her help opened a convenience store, which failed shortly thereafter. She then opened Crosstown Nails a year later, and the business has thrived.

The secret of Crosstown Nail's success is its ability to appeal to customers who lack excess disposable income and normally would not indulge in a professional manicure but are attracted by the convenience and price. Julia, a white bartender, commented,

> I'm kind of a ragamuffin, so it kind of surprises me that I get them done as often as I do, which is still much less than most people in the city. It's just so easy to do here, and cheap.

Julia's description of herself as a "ragamuffin" suggests that she does not adhere to strict codes of femininity in her dress or other beauty routines, as indicated by her casual peasant skirt and no makeup. Nonetheless, easy and cheap access draws her into purchasing regular manicures.

Many customers at Crosstown Nails seek manicures not as a pampering experience or as creative expression but as a utilitarian measure to enhance their self-presentation at work. Merna, an Afro-Caribbean clinical researcher, explained,

> I only get them done about every two months. I don't want to get attached to it. For some women it's such a ritual, it becomes a job—maintaining the tips and stuff. I'm presenting my hands all day long so it's worth it to me to spend some time and money to make sure they look good.

Merna regards manicured nails as a professional asset more than a core aspect of a gendered self. Thus, the style of her nails and the meaning she gives to them is more similar to the white middle-class customers at Crosstown Nails than to the Black working-class customers at Downtown Nails.

In general, middle-class Black customers like Merna mostly exhibited similar nail aesthetics to those of middle-class white women, suggesting the greater importance of class over race in influencing nail styles and expectations of body labor, particularly in routinized settings such as Crosstown Nails.

Discussion

The concept of emotional labor addresses how service providers present and manipulate their feelings to communicate a sense of caring and attentiveness to customers, or in Hochschild's (1983, 6) words, where "the emotional style of offering service is part of the service itself." This study of interactions in Korean-owned nail salons enriches the literature on emotional labor by expanding it to include embodied dimensions, or body labor. The embodied aspects of emotional labor by expanding it to include embodied dimensions, or body labor. The embodied aspects of emotional labor not only heighten the intensity of commercialized feeling exchanges but they also point out variation in these exchanges beyond the white middle-class settings explored by most researchers. Nail salon services, and body labor more generally are generated work processes, but they are enacted in different forms according to the influences of race and class.

In what ways is nail salon work gendered? In what ways are these gendered work processes remolded by race and class? Understanding the influence of race and class on the gendered performance of body labor in Korean-owned nail salons illuminates how gendered work processes reflect and reproduce racial and class inequalities at the level of social structures. Nail salon work is gendered in four major dimensions: (1) It involves mostly female actors, as both service providers and customers; (2) it focuses on the construction of beauty according to feminine norms; (3) it is situated in feminized, semiprivate spaces; and (4) it involves the gendered performance of emotional labor.

In describing each of these dimensions, I do not emphasize how socialized gender roles are acted out in these establishments, but rather how gender operates as a social institution that lays the groundwork for the very existence of these businesses and frames the interactions that occur within them. Thus, I conceptualize these small businesses according to the model of gendered institutions (Marx Ferree and Hall 1996) and examine how they are constructed from the group up through gendered ideologies, relations, and practices that sustain systematic gender inequality at the micro level of sex differences, at the meso level of group conflict, and [at] the macro levels of power, social control, and the division of labor. At the same time, I argue that as gendered institutions, they cannot be separated from forces of racial and class inequality.

If, as Paul Gilroy (1993, 85) asserted, "gender is the modality in which race is lived," then race, and I argue class as well, are lived in these nail salons and other body-service sites as differences in gendered styles of body labor. Interactions in Korean female immigrant—owned nail salons illustrate how the gendered practices of body labor become the locus of expressing and negotiating race and class hierarchies between white, Black, and Asian women. High-service body labor, as performed at Uptown Nails, is similar to the style of caring, attentive emotional labor, as performed at Uptown Nails, is similar to the style of caring, the emotional labor practiced by Hochschild's flight attendants and conforms to the feeling rules of white middle-class women. Expressive body labor focuses on the physical appearance and artistry of the nails and the communication of respect and fairness in serving mostly working- and lower-middle-class African American and Caribbean women customers at Downtown Nails. Routinized body labor stresses efficiency, predictability, affordability, and competency in physical labor and a courteous but no-frills style of emotional labor geared toward mostly lower-middle- and middle-class racially mixed female customers at Crosstown Nails.

These patterns of body labor conform to the racial and class positions of the customers and the associated feeling rules that define their service expectations. At Uptown Nails, race, gender, and class intersect to produce an emotionally and physically pampering form of body labor that conforms to the expectations of white, professional women for caring and attentive service. These women have high expectations regarding massages, cleanliness, sensitive touch, and friendly conversation while Black, working-class women at Downtown Nails expect minimal pampering and focus on the appearance, originality, and durability of the nails themselves. At Crosstown Nails, class prevails over race as both Black and white women of middling socioeconomic status view the nails instrumentally as a no-nonsense professional asset rather than conforming to traditional notions of pampered femininity. Thus, they trade off the physical pleasure and emotional attentiveness of high-service treatment for the convenience and price of routinized body labor.

Black middle-class women at Crosstown Nails share this instrumental view of nails and a preference for a routinized, hassle-free manicure. The style of nails and the meaning given to them by Black middle-class women radically differ from the working-class Black women at Downtown Nails, who value nail art as a form of self-expression and demand emotional labor that communicates respect and fairness. This contrast between the Black middle-class and working-class women customers at

Crosstown and Downtown Nails again suggests the greater salience of class over race in determining the type of body labor.

What structural factors explain the differences in the provision of body labor in these three sites? These body labor types, while enacted at the micro level, reflect the social conditions of the neighborhoods in which the salons are located and the clientele they serve. Because of the reliance on tips in white middle-class neighborhoods, service providers have greater incentive to cater to the emotional needs of customers such as those at Uptown Nails to increase their earnings. In the Black working-class neighborhoods where tipping is not a widespread practice, nail salon workers guarantee their economic livelihood by establishing a base of regular customers who seek them out for their technical and artistic abilities more than their emotional or physical attentiveness. In routinized body labor settings serving lower-middle-class women of mixed races, service providers maximize their earnings by generating a high turnover of customers who receive satisfactory but not special emotional and physical treatment.

These patterns of body labor service reflect and reproduce racial and class inequalities between women. Korean service providers learn to respond to white middle- and upper-class customers' emotional pampering and physical pleasure, thereby reinforcing the invisible sense of privilege claimed by these customers. The expressive practices of creating artful nails and troubleshooting potential problems with Black working-class customers, while helping to smooth relations, can also serve to emphasize racial meanings in these interactions and enforce a sense of difference. The routinized style of body labor reflects the generic social position of women whose bodies are neither privileged nor pathologized but simply treated with routine efficiency.

Conclusions

Exchanges of manicuring services set up complex emotional and embodied interactions between diverse women. In introducing and exploring the dimensions of body labor, this article challenges the scholarship on emotional labor, this article challenges the scholarship on emotional labor to take more seriously the growth in body-related service jobs and to address the differences in these service interactions not simply in terms of gendered processes but through the lens of race, gender, and class intersections. Thus, not only does the concept of body labor add embodied dimensions to emotional labor, but it also makes it more applicable to low-wage service work performed by immigrant women of color.

This study situates the practice of body labor in Korean-owned nail salons within the restructuring of the global economy and the transplantation of the practices of enhancing bodily appearance from private households into new forms of public urban space. A manicure is no longer something a woman gives herself, her daughter, or a girlfriend in the quiet of her own bathroom, but it is something that she increasingly purchases in a nail salon. In purchasing these services, she not only expands the boundaries of the service economy to include formerly private regimens of personal hygiene, but she also encounters the "other," often an immigrant woman of different racial and class background through physical contact that can generate highly charged feelings on both sides. These feelings manifest and are worked out differently in distinct styles of body labor that emerge through the intersection of gendered work processes with customers' racial and class positions and their associated service expectations.

Although so far I have drawn parallels between this process of exchanging body services for a wage with the commercialization of feelings in emotional labor, another parallel can be drawn to the encroachment of the capitalist system into the area of social reproduction. Nakano Glenn (1992) and others have illuminated how the performance of household work such as cleaning, cooking, and caring for children and the elderly has become increasingly part of the capitalist market, and these low-paying, unprotected jobs (nanny, elderly caregiver, nurses, aide) are most often filled by immigrant women of color. This study has illustrated how similar to these dynamics of commodifying reproductive labor and farming it out at low wages to less privileged women, body services and the emotional labor accompanying it (what I have conceptualized as body labor) have become increasingly commercialized and designated as racialized immigrant women's work.

While this article has concentrated on my case study of nail salons, the concept of body labor can be applied to many other occupations, especially female-dominated service professions in which service providers and customers are of different race and class origins, including hairdressers, masseuses, nannies, nurses, doctors, personal trainers, and prostitutes.

Finally, in mapping out the racial, gendered, and classed complexity of body labor, this article highlights a kernel of social change that lies in negotiating service interactions between women of different classes, racial and ethnic backgrounds, and immigrant statuses. While these interactions often mimic structures of power and privilege, they also create opportunities to contest these structures. The Korean salon owner of Downtown Nails learns to respect and show appreciation for Black working-class patrons. Korean manicurists at Uptown Nails assert their knowledge and expertise over their white middle-class customers. Routinized service at Crosstown Nails equalizes treatment of women across race and class.

From the customer's side, a weekly trip to the local nail salon can become a lesson in relating to a woman of a radically different social position, whom she would rarely encounter in her own milieu. As these emotional and embodied interactions reflect larger systems of status and power, by rewritting the unspoken feeling rules of these interactions, women can take small but important steps in the creation of more equal relations with other women. Nakano Gleen (2002, 16–17) wrote that "contesting race and gender hierarchies may involve challenging everyday assumptions and practices, take forms that do not involve direct confrontation, and occur in locations not considered political." Exchanges involving body labor in Korean-owned nail salons are one such location where these everyday assumptions and practices can be recognized and possibly renegotiated.

Acknowledgments

I would like to thank Catherine Berheide, C. N. Le, Jennifer Lee, Sara Lee, Susan Walzer and Chris Bose, Minjeong Kim, and the *Gender & Society* anonymous reviewers for valuable comments and suggestions. My dissertation committee at New York University, Craig Calhoun, Jeff Goodwin, and Ruth Horowitz, and readers,

Troy Duster and Kathleen Gerson, guided the theory and research design. Thanks to Liann Kang, Wi Jo Kang, Nora Choi-Lee, Junghwa Hwang, Eunja Lee, and especially Jiwon Lee for research assistance. Research was supported in part by New York University, the Social Science Research Council's Committee on International Migration, Skidmore College, and Grinnell College. By recognizing this study with the Cheryl Allyn Miller award, Sociologists for Women in Society provided encouragement and intellectual community. I am grateful to Myra Marx Ferree, Mitchell Duneier, and members of the Feminist Seminar and Race and Ethnicity Seminar for inviting me to present and for responding to an earlier version of this article at the University of Wisconsin—Madison, 2001.

References

Anderson, Margaret, and Patricia Hill Collins. 2001. *Race, class, and gender: An anthology*. Belmont, CA: Wadsworth.

Baca Zinn, Maxine. 1989. Family, race, and poverty in the eighties. *Signs: Journal of Women in Culture and Society* 14:856–74.

Banks, Ingrid. 2000. *Hair matters: Beauty, power, and Black women's consciousness*. New York: New York University Press.

Banner, Lois. 1983. *American beauty*. New York: Alfred A. Knopf.

Bordo, Susan. 1993. *Unbearable weight: Feminism, Western culture and the body*. Berkeley: University of California Press.

Burawoy, Michael. 1991. *Ethnography unbound*. Berkeley: University of California Press.

Chapkis, Wendy. 1986. *Beauty secrets*. Boston: South End.

Cheng, Lucie, and Edna Bonacich. 1984. *Labor immigration under capitalism: Asian workers in the United States before World War 2*. Berkeley: University of California Press.

Frank, Arthur W. 1990. Bringing bodies back in: A decade review. *Theory, Culture, and Society* 7:131–62.

Gilroy, Paul. 1993. *The Black Atlantic: Modernity and double consciousness*. Cambridge, MA: Harvard University Press.

Gimlan, Debra. 1996. Pamela's place: Power and negotiation in the hair salon. *Gender & Society* 10:505–26.

Hall, Elaine J. 1993. Waitering/waitressing: Engendering the work of table servers. *Gender & Society* 7:329–46.

Hill Collins, Patricia. 1991. *Black feminist thought: Knowledge, consciousness, and the politics of empowerment*. New York: Routledge.

Hochschild, Arlie. 1983. *The managed heart: The commercialization of human feeling*. Berkeley: University of California Press.

hooks, bell. 1981. *Ain't I a woman: Black women and feminism*. Boston: South End.

——. 1990. *Black looks: Race and representation*. Boston: South End.

Hu-DeHart, Evelyn. 1999. *Across the Pacific: Asian Americans and globalization*. Philadelphia: Temple University Press.

Hurtado, Aida. 1989. Relating to privilege: Seducation and rejection in the subordination of white women and women of color. *Signs: Journal of Women in Culture and Society* 14:833–55.

Kang, Miliann. 1997. Manicuring race, gender, and class Service interactions in New York City Korean nail salons. *Race, Gender, and Class* 4:143–64.

Kerner Furman, Frida. 1997. *Facing the mirror: Older women and the beauty shop culture*. New York: Routledge.

Lee, Jee-Young Jennifer. 2002. *Civility in the city: Blacks, Jews, and Koreans in urban America*. Cambridge. MA: Harvard University Press.

Leidner, Robin. 1993. *Fast food, fast talk: Service work and the routinization of everyday life*. Berkeley: University of California Press.

——. 1999. Emotional labor in service work. *Annals of the American Academy of Political and Social Science* 561:81–95.

Lively, Kathryn. 2000. Reciprocal emotion management: Working together to maintain stratification in private law firms. *Work and Occupations* 27:32–63.

Macdonald, Cameron. 1996. Shadow mothers: Nannies, au pairs, and invisible work. In *Working in the service society*, edited by Cameron Lynne Macdonald and Carmen Sirianni. Philadelphia: Temple University Press.

Marx Ferree, Myra, and Elaine J. Hall. 1996. Rethinking stratification from a feminist perspective: Gender, race, and class in mainstream textbooks. *American Sociological Review* 61:929–50.

Nakano Glenn, Evelyn. 1992. From servitude to service work: Historical continuities in the racial division of paid reproductive labor. *Signs: Journal of Women in Culture and Society* 18:1–43.

——. 2002. *Unequal freedom: How race and gender shaped American citizenship and labor*. Cambridge, MA: Harvard University Press.

Nagan-Ling Chow, Esther. 1994. Asian American women at work. In *Women of color in U.S. society*, edited by Maxine Baca Zinn and Bonnie Dill Thornton. Philadelphia: Temple University Press.

Ong, Aihwa. 1987. *Spirits of resistance and capitalist discipline: Factory women in Malaysia*. Albany: State University of New York Press.

Pierce, Jennifer L. 1995. *Gender trials: Emotional lives in contemporary law firms*. Berkeley: University of California Press.

Rooks, Noliwe. 1996. *Hair rising: Beauty, culture, and African American women*. New Brunswick. NJ: Rutgers University Press.

Schmitt, Frederika E., and Patricia Yancey Martin. 1999. Unobtrusive mobilization by an institutionalized rape crisis center: "All we do comes from victims." *Gender & Society* 13:364–84.

Smith, Dorothy. 1987. *The everyday world as problematic: A feminist sociology*. Boston: Northeastern University Press.

Steinberg, Ronnie, and Deborah Figart. 1999. Emotional labor since *The Managed Heart. Annals of the American Academy of Political and Social Science* 561:8–26.

Wharton, Amy. 1999. The psychological consequences of emotional labor. *Annals of the American Academy of Political and Social Science* 561:158–77.

Wolf, Naomi. 1991. *The beauty myth: How images of beauty are used against women*. New York: William Morrow.

Feminism Amplified (1996)

Kim France

In this 1996 selection from New York Magazine, *Kim France presents modern female musicians as leaders in the contemporary women's movement. Drawing parallels between 90s rockers like Alanis Morissette and Melissa Etheridge and feminist leaders like Gloria Steinem, France suggests that music can be a powerful vehicle for feminist thought. The style of performers and their emotional lyrics capture young women's struggle with identity and their often ambivalent feelings about sexuality.*

"Feminism Amplified—Led by Alanis Morissette and Courtney Love, a whole new breed of angry, funny, complicated women rockers with attitudes is standing atop the pop-culture heap. They are the real daughters of Germaine Greer and Gloria Steinhem."

If the true test of social change is whether it's reflected in the marketplace, then the 1996 Grammy Awards were pretty compelling proof that feminism—at least a certain kind of feminism—is not dead at all. There was Mariah Carey—the type of standard-

---

issue cream puff most commonly rewarded at this type of event—looking increasingly miffed as 21-year-old Alanis Morissette bounded onstage to receive five awards. Morissette's debut album, *Jagged Little Pill,* has spent almost a year on the *Billboard* charts. Her breakout single, "You Oughta Know," is a growly diatribe notable largely for stalkerlike lyrics that detail how she will make an ex-boyfriend pay for his betrayal. She is a woman who clearly has some issues with men, and she is beloved across the land.

Morissette's got little credibility with critics, who point out that she got her start as a fluffy, Debbie Gibson-style singer in her native Canada; that *Jagged Little Pill* was produced by cheesemeister Glen Ballard (whose résumé also includes such ultracommercial acts as Paula Abdul and Wilson Phillips); that she represents little more than a corporate expropriation of the kind of female-rage music that had been all but ignored by the music industry and the public for years. Whatever her musical pedigree, Morissette has inarguably marked the arrival to the mass-market of an entirely new female-rocker persona. A woman moving so far beyond delicate, weepy declarations of loss and longing to express explicit rage in the context of a sexual relationship does not, traditionally, a Top 40 single make. Susan Faludi has often pointed out that while our culture admires the angry young man, who is perceived as heroic and sexy, it can't find anything but scorn for the angry young woman, who is seen as emasculating and bitter. That is, unless she is the kind of angry woman who, à la Camille Paglia, reserves her contempt for other women. Says Andrea Juno, editor of the forthcoming anthology *Angry Women in Rock*: "In the back of women's heads, they were gonna be delibidinized: You're unsexy, you won't be loved, and you won't get screwed."

But with the unrepentantly unscrewed Morissette of "You Oughta Know," a whole new palette of female emotions hitherto confined to college and alternative audiences has become acceptable—even admirable—to the lowest-common-denominator record buyers whose tastes are reflected by the Grammys and the *Billboard* charts. The Morissette persona harks back to *Fatal Attraction,* says Nina Gordon of the female-fronted band Veruca Salt, but with a difference: "Nobody identified with the Glenn Close character—she was clearly the villain—whereas people are like, 'You go girl!' to Alanis."

This does not mean that women everywhere can dance a happy jig to the end of the anti-feminist backlash. "But I think it probably reflects some growth in the consciousness of the audience, which translates into sales," says Mercury Records president and CEO Danny Goldberg, whose own label has done brisk business this year with the bluesy folk-rocker Joan Osborne. "There's no question that record companies, like any other business, are driven by business." Shirley Manson, lead singer of the band Garbage, puts it a bit more bluntly. "Alanis," she says, "has wiped the floor with the music industry, and I think that's phenomenally exciting. Because I know now that there's hundreds of A&R men running around trying to find the next Alanis."

There have been certain moments in the past few decades when rebellion has been expressed most acutely through popular music, when artists have provided more complicated, pointed answers to what's going on in the culture than self-styled thinkers. You don't "read" pop music the way you read *The Beauty Myth*, of course, but Liz Phair—by design and by example—happens to be a much more interesting feminist thinker than, say, Rebecca Walker. So it makes a lot of sense that the generation that came of age in the shadow of feminism—that both reaped its rewards and paid for its shortcomings—is using rock as a vehicle to make some powerful and nuanced statements about gender.

I was born in 1964, which is long enough ago for me to have formed a vague firsthand impression of suburban, middle-class seventies feminism. I remember consciousness-raising groups, and the few daring wives in the neighborhood who insisted on being called "*Ms.*" I remember a book that my mother's friend had given her husband as a joke: The title was *What I Understand about Women*, and all the pages were blank. What *I* didn't understand about women—who as far as I could tell spent their days playing tennis and carpooling—was what they needed liberation from, except possibly boredom.

I was way too young to get it, of course, and by the time I got to my lefty college, I was reading the Robin Morgan anthology *Sisterhood Is Powerful* and going to Take Back the Night marches. But after graduation, I dropped any pretense of being part of a movement. I went to a Women's Action Committee meeting once but was bored and annoyed by the main order of business, which was agreeing on the design of the T-shirt that the group would wear to the big pro-choice march on Washington. Outside of the collegiate petri dish, Big-F Feminism was revealed to be a pallid little affair, like American communism in the forties, that had little direct relevance to life as it is actually lived.

I didn't realize it at the time, but a lot of what I—and other young lapsed feminists—thought and felt was reflected in the complexity and contradictions of pop music. And after a while I understood that it didn't matter that my generation had no Gloria Steinems, Germaine Greers, or even Nancy Fridays or Erica Jongs. Because we have the Breeders, PJ Harvey, Liz Phair, Morissette, Courtney Love, Veruca Salt, Joan Osborne, Elastica, Tori Amos, and Tracy Bonham.

If these women constitute a movement, it's a helter-skelter one. The Breeders are pool-playing, beer-drinking tough chicks, and they make music that rocks in a hard and murky way and top it off with pretty harmonies. Courtney Love is all about anger, excess, obsession, confession, and great melodies. Polly Jean Harvey is restrained, theatrical, a diva. All of them are dealing with issues that feminism has traditionally claimed but without trafficking in constricting, sexless Women's Studies 101 dogma (and anyone who's ever puzzled over why the talent booked at pro-choice rallies is so consistently lame can attest to the necessity for that). Eschewing the usual angry platitudes, they give full symphonic vent to the particular pleasures and terrors of being female. This is very good news indeed to those of us who love Liz Phair's frisky, do-me lyrics and *still* think date-rape apologist Katie Roiphe is full of it.

"The future of rock belongs to women," Kurt Cobain predicted in 1994, and it is partly due to him that this is turning out to be true. He not only redefined the genre but also provided an updated guy-in-rock prototype. First of all, he wasn't a goon: He was inward, vulnerable—he sometimes wore dresses!—and he didn't seem to be in it for the money or the fame. And instead of dating models, Cobain married Courtney, showing himself to be the kind of man whose idea of masculinity involved loving a strong, opinionated woman, and carrying their baby in a Snugli.

"People like Kurt Cobain, Eddie Vedder, Michael Stipe, and Billy Corgan are very, very different as symbols of maleness for adolescents than Axl Rose or Steven Tyler and some of the other more muscle-bound, macho figures that immediately preceded them," says Danny Goldberg, who was a close friend of Cobain's. "And I think that created a sort of consciousness on the part of the audience. Kurt was very outspoken about the need for women to be respected, and he was passionate in his belief in Courtney. I think what happened in male rock and roll five years earlier broke up the macho hegemony over the rock part of the culture and gave the oxygen for some of the women to find an audience."

Nirvana also fired the final shot at that lumbering beast known as classic rock. No longer were radio listeners exclusively showered with music by way-past-their-prime peacocks like the Rolling Stones and Rod Stewart: Stations that shifted to modern-rock playlists were freed up to play bands like the Breeders or Hole—along with the now inevitable Soundgarden and Stone Temple Pilots—without worrying quite so much that listeners would switch stations once they heard female vocals. "Radio had always been a little afraid of that before," says Joan Osborne. "You know, they would play one Melissa Etheridge song in a four-hour slot and think that that was all they could do. Audiences I don't think ever really cared that much about those kind of distinctions. They just want something good. But it took a while for the programmers and people like that to catch up to that idea."

Furthermore, girls who loved music but had been too intimidated to pick up instruments—having somehow internalized the information that one had to possess some special boy gene in order to get behind a drum set—were inspired by Nirvana's punk-rock do-it-yourself ethos. "People who couldn't play anyway—boys—were doing it, and once that opened up, there was no reason not to be a girl and do it," says Phair, whose career started after a tape of songs she'd recorded in her bedroom scored her a record deal. The band Veruca Salt, which is fronted by Gordon and Louise Post, inspired a major-label bidding war in 1994 when the single "Seether"—from a cheaply produced album on a tiny Chicago label—started getting radio play and heavy MTV rotation. They eventually signed with Geffen, which rereleased the album and sold 700,000 copies. "It is much less expensive to make a record than do anything else in the media, other than fanzines, but that doesn't have the potential to plug into the mainstream culture the way a record can," says Goldberg. "It's not a moral thing, it's not an aesthetic thing, it's just an economic reality that that doorway exists in music. The nature of the medium is less top-down, it's more decentralized, it's more a vehicle for personal visions, and one of these visions has been women."

> "When we first started getting written about, people kept saying we were 'angry post-feminists,' and we were like, 'Hmm . . . I guess, whatever.' It was like, 'Oh, thank you for reducing me to a little pat phrase that really means nothing to me.'"
>
> —Nina Gordon of Veruca Salt

A few years ago, I met some rock-critic friends for dinner before going to see a show at Irving Plaza. It was around the time PJ Harvey—who is sort of the Maria Callas of rock—released her first record, and we were talking about a profile in which she'd said she didn't consider herself a feminist. As it happened, I had interviewed Miss America just that afternoon for a piece I was writing about how the pageant was trying to update its image, and we agreed that it is a strange world we live in, where Miss America will say she's a feminist and PJ Harvey won't.

Actually, though, it's not so ironic. Increasingly, feminism itself has become a meaningless term: You're now a victim feminist, a do-me feminist, a womanist. Then there are people like Miss America and swimsuit models who fashion themselves as feminists as a defense mechanism because the alternative would be too hard to countenance. Who can blame PJ Harvey for not wanting to sign herself up for that team?

Rock succeeds where textbook feminism has stalled for a variety of reasons. A huge question that sixties feminism failed to answer had to do with sex: Could a healthy heterosexual libido be reconciled with good movement politics? Were we tools of the patriarchy just because we enjoyed renting the occasional porno movie with our boyfriends? Or if we read *Vogue* and profoundly believed in the magic of Maybelline? The Big Thinkers famously recused themselves from such mundanities.

In the meantime, rock started providing ad hoc, provisional answers. The medium permitted contradiction; you could change your mind without having to justify it. And the more you broke the rules, the more likely you'd be rewarded. New images of strength and sexuality emerged out of the pop-cultural ooze. There was leather-clad, eyelinered Chrissie Hynde of the Pretenders, who beginning in the eighties projected a tough, almost-but-not-quite-bulletproof cool. "The thing I found so fascinating about Chrissie Hynde when I was growing up was that I found her incredibly sexy but she also embodied what I found attractive about men," says Shirley Manson of Garbage. "She wasn't wearing pretty skirts and being a victim and talking about love. She was standing at that microphone with her legs spread, she was playing her guitar, and she was the coolest sight I'd ever seen in my life. It was the first time I really connected with a woman like that."

Exene Cervenka of the Los Angeles band X made it cool to be a punk chick; Cyndi Lauper made it okay to be a goofy party girl. And Madonna made it okay to be entirely about sex and still be in control. Though the brazen, brassiere-by-Gaultier look she presented ten years ago looks quaint by today's standards, and her appeal never had much to do with her musicianship or songwriting abilities, it is amazing how many young rock women today proudly cite her as a role model.

The change Madonna wrought has been most visible on MTV. For the network's first decade, the women shown in videos tended to be either big-hair pop goddesses like Taylor Dayne, or heavy-metal video extras, or Apollonia humping Prince's thigh, or the zombie-ish Robert Palmer girls. "There are these sort of low moments—and there are plenty of them, believe me—at MTV," says Judy McGrath, the network's president and one of the handful of genuinely powerful women in an industry that is still largely run by men. She recalls a 1988 staff meeting during which a video for the song "Wild Thing"—in which Sam Kinison mudwrestled a bikini-clad Jessica Hahn—was screened. "The level of despair on the faces of the women was beyond description," she says. "We haven't gotten a video in the door in years that made you feel that way."

"There's a certain exhilaration now, even from the guys here, about all these women," McGrath continues. "There's a guy in the music-programming department who is like, you know, he's Mr. Rock. And he always says, 'This rocks!' And if you go into his office, he has a nine-foot picture of PJ Harvey plastered to his wall. I've seen a change in that regard. It isn't like the Steven Tyler Hall of Fame in here anymore."

McGrath believes that the fact that so many of these artists are giving voice to so many different perspectives on the female experience—and not doing it under the banner of revolution—is precisely why fans are so attracted to it. "I think this is a watershed moment," she says. "When I was growing up, I knew the difference between Betty Friedan and Gloria Steinem and so on, and you had to line up in one of those camps or you weren't, you know, in the game. And now I think there are so many voices."

If a woman is acting dolled up and sexy in a video these days, chances are it's her own. But even when she's not dolled up and sexy, it's likely that she will be singing about sex in a way women have never sung about sex before. In one song, Elastica's Justine Frischmann, sounding very male, bemoans the guy who can't get it up when she's in the mood. Shirley Manson of Garbage vamped around the stage at Roseland with a pink feather puff attached to the mike stand at precisely crotch level. Tori Amos is famous for straddling the piano bench suggestively while she plays.

Not everyone is hailing this as tremendous social progress. "There was some article in one of the British magazines about one of our shows saying that we set feminism back ten years, because Louise [Post] applied lipstick onstage," says Veruca Salt's Gordon. "And I remember thinking, 'Who is this woman?'—it was a woman who wrote the article—'Who is this woman who thinks it's important to point that out?'"

She was probably a woman very much like Exene Cervenka, who doesn't understand why PJ Harvey performs in evening gowns, or why Liz Phair poses for pictures wearing nothing but a slip dress. "I kind of call it 'Rod Stewart Feminism,'" she says. "It's kind of the same mentality, which is if it's okay for guys to do it, it's okay for girls to do it. Tori Amos straddling a piano bench—is that empowering women or is that *Penthouse*-ing women? I don't know."

It's debatable whether men see this sexuality as edifying rather than merely hot. Writing about Maureen Dowd in *The New Yorker* a few weeks ago, James Wolcott bemoaned "one of the odd aftereffects of feminism . . . that it seems to have softened and juvenilized so much of women's journalistic swagger." He went on to cite other areas where he perceived the phenomenon to be occurring: "In pop music, a kooky singer-songwriter chick seems to surface every six months to be photographed barefoot for *Spin*." Wolcott, presumably, would prefer they pose in sackcloth and ashes or, alternatively, in nothing at all. Would that clear up the confusion?

Of course, women have been all over *Spin* recently, generally shod. Only one of the *Spin* cover girls, Tori Amos, could be considered kooky—she named her most recent album after the goddess of creation and destruction and has said she was a Viking in another life. But she has also never shied away from hard topics, writing smart, cant-free songs that deal with rape and the church's oppression of women. "Tori's no one to be messed or trifled with," says Phair, whose music could not possibly be more different from hers. "She's a goddess."

Amos is a minister's daughter—she's got a song, "Icicle," about being upstairs in her bedroom masturbating while the rest of the family is in the living room praying. The struggle to be at home with her sexuality has been too hard-won for her to care what anyone thinks about it. "Somebody made this really funny comment about me that I just giggled over: 'You can't fight the patriarchy in a tube top,'" she says. "So I went, 'Okay, so why don't I wait for that writer to fax me on what I should wear to fight the patriarchy?' To me, when you cut yourself off—mentally, emotionally, or physically—then you've just been dominated by somebody else's thought."

Joan Osborne, 33, is one of the few female rockers who go out of their way to call themselves feminists. She aligns herself with mainstream feminist causes like NARAL, and performed on *Saturday Night Live* in a CHOICE T-shirt. She's the most middle-of-the-road, VH-1–friendly artist of the group, and the sexuality she projects onstage and in videos is subdued. "Feminism as I always understood it—and I was somebody who read a lot of Germaine Greer and stuff like that—part of the manifesto was to find a way for women to reclaim their own sexuality, to not only be the object of male desire but discover what their own desire was about, and claim that for themselves," she says. "And of course, an ingredient of rock has always been this sexual display, and women have been more and more finding out a way that they can do that. Instead of just being the chick in the spandex with the teased-up hair that all the guys want to screw, it's more like, 'Yeah, this is how I'm going to project my sexuality, and these are my desires.'"

It's amazing how threatening that can still be to men. Liz Phair's first album was a godsend to female fans because it communicated so explicitly the ambivalent knot of feelings that coexist with sexual desire. That this clean-scrubbed college graduate from Winnetka could think as dirty as any man floored a lot of people. "I heard a lot of men saying that they were listening to my album because someone told them they should, then one day they suddenly heard the words and it flipped them out," says Phair. "They all expressed this powerful feeling of being both fired at and caught, like, for being what they are. And the women were like, 'Well, I heard the words from the beginning, and they made perfect sense to me.'" She says she was shocked that men were shocked. "For me what it highlighted was how very rarely they had felt that before. Because there wasn't anything that damning. And it just made me realize that women hadn't nailed them before."

Part of Liz Phair's appeal is how heady her lyrics are. She and many of the other women in rock right now are quite self-evidently overqualified for the job intellectually—though alternative rock these days seems increasingly to be performed by and for slumming grad students—and their songs have a truth-telling complexity and confidence that was hardly available on vinyl twenty years ago. Joni Mitchell was wonderful, but she has comparatively little to say to the proverbial just-dumped 16-year-old that Liz Phair cannot say better. Today's teenage girls simply have it over their elders in the tell-it-sister department. "I didn't have high self-esteem when I was a teenager," Morissette told the *New York Times*. "I used to think I was alone in that. Oh, man, I wish I had me to listen to when I was 14."

One of the best things about going to see PJ Harvey or Hole or Elastica or Veruca Salt is witnessing the hordes of teenage girls who force their way into the mosh pit. The fact that they're not climbing on their boyfriends' shoulders and whipping off their halter tops—but rocking out to a woman wailing on her guitar—changes everything. "It's like having someone in a movie that you can follow," says Phair. "It's like having a character you can live through. And for so long, they didn't. You go to a rock show because you want the guy to stare at you. You want to be noticed and singled out as an object. And this time, they are watching someone and pretending they are *her*. And that's a very good experience, I think, for the self-esteem of the young American girl."

Those looking for role models, however, will be as disappointed as basketball fans who wish Dennis Rodman would stop showing his butt to the kids. But since when have pop musicians had to be role models? (At precisely the same moment as women and rap stars started selling records, it would appear.) The personal has always made for better rock music than the straightforwardly political has, and that's a lesson these artists have taken to heart. "I don't want to be anyone's revolutionary," says Liz Phair. "I don't want to lead a movement. I mean, it turns me off so much. I never saw music as a way—and a lot of people do, especially riot grrrls—to make change happen. I never, ever saw it that way. I still don't. Anyone with any kind of sensitivity beyond their general age group knows you can't tidy life up like that."

No one is less tidy than Courtney Love. Experiencing Love, onstage or on CD, in the gossip pages or on the Internet (where, most recently, she has bitterly railed against Morissette), one can't help but notice that the line between her art and her life is hopelessly blurred. The raw, exposed manner in which she makes her music and conducts her affairs has made her the most loved/loathed figure in rock today. "I'm a huge admirer of Courtney Love," says Garbage's Manson. "She's vulnerable and I warm to that. She's incredibly intelligent and incredibly articulate and she's not afraid to open her mouth up and attack anybody and anything. She's neither black nor white and that's why, I think, she irritates a lot of people, but that's what I find endearing about her."

Cervenka, predictably, is not as impressed. "People who are pathologically insane don't interest me," she says. "Courtney has nothing to do with reality as far as I'm concerned. You've got to talk about people who are sober, who can raise their children, and who are not involved in all kinds of scandalous tabloid-style gimmicks in order to become famous."

Still, as wild as she's been, Courtney certainly hasn't done anything that would have raised eyebrows backstage at a Led Zeppelin show, and *those* guys just got inducted into the Rock and Roll Hall of Fame. Plus, she's a whole lot more interesting than Robert Plant. Love is a walking Rorschach test. Either a liberating angel or the Yoko Ono of alternative rock, she has quite improbably become an embodiment of all that is interesting, exciting, and depressing about being a young woman now. (Teenage boys in online chat groups, grossed out by her schizo aggressiveness and anti-pinup mien, often suggest that she has no right to be alive.)

Love is obviously well aware of her role. She has said that she was moved to name her band Hole by a line from Euripides' *Medea*: "There's a hole that pierces right through me." She once told a writer from *Spin* the band's name also refers to something her mother, a hippie feminist of the *Our Bodies, Ourselves* era, used to say: "You can't walk around with a big hole inside yourself."

Things are never that simple in Love-land. The song "Asking for It" was inspired, she told an interviewer, by the experience of stage-diving into the crowd at a show: "Suddenly, it was like my dress was being torn off me, my underwear was being torn off me, people were putting their fingers inside of me and grabbing my breasts really hard." The worst thing, she went on, was seeing a photograph of herself later "and I had a big smile on my face like I was pretending it wasn't happening. I can't compare it to rape because it isn't the same. But in a way it was. I was raped by an audience—figuratively, literally, and yet, was I asking for it?" The song is a more nuanced treatment than any ten essays about date rape of the way women can feel torn between the desire to be driven by their sexuality and the horror that the desire might ultimately degrade or even destroy them.

Love has also taken prototypically male gestures, transformed them into female ones, and made them powerful again and new. When a male artist, for instance, props his leg up on a monitor and launches into a guitar solo these days, he looks stupid—like he's playing in a Foghat cover band at some Bleecker Street tourist club. But when Love, wearing torn stockings, props a stiletto-heeled leg up on a monitor, the entire gesture changes—it is undeniably theatrical and brazen, but it's certainly interesting.

I share this theory of mine with Phair, who wonders whether I'm not getting a little carried away. "There is something that is rock itself, and it is an attitude that is genderless, and it is what is appealing about rock," she says. When Courtney does that thing with the monitor, she continues, "that's her just being infected with this thing called Rock. But probably I'm wrong, and she actually watched a million guys do that, sticking your foot up there, and she is saying, 'Fuck you, I'm the front guy; deal with my frontalness.'"

Phair pauses, then sighs, "I'm wondering, would Courtney Love really think about doing that gesture, or is it just like a way to really, you know, crunch into her guitar? . . . I'll bet she's just like, 'Why shouldn't I be right up at the edge of the stage?' She's just free in her mind. It's not so much that she has something. It's that she doesn't have something, which is the fear that traditionally keeps women in their place."

It's tempting, sometimes, to think that women are being allowed this moment only because we have seen every conceivable rock pose many times over from men, and the one thing that really feels fresh right now is a chick jabbing her stiletto heel into a monitor. And for all of their bravado, none of the artists I spoke to felt like a fundamental transformation had occurred; they thought the odds were about even that next year the charts will be ruled by guys again. "The industry still views bands fronted by women as novelties," says Nina Gordon. "It seems like to me that right now women are entitled to just one shining moment."

But Cervenka, the progressive-rock darling of 1982, was by far the most cold-eyed. "There's always some woman who is the new angry young woman," she said. "It was me, and it was someone else, and it was someone else. But as far as selling millions and millions of records, to me that's no validation whatsoever. It means nothing. If it means anything to me, it means it's *not* okay to be an angry young woman—it's cute to be an angry young woman; it's trendy to be an angry young woman." But is Love-ism really just the flavor of the month?

"I want to be the girl with the most cake," she sings on "Doll Parts." Women love that line: it's all about authorizing desire, and about winning, which remain as tricky as ever for a woman. And when I start thinking that *Ms.* magazine-era feminism has nothing to do with my life, I think about another person who wanted to be the girl with the most cake—Sylvia Plath's Esther, in *The Bell Jar*. There's that passage where she sees all of her options—wife and mother, famous writer, magazine editor—as figs on a tree. But she can choose only one, and she can't make up her mind, and the figs all wither and die.

Women, of course, have it better than they did when Plath wrote that book in 1963, but how much has really changed? You could argue that our culture still isn't rewarding women who try to stake out new territory. But Courtney Love is an object lesson in the punishments and rewards that come to a woman who tries. "Courtney's got the kind of ambition most people would associate with a male rock star," says Justine Frischmann. "One thing you have to admire her for is that she refuses—just refuses—to be overlooked in any way."

QUESTIONS

1. Describe France's writing style. Does her writing enhance, or distract from, her message in this essay? Who is her intended audience?
2. Who are some of the female rockers presented in this essay? How do their lyrics express feminist ideals, according to France? How do the rockers themselves define their

role in the women's movement? Do they consider themselves feminists?

3. How does the expression of feminist ideals through music differ from other modes of feminist expression? What advantages does music offer as a vehicle for the women's movement? What disadvantages does it pose?

4. What role does sexuality play in the performances and lyrics of female rockers? Are the messages about sexuality empowering for women? Disempowering? What arguments does France introduce on both sides of this issue?

Herstory of Women's Liberation and Feminism

DECLARATION OF SENTIMENTS AND RESOLUTIONS (1848)

The Seneca Falls Women's Rights Convention of 1848

This document, drawn in 1848, was a product of the first meeting on women's rights in the United States. Written in a style similar to the Declaration of Independence, *the document presents the many injustices women faced in the nineteenth century. From a contemporary viewpoint, the document provides important historical information on the origins of social movements seeking improvement in the quality of women's lives.*

When, in the course of human events, it becomes necessary for one portion of the family of man to assume among the people of the earth a position different from that which they have hitherto occupied, but one to which the laws of nature and of nature's God entitle them, a decent respect to the opinions of mankind requires that they should declare the causes that impel them to such a course.

"Declaration of Sentiments and Resolutions," from The Seneca Falls Women's Rights Convention of 1848.

We hold these truths to be self-evident: that all men and women are created equal; that they are endowed by their Creator with certain inalienable rights; that among these are life, liberty, and the pursuit of happiness; that to secure these rights governments are instituted, deriving their just powers from the consent of the governed. Whenever any form of government becomes destructive of these ends, it is the right of those who suffer from it to refuse allegiance to it, and to insist upon the institution of a new government, laying its foundation on such principles, and organizing its powers in such form, as to them shall seem most likely to effect their safety and happiness. Prudence, indeed, will dictate that governments long established should not be changed for light and transient causes; and accordingly all experience hath shown that mankind are more disposed to suffer, while evils are sufferable, than to right themselves by abolishing the forms to which they were accustomed. But when a long train of abuses and usurpations, pursuing invariably the same object evinces a design to reduce them under absolute despotism, it is their duty to throw off such government, and to provide new guards for their future security. Such has been the patient sufferance of the women under this government, and such is now the necessity which constrains them to demand the equal station to which they are entitled.

The history of mankind is a history of repeated injuries and usurpations on the part of man toward woman, having in direct object the establishment of an absolute tyranny over her. To prove this, let facts be submitted to a candid world.

He has never permitted her to exercise her inalienable right to the elective franchise.

He has compelled her to submit to laws, in the formation of which she had no voice.

He has withheld from her rights which are given to the most ignorant and degraded men—both natives and foreigners.

Having deprived her of this first right of a citizen, the elective franchise, thereby leaving her without representation in the halls of legislation, he has oppressed her on all sides.

He has made her, if married, in the eye of the law, civilly dead.

He has taken from her all right in property, even to the wages she earns.

He has made her, morally, an irresponsible being, as she can commit many crimes with impunity, provided they be done in the presence of her husband. In the covenant of marriage, she is compelled to promise obedience to her husband, he becoming, to all intents and purposes, her master—the law giving him power to deprive her of her liberty, and to administer chastisement.

He has so framed the laws of divorce, as to what shall be the proper causes, and in case of separation, to whom the guardianship of the children shall be given, as to be wholly regardless of the happiness of women—the law, in all cases, going upon a false supposition of the supremacy of man, and giving all power into his hands.

After depriving her of all rights as a married woman, if single, and the owner of property, he has taxed her to support a government which recognizes her only when her property can be made profitable to it.

He has monopolized nearly all the profitable employments, and from those she is permitted to follow, she receives but a scanty remuneration. He closes against her all the avenues to wealth and distinction which he considers most honorable to himself. As a teacher of theology, medicine, or law, she is not known.

He has denied her the facilities for obtaining a thorough education, all colleges being closed against her.

He allows her in Church, as well as State, but a subordinate position, claiming Apostolic authority for her exclusion from the ministry, and, with some exceptions, from any public participation in the affairs of the Church.

He has created a false public sentiment by giving to the world a different code of morals for men and women, by which moral delinquencies which exclude women from society, are not only tolerated, but deemed of little account in man.

He has usurped the prerogative of Jehovah himself, claiming it as his right to assign for her a sphere of action, when that belongs to her conscience and to her God.

He has endeavored, in every way that he could, to destroy her confidence in her own powers, to lessen her self-respect, and to make her willing to lead a dependent and abject life.

Now, in view of this entire disfranchisement of one-half the people of this country, their social and religious degradation—in view of the unjust laws above mentioned, and because women do feel themselves aggrieved, oppressed, and fraudulently deprived of their most sacred rights, we insist that they have immediate admission to all the rights and privileges which belong to them as citizens of the United States.

In entering upon the great work before us, we anticipate no small amount of misconception, misrepresentation, and ridicule; but we shall use every instrumentality within our power to effect our object. We shall employ agents, circulate tracts, petition the State and National legislatures, and endeavor to enlist the pulpit and the press in our behalf. We hope this Convention will be followed by a series of Conventions embracing every part of the country.

Resolutions

WHEREAS, The great precept of nature is conceded to be, that "man shall pursue his own true and substantial happiness." Blackstone in his Commentaries remarks, that this law of Nature being coeval with mankind, and dictated by God himself, is of course superior in obligation to any other. It is binding over all the globe, in all countries and at all times; no human laws are of any validity if contrary to this, and such of them as are valid, derive all their force, and all their validity, and all their authority, mediately and immediately, from this original; therefore,

Resolved, That such laws as conflict, in any way, with the true and substantial happiness of woman, are contrary to the great precept of nature and of no validity, for this is "superior in obligation to any other."

Resolved, That all laws which prevent woman from occupying such a station in society as her conscience shall dictate, or which place her in a position inferior to that of man, are contrary to the great precept of nature, and therefore of no force or authority.

Resolved, That woman is man's equal—was intended to be so by the Creator, and the highest good of the race demands that she should be recognized as such.

Resolved, That the women of this country ought to be enlightened in regard to the laws under which they live, that they may no longer publish their degradation by declaring themselves satisfied with their present position, nor their ignorance, by asserting that they have all the rights they want.

Resolved, That inasmuch as man, while claiming for himself intellectual superiority, does accord to woman moral superiority, it is pre-eminently his duty to encourage her to speak and teach, as she has an opportunity, in all religious assemblies.

Resolved, That the same amount of virtue, delicacy, and refinement of behavior that is required of woman in the social state, should also be required of man, and the same transgressions should be visited with equal severity on both man and woman.

Resolved, That the objection of indelicacy and impropriety, which is so often brought against woman when she addresses a public audience, comes with a very ill-grace from those who encourage, by their attendance, her appearance on the stage, in the concert, or in feats of the circus.

Resolved, That woman has too long rested satisfied in the circumscribed limits which corrupt customs and a perverted application of the Scriptures have marked out for her, and that it is time she should move in the enlarged sphere which her great Creator has assigned her.

Resolved, That it is the duty of the women of this country to secure to themselves their sacred right to the elective franchise.

Resolved, That the equality of human rights results necessarily from the fact of the identity of the race in capabilities and responsibilities.

Resolved, therefore, That, being invested by the Creator with the same capabilities, and the same consciousness of responsibility for their exercise, it is demonstrably the right and duty of woman, equally with man, to promote every righteous cause by every righteous means; and especially in regard to the great subjects of morals and religion, it is self-evidently her right to participate with her brother in teaching them, both in private and in public, by writing and by speaking, by any instrumentalities proper to be used, and in any assemblies proper to be held; and this being a self-evident truth growing out of the divinely implanted principles of human nature, any custom or authority adverse to it, whether modern or wearing the hoary sanction of antiquity, is to be regarded as a self-evident falsehood, and at war with mankind.

[At the last session Lucretia Mott offered and spoke to the following resolution:]

Resolved, That the speedy success of our cause depends upon the zealous and untiring efforts of both men and women, for the overthrow of the monopoly of the pulpit, and for the securing to woman an equal participation with men in the various trades, professions, and commerce.

Questions

1. Explain the significance of the author's decision to use the same format as the Declaration of Independence in this document. What might this choice of format have accomplished for women in a nineteenth century context? What were the goals of the authors? What might have been the response to the document?
2. What echoes from the Seneca Falls document do you hear in contemporary feminist concerns? What contemporary concerns were not relevant for inclusion in the document at that time? What social changes might account for both the echoes and the emergence of other concerns today?
3. Who does "women" refer to in this document? What language from the text leads you to these conclusions?
4. Why is this an important document in the history of the women's movement?

Ain't I a Woman? (1851)

Sojourner Truth

This eloquent 1851 address was given by Sojourner Truth at a women's convention in Akron, Ohio, and recorded by Frances Gage almost ten years later. Born into slavery around 1795, Truth spent years traveling and speaking on behalf of abolitionism and women's rights after she gained her freedom in 1827. Truth's extemporaneous speech responds to women's rights opponents of the Akron convention, and also reveals the inadequacy of the nineteenth century ideals like the "Cult of True Womanhood" to account for all women's experiences.

Well, children, where there is so much racket there must be something out of kilter. I think that 'twixt the negroes of the South and the women of the North, all talking about rights, the white men will be in a fix pretty soon. But what's all this here talking about?

That man over there says that women need to be helped into carriages, and lifted over ditches, and to have the best place everywhere. Nobody ever helps me into carriages, or over mud-puddles, or gives me any best place! An ain't I a woman? Look at me! Look at my arm! I have ploughed and planted, and gathered into barns, and no man could head me! And ain't I a woman? I could work as much and eat as much as a man—when I could get it— and bear the lash as well! And ain't I a woman? I have borne thirteen children, and seen them most all sold off to slavery, and when I cried out with my mother's grief, none but Jesus heard me! And ain't I a woman?

Then they talk about this thing in the head; what's this they call it? [Intellect, someone whispers.] That's it, honey. What's that got to do with women's rights or negro's rights? If my cup won't hold but a pint, and yours holds a quart, wouldn't you be mean not to let me have my little half-measure full?

Then that little man in black there, he says women can't have as much rights as men, 'cause Christ wasn't a woman! Where did your Christ come from? Where did your Christ come from? From God and a woman! Man had nothing to do with Him.

If the first woman God ever made was strong enough to turn the world upside down all alone, these women together ought to be able to turn it back, and get it right side up again! And now they is asking to do it, the men better let them.

Obliged to you for hearing me, and now old Sojourner ain't got nothing more to say.

Questions

1. What is Truth trying to accomplish in this speech? What is her speaking style? What arguments does she use to combat women's rights opponents? What sources does she draw from to make her points?

2. What might have been the audience reaction to Truth's speech? How would the speech have helped women's rights activists? How might it have hindered them?

3. How does Truth's speech contradict the "Cult of True Womanhood" as a feminine ideal? What issues does she introduce about race and class?

4. How does this address fit into the nineteenth century women's movement? Why does it remain a touchstone for twentieth century feminists?

National Organization for Women Statement of Purpose (1966) and Bill of Rights (1968)

In the 1960s a new wave of feminism surged through the United States. Underlying that development were broad social and economic forces, including changes in women's employment, education and childbearing patterns. More immediately, the resurgence of feminism owed much to the civil rights movement, which provided examples of activism and legal precedents while creating a political climate favorable to the discussion of rights. A broad range of women were drawn to feminism in the late 1960s and 1970s, and the issues they addressed included legal equality, reproductive freedom, violence against women, poverty among women, lesbian rights, pornography, and women in the military.

The National Organization for Women, founded in 1966, represented the first organizational manifestation of what came to be called the liberal or main-

stream branch of feminism. As feminism developed, its radical and moderate branches became less distinct, and NOW expanded its agenda to include broader and deeper changes in society. Within just two years after its founding, NOW embraced two new goals, both of which would become high priorities in the 1970s. The organization's statement of purpose and bill of rights, which follow, indicate the original issues that stirred women to feminism as well as how rapidly its agenda expanded.

NOW Statement of Purpose 1966

We, men and women who hereby constitute ourselves as the National Organization for Women, believe that the time has come for a new movement toward true equality for all women in America, and toward a fully equal partnership of the sexes, as part of the world-wide revolution of human rights now taking place within and beyond our national borders.

The purpose of NOW is to take action to bring women into full participation in the mainstream of American society now, exercising all the privileges and responsibilities thereof in truly equal partnership with men.

We believe the time has come to move beyond the abstract argument, discussion and symposia over the status and special nature of women which has raged in America in recent years; the time has come to confront, with concrete action, the conditions that now prevent women from enjoying the equality of opportunity and freedom of choice which is their right as individual Americans, and as human beings.

NOW is dedicated to the proposition that women first and foremost are human beings, who, like all other people in our society, must have the chance to develop their fullest human potential. We believe that women can achieve such equality only by accepting to the full the challenges and responsibilities they share with all other people in our society, as part of the decision-making mainstream of American political, economic and social life.

We organize to initiate or support action, nationally or in any part of this nation, by individuals or organizations, to break through the silken curtain of prejudice and discrimination against women in government, industry, the professions, the churches, the political parties, the judiciary, the labor unions, in education, science, medicine, law, religion and every other field of importance in American society.

Enormous changes taking place in our society make it both possible and urgently necessary to advance the unfinished revolution of women toward true equality, now. With a life span lengthened to nearly seventy-five years, it is no longer either necessary or possible for women to devote the greater part of their lives to child rearing; yet childbearing and rearing—which continues to be a most important part of most women's lives—is still used to justify barring women from equal professional and economic participation and advance.

Today's technology has reduced most of the productive chores which women once performed in the home and in mass production industries based upon routine unskilled labor. This same technology has virtually eliminated the quality of muscular strength as a criterion for filling most jobs, while intensifying American industry's need for creative intelligence. In view of this new industrial revolution created by automation in the mid-twentieth century, women can and must participate in old and new fields of society in full equality—or become permanent outsiders.

Despite all the talk about the status of American women in recent years, the actual position of women in the United States has declined, and is declining, to an alarming degree throughout the 1950s and 1960s. Although 46.4 percent of all American women between the ages of eighteen and sixty-five now work outside the home, the overwhelming majority—75 percent—are in routine clerical, sales, or factory jobs, or they are household workers, cleaning women, hospital attendants. About two-thirds of Negro women workers are in the lowest paid service occupations. Working women are becoming increasingly—not less—concentrated on the bottom of the job ladder. As a consequence, full-time women workers today earn on the average only 60 percent of what men earn, and that wage gap has been increasing over the past twenty-five years in every major industry group. In 1964, of all women with a yearly income, 89 percent earned under $5,000 a year; half of all full-time year-round women workers earned less than $3,690; only 1.4 percent of full-time year-round women workers had an annual income of $10,000 or more.

Further, with higher education increasingly essential in today's society, too few women are entering and finishing college or going on to graduate or professional school. Today women earn only one in three of the B.A.'s and M.A.'s granted, and one in ten of the Ph.D.'s.

In all the professions considered of importance to society, and in the executive ranks of industry and government, women are losing ground. Where they are present it is only a token handful. Women comprise less than 1 percent of federal judges; less than 4 percent of all lawyers; 7 percent of doctors. Yet women represent 53 percent of the U.S. population. And increasingly men are replacing women in the top positions in secondary and elementary schools, in social work, and in libraries—once thought to be women's fields.

Official pronouncements of the advance in the status of women hide not only the reality of this dangerous decline, but the fact that nothing is being done to stop it. The excellent reports of the President's Commission on the Status of Women and of the state commissions have not been fully implemented. Such commissions have power only to advise. They have no power to enforce their recommendations, nor have they the freedom to organize American women and men to press for action on them. The reports of these commissions have, however, created a basis upon which it is now possible to build.

Discrimination in employment on the basis of sex is now prohibited by federal law, in Title VII of the Civil Rights Act of 1964. But although nearly one-third of the cases brought before the Equal Employment Opportunity Commission during the first year dealt with sex discrimination and the proportion is increasing dramatically, the commission has not made clear its intention to enforce the law with the same seriousness on behalf of women as of other victims of discrimination. Many of these cases were

Negro women, who are the victims of the double discrimination of race and sex. Until now, too few women's organizations and official spokesmen have been willing to speak out against these dangers facing women. Too many women have been restrained by the fear of being called "feminist."

There is no civil rights movement to speak for women, as there has been for Negroes and other victims of discrimination. The National Organization for Women must therefore begin to speak.

WE BELIEVE that the power of American law, and the protection guaranteed by the U.S. Constitution to the civil rights of all individuals, must be effectively applied and enforced to isolate and remove patterns of sex discrimination, to ensure equality of opportunity in employment and education, and equality of civil and political rights and responsibilities on behalf of women, as well as for Negroes and other deprived groups.

We realize that women's problems are linked to many broader questions of social justice; their solution will require concerted action by many groups. Therefore, convinced that human rights for all are indivisible, we expect to give active support to the common cause of equal rights for all those who suffer discrimination and deprivation, and we call upon other organizations committed to such goals to support our efforts toward equality for women.

WE DO NOT ACCEPT the token appointment of a few women to high level positions in government and industry as a substitute for a serious continuing effort to recruit and advance women according to their individual abilities. To this end, we urge American government and industry to mobilize the same resources of ingenuity and command with which they have solved problems of far greater difficulty than those now impeding the progress of women.

WE BELIEVE that this nation has a capacity at least as great as other nations, to innovate new social institutions which will enable women to enjoy true equality of opportunity and responsibility in society, without conflict with their responsibilities as mothers and homemakers. In such innovations, America does not lead the Western world, but lags by decades behind many European countries. We do not accept the traditional assumption that a woman has to choose between marriage and motherhood, on the one hand, and serious participation in industry or the professions on the other. We question the present expectation that all normal women will retire from job or profession for ten or fifteen years, to devote their full time to raising children, only to reenter the job market at a relatively minor level. This in itself is a deterrent to the aspirations of women, to their acceptance into management or professional training courses, and to the very possibility of equality of opportunity or real choice, for all but a few women. Above all, we reject the assumption that these problems are the unique responsibility of each individual woman, rather than a basic social dilemma which society must solve. True equality of opportunity and freedom of choice for women requires such practical and possible innovations as a nationwide network of child-care centers, which will make it unnecessary for women to retire completely from society until their children are grown, and national programs to provide retraining for women who have chosen to care for their own children full time.

WE BELIEVE that it is as essential for every girl to be educated to her full potential of human ability as it is for every boy—with the knowledge that such education is the key to effective participation in today's economy and that, for a girl as for a boy, education can only be serious where there is expectation that it will be used in society. We believe that American educators are capable of devising means of imparting such expectations to girl students. Moreover, we consider the decline in the proportion of women receiving higher and professional education to be evidence of discrimination. This discrimination may take the form of quotas against the admission of women to colleges and professional schools; lack of encouragement by parents, counselors and educators; denial of loans or fellowships; or the traditional or arbitrary procedures in graduate and professional training geared in terms of men, which inadvertently discriminate against women. We believe that the same serious attention must be given to high school dropouts who are girls as to boys.

WE REJECT the current assumptions that a man must carry the sole burden of supporting himself, his wife, and family, and that a woman is automatically entitled to lifelong support by a man upon her marriage, or that marriage, home and family are primarily woman's world and responsibility—hers to dominate, his to support. We believe that a true partnership between the sexes demands a different concept of marriage, an equitable sharing of the responsibilities of home and children and of the economic burdens of their support. We believe that proper recognition should be given to the economic and social value of homemaking and child care. To these ends, we will seek to open a reexamination of laws and mores governing marriage and divorce, for we believe that the current state of "half-equality" between the sexes discriminates against both men and women, and is the cause of much unnecessary hostility between the sexes.

WE BELIEVE that women must now exercise their political rights and responsibilities as American citizens. They must refuse to be segregated on the basis of sex into separate-and-not-equal ladies' auxiliaries in the political parties, and they must demand representation according to their numbers in the regularly constituted party committees—at local, state, and national levels—and in the informal power structure, participating fully in the selection of candidates and political decision-making, and running for office themselves.

IN THE INTERESTS OF THE HUMAN DIGNITY OF WOMEN, we will protest and endeavor to change the false image of women now prevalent in the mass media, and in the texts, ceremonies, laws, and practices of our major social institutions. Such images perpetuate contempt for women by society and by women for themselves. We are similarly opposed to all policies and practices—in church, state, college, factory, or office—which, in the guise of protectiveness, not only deny opportunities but also foster in women self-denigration, dependence, and evasion of responsibility, undermine their confidence in their own abilities and foster contempt for women.

NOW WILL HOLD ITSELF INDEPENDENT OF ANY POLITICAL PARTY in order to mobilize the political power of all women and men intent on our goals. We will strive to ensure that no party, candidate, President, senator, governor, congressman, or any public official who betrays or ignores the principle of full equality between the sexes is elected or appointed to office. If it is necessary to mobilize the votes of men and women who believe in our cause, in order to win for women the final right to be fully free and equal human beings, we so commit ourselves.

WE BELIEVE THAT women will do most to create a new image of women by *acting* now, and by speaking out in behalf of their own equality, freedom, and human dignity—not in pleas for special privilege, nor in enmity toward men, who are also victims of the current half-equality between the sexes—but in an active, self-respecting partnership with men. By so doing, women will develop confidence in their own ability to determine actively, in partnership with men, the conditions of their life, their choices, their future and their society.

NOW Bill of Rights 1968

I Equal Rights Constitutional Amendment

II Enforce Law Banning Sex Discrimination in Employment

III Maternity Leave Rights in Employment and in Social Security Benefits

IV Tax Deduction for Home and Child Care Expenses for Working Parents

V Child Care Centers

VI Equal and Unsegregated Education

VII Equal Job Training Opportunities and Allowances for Women in Poverty

VIII The Right of Women to Control Their Reproductive Lives

WE DEMAND:

I. That the United States Congress immediately pass the Equal Rights Amendment to the constitution to provide that "Equality of rights under the law shall not be denied or abridged by the United States or by any State on account of sex," and that such then be immediately ratified by the several States.

II. That equal employment opportunity be guaranteed to all women, as well as men, by insisting that the Equal Employment Opportunity Commission enforces the prohibitions against sex discrimination in employment under Title VII

"1968—National Organization for Women Bill of Rights," reprinted by permission of the National Organization for Women.

of the Civil Rights Act of 1964 with the same vigor as it enforces the prohibitions against racial discrimination.

III. That women be protected by law to ensure their rights to return to their jobs within a reasonable time after childbirth without loss of seniority or other accrued benefits, and be paid maternity leave as a form of social security and/or employee benefit.

IV. Immediate revision of tax laws to permit the deduction of home and child care expenses for working parents.

V. That child care facilities be established by law on the same basis as parks, libraries, and public schools, adequate to the needs of children from the pre-school years through adolescence, as a community resource to be used by all citizens from all income levels.

VI. That the right of women to be educated to their full potential equally with men be secured by Federal and State Legislation, eliminating all discrimination and segregation by sex, written and unwritten, at all levels of education, including colleges, graduate and professional schools, loans and fellowships, and Federal and State training programs such as the Job Corps.

VII. The right of women in poverty to secure job training, housing and family allowances on equal terms with men, but without prejudice to a parent's right to remain at home to care for his or her children; revision of welfare legislation and poverty programs which deny women dignity, privacy and self-respect.

VIII. The right of women to control their own reproductive lives by removing from penal codes laws limiting access to contraceptive information and devices and laws governing abortion.

Questions

1. What issues appear in NOW's Bill of Rights that were not addressed in its founding Statement of Purpose? What does their addition suggest about how feminism was developing in the late 1960s?
2. What issues do these two documents have in common with the Seneca Falls Declaration of 1848? What issues does NOW address that were not included in the grievances and demands of the first women's rights movement?
3. Are NOW's concerns focused exclusively on women? To what extent does NOW address the particular needs of women of different economic classes, races, ethnicities, and sexualities?
4. What goals announced in the Statement of Purpose and Bill of Rights have not yet been achieved?

"A Day without Feminism" & "Third Wave Manifesta: A Thirteen-Point Agenda" (2000)

Jennifer Baumgardner and Amy Richards

What if the American women's movement never happened? What if conditions for women today resembled those of 1970? "A Day Without Feminism," prologue to the popular feminist text, Manifesta, *provides possible answers to these questions, describing a time when employment ads were segregated by sex, teachers could be demoted or fired for pregnancy, and women had little control over their own reproductive lives. Women today owe much to the changes activists initiated in the 1960s and 70s, a period of the women's movement commonly referred to as the "second wave." Yet as the authors' "Third Wave Manifesta" details— much work remains to be done.*

We were both born in 1970, the baptismal moment of a decade that would change dramatically the lives of American women. The two of us grew up thousands of miles apart, in entirely different kinds of families, yet we both came of age with the awareness that certain rights had been won by the women's movement. We've never doubted how important feminism is to people's lives—men's and women's. Both of our mothers went to consciousness-raising-type groups. Amy's mother raised Amy on her own, and Jennifer's mother, questioning the politics of housework, staged laundry strikes.

With the dawn of not just a new century but a new millennium, people are looking back and taking stock of feminism. Do we need new strategies? Is feminism dead? Has society changed so much that the idea of a feminist movement is obsolete? For us, the only way to answer these questions is to imagine what our lives would have been if the women's movement had never happened and the conditions for women had remained as they were in the year of our births.

Imagine that for a day it's still 1970, and women have only the rights they had then. Sly and the Family Stone and Dionne Warwick are on the radio, the kitchen appliances are Harvest Gold, and the name of your Whirlpool gas stove is Mrs. America. What is it like to be female?

Babies born on this day are automatically given their father's name. If no father is listed, "illegitimate" is likely to be typed on the birth certificate. There are virtually no child-care centers, so all preschool children are in the hands of their mothers, a baby-sitter, or an expensive nursery school. In elementary school, girls can't play in Little League and almost all of the teachers are female. (The latter is still true.) In a few states, it may be against the law for a male to teach grades lower than the sixth, on the basis that it's unnatural, or that men can't be trusted with young children.

In junior high, girls probably take home ec; boys take shop or small-engine repair. Boys who want to learn how to cook or sew on a button are out of luck, as are girls who want to learn how to fix a car. *Seventeen* magazine doesn't run feminist-influenced current columns like "Sex + Body" and "Traumarama." Instead the magazine encourages girls not to have sex; pleasure isn't part of its vocabulary. Judy Blume's books are just beginning to be published, and *Free to be . . . You and Me* does not exist. No one reads much about masturbation as a natural activity; nor do they learn that sex is for anything other than procreation. Girls do read mystery stories about Nancy Drew, for whom there is no sex, only her blue roadster and having "luncheon." (The real mystery is how Nancy gets along without a purse and manages to meet only white people.) Boys read about the Hardy Boys, for whom there are no girls.

In high school, the principal is a man. Girls have physical-education class and play half-court basketball, but not soccer, track, or cross country; nor do they have any varsity sports teams. The only prestigious physical activity for girls is cheerleading, or being a drum majorette. Most girls don't take calculus or physics; they plan the dances and decorate the gym. Even when girls get better grades than their male counterparts, they are half as likely to qualify for a National Merit Scholarship because many of the test questions favor boys. Standardized tests refer to males and male experiences much more than to females and their experiences.[1] If a girl "gets herself pregnant," she loses her membership in the National Honor Society (which is still true today) and is expelled.[2]

Girls and young women might have sex while they're unmarried, but they may be ruining their chances of landing a guy full-time, and they're probably getting a bad reputation. If a pregnancy happens, an enterprising gal can get a legal abortion only if she lives in New York or is rich enough to fly there, or to Cuba, London, or Scandinavia. There's also the Chicago-based Jane Collective, an underground abortion-referral service which can hook you up with an illegal or legal termination. (Any of these options are going to cost you. Illegal abortions average $300 to $500, sometimes as much as $2,000.) To prevent pregnancy, a sexually active woman might go to a doctor to be fitted for a diaphragm, or take the high-dose birth-control pill, but her doctor isn't likely to inform her of the possibility of deadly blood clots. Those who do take the Pill also may have to endure this contraceptive's crappy side effects: migraine headaches, severe weight gain, irregular bleeding, and hair loss (or gain), plus the possibility of an increased risk of breast cancer in the long run. It is unlikely that women or their male partners know much about the clitoris and its role in orgasm unless someone happens to fumble upon it. Instead, the myth that vaginal orgasms from penile penetration are the only "mature" (according to Freud) climaxes prevails.

Lesbians are rarely "out," except in certain bars owned by organized crime (the only businessmen who recognize this untapped market), and if lesbians don't know about the bars, they're less likely to know whether there are any other women like them. Radclyffe Hall's depressing early-twentieth-century novel *The Well of Loneliness* pretty much indicates their fate.

The Miss America Pageant is the biggest source of scholarship money for women.[3] Women can't be students at Dartmouth, Columbia, Harvard, West Point, Boston College, or the Citadel, among other all-male institutions. Women's colleges are referred to as "girls' schools." There are no Take Back the Night marches to protest women's lack of safety after dark, but that's okay because college girls aren't allowed out much after dark anyway. Curfew is likely to be midnight on Saturday and 9 or 10 p.m. the rest of the week. Guys get to stay out as late as they want. Women tend to major in teaching, home economics, English, or maybe a language—a good skill for translating someone else's words.[4] The women's studies major does not exist, although you can take a women's studies course at six universities, including Cornell and San Diego State College.[5] The absence of women's history, black history, Chicano studies, Asian-American history, queer studies, and Native American history from college curricula implies that they are not worth studying. A student is lucky if he or she learns that women were "given" the vote in 1920, just as Columbus "discovered" America in 1492. They might also learn that Sojourner Truth, Mary Church Terrell, and Fannie Lou Hamer were black abolitionists or civil-rights leaders, but not that they were feminists. There are practically no tenured female professors at any school, and campuses are not racially diverse. Women of color are either not there or they're lonely as hell. There is no nationally recognized Women's History Month or Black History Month. Only 14 percent of doctorates are awarded to women. Only 3.5 percent of MBAs are female.

Only 2 percent of everybody in the military is female, and these women are mostly nurses. There are no female generals in the U.S. Air Force, no female naval pilots, and no Marine brigadier generals. On the religious front, there are no female cantors or rabbis, Episcopal canons, or Catholic priests. (This is still true of Catholic priests.)

Only 44 percent of women are employed outside the home. And those women make, on average, fifty-two cents to the dollar earned by males. Want ads are segregated into "Help Wanted

Male" and "Help Wanted Female." The female side is preponderantly for secretaries, domestic workers, and other low-wage service jobs, so if you're a female lawyer you must look under "Help Wanted Male." There are female doctors, but twenty states have only five female gynecologists or fewer. Women workers can be fired or demoted for being pregnant, especially if they are teachers, since the kids they teach aren't supposed to think that women have sex. If a boss demands sex, refers to his female employee exclusively as "Baby," or says he won't pay her unless she gives him a blow job, she either has to quit or succumb—no pun intended. Women can't be airline pilots. Flight attendants are "stewardesses"—waitresses in the sky—and necessarily female. Sex appeal is a job requirement, wearing makeup is a rule, and women are fired if they exceed the age or weight deemed sexy. Stewardesses can get married without getting canned, but this is a new development. (In 1968 the Equal Employment Opportunity Commission—EEOC—made it illegal to forcibly retire stewardesses for getting hitched.) Less than 2 percent of dentists are women; 100 percent of dental assistants are women. The "glass ceiling" that keeps women from moving naturally up the ranks, as well as the sticky floor that keeps them unnaturally down in low-wage work, has not been named, much less challenged.

When a woman gets married, she vows to love, honor, and obey her husband, though he gets off doing just the first two to uphold his end of the bargain. A married woman can't obtain credit without her husband's signature. She doesn't have her own credit rating, legal domicile, or even her own name unless she goes to court to get it back. If she gets a loan with her husband—and she has a job—she may have to sign a "baby letter" swearing that she won't have one and have to leave her job.

Women have been voting for up to fifty years, but their turnout rate is lower than that for men, and they tend to vote right along with their husbands, not with their own interests in mind.[6] The divorce rate is about the same as it is in 2000, contrary to popular fiction's blaming the women's movement for divorce. However, divorce required that one person be at fault, therefore if you just want out of your marriage, you have to lie or blame your spouse. Property division and settlements, too, are based on fault. (And at a time when domestic violence isn't a term, much less a crime, women are legally encouraged to remain in abusive marriages.) If fathers ask for custody of their children, they get it in 60 to 80 percent of the cases. (This is still true.) If a husband or a lover hits his partner, she has no shelter to go to unless she happens to live near the one in northern California or the other in upper Michigan. If a woman is downsized from her role as a housewife (a.k.a. left by her husband), there is no word for being a displaced homemaker. As a divorcée, she may be regarded as a family disgrace or as easy sexual prey. After all, she had sex with one guy, so why not *all* guys?

If a woman is not a Mrs., she's a Miss. A woman without makeup and a hairdo is as suspect as a man with them. Without a male escort she may be refused service in a restaurant or a bar, and a woman alone is hard-pressed to find a landlord who will rent her an apartment. After all, she'll probably be leaving to get married soon, and, if she isn't, the landlord doesn't want to deal with a potential brothel.

Except among the very poor or in very rural areas, babies are born in hospitals. There are no certified midwives, and women are knocked out during birth. Most likely, they are also strapped down and lying down, made to have the baby against gravity for the doctor's convenience. If he has a schedule to keep, the likelihood of a cesarean is also very high. *Our Bodies, Ourselves* doesn't exist, nor does the women's health movement. Women aren't taught how to look at their cervixes, and their bodies are nothing to worry their pretty little heads about; however, they are supposed to worry about keeping their little heads pretty. If a woman goes under the knife to see if she has breast cancer, the surgeon won't wake her up to consult about her options before performing a Halsted mastectomy (a disfiguring radical procedure, in which the breast, the muscle wall, and the nodes under the arm, right down to the bone, are removed). She'll just wake up and find that the choice has been made for her.

Husbands are likely to die eight years earlier than their same-aged wives due to the stress of having to support a family and repress an emotional life, and a lot earlier than that if women have followed the custom of marrying older, authoritative, paternal men. The stress of raising kids, managing a household, and being undervalued by society doesn't seem to kill off women at the same rate. Upon a man's death, his beloved gets a portion of his Social Security. Even if she has worked outside the home for her entire adult life, she is probably better off with that portion than with hers in its entirety, because she has earned less and is likely to have taken time out for such unproductive acts as having kids.[7]

Has feminism changed our lives? Was it necessary? After thirty years of feminism, the world we inhabit barely resembles the world we were born into. And there's still a lot left to do.

Third Wave Manifesta: A Thirteen-Point Agenda

1. To out unacknowledged feminists, specifically those who are younger, so that Generation X can become a visible movement and, further, a voting block of eighteen- to forty-year-olds.
2. To safeguard a woman's right to bear or not to bear a child, regardless of circumstances, including women who are younger than eighteen or impoverished. To preserve this right throughout her life and support the choice to be childless.
3. To make explicit that the fight for reproductive rights must include birth control; the right for poor women and lesbians to have children; partner adoption for gay couples; subsidized fertility treatments for all women who choose them; and freedom from sterilization abuse. Furthermore, to support the idea that sex can be—and usually is—for pleasure, not procreation.
4. To bring down the double standard in sex and sexual health, and foster male responsibility and assertiveness in the following areas: achieving freedom from STDs; more fairly dividing the burden of family planning as well as responsibilities such as child care; and eliminating violence against women.
5. To tap into and raise awareness of our revolutionary history, and the fact that almost all movements began as youth movements. To have access to our intellectual feminist legacy and women's history; for the classics of radical feminism, womanism, *mujeristas*, women's liberation, and all our roots to remain in print; and to have women's history taught to men as well as women as a part of all curricula.
6. To support and increase the visibility and power of lesbians and bisexual women in the feminist movement, in high

schools, colleges, and the workplace. To recognize that queer women have always been at the forefront of the feminist movement, and that there is nothing to be gained—and much to be lost—by downplaying their history, whether inadvertently or actively.

7. To practice "autokeonony" ("self in community"): to see activism not as a choice between self and community but as a link between them that creates balance.
8. To have equal access to health care, regardless of income, which includes coverage equivalent to men's and keeping in mind that women use the system more often than men do because of our reproductive capacity.
9. For women who so desire to participate in all reaches of the military, including combat, and to enjoy all the benefits (loans, health care, pensions) offered to its members for as long as we continue to have an active military. The largest expenditure of our national budget goes toward maintaining this welfare system, and feminists have a duty to make sure women have access to every echelon.
10. To liberate adolescents from slut-bashing, listless educators, sexual harassment, and bullying at school, as well as violence in all walks of life, and the silence that hangs over adolescents' heads, often keeping them isolated, lonely, and indifferent to the world.
11. To make the workplace responsive to an individual's wants, needs, and talents. This includes valuing (monetarily) stay-at-home parents, aiding employees who want to spend more time with family and continue to work, equalizing pay for jobs of comparable worth, enacting a minimum wage that would bring a full-time worker with two children over the poverty line, and providing employee benefits for freelance and part-time workers.
12. To acknowledge that, although feminists may have disparate values, we share the same goal of equality, and of supporting one another in our efforts to gain the power to make our own choices.
13. To pass the Equal Rights Amendment so that we can have a constitutional foundation of righteousness and equality upon which future women's rights conventions will stand.

Notes

1. Phyllis Rosser pioneered the research that named the gender gap in SAT and PSAT scores. She wrote to us as we were finishing the book that in the past couple of years "the gender gap on the PSAT has narrowed from 45 to 20 points (in SAT terms). This means that women will achieve about $1,500,000 more in scholarship money in 2000 than in previous years." See Rosser's book, *The SAT Gender Gap: Identifying the Causes,* published by the center for Women's Policy Studies (1989) for more information.
2. In 1999, the Women's Rights Project of the American Civil Liberties Union (ACLU) won a landmark Title IX case. Two high-school girls from Covington, Kentucky, brought suit against the National Honor Society for ignoring their qualifying GPAs in light of their pregnancy and parental status. The school district argued that the girls weren't denied admission because of their parental status (and implicitly acknowledged that such a practice would be unlawful) but because "they engaged in premarital sex." The school relied solely on pregnancy as proof of sexual activity, though, a determining factor that can apply only to women. (No males had ever been excluded from the school's chapter of the National Honor Society on grounds of having had sex—Title IX prevailed!)
3. Beauty contests are still the largest source of college scholarships for women. For example, the Miss America winner receives upward of $50,000, and the Miss America Organization has given more than $100 million in grants since 1945, when it began awarding scholarships. It remains the largest "scholarship organization" in the world.
4. Anonymous was a woman, as were the translators of most "great" works. For instance, the first English translation of *The Communist Manifesto* was done by a woman, Helen McFarlane. We intend to have any translations of *Manifesta* done by a man.
5. Before 1969, there were no women's studies departments, and very few individual courses. As of 2000, the National Women's Studies Association counted 728 women's studies courses in their database in the United States alone.
6. The McGovern-Nixon election of 1972 marked the emergence of a "gender gap," the first election in which there was a clear difference between men's and women's voting patterns. During the 1980 Carter-Reagan election, the gap had become wide enough for politicians to worry about getting the women's vote. (Only 46 percent of

women voted for Reagan, according to the Gallup poll, but 54 percent of men did.)

7. Statistics and facts from "A Day without Feminism" come from a few sources: *The American Woman 1994–95: Where We Stand, Women and Health,* edited by Cynthia Costello and Anne J. Stone for the Women's Research and Education Institute (New York: W. W. Norton, 1994); *The Book of Women's Firsts,* by Phyllis J. Read and Bernard L. Witlieb (New York: Random House, 1992); *Mother's on Trial: The Battle for Children and Custody,* by Phyllis Chesler; *The Reader's Companion to U.S. Women's History;* and the U.S. Bureau of Labor Statistics. (For full citations of all other books mentioned, see the Bibliography.)

QUESTIONS

1. Why might the authors have chosen the term "Manifesta" for their book? How does the tone of the "thirteen-point agenda" compare with documents from other periods in the women's movement?
2. How did conditions in the pre-feminist world prevent the achievement of equality between men and women and limit women's opportunities and growth? What educational inequalities do the authors describe? What economic distinctions are detailed? Which of these conditions still exist for women today?
3. What conditions described in "A Day Without Feminism" surprised you? Why?
4. What kind of list might women write 30 years from now about today's social conditions? What conditions, according to the authors, still need to be changed?

Becoming the Third Wave (1992)

Rebecca Walker

Rebecca Walker is the editor of To Be Real *(1995) and co-founder of the Third Wave Direct Action Corporation, a national non-profit organization that promotes young women's leadership and activism in the United States. In this 1992 selection, Walker explores what it means to be part of Third Wave feminism. In her first person narrative, she insists on the need to move beyond political theory and toward "tangible action."*

I am not one of the people who sat transfixed before the television, watching the Senate hearings. I had classes to go to, papers to write, and frankly, the whole thing was too painful. A black man grilled by a panel of white men about his sexual deviance. A black woman claiming harassment and being discredited by other women. . . . I could not bring myself to watch that sensationalized assault [of] the human spirit.

To me, the hearings were not about determining whether or not Clarence Thomas did in fact harass Anita Hill. They were about checking and redefining the extent of women's credibility and power.

"Becoming the Third Wave," by Rebecca Walker, reprinted from *Ms. Magazine*, January/February 1992.

Can a woman's experience undermine a man's career? Can a woman's voice, a woman's sense of self-worth and injustice, challenge a structure predicated upon the subjugation of our gender? Anita Hill's testimony threatened to do that and more. If Thomas had not been confirmed, every man in the United States would be at risk. For how many senators never told a sexist joke? How many men have not used their protected male privilege to thwart in some way the influence or ideas of a woman colleague, friend, or relative?

For those whose sense of power is so obviously connected to the health and vigor of the penis, it would have been a metaphoric castration. Of course, this is too great a threat.

While some may laud the whole spectacle for the consciousness it raised around sexual harassment, its very real outcome is more informative. He was promoted. She was repudiated. Men were assured of the inviolability of their penis/power. Women were admonished to keep their experiences to themselves.

The backlash against U.S. women is real. As the misconception of equality between the sexes becomes more ubiquitous, so does the attempt to restrict the boundaries of women's personal and political power. Thomas's confirmation, the ultimate rally of support for the male paradigm of harassment, sends a clear message to women: "Shut up! Even if you speak, we will not listen."

I will not be silenced.

I acknowledge the fact that we live under siege. I intend to fight back. I have uncovered and unleashed more repressed anger than I thought possible. For the umpteenth time in my 22 years, I have been radicalized, politicized, shaken awake. I have come to voice again, and this time my voice is not conciliatory.

The night after Thomas' confirmation I ask the man I am intimate with what he thinks of the whole mess. His concern is primarily with Thomas' propensity to demolish civil rights and opportunities for people of color. I launch into a tirade. "When will progressive black men prioritize my rights and well-being? When will they stop talking so damn much about 'the race' as if it revolved exclusively around them?" He tells me I wear my emotions on my sleeve. I scream "I need to know, are you with me or are you going to help them try to destroy me?"

A week later I am on a train to New York. A beautiful mother and daughter, both wearing green outfits, sit across the aisle from me. The little girl has tightly plaited braids. Her brown skin is glowing and smooth, her eyes bright as she chatters happily while looking out the window. Two men get on the train and sit directly behind me, shaking my seat as they thud into place. I bury myself in *The Sound and the Fury*. Loudly they begin to talk about women. "Man, I fucked that bitch all night and then I never called her again." "Man, there's lots of girlies over there, you know that ho, live over there by Tyrone? Well, I snatched that shit up."

The mother moves closer to her now quiet daughter. Looking at her small back I can see that she is listening to the men. I am thinking of how I can transform the situation, of all the people in the car whose silence makes us complicit.

Another large man gets on the train. After exchanging loud greetings with the two men, he sits next to me. He tells them he is going to Philadelphia to visit his wife and child. I am suckered into thinking that he is different. Then, "Man, there's a ton of females in Philly, just waitin' for you to give 'em some." I turn my head and allow the fire in my eyes to burn into him. He takes up two seats and has hands with huge swollen knuckles. I imagine the gold rings on his fingers slamming into my face. He senses something, "What's your name, sweetheart?" The other men lean forward over the seat.

A torrent explodes: "I ain't your sweetheart, I ain't your bitch, I ain't your baby. How dare you have the nerve to sit up here and talk about women that way, and then try to speak to me." The woman/mother chimes in to the beat with claps of sisterhood. The men are momentarily stunned. Then the comeback: "Aw, bitch, don't play that woman shit over here 'cause that's bullshit." He slaps the back of one hand against the palm of the other. I refuse to back down. Words fly.

My instinct kicks in, telling me to get out. "Since I see you all are not going to move, I will." I move to the first car. I am so angry that thoughts of murder, of physically retaliating against them, of separatism, engulf me. I am almost out of body, just shy, of being pure force. I am sick of the way women are negated, violated, devalued, ignored. I am livid, unrelenting in my anger at those who invade my space, who wish to take away my rights, who refuse to hear my voice.

As the days pass, I push myself to figure out what it means to be a part of the Third Wave of feminism. I begin to realize that I owe it to myself, to my little sister on the train, to all of the daughters yet to be born, to push beyond my rage and articulate an agenda. After battling with ideas of separatism and militancy, I connect with my own feelings of powerlessness. I realize that I must undergo a transformation if I am truly committed to women's empowerment. My involvement must reach beyond my own voice in discussion, beyond voting, beyond reading feminist theory. My anger and awareness must translate into tangible action.

I am ready to decide, as my mother decided before me, to devote much of my energy to the history, health, and healing of women. Each of my choices will have to hold to my feminist standard of justice.

To be a feminist is to integrate an ideology of equality and female empowerment into the very fiber of my life. It is to search for personal clarity in the midst of systemic destruction, to join in sisterhood with women when often we are divided, to understand power structures with the intention of challenging them.

While this may sound simple, it is exactly the kind of stand that many of my peers are unwilling to take. So I write this as a plea to all women, especially the women of my generation: Let Thomas' confirmation serve to remind you, as it did me, that the fight is far from over. Let this dismissal of a woman's experience move you to anger. Turn that outrage into political power. Do not vote for them unless they work for us. Do not have sex with them, do not break bread with them, do not nurture them if they do not prioritize our freedom to control our bodies and our lives.

I am not a postfeminism feminist. I am the Third Wave.

QUESTIONS

1. What characteristics of third wave feminism are evident in Walker's article? How does Walker see these characteristics as different from previous concerns of the women's movement?

2. Why does Walker begin and end the article with references to the Hill/Thomas decision? What effects of sexism are evident in that decision?

3. How does Walker's story of her train ride through New York support the idea that words are powerful actions? How do the other riders on the train illustrate the effects of sexism?

A Black Feminist Statement (1977)

The Combahee River Collective

The Combahee River Collective was a black feminist group that was formed in 1974 during the second wave of the feminist movement. The distinctive name was taken from a South Carolina river where Harriet Tubman led an effort to free 750 slaves during the Civil War. In 1977, the group released a statement of purpose, printed below, that articulates its philosophy and the importance of the women's liberation movement for women of color. The manifesto—a classic in movement history—describes the development of black feminism and the importance of addressing the issue of homophobia within the black feminist community.

We are a collective of black feminists who have been meeting together since 1974.[1] During that time we have been involved in the process of defining and clarifying our politics, while at the same time doing political work within our own group and in coalition with other progressive organizations and movements. The most general statement of our politics at the present time would be that we are actively committed to struggling against racial, sexual, heterosexual, and class oppression and see as our particular task the development of integrated analysis and practice based upon the fact that the major systems of oppression are interlocking. The synthesis of these oppressions creates the conditions of our lives. As black women we see black feminism as the logical political movement to combat the manifold and simultaneous oppressions that all women of color face.

We will discuss four major topics in the paper that follows: (1) The genesis of contemporary black feminism; (2) what we believe, i.e., the specific province of our politics; (3) the problems in organizing black feminists, including a brief herstory of our collective; and (4) black feminist issues and practice.

1. The Genesis of Contemporary Black Feminism

Before looking at the recent development of black feminism, we would like to affirm that we find our origins in the historical reality of Afro-American women's continuous life-and-death struggle for survival and liberation. Black women's extremely negative relationship to the American political system (a system of white male rule) has always been determined by our membership in two oppressed racial and sexual castes. As Angela Davis points out in "Reflections on the Black Woman's Role in the Community of Slaves," black women have always embodied, if only in their physical manifestation, an adversary stance to white male rule and have actively resisted its inroads upon them and their communities in both dramatic and subtle ways. There have always been black women activists—some known, like Sojourner Truth, Harriet Tubman, Frances E. W. Harper, Ida B. Wells Barnett, and Mary Church Terrell, and thousands upon thousands unknown—who had a shared awareness of how their sexual identity combined with their racial identity to make their whole life situation and the focus of their political struggles unique. Contemporary black feminism is the outgrowth of countless generations of personal sacrifice, militancy, and work by our mothers and sisters.

A black feminist presence has evolved most obviously in connection with the second wave of the American women's movement beginning in the late 1960s. Black, other Third World, and working women have been involved in the feminist movement from its start, but both outside reactionary forces and racism and elitism within the movement itself have served to obscure our participation. In 1973 black feminists, primarily located in New York, felt the necessity of forming a separate black feminist group. This became the National Black Feminist Organization (NBFO).

Black feminist politics also have an obvious connection to movements for black liberation, particularly those of the 1960s and 1970s. Many of us were active in those movements (civil rights, black nationalism, the Black Panthers), and all of our lives were greatly affected and changed by their ideology, their goals, and the tactics used to achieve their goals. It was our experience and disillusionment within these liberation movements, as well as experience on the periphery of the white male left, that led to the need to develop a politics that was antiracist, unlike those of white women, and antisexist, unlike those of black and white men.

There is also undeniably a personal genesis for black feminism, that is, the political realization that comes from the seemingly personal experiences of individual black women's lives. Black feminists and many more black women who do not define themselves as feminists have all experienced sexual oppression as a constant factor in our day-to-day existence.

Black feminists often talk about their feelings of craziness before becoming conscious of the concepts of sexual politics, patriarchal rule, and, most importantly, feminism, the political analysis and practice that we women use to struggle against our oppression. The fact that racial politics and indeed racism are pervasive factors in our lives did not allow us, and still does not allow most black women, to look more deeply into our own experiences and define those things that make our lives what they are and our oppression specific to us. In the process of consciousness-raising, actually life-sharing, we began to recognize the commonality of our experiences and, from that sharing and growing consciousness, to build a politics that will change our lives and inevitably end our oppression.

Our development also must be tied to the contemporary economic and political position of black people. The post-World War II generation of black youth was the first to be able to minimally partake of certain educational and employment options, previously closed completely to black people. Although our economic position is still at the very bottom of the American capitalist economy, a handful of us have been able to gain certain tools as a result of tokenism in education and employment which potentially enable us to more effectively fight our oppression.

A combined antiracist and antisexist position drew us together initially, and as we developed politically we addressed ourselves to heterosexism and economic oppression under capitalism.

2. WHAT WE BELIEVE

Above all else, our politics initially sprang from the shared belief that black women are inherently valuable, that our liberation is a necessity not as an adjunct to somebody else's but because of our need as human persons for autonomy. This may seem so obvious as to sound simplistic, but it is apparent that no other ostensibly progressive movement has ever considered our specific oppression a priority or worked seriously for the ending of that oppression. Merely naming the pejorative stereotypes attributed to black women (e.g., mammy, matriarch, Sapphire, whore, bulldagger), let alone cataloguing the cruel, often murderous, treatment we receive, indicates how little value has been placed upon our lives during four centuries of bondage in the Western hemisphere. We realize that the only people who care enough about us to work consistently for our liberation is us. Our politics evolve from a healthy love for ourselves, our sisters, and our community which allows us to continue our struggle and work.

This focusing upon our own oppression is embodied in the concept of identity politics. We believe that the most profound and potentially the most radical politics come directly out of our own identity, as opposed to working to end somebody else's oppression. In the case of black women this is a particularly repugnant, dangerous, threatening, and therefore revolutionary concept because it is obvious from looking at all the political movements that have preceded us that anyone is more worthy of liberation than ourselves. We reject pedestals, queenhood, and walking ten paces behind. To be recognized as human, levelly human, is enough.

We believe that sexual politics under patriarchy is as pervasive in black women's lives as are the politics of class and race. We also often find it difficult to separate race from class from sex oppression because in our lives they are most often experienced simultaneously. We know that there is such a thing as racial-sexual oppression which is neither solely racial nor solely sexual, e.g., the history of rape of black women by white men as a weapon of political repression.

Although we are feminists and lesbians, we feel solidarity with progressive black men and do not advocate the fractionalization that white women who are separatists demand. Our situation as black people necessitates that we have solidarity around the fact of race, which white women of course do not need to have with white men, unless it is their negative solidarity as racial oppressors. We struggle together with black men against racism, while we also struggle with black men about sexism.

We realize that the liberation of all oppressed peoples necessitates the destruction of the political-economic systems of capitalism and imperialism as well as patriarchy. We are socialists because we believe the work must be organized for the collective benefit of those who do the work and create the products and not for the profit of the bosses. Material resources must be equally distributed among those who create these resources. We are not convinced, however, that a socialist revolution that is not also a feminist and antiracist revolution will guarantee our liberation. We have arrived at the necessity for developing an understanding of class relationships that takes into account the specific class position of black women who are generally marginal in the labor force, while at this particular time some of us are temporarily viewed as doubly desirable tokens at white-collar and professional levels. We need to articulate the real class situation of persons who are not merely raceless, sexless workers, but for whom racial and sexual oppression are significant determinants in their working/economic lives. Although we are in essential agreement with Marx's theory as it applied to the very specific economic relationships he analyzed, we know that this analysis must be extended further in order for us to understand our specific economic situation as black women.

A political contribution which we feel we have already made is the expansion of the feminist principle that the personal is political. In our consciousness-raising sessions, for example, we have in many ways gone beyond white women's revelations because we are dealing with the implications of race and class as well as sex. Even our black women's style of talking/testifying in black language about what we have experienced has a resonance that is both cultural and political. We have spent a great deal of energy delving into the cultural and experiential nature of our oppression out of necessity because none of these matters have ever been looked at before. No one before has ever examined the multilayered texture of black women's lives.

As we have already stated, we reject the stance of lesbian separatism because it is not a viable political analysis or strategy for us. It leaves out far too much and far too many people, particularly black men, women, and children. We have a great deal of criticism and loathing for what men have been socialized to be in this society: what they support, how they act, and how they oppress. But we do not have the misguided notion that it is their maleness, per se—i.e., their biological maleness—that makes them what they are. As black women we find any type of biological determinism a particularly dangerous and reactionary basis upon which to build a politic. We must also question whether lesbian separatism is an adequate and progressive political analysis and strategy, even for those who practice it, since it so completely denies any but the sexual sources of women's oppression, negating the facts of class and race.

3. Problems in Organizing Black Feminists

During our years together as a black feminist collective we have experienced success and defeat, joy and pain, victory and failure. We have found that it is very difficult to organize around black feminist issues, difficult even to announce in certain contexts that we *are* black feminists. We have tried to think about the reasons for our difficulties, particularly since the white women's movement continues to be strong and to grow in many directions. In this section we will discuss some of the general reasons for the organizing problems we face and also talk specifically about the stages in organizing our own collective.

The major source of difficulty in our political work is that we are not just trying to fight oppression on one front or even two, but instead to address a whole range of oppressions. We do not have racial, sexual, heterosexual, or class privilege to rely upon, nor do we have even the minimal access to resources and power that groups who possess any one of these types of privilege have.

The psychological toll of being a black woman and the difficulties this presents in reaching political consciousness and doing political work can never be underestimated. There is a very low value placed upon black women's psyches in this society, which is both racist and sexist. As an early group member once said, "We are all damaged people merely by virtue of being black women." We are dispossessed psychologically and on every other level, and yet we feel the necessity to struggle to change our condition and the condition of all black women. In "A Black Feminist's Search for Sisterhood," Michele Wallace arrives at this conclusion:

> We exist as women who are black who are feminists, each stranded for the moment, working independently because there is not yet an environment in this society remotely congenial to our struggle—because, being on the bottom, we would have to do what no one else has done: we would have to fight the world.[2]

Wallace is not pessimistic but realistic in her assessment of black feminists' position, particularly in her allusion to the nearly classic isolation most of us face. We might use our position at the bottom, however, to make a clear leap into revolutionary action. If black women were free, it would mean that everyone else would have to be free since our freedom would necessitate the destruction of all the systems of oppression.

Feminism is, nevertheless, very threatening to the majority of black people because it calls into question some of the most basic assumptions about our existence, i.e., that gender should be a determinant of power relationships. Here is the way male and female roles were defined in a black nationalist pamphlet from the early 1970s.

> We understand that it is and has been traditional that the man is the head of the house. He is the leader of the house/nation because his knowledge of the world is broader, his awareness is greater, his understanding is fuller and his application of this

> information is wiser. . . . After all, it is only reasonable that the man be the head of the house because he is able to defend and protect the development of his home. . . . Women cannot do the same things as men—they are made by nature to function differently. Equality of men and women is something that cannot happen even in the abstract world. Men are not equal to other men, i.e., ability, experience, or even understanding. The value of men and women can be seen as in the value of gold and silver—they are not equal but both have great value. We must realize that men and women are a complement to each other because there is no house/family without a man and his wife. Both are essential to the development of any life.[3]

The material conditions of most black women would hardly lead them to upset both economic and sexual arrangements that seem to represent some stability in their lives. Many black women have a good understanding of both sexism and racism, but because of the everyday constrictions of their lives cannot risk struggling against them both.

The reaction of black men to feminism has been notoriously negative. They are, of course, even more threatened than black women by the possibility that black feminists might organize around our own needs. They realize that they might not only lose valuable and hard-working allies in their struggles but that they might also be forced to change their habitually sexist ways of interacting with and oppressing black women. Accusations that black feminism divides the black struggle are powerful deterrents to the growth of an autonomous black women's movement.

Still, hundreds of women have been active at different times during the three-year existence of our group. And every black women who came, came out of a strongly felt need for some level of possibility that did not previously exist in her life.

When we first started meeting early in 1974 after the NBFO first eastern regional conference, we did not have a strategy for organizing, or even a focus. We just wanted to see what we had. After a period of months of not meeting, we began to meet again late in the year and started doing an intense variety of consciousness-raising. The overwhelming feeling that we had is that after years and years we had finally found each other. Although we were not doing political work as a group, individuals continued their involvement in lesbian politics, sterilization abuse and abortion rights work, Third World Women's International Women's

Day activities, and support activity for the trials of Dr. Kenneth Edelin, Joan Little, and Inez Garcia. During our first summer, when membership had dropped off considerably, those of us remaining devoted serious discussion to the possibility of opening a refuge for battered women in a black community. (There was no refuge in Boston at that time.) We also decided around that time to become an independent collective since we had serious disagreements with NBFOs bourgeois-feminist stance and their lack of a clear political focus.

We also were contacted at that time by socialist feminists, with whom we had worked on abortion rights activities, who wanted to encourage us to attend the National Socialist Feminist Conference in Yellow Springs. One of our members did attend and despite the narrowness of the ideology that was promoted at that particular conference, we became more aware of the need for us to understand our own economic situation and to make our own economic analysis.

In the fall, when some members returned, we experienced several months of comparative inactivity and internal disagreements which were first conceptualized as a lesbian-straight split but which were also the result of class and political differences. During the summer those of us who were still meeting had determined the need to do political work and to move beyond consciousness-raising and serving exclusively as an emotional support group. At the beginning of 1976, when some of the women who had not wanted to do political work and who also had voiced disagreements stopped attending of their own accord, we again looked for a focus. We decided at that time, with the addition of new members, to become a study group. We had always shared our reading with each other, and some of us had written papers on black feminism for group discussion a few months before this decision was made. We began functioning as a study group and also began discussing the possibility of starting a black feminist publication. We had a retreat in the late spring which provided a time for both political discussion and working out interpersonal issues. Currently we are planning to gather together a collection of black feminist writing. We feel that it is absolutely essential to demonstrate the reality of our politics to other black women and believe that we can do this through writing and distributing our work. The fact that individual black feminists are living in isolation all over the country, that our own numbers are small, and that we have some skills in writing, printing, and publishing makes us want to carry out these kinds of projects as a means of organizing black feminists as we continue to do political work in coalition with other groups.

4. Black Feminist Issues and Practice

During our time together we have identified and worked on many issues of particular relevance to black women. The inclusiveness of our politics makes us concerned with any situation that impinges upon the lives of women, Third World, and working people. We are of course particularly committed to working on those struggles in which race, sex, and class are simultaneous factors in oppression. We might, for example, become involved in workplace organizing at a factory that employs Third World women or picket a hospital that is cutting back on already inadequate health care to a Third World community, or set up a rape crisis center in a black neighborhood. Organizing around welfare or daycare concerns might also be a focus. The work to be done and the countless issues that this work represents merely reflect the pervasiveness of our oppression.

Issues and projects that collective members have actually worked on are sterilization abuse, abortion rights, battered women, rape, and health care. We have also done many workshops and educationals on black feminism on college campuses, at women's conferences, and most recently for high school women.

One issue that is of major concern to us and that we have begun to publicly address is racism in the white women's movement. As black feminists we are made constantly and painfully aware of how little effort white women have made to understand and combat their racism, which requires among other things that they have a more than superficial comprehension of race, color, and black history and culture. Eliminating racism in the white women's movement is by definition work for white women to do, but we will continue to speak to and demand accountability on this issue.

In the practice of our politics we do not believe that the end always justifies the means. Many reactionary and destructive acts have been done in the name of achieving "correct" political goals. As feminists we do not want to mess over people in the name of politics. We believe in collective process and a nonhierarchical distribution of power within our own group and in our vision of a revolutionary society. We are committed to a continual examination of our politics as they develop through criticism and self-criticism as an essential aspect of our practice. As black feminists and lesbians we know that we have a very definite revolutionary task to perform and we are ready for the lifetime of work and struggle before us.

Notes

1. This statement is dated April 1977.
2. Michele Wallace, "A Black Feminist's Search for Sisterhood," *The Village Voice*, 28 July 1975, pp. 6–7.
3. Mumininas of Committee for Unified Newark, *Mwanamke Mwananchi* (*The Nationalist Woman*), Newark, N.J., © 1971, pp. 4–5.

Questions

1. How did Black feminism develop? Why is it needed? Why isn't just "feminism" enough? What do the authors mean by the statement that the "personal is political"?
2. What specific concerns do black feminists have that the women's liberation movement has not adequately addressed? What do the authors mean by black women's "multiplicity of oppressions"?
3. Why do the authors of this piece believe that lesbian separatism is not an acceptable answer to the challenges black lesbians face?

4. Why do the authors believe that black women need to feel solidarity with progressive black men around the subject of race?
5. What challenges to organizing do black women face? Why is political work nevertheless so vital to the position of black women?

"Womanist" from *In Search of Our Mothers' Gardens* (1983)

Alice Walker

Alice Walker is an activist, a poet, and a Pulitzer Prize winning novelist. Born in Georgia in 1944, Walker attended Sarah Lawrence College, and began publishing poetry after she became active in both the voter registration movement and the welfare rights movement in the 1960s. She has published numerous novels over the course of her career, including The Third Life of Grange Copeland *(1970),* In Love and Trouble *(1973),* Meridian *(1976),* The Color Purple *(1982),* In the Temple of My Familiar *(1989),* Possessing the Secret of Joy *(1992) and* Warrior Marks *(1995).*

Since Walker's coining of the term "womanist," womanism has evolved into an academic, political and spiritual framework. The following selection presents her definition of "womanist," capturing the unique-

ness and importance of Black feminism in the United States.

Womanist 1. From *womanish.* (Opp. of "girlish," i.e., frivolous, irresponsible, not serious.) A black feminist or feminist of color. From the black folk expression of mothers to female children, "You acting womanish," i.e., like a woman. Usually referring to outrageous, audacious, courageous or *willful* behavior. Wanting to know more and in greater depth than is considered "good" for one. Interested in grown-up doings. Acting grown up. Being grown up. Interchangeable with another black folk expression: "You trying to be grown." Responsible. In charge. *Serious.*

2. *Also*: A woman who loves other women, sexually and/or nonsexually. Appreciates and prefers women's culture, women's emotional flexibility (values tears as natural counterbalance of laughter), and women's strength. Sometimes loves individual men, sexually and/or nonsexually. Committed to survival and wholeness of entire people, male *and* female. Not a separatist, except periodically, for health. Traditionally universalist as in: "Mama, why are we brown, pink, and yellow, and our cousins are white, beige, and black?" Ans.: "Well, you know the colored race is just like a flower garden, with every color flower represented." Traditionally capable, as in: "Mama, I'm walking to Canada and I'm taking you and a bunch of other slaves with me." Reply: "It wouldn't be the first time."

3. Loves music. Loves dance. Loves the moon. *Loves* the Spirit. Loves love and food and roundness. Loves struggle. *Loves* the Folk. Loves herself. *Regardless.*

4. Womanist is to feminist as purple to lavender.

Questions

---

1. What is the significance of the final line of Walker's definition? How does Walker distinguish a womanist and a feminist? What evidence from the definition can you offer to support your interpretation?

2. What is significant about the format Walker has chosen for this presentation of the definition womanist? Why?

In Pursuit of Latina Liberation (1995)

Elizabeth Martínez

Elizabeth Martinez is the author of numerous books and articles on social movements based, in part, on her own activism spanning the past thirty years. Her most recent book is the bilingual 500 Years of Chicano History in Pictures *(1991). She has worked as an instructor in ethnic studies and women's studies in various California schools and is currently the editor of* CrossRoads *magazine. Here, Martinez discusses the growth and development of Chicana feminism and the struggles of Latinas against sexism. She situates her analysis in the broader context of conquest, colonization and Chicano liberation.*

Who and what is a Latina? Ignorance, confusion, and often impassioned controversy make it necessary to begin this commentary with such basic questions. Latinas, like Latinos, are in general a *mestizo* or mixed people. They combine, in varying degrees, indigenous (from pre-Columbian times), European (from Spain's invasion of the Americas), and African roots (from the millions of slaves brought to the Americans, including at least two hundred thousand to Mexico alone). Today in the United States, Latinas include women whose background links them to some twenty countries and going back one, two, or ten generations.

The term "Latina," used here, is problematic but preferable to the totally Eurocentric label "Hispanic" with its obliteration of our indigenous heritage. "Hispanic" also carries the disadvantage of being a term that did not emerge from the community itself but has been imposed by the dominant society, in particular by its census bureau and other bureaucracies, during the 1970s. (People from Brazil, of course, reject the term "Hispanic" because it replaces Portugal with Spain in their history; this is just one example of the many existing complexities and problems related to terminology. Such distinctions concern not only scholars but also organizers and activists like myself.)

To many of us in the United States, *La Raza* or simply *Raza*, meaning the People, is a better name than either Hispanic or Latina/o; it dates back many years in the community. In the end, the least controversial and most common form of identification is by specific nationality: Mexican, Guatemalan, Colombian, and so forth. "Chicana/o," a term for Mexican Americans, became popular during the 1960s and 1970s movement years for its strong message of pride in one's peoplehood. In essence a political term of affirmation, it continues to be widely used, especially among youth.

Whatever the terminology, Latino peoples in this country have in their historical background a deep experience with colonization, direct or indirect, and mainly by two countries: first, Spain (or Portugal), and later the United States. Among Latina/os, it is Mexicans in what we now call the Southwest who have experienced U.S. colonialism the longest and most directly, with Puerto Ricans not far behind. Almost one-third of today's United States was the home of Mexicans as far back as the 1500s, until Anglos seized it by war in 1848 and treated its population as conquered subjects (The Mexicans, of course, themselves occupied lands that had been seized by Spain from Native Americans.) This treatment occurred despite the Treaty of Guadalupe Hidalgo, which ended the 1846–48 war and promised respect for the civil and property rights of Mexicans remaining in the Southwest.

The imposition of U.S. rule included taking over millions of acres of Mexican-held land by trickery and violence. Colonization also brought the imposition of Anglo values and institutions at the expense of Mexican culture, including use of the Spanish language. Anglos lynched many Mexicans in ways similar to the lynching of Southern blacks.

In the early 1900s, even as the process of colonization continued, the original Mexican population of the Southwest was greatly increased by an immigration that continues today. This combination of centuries-old roots with relatively recent ones gives the Mexican American people a rich and varied cultural heritage. At the same time, the institutionalized racism imposed by U.S. colonization confronts the entire population to one degree or another, regardless of when any sector arrived.

But we cannot understand all that history simply in terms of victimization: popular resistance is its other face. Resistance, which took the form of organized armed struggle in the Southwest during the last century, continues today in many ways. These include resistance to what we can call the colonized mentality: that process of internalizing belief in the master's superiority and our inferiority. (As a resident of California and a Chicana, I am drawing primarily on the experience of Mexican/Chicana and Central American women, who predominate among Latinas here.)

Advances by Women

Without attempting to review the history of Latina feminist struggle in these few pages, it should be noted that such a tradition does exist despite the stereotype of the passive Latin woman. The historical landmarks in Mexico are numerous, from the seventeenth-century feminist thinker Sor Juana Inés de La Cruz, a nun, to the first feminist congress of 1911 and the suffrage movement of the 1930s. Cultural mainstays like the powerful pre-Columbian queens and goddesses who ruled alongside male deities and the timeless *curandera* or healer demonstrate the power of women's historical presence. The many women who participated in the Mexican war of independence from Spain (1810–21) and the Mexican Revolution may or may not have been consciously feminist, yet their collective image resonates with strength and courage.

We also note a growing feminism and advances over sexism by Mexican and Chicana women in recent years. During the Chicano liberation movement of 1965–75, open challenges to male supremacy began to be heard from Chicana participants. As sociologist Alma García tells us in "The Development of Chicana Feminist Discourse, 1970–1980" (1990) and as confirmed by my personal experience, the contradiction of encountering male supremacist practices within a movement supposedly fighting for social justice spurred many Chicanas to new consciousness. In the process they made minimal feminist demands. (Women in the African American and Asian American movements of the 1960s and early 1970s were similarly encouraged in a feminist direction by experiencing sexism inside their movements.)

In response, male supremacy hurled two weapons at such Chicanas. The first was the accusation that "you're acting like a white woman" [*agringada*]. In other words, you're a traitor to your people, your culture. This could be devastating to Chicana activists, given that a central goal of the *movimiento* was liberation for brown people from Anglo-imposed domination and its values. In effect, the charge accused women of undermining ethnicity as a unifying force.

The second counterinsurgent weapon was the accusation, "You're being divisive." It could be equally devastating, because unity and the sense of *Raza* as family were so important to the movement. What could be worse, in a hostile society, than to be divisive among your own people? That charge also resonated with certain realities about the women's liberation movement as Chicanas saw it then, including many strong activists. As a participant in New York Radical Women in 1968 (the only Latina member, I believe), I shared the powerful sense of feminist discovery that illuminated those years yet also came to understand why so many Chicanas in the Southwest saw the women's movement then as irrelevant because it was overwhelmingly Anglo and middle-class. Again, like many African American and Native American women, Chicana activists believed that the women's movement saw men as the enemy, a view they could not accept because *Raza* were fighting racism and oppression as a people; men suffered from those same forces. To focus on women's oppression alone and to discount racial and class oppression, as the national women's movement often did, contradicted our perception. This sense of clashing worldviews, which resulted from having such different historical experiences, became a major reason why only a few Chicanas looked for lessons that could be learned or alliances that could be forged with Euramerican feminists.

In the next twenty years a self-defined Chicana feminism flowered, mainly in academia and most visibly among young faculty and graduate students. Under pressure, the National Association for Chicano Studies (NACS) established a women's caucus at its 1985 meeting in Sacramento, California. A lesbian caucus was formalized at its 1992 meeting in Alburquerque, New Mexico, which established an active rejection of homophobia in NACS toward lesbians. Another organization, Mujeres Activas en Letras y Cambio Social (MALCS), emerged in the 1980s as the locus of Latina feminist academics' work for social change that prioritizes mentoring young Chicanas in their scholarly development. Its initial leadership came from Adaljiza Sosa Riddell at the University of California, Davis, and the University of California, Berkeley's Mujeres en Marcha, a graduate student women's group.

At the undergraduate level, signs of growing feminism exist alongside visible hesitation about being labeled "feminist." As elsewhere, symbols and terminology often define the debate; changing the name "Chicano Studies" to "Chicano and Chicana Studies" (or some similarly inclusive phrase, necessitated by a gendered language) has become common on California campuses. At the same time, when I speak about feminism as such to Latina and Latino undergraduate students, I frequently encounter a telling combination of reactions from mixed audiences. Few Chicanas in the audience support my ideas publicly or declare themselves feminist; few if any men are sympathetic, and many air sexist attitudes or make such statements as, "I believe in equal rights for women but not in feminism"; and several Chicanas express agreement after the event, in private. As might be expected, feminist expression intensifies in any all-women's gathering, where Chicana students analyze and grapple with issues of patriarchy and sexist practice.

These developments suggest two realities. First, the women's movement of the 1960s has had positive effects, despite its racial and class biases. The idea of separate women's organizing, once anathema to *Raza* activists and energetically opposed by the men, has become widely accepted. Latina lesbians would have stayed in the closet longer without the national women's movement to encourage them out, I believe. The articulation of concerns common to almost all women, such as health, child care, and reproductive rights, is much more frequent than it was two decades ago.

Our second reality is that Latina feminism, like other forms of feminism, has been sabotaged by backlash forces that rage everywhere. We can thank those forces for making the term "feminist" so unpopular, for making so many Chicanas and Chicanos buy today's bra-burning, manhating images. In the case of Chicanas, another political trend sometimes strengthens the general assault on feminism: a nationalism that has intensified in direct relation to the racist backlash of the last twenty years and especially since President Reagan's election in 1980. That nationalism, for all its other positive effects, is often accompanied by sexist forms of pride in one's peoplehood that leave women in stereotyped and inferior places. (Much more research and analysis needs to be done on the relationship between nationalism and sexism.)

The present picture, then, can seem almost surreal in its contradictions. One can observe young Chicanas who will unequivocally distance themselves from the word "feminist" but who act in ways that objectively are so very feminist.

Who Says Teenagers Aren't Feminist?

Portents of change can often be found. For example, the California division of the Chicano student organization Movimiento Estudiantil Chicano de Aztlan (MEChA) declined a few years ago to establish a Chicana caucus, despite urging from a women's workshop I attended. It now has such a caucus. More than a few MEChA chapters in California are formally headed by women, which rarely happened ten or fifteen years ago (although women may well have been the real leaders in practice).

In the 1993 hunger strike to win departmental status for Chicana/o studies at the University of California, Los Angeles, half of the strikers were women students. In 1994 women also formed a major part of the hunger strikes for similar causes at the University of California, Santa Barbara, and the University of Colorado in Boulder. In the May 1994 Stanford University hunger strike for Chicana/o studies classes and other demands, the fasters were four Chicanas. Through such experiences, women have often developed new attitudes toward themselves—perhaps the most subversive change of all. This has taken concrete form in networking; the fasters and supporters from Boulder, for example, came to Santa Barbara to express their solidarity with the fasters there.

As for the reactions of Latino men on California campuses, contradiction is often written across their faces. The same Chicano student who articulates extremely backward ideas about women may also recognize that change is blowing in the wind and that he cannot oppose it in obvious ways. A day or week devoted to "La Chicana" or Latinas in general is institutionalized on many campuses. Unfortunately, this is less true with respect to gays and lesbians; among Latino college students, homophobia still runs more freely than sexism toward women.

At the level of secondary school in California, one can find an even stronger current of self-conscious feminism (without the word being used) than at the college level. Last year I spoke before six hundred Latina/o high school seniors who had come for "Raza Day" at the University of California, Berkeley, when students visit Cal as a college they might want to attend. My talk was about Latina women's history. I began by describing how, at marches and other demonstrations, you could hear cheers for this man or that—"Viva Zapata! Viva César Chávez!"—by name. "And then," I said, "we hear 'Viva la mujer'—Long live women!" I was going to make the point that it is rare to hear a women's actual name cheered and to ask why women, unlike men, were celebrated anonymously. But this audience upstaged me with thunderous applause and cheers shaking the auditorium: "Viva la mujer!" Dozens of young women were jumping in their seats.

More examples have accumulated since then, during various encounters with junior high and high school girls. In an era when we are told that feminism does not appeal to young women, the opposite seems true, at least for working-class or lower-middle class Chicanas in the San Francisco Bay Area, and at least if the "F word" is not used. Last April 22, Latina/o and other students from thirty-eight schools in eleven Bay Area towns held walkouts—called blowouts—or similar protests. They demanded educational reforms: more bilingual counselors, more retention programs, no more cutbacks, a relevant multicultural curriculum. At the staging-area rally, during the march downtown, and at the main rally facing City Hall, a good half of the speakers were female. That would have been unthinkable during the 1960s movement years.

During the San Francisco walkouts, it was the women who called loudest and most clearly for unity and peace among their peers rather than gang warfare over "colors." One moment that vividly demonstrated this concern came when the marching crowd was shouting a chant against Governor Pete Wilson's educational cutbacks: "Wilson, Wilson, *a la chingada!* Viva, viva Che Guevara!" I overheard one young woman say to another, "We have to change that chant—the kids from Wilson High will think it's about them." So they started shouting, "Pete Wilson, *a la chingada* . . ." to make sure listeners knew they were trashing the governor and not their peers.

The April 22 blowouts, which formed the third wave of such actions in less than a year, involved five to six hundred high school students in San Francisco and environs plus another thousand in nearby Hayward (just to mention two areas). They had been organized by different groups. Several have a fifty-fifty rule on male-female participation in leadership, handling the press, and so forth. During the summer of 1994 I saw key organizers meet weekly to develop a structure, program, and outreach for ongoing work in 1994–95; they took the fifty-fifty rule seriously.

All this anecdotal evidence leaves many questions, such as how deep the teenage women's feminism runs—that is, does it operate at home when mother tells daughter, "Make your brother's bed"? Perhaps, perhaps not. Two Latinas aged thirteen and fourteen who had participated in the blowouts told me that "in this protest we do not feel put down": "boys have not put down girls for being leaders." On the personal relations level, however, "We get called 'ho' if we have sex but for a boy, it makes him a man." Despite these and other contradictions, the evidence of a Latina feminist consciousness evolving among young women has been too constant, too strong, for me to doubt its existence.

In the provocation and shaping of that consciousness, Chicana artists and writers have had great influence. We would not be as far along as we are today without the beautifully bold writing of lesbian authors Cherríe Moraga, Gloria Anzaldúa, and others or the performance art of lesbian comedians like Marga Gómez and Monica Palacios. We would not be as far along as we are today without the heretical work of painters Yolanda López and Ester Hernández, whose feminist transformations of the Virgin of Guadalupe offer a liberation never before available. We would not be this far along without some biting poems from Sandra Cisneros, the multifaceted work of feminist writer Ana Castillo, and painter Juana Alicia's images of Latina women as strong survivors all. So many more names could be set down; all have nurtured the feminist impulse of young Chicanas, especially those in their upper teens and/or college students.

Working Women Speak Feminist Tongues

Chicana workers and other community women who do not define themselves as feminists but lead objectively feminist lives have been among us since the United States took half of Mexico by war in 1848. Often this feminist practice resulted from their becoming involved in labor organizing and other forms of collective struggle. They have provided the backbone of male-dominated groups but also formed all-women's groups. Today various Latina labor organizations offer shining examples of such activism.

Look at Fuerza Unida (United Force, or Strength), formed in San Antonio, Texas, when Levi Straus laid off eleven hundred garment workers there in 1990 and moved the plant to Costa Rica for cheaper labor. Angered by their experience of lies, broken promises, inadequate compensation, pathetic retraining, and no special aid to workers crippled with carpal tunnel syndrome, the former Chicana and Mexican employees have still not given up five years later. From often being shy or nervous because of their lack of formal, higher education, Fuerza Unida women have become administrators and amateur labor lawyers, steadily developing as leaders. In 1994 they opened an office in San Francisco, home to Levi's international headquarters, and held a three-week "fast for justice" in Levi's face. Fuerza Unida has become an inspiration for women workers everywhere. So has Mujer Obrera (Working Woman), founded in El Paso by garment workers who demanded thousands of dollars in back pay and won some of it with such bold tactics as chaining themselves to their sewing machines. The garment industry is one arena in which Latinas are superexploited; another is the *maquiladoras*, plants in the U.S.-Mexico border zone where workers assembled everything from bikinis to transistors. Thousands of *maquila* women have been organizing steadily for a decade. The plants' deliberate employment of very young, preferably teenage, Latinas reeks of cynical exploitation. The corporate goal: hire them young, suck out the best of their energy, exploit their inexperience as workers and their fear of angering the boss—then toss them aside like so many rag dolls when they become pregnant, injured, or "troublemakers." But these women are fighting back, often with a clear sense of being a class unto themselves as *maquila* women.

Then look at the first statewide gathering of Latina farmworkers in August 1993 at Fresno, California, where a hundred women came together from all over the state as part of the new Farmworker Women's Leadership Development Project. They discussed not only labor issues like wages, pesticide poisoning, and contracts but also sexual harassment, domestic violence, and sexual discrimination. In those workshops you could sense the women's desire to talk, to tell their stories, along with their feelings of awkwardness and perhaps fear.

At the beginning I was concerned that only the workshop facilitators and other prepared participants would feel able to talk. Wrong: as one spoke, another gathered strength to open up on painful subjects, and then another. Very few outsiders like myself had been allowed in the room, and we were wisely assigned to sit on the outer edges. Millie Treviño is director of the project and a former farmworker herself; a second statewide conference took place in 1994 at Irvine, California, with ongoing discussion of those thorny topics.

Indeed, across this state our moon is rising!

Back to the Word "Feminism"

Like other women of color, most Latinas have rejected any feminism shaped by an exclusively white middle-class perspective that denies the racist, classist oppression of Latino men alongside the women. Such a feminism does not understand how, for a colonized racial/ethnic people, cultural integrity is profoundly interwoven with survival. Or how the family can be seen primarily as a key weapon of self-defense in a hostile world rather than

as an oppressive institution. Thus we had to define our own Chicana feminism in the 1970s.
The problem continues today. We still find some Anglo leaders of the pro-choice movement, for example, who defensively refuse to yield control of the agenda or to prioritize the women-of-color perspective that demands reproductive choice in every sense of the term, including adequate prenatal care and freedom from forced sterilization. In a white supremacist world where so many women are of color and poor, it should be obvious that any true feminist must be constantly and passionately antiracist and anticlassist. The times cry out for work by Anglo women that combines resistance to oppression based on race and class as well as on gender.

Today the need to build bridges among all women could not be greater. Xenophobic immigrant bashing reaches new and frightening heights as the corporate elite scapegoats working-class people of color—primarily Latina/os and Asians—for the ongoing economic crisis. We would all do well to remember: there is no more exploited, vulnerable person in the United States today than the undocumented woman worker of color. Her lack of papers means she can almost never fight back, no matter how vilely she has been abused.

Evidence of that exploitation and abuse has come to public attention sharply in recent years. In March 1993, Latinas presented a full day of testimony in San Francisco about how they had been recruited from their home countries to serve as housekeepers or in similar positions for professional families in the Bay Area. They gave chilling, detailed accounts of being raped on their first day at work; of being kept on duty around the clock as housekeeper, nursemaid, cook, laundress, cleaning woman, babysitter, and personal maid; of not being paid for months at a time; of being locked up in their employers' homes; and of being kept ignorant about how to seek help in a strange land, or being too terrorized to try. Their treatment in the United States of the late twentieth century is simply barbarous.

Yet even these Latinas are no longer silent, no longer invisible. The moon is rising even as the sky fills with new storm clouds. Time for sharp eyes, open minds, and the tenacity that has stamped our historic Latina heritage.

San Francisco, California

Afterword about sources

This article draws on interviews, personal experience as an activist, lecturing, and reading over many years. Without pretending to offer a full list, here are some titles or authors relevant to the article.

Two useful readings about early Chicana feminism:

Cotera, Marta. 1989. "The Chicana Feminist." Austin, Tex.: Information Systems Development.

García. Alma. 1990. "The Development of Chicana Feminist Discourse, 1970–1980." In *Unequal Sisters: A Multicultural Reader in U.S. Women's History*, ed. Ellen Carol DuBois and Vicki L. Ruiz. New York: Routledge.

A few general titles and authors important to my own development:

Mora, Magadalena, and Adelaida R. Del Castillo, eds. 1980. *Mexican Women in the United States*. Los Angeles: Chicano Studies Research Center Publications, University of California.

Ruiz, Vicki L. 1987. *Cannery Women/Cannery Lives: Mexican Women, Unionization and the California Food Processing Industry, 1930–1950*. Albuquerque: University of New Mexico Press.

Del Castillo, Adelaida R., ed. 1990. *Between Borders: Essays on Mexicana/Chicana History*. Encino, Calif.: Floricanto.

A few titles that could introduce readers to Chicana writing referred to in this article (all of these authors have published other important work):

Anzaldúa, Gloria. 1987. *Borderlands/La Frontera*. San Francisco: Spinsters/Aunt Lute.

Martínez, Demetria. 1994. *Mother Tongue*. Tempe, Ariz.: Bilingual.

Moraga, Cherríe. 1993. *The Last Generation*. Boston: South End.

Cisneros, Sandra. 1994. *Loose Woman*. New York: Knopf.

Castillo, Ana. 1994. *Massacre of the Dreamers*. Albuquerque: University of New Mexico Press.

I have found many works by the following scholars useful and interesting: Maxine Baca Zinn, who writes extensively on Chicana sociological issues; Julia Curry, on Mexican immigrant women; María Lugones, on racism/ethnocentrism; Ana Nieto Gomez, one of the earliest Chicana feminists; Mary Pardo, on contemporary Chicana activism. Marta López Garza and Gloria Romero are Chicana scholars trained in sociology and psychology, respectively, whose work often offers a valuable and progressive feminist perspective.

Original research on the California student walkouts has been published in "Be Down with the Brown," by Elizabeth Martínez (Z [November 1994]).

Questions

1. What is the significance and meaning of the term *La Raza*? For Latinas, how does their identity as women intersect with their ethnic and cultural identities? How do Latina lesbians confront the challenges of integrating all of their identities?
2. What are some of the ideas, issues and activities characteristic of Chicana feminism? How do cultural artists and writers contribute to the development of a political consciousness among Latinas?
3. Why are Latinas careful about how they use the term feminism? What are some of the obstacles they face as feminists? What are their concerns about feminism? Discuss how women who do not define themselves as feminist still lead lives as feminists. What are some of the parallels between Chicana feminism and the type of feminism developed by other women of color?

La conciencia de la mestiza: Towards a New Consciousness

Gloria Anzaldúa

Por la mujer de mi raza hablará el espíritu.[1]

Jose Vasconcelos, Mexican philosopher, envisaged *una raza mestiza, una mezcla de razas afines, una raza de color—la primera raza síntesis del globo.* He called it a cosmic race, *la raza cósmica,* a fifth race embracing the four major races of the world.[2] Opposite to the theory of the pure Aryan, and to the policy of racial purity that white America practices, his theory is one of inclusivity. At the confluence of two or more genetic streams, with chromosomes constantly "crossing over," this mixture of races, rather than resulting in an inferior being, provides hybrid progeny, a mutable, more malleable species with a rich gene pool. From this racial, ideological, cultural and biological cross-pollinization, an "alien" consciousness is presently in the making—a new *mestiza* consciousness, *una conciencia de mujer.* It is a consciousness of the Borderlands.

Una lucha de fronteras/A Struggle of Borders

> Because I, a *mestiza,*
> continually walk out of one culture
> and into another,
> because I am in all cultures at the same time,
> *alma entre dos mundos, tres, cuatro,*
> *me zumba la cabeza con lo contradictorio.*

Reprinted from *Making Face, Making Soul: Haciendo Caras,* Aunt Lute Books.

> *Estoy norteada por todas las voces que me hablan simultáneamente.*

The ambivalence from the clash of voices results in mental and emotional states of perplexity. Internal strife results in insecurity and indecisiveness. The *mestiza*'s dual or multiple personality is plagued by psychic restlessness.

In a constant state of mental nepantilism, an Aztec word meaning torn between ways, *la mestiza* is a product of the transfer of the cultural and spiritual values of one group to another. Being tricultural, monolingual, bilingual or multilingual, speaking a patois, and in a state of perpetual transition, the *mestiza* faces the dilemma of the mixed breed: which collectivity does the daughter of a darkskinned mother listen to?

El choque de un alma atrapado entre el mundo del espíritu y el mundo de la técnica a veces la deja entullada. Cradled in one culture, sandwiched between two cultures, straddling all three cultures and their value systems, *la mestiza* undergoes a struggle of flesh, a struggle of borders, an inner war. Like all people, we perceive the version of reality that our culture communicates. Like others having or living in more than one culture, we get multiple, often opposing messages. The coming together of two self-consistent but habitually incompatible frames of reference[3] causes *un choque*, a cultural collision.

Within us and within *la cultura chicana*, commonly held beliefs of the white culture attack commonly held beliefs of the Mexican culture, and both attack commonly held beliefs of the indigenous culture. Subconsciously, we see an attack on ourselves and our beliefs as a threat and we attempt to block with a counterstance.

But it is not enough to stand on the opposite river bank, shouting questions, challenging patriarchical, white conventions. A counterstance locks one into a duel of oppressor and oppressed; locked in mortal combat, like the cop and the criminal, both are reduced to a common denominator of violence. The counterstance refutes the dominant culture's views and beliefs, and, for this, it is proudly defiant. All reaction is limited by, and dependent on, what it is reacting against. Because the counterstance stems from a problem with authority—outer as well as inner—it's a step towards liberation from cultural domination. But it is not a way of life. At some point, on our way to a new consciousness, we will have to leave the opposite bank, the split between the two mortal combatants somehow healed so that we are on both shores at once and, at once, see through serpent and eagle eyes. Or perhaps we will decide to disengage from the dominant culture, write it off altogether as a lost cause, and cross the border into a wholly new and separate territory. Or we might go another route. The possibilities are numerous once we decide to act and not react.

A Tolerance For Ambiguity

These numerous possibilities leave *la mestiza* floundering in uncharted seas. In perceiving conflicting information and points of view, she is subjected to a swamping of her psychological borders. She has discovered that she can't hold concepts or ideas in rigid boundaries. The borders and walls that are supposed to keep the undesirable ideas out are entrenched habits and patterns of behavior; these habits and patterns are the enemy within. Rigidity means death. Only by remaining flexible is she able to stretch the psyche horizontally and vertically. *La mestiza* constantly has to shift out of habitual formations; from convergent thinking, analytical reasoning that tends to use rationality to move toward a single goal (a Western mode), to divergent thinking,[4] characterized by movement away from set patterns and goals and toward a more whole perspective, one that includes rather than excludes.

The new *mestiza* copes by developing a tolerance for contradictions, a tolerance for ambiguity. She learns to be an Indian in Mexican culture, to be Mexican from an Anglo point of view. She learns to juggle cultures. She has a plural personality, she operates in a pluralistic mode—nothing is thrust out, the good, the bad and the ugly, nothing rejected, nothing abandoned. Not only does she sustain contradictions, she turns the ambivalence into something else.

She can be jarred out of ambivalence by an intense, and often painful, emotional event which inverts or resolves the ambivalence. I'm not sure exactly how. The work takes place underground—subconsciously. It is work that the soul performs. That focal point or fulcrum, that juncture where the *mestiza* stands, is where phenomena tend to collide. It is where the possibility of uniting all that is separate occurs. This assembly is not one where severed or separated pieces merely come together. Nor is it a balancing of opposing powers. In attempting to work out a synthesis, the self has added a third element which is greater than the sum of its severed parts. That third element is a new consciousness—a *mestiza* consciousness—and though it is a source of intense pain, its energy comes from a continual creative motion that keeps breaking down the unitary aspect of each new paradigm.

En unas pocas centurias, the future will belong to the *mestiza.* Because the future depends on the breaking down of paradigms, it depends on the straddling of two or more cultures. By creating a new mythos—that is, a change in the way we perceive reality, the way we see ourselves and the ways we behave—*la mestiza* creates a new consciousness.

The work of *mestiza* consciousness is to break down the subject-object duality that keeps her a prisoner and to show in the flesh and through the images in her work how duality is transcended. The answer to the problem between the white race and the colored, between males and females, lies in healing the split that originates in the very foundation of our lives, our culture, our languages, our thoughts. A massive uprooting of dualistic thinking in the individual and collective consciousness is the beginning of a long struggle, but one that could, in our best hopes, bring us to the end of rape, of violence, of war.

La encrucijada/The Crossroads

> A chicken is being sacrificed
> at a crossroads, a simple mound of earth
> a mud shrine for *Eshu,*
> *Yoruba* god of indeterminacy,
> who blesses her choice of path.
> She begins her journey.

Su cuerpo es una bocacalle. La mestiza has gone from being the sacrificial goat to becoming the officiating priestess at the crossroads.

As a *mestiza* I have no country, my homeland cast me out; yet all countries are mine because I am every woman's sister or potential lover. (As a lesbian I have no race, my own people disclaim me; but I am all races because there is the queer of me in all races.) I am cultureless because, as a feminist, I challenge the collective cultural/religious male-derived beliefs of Indo-Hispanics and Anglos; yet I am cultured because I am participating in the creation of yet another culture, a new story to explain the world and our participation in it, a new value system with images and symbols that connect us to each other and to the planet. *Soy un amasamiento,* I am an act of kneading, of uniting and joining that not only has produced both a creature of darkness and a creature of light, but also a creature that questions the definitions of light and dark and gives them new meanings.

We are the people who leap in the dark, we are the people on the knees of the gods. In our flesh, (r)evolution works out the clash of cultures. It makes us crazy constantly, but if the center holds, we've made some kind of evolutionary step forward. *Nuestra alma el trabajo,* the opus, the great alchemical work; spiritual *mestizaje,* a "morphogenesis,"* an inevitable unfolding. We have become the quickening serpent movement.

Indigenous like corn, like corn, the *mestiza* is a product of crossbreeding, designed for preservation under a variety of conditions. Like an ear of corn—a female seed-bearing organ—the *mestiza* is tenacious, tightly wrapped in the husks of her culture. Like kernels she clings to the cob; with thick stalks and strong brace roots, she holds tight to the earth—she will survive the crossroads.

*Lavando y remojando el maíz en agua de cal, despojando el pellejo. Moliendo, mixteando, amasando, haciendo tortillas de masa.*** She steeps the corn in lime, it swells, softens. With stone roller on *metate,* she grinds the corn, then grinds again. She kneads and moulds the dough, pats the round balls into *tortillas.*

> We are the porous rock in the stone *metate*
> squatting on the ground.
> We are the rolling pin, *el maíz y agua,*
> *la masa harina. Somos el amasijo.*
> *Somos lo molido en el metate.*
> We are the *comal* sizzling hot,
> the hot *tortilla,* the hungry mouth.
> We are the coarse rock.

---

*To borrow chemist Ilya Prigogine's theory of "dissipative structures." Prigogine discovered that substances interact not in predictable ways as it was taught in science, but in different and fluctuating ways to produce new and more complex structures, a kind of birth he called "morphogenesis," which created unpredictable innovations.[5]

***Tortillas de masa harina*: corn tortillas are of two types, the smooth uniform ones made in a tortilla press and usually bought at a tortilla factory or supermarket, and *gorditas,* made by mixing *masa* with lard or shortening or butter (my mother sometimes puts in bits of bacon or *chicharrones*).

We are the grinding motion,
the mixed potion, *somos el molcajete.*
We are the pestle, the *comino, ajo, pimienta,*
We are the *chile colorado,*
the green shoot that cracks the rock.
We will abide.

El camino de la mestiza/The *Mestiza* Way

Caught between the sudden contraction, the breath sucked in and the endless space, the brown woman stands still, looks at the sky. She decides to go down, digging her way along the roots of trees. Sifting through the bones, she shakes them to see if there is any marrow in them. Then, touching the dirt to her forehead, to her tongue, she takes a few bones, leaves the rest in their burial place.
She goes through her backpack, keeps her journal and address book, throws away the muni-bart metromaps. The coins are heavy and they go next, then the greenbacks flutter through the air. She keeps her knife, can opener and eyebrow pencil. She puts bones, pieces of bark, *hierbas,* eagle feather, snakeskin, tape recorder, the rattle and drum in her pack and she sets out to become the complete *tolteca.*

Her first step is to take inventory. *Despojando, desgranando, quitando paja.* Just what did she inherit from her ancestors? This weight on her back—which is the baggage from the Indian mother, which the baggage from the Spanish father, which the baggage from the Anglo?

Pero es difícil differentiating between *lo heredado, lo adquirido, lo impuesto.* She puts history through a sieve, winnows out the lies, looks at the forces that we as a race, as women, have been a part of. *Luego bota lo que no vale, los desmientos, los desencuentos, el embrutecimiento. Aguarda el juicio, hondo y enraízado, de la gente antigua.* This step is a conscious rupture with all oppressive traditions of all cultures and religions. She communicates that rupture, documents the struggle. She reinterprets history and, using new symbols, she shapes new myths. She adopts new perspectives toward the darkskinned, women and queers. She strengthens her tolerance (and intolerance) for ambiguity. She is willing to share, to make herself vulnerable to foreign ways of seeing and thinking.

She surrenders all notions of safety, of the familiar. Deconstruct, construct. She becomes a *nahual,* able to transform herself into a tree, a coyote, into another person. She learns to transform the small "I" into the total Self. *Se hace moldeadora de su alma. Según la concepción que tiene de sí misma, así será.*

Que no se nos olvide los hombres

> "Tú no sirves pa' nada—
> you're good for nothing.
> *Eres pura vieja.*"

"You're nothing but a woman" means you are defective. Its opposite is to be *un macho.* The modern meaning of the word "machismo," as well as the concept, is actually an Anglo invention. For men like my father, being "macho" meant being strong enough to protect and support my mother and us, yet being able to show love. Today's macho has doubts about his ability to feed and protect his family. His "machismo" is an adaptation to oppression and poverty and low self-esteem. It is the result of hierarchical male dominance. The Anglo, feeling inadequate and inferior and powerless, displaces or transfers these feeling to the Chicano by shaming him. In the Gringo world, the Chicano suffers from excessive humility and self-effacement, shame of self and self-deprecation. Around Latinos he suffers from a sense of language inadequacy and its accompanying discomfort; with Native Americans he suffers from a racial amnesia which ignores our common blood, and from guilt because the Spanish part of him took their land and oppressed them. He has an excessive compensatory hubris when around Mexicans from the other side. It overlays a deep sense of racial shame.

The loss of a sense of dignity and respect in the macho breeds a false machismo which leads him to put down women and even to brutalize them. Coexisting with his sexist behavior is a love for the mother which takes precedence over that of all others. Devoted son, macho pig. To wash down the shame of his acts, of his very being, and to handle the brute in the mirror, he takes to the bottle, the snort, the needle and the fist.

Though we "understand" the root causes of male hatred and fear, and the subsequent wounding of women, we do not excuse, we do not condone and we will not longer put up with it. From the men of our race, we demand the admission/acknowledgement/disclosure/testimony that they wound us, violate us, are afraid of us and of our power. We need them to say they will begin to eliminate their hurtful put-down ways. But more than the words, we demand acts. We say to them: we will develop equal power with you and those who have shamed us.

It is imperative that *mestizas* support each other in changing the sexist elements in the Mexican-Indian culture. As long as woman is put down, the Indian and the Black in all of us is put down. The struggle of the *mestiza* is above all a feminist one. As long as *los hombres* think they have to *chingar mujeres* and each other to be men, as long as men are taught that they are superior and therefore culturally favored over *la mujer*, as long as to be a *vieja* is a thing of derision, there can be no real healing of our psyches. We're halfway there—we have such love of the Mother, the good mother. The first step is to unlearn the *puta/virgen* dichotomy and to see *Coatlapopeuh—Coatlicue* in the Mother, *Guadalupe*.

Tenderness, a sign of vulnerability, is so feared that it is showered on women with verbal abuse and blows. Men, even more than women, are fettered to gender roles. Women at least have had the guts to break out of bondage. Only gay men have had the courage to expose themselves to the woman inside them and to challenge the current masculinity. I've encountered a few scattered and isolated gentle straight men, the beginnings of a new breed, but they are confused, and entangled with sexist behaviors that they have not been able to eradicate. We need a new masculinity and the new man needs a movement.

Lumping the males who deviate from the general norm with man, the oppressor, is a gross injustice. *Asombra pensar que nos hemos quedado en ese pozo oscuro donde el mundo encierra a las lesbianas. Asombra pensar que hemos, como femenistas y lesbianas, cerrado nuestros corazónes a los hombres, a nuestros hermanos los jotos, desheredados y marginales como nosotros.* Being the supreme crossers of cultures, homosexuals have strong bonds with the queer white, Black, Asian, Native American, Latino and with the queer in Italy, Australia and the rest of the planet. We come from all colors, all classes, all races, all time periods. Our role is to link people with each other—the Blacks with Jews with Indians with Asians with whites with extraterrestrials. It is to transfer ideas and information from one culture to another. Colored homosexuals have more knowledge of other cultures; have always been at the forefront (although sometimes in the closet) of all liberation struggles in this country; have suffered more injustices and have survived them despite all odds. Chicanos need to acknowledge the political and artistic contributions of their queer. People, listen to what your *jotería* is saying.

The *mestizo* and the queer exist at this time and point on the evolutionary continuum for a purpose. We are a blending that proves that all blood is intricately woven together, and that we are spawned out of similar souls.

Somos una genta

> *Hay tantísimas fronteras*
> que dividen a la gente,
> pero por cada frontera
> existe también un puente.
> —GINA VALDÉS[6]

Divided Loyalties. Many women and men of color do not want to have any dealings with white people. It takes too much time and energy to explain to the downwardly mobile, white middle-class women that it's okay for us to want to own "possesions," never having had any nice furniture on our dirt floors or "luxuries" like washing machines. Many feel that whites should help their own people rid themselves of race hatred and fear first. I, for one, choose to use some of my energy to serve as mediator. I think we need to allow whites to be our allies. Through our literature, art, *corridos* and folktales we must share our history with them so when they set up committees to help Big Mountain Navajos or the Chicano farmworkers or *los Nicaragüenses* they won't turn people away because of their racial fears and ignorances. They will come to see that they are not helping us but following our lead.

Individually, but also as a racial entity, we need to voice our needs. We need to say to white society: we need you to accept the fact that Chicanos are different, to acknowledge your rejection and negation of us. We need you to own the fact that you looked upon us as less than human, that you stole our lands, our personhood, our self-respect. We need you to make public restitution: to say that, to compensate for your own sense of defectiveness, you strive for power over us, you erase our history and our experience because it makes you feel guilty—you'd rather forget your brutish acts. To say you've split yourself from minority groups, that you disown us, that your dual consciousness splits off parts of yourself, transferring the "negative" parts onto us. (Where there is persecution of minorities, there is shadow projection. Where there is violence and war, there is repression of shadow.) To say that you are afraid of us, that to put distance between us, you wear the mask of contempt. Admit that Mexico is your double, that she exists in the shadow of this country, that we are irrevocably tied to her. Gringo, accept the doppelganger in your psyche. By taking back your collective shadow the intracultural split will heal. And finally, tell us what you need from us.

By Your True Faces We Will Know You

I am visible—see this Indian face—yet I am invisible. I both blind them with my beak nose and am their blind spot. But I exist, we exist. They'd like to think I have melted in the pot. But I haven't, we haven't.

The dominant white culture is killing us slowly with its ignorance. By taking away our self-determination, it has made us weak and empty. As a people we have resisted and we have taken expedient positions, but we have never been allowed to develop unencumbered—we have never been allowed to be fully ourselves. The whites in power want us people of color to barricade ourselves behind our separate tribal walls so they can pick us off one at a time with their hidden weapons; so they can whitewash and distort history. Ignorance splits people, creates prejudices. A misinformed people is a subjugated people.

Before the Chicano and the undocumented worker and the Mexican from the other side can come together, before the Chicano can have unity with Native Americans and other groups, we need to know the history of their struggle and they need to know ours. Our mothers, our sisters and brothers, the guys who hang out on street corners, the children in the playgrounds, each of us must know our Indian lineage, our afro-*mestisaje*, our history of resistance.

To the immigrant *mexicano* and the recent arrivals we must teach our history. The 80 million *mexicanos* and the Latinos from Central and South America must know of our struggles. Each one of us must know basic facts about Nicaragua, Chile and the rest of Latin America. The Latinoist movement (Chicanos, Puerto Ricans,

Cubans and other Spanish-speaking people working together to combat racial discrimination in the market place) is good but it is not enough. Other than a common culture we will have nothing to hold us together. We need to meet on a broader communal ground.

The struggle is inner: Chicano, *indio*, American Indian, *mojado, mexicano*, immigrant Latino, Anglo in power, working class Anglo, Black, Asian—our psyches resemble the bordertowns and are populated by the same people. The struggle has always been inner, and is played out in the outer terrains. Awareness of our situation must come before inner changes, which in turn come before changes in society. Nothing happens in the "real" world unless it first happens in the images in our heads.

El día de la Chicana

> I will not be shamed again
> Nor will I shame myself.

I am possessed by a vision: that we Chicanas and Chicanos have taken back or uncovered our true faces, our dignity and self-respect. It's a validation vision.

Seeing the Chicana anew in light of her history. I seek an exoneration, a seeing through the fictions of white supremacy, a seeing of ourselves in our true guises and not as the false racial personality that has been given to us and that we have given to ourselves. I seek our woman's face, our true features, the positive and the negative seen clearly, free of the tainted biases of male dominance. I seek new images of identity, new beliefs about ourselves, our humanity and worth no longer in question.

Estamos viviendo en la noche de la Raza, un tiempo cuando el trabajo se hace a lo quieto, en el oscuro. El día cuando aceptamos tal y como somos y para en donde vamos y porque—ese día será el día de la Raza. Yo tengo el conpromiso de expresar mi visión, mi sensibilidad, mi percepción de la revalidación de la gente mexicana, su mérito, estimación, honra, aprecio y validez.

On December 2nd when my sun goes into my first house, I celebrate *el día de la Chicana y el Chicano*. On that day I clean my altars, light my *Coatlalopeuh* candle, burn sage and copal, take *el baño para espantar basura*, sweep my house. On that day I bare my soul, make myself vulnerable to friends and family by expressing my feelings. On that day I affirm who we are.

On that day I look inside our conflicts and our basic introverted racial temperament. I identify our needs, voice them. I acknowledge that the self and the race have been wounded. I recognize the need to take care of our personhood, of our racial self. On that day I gather the splintered and disowned parts of *la gente mexicana* and hold them in my arms. *Todas las partes de nosotros valen.*

On that day I say, "Yes, all you people wound us when you reject us. Rejection strips us of self-worth; our vulnerability exposes us to shame. It is our innate identity you find wanting. We are ashamed that we need your good opinion, that we need your acceptance. We can no longer camouflage our needs, can no longer let defenses and fences sprout around us. We can no longer withdraw. To rage and look upon you with contempt is to rage and be contemptuous of ourselves. We can no longer blame you, nor disown the white parts, the male parts, the pathological parts, the queer parts, the vulnerable parts. Here we are weaponless with open arms, with only our magic. Let's try it our way, the *mestiza* way, the Chicana way, the woman way.

On that day, I search for our essential dignity as a people, a people with a sense of purpose—to belong and contribute to something greater than our *pueblo*. On that day I seek to recover and reshape my spiritual identity. *Anímate! Raza, a celebrar el día de la Chicana.*

El retorno

> All movements are accomplished in six stages,
> and the seventh brings return.
>
> —I CHING[7]
>
> *Tanto tiempo sin verte casa mía,*
> mi cuna, mi hondo nido de la huerta.
>
> —"SOLEDAD"[8]

I stand at the river, watch the curving, twisting serpent, a serpent nailed to the fence where the mouth of the Rio Grande empties into the Gulf.

I have come back. *Tanto dolor me costó el alejamiento.* I shade my eyes and look up. The bone beak of a hawk slowly circling over me, checking me out as potential carrion. In its wake a little bird flickering its wings, swimming sporadically like a fish. In the distance the expressway and the slough of traffic like an irritated sow. The sudden pull in my gut, *la tierra, los aguaceros*. My land, *el viento soplando la arena, el lagartijo debajo de un nopalito. Me acuerdo como era antes. Una región desértica de vasta llanuras, costeras de baja altura, de escasa lluvia, de chaparrales formados por mesquites y huizaches*. If I look real hard I can almost see the Spanish fathers who were called "the cavalry of Christ" enter this valley riding their burros, see the clash of cultures commence.

Tierra natal. This is home, the small towns in the Valley, *los pueblitos* with chicken pens and goats picketed to mesquite shrubs. *En las colonias* on the other side of the tracks, junk cars line the front yards of hot pink and lavender-trimmed houses—Chicano architecture we call it, self-consciously. I have missed the TV shows where hosts speak in half and half, and where awards are given in the category of Tex-Mex music. I have missed the Mexican cemeteries blooming with artificial flowers, the fields of aloe vera and red pepper, rows of sugar cane, of corn hanging on the stalks, the cloud of *polvareda* in the dirt roads behind a speeding truck, *el sabor de tamales de rez y venado*. I have missed *la yequa colorada* gnawing the wooden gate of her stall, the smell of horse flesh from Carito's corrals. *He hecho menos las noches calientes sin aire, noches de linternas y lechuzas* making holes in the night.

I still feel the old despair when I look at the unpainted, dilapidated, scrap lumber houses consisting mostly of corrugated aluminum. Some of the poorest people in the U.S. live in the Lower Rio Grande Valley, an arid and semi-arid land of irrigated farming, intense sunlight and heat, citrus groves next to chaparral and cactus. I walk through the elementary school I attended so long ago, that remained segregated until recently. I remember how the white teachers used to punish us for being Mexican.

How I love this tragic valley of South Texas, as Ricardo Sánchez calls it; this borderland between the Nueces and the Rio Grande. This land has survived possession and ill-use by five countries: Spain, Mexico, the Republic of Texas, the Confederacy, and the U.S. again. It has survived Anglo-Mexican blood feuds, lynchings, burnings, rapes, pillage.

Today I see the Valley still struggling to survive. Whether it does or not, it will never be as I remember it. The borderlands depression that was set off by the 1982 peso devaluation in Mexico resulted in the closure of hundreds of Valley businesses. Many people lost their homes, cars, land. Prior to 1982, U.S. store owners thrived on retail sales to Mexicans who came across the borders for groceries and clothes and appliances. While goods on the U.S. side have become 10, 100, 1000 times more expensive for Mexican buyers, goods on the Mexican side have become 10, 100, 1000 times cheaper for Americans. Because the Valley is heavily dependent on agriculture and Mexican retail trade, it has the highest unemployment rates along the entire border region; it is the Valley that has been hardest hit.*

"It's been a bad year for corn," my brother, Nune, says. As he talks, I remember my father scanning the sky for a rain that would end the drought, looking up into the sky, day after day, while the corn withered on its stalk. My father has been dead for 29 years, having worked himself to death. The life span of a Mexican farm laborer is 56—he lived to be 38. It shocks me that I am older than he. I, too, search the sky for rain. Like the ancients, I worship the rain god and the maize goddess, but unlike my father I have recovered their names. Now for rain (irrigation) one offers not a sacrifice of blood, but of money.

"Farming is in a bad way," my brother says. "Two to three thousand small and big farmers went bankrupt in this country last year. Six years ago the price of corn was $8.00 per hundred pounds," he goes on. "This year it is $3.90 per hundred pounds." And, I think to myself, after taking inflation into account, not planting anything puts you ahead.

I walk out to the back yard, stare at *los rosales de mamá*. She wants me to help her prune the rose bushes, dig out the carpet grass that is choking them. *Mamagrande Ramona también tenía rosales*. Here every Mexican grows flowers. If they don't have a piece of dirt, they use car tires, jars, cans, shoe boxes. Roses are the Mexican's favorite flower. I think, how symbolic—thorns and all.

Yes, the Chicano and Chicana have always taken care of growing things and the land. Again I see the four of us kids getting off the school bus, changing into our work clothes, walking

---

*Out of the twenty-two border counties in the four border states, Hidalgo County (named for Father Hidalgo who was shot in 1810 after instigating Mexico's revolt against Spanish rule under the banner of *la Virgen de Guadalupe*) is the most poverty-stricken county in the nation as well as the largest home base (along with Imperial in California) for migrant farmworkers. It was here that I was born and raised, I am amazed that both it and I have survived.

into the field with Papí and Mamí, all six of us bending to the ground. Below our feet, under the earth lie the watermelon seeds. We cover them with paper plates, putting *terremotes* on top of the plates to keep them from being blown away by the wind. The paper plates keep the freeze away. Next day or the next, we remove the plates, bare the tiny green shoots to the elements. They survive and grow, give fruit hundreds of times the size of the seed. We water them and hoe them. We harvest them. The vines dry, rot, are plowed under. Growth, death, decay, birth. The soil prepared again and again, impregnated, worked on. A constant changing of forms, *renacimientos de la tierra madre.*

> This land was Mexican once
> was Indian always
> and is.
> And will be again.

—From *Borderlands/La Frontera: The New Mestiza*

Notes

1. This is my own "take-off" on Jose Vasconcelos' idea. Jose Vasconcelos, *La Raza Cósmica: Missión de la Raza Ibero-Americana* (México: Aguilar S.A. de Ediciones, 1961).
2. Vasconcelos.
3. Arthur Koestler termed this "bisociation." Albert Rothenberg, *The Creative Process in Art, Science, and Other Fields* (Chicago, IL: University of Chicago Press, 1979), 12.
4. In part, I derive my definitions for "convergent" and "divergent" thinking from Rothenberg, 12–13.
5. Harold Gilliam, "Searching for a New World View," *This World* (January, 1981), 23.
6. Gina Valdés, *Puentes y Fronteras: Coplas Chicanas* (Los Angeles, CA: Castle Lithograph, 1982), 2.
7. Richard Wilhelm, *The I Ching or Book of Changes*, trans. Cary F. Baynes (Princeton, NJ: Princeton University Press, 1950), 98.
8. *"Soledad"* is sung by the group Haciendo Punto en Otro Son.

Theorizing Difference From Multiracial Feminism (1996)

Maxine Baca Zinn and Bonnie Thornton Dill

In "Theorizing Difference from Multiracial Feminism," Maxine Baca Zinn and Bonnie Thornton Dill articulate a working definition of multiracial feminism, tracing its roots in socialist feminism and race/ethnic studies, explaining its underlying premises, and differentiating it from other modes of feminist thinking. While Baca Zinn and Thornton Dill affirm that multiracial feminism is an evolving conceptual framework, they nevertheless identify principles crucial to this approach—the role of race and institutionalized racism in shaping social, cultural and group differences and the "interlocking inequalities" that produce socially-constructed differences like gender. Multiracial feminism begins with race and utilizes it as a lens to analyze other social constructs and inequalities that influence women's lives.

Women of color have long challenged the hegemony of feminisms constructed primarily around the lives of white middle-class women. Since the late 1960s, U.S. women of color have taken issue with unitary theories of gender. Our critiques grew out of the widespread concern about the exclusion of women of color from feminist scholarship and the misinterpretation of our experiences,[1] and ultimately "out of the very discourses, denying, permitting, and producing difference."[2] Speaking simultaneously from "within and against" *both* women's liberation *and* antiracist movements, we have insisted on the need to challenge systems of domination,[3] not merely as gendered subjects but as women whose lives are affected by our location in multiple hierarchies.

Recently, and largely in response to these challenges, work that links gender to other forms of domination is increasing. In this article, we examine this connection further as well as the ways in which difference and diversity infuse contemporary feminist studies. Our analysis draws on a conceptual framework that we refer to as "multiracial feminism."[4] This perspective is an attempt to go beyond a mere recognition of diversity and difference among women to examine structures of domination, specifically the importance of race in understanding the social construction of gender. Despite the varied concerns and multiple intellectual stances which characterize the feminisms of women of color, they share an emphasis on race as a primary force situating genders differently. It is the centrality of race, of institutionalized racism, and of struggles against racial oppression that link the various feminist perspectives within this framework. Together, they demonstrate that racial meanings offer new theoretical directions for feminist thought.

Tensions in Contemporary Difference Feminism

Objections to the false universalism embedded in the concept "woman" emerged within other discourses as well as those of women of color.[5] Lesbian feminists and postmodern feminists put

"Theorizing Difference from Multiracial Feminism," by Maxine Baca Zinn and Bonnie Thornton Dill. This article is reprinted from *Feminist Studies*, Volume 22, Number 2 (Summer 1996): 321-331, by permission of the publisher, Feminist Studies, Inc., c/o Department of Women's Studies, University of Maryland, College Park, MD 20742.

forth their own versions of what Susan Bordo has called "gender skepticism."[6]

Many thinkers within mainstream feminism have responded to these critiques with efforts to contextualize gender. The search for women's "universal" or "essential" characteristics is being abandoned. By examining gender in the context of other social divisions and perspectives, difference has gradually become important—even problematizing the universal categories of "women" and "men." Sandra Harding expresses the shift best in her claim that "there are no gender relations *per se*, but only gender relations as constructed by and between classes, races, and cultures."[7]

Many feminists now contend that difference occupies center stage as *the* project of women studies today.[8] According to one scholar, "difference has replaced equality as the central concern of feminist theory."[9] Many have welcomed the change, hailing it as a major revitalizing force in U.S. feminist theory.[10] But if *some* priorities within mainstream feminist thought have been refocused by attention to difference, there remains an "uneasy alliance"[11] between women of color and other feminists.

If difference has helped revitalize academic feminisms, it has also "upset the apple cart" and introduced new conflicts into feminist studies.[12] For example, in a recent and widely discussed essay, Jane Rowland Martin argues that the current preoccupation with difference is leading feminism into dangerous traps. She fears that in giving privileged status to a predetermined set of analytic categories (race, ethnicity, and class), "we affirm the existence of nothing but difference." She asks, "How do we know that for us, difference does not turn on being fat, or religious, or in an abusive relationship?"[13]

We, too, see pitfalls in some strands of the difference project. However, our perspectives take their bearings from social relations. Race and class differences are crucial, we argue, not as individual characteristics (such as being fat) but insofar as they are primary organizing principles of a society which locates and positions groups within that society's opportunity structures.

Despite the much-heralded diversity trend within feminist studies, difference is often reduced to mere pluralism: a "live and let live" approach where principles of relativism generate a long list of diversities which begin with gender, class, and race and continue through a range of social structural as well as personal characteristics.[14] Another disturbing pattern, which bell hooks refers to as "the commodification of difference," is the representation of diversity as a form of exotica, "a spice, seasoning that livens up the dull dish that is mainstream white culture."[15] The major limitation of these approaches is the failure to attend to the power relations that accompany difference. Moreover, these approaches ignore the inequalities that cause some characteristics to be seen as "normal" while others are seen as "different" and thus, deviant.

Maria C. Lugones expresses irritation at those feminists who see only the *problem* of difference without recognizing *difference*.[16] Increasingly, we find that difference *is* recognized. But this in no way means that difference occupies a "privileged" theoretical status. Instead of using difference to rethink the category of women, difference is often a euphemism for women who differ from the traditional norm. Even in purporting to accept difference, feminist pluralism often creates a social reality that reverts to universalizing women:

> So much feminist scholarship assumes that when we cut through all of the diversity among women created by differences of racial classification, ethnicity, social class, and sexual orientation, a "universal truth" concerning women and gender lies buried underneath. But if we can face the scary possibility that no such certainty exists and that persisting in such a search will always distort or omit someone's experiences, with what do we replace this old way of thinking? Gender differences and gender politics begin to look very different if there is no essential woman at the core.[17]

What is Multiracial Feminism?

A new set of feminist theories have emerged from the challenges put forth by women of color. Multiracial feminism is an evolving body of theory and practice informed by wide-ranging intellectual traditions. This framework does not offer a singular or unified feminism but a body of knowledge situating women and men in multiple systems of domination. U.S. multiracial feminism encompasses several emergent perspectives developed primarily by women of color: African Americans, Latinas, Asian Americans, and Native Americans, women whose analyses are shaped by their unique perspectives as "outsiders within"—marginal intellectuals whose social locations provide them with a particular perspective on self and society.[18] Although U.S. women of color represent many races and ethnic backgrounds—with different histories and cultures—our feminisms cohere in their treatment of race as a basic social division, a structure of power, a focus of political struggle, and hence a fundamental force in shaping women's and men's lives.

This evolving intellectual and political perspective uses several controversial terms. While we adopt the label "multiracial," other terms have been used to describe this broad framework. For example, Chela Sandoval refers to "U.S. Third World feminisms,"[19] while other scholars refer to "indigenous feminisms." In their theory text-reader, Alison M. Jagger and Paula M. Rothenberg adopt the label "multicultural feminism."[20]

We use "multiracial" rather than "multicultural" as a way of underscoring race as a power system that interacts with other structured inequalities to shape genders. Within the U.S. context, race, and the system of meanings and ideologies which accompany it, is a fundamental organizing principle of social relationships.[21] Race affects all women and men, although in different ways. Even cultural and group differences among women are produced through interaction within a racially stratified social order. Therefore, although we do not discount the importance of culture, we caution that cultural analytic frameworks that ignore race tend to view women's differences as the product of group-specific values and practices that often result in the marginalization of cultural groups which are then perceived as exotic expressions of a normative center. Our focus on race stresses the social construction of differently situated social groups and their varying degrees of advantage and power. Additionally, this emphasis on race takes on increasing political importance in an era where discourse about race is governed by color-evasive language[22] and a preference for individual rather than group remedies for social inequalities. Our analyses insist upon the primary and pervasive nature of race in contemporary U.S. society while at the same time acknowledging how race both shapes and is shaped by a variety of other social relations.

In the social sciences, multiracial feminism grew out of socialist feminist thinking. Theories about how political economic forces shape women's lives were influential as we began to uncover the social causes of racial ethnic women's subordination. But socialist feminism's concept of capitalist patriarchy, with its focus on women's unpaid (reproductive) labor in the home failed to address racial differences in the organization of reproductive labor. As feminists of color have argued, "reproductive labor has divided along racial as well as gender lines, and the specific characteristics have varied regionally and changed over time as capitalism has reorganized."[23] Despite the limitations of socialist feminism, this body of literature has been especially useful in pursuing questions about the interconnections among systems of domination.[24]

Race and ethnic studies was the other major social scientific source of multiracial feminism. It provided a basis for comparative analyses of groups that are socially and legally subordinated and remain culturally distinct within U.S. society. This includes the systematic discrimination of socially constructed racial groups and their distinctive cultural arrangements. Historically, the categories of African American, Latino, Asian American, and Native American were constructed as both racially and culturally distinct. Each group has a distinctive culture, shares a common heritage, and has developed a common identity within a larger society that subordinates them.[25]

We recognize, of course, certain problems inherent in an uncritical use of the multiracial label. First, the perspective can be hampered by a biracial model in which only African Americans and whites are seen as racial categories and all other groups are viewed through the prism of cultural differences. Latinos and Asians have always occupied distinctive places within the racial hierarchy, and current shifts in the composition of the U.S. population are racializing these groups anew.[26]

A second problem lies in treating multiracial feminism as a single analytical framework, and its principle architects, women of color, as an undifferentiated category. The concepts "multiracial feminism," "racial ethnic women," and "women of color" "homogenize quite different experiences and can falsely universalize experiences across race, ethnicity, sexual orientation, and age."[27] The feminisms created by women of color exhibit a plurality of intellectual and political positions. We speak in many voices, with inconsistencies that are born of our different social locations. Multiracial feminism embodies this plurality and richness. Our intent is not to falsely universalize women of color. Nor do we wish to promote a new racial essentialism in place of the old gender essentialism. Instead, we use these concepts to examine the structures and experiences produced by intersecting forms of race and gender.

It is also essential to acknowledge that race is a shifting and contested category whose meanings construct definitions of all aspects of social life.[28] In the United States it helped define citizenship by excluding everyone who was not a white, male property owner. It defined labor as slave or free, coolie or contract, and family as available only to those men whose marriages were recognized or whose wives could immigrate with them. Additionally, racial meanings are contested both within groups and between them.[29]

Although definitions of race are at once historically and geographically specific, they are also transnational, encompassing diasporic groups and crossing traditional geographic boundaries. Thus, while U.S. multiracial feminism calls attention to the fundamental importance of race, it must also locate the meaning of race within specific national traditions.

The Distinguishing Features of Multiracial Feminism

By attending to these problems, multiracial feminism offers a set of analytic premises for thinking about and theorizing gender. The following themes distinguish this branch of feminist inquiry.

First, multiracial feminism asserts that gender is constructed by a range of interlocking inequalities, what Patricia Hill Collins calls a "matrix of domination."[30] The idea of a matrix is that several fundamental systems work with and through each other. People experience race, class, gender, and sexuality differently depending upon their social location in the structures of race, class, gender, and sexuality. For example, people of the same race will experience race differently depending upon their location in the class structure as working class, professional managerial class, or unemployed; in the gender structure as female or male; and in structures of sexuality as heterosexual, homosexual, or bisexual.

Multiracial feminism also examines the simultaneity of systems in shaping women's experience and identity. Race, class, gender, and sexuality are not reducible to individual attributes to be measured and assessed for their separate contribution in explaining given social outcomes, an approach that Elizabeth Spelman calls "popbead metaphysics," where a women's identity consists of the sum of parts neatly divisible from one another.[31] The matrix of domination seeks to account for the multiple ways that women experience themselves as gendered, raced, classed, and sexualized.

Second, multiracial feminism emphasizes the intersectional nature of hierarchies at all levels of social life. Class, race, gender, and sexuality are components of both social structure and social interaction. Women and men are differently embedded in locations created by these cross-cutting hierarchies. As a result, women and men throughout the social order experience different forms of privilege and subordination, depending on their race, class, gender, and sexuality. In other words, intersecting forms of domination produce *both* oppression *and* opportunity. At the same time that structures of race, class, and gender create disadvantages for women of color, they provide unacknowledged benefits for those who are at the top of these hierarchies—whites, members of the upper classes, and males. Therefore, multiracial feminism applies not only to racial ethnic women but also to women and men of all races, classes, and genders.

Third, multiracial feminism highlights the relational nature of dominance and subordination. Power is the cornerstone of women's differences.[32] This means that women's differences are *connected* in systematic ways.[33] Race is a vital element in the pattern of relations among minority and white women. As Linda Gordon argues, the very meanings of being a white woman in the United States have been affected by the existence of subordinated women of color: "They intersect in conflict and in occasional cooperation, but always in mutual influence."[34]

Fourth, multiracial feminism explores the interplay of social structure and women's agency. Within the constraints of race, class, and gender oppression, women create viable lives for themselves, their families, and their communities. Women of color have resisted and often undermined the forces of power that control them. From acts of quiet dignity and steadfast determination to involvement in revolt and rebellion, women struggle to shape their own lives. Racial oppression has been a common focus of the "dynamic of oppositional agency" of women of color. As

Chandra Talpade Mohanty points out, it is the nature and organization of women's opposition which mediates and differentiates the impact of structures of domination.[35]

Fifth, multiracial feminism encompasses wide-ranging methodological approaches, and like other branches of feminist thought, relies on varied theoretical tools as well. Ruth Frankenberg and Lata Mani identify three guiding principles of inclusive feminist inquiry: "building complex analyses, avoiding erasure, specifying location."[36] In the last decade, the opening up of academic feminism has focused attention on social location in the production of knowledge. Most basically, research by and about marginalized women has destabilized what used to be considered as universal categories of gender. Marginalized locations are well suited for grasping social relations that remained obscure from more privileged vantage points. Lived experience, in other words, creates alternative ways of understanding the social world and the experience of different groups of women within it. Racially informed standpoint epistemologies have provided new topics, fresh questions, and new understandings of women and men. Women of color have, as Norma Alarçon argues, asserted ourselves as subjects, using our voices to challenge dominant conceptions of truth.[37]

Sixth, multiracial feminism brings together understandings drawn from the lived experiences of diverse and continuously changing groups of women. Among Asian Americans, Native American, Latinas, and Blacks are many different national cultural and ethnic groups. Each one is engaged in the process of testing, refining, and reshaping these broader categories in its own image. Such internal differences heighten awareness of and sensitivity to both commonalities and differences, serving as a constant reminder of the importance of comparative study and maintaining a creative tension between diversity and universalization.

Difference and Transformation

Efforts to make women's studies less partial and less distorted have produced important changes in academic feminism. Inclusive thinking has provided a way to build multiplicity and difference into our analyses. This has led to the discovery that race matters for everyone. White women, too, must be reconceptualized as a category that is multiply defined by race, class, and other differences. As Ruth Frankenberg demonstrates in a study of whiteness among contemporary women, all kinds of social relations, even those that appear neutral, are, in fact, racialized. Frankenberg further complicates the very notion of a unified white identity by introducing issues of Jewish identity.[38] Therefore, the lives of women of color cannot be seen as a *variation on* a more general model of white American womanhood. The model of womanhood that feminist social science once held as "universal" is also a product of race and class.

When we analyze the power relations constituting all social arrangements and shaping women's lives in distinctive ways, we can begin to grapple with core feminist issues about how genders are socially constructed and constructed differently. Women's difference is built into our study of gender. Yet this perspective is quite far removed from the atheoretical pluralism implied in much contemporary thinking about gender.

Multiracial feminism, in our view, focuses not just on differences but also on the way in which differences and domination intersect and are historically and socially constituted. It challenges feminist scholars to go beyond the mere recognition and inclusion of difference to reshape the basic concepts and theories of our disciplines. By attending to women's social location based on race, class, and gender, multiracial feminism seeks to clarify the structural sources of diversity. Ultimately, multiracial feminism forces us to see privilege and subordination as interrelated and to pose such questions as: How do the existences and experiences of all people—women and men, different racial-ethnic groups, and different classes—shape the experiences of each other? How are those relationships defined and enforced through social institutions that are the primary sites for negotiating power within society? How do these differences contribute to the construction of both individual and group identity? Once we acknowledge that all women are affected by the racial order of society, then it becomes clear that the insights of multiracial feminism provide an analytical framework, not solely for understanding the experiences of women of color but for understanding *all* women, and men, as well.

NOTES

1. Maxine Baca Zinn, Lynn Weber Cannon, Elizabeth Higginbotham, and Bonnie Thornton Dill, "The Costs of Exclusionary Practices in Women's Studies," *Signs* 11 (Winter 1986): 290–303.
2. Chela Sandoval, "U.S. Third World Feminism: The Theory and Method of Oppositional Consciousness in the Postmodern World," *Genders* (spring 1991): 1–24.
3. Ruth Frankenberg and Lata Mani, "Cross Currents, Crosstalk: Race, 'Postcoloniality,' and the Politics of Location," *Cultural Studies* 7 (May 1993): 292–310.
4. We use the term "multiracial feminism" to convey the multiplicity of racial groups and feminist perspectives.
5. A growing body of work on difference in feminist thought now exists. Although we cannot cite all the current work, the following are representative: Michèle Barrett, "The Concept of Difference," *Feminists Review* 26 (July 1987): 29–42; Christina Crosby, "Dealing with Difference," in *Feminists Theorize the Political*, ed. Judith Butler and Joan W. Scott (New York: Routledge, 1992), 130–43; Elizabeth Fox-Genovese, "Difference, Diversity, and Divisions in an Agenda for the Women's Movement," in *Color, Class, and Country: Experiences of Gender*, ed. Gay Young and Bette J. Dickerson (London: Zed Books, 1994), 232–48; Nancy A. Hewitt, "Compounding Differences," *Feminist Studies* 18 (summer 1992): 313–26; Maria C. Lugones, "On the Logic of Feminist Pluralism," in *Feminist Ethics*, ed. Claudia Card (Lawrence: University of Kansas Press, 1991), 35–44; Rita S. Gallin and Anne Ferguson, "The Plurality of Feminism: Rethinking 'Difference,'" in *The Woman and International Development Annual* (Boulder: Westview Press, 1993), 3: 1–16; and Linda Gordon, "On Difference," *Genders* 10 (spring 1991): 91–111.
6. Susan Bordo, "Feminism, Postmodernism, and Gender Skepticism," in *Feminism/Postmodernism*, ed. Linda J. Nicholson (London: Routledge, 1990), 133–56.
7. Sandra G. Harding, *Whose Science? Whose Knowledge? Thinking from Women's Lives* (Ithaca: Cornell University Press, 1991), 179.
8. Crosby, 131.
9. Fox-Genovese, 232.

10. Faye Ginsberg and Anna Lowenhaupt Tsing, Introduction to *Uncertain Terms, Negotiating Gender in American Culture*, ed. Faye Ginsberg and Anna Lowenhaupt Tsing (Boston: Beacon Press, 1990), 3.

11. Sandoval, 2.

12. Sandra Morgan, "Making Connections: Socialist-Feminist Challenges to Marxist Scholarship," in *Women and a New Academy: Gender and Cultural Contexts*, ed. Jean F. O'Barr (Madison: University of Wisconsin Press, 1989), 149.

13. Jane Rowland Martin, "Methodological Essentialism, False Difference, and Other Dangerous Traps," *Signs* 19 (Spring 1994): 647.

14. Barrett, 32.

15. bell hooks, *Black Looks: Race and Representaton* (Boston: South End Press, 1992), 21.

16. Lugones, 35–44.

17. Patricia Hill Collins, Foreword to *Women of Color in U.S. Society*, ed. Maxine Baca Zinn and Bonnie Thornton Dill (Philadelphia: Temple University Press, 1994), xv.

18. Patricia Hill Collins, "Learning from the Outsider Within: The Sociological Significance of Black Feminist Thought," *Social Problems* 33 (December 1986): 514–32.

19. Sandoval, 1.

20. Alison M. Jagger and Paula S. Rothenberg, *Feminist Frameworks: Alternative Theoretical Accounts of the Relations between Women and Men*, 3d ed. (New York: McGraw-Hill, 1993).

21. Michael Omi and Howard Winant, *Racial Formation in the United States: From the 1960s to the 1980s*, 2d ed. (New York: Routledge, 1994).

22. Ruth Frankenberg, *The Social Construction of Whiteness: White Women, Race Matters* (Minneapolis: University of Minnesota Press, 1993).

23. Evelyn Nakano Glenn, "From Servitude to Sevice Work: Historical Continuities in the Racial Division of Paid Reproductive Labor," *Signs* 18 (autumn 1992): 3. See also Bonnie Thornton Dill, "Our Mothers' Grief: Racial-Ethnic Women and the Maintenance of Families," *Journal of Family History* 13, no. 4 (1988): 415–31.

24. Morgan, 146.

25. Maxine Baca Zinn and Bonnie Thornton Dill, "Difference and Domination," in *Women of Color in U.S. Society*, 11–12.

26. See Omi and Winant, 53–76, for a discussion of racial formation.
27. Margaret L. Andersen and Patricia Hill Collins, *Race, Class, and Gender: An Anthology* (Belmont, Calif.: Wadsworth, 1992), xvi.
28. Omi and Winant.
29. Nazli Kibria, "Migration and Vietnamese American Women: Remaking Ethnicity," in *Women of Color in U.S. Society*, 247–61.
30. Patricia Hill Collins, *Black Feminist Thought: Knowledge, Consciousness, and the Politics of Empowerment* (Boston: Unwin Hyman, 1990).
31. Elizabeth Spelman, *Inessential Women: Problems of Exclusion in Feminist Thought* (Boston: Beacon Press, 1988), 136.
32. Several discussions of difference make this point. See Baca Zinn and Dill, 10; Gordon, 106; and Lynn Weber, in the "Symposium on West and Fenstermaker's 'Doing Difference,'" *Gender & Society* 9 (August 1995): 515–19.
33. Glenn, 10.
34. Gordon, 106.
35. Chandra Talpade Mohanty, "Cartographies of Struggle: Third World Women and the Politics of Feminism," in *Third World Women and the Politics of Feminism*, ed. Chandra Talpade Mohanty, Ann Russo, and Lourdes Torres (Bloomington: Indiana University Press, 1991), 13.
36. Frankenberg and Mani, 306.
37. Norma Alarçon, "The Theoretical Subject(s) of *This Bridge Called My Back* and Anglo-American Feminism," in *Making Face, Making Soul, Haciendo Caras: Creative and Critical Perspectives by Women of Color*, ed. Gloria Anzaldúa (San Francisco: Aunt Lute, 1990), 356.
38. Frankenberg. See also Evelyn Torton Beck, "The Politics of Jewish Invisibility," *NWSA Journal* (fall 1988): 93–102.

QUESTIONS

1. What is multiracial feminism? How does it differ from other modes of feminist thinking? According to the authors, what are the major limitations of "pluralism" and the "commodification of difference" as approaches attempting to deal with race and racism?

2. To what are Baca Zinn and Thornton Dill referring when they speak of "socially constructed racial groups"? What does this terminology mean and why is it important to their argument? How can race be "a shifting and contested category" and still be powerful enough to "construct definitions of all aspects of social life"?

3. According to the authors, how do intersecting systems of domination "produce *both* oppression *and* opportunity"? How can domination and inequality possibly provide opportunity, and for whom? How does this article add to your thinking about power? How does it add to your thinking about the variety of ways feminism is expressed?

Theories of Socialization & Hierarchies of Identity

White Privilege: Unpacking the Invisible Knapsack (1989)

Peggy McIntosh

This well-known consciousness-raising essay, written in 1988, examines the advantages that can come from being white in U.S. society. Although often unrecognized or unacknowledged, these advantages have a direct relationship to the disadvantages and oppression people of color face. McIntosh pinpoints concrete examples from her own experience that illustrate how even daily activities of white people reflect invisible privileges upon which other racial groups cannot depend. Peggy McIntosh, an educator and activist, is the Associate Director of the Center for Research on Women at Wellesley College.

Through work to bring materials from women's studies into the rest of the curriculum, I have often noticed men's unwillingness to grant that they are overprivileged, even though they may grant that women are disadvantaged. They may say they will work to improve women's status, in the society, the university, or the

"White Privilege: Unpacking the Invisible Knapsack," by Peggy McIntosh, reprinted from *Independent School*, Winter, 1990.

curriculum, but they can't or won't support the idea of lessening men's. Denials that amount to taboos surround the subject of advantages that men gain from women's disadvantages. These denials protect male privilege from being fully acknowledged, lessened, or ended.

Thinking through unacknowledged male privilege as a phenomenon, I realized that, since hierarchies in our society are interlocking, there was most likely a phenomenon of white privilege that was similarly denied and protected. As a white person, I realized I had been taught about racism as something that puts others at a disadvantage, but had been taught not to see one of its corollary aspects, white privilege, which puts me at an advantage.

I think whites are carefully taught not to recognize white privilege, as males are taught not to recognize male privilege. So I have begun in an untutored way to ask what it is like to have white privilege. I have come to see white privilege as an invisible package of unearned assets that I can count on cashing in each day, but about which I was "meant" to remain oblivious. White privilege is like an invisible weightless knapsack of special provisions, maps, passports, codebooks, visas, clothes, tools, and blank checks.

Describing white privilege makes one newly accountable. As we in women's studies work to reveal male privilege and ask men to give up some of their power, so one who writes about having white privilege must ask. "Having described it, what will I do to lessen or end it?"

After I realized the extent to which men work from a base of unacknowledged privilege, I understood that much of their oppressiveness was unconscious. Then I remembered the frequent charges from women of color that white women whom they encounter are oppressive. I began to understand why we are justly seen as oppressive, even when we don't see ourselves that way. I began to count the ways in which I enjoy unearned skin privilege and have been conditioned into oblivion about its existence.

My schooling gave me no training in seeing myself as an oppressor, as an unfairly advantaged person, or as a participant in a damaged culture. I was taught to see myself as an individual whose moral state depended on her individual moral will. My schooling followed the pattern my colleague Elizabeth Minnich has pointed out: whites are taught to think of their lives as morally neutral, normative, and average, and also ideal, so that when we work to benefit others, this is seen as work that will allow "them" to be more like "us."

DAILY EFFECTS OF WHITE PRIVILEGE

I decided to try to work on myself at least by identifying some of the daily effects of white privilege in my life. I have chosen those conditions that I think in my case *attach somewhat more to skin-color privilege* than to class, religion, ethnic status, or geographic location, though of course all these other factors are intricately intertwined. As far as I can tell, my African American coworkers, friends, and acquaintances with whom I come into daily or frequent contact in this particular time, place, and line of work cannot count on most of these conditions.

1. I can, if I wish, arrange to be in the company of people of my race most of the time.
2. If I should need to move, I can be pretty sure of renting or purchasing housing in an area that I can afford and in which I would want to live.
3. I can be pretty sure that my neighbors in such a location will be neutral or pleasant to me.
4. I can go shopping alone most of the time, pretty well assured that I will not be followed or harassed.
5. I can turn on the television or open to the front page of the paper and see people of my race widely represented.
6. When I am told about our national heritage or about "civilization," I am shown that people of my color made it what it is.
7. I can be sure that my children will be given curricular materials that testify to the existence of their race.
8. If I want to, I can be pretty sure of finding a publisher for this piece on white privilege.

9. I can go into a music shop and count on finding the music of my race represented, into a supermarket and find the staple foods that fit with my cultural traditions, into a hairdresser's shop and find someone who can deal with my hair.
10. Whether I use checks, credit cards, or cash, I can count on my skin color not to work against the appearance of financial reliability.
11. I can arrange to protect my children most of the time from people who might not like them.
12. I can swear, or dress in second-hand clothes, or not answer letters without having people attribute these choices to the bad morals, the poverty, or the illiteracy of my race.
13. I can speak in public to a powerful male group without putting my race on trial.
14. I can do well in a challenging situation without being called a credit to my race.
15. I am never asked to speak for all the people of my racial group.
16. I can remain oblivious of the language and customs of persons of color, who constitute the world's majority, without feeling in my culture any penalty for such oblivion.
17. I can criticize our government and talk about how much I fear its policies and behavior without being seen as a cultural outsider.
18. I can be pretty sure that if I ask to talk to "the person in charge" I will be facing a person of my race.
19. If a traffic cop pulls me over, or if the IRS audits my tax return, I can be sure I haven't been singled out because of my race.
20. I can easily buy posters, postcards, picture books, greeting cards, dolls, toys, and children's magazines featuring people of my race.
21. I can go home from most meetings of organizations I belong to feeling somewhat tied in rather than isolated, out

of place, outnumbered, unheard, held at a distance, or feared.

22. I can take a job with an affirmative action employer without having coworkers on the job suspect that I got it because of race.
23. I can choose public accommodation without fearing that people of my race cannot get in or will be mistreated in the places I have chosen.
24. I can be sure that if I need legal or medical help my race will not work against me.
25. If my day, week, or year is going badly, I need not ask of each negative episode or situation whether it has racial overtones.
26. I can choose blemish cover or bandages in "flesh" color that more or less match my skin.

Elusive and Fugitive

I repeatedly forgot each of the realizations on this list until I wrote it down. For me white privilege has turned out to be an elusive and fugitive subject. The pressure to avoid it is great, for in facing it I must give up the myth of meritocracy. If these things are true, this is not such a free country; one's life is not what one makes it; many doors open for certain people through no virtues of their own.

In unpacking this invisible knapsack of white privilege, I have listed conditions of daily experience that I once took for granted. Nor did I think of any of these perquisites as bad for the holder. I now think that we need a more finely differentiated taxonomy of privilege, for some of these varieties are only what one would want for everyone in a just society, and others give license to be ignorant, oblivious, arrogant, and destructive.

I see a pattern running through the matrix of white privilege, a pattern of assumptions that were passed on to me as a white person. There was one main piece of cultural turf; it was my own turf, and I was among those who could control the turf. *My skin color was an asset for any move I was educated to want to make.* I could think of myself as belonging in major ways and of making social systems work for me. I could freely disparage, fear, neglect, or be oblivious to anything outside of the dominant cultural forms. Being of the main culture, I could also criticize it fairly freely.

In proportion as my racial group was being made confident, comfortable, and oblivious, other groups were likely being made unconfident, uncomfortable, and alienated. Whiteness protected me from many kinds of hostility, distress, and violence, which I was being subtly trained to visit, in turn, upon people of color.

For this reason, the word "privilege" now seems to me misleading. We usually think of privilege as being a favored state, whether earned or conferred by birth or luck. Yet some of the conditions I have described here work systematically to overempower certain groups. Such privilege simply *confers dominance* because of one's race or sex.

EARNED STRENGTH, UNEARNED POWER

I want, then, to distinguish between earned strength and unearned power conferred systemically. Power from unearned privilege can look like strength when it is in fact permission to escape or to dominate. But not all of the privileges on my list are inevitably damaging. Some, like the expectation that neighbors will be decent to you, or that your race will not count against you in court, should be the norm in a just society. Others, like the privilege to ignore less powerful people, distort the humanity of the holders as well as the ignored groups.

We might at least start by distinguishing between positive advantages, which we can work to spread, and negative types of advantage, which unless rejected will always reinforce our present hierarchies. For example, the feeling that one belongs within the human circle, as Native Americans say, should not be seen as privilege for a few. Ideally it is an *unearned entitlement*. At present, since only a few have it, it is an *unearned advantage* for them. This paper results from a process of coming to see that some of the power that I originally saw as attendant on being a human being in the United States consisted in *unearned advantage* and *conferred dominance*.

I have met very few men who are truly distressed about systemic, unearned male advantage and conferred dominance. And so one question for me and others like me is whether we will be like them, or whether we will get truly distressed, even outraged, about unearned race advantage and conferred dominance, and, if so, what we will do to lessen them. In any case, we need to do more work in identifying how they actually affect our daily lives. Many, perhaps most, of our white students in the United States think that racism doesn't affect them because they are not people of color; they do not see "whiteness" as a racial identity. In addition, since race and sex are not the only advantaging systems at work, we need similarly to examine the daily experience of having age advantage, or ethnic advantage, or physical ability, or advantage related to nationality, religion, or sexual orientation.

Difficulties and dangers surrounding the task of finding parallels are many. Since racism, sexism, and heterosexism are not the same, the advantages associated with them should not be seen as the same. In addition, it is hard to disentangle aspects of unearned advantage that rest more on social class, economic class, race, religion, sex, and ethnic identity than on other factors. Still, all of the oppressions are interlocking, as the members of the Combahee River collective pointed out in their "Black Feminist Statement" of 1977.

One factor seems clear about all of the interlocking oppressions. They take both active forms, which we can see, and embedded forms, which as a member of the dominant group one is taught not to see. In my class and place, I did not see myself as a racist because I was taught to recognize racism only in individual acts of meanness by members of my group, never in invisible systems conferring unsought racial dominance on my group from birth.

Disapproving of the systems won't be enough to change them. I was taught to think that racism could end if white individuals changed their attitudes. But a "white" skin in the United States opens many doors for whites whether or not we approve of the way dominance has been conferred on us. Individual acts can palliate, but cannot end, these problems.

To redesign social systems we need first to acknowledge their colossal unseen dimensions. The silences and denials surrounding privilege are the key political tool here. They keep the thinking about equality or equity incomplete, protecting unearned advantage and conferred dominance by making these subjects taboo. Most talk by whites about equal opportunity seems to me now to be about equal opportunity to try to get into a position of dominance while denying that *systems* of dominance exist.

It seems to me that obliviousness about white advantage, like obliviousness about male advantage, is kept strongly inculturated in the United States so as to maintain the myth of meritocracy, the myth that democratic choice is equally available to all. Keeping most people unaware that freedom of confident action is there for just a small number of people props up those in power and serves to keep power in the hands of the same groups that have most of it already.

Although systemic change takes many decades, there are pressing questions for me and, I imagine, for some others like me if we raise our daily consciousness on the perquisites of being light-skinned. What will we do with such knowledge? As we know from watching men, it is an open question whether we will choose to use unearned advantage to weaken hidden systems of advantage, and whether we will use any of our arbitrarily awarded power to try to reconstruct power systems on a broader base.

QUESTIONS

1. What is "white privilege"? How is white privilege connected to the disadvantages and oppression people of color face? What distinction does McIntosh make between "positive" and "negative" advantages?
2. How do racism and white privilege differ? How do individual and institutional racism differ?
3. Why is whiteness, and the advantages that come from being white, so often unrecognized? What examples does McIntosh offer that resonate with your experience?

"Night to His Day": The Social Construction of Gender (1994)

Judith Lorber

In this essay from Paradoxes of Gender, *sociologist Judith Lorber presents us with a new way to think about something we all take for granted—gender. She argues that gender is a paradox: something that is culturally assigned to us at birth and at the same time something we actively create throughout our lives. Gender organizes our social relations and our basic institutions, like religion, education, work and the state. We understand the cultural significance of gender only when our expectations about gender are disrupted in some way.*

Talking about gender for most people is the equivalent of fish talking about water. Gender is so much the routine ground of everyday activities that questioning its taken-for-granted assumptions and presuppositions is like thinking about whether the sun will come up.[1] Gender is so pervasive that in our society we assume it is bred into our genes. Most people find it hard to believe that gender is constantly created and re-created out of human interaction, out of social life, and is the texture and order of that social life. Yet gender, like culture, is a human production that depends on everyone constantly "doing gender" (West and Zimmerman 1987).

And everyone "does gender" without thinking about it. Today, on the subway, I saw a well-dressed man with a year-old child in a stroller. Yesterday, on a bus, I saw a man with a tiny baby in a carrier on his chest. Seeing men taking care of small children in public is increasingly common—at least in New York City. But both men were quite obviously stared at—and smiled at, approvingly. Everyone was doing gender—the men who were changing the role of fathers and the other passengers, who were applauding them silently. But there was more gendering going on that probably fewer people noticed. The baby was wearing a white crocheted cap and white clothes. You couldn't tell if it was a boy or a girl. The child in the stroller was wearing a dark blue T-shirt and dark print pants. As they started to leave the train, the father put a Yankee baseball cap on the child's head. Ah, a boy, I thought. Then I noticed the gleam of tiny earrings in the child's ears, and as they got off, I saw the little flowered sneakers and lace-trimmed socks. Not a boy after all. Gender done.

Gender is such a familiar part of daily life that it usually takes a deliberate disruption of our expectations of how women and men are supposed to act to pay attention to how it is produced. Gender signs and signals are so ubiquitous that we usually fail to note them—unless they are missing or ambiguous. Then we are uncomfortable until we have successfully placed the other person in a gender status; otherwise, we feel socially dislocated. In our society, in addition to man and woman, the status can be *transvestite* (a person who dresses in opposite gender clothes) and *transsexual* (a person who has had sex-change surgery). Transvestites and transsexuals carefully construct their gender status by dressing, speaking, walking, gesturing in the ways prescribed for women or men—whichever they want to be taken for—and so does any "normal" person.

For the individual, gentler construction starts with assignment to a sex category on the basis of what the genitalia look like at birth.[2] Then babies are dressed or adorned in a way that displays the category because parents don't want to be constantly asked whether their baby is a girl or a boy. A sex category becomes a gentler status through naming, dress, and the use of other gender markers. Once a child's gender is evident, others treat those in one gender differently from those in the other, and the children respond to the different treatment by feeling different and behaving differently. As soon as they can talk, they start to refer to themselves as members of their gender. Sex doesn't come into play again until puberty, but by that time, sexual feelings and desires and practices have been shaped by gendered norms and expectations. Adolescent boys and girls approach and avoid each other in an elaborately scripted and gendered mating dance. Parenting is gendered, with different expectations for mothers and for fathers, and people of different genders work at different kinds of jobs. The work adults do as mothers and fathers and as low-level workers and high-level bosses, shapes women's and men's life experiences, and these experiences produce different feelings, consciousness, relationships, skills—ways of being that we call feminine or masculine.[3] All of these processes constitute the social construction of gender.

Gendered roles change—today fathers are taking care of little children, girls and boys are wearing unisex clothing and getting the same education, women and men are working at the same jobs. Although many traditional social groups are quite strict about maintaining gender differences, in other social groups they seem to be blurring. Then why the one-year-old's earrings? Why is it still so important to mark a child as a girl or a boy, to make sure she is not taken for a boy or he for a girl? What would happen if they were? They would, quite literally, have changed places in their social world.

To explain why gendering is done from birth, constantly and by everyone, we have to look not only at the way individuals experience gender but at gender as a social institution. As a social institution, gender is one of the major ways that human beings organize their lives. Human society depends on a predictable division of labor, a designated allocation of scarce goods, assigned responsibility for children and others who cannot care for themselves, common values and their systematic transmission to new members, legitimate leadership, music, art, stories, games, and other symbolic productions. One way of choosing people for the different tasks of society is on the basis of their talents, motivations, and competence—their demonstrated achievements. The other way is on the basis of gender, race, ethnicity—ascribed membership in a category of people. Although societies vary in the extent to which they use one or the other of these ways of allocating people to work and to carry out other responsibilities, every society uses gender and age grades. Every society classifies people as "girl and boy children," "girls and boys ready to be married," and "fully adult women and men," constructs similarities among them and differences between them, and assigns them to different roles and responsibilities. Personality characteristics, feelings, motivations, and ambitions flow from these different life experiences so that the members of these different groups become different kinds of people. The process of gendering and its outcome are legitimated by religion, law, science, and the society's entire set of values. . . .

Western society's values legitimate gendering by claiming that it all comes from physiology—female and male procreative differences. But gender and sex are not equivalent, and gender as a social construction does not flow automatically from genitalia and reproductive organs, the main physiological differences of females and males. In the construction of ascribed social statuses, physiological differences such as sex, stage of development, color of skin, and size are crude markers. They are not the source of the social statuses of gender, age, grade, and race. Social statuses are carefully constructed through prescribed processes of teaching, learning, emulation, and enforcement. Whatever genes, hormones, and biological evolution contribute to human social institutions is materially as well as qualitatively transformed by social practices. Every social institution has a material base, but culture and social practices transform that base into something with qualitatively different patterns and constraints. The economy is much more than producing food and goods and distributing them to eaters and users; family and kinship are not the equivalent of having sex and procreating; morals and religions cannot be equated with the fears and ecstasies of the brain; language goes far beyond the sounds produced by tongue and larynx. No one eats "money" or "credit"; the concepts of "god" and "angels" are the subjects of theological disquisitions; not only words but objects, such as their flag, "speak" to the citizens of a country.

Similarly, gender cannot be equated with biological and physiological differences between human females and males. The building blocks of gender are *socially constructed statuses.* Western societies have only two genders, "man" and "woman." Some societies have three genders—men, women, and *berdaches* or *hijras* or *xaniths*. Berdaches, hijras, and xaniths are biological males who behave, dress, work, and are treated in most respects as social women; they are therefore not men, nor are they female women; they are, in our language, "male women."[4] There are African and American Indian societies that have a gender status called *manly hearted women*—biological females who work, marry, and parent as men; their social status is "female men" (Amadiume 1987; Blackwood 1984). They do not have to behave or dress as men to have the social responsibilities and prerogatives of husbands and fathers; what makes them men is enough wealth to buy a wife.

Modern Western societies' *transsexuals* and *transvestites* are the nearest equivalent of these crossover genders, but they are not institutionalized as third genders (Bolin 1987). Transsexuals are biological males and females who have sex-change operations to alter their genitalia. They do so in order to bring their physical anatomy in congruence with the way they want to live and with their own sense of gender identity. They do not become a third gender; they change genders. Transvestites are males who live as women and females who live as men but do not intend to have sex-change surgery. Their dress, appearance, and mannerisms fall within the range of what is expected from members of the opposite gender, so that they "pass." They also change genders, sometimes temporarily, some for most of their lives. Transvestite women have fought in wars as men soldiers as recently as the nineteenth century; some married women, and others went back to being women and married men once the war was over.[5] Some were discovered when their wounds were treated; others not until they died. In order to work as a jazz musician, a man's occupation, Billy Tipton, a woman, lived most of her life as a man. She died recently at seventy-four, leaving a wife and three adopted sons for whom she was husband and father, and musicians with whom she had played and traveled, for whom she was "one of the boys" (*New York Times* 1989).[6] There have been many other such occurrences of women passing as men to do more prestigious or lucrative men's work (Matthaei 1982, 192–93).[7]

Genders, therefore, are not attached to a biological substratum. Gender boundaries are breachable, and individual and socially organized shifts from one gender to another call attention to "cultural, social, or aesthetic dissonances" (Garber 1992, 16). These odd or deviant or third genders show us what we ordinarily take for granted—that people have to learn to be women and men. Men who cross-dress for performances or for pleasure often learn from women's magazines how to "do femininity" convincingly (Garber 1992, 41–51). Because transvestism is direct evidence of how gender is constructed, Marjorie Garber claims it has "extraordinary power . . . to disrupt, expose, and challenge, putting in question the very notion of the 'original' and of stable identity" (1992, 16).

GENDER BENDING

It is difficult to see how gender is constructed because we take it for granted that it's all biology, or hormones, or human nature. The differences between women and men seem to be self-evident, and we think they would occur no matter what society did. But in actuality, human females and males are physiologically more similar in appearance than are the two sexes of many species of animals and are more alike than different in traits and behavior (C. F. Epstein 1988). Without the deliberate use of gendered clothing, hairstyles, jewelry, and cosmetics, women and men would look far more alike.[8] Even societies that do not cover women's breasts have gender-identifying clothing, scarification, jewelry, and hairstyles.

The ease with which many transvestite women pass as men and transvestite men as women is corroborated by the common gender misidentification in Westernized societies of people in jeans, T-shirts, and sneakers. Men with long hair may be addressed as "miss," and women with short hair are often taken for men unless they offset the potential ambiguity with deliberate gender markers (Devor 1987, 1989). Jan Morris, in *Conundrum*, an autobiographical account of events just before and just after a sex-change operation, described how easy it was to shift back and forth from being a man to being a woman when testing how it would feel to change gender status. During this time, Morris still had a penis and wore more or less unisex clothing; the context alone made the man and the woman:

> Sometimes the arena of my ambivalence was uncomfortably small. At the Travellers' Club, for example, I was obviously known as a man of sorts—women were only allowed on the

> premises at all during a few hours of the day, and even then were hidden away as far as possible in lesser rooms or alcoves. But I had another club, only a few hundred yards away, where I was known only as a woman, and often I went directly from one to the other, imperceptibly changing roles on the way—"Cheerio, sir," the porter would say at one club, and "Hello, madam," the porter would greet me at the other. (1975, 132)

Gentler shifts are actually a common phenomenon in public roles as well. Queen Elizabeth II of England bore children, but when she went to Saudi Arabia on a state visit, she was considered an honorary man so that she could confer and dine with the men who were heads of a state that forbids unrelated men and women to have face-to-unveiled-face contact. In contemporary Egypt, lower-class women who run restaurants or shops dress in men's clothing and engage in unfeminine aggressive behavior, and middle-class educated women of professional or managerial status can take positions of authority (Rugh 1986, 131). In these situations, there is an important status change: These women are treated by the others in the situation as if they are men. From their own point of view, they are still women. From the social perspective, however, they are men.[9]

In many cultures, gender bending is prevalent in theater or dance—the Japanese kabuki are men actors who play both women and men; in Shakespeare's theater company, there were no actresses. Juliet and Lady Macbeth were played by boys. Shakespeare's comedies are full of witty comments on gender shifts. Women characters frequently masquerade as young men, and other women characters fall in love with them; the boys playing these masquerading women, meanwhile, are acting out pining for the love of men characters.[10] . . .

But despite the ease with which gender boundaries can be traversed in work, in social relationship, and in cultural productions, gender statuses remain. Transvestites and transsexuals do not challenge the social construction of gender. Their goal is to be feminine women and masculine men. (Kando 1973). Those who do not want to change their anatomy but do want to change their gender behavior fare less well in establishing their social identity.

Paradoxically, then, bending gender rules and passing between genders does not erode but rather preserves gender boundaries. In societies with only two genders, the gender dichotomy is not disturbed by transvestites, because others feel that a transvestite is only transitorily ambiguous—is "really a man or woman underneath." After sex change surgery, transsexuals end up in a conventional gender status—a "man" or a "woman" with the appropriate genitals (Eichler 1989). When women dress as men for business reasons, they are indicating that in that situation, they want to be treated the way men are treated; when they dress as women, they want to be treated as women:

> By their male dress, female entrepreneurs signal their desire to suspend the expectations of accepted feminine conduct without losing respect and reputation. By wearing what is "unattractive" they signify that they are not intending to display their physical charms while engaging in public activity. Their loud, aggressive banter contrasts with the modest demeanor that attracts men. . . . Overt signalling of a suspension of the rules preserves normal conduct from eroding expectations. (Rugh 1986, 131)

FOR INDIVIDUALS, GENDER MEANS SAMENESS

Although the possible combinations of genitalia, body shapes, clothing, mannerisms, sexuality, and roles could produce infinite varieties in human beings, the social institution of gender depends on the production and maintenance of a limited number of gender statuses and of making the members of these statuses similar to each other. Individuals are born sexed but not gendered, and they have to be taught to be masculine or feminine.[11] As Simone de Beauvoir said: "One is not born, but rather becomes, a woman . . . ; it is civilization as a whole that produces this creature . . . which is described as feminine." (1952, 267).

Children learn to walk, talk, and gesture the way their social group says girls and boys should. Ray Birdwhistell, in his analysis of body motion as human communication, calls these learned gender displays *tertiary* sex characteristics and argues that they are needed to distinguish genders because humans are a weakly dimorphic species—their only sex markers are genitalia (1970, 39–46). Clothing, paradoxically, often hides the sex but displays the gender.

In early childhood, humans develop gendered personality structures and sexual orientations through their interactions with parents of the same and opposite gender. As adolescents, they conduct their sexual behavior according to gendered scripts. Schools, parents, peers, and the mass media guide young people into gendered work and family roles. As adults, they take on a gendered social status in their society's stratification system. Gender is thus both ascribed and achieved (West and Zimmerman 1987).

The achievement of gender was most dramatically revealed in a case of an accidental transsexual—a baby boy whose penis was destroyed in the course of a botched circumcision when he was seven months old (Money and Ehrhardt 1972, 118–23). The child's sex category was changed to "female," and a vagina was surgically constructed when the child was seventeen months old. The parents were advised that they could successfully raise the child, one of identical twins, as a girl. Physicians assured them that the child was too young to have formed a gender identity. Children's sense of which gender they belong to usually develops around the age of three, at the time that they start to group objects and recognize that the people around them also fit into categories big, little; pink-skinned, brown-skinned; boys, girls. Three has also been the age when children's appearance is ritually gendered, usually by cutting a boy's hair or dressing him in distinctively masculine clothing. In Victorian times, English boys wore dresses up to the age of three, when they were put into short pants (Garber 1992, 1–2).

The parents of the accidental transsexual bent over backward to feminize the child—and succeeded. Frilly dresses, hair ribbons, and jewelry created a pride in looks, neatness, and "daintiness." More significant, the child's dominance was also feminized:

> The girl had many tomboyish traits, such as abundant physical energy, a high level of activity, stubbornness, and being often the dominant one in a girls' group. Her mother tried to modify her tomboyishness: " . . . I teach her to be more polite and quiet. I always wanted those virtues. I never did manage, but I'm going to try to manage them—to my daughter—to be more quiet and ladylike." From the beginning the girl had been the dominant twin. By the age of three, her dominance over her brother was, as her mother described it, that of a mother hen. The boy in turn took up for his sister, if anyone threatened her. (Money and Ehrhardt 1972, 122).

This child was not a tomboy because of male genes or hormones; according to her mother, she herself had also been a tomboy. What the mother had learned poorly while growing up as a "natural" female she insisted that her physically reconstructed son-daughter learn well. For both mother and child, the social construction of gender overrode any possibly inborn traits.

People go along with the imposition of gender norms because the weight of morality as well as immediate social pressure enforces them. Consider how many instructions for properly gendered behavior are packed into this mother's admonition to her daughter: "This is how to hem a dress when you see the hem coming down and so to prevent yourself from looking like the slut I know you are so bent on becoming" (Kincaid 1978).

Gender norms are inscribed in the way people move, gesture, and even eat. In one African society, men were supposed to eat with their "whole mouth, wholeheartedly, and not, like women, just with the lips, that is halfheartedly, with reservation and restraint" (Bourdieu [1980], 1990, 70). Men and women in this society learned to walk in ways that proclaimed their different positions in the society:

> The manly man . . . stands up straight into the face of the person he approaches, or wishes to welcome. Ever on the alert, because ever threatened, he misses nothing of what happens around him. . . . Conversely, a well brought-up woman . . . is expected to walk with a slight stoop, avoiding every misplaced movement of her body, her head or her arms, looking down, keeping her eyes on the spot where she will next put her foot, especially if she happens to have to walk past the men's assembly. (70)

Many cultures go beyond clothing, gestures, and demeanor in gendering children. They inscribe gender directly into bodies. In traditional Chinese society, mothers bound their daughters' feet into three-inch stumps to enhance their sexual attractiveness. Jewish fathers circumcise their infant sons to show their covenant with God. Women in African societies remove the clitoris of prepubescent girls, scrape their labia, and make the lips grow together to preserve their chastity and ensure their marriageability. In Western societies, women augment their breast size with silicone and reconstruct their faces with cosmetic surgery to conform to cultural ideals of feminine beauty. . . .

Most parents create a gendered world for their newborn by naming, birth announcements, and dress. Children's relationships with same-gendered and different-gendered caretakers structure their self-identifications and personalities. Through cognitive development, children extract and apply to their own actions the appropriate behavior for those who belong in their own gender, as well as race, religion, ethnic group, and social class, rejecting what is not appropriate. If their social categories are highly valued, they value themselves highly; if their social categories are low status, they lose self-esteem (Chodorow 1974). Many feminist parents who want to raise androgynous children soon lose their children to the pull of gendered norms (T. Gordon 1990, 87–90). My son attended a carefully nonsexist elementary school, which didn't even have girls' and boys' bathrooms. When he was seven or eight years old, I attended a class play about "squares" and "circles" and their need for each other and noticed that all the girl squares and circles wore makeup, but none of the boy squares and circles did. I asked the teacher about it after the play, and she said, "Bobby said he was not going to wear makeup, and he is a powerful child, so none of the boys would either." In a long discussion about conformity, my son confronted me with the question of who the conformists were, the boys who followed their leader or the girls who listened to the woman teacher. In actuality, they both were, because they both followed same-gender leaders and acted in gender-appropriate ways. (Actors may wear makeup, but real boys don't.)

For human beings there is no essential femaleness or maleness, femininity or masculinity, womanhood or manhood, but once gender is ascribed, the social order constructs and holds individuals to strongly gendered norms and expectations. Individuals may vary on many of the components of gender and may shift genders temporarily or permanently, but they must fit into the limited number of gender statuses their society recognizes. In the process, they re-create their society's version of women and men: "If we do gender appropriately, we simultaneously sustain, reproduce, and render legitimate the institutional arrangements. . . . If we fail to do gender appropriately, we as individuals—not the institutional arrangements—may be called to account (for our character, motives, and predispositions)" (West and Zimmerman 1987, 146).

The gendered practices of everyday life reproduce a society's view of how women and men should act (Bourdieu [1980] 1990). Gendered social arrangements are justified by religion and cultural productions and backed by law, but the most powerful means of sustaining the moral hegemony of the dominant gender ideology is that the process is made invisible; any possible alternatives are virtually unthinkable (Foucault 1972; Gramsci 1971).[12]

FOR SOCIETY, GENDER MEANS DIFFERENCE

The pervasiveness of gender as a way of structuring social life demands that gender statuses be clearly differentiated. Varied talents, sexual preferences, identities, personalities, interests, and ways of interacting fragment the individual's bodily and social experiences. Nonetheless, these are organized in Western cultures into two and only two socially and legally recognized gender statuses, "man" and "woman."[13] In the social construction of gender, it does not matter what men and women actually do; it does not even matter if they do exactly the same thing. The social institution of gender insists only that what they do is *perceived* as different.

If men and women are doing the same tasks, they are usually spatially segregated to maintain gender separation, and often the tasks are given different job titles as well, such as executive secretary and administrative assistant (Reskin 1988). If the differences between women and men begin to blur, society's "sameness taboo" goes into action (G. Rubin 1975, 178). At a rock and roll dance at West Point in 1976, the year women were admitted to the prestigious military academy for the first time, the school's administrators "were reportedly perturbed by the sight of mirror-image couples dancing in short hair and dress gray trousers," and a rule was established that women cadets could dance at these events only if they wore skirts (Barkalow and Raab 1990, 53).[14] Women recruits in the U.S. Marine Corps are required to wear makeup—at a minimum, lipstick and eye shadow—and they have to take classes in makeup, hair care, poise, and etiquette. This feminization is part of a deliberate policy of making them clearly distinguishable from men Marines. Christine Williams quotes a twenty-five-year-old woman drill instructor as saying: "A lot of the recruits who come here don't wear makeup; they're tomboyish or athletic. A lot of them have the preconceived idea that going into the military means they can still be a tomboy. They don't realize that you are a *Woman* Marine" (1989, 76–77).[15]

If gender differences were genetic, physiological, or hormonal, gender bending and gender ambiguity would occur only in hermaphrodites, who are born with chromosomes and genitalia that are not clearly female or male. Since gender differences are socially constructed, all men and all women can enact the behavior of the other, because they know the other's social script: "'Man' and 'woman' are at once empty and overflowing categories. Empty because they have no ultimate, transcendental meaning. Overflowing because even when they appear to be fixed, they still contain within them alternative, denied, or suppressed definitions." (J. W. Scott 1988a, 49). Nonetheless, though individuals may be able to shift gender statuses, the gender boundaries have to hold, or the whole gendered social order will come crashing down.

Pardoxically, it is the social importance of gender statuses and their external markers—clothing, mannerisms, and spatial segregation—that makes gender bending or gender crossing possible—or even necessary. The social viability of differentiated gender statuses produces the need or desire to shift statuses. Without gender differentiation, transvestism and transsexuality would be meaningless. You couldn't dress in the opposite gender's clothing if all clothing were unisex. There would be no need to reconstruct genitalia to match identity if interests and life-styles were not gendered. There would be no need for women to pass as men to do certain kinds of work if jobs were not typed as "women's work" and "men's work." Women would not have to dress as men in public life in order to give orders or aggressively bargain with customers.

Gender boundaries are preserved when transsexuals create congruous autobiographies of always having felt like what they are now. The transvestite's story also "recuperates social and sexual norms" (Garber 1992, 69). In the transvestite's normalized narrative, he or she "is 'compelled' by social and economic forces to disguise himself or herself in order to get a job, escape repression, or gain artistic or political 'freedom'" (Garber 1992, 70). The "true identity" when revealed, causes amazement over how easily and successfully the person passed as a member of the opposite gender, not a suspicion that gender itself is something of a put on. . . .

Notes

1. Gender is, in Erving Goffman's words, an aspect of *Felicity's Condition:* "any arrangement which leads us to judge an individual's . . . acts not to be a manifestation of strangeness. Behind *Felicity's Condition* is our sense of what it is to be sane" (1983, 27). Also see Bem 1993; Frye 1983, 17–40; Goffman 1977.
2. In cases of ambiguity in countries with modern medicine, surgery is usually performed to make the genitalia more clearly male or female.
3. See J. Butler 1990 for an analysis of how doing gender *is* gender identity.
4. On the hijras of India, see Nanda 1990; on the xaniths of Oman, Wikan 1982, 168–86; on the American Indian berdaches, W. L. Williams 1986. Other societies that have similar institutionalized third-gender men are the Koniag of Alaska, the Tanala of Madagascar, the Mesakin of Nuba, and the Chukchee of Siberia (Wikan 1982, 170).
5. Durova 1989; Freeman and Bond 1992; Wheelwright 1989.
6. Gender segregation of work in popular music still has not changed very much, according to Groce and Cooper 1989, despite considerable androgyny in some very popular figures. See Garber 1992 on the androgyny. She discusses Tipton on pp. 67–70.
7. In the nineteenth century, not only did these women get men's wages, but they also "had male privileges and could do all manner of things other women could not: open a bank account, write checks, own property, go anywhere unaccompanied, vote in elections" (Faderman 1991, 44).
8. When unisex clothing and men wearing long hair came into vogue in the United States in the mid-1960s, beards and mustaches for men also came into style again as gender identifications.

9. For other accounts of women being treated as men in Islamic countries, as well as accounts of women and men cross-dressing in these countries, see Garber 1992, 304–52.

10. Dollimore 1986; Garber 1992, 32–40; Greenblatt 1987, 66–93; Howard 1988. For Renaissance accounts of sexual relations with women and men of ambiguous sex, see Laqueur 1990a, 134–39. For modern accounts of women passing as men that other women find sexually attractive, see Devor 1989, 136–37; Wheelwright 1989, 53–59.

11. For an account of how a potential man-to-woman transsexual learned to be feminine, see Garfinkel 1967, 116–85, 285–88. For a gloss on this account that points out how, throughout his encounters with Agnes, Garfinkel failed to see how he himself was constructing his own masculinity, see Rogers 1992.

12. The concepts of moral hegemony, the effects of everyday activities (praxis) on thought and personality, and the necessity of consciousness of these processes before political change can occur are all based on Marx's analysis of class relations.

13. Other societies recognize more than two categories, but usually no more than three or four (Jacobs and Roberts 1989).

14. Carol Barkalow's book has a photograph of eleven first-year West Pointers in a math class, who are dressed in regulation pants, shirts, and sweaters, with short haircuts. The caption challenges the reader to locate the only woman in the room.

15. The taboo on males and females looking alike reflects the U.S. military's homophobia (Bérubé 1989). If you can't tell those with a penis from those with a vagina, how are you going to determine whether their sexual interest is heterosexual or homosexual unless you watch them having sexual relations?

Questions

1. What is the first question we ask about the newborn? Why is this important knowledge? What is the relationship between sex and gender? Between biology and culture?

2. What does it mean to say gender is socially constructed? How do individuals "do" gender? Is it possible to change the way you do gender? What are the consequences? How does gender get inscribed on the body?

3. What does gender bending or gender crossing teach us about gender categories and boundaries? What makes gender shifts possible? Have you ever been in a circumstance where you have violated the taken-for-granted norms about your gender? Describe what happened.

4. How does the author interpret the words of Simone de Beauvoir, "One is not born, but rather becomes, a woman"?

5. According to Lorber, "man" and "woman" are at once "empty and overflowing" categories. Discuss what you think she means? Why does she put quotation marks around the words man and woman? Why are they often defined as opposites?

Heterosexual Privilege: Owning My Advantage, Uncovering My Collusion (1997)

Judith H. Katz

Judith Katz uses the conceptual framework established in Peggy McIntosh's popular essay on white racial privilege to identify advantages that can accrue from heterosexual identity. Millions of gays, lesbians and bisexuals do not have access to the array of privileges that heterosexuals experience on a daily basis. Katz lists twenty such advantages and encourages us to consider how our culture unfairly puts sexual minorities at a disadvantage.

Owning the ways in which we hold privilege can be as difficult as seeing air. Consciously or unconsciously, we white middle-class heterosexuals accept our privileged positions in society and organizations as part of the natural order. We assume we gained our status strictly on our own merit and that we just work harder and enjoy better luck than individuals from other identity groups.

We have no trouble noticing oppression when we bump up against it. We immediately see the unfairness when our talents are diminished, overlooked, and unheard. But we rarely see how we exhibit those same behaviors toward others, or how we collude with those behaviors.

Peggy McIntosh's work on White privilege was, and continues to be, a valuable tool and resource for me. This piece was inspired by her article "White Privilege: Unpacking the Invisible Knapsack" (Peace and Freedom, July/August 1989). Her work has opened new doors to continue my own learning and to explore more deeply the ways in which I collude with and unconsciously support oppression. I am struck by the parallels that can be drawn to other instances of prejudice, discrimination, and dehumanization.

Issues of privilege based on differences don't stop with race. There are many kinds of privilege that set us apart and keep us apart. Seeking to discover different ways in which I hold privilege led me to examine my experience of life through the lens of my heterosexism, and to contrast my experience with that of friends who are lesbian, gay, and bi-sexual.

In identifying the privileges I enjoy as a heterosexual, I was struck by the sheer weight of the barriers my non-heterosexual friends face. I was surprised at how easy it is to take these unearned advantages for granted, how easy not to notice the ways my life is made easier because I am in the "one-up" group.

A Partial List of Heterosexual Privileges

1. I can legally marry the person I love.
2. I can find greeting cards for the person I love for any occasion in any card store.
3. I can hold hands, touch, and dance with the person I love in public without fear of others' reactions.
4. I can share openly with colleagues, friends and family the news of falling in love, anniversaries, details of our vacation, or what I did last weekend.
5. I can talk about the person I love without fear of losing my job.

6. I can, in many organizations, if considered for a transfer, have the organization assist the person I love in finding employment.
7. I do not have to fear that someone will find out that I am heterosexual and risk being fired, dead ended in my career, or shunned by my friends.
8. I will not be discriminated against in finding a place to live because I am heterosexual.
9. I don't have to fear that my child will be taken away from me because of loving the person I love.
10. I can adopt a child, knowing that my sexual orientation will not disqualify me.
11. I do not have to experience, on a daily basis, the jokes, slurs, and outright hatred directed towards people of my sexual orientation.
12. I can keep pictures of the person I love on my desk without fear of reprisal, harassment, or being accused of flaunting my sexuality.
13. If a friend of mine is dying of AIDS, I can talk about it freely without worrying about how I'll be seen.
14. I don't fear that I'll be attacked or beaten because of whom I love.
15. If the person I love dies, I can openly share my sorrow.
16. I will not be turned away from my house of worship because of whom I love.
17. I am constantly reminded that my sexuality is normal—and I see a range of couples and role models on TV, in the movies, and everywhere I turn.
18. I do not have to live my life in secret, lie to people I love, fear being rejected and condemned by my parents or family for loving the person I love.
19. I do not have to worry that when the person I love goes out of the house he or she will be beaten because of loving me.
20. I can live life fully and openly with my family and friends.

I feel it is important to continually challenge my own thinking and awareness of these advantages. Each time I review them, I think of others—additional privileges I receive, additional barriers faced by people simply because of a difference.

To break down the barriers and eliminate oppression, we must acknowledge the privileges we receive, invisible though they may be. We must be willing to re-examine our perceptions about merit—our own and that of others. And we must be ready to challenge the barriers that exist so we can all live freer lives.

QUESTIONS

1. What is heterosexism? How does it differ from heterosexuality?
2. Why does Katz believe "owning" her heterosexual advantage is important?
3. Which of the heterosexual privileges on Katz's list are legal advantages? Which are social advantages? Which are economic?
4. How is heterosexuality affirmed in our culture in ways that gay, lesbian and bisexual (GLBT) identities are not? Why might this matter?
5. Which of the advantages on Katz's list most surprise you? Which might affect GLBT people's daily lives and choices most significantly? What advantages would you add to Katz's list?
6. Why do the legal and economic rights and daily experiences of people in the United States differ greatly based on sexuality? Doesn't the Constitution of the United States declare that "all men are created equal"?

The Other Body: Reflections on Difference, Disability, and Identity Politics (1993)

Ynestra King

As Ynestra King suggests in the following 1993 essay, disability is the only category of "difference" that "can happen to anyone in an instant, transforming that person's life and identity forever." A troubling idea in a culture that views "autonomy" and disability as opposites, King demonstrates through her own experiences with disability how fears and cultural expectations about the human body shape the way women with disabilities are treated.

Disabled people rarely appear in popular culture. When they do, their disability must be a continuous preoccupation overshadowing all other areas of their character. Disabled people are disabled. That is what they "do." That is what they "are."

My own experience with a mobility impairment that is only minorly disfiguring is that one must either be a creature of the disability, or have transcended it entirely. For me, like most disabled people (and this of course depends on relative severity), neither extreme is true. It is an organic, literally embodied fact that will not change—like being a woman. While it may be possible to "do gender," one does not "do disability." But there is an organic base to both conditions that extends far into culture, and the meaning that "nature" has. Unlike being a woman, being disabled is not a socially constructed condition. It is a tragedy of nature, of a kind that will always exist. The very condition of disability provides a vantage point of a certain lived experience in the body, a lifetime of opportunity for the observation of reaction to bodily deviance, a testing ground for reactions to persons who are readily perceived as having something wrong or being different. It is fascinating, maddening, and disorienting. It defies categories of "sickness" and "health," "broken" and "whole." It is in between.

Meeting people has an overlay: I know what they notice first is that I am different. And there is the experience of the difference in another person's reaction who meets me sitting down (when the disability is not apparent), and standing up and walking (when the infirmity is obvious). It is especially noticeable when another individual is flirting and flattering, and has an abrupt change in affect when I stand up. I always make sure that I walk around in front of someone before I accept a date, just to save face for both of us. Once the other person perceives the disability, the switch on the sexual circuit breaker often pops off—the connection is broken. "Chemistry" is over. I have a lifetime of such experiences, and so does every other disabled woman I know.

White middle-class people—especially white men—in the so-called First World have the most negative reactions. And I always recognize studied politeness, the attempt to pretend that there's nothing to notice (this is the liberal response—Oh, You're black? I hadn't noticed). Then there's the do-gooder response, where the person falls all over her/himself, insisting on doing everything for you; later they hate you; it's a form of objectification. It conveys to you that that is all they see, rather like a man who can't quit talking with a woman about sex.

In the era of identity politics in feminism, disability has not only been an added cross to bear, but an added "identity" to take on—with politically correct positions, presumed instant alliances, caucuses to join, and closets to come out of. For example, I was once dragged across a room to meet someone. My friend, a very politically correct lesbian feminist, said, "She's disabled, too. I thought you'd like to meet her." Rather than argue—what would I say? "I'm not interested in other disabled people," or "This is my night off"? (The truth in that moment was like the truth of this experience in every other moment, complicated and difficult to explain.)—I went along to find myself standing before someone strapped in a wheelchair she propels by blowing into a tube with a respirator permanently fastened to the back of the chair. To suggest that our relative experience of disability is something we could casually compare (as other people stand by!) demonstrates the crudity of perception about the complex nature of bodily experience.

My infirmity is partial leg paralysis. I can walk anywhere, climb stairs, drive a car, ride a horse, swim, hang-glide, fly a plane, hike in the wilderness, go to jail for my political convictions, travel alone, and operate heavy equipment. I can earn a living, shop, cook, eat as I please, dress myself, wash and iron my own clothes, clean my house. The woman in that wheelchair can do none of these fundamental things, much less the more exotic ones. On a more basic human level I can spontaneously get my clothes off if I decide to make love. Once in bed my lover and I can forget my disability. None of this is true of the woman in the wheelchair. There is no bodily human activity that does not have to be specially negotiated, none in which she is not absolutely "different." It would take a very long time, and a highly nuanced conversation, for us to be able to share experiences as if they were common. The experience of disability for the two of us was more different than my experience is from the daily experience of people who are not considered disabled. So much for disability solidarity.

With disability, one is somewhere on a continuum between total bodily dysfunction—or death—and complete physical wholeness. In some way, this probably applies to every living person. So when is it that we call a person "disabled"? When do they become "other"? There are "minor" disabilities that are nonetheless significant for a person's life. Color blindness is one example. But in our culture, color blindness is considered an inconvenience rather than a disability.

The ostracization, marginalization, and distorted response to disability are not simply issues of prejudice and denial of civil rights. They reflect attitudes toward bodily life, an unease in the human skin, an inability to cope with contingency, ambiguity, flux, finitude, and death.

Visibly disabled people (like women) in this culture are the scapegoats for resentments of the limitations of organic life. I had polio when I was seven, finishing second grade. I had excelled in everything, and rarely missed school. I had one bad conduct notation—for stomping on the boys' blocks when they wouldn't let me play with them. Although I had leg braces and crutches when I was ready to start school next year, I wanted desperately to go back and resume as much of the same life as I could. What I was not prepared for was the response of the school system. They insisted that I was now "handicapped" and should go into what they called "special education." This was a program aimed primarily at multiply disabled children, virtually all of whom were mentally retarded as well as physically disabled. It was in a separate wing of another school, and the children were completely segregated from the "normal" children in every aspect of the school day, including lunch and recreational activities. I was fortunate enough to have educated, articulate parents and an especially aggressive mother; she went to the school board and waged a tireless campaign to allow me to come back to my old school on a trial basis—the understanding being that the school could send me to special education if things "didn't work out" in the regular classroom.

And so began my career as an "exceptional" disabled person, not like the *other* "others." And I was glad. I didn't want to be associated with those others either. Apart from the objective limitations caused by the polio, the transformation in identity—the difference in worldly reception—was terrifying and embarrassing, and it went far beyond the necessary considerations my limitations required.

My experience as "other" is much greater and more painful as a disabled person than as a woman. Maybe the most telling dimension of this knowledge is my observation of the reactions of others over the years, of how deeply afraid people are of being outside the normative appearance (which is getting narrower as capitalism exaggerates patriarchy). It is no longer enough to be thin; one must have ubiquitous muscle definition, nothing loose, flabby, or ill defined, no fuzzy boundaries. And of course, there's the importance of control. Control over aging, bodily process, weight, fertility, muscle tone, skin quality, and movement. Disabled women, regardless of how thin, are without full bodily control.

I see disabled women fight these normative standards in different ways, but never get free of negotiating and renegotiating them. I did it by constructing my life around other values and, to the extent possible, developing erotic attachments to people who had similar values, and for whom my compensations were more than adequate. But at one point, after two disastrous but steamy liaisons with a champion athlete and a dancer (during which my friends pointed out the obvious unkind truth and predicted painful endings), I discovered the worlds I have tried to protect myself from: the disastrous attraction to "others" to complete oneself. I have seen disabled women endure unspeakably horrible relationships because they were so flattered to have such a conventionally attractive individual in tow.

And then there's the weight issue. I got fat by refusing to pay attention to my body. Now that I'm slimming down again, my old vanities and insecurities are surfacing. The battle of dieting can be especially fraught for disabled women. It is more difficult because exercising is more difficult, as is traveling around to get the proper foods, and then preparing them. But the underlying rage at the system that makes you feel as if you *are* your body (female, infirm) and that everything else is window dressing—this also undermines the requisite discipline. A tempting response is to resort to an ideal of self as bodiless essence in which the body is completely incidental, and irrelevant.

The wish that the body should be irrelevant has been one of my most fervent lifelong wishes. The knowledge that it isn't is my most intense lifelong experience.

I have seen other disabled women wear intentionally provocative clothes, like the woman in the wheelchair on my bus route to work. She can barely move. She has a pretty face, and tiny legs she could not possibly walk on. Yet she wears black lace stockings and spike high heels. The other bus occupants smile condescendingly, or pretend not to notice, or whisper in appalled disbelief that this woman could represent herself as having a sexual self. That she could "flaunt" her sexual being violates the code of acceptable appearance for a disabled woman. This woman's apparel is no more far out than that of many other women on our bus—but she refuses to fold up and be a good little asexual handicapped person.

The well-intentioned liberal new campaigns around "hire the handicapped" are oppressive in related ways. The Other does not only have to demonstrate her competence on insider terms; she must be better, by way of apologizing for being different and rewarding the insiders for letting her in. And the happy handicapped person, who has had faith placed in her/him, must vindicate "the race" because the politics of tokenism assumes that there are in fact other qualifications than doing the job.

This is especially prejudicial in a recession, where there are few social services, where it is "every man for himself." Disabled people inevitably have greater expenses, since assistance must often be paid for privately. In the U.S., public construction of the disabled body is that one either is fully disabled and dysfunctional/unemployable (and therefore eligible for public welfare) or totally on one's own. There is no in-between—the possibility of a little assistance, or exceptions in certain areas. Disabled people on public assistance cannot work or they will lose their benefits. (In the U.S. ideology that shapes public attitudes and public policy, one is either fully dependent or fully autonomous.) But the reality of human organic life is that everyone is different in some way; there is no such thing as a totally autonomous individual. Yet the mythology of autonomy perpetuates in terrible ways the oppression of the disabled. It also perpetuates misogyny—and the destruction of the planet.

It may be that this clear lack of autonomy—this reminder of mortal finitude and contingency and embeddedness of nature and the body—is at the root of the hatred of the disabled. On the continuum of autonomy and dependence, disabled people need help. To need help is to feel humiliated, to have failed. I think this "help" issue must be even harder for men than women. But any disabled person is always negotiating both the provisionality of autonomy and the rigidity of physical norms.

From the vantage point of disability, there are some objective and desirable aspects of autonomy. But they have to do with independence. The preferred protocol is that the attendant or friend perform the task that the disabled person needs done in the way the disabled person *asks it to be done.* Assistance from friends and family is a negotiated process, and often maddening. For that reason most disabled people prefer to live in situations where they can do all the basic functions themselves, with whatever special equipment or built-ins are required.

It's a dreadful business, this needing help. And it's more dreadful in the U.S. than in any place in the world, because our heroes are dynamic overcomers of adversity, and there is an inevitable cultural contempt for weakness.

Autonomy is on a continuum toward dependency and death. And the idea that dependency could come at any time, that one could die at any time, or be dismembered or disfigured, and still have to live (maybe even *want to live*) is unbearable in a context that understands and values autonomy in the way we moderns do.

I don't want to depict this experience of unbearability as strictly cultural. The compromising of the human body before its natural time is tragic. It forces terrible hardship on the individual to whom it occurs. But the added overlay of oppression on the disabled is intimately related to the fear of death, and the acknowledgment of our embeddedness in organic nature. We are finite, contingent, dependent creatures by our very nature; we will all eventually die. We will all experience compromises to our physical integrity. The aspiration to human wholeness is an oppressive idealism. Socially, it is deeply infantilizing.

It promotes a simplistic view of the human person, a static notion of human life that prevents the maturity and social wisdom that might allow human beings to more fully apprehend the human condition. It marginalizes the "different," those perceived as hopelessly wedded to organic existence—women and the disabled. The New Age "human potential movement"—in the name of maximizing human growth—is one of the worst offenders in obscuring the kind of human growth I am suggesting.

I too believe that the potential for human growth and creativity is infinite—but it is not groundless. The common ground for the person—the human body—is a place of shifting sand that can fail us at any time. It can change shape and properties without warning; this is an essential truth of embodied existence.

Of all the ways of becoming "other" in our society, disability is the only one that can happen to anyone, in an instant, transforming that person's life and identity forever.

Questions

1. What is King's disability? How is King not like the other "others"? How does she feel about her experiences with disability? How does she feel about identity politics?
2. In what ways is the experience of being a woman similar to being disabled? In what ways are these experiences different? What are some of the unique issues women *with* disabilities face?
3. According to King, disability is more than a civil rights issue. What does she mean by this? Where does she root cultural anxieties about disability? What role does control play?

The Social Construction of Disability

Susan Wendell

I maintain that the distinction between the biological reality of a disability and the social construction of a disability cannot be made sharply, because the biological and the social are interactive in creating disability. They are interactive not only in that complex interactions of social factors and our bodies affect health and functioning, but also in that social arrangements can make a biological condition more or less relevant to almost any situation. I call the interaction of the biological and the social to create (or prevent) disability "the social construction of disability."

Disability activists and some scholars of disability have been asserting for at least two decades that disability is socially constructed. Moreover, feminist scholars have already applied feminist analyses of the social construction of the experience of being female to their analyses of disability as socially constructed. Thus I am saying nothing new when I claim that disability, like gender, is socially constructed. Nevertheless, I understand that such an assertion may be new and even puzzling to many readers, and that not everyone who says that disability is socially constructed means the same thing by it. Therefore, I will explain what I mean in some detail.

I see disability as socially constructed in ways ranging from social conditions that straightforwardly create illnesses, injuries,

Reprinted from *The Rejected Body* (1996), Taylor & Francis Books Ltd.

and poor physical functioning, to subtle cultural factors that determine standards of normality and exclude those who do not meet them from full participation in their societies. I could not possibly discuss all the factors that enter into the social construction of disability here, and I feel sure that I am not aware of them all, but I will try to explain and illustrate the social construction of disability by discussing what I hope is a representative sample from a range of factors.

Social Factors That Construct Disability

First, it is easy to recognize that social conditions affect people's bodies by creating or failing to prevent sickness and injury. Although, since disability is relative to a person's physical, social, and cultural environment, none of the resulting physical conditions is necessarily disabling, many do in fact cause disability given the demands and lack of support in the environments of the people affected. In this direct sense of damaging people's bodies in ways that are disabling in their environments, much disability is created by the violence of invasions, wars, civil wars, and terrorism, which cause disabilities not only through direct injuries to combatants and noncombatants, but also through the spread of disease and the deprivations of basic needs that result from the chaos they create. In addition, although we more often hear about them when they cause death, violent crimes such as shootings, knifings, beatings, and rape all cause disabilities, so that a society's success or failure in protecting its citizens from injurious crimes has a significant effect on its rates of disability.

The availability and distribution of basic resources such as water, food, clothing, and shelter have major effects on disability, since much disabling physical damage results directly from malnutrition and indirectly from diseases that attack and do more lasting harm to the malnourished and those weakened by exposure. Disabling diseases are also contracted from contaminated water when clean water is not available. Here too, we usually learn more about the deaths caused by lack of basic resources than the (often life-long) disabilities of survivors.

Many other social factors can damage people's bodies in ways that are disabling in their environments, including (to mention just a few) tolerance of high-risk working conditions, abuse and neglect of children, low public safety standards, the degradation of the environment by contamination of air, water, and food, and the overwork, stress, and daily grinding deprivations of poverty. The social factors that can damage people's bodies almost always affect some groups in a society more than others because of racism, sexism, heterosexism, ageism, and advantages of class background, wealth, and education.

Medical care and practices, traditional and Western-scientific, play an important role in both preventing and creating disabling physical damage. (They also play a role in defining disability. . . .) Lack of good prenatal care and dangerous or inadequate obstetrical practices cause disabilities in babies and in the women giving birth to them. Inoculations against diseases such as polio and measles prevent quite a lot of disability. Inadequate medical care of those who are already ill or injured results in unnecessary disablement. On the other hand, the rate of disability in a society increases with improved medical capacity to save the lives of people who are dangerously ill or injured in the absence of the capacity to prevent or cure all the physical damage they have incurred. Moreover, public health and sanitation measures that increase the average lifespan also increase the number of old people with disabilities in a society, since more people live long enough to become disabled.

The *pace of life* is a factor in the social construction of disability that particularly interests me, because it is usually taken for granted by non-disabled people, while many people with disabilities are acutely aware of how it marginalizes or threatens to marginalize us. I suspect that increases in the pace of life are important social causes of damage to people's bodies through rates of accident, drug and alcohol abuse, and illnesses that result from people's neglecting their needs for rest and good nutrition. But the pace of life also affects disability as a second form of social construction, the social construction of disability through expectation of performance.

When the pace of life in a society increases, there is a tendency for more people to become disabled, not only because of physically damaging consequences of efforts to go faster, but also because fewer people can meet expectations of 'normal' performance; the physical (and mental) limitations of those who cannot meet the new pace become conspicuous and disabling, even though the same limitations were inconspicuous and irrelevant to full participation in the slower-paced society. Increases in the pace of life can be counterbalanced for some people by improvements in accessibility, such as better transportation and easier communication, but for those who must move or think slowly, and for those whose energy is severely limited, expectations of pace can make work, recreational, community, and social activities inaccessible.

Let me give a straightforward, personal illustration of the relationship between pace and disability. I am currently just able (by doing very little else) to work as a professor three-quarter time, on one-quarter disability leave. There has been much talk recently about possible increases in the teaching duties of professors at my university, which would not be accompanied by any reduction in expectations for the other two components of our jobs, research and administration. If there were to be such an increase in the pace of professors' work, say by one additional course per term, I would be unable to work more than half-time (by the new standards) and would have to request half-time disability leave, even though there had been no change in my physical condition. Compared to my colleagues, I would be more work-disabled than I am now. Some professors with less physical limitation than I have, who now work full-time, might be unable to work at the new full-time pace and be forced to go on part-time disability leave. This sort of change could contribute to disabling anyone in any job.

Furthermore, even if a person is able to keep up with an increased pace of work, any increase in the pace of work will decrease the energy available for other life activities, which may upset the delicate balance of energy by which a person manages to participate in them and eventually exclude her/him from those activities. The pace of those other activities may also render them inaccessible. For example, the more the life of a society is conducted on the assumption of quick travel, the more disabling are those physical conditions that affect movement and travel, such as needing to use a wheelchair or having a kind of epilepsy that prevents one from driving a car, unless compensating help is provided. These disabling effects extend into people's family, social, and sexual lives and into their participation in recreation, religious life, and politics.

Pace is a major aspect of expectations of performance; non-disabled people often take pace so much for granted that they feel and express impatience with the slower pace at which some people with disabilities need to operate, and accommodations of pace are often crucial to making an activity accessible to people with a wide range of physical and mental abilities. Nevertheless, expectations of pace are not the only expectations of performance that contribute to disability. For example, expectations of individual productivity can eclipse the actual contributions of people who cannot meet them, making people unemployable when they can in fact do valuable work. There are often very definite expectations about *how* tasks will be performed (not the standards of performance, but the methods). For example, many women with disabilities are discouraged from having children because other people can only imagine caring for children in ways that are impossible for women with their disabilities, yet everything necessary could be done in other ways, often with minor accommodations. Furthermore, the expectation that many tasks will be performed by individuals on their own can create or expand the disability of those who can perform the tasks only in cooperative groups or by instructing a helper.

Expectations of performance are reflected, because they are assumed, in the social organization and physical structure of a society, both of which create disability. Societies that are physically constructed and socially organized with the unacknowledged assumption that everyone is healthy, non-disabled, young but adult, shaped according to cultural ideals, and, often, male, create a great deal of disability through sheer neglect of what most people need in order to participate fully in them.

Feminists talk about how the world has been designed for the bodies and activities of men. In many industrialized countries, including Canada and the United States, life and work have been structured as though no one of any importance in the public world, and certainly no one who works outside the home for wages, has to breast-feed a baby or look after a sick child. Common colds can be acknowledged publicly, and allowances are made for them, but menstruation cannot be acknowledged and allowances are not made for it. Much of the public world is also structured as though everyone were physically strong, as though all bodies were shaped the same, as though everyone could walk, hear, and see well, as though everyone could work and play at a pace that is not compatible with any kind of illness or pain, as though no one were ever dizzy or incontinent or simply needed to sit or lie down. (For instance, where could you rest for a few minutes in a supermarket if you needed to?) Not only the architecture, but the entire physical and social organization of life tends to assume that we are either strong and healthy and able to do what the average young, non-disabled man can do or that we are completely unable to participate in public life.

A great deal of disability is caused by this physical structure and social organization of society. For instance, poor architectural planning creates physical obstacles for people who use wheelchairs, but also for people who can walk but cannot walk far or cannot climb stairs, for people who cannot open doors, and for people who can do all of these things but only at the cost of pain or an expenditure of energy they can ill afford. Some of the same architectural flaws cause problems for pregnant women, parents with strollers, and young children. This is no coincidence. Much architecture has been planned with a young adult, non-disabled male paradigm of humanity in mind. In addition, aspects of social organization that take for granted the social expectations of performance and productivity, such as inadequate public transportation (which I believe assumes that no one who is needed in the public world needs public transportation), communications systems that are inaccessible to people with visual or hearing impairments, and inflexible work arrangements that exclude part-time work or rest periods, create much disability.

When public and private worlds are split, women (and children) have often been relegated to the private, and so have the disabled, the sick, and the old. The public world is the world of strength, the positive (valued) body, performance and production, the non-disabled, and young adults. Weakness, illness, rest and recovery, pain, death, and the negative (devalued) body are private, generally hidden, and often neglected. Coming into the public world with illness, pain, or a devalued body, people encounter resistance to mixing the two worlds; the split is vividly revealed. Much of the experience of disability and illness goes underground, because there is no socially acceptable way of expressing it and having the physical and psychological experience acknowledged. Yet acknowledgement of this experience is exactly what is required for creating accessibility in the public world. The more a society regards disability as a private matter, and people with disabilities as belonging in the private sphere, the more disability it creates by failing to make the public sphere accessible to a wide range of people.

Disability is also socially constructed by the failure to give people the amount and kind of help they need to participate fully in all major aspects of life in the society, including making a significant contribution in the form of work. Two things are important to remember about the help that people with disabilities may need. One is that most industrialized societies give non-disabled people (in different degrees and kinds, depending on class, race, gender, and other factors) a lot of help in the form of education, training, social support, public communication and transportation facilities, public recreation, and other services. The help that non-disabled people receive tends to be taken for granted and not considered help but entitlement, because it is offered to citizens who fit the social paradigms, who by definition are not considered dependent on social help. It is only when people need a different kind or amount of help than that given to 'paradigm' citizens that it is considered help at all, and they are considered socially dependent. Second, much, though not all, of the help that people with disabilities need is required because their bodies were damaged by social conditions, or because they cannot meet social expectations of performance, or because the narrowly-conceived physical structure and social organization of society have placed them at a disadvantage; in other words, it is needed to overcome problems that were created socially.

Thus disability is socially constructed through the failure or unwillingness to create ability among people who do not fit the physical and mental profile of 'paradigm' citizens. Failures of social support for people with disabilities result in inadequate rehabilitation, unemployment, poverty, inadequate personal and medical care, poor communication services, inadequate training and education, poor protection from physical, sexual, and emotional abuse, minimal opportunities for social learning and interaction, and many other disabling situations that hurt people with disabilities and exclude them from participation in major aspects of life in their societies.

...

Cultural Construction of Disability

Culture makes major contributions to disability. These contributions include not only the omission of experiences of disability from cultural respresentations of life in a society, but also the cultural stereotyping of people with disabilities, the selective stigmatization of physical and mental limitations and other differences (selective because not all limitations and differences are stigmatized, and different limitations and differences are stigmatized in different societies), the numerous cultural meanings attached to various kinds of disability and illness, and the exclusion of people with disabilities from the cultural meanings of activities they cannot perform or are expected not to perform.

The lack of realistic cultural representations of experiences of disability not only contributes to the 'Otherness' of people with disabilities by encouraging the assumption that their lives are inconceivable to non-disabled people but also increases non-disabled people's fear of disability by suppressing knowledge of how people live with disabilities. Stereotypes of disabled people as dependent, morally depraved, super-humanly heroic, asexual, and/or pitiful are still the most common cultural portrayals of people with disabilities. Stereotypes repeatedly get in the way of full participation in work and social life. For example, Francine Arsenault, whose leg was damaged by childhood polio and later by gangrene, describes the following incident at her wedding:

> When I got married, one of my best friends came to the wedding with her parents. I had known her parents all the time I was growing up; we visited in each other's homes and I thought that they knew my situation quite well.
>
> But as the father went down the reception line and shook hands with my husband, he said, "You know, I used to think that Francine was intelligent, but to put herself on you as a burden like this shows that I was wrong all along."

Here the stereotype of a woman with a disability as a helpless, dependent burden blots out, in the friend's father's consciousness, both the reality that Francine simply has one damaged leg and the probability that her new husband wants her for her other qualities. Moreover, the man seems to take for granted that the new husband sees Francine in the same stereotyped way (or else he risks incomprehension or rejection), perhaps because he counts on the cultural assumptions about people with disabilities. I think both the stigma of physical 'imperfection' (and possibly the additional stigma of having been damaged by disease) and the cultural meanings attached to the disability contribute to the power of the stereotype in situations like this. Physical 'imperfection' is more likely to be thought to 'spoil' a woman than a man by rendering her unattractive in a culture where her physical appearance is a large component of a woman's value; having a damaged leg probably evokes the metaphorical meanings of being 'crippled,' which include helplessness, dependency, and pitifulness. Stigma, stereotypes, and cultural meanings are all related and interactive in the cultural construction of disability. . . .

Social Deconstruction of Disability

In my view, then, disability is socially constructed by such factors as social conditions that cause or fail to prevent damage to people's bodies; expectations of performance; the physical and social organization of societies on the basis of a young, non-disabled, 'ideally shaped,' healthy adult male paradigm of citizens; the failure or unwillingness to create ability among citizens who do not fit the paradigm; and cultural representations, failures of representation, and expectations. Much, but perhaps not all, of what can be socially constructed can be socially (and not just intellectually) deconstructed, given the means and the will.

A great deal of disability can be prevented with good public health and safety standards and practices, but also by relatively minor changes in the built environment that provide accessibility to people with a wide range of physical characteristics and abilities. Many measures that are usually regarded as helping or accommodating people who are now disabled, such as making buildings and public places wheelchair accessible, creating and respecting parking spaces for people with disabilities, providing American Sign Language translation, captioning, and Telephone Devices for the Deaf, and making tapes and Descriptive Video services available for people who are visually impaired, should be seen as preventive, since a great deal of disability is created by building and organizing environments, objects, and activities for a too-narrow range of people. Much more could be done along the same lines by putting people with a wide variety of physical abilities and characteristics in charge of deconstructing disability. People with disabilities should be in charge, because people without disabilities are unlikely to see many of the obstacles in their environment. Moreover, they are likely not to see them *as obstacles* even when they are pointed out, but rather as 'normal' features of the built environment that present difficulties for 'abnormal' people.

Disability cannot be deconstructed by consulting a few token disabled representatives. A person with a disability is not likely to see all the obstacles to people with disabilities different from her/his own, although s/he is likely to be more aware of potential inaccessibility. Moreover, people with disabilities are not always aware of the obstacles in our environment *as obstacles*, even when they affect us. The cultural habit of regarding the condition of the person, not the built environment or the social organization of activities, as the source of the problem, runs deep. For example, it took me several years of struggling with the heavy door to my building, sometimes having to wait until someone stronger came along, to realize that the door was an accessibility problem, not only for me, but for others as well. And I did not notice, until one of my students pointed it out, that the lack of signs that could be read from a distance at my university forced people with mobility impairments to expend a lot of energy unnecessarily, searching for rooms and offices. Although I have encountered this difficulty myself on days when walking was exhausting to me, I interpreted it, automatically, as a problem arising from my illness (as I did with the door), rather than as a problem arising from the built environment having been created for too narrow a range of people and situations. One of the most crucial factors in the deconstruction of disability is the change of perspective that causes us to look in the environment for both the source of the problem and the solutions.

...

Obstacles to the Deconstruction of Disability

...

Attitudes that disability is a personal or family problem (of biological or accidental origin), rather than a matter of social responsibility, are cultural contributors to disability and powerful factors working against social measures to increase ability. The attitude that disability is a personal problem is manifested when people with disabilities are expected to overcome obstacles to their participation in activities by their own extraordinary efforts. The public adoration of a few disabled heroes who are believed to have 'overcome their handicaps' against great odds both demonstrates and contributes to this expectation. The attitude that disability is a family matter is manifested when the families of people with disabilities are expected to provide whatever they need, even at great personal sacrifice by other family members. Barbara Hillyer describes the strength of expectations that mothers and other caregivers will do whatever is necessary to 'normalize' the lives of family members, especially children, with disabilities—not only providing care, but often doing the work of two people to maintain the illusion that there is nothing 'wrong' in the family.

These attitudes are related to the fact that many modern societies split human concerns into public and private worlds. Typically, those with disabilities and illnesses have been relegated to the private realm, along with women, children, and the old. This worldwide tendency creates particularly intractable problems for women with disabilities; since they fit two 'private' categories, they are often kept at home, isolated and overprotected. In addition, the confinement of people with disabilities in the private realm exploits women's traditional caregiving roles in order to meet the needs of people with disabilities, and it hides the need for measures to make the public realm accessible to everyone.

There also seem to be definite material advantages for some people (people without disabilities who have no disabled friends or relatives for whom they feel responsible) to seeing disability as a biological misfortune, the bad luck of individuals, and a personal or family problem. Accessibility and creating ability cost time, energy, and/or money. Charities for people with disabilities are big businesses that employ a great many non-disabled professionals; these charities depend upon the belief that responding to the difficulties faced by people with disabilities is superogatory for people who are not members of the family—not a social responsibility to be fulfilled through governments, but an act of kindness. Moreover, both the charities and most government bureaucracies (which also employ large numbers of non-disabled professionals) hand out help which would not be needed in a society that was planned and organized to include people with a wide range of physical and mental abilities. The potential resistance created by these vested interests in disability should not be underestimated.

The 'personal misfortune' approach to disability is also part of what I call the 'lottery' approach to life, in which individual good fortune is hoped for as a substitute for social planning that deals realistically with everyone's capabilities, needs and limitations, and the probable distribution of hardship. In Canada and the United States, most people reject the 'lottery' approach to such matters as acute health care for themselves and their families or basic education for their children. We expect it to be there when we need it, and we are (more or less) willing to pay for it to be there. I think the lottery approach persists with respect to disability partly because *fear*, based on ignorance and false beliefs about disability, makes it difficult for most non-disabled people to identify with people with disabilities. If the non-disabled saw the disabled as potentially themselves or as their future selves, they would want their societies to be fully accessible and to invest the resources necessary to create ability wherever possible. They would feel that 'charity' is as inappropriate a way of thinking about resources for people with disabilities as it is about emergency medical care or basic education.

The philosopher Anita Silvers maintains that it is probably impossible for most non-disabled people to imagine what life is like with a disability, and that their own becoming disabled is unthinkable to them. Certainly many people without disabilities believe that life with a disability would not be worth living. This is reflected in the assumption that potential disability is a sufficient reason for aborting a fetus, as well as in the frequent statements by non-disabled people that they would not want to live if they had to use a wheelchair, lost their eyesight, were dependent on others for care, and so on. The belief that life would not be worth living with a disability would be enough to prevent them from imagining their own disablement. This belief is fed by stereotypes and ignorance of the lives of people with disabilities. For example, the assumption that permanent, global incompetence results from any major disability is still prevalent; there is a strong presumption that competent people either have no major physical or mental limitations or are able to hide them in public and social life.

It seems that the cultural constructions of disability, including the ignorance, stereotyping, and stigmatization that feed fears of disability, have to be at least partly deconstructed before disability can be seen by more people as a set of social problems and social responsibilities. Until that change in perspective happens, people with disabilities and their families will continue to be given too much individual responsibility for 'overcoming' disabilities, expectations for the participation of people with disabilities in public life will be far too low, and social injustices that are recognized now (at least in the abstract), such as discrimination against people with disabilities, will be misunderstood.

To illustrate, let me look briefly at the problem of discrimination. Clearly, when considering whether some action or situation is an instance of discrimination on the basis of ability, the trick is to distinguish ability to do the relevant things from ability to do irrelevant things. But, given that so many places and activities are structured for people with a narrow range of abilities, telling the two apart is not always easy. No one has to walk to be a typist, but if a company is housed in a building that is inaccessible to wheelchairs, and therefore refuses to hire a competent typist who uses a wheelchair because it would be expensive to fix the building, has it discriminated against her on the basis of her disability? Laws may say yes, but people will resist the laws unless they can see that the typist's inability to work in that office is not solely a characteristic of her as an individual. Most people will be ready to recognize refusal to hire her to work in a wheelchair-accessible office, provided she is the most competent typist who applied, as discrimination against her because of her disability; they will regard her disability (like her race) as a personal characteristic irrelevant in the circumstances. But will they be ready to require a company to create wheelchair accessibility so that it can hire her? This is being tested now in the United States by the 1990 Americans with Disabilities Act. Although I expect the Act to have an invaluable educational function, I predict that it will be very difficult to enforce until more people see accessibility as a public responsibility. Only then will they be able to recognize inabilities that are created by faulty planning and organization as irrelevant.

Consider these sentiments expressed in the Burger King case, as described in *The Disability Rag and Resource:*

> When deaf actress Terrylene Sacchetti sued Burger King under the ADA for refusing to serve her when she handed the cashier a written order at the pickup window instead of using the intercom, Stan Kyker, executive vice-president of the California Restaurant Association, said that those "people (with disabilities) are going to have to accept that they are not 100 percent whole and they can't be made 100 percent whole in everything they do in life."

Had a woman been refused service because she used a cane to walk up to the counter, her treatment would, I think, have been recognized at once as discrimination. But since Ms. Sacchetti was refused service because she was unable to perform the activity (ordering food) in the way (orally) that the restaurant required it to be performed, the refusal to serve her was not immediately recognized as discrimination. Indeed, the representative of the restaurant association apparently felt comfortable defending it on the grounds that her individual characteristics were the obstacles to Ms. Sacchetti's being served.

When I imagine a society without disabilities, I do not imagine a society in which every physical and mental 'defect' or 'abnormality' can be cured. On the contrary, I believe the fantasy that someday everything will be 'curable' is a significant obstacle to the social deconstruction of disability. Instead, I imagine a fully accessible society, the most fundamental characteristic of which is universal recognition that all structures have to be built and all activities have to be organized for the widest practical range of human abilities. In such a society, a person who cannot walk would not be disabled, because every major kind of activity that is accessible to someone who can walk would be accessible to someone who cannot, and likewise with seeing, hearing, speaking, moving one's arms, working for long stretches of time without rest, and many other physical and mental functions. I do not mean that everyone would be able to do everything, but rather that, with respect to the major aspects of life in the society, the differences in ability between someone who can walk, or see, or hear, and someone who cannot would be no more significant than the differences in ability among people who can walk, see, or hear. Not everyone who is not disabled now can play basketball or sing in a choir, but everyone who is not disabled now can participate in sports or games and make art, and that sort of general ability should be the goal in deconstructing disability.

I talk about accessibility and ability rather than independence or integration because I think that neither independence nor integration is always an appropriate goal for people with disabilities. Some people cannot live independently because they will always need a great deal of help from caregivers, and some people with disabilities, for example the Deaf, do not want to be integrated into non-disabled society; they prefer their own, separate social life. Everyone should, however, have access to *opportunities* to develop their abilities, to work, and to participate in the full range of public and private activities available to the rest of society.

A Question of Class (1994)

Dorothy Allison

For acclaimed author Dorothy Allison, growing up in a poor, white "trash" family from South Carolina was the greatest shame but also the greatest force in her life. To be poor in a world that considers poverty to be "contemptible and somehow deserved" and to be a lesbian in a "world that hates queers" required that Allison conceal her identity to survive. Becoming a writer was a method of resisting her fear and speaking about the aspects of her identity that she both cherished and despised. Allison's works include Trash *(1989),* Bastard Out of Carolina *(1992),* Skin *(1994), and* Two or Three Things I Know For Sure *(1995).*

The first time I heard, "They're different than us, don't value human life the way we do," I was in high school in Central Florida. The man speaking was an army recruiter talking to a bunch of boys, telling them what the army was really like, what they could expect overseas. A cold angry feeling swept over me. I

"A Question of Class," by Dorothy Allison, reprinted from *Skin: Talking About Sex, Class & Literature*, 1994, Firebrand Books.

had heard the word *they* pronounced in that same callous tone before. *They*, those people over there, those people who are not us, they die so easily, kill each other so casually. They are different. *We*, I thought. *Me.*

When I was six or eight back in Greenville, South Carolina, I had heard that same matter-of-fact tone of dismissal applied to me. "Don't you play with her. I don't want you talking to them." Me and my family, we had always been *they*. Who am I? I wondered, listening to that recruiter. Who are my people? We die so easily, disappear so completely—we/they, the poor and the queer. I pressed my bony white trash fists to my stubborn lesbian mouth. The rage was a good feeling, stronger and purer than the shame that followed it, the fear and the sudden urge to run and hide, to deny, to pretend I did not know who I was and what the world would do to me.

My people were not remarkable. We were ordinary, but even so we were mythical. We were the *they* everyone talks about—the ungrateful poor. I grew up trying to run away from the fate that destroyed so many of the people I loved, and having learned the habit of hiding, I found I had also learned to hide from myself. I did not know who I was, only that I did not want to be *they*, the ones who are destroyed or dismissed to make the "real" people, the important people, feel safer. By the time I understood that I was queer, that habit of hiding was deeply set in me, so deeply that it was not a choice but an instinct. Hide, hide to survive, I thought, knowing that if I told the truth about my life, my family, my sexual desire, my history, I would move over into that unknown territory, the land of they, would never have the chance to name my own life, to understand it or claim it.

Why are you so afraid? my lovers and friends have asked me the many times I have suddenly seemed a stranger, someone who would not speak to them, would not do the things they believed I should do, simple things like applying for a job, or a grant, or some award they were sure I could acquire easily. Entitlement, I have told them, is a matter of feeling like we rather than they. You think you have a right to things, a place in the world, and it is so intrinsically a part of you that you cannot imagine people like me, people who seem to live in your world, who don't have it. I have explained what I know over and over, in every way I can, but I have never been able to make clear the degree of my fear, the extent to which I feel myself denied: not only that I am queer in a world that hates queers, but that I was born poor into a world that despises the poor. The need to make my world believable to people who have never experienced it is part of why I write fiction. I know that some things must be felt to be understood, that despair, for example, can never be adequately analyzed; it must be lived. But if I can write a story that so draws the reader in that she imagines herself like my characters, feels their sense of fear and uncertainty, their hopes and terrors, then I have come closer to knowing myself as real, important as the very people I have always watched with awe.

I have known I was a lesbian since I was a teenager, and I have spent a good twenty years making peace with the effects of incest and physical abuse. But what may be the central fact of my life is that I was born in 1949 in Greenville, South Carolina, the bastard daughter of a white woman from a desperately poor family, a girl who had left the seventh grade the year before, worked as a waitress, and was just a month past fifteen when she had me. That fact, the inescapable impact of being born in a condition of poverty that this society finds shameful, contemptible, and somehow deserved, has had dominion over me to such an extent that I have spent my life trying to overcome or deny it. I have learned with great difficulty that the vast majority of people believe that poverty is a voluntary condition.

I have loved my family so stubbornly that every impulse to hold them in contempt has sparked in me a countersurge of pride—complicated and undercut by an urge to fit us into the acceptable myths and theories of both mainstream society and a lesbian-feminist reinterpretation. The choice becomes Steven Spielberg movies or Erskine Caldwell novels, the one valorizing and the other caricaturing, or the patriarchy as villain, trivializing the choices the men and women of my family have made. I have had to fight broad generalizations from every theoretical viewpoint.

Traditional feminist theory has had a limited understanding of class differences and of how sexuality and self are shaped by both desire and denial. The ideology implies that we are all sisters who should only turn our anger and suspicion on the world outside the lesbian community. It is easy to say that the patriarchy did it, that poverty and social contempt are products of the world of the fathers, and often I felt a need to collapse my sexual history into what I was willing to share of my class background, to pretend that my life both as a lesbian and as a working-class escapee was constructed by the patriarchy. Or conversely, to ignore how much my life was shaped by growing up poor and talk only about what incest did to my identity as a woman and as a lesbian. The difficulty is that I can't ascribe everything that has been problematic about my life simply and easily to the patriarchy, or to incest, or even to the invisible and much denied class structure of our society.

In my lesbian-feminist collective we had long conversations about the mind/body split, the way we compartmentalize our lives to survive. For years I thought that that concept referred to the way I had separated my activist life from the passionate secret life in which I acted on my sexual desires. I was convinced that the fracture was fairly simple, that it would be healed when there was time and clarity to do so—at about the same point when I might begin to understand sex. I never imagined that it was not a split but a splintering, and I passed whole portions of my life—days, months, years—in pure directed progress, getting up every morning and setting to work, working so hard and so continually that I avoided in any way what I knew about my life. Busywork became a trance state. I ignored who I really was and how I became that person, continued in that daily progress, became an automaton who was what she did.

I tried to become one with the lesbian-feminist community so as to feel real and valuable. I did not know that I was hiding, blending in for safety just as I had done in high school, in college. I did not recognize the impulse to forget. I believed that all those things I did not talk about, or even let myself think too much about, were not important, that none of them defined me. I had constructed a life, an identity in which I took pride, an alternative lesbian family in which I felt safe, and I did not realize that the fundamental me had almost disappeared.

It is surprising how easy it was to live that life. Everyone and everything cooperated with the process. Everything in our culture—books, television, movies, school, fashion—is presented as if it is being seen by one pair of eyes, shaped by one set of hands, heard by one pair of ears. Even if you know you are not part of that imaginary creature—if you like country music not symphonies, read books cynically, listen to the news unbelievingly, are lesbian not heterosexual, and surround yourself with your own small deviant community—you are still shaped by that hegemony, or your resistance to it. The only way I found to resist that homogenized view of the world was to make myself part of something larger than myself. As a feminist and a radical lesbian organizer, and later as a sex radical (which eventually became the term, along with pro-sex feminist, for those who were not anti-pornography but anti-censorship, those of us arguing for sexual diversity), the need to belong, to feel safe, was just as important for me as for any heterosexual, nonpolitical citizen, and sometimes even more important because the rest of my life was so embattled.

The first time I read the Jewish lesbian Irena Klepfisz's poems,[1] I experienced a frisson of recognition. It was not that my people had been "burned off the map" or murdered as hers had. No, we had been encouraged to destroy ourselves, made invisible because we did not fit the myths of the noble poor generated by the middle class. Even now, past forty and stubbornly proud of my family, I feel the draw of that mythology, that romanticized, edited version of the poor. I find myself looking back and wondering what was real, what was true. Within my family, so much was lied about, joked about, denied, or told with deliberate indirection, an undercurrent of humiliation or a brief pursed grimace that belied everything that had been said. What was real? The poverty depicted in books and movies was romantic, a backdrop for the story of how it was escaped.

The poverty portrayed by left-wing intellectuals was just as romantic, a platform for assailing the upper and middle classes, and from their perspective, the working-class hero was invariably male, righteously indignant, and inhumanly noble. The reality of self-hatred and violence was either absent or caricatured. The poverty, I knew was dreary, deadening, shameful, the women powerful in ways not generally seen as heroic by the world outside the family.

My family's lives were not on television, not in books, not even comic books. There was a myth of the poor in this country, but it did not include us, no matter how hard I tried to squeeze us in. There was an idea of the good poor—hard-working, ragged but clean, and intrinsically honorable. I understood that we were the bad poor: men who drank and couldn't keep a job; women, invariably pregnant before marriage, who quickly became worn, fat, and old from working too many hours and bearing too many children; and children with runny noses, watery eyes, and the wrong attitudes. My cousins quit school, stole cars, used drugs, and took dead-end jobs pumping gas or waiting tables. We were not noble, not grateful, not even hopeful. We knew ourselves despised. My family was ashamed of being poor, of feeling hopeless. What was there to work for, to save money for, to fight for or struggle against? We had generations before us to teach us that nothing ever changed, and that those who did try to escape failed.

My mama had eleven brothers and sisters, of whom I can name only six. No one is left alive to tell me the names of the others. It was my grandmother who told me about my real daddy, a shiftless pretty man who was supposed to have married, had six children, and sold cut-rate life insurance to poor Black people. My mama married when I was a year old, but her husband died just after my little sister was born a year later.

When I was five, Mama married the man she lived with until she died. Within the first year of their marriage Mama miscarried, and while we waited out in the hospital parking lot, my stepfather molested me for the first time, something he continued to do until I was past thirteen. When I was eight or so, Mama took us away to a motel after my stepfather beat me so badly it caused a family scandal, but we returned after two weeks. Mama told me that she really had no choice: she could not support us alone. When I was eleven I told one of my cousins that my stepfather was molesting me. Mama packed up my sisters and me and took us away for a few days, but again, my stepfather swore he would stop, and again we went back after a few weeks. I stopped talking for a while, and I have only vague memories of the next two years.

My stepfather worked as a route salesman, my mama as a waitress, laundry worker, cook, or fruit packer. I could never understand, since they both worked so hard and such long hours, how we never had enough money, but it was also true of my mama's brothers and sisters who worked hard in the mills or the furnace industry. In fact, my parents did better than anyone else in the family. But eventually my stepfather was fired and we hit bottom—nightmarish months of marshals at the door, repossessed furniture, and rubber checks. My parents worked out a scheme so that it appeared my stepfather had abandoned us, but instead he went down to Florida, got a new job, and rented us a house. He returned with a U-Haul trailer in the dead of night, packed us up, and moved us south.

The night we left South Carolina for Florida, my mama leaned over the backseat of her old Pontiac and promised us girls, "It'll be better there." I don't know if we believed her, but I remember crossing Georgia in the early morning, watching the red clay hills and swaying grey blankets of moss recede through the back window. I kept looking at the trailer behind us, ridiculously small to contain everything we owned. Mama had packed nothing that wasn't fully paid off, which meant she had only two things of worth: her washing and sewing machines, both of them tied securely to the trailer walls. Throughout the trip I fantasized an accident that would burst that trailer, scattering old clothes and cracked dishes on the tarmac.

I was only thirteen. I wanted us to start over completely, to begin again as new people with nothing of the past left over. I wanted to run away from who we had been seen to be, who we had been. That desire is one I have seen in other members of my family. It is the first thing I think of when trouble comes—the geographic solution. Change your name, leave town, disappear, make yourself over. What hides behind that impulse is the conviction that the life you have lived, the person you are, is valueless, better off abandoned, that running away is easier than trying to change things that change itself is not possible. Sometimes I think it is this conviction—more seductive than alcohol or violence, more subtle than sexual hatred or gender injustice—that has dominated my life and made real change so painful and difficult.

Moving to Central Florida did not fix our lives. It did not stop my stepfather's violence, heal my shame, or make my mother happy. Once there, our lives became controlled by my mother's illness and medical bills. She had a hysterectomy when I was about eight and endured a series of hospitalizations for ulcers and a chronic back problem. Through most of my adolescence she superstitiously refused to allow anyone to mention the word *cancer.* When she was not sick, Mama and my stepfather went on working, struggling to pay off what seemed an insurmountable load of debts.

By the time I was fourteen, my sisters and I had found ways to discourage most of our stepfather's sexual advances. We were not close, but we united against him. Our efforts were helped along when he was referred to a psychotherapist after he lost his temper at work, and was prescribed drugs that made him sullen but less violent. We were growing up quickly, my sisters moving toward dropping out of school while I got good grades and took every scholarship exam I could find I was the first person in my family to graduate from high school, and the fact that I went on to college was nothing short of astonishing.

We all imagine our lives are normal, and I did not know my life was not everyone's. It was in Central Florida that I began to realize just how different we were. The people we met there had not been shaped by the rigid class structure that dominated the South Carolina Piedmont. The first time I looked around my junior high classroom and realized I did not know who those people were—not only as individuals but as categories, who their people were and how they saw themselves—I also realized that they did not know me. In Greenville, everyone knew my family, knew we were trash, and that meant we were supposed to be poor, supposed to have grim low-paid jobs, have babies in our teens, and never finish school. But Central Florida in the 1960s was full of runaways and immigrants, and our mostly white working-class suburban school sorted us out not by income and family background but by intelligence and aptitude tests. Suddenly I was boosted into the college-bound track, and while there was plenty of contempt for my inept social skills, pitiful wardrobe, and slow drawling accent, there was also something I had never experienced before: a protective anonymity, and a kind of grudging respect and curiosity about who I might become. Because they did not see poverty and hopelessness as a foregone conclusion for my Iife, I could begin to imagine other futures for myself.

In that new country, we were unknown. The myth of the poor settled over us and glamorized us. I saw it in the eyes of my teachers, the Lion's Club representative who paid for my new glasses, and the lady from the Junior League who told me about the scholarship I had won. Better, far better, to be one of the mythical poor than to be part of the *they* I had known before. I also experienced a new level of fear, a fear of losing what had never before been imaginable. Don't let me lose this chance, I prayed, and lived in terror that I might suddenly be seen again as what I knew myself to be.

As an adolescent I thought that my family's escape from South Carolina played like a bad movie. We fled the way runaway serfs might have done, with the sheriff who would have arrested my stepfather the imagined border guard. I am certain that if we had remained in South Carolina, I would have been trapped by my family's heritage of poverty, jail, and illegitimate children—that even being smart, stubborn, and a lesbian would have made no difference.

My grandmother died when I was twenty, and after Mama went home for the funeral, I had a series of dreams in which we still lived up in Greenville, just down the road from where Granny died. In the dreams I had two children and only one eye, lived in a trailer, and worked at the textile mill. Most of my time was taken up with deciding when I would finally kill my children and myself. The dreams were so vivid, I became convinced they were about the life I was meant to have had, and I began to work even harder to put as much distance as I could between my family and me. I copied the dress, mannerisms, attitudes, and ambitions of the girls I met in college, changing or hiding my own tastes, interests, and desires. I kept my lesbianism a secret, forming a relationship with an effeminate male friend that served to shelter and disguise us both. I explained to friends that I went home so rarely because my stepfather and I fought too much for me to be comfortable in his house. But that was only part of the reason I avoided home, the easiest reason. The truth was that I feared the person I might become in my mama's house, the woman of my dreams—hateful, violent, and hopeless.

It is hard to explain how deliberately and thoroughly I ran away from my own life. I did not forget where I came from, but I gritted my teeth and hid it. When I could not get enough scholarship money to pay for graduate school, I spent a year of rage working as a salad girl, substitute teacher, and maid. I finally managed to find a job by agreeing to take any city assignment where the Social Security Administration needed a clerk. Once I had a job and my own place far away from anyone in my family, I became sexually and politically active, joining the Women's Center support staff and falling in love with a series of middle-class women who thought my accent and stories thoroughly charming. The stories I told about my family, about South Carolina, about being poor itself, were all lies, carefully edited to seem droll or funny. I knew damn well that no one would want to hear the truth about poverty, the hopelessness and fear, the feeling that nothing I did would ever make any difference and the raging resentment that burned beneath my jokes. Even when my lovers and I formed an alternative lesbian family, sharing what we could of our resources, I kept the truth about my background and who I knew myself to be a carefully obscured mystery. I worked as hard as I could to make myself a new person, an emotionally healthy radical lesbian activist, and I believed completely that by remaking myself I was helping to remake the world.

For a decade, I did not go home for more than a few days at a time.

When in the 1980s I ran into the concept of feminist sexuality, I genuinely did not know what it meant. Though I was, and am, a feminist, and committed to claiming the right to act on my sexual desires without tailoring my lust to a sex-fearing society, demands that I explain or justify my sexual fantasies have left me at a loss. How does anyone explain sexual need?

The Sex Wars are over, I've been told, and it always makes me want to ask who won. But my sense of humor may be a little obscure to women who have never felt threatened by the way most lesbians use and mean the words *pervert* and *queer*. I use the word queer to mean more than lesbian. Since I first used it in 1980 I have always meant it to imply that I am not only a lesbian but a transgressive lesbian-femme, masochistic, as sexually aggressive as the women I seek out, and as pornographic in my imagination and sexual activities as the heterosexual hegemony has ever believed.

My aunt Dot used to joke, "There are two or three things I know for sure, but never the same things and I'm never as sure as I'd like." What I know for sure is that class, gender, sexual preference, and prejudice—racial, ethnic, and religious—form an intricate lattice that restricts and shapes our lives, and that resistance to hatred is not a simple act. Claiming your identity in the cauldron of hatred and resistance to hatred is infinitely complicated, and worse, almost unexplainable.

I know that I have been hated as a lesbian both by "society" and by the intimate world of my extended family, but I have also been hated or held in contempt (which is in some ways more debilitating and slippery than hatred) by lesbians for behavior and sexual practices shaped in large part by class. My sexual identity is intimately constructed by my class and regional background, and much of the hatred directed at my sexual preferences is class hatred—however much people, feminists in particular, like to pretend this is not a factor. The kind of woman I am attracted to is invariably the kind of woman who embarrasses respectably middle- class, politically aware lesbian feminists. My sexual ideal is butch, exhibitionistic, physically aggressive, smarter than she wants you to know, and proud of being called a pervert. Most often she is working class, with an aura of danger and an ironic sense of humor. There is a lot of contemporary lip service paid to sexual tolerance, but the fact that my sexuality is constructed within, and by, a butch/femme and leather fetishism is widely viewed with distaste or outright hatred.

For most of my life I have been presumed to be misguided, by incest and childhood physical abuse, or deliberately indulging in hateful and retrograde sexual practices out of a selfish concentration on my own sexual satisfaction. I have been expected to abandon my desires, to become the normalized woman who flirts with fetishization, who plays with gender roles and treats the historical categories of deviant desire with humor or gentle contempt but never takes any of it so seriously as to claim a sexual identity based on these categories. It was hard enough for me to shake off demands when they were made by straight society. It was appalling when I found the same demands made by other lesbians.

One of the strengths I derive from my class background is that I am accustomed to contempt. I know that I have no chance of becoming what my detractors expect of me, and I believe that even the attempt to please them will only further engage their contempt, and my own self-contempt as well. Nonetheless, the relationship between the life I have lived and the way that life is seen by strangers has constantly invited a kind of self-mythologizing fantasy. It has always been tempting for me to play off of the stereotypes and misconceptions of mainstream culture, rather than describe a difficult and sometimes painful reality.

I am trying to understand how we internalize the myths of our society even as we resist them. I have felt a powerful temptation to write about my family as a kind of morality tale, with us as the heroes and middle and upper classes as the villains. It would be within the romantic myth, for example, to pretend that we were the kind of noble Southern whites portrayed in the movies, mill workers for generations until driven out by alcoholism and a family propensity for rebellion and union talk. But that would be a lie. The truth is that no one in my family ever joined a union.

Taken to its limits, the myth of the poor would make my family over into union organizers or people broken by the failure of the unions. As far as my family was concerned union organizers, like preachers, were of a different class, suspect and hated however much they might be admired for what they were supposed to be to trying to achieve. Nominally Southern Baptist, no one in my family actually paid much attention to preachers, and only little children went to Sunday school. Serious belief in anything—any political ideology, any religious system, or any theory of life's meaning and purpose—was seen as unrealistic. It was an attitude that bothered me a lot when I started reading the socially conscious novels I found in the paperback racks when I was eleven or so. I particularly loved Sinclair Lewis's novels and wanted to imagine my own family as part of the working man's struggle.

"We were not joiners," my aunt Dot told me with a grin when I asked her about the union. My cousin Butch laughed at that, told me the union charged dues, and said, "Hell, we can't even be persuaded to toss money in the collection plate. An't gonna give it to no union man." It shamed me that the only thing my family wholeheartedly believed in was luck and the waywardness of fate. They held the dogged conviction that the admirable and wise thing to do was keep a sense of humor, never whine or cower, and trust that luck might someday turn as good as it had been bad—and with just as much reason. Becoming a political activist with an almost religious fervor was the thing I did that most outraged my family and the Southern working-class community they were part of.

Similarly, it was not my sexuality, my lesbianism, that my family saw as most rebellious; for most of my life, no one but my mama took my sexual preference very seriously. It was the way I thought about work, ambition, and self-respect. They were waitresses, laundry workers, counter girls. I was the one who went to work as a maid, something I never told any of them. They would have been angry if they had known. Work was just work for them, necessary. You did what you had to do to survive. They did not so much believe in taking pride in doing your job as in stubbornly enduring hard work and hard times. At the same time, they held that there were some forms of work, including maid's work, that were only for Black people, not white, and while I did not share that belief, I knew how intrinsic it was to the way my family saw the world. Sometimes I felt as if I straddled cultures and belonged on neither side. I would grind my teeth at what I knew was my family's unquestioning racism while continuing to respect their pragmatic endurance. But more and more as I grew older, what I felt was a deep estrangement from their view of the world, and gradually a sense of shame that would have been completely incomprehensible to them.

"Long as there's lunch counters, you can always find work," I was told by my mother and my aunts. Then they'd add, "I can get me a little extra with a smile." It was obvious there was supposed to be nothing shameful about it, that needy smile across a lunch counter, that rueful grin when you didn't have rent, or the half-provocative, half-pleading way my mama could cajole the man at the store to give her a little credit. But I hated it, hated the need for it and the shame that would follow every time I did it myself. It was begging, as far as I was concerned, a quasi-prostitution that I despised even while I continued to rely on it. After all, I needed the money.

"Just use that smile," my girl cousins used to joke, and I hated what I knew they meant. After college, when I began to support myself and study feminist theory, I became more contemptuous rather than more understanding of the women in my family. I told myself that prostitution is a skilled profession and my cousins were never more than amateurs. There was a certain truth in this, though like all cruel judgments rendered from the outside, it ignored the conditions that made it true. The women in my family, my mother included, had sugar daddies, not johns, men who slipped them money because they needed it so badly. From their point of view they were nice to those men because the men were nice to them, and it was never so direct or crass an arrangement that they would set a price on their favors. Nor would they have described what they did as prostitution. Nothing made them angrier than the suggestion that the men who helped them out did it just for their favors. They worked for a living, they swore, but this was different.

I always wondered if my mother hated her sugar daddy, or if not him then her need for what he offered her, but it did not seem to me in memory that she had. He was an old man, half-crippled, hesitant and needy, and he treated my mama with enormous consideration and, yes, respect. The relationship between them was painful, and since she and my stepfather could not earn enough to support the family, Mama could not refuse her sugar daddy's money. At the same time the man made no assumptions about that money buying anything Mama was not already offering. The truth was, I think, that she genuinely liked him, and only partly because he treated her so well.

Even now, I am not sure whether there was a sexual exchange between them. Mama was a pretty woman, and she was kind to him, a kindness he obviously did not get from anyone else in his life. Moreover, he took extreme care not to cause her any problems with my stepfather. As a teenager, with a teenager's contempt for moral failings and sexual complexity of any kind, I had been convinced that Mama's relationship with that old man was contemptible. Also, that I would never do such a thing. But the first time a lover of mine gave me money and I took it, everything in my head shifted. The amount was not much to her, but it was a lot to me and I needed it. While I could not refuse it, I hated myself for taking it and I hated her for giving it. Worse, she had much less grace about my need than my mama's sugar daddy had displayed toward her. All that bitter contempt I felt for my needy cousins and aunts raged through me and burned out the love. I ended the relationship quickly, unable to forgive myself for selling what I believed should only be offered freely—not sex but love itself.

When the women in my family talked about how hard they worked, the men would spit to the side and shake their heads. Men took real jobs—harsh, dangerous, physically daunting work. They went to jail, not just the cold-eyed, careless boys who scared me with their brutal hands, but their gentler, softer brothers. It was another family thing, what people expected of my mama's people, mine. "His daddy's that one was sent off to jail in Georgia, and his uncle's another. Like as not, he's just the same," you'd hear people say of boys so young they still had their milk teeth. We were always driving down to the county farm to see somebody, some uncle, cousin, or nameless male relation. Shaven-headed, sullen, and stunned, they wept on Mama's shoulder or begged my aunts to help. "I didn't do nothing, Mama" they'd say, and it might have been true, but if even we didn't believe them, who would? No one told the truth, not even about how their lives were destroyed.

One of my favorite cousins went to jail when I was eight years old, for breaking into pay phones with another boy. The other boy was returned to the custody of his parents. My cousin was sent to the boys' facility at the county farm. After three months, my mama took us down there to visit, carrying a big basket of fried chicken, cold cornbread, and potato salad. Along with a hundred others we sat out on the lawn with my cousin and watched him eat like he hadn't had a full meal in the whole three months. I stared at his near-bald head and his ears marked with fine blue scars from the carelessly handled razor. People were laughing, music was playing, and a tall, lazy, uniformed man walked past us chewing on toothpicks and watching us all closely. My cousin kept his head down, his face hard with hatred, only looking back at the guard when he turned away.

"Sons-a-bitches," he whispered, and my mama shushed him. We all sat still when the guard turned back to us. There was a long moment of quiet, and then that man let his face relax into a big wide grin.

"Uh-huh," he said. That was all he said. Then he turned and walked away. None of us spoke. None of us ate. He went back inside soon after, and we left. When we got back to the car, my mama sat there for a while crying quietly. The next week my cousin was reported for fighting and had his stay extended by six months.

My cousin was fifteen. He never went back to school, and after jail he couldn't join the army. When he finally did come home we never talked, never had to. I knew without asking that the guard had had his little revenge, knew too that my cousin would break into another phone booth as soon as he could, but do it sober and not get caught. I knew without asking the source of his rage, the way he felt about clean, well-dressed, contemptuous people who looked at him like his life wasn't as important as a dog's. I knew because I felt it too. That guard had looked at me and Mama with the same expression he used on my cousin. We were trash. We were the ones they built the county farm to house and break. The boy who was sent home was the son of a deacon in the church, the man who managed the hardware store.

As much as I hated that man, and his boy, there was a way in which I also hated my cousin. He should have known better, I told myself, should have known the risk he ran. He should have been more careful. As I grew older and started living on my own, it was a litany I used against myself even more angrily than I used it against my cousin. I knew who I was, knew that the most important thing I had to do was protect myself and hide my despised identity, blend into the myth of both the good poor and the reasonable lesbian. When I became a feminist activist, that litany went on reverberating in my head, but by then it had become a groundnote, something so deep and omnipresent I no longer heard it, even when everything I did was set to its cadence.

By 1975 I was earning a meager living as a photographer's assistant in Tallahassee, Florida. But the real work of my life was my lesbian-feminist activism, the work I did with the local women's center and the committee to found a women's studies program at Florida State University. Part of my role, as I saw it, was to be a kind of evangelical lesbian feminist, and to help develop a political analysis of this woman-hating society. I did not talk about class, except to give lip service to how we all needed to think about it, the same way I thought we all needed to think about racism. I was a determined person, living in a lesbian collective—all of us young and white and serious—studying each new book that purported to address feminist issues, driven by what I saw as a need to revolutionize the world.

Years later it's difficult to convey just how reasonable my life seemed to me at that time. I was not flippant, not consciously condescending, not casual about how tough a struggle remaking social relations would be, but like so many women of my generation, I believed absolutely that I could make a difference with my life, and I was willing to give my life for the chance to make that difference. I expected hard times, long slow periods of self-sacrifice and grinding work, expected to be hated and attacked in public, to have to set aside personal desire, lovers, and family in order to be part of something greater and more important than my individual concerns. At the same time, I was working ferociously to take my desires, my sexuality, my needs as a woman and a lesbian more seriously. I believed I was making the personal political revolution with my life every moment, whether I was scrubbing the floor of the childcare center, setting up a new budget for the women's lecture series at the university, editing the local feminist magazine or starting a women's bookstore. That I was constantly exhausted and had no health insurance, did hours of dreary unpaid murk and still sneaked out of the collective to date butch women my housemates thought retrograde and sexist never interfered with my sense of total commitment to the feminist revolution. I was not living in a closet: I had compartmentalized my own mind to such an extent that I never questioned why I did what I did. And I never admitted what lay behind all my feminist convictions—a class-constructed distrust of change, a secret fear that someday I would be found out for who I really was, found out and thrown out. If I had not been raised to give my life away, would I have made such an effective, self-sacrificing revolutionary?

The narrowly focused concentration of a revolutionary shifted only when I began to write again. The idea of writing stories seemed frivolous when there was so much work to be done, but everything changed when I found myself confronting emotions and ideas that could not be explained away or postponed until after the revolution. The way it happened was simple and unexpected. One week I was asked to speak to two completely different groups: an Episcopalian Sunday school class and a juvenile detention center. The Episcopalians were all white, well-dressed, highly articulate, nominally polite, and obsessed with getting me to tell them (without their having to ask directly) just what it was that two women did together in bed. The delinquents were all women, 80 percent Black and Hispanic, wearing green uniform dresses or blue jeans and workshirts, profane, rude, fearless, witty, and just as determined to get me to talk about what it was that two women did together in bed.

I tried to have fun with the Episcopalians, teasing them about their fears and insecurities, and being as bluntly honest as I could about my sexual practices. The Sunday school teacher, a man who had assured me of his liberal inclinations, kept blushing and stammering as the questions about my growing up and coming out became more detailed. I stepped out into the sunshine when the meeting was over, angry at the contemptuous attitude implied by all their questioning, and though I did not know why, so deeply depressed I couldn't even cry.

The delinquents were another story. Shameless, they had me blushing within the first few minutes, yelling out questions that were part curiosity and partly a way of boasting about what they already knew. "You butch or femme?" "You ever fuck boys?" "You ever want to?" "You want to have children?" "What's your girlfriend like?" I finally broke up when one very tall, confident girl leaned way over and called out, "Hey, girlfriend! I'm getting out of here next weekend. What you doing that night?" I laughed so hard I almost choked. I laughed until we were all howling and giggling together. Even getting frisked as I left didn't ruin my mood. I was still when I climbed into the waterbed with my lover that night, right up to the moment when she wrapped her arms around me and I burst into tears.

That night I understood, suddenly, everything that had happened to my cousins and me, understood it from a wholly new and agonizing perspective, one that made clear how brutal I had been to both my family and myself. I grasped all over again how we had been robbed and dismissed, and why I had worked so hard not to think about it. I had learned as a child that what could not be changed had to go unspoken, and worse, that those who cannot change their own lives have every reason to be ashamed of that fact and to hide it. I had accepted that shame and believed in it, but why? What had I or my cousins done to deserve the contempt directed at us? Why had I always believed us contemptible by nature? I wanted to talk to someone about all the things I was thinking that night, but I could not. Among the women I knew there was no one who would have understood what I was thinking, no other working-class woman in the women's collective where I was living. I began to suspect that we shared no common language to speak those bitter truths.

In the days that followed I found myself remembering that afternoon long ago at the county farm, that feeling of being the animal in the zoo, the thing looked at and laughed at and used by the real people who watched us. For all his liberal convictions, that Sunday school teacher had looked at me with the eyes of my cousin's long ago guard. I felt thrown back into my childhood, into all the fears I had tried to escape. Once again I felt myself at the mercy of the important people who knew how to dress and talk, and would always be given the benefit of the doubt, while my family and I would not.

I experienced an outrage so old I could not have traced all the ways it shaped my life. I realized again that some are given no quarter, no chance, that all their courage, humor, and love for each other is just a joke to the ones who make the rules, and I hated the rule-makers. Finally, I recognized that part of my grief came from the fact that I no longer knew who I was or where I belonged. I had run away from my family, refused to go home to visit, and tried in every way to make myself a new person. How could I be working class with a college degree? As a lesbian activist? I thought about the guards at the detention center. They had not stared at me with the same picture-window emptiness they turned on the girls who came to hear me, girls who were closer to the life I had been meant to live than I could bear to examine. The contempt in their eyes was contempt for me as a lesbian, different and the same, but still contempt.

While I raged, my girlfriend held me and comforted me and tried to get me to explain what was hurting me so bad, but I could not. She had told me so often about her awkward relationship with her own family, the father who ran his own business and still sent her checks every other month. She knew almost nothing about my family, only the jokes and careful stories I had given her. I felt so alone and at risk lying in her arms that I could not have explained anything at all. I thought about those girls in the detention center and the stories they told in brutal shorthand about their sisters, brothers, cousins, and lovers. I thought about their one-note references to those they had lost, never mentioning the loss of their own hopes, their own futures, the bent and painful shape of their lives when they would finally get free. Cried-out and dry-eyed, I lay watching my sleeping girlfriend and thinking about what I had not been able to say to her. After a few hours I got up and made some notes for a poem I wanted to write, a bare, painful litany of loss shaped as a conversation between two women, one who cannot understand the other, and one who cannot tell all she knows.

It took me a long time to take that poem from a raw lyric of outrage and grief to a piece of fiction that explained to me something I had never let myself see up close before—the whole process of running away, of closing up inside yourself, of hiding. It has taken me most of my life to understand that, to see how and why those of us who are born poor and different are so driven to give ourselves away or lose ourselves, but most of all, simply to disappear as the people we really are. By the time that poem became the story "River of Names"[2] I had made the decision to reverse that process: to claim my family, my true history, and to tell the truth not only about who I was but about the temptation to lie.

By the time I taught myself the basics of storytelling on the page, I knew there was only one story that would haunt me until I understood how to tell it—the complicated, painful story of how my mama had, and had not, saved me as a girl. Writing *Bastard Out of Carolina*[3] became, ultimately, the way to claim my family's pride and tragedy, and the embattled sexuality I had fashioned on a base of violence and abuse.

The compartmentalized life I had created burst open in the late 1970s after I began to write what I really thought about my family. I lost patience with my fear of what the women I worked with, lesbians, thought of who I slept with and what we did together. When schisms developed within my community; when I was no longer able to hide within the regular dyke network; when I could not continue to justify my life by constant political activism or distract myself by sleeping around; when my sexual promiscuity, butch/femme orientation, and exploration of sadomasochistic sex became part of what was driving me out of my community of choice—I went home again. I went home to my mother and my sisters, to visit, talk, argue, and begin to understand.

Once home I saw that as far as my family was concerned, lesbians were lesbians whether they wore suitcoats or leather jackets. Moreover, in all that time when I had not made peace with myself, my family had managed to make a kind of peace with me. My girlfriends were treated like odd versions of my sisters' husbands, while I was simply the daughter who had always been difficult but was still a part of their lives. The result was that I started trying to confront what had made me unable really to talk to my sisters for so many years. I discovered that they no longer knew who I was either, and it took time and lots of listening to each other to rediscover my sense of family, and my love for them.

It is only as the child of my class and my unique family background that I have been able to put together what is for me a meaningful politics, to regain a sense of why I believe in activism, why self-revelation is so important for lesbians. There is no all-purpose feminist analysis that explains the complicated ways our sexuality and core identity are shaped, the way we see ourselves as parts of both our birth families and the extended family of friends and lovers we invariably create within the lesbian community. For me, the bottom line has simply become the need to resist that omnipresent fear, that urge to hide and disappear, to disguise my life, my desires, and the truth about how little any of us understand—even as we try to make the world a more just and human place. Most of all, I have tried to understand the politics of *they*, why human beings fear and stigmatize the different while secretly dreading that they might be one of the different themselves. Class, race, sexuality, gender—and all the other categories by which we categorize and dismiss each other—need to be excavated from the inside.

The horror of class stratification, racism, and prejudice is that some people begin to believe that the security of their families and communities depends on the oppression of others, that for some to have good lives there must be others whose lives are truncated and brutal. It is a belief that dominates this culture. It is what makes the poor whites of the South so determinedly racist and the middle class so contemptuous of the poor. It is a myth that allows some to imagine that they build their lives on the ruin of others, a secret core of shame for the middle class, a goad and a spur to the marginal working class, and cause enough for the homeless and poor to feel no constraints on hatred or violence. The power of the myth is made even more apparent when we examine how, within the lesbian and feminist communities where we have addressed considerable attention to the politics of marginalization, there is still so much exclusion and fear, so many of us who do not feel safe.

I grew up poor, hated, the victim of physical, emotional, and sexual violence, and I know that suffering does not ennoble. It destroys. To resist destruction, self-hatred, or lifelong hopelessness, we have to throw off the conditioning of being despised, the fear of becoming the *they* that is talked about so dismissively, to refuse lying myths and easy moralities, to see ourselves as human, flawed, and extraordinary. All of us—extraordinary.

Notes

1. *A Few Words in the Mother Tongue: Poems, Selected and New* (Eighth Mountain Press: Portland, Oregon, 1990)
2. Trash (Firebrand Books: Ithaca, New York, 1988)
3. Dutton: New York, 1992

Questions

1. In what ways has Allison felt "despised"? Why has she had trouble feeling a sense of belonging? Why did Allison feel compelled to hide the truth about her childhood? How does membership in the "mythical poor" differ from being part of the "despised" poor? How has Allison's life differed from other members of her family?
2. Why was it easier for Allison to publicly claim her identity as a lesbian during her years as an activist than her identity as poor? Why has Allison sometimes felt alienated in the lesbian community? Why have other lesbians felt uncomfortable with some of her sexual practices? How has class shaped Allison's sexual identity?
3. What does Allison mean when she asserts that she will not "tailor her lust to a sex-fearing society"? What evidence can you offer that our society "fears" sex?
4. Why is this passage significant: "I had learned as a child that what could not be changed had to go unspoken, and worse, that those who cannot change their own lives have every reason to be ashamed of that fact and to hide it"? What connections exist between shame and silence? Between voice and empowerment? Why did Allison feel compelled to write?
5. How did Allison both internalize—and resist—the myths of society? Can you think of examples of myths that individuals both internalize and resist?

An earlier version of this essay appeared in *Sisters, SexPerts, Queers,* edited by Arlene Stein (Penguin/plume: New York, 1993).

Confessions of a Recovering Misogynist (2000)

Kevin Powell

Kevin Powell takes an honest, critical look at his own upbringing as a sexist male. His education, his family, his church and his peers all played roles in training him to act aggressively and disdainfully toward women until a traumatic event forced him to take a hard look at his behavior. Powell's narrative reflects the power of male gender socialization and the particular vulnerability of black men in our racist culture. Men can play significant roles in the feminist movement by facing their own complicity in the system of sexism and by publicly acknowledging their struggles and reaching out to other men.

I AM A SEXIST MALE. I take no great pride in saying this, I am merely stating a fact. It is not that I was born this way—rather, I was born into this male-dominated society, and consequently, from the very moment I began forming thoughts, they formed in a

"Confessions of a Recovering Misogynist," by Kevin Powell. Reprinted from *Ms.* Magazine,, April/May 2000, pp. 72–77

decidedly male-centered way. My "education" at home with my mother, at school, on my neighborhood playgrounds, and at church, all placed males in the middle of the universe. My digestion of 1970s American popular culture in the form of television, film, ads, and music only added to my training, so that by as early as age nine or ten I saw females, including my mother, as nothing more than the servants of males. Indeed, like the Fonz, I thought I could snap my fingers and girls would come running.

My mother, working-poor and a product of the conservative and patriarchal South, simply raised me as most women are taught to raise boys: the world was mine; there were no chores to speak of; and my aggressions were considered somewhat normal, something that we boys carry out as a rite of passage. Those "rites" included me routinely squeezing girls' butts on the playground. And it was at school that boys were encouraged to do "boy" things: work and build with our hands, fight each other, and participate in the most daring activities during our gym time. Meanwhile, the girls were relegated to home economics, drawing cute pictures, and singing in the school choir. Now that I think about it, school was the place that spearheaded the omission of women from my world view. Save Betsy Ross (whom I remember chiefly for sewing a flag), I recall virtually no women making appearances in my American history classes.

The church my mother and I attended, like most black churches, was peopled mainly by black women, most of them single parents, who dragged their children along for the ride. Not once did I see a preacher who was anything other than an articulate, emotionally charged, well-coiffed, impeccably suited black man running this church and, truly, these women. And behind the pulpit of this black man, where he convinced us we were doomed to hell if we did not get right with God, was the image of our savior, a male, always white, named Jesus Christ.

Not surprisingly, the "savior" I wanted in my life was my father. Ten years her senior, my father met my mother, my father wooed my mother, my father impregnated my mother, and then my father—as per his socialization—moved on to the next mating call. Responsibility was about as real to him as a three-dollar bill. When I was eight, my father flatly told my mother, via a payphone, that he felt she had lied, that I was not his child, and that he would never give her money for me again. The one remotely tangible image of maleness in my life was gone for good.

Both my mother and I were devastated, albeit for different reasons. I longed for my father's affections. And my mother longed to be married. Silently, I began to blame my mother for my father's disappearance. Reacting to my increasingly bad behavior, my mother turned resentful and her beatings became more frequent, more charged. I grew to hate her and all females, for I felt it was women who made men act as we do.

At the same time, my mother, a fiercely independent and outspoken woman despite having only a grade-school education and being poor, planted within me the seeds of self-criticism, of shame for wrongful behavior—and, ultimately, of feminism. Clear that she alone would have to shape me, my mother spoke pointedly about my father for many years after that call, demanding that I not grow up to "be like him." And I noted the number of times my mother rejected low-life male suitors, particularly the ones who wanted to live with us free of charge. I can see now that my mother is a feminist, although she is not readily familiar with the term. Like many women before and since, she fell hard for my father, and only through enduring immense pain did she realize the power she had within herself.

I ONCE HATED WOMEN, AND I TAKE NO PRIDE IN THIS CONFESSION. I entered Rutgers University in the mid-1980s and my mama's-boy demeanor advanced to that of pimp. I learned quickly that most males in college are some variety of pimp. Today I lecture regularly, from campus to campus, all over the country, and I see that not much has changed. For college is simply a place where we men, irrespective of race or class, can—and do—act out the sexist attitudes entrenched since boyhood. Rape, infidelity, girlfriend beat downs, and emotional abuse are common, and pimpdom reigns supreme. There is the athlete-pimp, the fratboy-pimp, the independent-pimp, and the college-professor-pimp. Buoyed by the anti apartheid movement and the presidential bids of Jesse Jackson, my social consciousness blossomed along racial lines and, behold, the student-leader-pimp was born.

Blessed with a gift for gab, a poet's sensibility, and an acute memory for historical facts, I baited women with my self-righteousness by quoting Malcolm X, Fratz Fanon, Machiavelli, and any other figure I was sure they had not studied. It was a polite form of sexism, for I was always certain to say "My sister" when I addressed women at Rutgers. But my politeness did not lend me tolerance for women's issues, nor did my affiliation with a variety of black nationalist organizations, especially the Nation of Islam. Indeed, whenever women in our African Student Congress would question the behavior and attitudes of men, I would scream, "We don't have time for them damn lesbian issues!" My scream was violent, mean-spirited, made with the intention to wound. I don't think it is any coincidence that during my four years in college I did not have one relationship with a woman that lasted more than three or four months. For every friend or girlfriend who would dare question my behavior, there were literally hundreds of others who acquiesced to the ways of us men, making it easy for me to ignore the legitimate cries of the feminists. Besides, I had taken on the demanding role of pimp, of conqueror, of campus revolutionary, and there was little time, or room, for real intimacy, and even less time for self-reflection.

CONFESSIONS ARE DIFFICULT BECAUSE THEY FORCE ME TO VISIT GHETTOES IN THE MIND I THOUGHT I HAD LONG ESCAPED. I was kicked out of college at the end of my fourth year because I drew a knife on a female student. We were both members of the African Student Congress and she was one of the many "subversive" female leaders I had sought to purge from the organization. She had left but for some reason was in our office a few days after we had brought Louis Farrakhan to speak at Rutgers. Made tense by her presence, I ignored her and turned to a male student asking him, as she stood there, to ask her to jet. As she was leaving, she turned and charged toward me. My instincts nurtured by my inner-city upbringing and several months of receiving anonymous threats as the Farrakhan talk neared, caused me to reach inside my pocket and pull out a knife.

My intent was to scare her into submission. The male student panicked and knocked the knife from my hand, believing I was going to stab this woman. I would like to believe that that is not the case. It does not matter. This woman pressed charges on and off campus, and my college career, the one I took on for myself, my undereducated mother, and my illiterate grandparents, came to a screeching halt.

IT IS NOT EASY FOR ME TO ADMIT I HAVE A PROBLEM. Before I could be readmitted to school I had to see a therapist. I went, grudgingly, and agonized over my violent childhood, my hatred of my mother, my many problems with women, and the nauseating torment of poverty and instability. But then it was done. I did not bother to try to return to college, and I found myself again using women for money, for sex, for entertainment. When I moved to New York City in August of 1990, my predator mentality was still in full effect. I met a woman, persuaded her to allow me to live with her, and then mentally abused her for nearly a year, cutting off her friends, her peace of mind, her spirit, and eventually pushing her into a bathroom door when she blew up my spot, challenging me and my manhood.

I do not want to recount the details of "the incident" here. What I will say is that I, like most black men I know, have spent much of my life living in fear. Fear of white racism, fear of the circumstances that gave birth to me, fear of walking out my door wondering what humiliation will be mine today. Fear of black women—of their mouths, of their bodies, of their attitudes, of their hurts, of their fear of us black men. I felt fragile, as fragile as a bird with clipped wings, that day my ex-girlfriend stepped up her game and spoke back to me. Nothing in my world, nothing in my self-definition prepared me for dealing with a woman as an equal. My world said women were inferior, that they must, at all costs, be put in their place, and my instant reaction was to do that. When it was over, I found myself dripping with sweat, staring at her back as she ran barefoot out of the apartment.

Guilt consumed me after the incident. The women I knew through my circle of poet and writer friends begged me to talk through what I had done, to get counseling, to read the books of bell hooks, Pearl Cleage's tiny tome, *Mad at Miles*, the poetry of Audre Lorde, the many meditations of Gloria Steinem. I resisted at first, but eventually I began to listen and read, feeling electric shocks running through my body when I realized these women, in describing abusive, oppressive men, were talking about me. Me, who thought I was progressive. Me, who claimed to be a revolutionary. Me, who still felt women were on the planet to take care of men.

During this time I did restart therapy sessions. I did, also, spend a good deal of time talking with young feminist women—some friends, some not. Some were soothing and understanding, some berated me and all men. I also spent a great deal of time alone, replaying my life in my mind: my relationship with my mother, how my mother responded to my father's behavior, how I responded to my mother's response to my father. I thought of my education, of the absence of women in it. How I managed to attend a major university affiliated with one of the oldest women's college in America, Douglass College, and visit that campus only in pursuit of sex. I thought of the older men I had encountered in my life—the ministers, the high school track coach, the street hustlers, the local businessmen, the college professors—and realized that many of the ways I learned to relate to women came from listening to and observing those men. Yeah, I grew up after women's studies classes had appeared in most of the major colleges in America, but that does not mean that feminism actually reached the people it really needed to reach: average, everyday American males.

The incident, and the remorse that followed, brought about something akin to a spiritual epiphany. I struggled, mightily, to rethink the context that created my mother. And my aunts. And my grandmother. And all the women I had been intimate with, either physically or emotionally or both. I struggled to understand terms like "patriarchy," "misogyny," "gender oppression." A year after the incident I penned a short essay for *Essence* magazine called simply, "The Sexist in Me," because I wanted to be honest in the most public forum possible, and because I wanted to reach some men, some young black men, who needed to hear from another male that sexism is as oppressive as racism. And at times, worse.

I AM NO HERO. I AM NO SAINT. I REMAIN A SEXIST MALE. But one who is now conscious of it and who has been waging an internal war for several years. Some days I am incredibly progressive, other days I regress. It is very lonely to swim against the stream of American male-centeredness, of black-man bravado and nut-grabbing. It is how I was molded, it is what I know, and in rejecting it I often feel mad naked and isolated. For example, when I publicly opposed the blatantly sexist and patriarchal rhetoric and atmosphere of the Million Man March, I was attacked by black men, some questioning my sanity, some accusing me of being a dupe for the white man, and some wondering if I was just "trying' to get some pussy from black women."

Likewise, I am a hip-hop head. Since adolescence I have been involved in rap culture as a dancer, a graffiti writer, an activist, a concert organizer, and most prominently, a hip-hop journalist. Indeed, as a journalist at *Vibe* magazine, I found myself interviewing rap icons like Dr. Dre, Snoop Dogg, and the late Tupac Shakur. And although I did ask Snoop and Tupac some pointed questions about their sexism, I still feel I dropped the ball. We black men often feel so powerless, so sure the world—politically, economically, spiritually, and psychologically—is aligned against us. The last thing any of us want is for another man to question how we treat women. Aren't we, black men, the endangered species anyhow? This is how many of us think.

While I do not think hip-hop is any more sexist or misogynist than other forms of American culture, I do think it is the most explicit form of misogyny around today. It is also a form of sexism that gets more than its share of attention, because hip-hop—now a billion-dollar industry—is the soundtrack for young America, regardless of race or class. What folks don't understand is that hip-hop was created on the heels of the civil rights era by impoverished black men and Latinos, who literally made something out of nothing. But in making that something out of nothing, many of us men of color have held tightly to white patriarchal notions of manhood—that is, the way to be a man is to have power. Within hip-hop culture, in our lyrics, in our videos, and on our tours, that power translates into material possessions, provocative and often foul language, flashes of violence, and blatant objectification of and disrespect for women. Patriarchy, as manifested in hip-hop, is where we can have our version of power within this very oppressive society. Who would want to even consider giving that up?

Well, I have, to a large extent, and these days I am a hip-hopper-in-exile. I dress, talk, and walk like a hip-hopper, yet I cannot listen to rap radio or digest music videos without commenting on the pervasive sexism. Moreover, I try to drop seeds, as we say, about sexism, whenever and wherever I can, be it a community forum or on a college campus. Some men, young and old alike, simply cannot deal with it and walk out. Or there is the nervous shifting in seats, the uneasy comments during the question-and-answer sessions, generally in the form of "Why you gotta pick on the men, man?" I constantly "pick on the men" and myself, because I truly wonder how many men actually listen to the concerns of women. Just as I feel it is whites who need to be more vociferous about racism in their communities, I feel it is men who need to speak long and loud about sexism among each other.

I AM A RECOVERING MISOGYNIST. I do not say this with pride. Like a recovering alcoholic or a crack fiend who has righted her on his ways, I am merely cognizant of the fact that I have had some serious problems in my life with and in regard to women. I am also aware of the fact that I can lapse backward—and have—at any time. My relationship with my mother is better than it has ever been, though there are days when speaking with her turns me back into that little boy, cowering beneath the belt and tongue of a woman deeply wounded by my father, by poverty, by her childhood, by the sexism that had dominated her life. My relationships since the incident with my ex-girlfriend have been better, no doubt, but not the bomb.

So I flow solo, and have done so for some time. For sure, I now count among my friends, peers, and mentors feminist women like bell hooks and Johnnetta B. Cole, and young feminists like Nikki Stewart, a girls' rights advocate in Washington, D.C., and Aishah Simmons, who is currently putting together a documentary on rape within the black community. I do not always agree with these women, but I also know that if I do not struggle, hard and constantly, backsliding is real. This is made worse by the fact that outside of a handful of male friends, there are no young men I know—and I know many people around the country—who I can speak with regarding sexism as easily as I do with women. So few of us actually believe there is a problem.

The fact is there was a blueprint handed to me in childhood telling me this is the way a man should behave, and I unwittingly followed the script verbatim. There was no blueprint handed to me about how to begin to wind myself out of sexism as an adult, but maybe there should have been. Everyday I struggle within myself not to use the language of gender oppression, to see the sexism inherent in every aspect of America, to challenge all injustices, not just those that are convenient for me. I am ashamed of my ridiculously sexist life, of raising my hand to my girlfriend. But with that shame has come a consciousness and, as the activists said during the civil rights movement, this consciousness, this knowing, is a river of no return. I have finally learned how to swim, I have finally learned how to push forward. I may become tired, I may lose my breath, I may hit a rock from time to time and become cynical, but I am not going to drown this time around.

QUESTIONS

1. What does Powell mean by "misogynist"? What sort of "training" did he receive to become this way? What type of behavior and feelings does Powell characterize as sexist or misogynistic? Give examples from the selection.
2. Why does he use the language of misogynist "in recovery"? What does it mean to be in "recovery"?
3. What events and feelings led Powell to face his issues with women and sexism? How was feminism helpful to him in thinking about his own gender socialization?
4. According to Powell, how can sexism be as oppressive as racism? How does the particular position of black men complicate the issue of living in a sexist culture?
5. How does Powell address his sexism? How does he recommend other men deal with their sexism? What obstacles exist in our culture to the honest discussion of masculinity, sexism and gender socialization issues among men?
6. Do you think Powell is overstating men's sexism in our culture? Why or why not?

Gender and Sexualities

We Are All Works in Progress

Leslie Feinberg

The sight of pink-blue gender-coded infant outfits may grate on your nerves. Or you may be a woman or a man who feels at home in those categories. Trans liberation defends you both.

Each person should have the right to *choose* between pink or blue tinted gender categories, as well as all the other hues of the palette. At this moment in time, that right is denied to us. But together, we could make it a reality.

And that's what this book is all about.

I am a human being who would rather not be addressed as Ms. or Mr., ma'am or sir. I prefer to use gender-neutral pronouns like *sie* (pronounced like "*see*") and *hir* (pronounced like "*here*") to describe myself. I am a person who faces almost insurmountable difficulty when instructed to check off an "F" or an "M" box on identification papers.

I'm not at odds with the fact that I was born female-bodied. Nor do I identify as an intermediate sex. I simply do not fit the prevalent Western concepts of what a woman or a man "should" look like. And that reality has dramatically directed the course of my life.

I'll give you a graphic example. From December 1995 to December 1996, I was dying of endocarditis—a bacterial infection that lodges and proliferates in the valves of the heart. A simple blood culture would have immediately exposed the root cause of my raging fevers. Eight weeks of 'round-the-clock intravenous antibiotic drips would have eradicated every last seedling of

Reprinted from *TransLiberation: Beyond Pink or Blue*, Beacon Press.

bacterium in the canals of my heart. Yet I experienced such hatred from some health practitioners that I very nearly died.

I remember late one night in December my lover and I arrived at a hospital emergency room during a snowstorm. My fever was 104 degrees and rising. My blood pressure was pounding dangerously high. The staff immediately hooked me up to monitors and worked to bring down my fever. The doctor in charge began physically examining me. When he determined that my anatomy was female, he flashed me a mean-spirited smirk. While keeping his eyes fixed on me, he approached one of the nurses, seated at a desk, and began rubbing her neck and shoulders. He talked to her about sex for a few minutes. After his pointed demonstration of "normal sexuality," he told me to get dressed and then he stormed out of the room. Still delirious, I struggled to put on my clothes and make sense of what was happening.

The doctor returned after I was dressed. He ordered me to leave the hospital and never return. I refused. I told him I wouldn't leave until he could tell me why my fever was so high. He said, "You have a fever because you are a very troubled person."

This doctor's prejudices, directed at me during a moment of catastrophic illness, could have killed me. The death certificate would have read: Endocarditis. By all rights it should have read: Bigotry.

As my partner and I sat bundled up in a cold car outside the emergency room, still reverberating from the doctor's hatred, I thought about how many people have been turned away from medical care when they were desperately ill—some because an apartheid "whites only" sign hung over the emergency room entrance, or some because their visible Kaposi's sarcoma lesions kept personnel far from their beds. I remembered how a blemish that wouldn't heal drove my mother to visit her doctor repeatedly during the 1950s. I recalled the doctor finally wrote a prescription for Valium because he decided she was a hysterical woman. When my mother finally got to specialists, they told her the cancer had already reached her brain.

Bigotry exacts its toll in flesh and blood. And left unchecked and unchallenged, prejudices create a poisonous climate for us all. Each of us has a stake in the demand that every human being has a right to a job, to shelter, to health care, to dignity, to respect.

I am very grateful to have this chance to open up a conversation with you about why it is so vital to also defend the right of individuals to express and define their sex and gender, and to control their own bodies. For me, it's a life-and-death question. But I also believe that this discussion will have great meaning for you. All your life you've heard such dogma about what it means to be a "real" woman or a "real" man. And chances are you've choked on some of it. You've balked at the idea that being a woman means having to be thin as a rail, emotionally nurturing, and an airhead when it comes to balancing her checkbook. You know in your guts that being a man has nothing to do with rippling muscles, innate courage, or knowing how to handle a chain saw. These are really caricatures. Yet these images have been drilled into us through popular culture and education over the years. And subtler, equally insidious messages lurk in the interstices of these grosser concepts. These ideas of what a "real" woman or man should be straightjacket the freedom of individual self-expression. These gender messages play on and on in a continuous loop in our brains, like commercials that can't be muted.

But in my lifetime I've also seen social upheavals challenge this sex and gender doctrine. As a child who grew up during the McCarthyite, Father-Knows-Best 1950s, and who came of age during the second wave of women's liberation in the United States, I've seen transformations in the ways people think and talk about what it means to be a woman or a man.

Today the gains of the 1970s women's liberation movement are under siege by right-wing propagandists. But many today who are too young to remember what life was like before the women's movement need to know that this was a tremendously progressive development that won significant economic and social reforms. And this struggle by women and their allies swung human consciousness forward like a pendulum.

The movement replaced the common usage of vulgar and diminutive words to describe females with the word *woman* and infused that word with strength and pride. Women, many of them formerly isolated, were drawn together into consciousness-raising groups. Their discussions—about the root of women's oppression and how to eradicate it—resonated far beyond the rooms in which they took place. The women's liberation movement sparked a mass conversation about the systematic degradation, violence, and discrimination that women faced in this society. And this consciousness raising changed many of the ways women and men thought about themselves and their relation to each other. In retrospect, however, we must not forget that these widespread discussions were not just organized to *talk* about oppression. They were a giant dialogue about how to take action to fight institutionalized anti-woman attitudes, rape and battering, the illegality of abortion, employment and education discrimination, and other ways women were socially and economically devalued.

This was a big step forward for humanity. And even the period of political reaction that followed has not been able to overturn all the gains made by that important social movement.

Now another movement is sweeping onto the stage of history: Trans liberation. We are again raising questions about the societal treatment of people based on their sex and gender expression. This discussion will make new contributions to human consciousness. And trans communities, like the women's movement, are carrying out these mass conversations with the goal of creating a movement capable of fighting for justice—of righting the wrongs.

We are a movement of masculine females and feminine males, cross-dressers, transsexual men and women, intersexuals born on the anatomical sweep between female and male, gender-blenders, many other sex and gender-variant people, and our significant others. All told, we expand understanding of how many ways there are to be a human being.

Our lives are proof that sex and gender are much more complex than a delivery room doctor's glance at genitals can determine, more variegated than pink or blue birth caps. We are oppressed for not fitting those narrow social norms. We are fighting back.

Our struggle will also help expose some of the harmful myths about what it means to be a woman or a man that have compartmentalized and distorted your life, as well as mine. Trans liberation has meaning for you—no matter how you define or express your sex or your gender.

If you are a trans person, you face horrendous social punishments—from institutionalization to gang rape, from beatings to denial of child visitation. This oppression is faced, in varying degrees, by all who march under the banner of trans liberation. This brutalization and degradation strips us of what we could achieve with our individual lifetimes.

And if you do not identify as transgender or transsexual or intersexual, your life is diminished by our oppression as well. Your own choices as a man or a woman are sharply curtailed.

Your individual journey to express yourself is shunted into one of two deeply carved ruts, and the social baggage you are handed is already packed.

So the defense of each individual's right to control their own body, and to explore the path of self-expression, enhances your own freedom to discover more about yourself and your potentialities. This movement will give you more room to breathe—to be yourself. To discover on a deeper level what it means to be your self.

Together, I believe we can forge a coalition that can fight on behalf of your oppression as well as mine. Together, we can raise each other's grievances and win the kind of significant change we all long for. But the foundation of unity is understanding. So let me begin by telling you a little bit about myself.

I am a human being who unnerves some people. As they look at me, they see a kaleidoscope of characteristics they associate with both males and females. I appear to be a tangled knot of gender contradictions. So they feverishly press the question on me: woman or man? Those are the only two words most people have as tools to shape their question.

"Which sex are you?" I understand their question. It sounds so simple. And I'd like to offer them a simple resolution. But merely answering woman or man will not bring relief to the questioner. As long as people try to bring me into focus using only those two lenses, I will always appear to be an enigma.

The truth is I'm no mystery. I'm a female who is more masculine than those prominently portrayed in mass culture. Millions of females and millions of males in this country do not fit the cramped compartments of gender that we have been taught are "natural" and "normal." For many of us, the words *woman* or *man*, *ma'am* or *sir, she* or *he*—in and of themselves—do not total up the sum of our identities or of our oppressions. Speaking for myself, my life only comes into focus when the word *transgender* is added to the equation.

Simply answering whether I was born female or male will not solve the conundrum. Before I can even begin to respond to the question of my own birth sex, I feel it's important to challenge the assumption that the answer is always as simple as either-or. I believe we need to take a critical look at the assumption that is built into the seemingly innocent question: "What a beautiful baby—is it a boy or a girl?"

The human anatomical spectrum can't be understood, let alone appreciated, as long as female or male are considered to be all that exists. "Is it a boy or a girl?" Those are the only two categories allowed on birth certificates.

But this either-or leaves no room for intersexual people, born between the poles of female and male. Human anatomy continues to burst the confines of the contemporary concept that nature delivers all babies on two unrelated conveyor belts. So are the birth certificates changed to reflect human anatomy? No, the U.S. medical establishment hormonally molds and shapes and surgically hacks away at the exquisite complexities of intersexual infants until they neatly fit one category or the other.

A surgeon decides whether a clitoris is "too large" or a penis is "too small." That's a highly subjective decision for anyone to make about another person's body. Especially when the person making the arbitary decision is scrubbled up for surgery! And what is the criterion for a penis being "too small"? Too small for successful heterosexual intercourse. Intersexual infants are already being tailored for their sexuality, as well as their sex. The infants have no say over what happens to their bodies. Clearly the struggle against genital mutilation must begin here, within the borders of the United States.

But the question asked of all new parents: "Is it a boy or a girl?" is not such a simple question when transsexuality is taken into account, either. Legions of out-and-proud transsexual men and women demonstrate that individuals have a deep, developed, and valid sense of their own sex that does not always correspond to the cursory decision made by a delivery-room obstetrician. Nor is transsexuality a recent phenomenon. People have undergone social sex reassignment and surgical and hormonal sex changes throughout the breadth of oral and recorded human history.

Having offered this view of the complexities and limitations of birth classification, I have no hesitancy in saying I was born female. But that answer doesn't clear up the confusion that drives some people to ask me "Are you a man or a woman?" The problem is that they are trying to understand my gender expression by determining my sex—and therein lies the rub! Just as most of us grew up with only the concepts of *woman* and *man*, the terms *feminine* and *masculine* are the only two tools most people have to talk about the complexities of gender expression.

That pink-blue dogma assumes that biology steers our social destiny. We have been taught that being born female or male will determine how we will dress and walk, whether we will prefer our hair shortly cropped or long and flowing, whether we will be emotionally nurturing or repressed. According to this way of thinking, masculine females are trying to look "like men," and feminine males are trying to act "like women."

But those of us who transgress those gender assumptions also shatter their inflexibility.

So why do I sometimes describe myself as a masculine female? Isn't each of those concepts very limiting? Yes. But placing the two words together is incendiary, exploding the belief that gender expression is linked to birth sex like horse and carriage. It is the social contradiction missing from Dick-and-Jane textbook education.

I actually chafe at describing myself as masculine. For one thing, masculinity is such an expansive territory, encompassing boundaries of nationality, race, and class. Most importantly, individuals blaze their own trails across this landscape.

And it's hard for me to label the intricate matrix of my gender as simply masculine. To me, branding individual self-expression as simply feminine or masculine is like asking poets: Do you write in English or Spanish? The question leaves out the possibilities that the poetry is woven in Cantonese or Ladino, Swahili or Arabic. The question deals only with the system of language that the poet has been taught. It ignores the words each writer hauls up, hand over hand, from a common well. The music words make when finding themselves next to each other for the first time. The silences echoing in the space between ideas. The powerful winds of passion and belief that move the poet to write.

That is why I do not hold the view that gender is simply a social construct—one of two languages that we learn by rote from early age. To me, gender is the poetry each of us makes out of the language we are taught. When I walk through the anthology of the world, I see individuals express their gender in exquisitely complex and ever-changing ways, despite the laws of pentameter.

So how can gender expression be mandated by edict and enforced by law? Isn't that like trying to handcuff a pool of mercury? It's true that human self-expression is diverse and is often expressed in ambiguous or contradictory ways. And what degree of gender expression is considered "acceptable" can depend on your social situation, your race and nationality, your class, and whether you live in an urban or rural environment.

But no one can deny that rigid gender education begins early on in life—from pink and blue color-coding of infant outfits to gender-labeling toys and games. And those who overstep these arbitrary borders are punished. Severely. When the steel handcuffs tighten, it is human bones that crack. No one knows how many trans lives have been lost to police brutality and street-corner bashing. The lives of trans people are so depreciated in this society that many murders go unreported. And those of us who have survived are deeply scarred by daily run-ins with hate, discrimination, and violence.

Trans people are still literally social outlaws. And that's why I am willing at times, publicly, to reduce the totality of my self-expression to descriptions like masculine female, butch, bulldagger, drag king, cross-dresser. These terms describe outlaw status. And I hold my head up proudly in that police lineup. The word *outlaw* is not hyperbolic. I have been locked up in jail by cops because I was wearing a suit and tie. Was my clothing really a crime? Is it a "man's" suit if I am wearing it? At what point—from field to rack—is fiber assigned a sex?

The reality of why I was arrested was as cold as the cell's cement floor: I am considered a masculine female. That's a *gender* violation. My feminine drag queen sisters were in nearby cells, busted for wearing "women's" clothing. The cells that we were thrown into had the same design of bars and concrete. But when we—gay drag kings and drag queens—were thrown into them, the cops referred to the cells as bull's tanks and queen's tanks. The cells were named after our crimes: gender transgression. Actual statutes against cross-dressing and cross-gendered behavior still exist in written laws today. But even where the laws are not written down, police, judges, and prison guards are empowered to carry out merciless punishment for sex and gender "difference."

I believe we need to sharpen our view of how repression by the police, courts, and prisons, as well as all forms of racism and bigotry, operates as gears in the machinery of the economic and social system that governs our lives. As all those who have the least to lose from changing this system get together and examine these social questions, we can separate the wheat of truths from the chaff of old lies. Historic tasks are revealed that beckon us to take a stand and to take action.

That moment is now. And so this conversation with you takes place with the momentum of struggle behind it.

What will it take to put a halt to "legal" and extralegal violence against trans people? How can we strike the unjust and absurd laws mandating dress and behavior for females and males from the books? How can we weed out all the forms of trans-phobic and gender-phobic discrimination?

Where does the struggle for sex and gender liberation fit in relation to other movements for economic and social equality? How can we reach a point where we appreciate each other's differences, not just tolerate them? How can we tear down the electrified barbed wire that has been placed between us to keep us separated, fearful and pitted against each other? How can we forge a movement that can bring about profound and lasting change—a movement capable of transforming society?

These questions can only be answered when we begin to organize together, ready to struggle on each other's behalf. Understanding each other will compel us as honest, caring people to fight each other's oppression as though it was our own.

This book is one of my contributions to this societal discussion. Many of the chapters are adaptations of talks I gave in the spring of 1997, as I set out on the rocky road to recover my health. In the weeks after the last intravenous tubes were removed from my arms and chest, I emerged from illness like a resistance fighter climbing up from a sewer into the sunlight. I faced a calendar filled with opportunities to speak with people at universities, conferences, and rallies. That particular spring was a precious gift I could not take for granted. I'd fought so hard to live.

I remember the enormous physical effort it took to lug my suitcase off a conveyorbelt, to walk long distances through crowded airports. But I also remember amazing conversations I had with many wonderful individuals. I found people were ready to talk about sex and gender liberation in every part of the United States I visited—from Manhattan to Tallahassee, from Birmingham to Denver. I was moved by the emotional and enthusiastic responses I received from audiences in Berlin, Leipzig, Köln, and Hamburg, Germany.

Some of those speeches are included in this book. I've prefaced them with a description of the circumstances, audiences, and surroundings, so that you can feel yourself a part of it. I've also included the voices of other trans people—each of whom I deeply respect. These trans people have different identities, experiences, and viewpoints from mine, so you can hear the wider conversation that is now underway.

The poet Rainer Maria Rilke wrote, "Be conversant with transformation." This book is my voice in this conversation. I look forward to hearing yours.

OPPRESSION (1983)

Marilyn Frye

Marilyn Frye is a philosopher and the author of numerous articles, essays and books including Willful Virgin: Essays in Feminism *(1992) and* The Politics of Reality: Essays in Feminist Theory *(1983). In this 1983 essay, Frye attempts to clarify the meaning of the term "oppression"—a forceful, value-laden term that is nonetheless significant for understanding women's experiences. Most illuminating in Frye's essay is her use of several metaphors and images to illustrate the complex nature of oppression. Through these key metaphors, Fry emphasizes how multiple factors intersect to place individuals in oppressive situations.*

It is a fundamental claim of feminism that women are oppressed. The word 'oppression' is a strong word. It repels and attracts. It is dangerous and dangerously fashionable and endangered. It is much misused, and sometimes not innocently.

"Oppression," by Marilyn Frye, reprinted from *The Politics of Reality: Essays in Feminist Theory*, 1983, by permission of Crossing Press.

The statement that women are oppressed is frequently met with the claim that men are oppressed too. We hear that oppressing is oppressive to those who oppress as well as to those they oppress. Some men cite as evidence of their oppression their much-advertised inability to cry. It is tough, we are told, to be masculine. When the stresses and frustrations of being a man are cited as evidence that oppressors are oppressed by their oppressing, the word 'oppression' is being stretched to meaninglessness; it is treated as though its scope includes any and all human experience of limitation or suffering, no matter the cause, degree or consequence. Once such usage has been put over on us, then if ever we deny that any person or group is oppressed, we seem to imply that we think they never suffer and have no feelings. We are accused of insensitivity; even of bigotry. For women, such accusation is particularly intimidating, since sensitivity is one of the few virtues that has been assigned to us. If we are found insensitive, we may fear we have no redeeming traits at all and perhaps are not real women. Thus are we silenced before we begin: the name of our situation drained of meaning and our guilt mechanisms tripped.

But this is nonsense. Human beings can be miserable without being oppressed, and it is perfectly consistent to deny that a person or group is oppressed, without denying that they have feelings or that they suffer.

We need to think clearly about oppression, and there is much that mitigates against this. I do not want to undertake to prove that women are oppressed (or that men are not), but I want to make clear what is being said when we say it. We need this word, this concept, and we need it to be sharp and sure.

I

The root of the word 'oppression' is the element 'press.' *The press of the crowd; pressed into military service; to press a pair of pants; printing press; press the button.* Presses are used to mold things or flatten them or reduce them in bulk, sometimes to reduce them by squeezing out the gasses or liquids in them. Something pressed is something caught between or among forces and barriers which are so related to each other that jointly they restrain, restrict or prevent the thing's motion or mobility. Mold. Immobilize. Reduce.

The mundane experience of the oppressed provides another clue. One of the most characteristic and ubiquitous features of the world as experienced by oppressed people is the double bind—situations in which options are reduced to a very few and all of them expose one to penalty, censure or deprivation. For example, it is often a requirement upon oppressed people that we smile and be cheerful. If we comply, we signal our docility and our acquiescence in our situation. We need not, then, be taken note of. We acquiesce in being made invisible, in our occupying no space. We participate in our own erasure. On the other hand, anything but the sunniest countenance exposes us to being perceived as mean, bitter, angry or dangerous. This means, at the least, that we may be found "difficult" or unpleasant to work with, which is enough to cost one one's livelihood; at worst, being seen as mean, bitter, angry or dangerous has been known to result in rape, arrest, beating and murder. One can only choose to risk one's preferred form and rate of annihilation.

Another example: It is common in the United States that women, especially younger women, are in a bind, where neither sexual activity nor sexual inactivity is all right. If she is heterosexually active, a woman is open to censure and punishment for being loose, unprincipled or a whore. The "punishment" comes in the form of criticism, snide and embarrassing remarks, being treated as an easy lay by men, scorn from her more restrained female friends. She may have to lie and hide her behavior from her parents. She must juggle the risks of unwanted pregnancy and dangerous contraceptives. On the other hand, if she refrains from heterosexual activity, she is fairly constantly harassed by men who try to persuade her into it and pressure her to "relax" and "let her hair down"; she is threatened with labels like "frigid," "uptight," "man-hater," "bitch" and "cocktease." The same parents who would be disapproving of her sexual activity may be worried by her inactivity because it suggests she is not or will not be popular, or is not sexually normal. She may be charged with lesbianism. If a woman is raped, then if she has been heterosexually active she is subject to the presumption that she liked it (since her activity is presumed to show that she likes sex), and if she has not been heterosexually active, she is subject to the presumption that she liked it (since she is supposedly "repressed and frustrated"). Both heterosexual activity and heterosexual nonactivity are likely to be taken as proof that you wanted to be raped, and hence, of course, weren't *really* raped at all. You can't win. You are caught in a bind, caught between systematically related pressures.

Women are caught like this, too, by networks of forces and barriers that expose one to penalty, loss or contempt whether one works outside the home or not, is on welfare or not, bears children or not, raises children or not, marries or not, stays married or not, is heterosexual, lesbian, both or neither. Economic necessity; confinement to racial and/or sexual job ghettos; sexual harassment; sex discrimination; pressures of competing expectations and judgments about *women, wives,* and *mothers* (in the society at large, in racial and ethnic subcultures and in one's own mind); dependence (full or partial) on husbands, parents or the state; commitment to political ideas; loyalties to racial or ethnic or other "minority" groups; the demands of self-respect and responsibilities to others. Each of these factors exists in complex tension with every other, penalizing or prohibiting all of the apparently available options. And nipping at one's heels, always, is the endless pack of little things. If one dresses one way, one is subject to the assumption that one is advertising one's sexual availability; if one dresses another way, one appears to "not care about oneself " or to be "unfeminine." If one uses "strong language," one invites categorization as a whore or slut; if one does not, one invites categorization as a "lady"—one too delicately constituted to cope with robust speech or the realities to which it presumably refers.

The experience of oppressed people is that the living of one's life is confined and shaped by forces and barriers which are not accidental or occasional and hence avoidable, but are systematically related to each other in such a way as to catch one between and among them and restrict or penalize motion in any direction. It is the experience of being caged in: all avenues, in every direction, are blocked or booby trapped.

Cages. Consider a birdcage. If you look very closely at just one wire in the cage, you cannot see the other wires. If your conception of what is before you is determined by this myopic focus, you could look at that one wire, up and down the length of it, and be unable to see why a bird would not just fly around the wire any time it wanted to go somewhere. Furthermore, even if, one day at a time, you myopically inspected each wire, you still could not see why a bird would have trouble going past the wires to get anywhere. There is no physical property of any one wire, *nothing* that the closest scrutiny could discover, that will reveal how a bird could be inhibited or harmed by it except in the most accidental way. It is only when you step back, stop looking at the wires one by one, microscopically, and take a macroscopic view of the whole cage, that you can see why the bird does not go anywhere; and then you will see it in a moment. It will require no great subtlety of mental powers. It is perfectly *obvious* that the bird is surrounded by a network of systematically related barriers, no one of which would be the least hindrance to its flight, but which, by their relations to each other, are as confining as the solid walls of a dungeon.

It is now possible to grasp one of the reasons why oppression can be hard to see and recognize: one can study the elements of an oppressive structure with great care and some good will without seeing the structure as a whole, and hence without seeing or being able to understand that one is looking at a cage and that there are people there who are caged, whose motion and mobility are restricted, whose lives are shaped and reduced.

The arresting of vision at a microscopic level yields such common confusion as that about the male door-opening ritual. This ritual, which is remarkably widespread across classes and races, puzzles many people, some of whom do and some of whom do not find it offensive. Look at the scene of the two people approaching a door. The male steps slightly ahead and opens the door. The male holds the door open while the female glides through. Then the male goes through. The door closes after them. "Now how," one innocently asks, "can those crazy womens-libbers say that is oppressive? The guy *removed* a barrier to the lady's smooth and unruffled progress." But each repetition of this ritual has a place in a pattern, in fact in several patterns. One has to shift the level of one's perception in order to see the whole picture.

The door-opening pretends to be a helpful service, but the helpfulness is false. This can be seen by noting that it will be done whether or not it makes any practical sense. Infirm men and men burdened with packages will open doors for able-bodied women who are free of physical burdens. Men will impose themselves awkwardly and jostle everyone in order to get to the door first. The act is not determined by convenience or grace. Furthermore, these very numerous acts of unneeded or even noisome "help" occur in counterpoint to a pattern of men not being helpful in many practical ways in which women might welcome help. What *women* experience is a world in which gallant princes charming commonly make a fuss about being helpful and providing small services when help and services are of little or no use, but in which there are rarely ingenious and adroit princes at hand when substantial assistance is really wanted either in mundane affairs or in situations of threat, assault or terror. There is no help with the (his) laundry; no help typing a report at 4:00 a.m.; no help in mediating disputes among relatives or children. There is nothing but advice that women should stay indoors after dark, be chaperoned by a man, or when it comes down to it, "lie back and enjoy it."

The gallant gestures have no practical meaning. Their meaning is symbolic. The door-opening and similar services provided are services which really are needed by people who are for one reason or another incapacitated—unwell, burdened with parcels, etc. So the message is that women are incapable. The detachment of the acts from the concrete realities of what women need and do not need is a vehicle for the message that women's actual needs and interests are unimportant or irrelevant. Finally, these gestures imitate the behavior of servants toward masters and thus mock women, who are in most respects the servants and caretakers of men. The message of the false helpfulness of male gallantry is female dependence, the invisibility or insignificance of women, and contempt for women.

One cannot see the meanings of these rituals if one's focus is riveted upon the individual event in all its particularity, including the particularity of the individual man's present conscious intentions and motives and the individual woman's conscious perception of the event in the moment. It seems sometimes that people take a deliberately myopic view and fill their eyes with things seen microscopically in order not to see macroscopically. At any rate, whether it is deliberate or not, people can and do fail to see the oppression of women because they fail to see macroscopically and hence fail to see the various elements of the situation as systematically related in larger schemes.

As the cageness of the birdcage is a macroscopic phenomenon, the oppressiveness of the situations in which women live our various and different lives is a macroscopic phenomenon. Neither can be *seen* from a microscopic perspective. But when you look macroscopically you can see it—a network of forces and barriers which are systematically related and which conspire to the immobilization, reduction and molding of women and the lives we live.

II

The image of the cage helps convey one aspect of the systematic nature of oppression. Another is the selection of occupants of the cages, and analysis of this aspect also helps account for the invisibility of the oppression of women.

It is as a woman (or as a Chicana/o or as a Black or Asian or lesbian) that one is entrapped.

> "Why can't I go to the park; you let Jimmy go!"
>
> "Because it's not safe for girls."

> "I want to be a secretary, not a seamstress; I don't want to learn to make dresses."
>
> "There's no work for negroes in that line; learn a skill where you can earn your living."[1]

When you question why you are being blocked, why this barrier is in your path, the answer has not to do with individual talent or merit, handicap or failure; it has to do with your membership in some category understood as a "natural" or "physical" category. The "inhabitant" of the "cage" is not an individual but a group, all those of a certain category. If an individual is oppressed, it is in virtue of being a member of a group or category of people that is systematically reduced, molded, immobilized. Thus, to recognize a person as oppressed, one has to see that individual as belonging to a group of a certain sort.

There are many things which can encourage or inhibit perception of someone's membership in the sort of group or category in question here. In particular, it seems reasonable to suppose that if one of the devices of restriction and definition of the group is that of physical confinement or segregation, the confinement and separation would encourage recognition of the group as a group. This in turn would encourage the macroscopic focus which enables one to recognize oppression and encourages the individuals' identification and solidarity with other individuals of the group or category. But physical confinement and segregation of the group as a group is not common to all oppressive structures, and when an oppressed group is geographically and demographically dispersed the perception of it as a group is inhibited. There may be little or nothing in the situations of the individuals encouraging the macroscopic focus which would reveal the unity of the structure bearing down on all members of that group.[2]

A great many people, female and male and of every race and class, simply do not believe that *woman* is a category of oppressed people, and I think that this is in part because they have been fooled by the dispersal and assimilation of women throughout and into the systems of class and race which organize men. Our simply being dispersed makes it difficult for women to have knowledge of each other and hence difficult to recognize the shape of our common cage. The dispersal and assimilation of women throughout economic classes and races also divides us against each other practically and economically and thus attaches *interest* to the inability to see: for some, jealousy of their benefits, and for some, resentment of the others' advantages.

To get past this, it helps to notice that in fact women of all races and classes *are* together in a ghetto of sorts. There is a women's place, a sector, which is inhabited by women of all classes and races, and it is not defined by geographical boundaries but by function. The function is the service of men and men's interests as men define them, which includes the bearing and rearing of children. The details of the service and the working conditions vary by race and class, for men of different races and classes have different interests, perceive their interests differently, and express their needs and demands in different rhetorics, dialects and languages. But there are also some constants.

Whether in lower, middle or upper-class home or work situations, women's service work always includes personal service (the work of maids, butlers, cooks, personal secretaries),[3] sexual service (including provision for his genital sexual needs and bearing his children, but also including "being nice," "being attractive for him," etc.), and ego service (encouragement, support, praise, attention). Women's service work also is characterized everywhere by the fatal combination of responsibility and powerlessness: we are held responsible and we hold ourselves responsible for good outcomes for men and children in almost every respect though we have in almost no case power adequate to that project. The details of the subjective experience of this servitude are local. They vary with economic class and race and ethnic tradition as well as the personalities of the men in question. So also are the details of the forces which coerce our tolerance of this servitude particular to the different situations in which different women live and work.

All this is not to say that women do not have, assert and manage sometimes to satisfy our own interests, nor to deny that in some cases and in some respects women's independent interests do overlap with men's. But at every race/class level and even across race/class lines men do not serve women as women serve men. "Women's sphere" may be understood as the "service sector," taking the latter expression much more widely and deeply than is usual in discussions of the economy.

III

It seems to be the human condition that in one degree or another we all suffer frustration and limitation, all encounter unwelcome barriers, and all are damaged and hurt in various ways. Since we are a social species, almost all of our behavior and activities are structured by more than individual inclination and the conditions of the planet and its atmosphere. No human is free of social structures, nor (perhaps) would happiness consist in such freedom. Structure consists of boundaries, limits and barriers; in a structured whole, some motions and changes are possible, and others are not. If one is looking for an excuse to dilute the word 'oppression,' one can use the fact of social structure as an excuse and say that everyone is oppressed. But if one would rather get clear about what oppression is and is not, one needs to sort out the sufferings, harms and limitations and figure out which are elements of oppression and which are not.

From what I have already said here, it is clear that if one wants to determine whether a particular suffering, harm or limitation is part of someone's being oppressed, one has to look at it *in context* in order to tell whether it is an element in an oppressive structure: one has to see if it is part of an enclosing structure of forces and barriers which tends to the immobilization and reduction of a group or category of people. One has to look at how the barrier or force fits with others and to whose benefit or detriment it works.

As soon as one looks at examples, it becomes obvious that not everything which frustrates or limits a person is oppressive, and not every harm or damage is due to or contributes to oppression.

If a rich white playboy who lives off income from his investments in South African diamond mines should break a leg in a skiing accident at Aspen and wait in pain in a blizzard for hours before he is rescued, we may assume that in that period he suffers. But the suffering comes to an end; his leg is repaired by the best surgeon money can buy and he is soon recuperating in a lavish suite, sipping Chivas Regal. Nothing in this picture suggests a structure of barriers and forces. He is a member of several oppressor groups and does not suddenly become oppressed because he is injured and in pain. Even if the accident was caused by someone's malicious negligence, and hence someone can be blamed for it and morally faulted, that person still has not been an agent of oppression.

Consider also the restriction of having to drive one's vehicle on a certain side of the road. There is no doubt that this restriction is almost unbearably frustrating at times, when one's lane is not moving and the other lane is clear. There are surely times, even, when abiding by this regulation would have harmful consequences. But the restriction is obviously wholesome for most of us most of the time. The restraint is imposed for our benefit, and does benefit us; its operation tends to encourage our *continued* motion, not to immobilize us. The limits imposed by traffic regulations are limits most of us would cheerfully impose on ourselves given that we knew others would follow them too. They are part of a structure which shapes our behavior, not to our reduction and immobilization, but rather to the protection of our continued ability to move and act as we will.

Another example: The boundaries of a racial ghetto in an American city serve to some extent to keep white people from going in, as well as to keep ghetto dwellers from going out. A particular white citizen may be frustrated or feel deprived because s/he cannot stroll around there and enjoy the "exotic" aura of a "foreign" culture, or shop for bargains in the ghetto swap shops. In fact, the existence of the ghetto, of racial segregation, does deprive the white person of knowledge and harm her/his character by nurturing unwarranted feelings of superiority. But this does not make the white person in this situation a member of an oppressed race or a person oppressed because of her/ his race.

One must look at the barrier. It limits the activities and the access of those on both sides of it (though to different degrees). But it is a product of the intention, planning and action of whites for the benefit of whites, to secure and maintain privileges that are available to whites generally, as members of the dominant and privileged group. Though the existence of the barrier has some bad consequences for whites, the barrier does not exist in systematic relationship with other barriers and forces forming a structure oppressive to whites; quite the contrary. It is part of a structure which oppresses the ghetto dwellers and thereby (and by white intention) protects and furthers white interests as dominant white culture understands them. This barrier is not oppressive to whites, even though it is a barrier to whites.

Barriers have different meanings to those on opposite sides of them, even though they are barriers to both. The physical walls of a prison no more dissolve to let an outsider in than to let an insider out, but for the insider they are confining and limiting while to the outsider they may mean protection from what s/he takes to be threats posed by insiders—freedom from harm or anxiety. A set of social and economic barriers and forces separating two groups may be felt, even painfully, by members of both groups and yet may mean confinement to one and liberty and enlargement of opportunity to the other.

The service sector of the wives/mommas/assistants/girls is almost exclusively a woman-only sector; its boundaries not only enclose women but to a very great extent keep men out. Some men sometimes encounter this barrier and experience it as a restriction on their movements, their activities, their control or their choices of "lifestyle." Thinking they might like the simple nurturant life (which they may imagine to be quite free of stress, alienation and hard work), and feeling deprived since it seems closed to them, they thereupon announce the discovery that they are oppressed, too, by "sex roles." But that barrier is erected and maintained by men, for the benefit of men. It consists of cultural and economic forces and pressures in a culture and economy controlled by men in which, at every economic level and in all racial and ethnic subcultures, economy, tradition—and even ideologies of liberation—work to keep at least local culture and economy in male control.[4]

The boundary that sets apart women's sphere is maintained and promoted by men generally for the benefit of men generally, and men generally do benefit from its existence, even the man who bumps into it and complains of the inconvenience. That barrier is protecting his classification and status as a male, as superior, as having a right to sexual access to a female or females. It protects a kind of citizenship which is superior to that of females of his class and race, his access to a wider range of better paying and higher status work, and his right to prefer unemployment to the degradation of doing lower status or "women's" work.

If a person's life or activity is affected by some force or barrier that person encounters, one may not conclude that the person is oppressed simply because the person encounters that barrier or force; nor simply because the encounter is unpleasant, frustrating or painful to that person at that time; nor simply because the existence of the barrier or force, or the processes which maintain or apply it, serve to deprive that person of something of value. One must look at the barrier or force and answer certain questions about it. Who constructs and maintains it? Whose interests are served by its existence? Is it part of a structure which tends to confine, reduce and immobilize some group? Is the individual a member of the confined group? Various forces, barriers and limitations a person may encounter or live with may be part of an oppressive structure or not, and if they are, that person may be on either the oppressed or the oppressor side of it. One cannot tell which by how loudly or how little the person complains.

IV

Many of the restrictions and limitations we live with are more or less internalized and self-monitored, and are part of our adaptations to the requirements and expectations imposed by the needs and tastes and tyrannies of others. I have in mind such things as women's cramped postures and attenuated strides and men's restraint of emotional self-expression (except for anger). Who gets what out of the practice of those disciplines, and who imposes what penalties for improper relaxations of them? What are the rewards of this self-discipline?

Can men cry? Yes, in the company of women. If a man cannot cry, it is in the company of men that he cannot cry. It is men, not women, who require this restraint; and men not only require it, they reward it. The man who maintains a steely or tough or laid-back demeanor (all are forms which suggest invulnerability) marks himself as a member of the male community and is esteemed by other men. Consequently, the maintenance of that demeanor contributes to the man's self-esteem. It is felt as good, and he can feel good about himself. The way this restriction fits into the structures of men's lives is as one of the socially required behaviors which, if carried off, contribute to their acceptance and respect by significant others and to their own self-esteem. It is to their benefit to practice this discipline.

Consider, by comparison, the discipline of women's cramped physical postures and attenuated stride. This discipline can be relaxed in the company of women; it generally is at its most strenuous in the company of men.[5] Like men's emotional restraint, women's physical restraint is required by men. But unlike the case of men's emotional restraint, women's physical restraint is not rewarded. What do we get for it? Respect and esteem and acceptance? No. They mock us and parody our mincing steps. We look silly, incompetent, weak and generally contemptible. Our exercise of this discipline tends to low esteem and low self-esteem. It does not benefit us. It fits in a network of behaviors through which we constantly announce to others our membership in a lower caste and our unwillingness and/or inability to defend our bodily or moral integrity. It is degrading and part of a pattern of degradation.

Acceptable behavior for both groups, men and women, involves a required restraint that seems in itself silly and perhaps damaging. But the social effect is drastically different. The woman's restraint is part of a structure oppressive to women; the man's restraint is part of a structure oppressive to women.

V

One is marked for application of oppressive pressures by one's membership in some group or category. Much of one's suffering and frustration befalls one partly or largely because one is a member of that category. In the case at hand, it is the category, *woman*. Being a woman is a major factor in my not having a better job than I do; being a woman selects me as a likely victim of sexual assault or harassment; it is my being a woman that reduces the power of my anger to a proof of my insanity. If a woman has little or no economic or political power, or achieves little of what she wants to achieve, a major causal factor in this is that she is a woman. For any woman of any race or economic class, being a woman is significantly attached to whatever disadvantages and deprivations she suffers, be they great or small.

None of this is the case with respect to a person's being a man. Simply being a man is not what stands between him and a better job; whatever assaults and harassments he is subject to, being male is not what selects him for victimization; being male is not a factor which would make his anger impotent—quite the opposite. If a man has little or no material or political power, or achieves little of what he wants to achieve, his being male is no part of the explanation. Being male is something he has going *for* him, even if race or class or age or disability is going against him.

Women are oppressed, *as women*. Members of certain racial and/or economic groups and classes, both the males and the females, are oppressed *as* members of those races and/or classes. But men are not oppressed *as men*.

. . . and isn't it strange that any of us should have been confused and mystified about such a simple thing?

Notes

1. This example is derived from *Daddy Was A Number Runner*, by Louise Meriwether (Prentice-Hall, Englewood Cliffs, New Jersey, 1970), p. 144.
2. Coerced assimilation is in fact one of the *policies* available to an oppressing group in its effort to reduce and/or annihilate another group. This tactic is used by the U.S. government, for instance, on the American Indians.
3. At higher class levels women may not *do* all these kinds of work, but are generally still responsible for hiring and supervising those who do it. These services are still, in these cases, women's responsibility.
4. Of course this is complicated by race and class. Machismo and "Black manhood" politics seem to help keep Latin or Black men in control of

more cash than Latin or Black women control; but these politics seem to me also to ultimately help keep the larger economy in *white* male control.

5. Cf. *Let's Take Back Our Space: "Female" and "Male" Body Language as a Result of Patriarchal Structures*, by Marianne Wex (Frauenliterature-verlag Hermine Fees, West Germany 1979), especially p. 173. This remarkable book presents literally thousands of candid photographs of woman and men, in public, seated, standing and lying down. It vividly demonstrates the very systematic differences in women's and men's postures and gestures.

QUESTIONS

1. What are some of the connotations of the word "oppression"? Why does Frye believe that "oppression" is an important word, one that should be defined and used precisely?
2. What metaphors does Frye employ to convey the complicated nature of oppression? What is a "double-bind" and how does it illustrate oppression?
3. How does Frye distinguish between suffering and oppression? Why is this difference significant? What is the difference between barriers experienced by individuals and barriers experienced because of individual membership in a group? What does Frye mean when she argues that women are oppressed *as women*, but men are not oppressed *as men*? Do this mean that no men are ever oppressed?
4. How do differences among women complicate the issue of considering women as an oppressed group? Does Frye address diversity among women in her essay, explicitly or implicitly?
5. How does Frye's essay reflect the time period in which she wrote? Can you think of some contemporary examples of oppression?

It's Your Gender, Stupid!

Riki Anne Wilchins

Take Me to Your Gender

Gender. Everyone talks about it, but no one knows what it is or agrees on a definition. Gender *identity*? Gender *expression*? Gender *characteristics*? The gender *system*? A softer synonym for "sex"? *Gender* never stands alone, but always seems to need a noun to refer to.

So, it seems strange in a book devoted to gender that no writer takes the space to define what *gender* means. We assume that it's a common term of meaning, although it appears to be anything but. As with pornography, we may not be able to define it, but we know it when we see it.

The fact that *gender* is used in so many different but related contexts hints that we've touched on something very basic and pervasive in the human condition. So does the fact that we "know it when we see it." But I believe all the confusion surrounding gender means that perhaps just the opposite is the case: that gender is a set of meanings, and so like children learning to tell Daddy from Mommy and little boys from little girls, we see it once we know it.

Early Morning Do

The most popular conception of gender is as a sort of inner substance, an essence we all carry within us, that is always conve-

Reprinted from *Genderqueer: Voices from Beyond the Sexual Binary*, Alyson Publications.

niently binary and, except in the case of transexuals, matched to our physical sex. It is the "expression" of this gendered core that leads us to various gender behaviors: from wearing dresses or ties to displaying dominance or vulnerability during sex.

But according to theorist Judith Butler, gender refers not to something we *are* but to something we *do*, which, through extended repetition and because of the vigorous suppression of all exceptions, achieves the appearance of a sort of coherent psychic substance.

In this view, there is no doer behind the deed, no gendered identity behind the acts that we say result from it. The acts are all there is, and it is the strict regulation of these acts within the binary—females must produce feminine behaviors and males masculine—that produces the appearance of two coherent and universal genders.

Thus, I don't pull on certain clothes in the morning or style my hair a particular way because of something within me. I do these acts in a manner consistent with either masculine or feminine norms because to do otherwise would render me socially unintelligible. People wouldn't know what I was or how to treat me, and I would be the target of a great deal of hostility.

My achieving a consistent appearance and behavior is then offered as proof of a binary gender inside me.

If my gender is a doing that has to be redone each day just like I pull on those clothes each morning, that would help explain why sometimes my gender "fails": Even though I've felt like a man (and then later like a woman), people didn't always recognize me as such. Even I couldn't always recognize myself as such.

Better Dead Than Read

If I can "fail" accidentally, maybe there are ways I can fail on purpose that will create room for me to grow, to find new ways of expression that resonate more deeply. If gender is a doing and a reading of that doing, a call-and-response that must be continually done and redone, then it's also unstable, and there are ways I can disrupt it. Maybe universal and binary genders are not so inevitable after all.

This is an attractive line of thinking, especially for anyone who has found themselves transcending narrow, outdated, 20th-century gender norms. Which is to say, all the writers in this book and most of its readers.

But how do we square this with some of the facts? For instance, transexuality. It is undoubtedly true that some people (the author included) have, or do, feel profound sense of discomfort at being confined to one sex and gender instead of another. If gender is a *doing*, does that imply that the transexual in distress is somehow reenacting his or her own pain each morning in a repeated series of gendered acts?

And transexuality aside, most people do report experiencing a stable, long-term sense of identification with either male or female, man or woman. That would seem to constitute pretty good evidence of gendered identities.

But then again, there are only two types of identities one can report experiencing. For instance, I said, "I feel like a woman trapped in a man's body," and my doctors understood and shipped me off to surgery. But if I'd worn my Intersex Society of North America HERMAPHRODITES WITH ATTITUDE T-shirt and told them, "I feel like a herm trapped in a man's body," they wouldn't have understood and would have shipped me off to a rubber room.

Moreover, paradoxical as it sounds, there is room to question whether any identification, however stable and long-term, actually constitutes *having* an identity. Identification is always an act, a repetition, a name we give to a collection of discrete traits, behaviors, urges, and empathies.

A System of Meanings

Let me repeat something from the introduction: Gender is a system of meanings and symbols—and the rules, privileges, and punishments pertaining to their use—for power and sexuality: masculinity and femininity, strength and vulnerability, action and passivity, dominance and weakness.

To gender something simply means investing it with one of two meanings. So anything and everything can be gendered, for example: ships, clothing, sexual positions, pens, bowls, hand positions, head tilts, vocal inflections, body hair, and different sports. Indeed, in many romance languages, every object is given a gender (*vive la difference*, Le Monde, *la dolce vita, el toro, el Riki*).

Because being gay itself is a transgression of the rules of gender, because those rules heavily disfavor femininity, gay and feminist (and lately transgendered) critics have tended to focus on gender's many repressive aspects.

The punishments we exact for using the "wrong" words cross from the mundane to the fatal, including hostile stares in the women's room, being humiliated after gym class for being a "sissy" or a "dyke," unfair termination for being a "ball-buster," assault for being a "faggot," arrest for "impersonating a woman," rape for being "too sexy," forced psychiatric treatment for gender identity disorder, genital mutilation for inter-sexed infants, and, of course, murder.

But like any language, gender's primary effect is not repressive but productive: It produces meanings. These are created through a vast and visible top-down structure: binary birth certificates, restrooms, adoption policies, immigration laws, passports, and marriage laws. But they are also produced and maintained from the bottom up, through thousands of small, everyday acts—interactions that create and destroy gendered meanings in every moment. These microexchanges of meaning—in an elevator, over a meal, while buying a newspaper, when answering the phone—stamp us with our gender, bind us to it, and require us to answer to it in order to interact with other people.

Thus not only does gender restrain us as individuals, but it is through the language of gender that we become who we are, that we come to recognize ourselves—and be recognized by others—as men and women, and only as men and women.

As an academic concept, gender has been remarkably productive. Every year witnesses a new crop of articles, books, and theory about gender. Yet as a civil rights cause, gender is just beginning.

One can see in it the outlines of something that links misogyny, homophobia, transphobia, and the restricted way we raise our youth. Indeed, a widespread understanding of gender would have enormous potential to transform society and remove inequity and violence.

A Sex by Any Other Name Would Still Smell as Sweet

If gender is a system of meanings, then what are we to make of the recent and remarkable degree to which "gender" is replacing "sex" to refer not only to men and women but also male and female? Perhaps this is only a way to avoid saying the overloaded word "sex," which also means intercourse, in public speech.

Yet it also seems to contradict the widely accepted notion that sex is a natural, physical property of bodies, while gender is something culturally derived from sex. In Butler's formulation, sex (male/female) is to "raw" as gender (man/women) is to "cooked." Sex is there "on the far side of language," while gender is something added on afterward.

The increasing use of gender to replace sex may be an acknowledgment, if only unconsciously, that once you start looking there is nothing, or at least very little, on the far side of language. As an experiment, I recently asked a large group of very hip queer youths to list on a blackboard all the attributes that made up a "real man" and "real woman." Interestingly, on the list beneath "real man" was "has a penis"; the list beneath "real woman" included "doesn't have a penis." Not one person in the entire group thought to list "doesn't have a vagina" or even "has a vagina" as an identifying trait of bodies. I take from this that although the body's moving parts may all be "over there" on the far side of language, nearly everything we make of them to render them meaningful to us is right here, in our laps.

I'd Like to Buy a Women's Dictionary

Gender as a language is at once terribly simple, because it has only two meanings, and terribly complex, because it touches us across the entire plane of contact between our bodies and society. In most languages, words can be used by anyone who can master them. But gender is a language that creates and sustains binary difference. To achieve this, gendered signs must be highly regulated so they don't fall into the wrong hands, as if certain dictionary words were colored blue for boys and pink for girls. Wearing a skirt, smoking a pipe, crying in public, moaning during sex, scratching your crotch, describing anything (but God) as divine: These are some of the signs that may be given by only one half of the population or the other.

20/20 Hind-Cite

If gender is a system of meanings, then, in a book of the same name, what is meant by "genderqueer"? For one thing, it brings back together those two things that have been wrongly separated: gender and gayness.

For Butler, "successful" genders are those that cite other earlier examples. Thus we learn to become men and women and to be recognized as such by copying other examples. In popular thought, men and women are considered examples of "real" genders, and drag, transexuals, and butch/femme couples are considered copies. Thus drag is to copy as woman is to real. Drag imitates real life.

But if Butler is right, if gender is always an artifice that copies something else, then all gender is a reuse of familiar stereotypes according to the rules for their use. All gender is drag. And those that fail, that are read as "queer," are simply those that break the rules. Thus neither a Streisand drag queen doing "Barbra" nor Barbra herself doing "woman" is any more or less real. There is no real gender to which they might be compared. Both use common symbols to achieve a visual meaning. The drag queen appears "false" because we don't grant her access to those symbols.

Considering gender as a language, I would approach queerness somewhat differently. What did I mean when I told my doctors that I felt "like a woman?" How was it possible for me to feel like anything other than myself? Perhaps I only meant that I was feminine. But although one can be seen as feminine, feel feminine feelings, or to express femininity through our clothing, hairstyle, and posture, can anyone really *be* feminine?

Achieving femininity sounds like a lot of work: how I feel, how I express myself to others, and how they perceive me. It's one thing to feel consistently male or feminine or like a boy, but keeping all that feeling/expressing/being-perceived continuously intact must take a lot of concentration. Having any gender at all is really a sort of accomplishment, a sustained effort.

Genderqueers are people for whom some link in the feeling/expressing/being-perceived fails. For example, a stone butch may feel masculine and embody—in his own mind and behavior—masculinity. Yet because of his sex (the pronoun strains here), she might still be read as womanly, like a girl trying on her boyfriend's clothes, especially if she is large-breasted and large-hipped.

If genderqueer bodies are those that fail because they don't follow the rules, the grammar of gender-as-language, then what are the boundaries of such a term and what are its exclusions? Is a lesbian femme harassed for her miniskirt and fuck-me pumps genderqueer? Is a 3-year-old who tries on his sister's dress or a 40-year-old who loses a promotion because her boss believes women should be seen but not promoted? What about a football captain who's humiliated by his coach because he wept after a tough loss?

If genderqueerness is not something we do but an identity we are, then none of these people would seem to be candidates. So one of the problems is that a narrow definition will exclude the millions of people who rub up against gender norms but don't step all the way out.

Some feminist theorists have questioned the queerness and radicalness of any sort of gender that doesn't do just that: leave norms behind. They consider transexuals, butch/femmes, and drag queens as not only not genderqueer but actually gender-conforming, because they partake of binary stereotypes. For them, the only "radical" choice is adopting more androgynous genders that fall totally off the binary map.

But how are we to tell someone who faces discrimination or violence that they aren't really queer? Surely their attackers think they are.

Using queerness itself as a category of analysis seems to invite a new round of debate devoted to who is "really queer." A voice that originated from one set of margins begins to create its own marginalized voices. These twin problems of identities—boundaries and hierarchies—emerge whenever we try to base politics on identity.

It's Not Me, I'm Just on Loan

If gender is always a bending of self toward prevailing norms, then gender is always a kind of displacement, from which not even genderqueers are immune.

For instance, Clare Howell recently said to me, "I know I sound like a man." This kind of displacement repositions her voice as coming from somewhere else. This is like the cross-dresser who declares, "I like wearing *women's* clothes." It's safe to say that no cross-dresser ever wore "women's clothes." If the bill came to him, they're his clothes, he bought them: They're obviously *men's clothes*. The displacement in naming them "women's clothes" prevents us from getting outside the terms of the language, from getting to something new that might redefine skirts or dresses or femininity as being about men.

Many cross-dressers would reply that the point of dressing for them is that these *are* women's clothes. It is the otherness of the clothing, the fact that they are "women's," that is precisely what allows them to feel feminine. But once again, we can't get to someplace new, where femininity might be something about men that is not anchored in Woman (or vice versa).

(I remember telling my therapist one day in what felt like a break-through: If I'm a woman and I haven't had surgery, then this must be a woman's penis. Wet dreams must be part of women's experience. However, I would be slow to make this argument at the next feminist conference.)

I don't mean to fall into the familiar trap of criticizing those who want to eat their cake but not have it. Some genderqueers, including cross-dressers, are not interested in that "something new." They will always enjoy appropriation *as* appropriation for its own sake. These strategic displacements renounce ownership and participation. They announce that "this part of my gender isn't me, it belongs to someone else, and I only appropriate/approximate it." They announce an acceptance of a particular gender's rules of access, who "owns" which words and who is allowed to use them. For instance, it's not possible for Clare to declare, "I sound like other men with breasts" or "I sound like other women trapped in male impersonators' bodies" or "I sound like a Clare," because those are not legitimate categories of description. By definition Clare must sound like something else, because her own body is not among the available choices.

Jenell, one of my favorite cross-dressers, always reminds me that hir enjoyment *is* transgression itself. If microminiskirts ever become fashionable for men, she'll have to decamp and find something else that is queer. In this sense, we are working somewhat at cross purposes. We both want to end the intolerable discrimination suffered by those who transcend gender stereotypes. But while I want to empty out those margins and bring queerness into the mainstream, she'd rather keep transgression in place, where s/he can enjoy it, but end its stigmatization. In retrospect, I think we both are right.

You Make Me Feel Like a Natural Woman Impersonator

Why do most genderqueers perceive themselves as falling within a long succession of binaries: female/male, butch/femme, top/bottom, boy/girl? Just as when we were children, we all learned to distinguish binary mommy from binary daddy, brother from sister, and little girls from little boys, it seems that like everyone else, genderqueers see in twos.

It is popular to explain genderqueerness as resulting from a "spectrum of gender" along which all individuals—queer and nonqueer—fall. This is presented as a more enlightened and inclusive approach to bodies. Yet when you look closer, every spectrum turns out to be anchored by the same familiar two poles—male/female, man/woman, gay/straight. The rest of us are just strung out between them, like damp clothes drying on the line. The spectrum of gender turns out to be a spectrum of heterosexual norms, only slightly less oppressive but not less binary than its predecessors. Maybe the problem is that gender is a way of seeing: black-and-white glasses through which we view a Technicolor world. Wherever we look, no matter what is "out there," we see only black and white.

There is an apocryphal story of an American anthropologist who visited a remote island where natives had 17 genders. Upon his return, he reported to the anthropological society that, "like all others we've studied, this culture also has only men and women."

We Are Men With Breasts. We Come in Peace.

I recently spent a week at a large queer activist conference in the Midwest. I was dressed in my best Banana Republic menswear and looking, if I may say, pretty phat for a woman trapped in a six-foot male impersonator's body. I went across the street to a sports bar to get some change, and when I entered the whole room just seemed to stop: woman *and* men turned from the immense TV screen showing the Sunday NFL game to watch me. It was intimidating. I got suddenly very nervous and self-conscious. I knew, for these people, I might just as well have landed from Mars. Before I knew it I was raising my voice, feminizing my stance, and trying to blend in a little.

I try to remind myself that if we can hold our course, it is at precisely such moments that we create a certain kind of freedom. It's a hard thing to keep in mind when you're afraid, that at these times we are doing the best and the most anonymous kind of activism.

What, I always wonder, did those people see? I asked my lover on one such occasion what she thought people were seeing and she replied, "Well, you do look like a man with breasts." Which, fortunately, was exactly the gender I was trying to do that day. As if that were possible. I only wish that option were available. Mostly I think people just try to figure out *what* in the world I am.

Don't Fuck With Mother Nature

But there are lots of things about bodies and genders that don't fit the binary model into which we try to force them, even that most unassailable of binaries: biological sex. Biological sex is considered to be the most basic and natural product of bodies. All creatures reproduce, and to reproduce—unless you're an amoeba—requires two sexes. But consider the lowly seahorse, a creature that is said to "switch sexes." (No, not with the help of a little aquatic seahorse surgeon.) We say it changes "from male to female" because what else could it change from or to?

And the "female" hyena, which not only dominates its species like a male but also has what any decent biologist would admit is a penis. Yet it must be a female, because it bears young. Or the male garter snake, which often morphs into a female after birth to attract male snakes to keep it warm. Something I might try during the next snowstorm.

But what if reproduction doesn't have to include two sexes? Or what if there are other sexes, and they can reproduce as well? But that's not possible, is it? Because any creatures that can reproduce must be either male and female—*by definition*. Hence surgeons' frantic search to locate the "real" sex of intersexed infants before their genitals are cut up to resemble "normal" male or female. The infant's "real sex," *by definition*, cannot be intersex, cannot be whatever it is. Any sex but binary male or female is pathology, unnatural, and unreal, to be discarded and corrected with the knife. We say two sexes is "nature's way." But Man produces this feminine version of Mother Nature—passive, pure, and reserved—when we need her, and then pushes Her aside when the facts don't fit His needs.

The debate over the naturalness of binary sex is circular: Whatever reproduces must be one of two sexes because there are only two sexes to be. Thus it is gender as a system of meaning that produces the "natural" Mother Nature, male and female sexes, and the gender binary that establishes what is genderqueer.

Homophobia: A Weapon of Sexism (1988)

Suzanne Pharr

By considering the relationship of sexism to negative responses to homosexuality, Suzanne Pharr offers an additional perspective on the forces of propelling homophobia. Based on personal experiences and her direction of numerous workshops across the country, Pharr suggests that we must examine the social structures contributing to sexism and their relationship to homophobia in order to visualize a world that is free from inequality. Suzanne Pharr is the director of the Arkansas-based Women's Project, a social justice organization, and the author of In the Time of the Right *and* Homophobia: A Weapon of Sexism, *from which this selection was taken.*

Homophobia—the irrational fear and hatred of those who love and sexually desire those of the same sex. Though I intimately knew its meaning, the word homophobia was unknown to me

Excerpt from *Homophobia: A Weapon of Sexism*, by Suzanne Pharr, 1988, reprinted by permission of Chardon Press. Distributed by The Women's Project, 2224 Main Street, Little Rock, AR, 72206.

until the late 1970s, and when I first heard it, I was struck by how difficult it is to say, what an ugly word it is, equally as ugly as its meaning. Like racism and anti-Semitism, it is a word that calls up images of loss of freedom, verbal and physical violence, death.

In my life I have experienced the effects of homophobia through rejection by friends, threats of loss of employment, and threats upon my life; and I have witnessed far worse things happening to other lesbian and gay people: loss of children, beatings, rape, death. Its power is great enough to keep ten to twenty percent of the population living lives of fear (if their sexual identity is hidden) or lives of danger (if their sexual identity is visible) or both. And its power is great enough to keep the remaining eighty to ninety percent of the population trapped in their own fears.

Long before I had a word to describe the behavior, I was engaged in a search to discover the source of its power, the power to damage and destroy lives. The most common explanations were that to love the same sex was either abnormal (sick) or immoral (sinful).

My exploration of the sickness theory led me to understand that homosexuality is simply a matter of sexual identity, which, along with heterosexual identity, is formed in ways that no one conclusively understands. The American Psychological Association has said that it is no more abnormal to be homosexual than to be left-handed. It is simply that a certain percentage of the population *is*. It is not healthier to be heterosexual or right-handed. What is unhealthy—and sometimes a source of stress and sickness so great it can lead to suicide—is homophobia, that societal disease that places such negative messages, condemnation, and violence on gay men and lesbians that we have to struggle throughout our lives for self-esteem.

The sin theory is a particularly curious one because it is expressed so often and with such hateful emotion both from the pulpit and from lay people who rely heavily upon the Bible for evidence. However, there is significant evidence that the approximately eight references to homosexuality in the Bible are frequently read incorrectly, according to Dr. Virginia Ramey Mollenkott in an essay in *Christianity and Crisis*:

> Much of the discrimination against homosexual persons is justified by a common misreading of the Bible. Many English translations of the Bible contain the word homo-

> sexual in extremely negative contexts. But the fact is that the word *homosexual* does not occur anywhere in the Bible. No extant text, no manuscript, neither Hebrew nor Greek, Syriac, nor Aramaic, contains the word. The terms *homosexual* and *heterosexual* were not developed in any language until the 1890's, when for the first time the awareness developed that there are people with a lifelong, constitutional orientation toward their own sex. Therefore the use of the word *homosexuality* by certain English Bible translators is an example of the extreme bias that endangers the human and civil rights of homosexual persons. (*pp. 383–384, Nov. 9, 1987*)

Dr. Mollenkott goes on to add that two words in I Corinthians 6:9 and one word in Timothy 1:10 have been used as evidence to damn homosexuals but that well into the twentieth century the first of these was understood by everyone to mean masturbation, and the second was known to refer to male prostitutes who were available for hire by either women or men. There are six other Biblical references that are thought by some to refer to homosexuals but each of these is disputed by contemporary scholars. For instance, the sin in the Sodom and Gommorah passage (Genesis 19:1–10) is less about homosexuality than it is about inhospitality and gang rape. The law of hospitality was universally accepted and Lot was struggling to uphold it against what we assume are heterosexual townsmen threatening gang rape to the two male angels in Lot's home. While people dwell on this passage as a condemnation of homosexuality, they bypass what I believe is the central issue or, if you will, *sin*; Lot's offering his two virgin daughters up to the men to be used as they desired for gang rape. Here is a perfectly clear example of devaluing and dehumanizing and violently brutalizing women.

The eight Biblical references (and not a single one by Jesus) to alleged homosexuality are very small indeed when compared to the several hundred references (and many by Jesus) to money and the necessity for justly distributing wealth. Yet few people go on a rampage about the issue of a just economic system, using the Bible as a base.

Finally, I came to understand that homosexuality, heterosexuality, bisexuality are *morally neutral*. A particular sexual identity is not an indication of either good or evil. What is important is not the gender of the two people in relationship with each other but the content of that relationship. Does that relationship contain violence, control of one person by the other? Is the relationship a growthful place for the people involved? It is clear that we must hold all relationships, whether opposite sex or same sex, to these standards.

The first workshops that I conducted were an effort to address these two issues, and I assumed that if consciousness could be raised about the invalidity of these two issues then people would stop feeling homophobic and would understand homophobia as a civil rights issue and work against it. The workshops took a high moral road, invoking participants' compassion, understanding, and outrage at injustice.

The eight-hour workshops raised consciousness and increased participants' commitment to work against homophobia as one more oppression in a growing list of recognized oppressions, but I still felt something was missing. I felt there was still too much unaccounted for power in homophobia even after we looked at the sick and sinful theories, at how it feels to be a lesbian in a homophobic world, at why lesbians choose invisibility, at how lesbian existence threatens male dominance. All of the pieces seemed available but we couldn't sew them together into a quilt.

As I conducted more workshops over the years I noticed several important themes that led to the final piecing together:

1. Women began to recognize that economics was a central issue connecting various oppressions;
2. Battered women began talking about how they had been called lesbians by their batterers;
3. Both heterosexual and lesbian women said they valued the workshops because in them they were given the rare opportunity to talk about their own sexuality and also about sexism in general.

Around the same time (1985–1986), the National Coalition Against Domestic Violence (NCADV) entered into a traumatic relationship with the U.S. Department of Justice (DOJ), requesting a large two-year grant to provide domestic violence training and information nationally. At the time the grant was to be announced, NCADV was attacked by conservative groups such as the Heritage Foundation as a "pro-lesbian, pro-feminist, anti-family" organization. In response to these attacks, the DOJ decided not to award a grant; instead they formulated a "cooperative agreement" that allowed them to monitor and approve all work, and they assured conservative organizations that the work would not be pro-lesbian and anti-family. The major issue between NCADV and the DOJ became whether NCADV would let an outside agency define and control its work, and finally, during never-ending concern from the DOJ about "radical" and "lesbian" issues, the agreement was terminated by NCADV at the end of the first year. Throughout that year, there were endless statements and innuendoes from the DOJ and some members of NCADV's membership about NCADV's lesbian leadership and its alleged concern for only lesbian issues. Many women were damaged by the crossfire, NCADV's work was stopped for a year, and the organization was split from within. It was lesbian baiting at its worst.

As one of NCADV's lesbian leadership during that onslaught of homophobic attacks, I was still giving homophobia workshops around the country, now able to give even more personal witness to the virulence of the hatred and fear of lesbians and gay men within both institutions and individuals. It was a time of pain and often anger for those of us committed to creating a world free of violence, and it was a time of deep distress for those of us under personal attack. However, my mother, like many mothers, had always said, "All things work for the good," and sure enough, it was out of the accumulation of these experiences that the pieces began coming together to make a quilt of our understanding.

On the day that I stopped reacting to attacks and gave my time instead to visioning, this simple germinal question came forth for the workshops: "What will the world be like without homophobia in it—for everyone, female and male, whatever sexual identity?" Simple though the question is, it was at first shocking because those of us who work in the anti-violence movement spend most of our time working with the damaging, negative results of violence and have little time to vision. It is sometimes difficult to create a vision of a world we have never experienced, but without such a vision, we cannot know clearly what we are working toward in our social change work. From this question, answer led to answer until a whole appeared of our collective making, from one workshop to another.

Here are some of the answers women have given:

- Kids won't be called tomboys or sissies; they'll just be who they are, able to do what they wish.
- People will be able to love anyone, no matter what sex; the issue will simply be whether or not she/he is a good human being, compatible, and loving.
- Affection will be opened up between women and men, women and women, men and men, and it won't be centered on sex; people won't fear being called names if they show affection to someone who isn't a mate or potential mate.
- If affection is opened up, then isolation will be broken down for all of us, especially for those who generally experience little physical affection, such as unmarried old people.
- Women will be able to work whatever jobs we want without being labeled masculine.
- There will be less violence if men do not feel they have to prove and assert their manhood. Their desire to dominate and control will not spill over from the personal to the level of national and international politics and the use of bigger and better weapons to control other countries.
- People will wear whatever clothes they wish, with the priority being comfort rather than the display of femininity or masculinity.
- There will be no gender roles.

It is at this point in the workshops—having imagined a world without homophobia—that the participants see the analysis begin to fall into place. Someone notes that all the things we have been talking about relate to sexual gender roles. It's rather like the beginning of a course in Sexism 101. The next question is "Imagine the world with no sex roles—sexual identity, which may be in flux, but no sexual gender roles." Further: imagine a world in which opportunity is not determined by gender or race. Just the imagining makes women alive with excitement because it is a vision of freedom, often just glimpsed but always known deep down as truth. Pure joy.

We talk about what it would be like to be born in a world in which there were no expectations or treatment based on gender but instead only the expectation that each child, no matter what race or sex, would be given as many options and possibilities as society could muster. Then we discuss what girls and boys would be like at puberty and beyond if sex role expectations didn't come crashing down on them with girls' achievement levels beginning to decline thereafter; what it would be for women to have the training and options for economic equity with men; what would happen to issues of power and control, and therefore violence, if there were real equality. To have no prescribed sex roles would open the possibility of equality. It is a discussion women find difficult to leave. Freedom calls.

Patriarchy—an enforced belief in male dominance and control—is the ideology and sexism the system that holds it in place. The catechism goes like this: Who do gender roles serve? Men and the women who seek power from them. Who suffers from gender roles? Women most completely and men in part. How are gender roles maintained? By the weapons of sexism: economics, violence, homophobia.

Why then don't we ardently pursue ways to eliminate gender roles and therefore sexism? It is my profound belief that all people have a spark in them that yearns for freedom, and the history of the world's atrocities—from the Nazi concentration camps to white dominance in South Africa to the battering of women—is the story of attempts to snuff out that spark. When that spark doesn't move forward to full flame, it is because the weapons designed to control and destroy have wrought such intense damage over time that the spark has been all but extinguished.

Sexism, that system by which women are kept subordinate to men, is kept in place by three powerful weapons designed to cause or threaten women with pain and loss. As stated before, the three are economics, violence, and homophobia. The stories of women battered by men, victims of sexism at its worst, show these three forces converging again and again. When battered women tell why they stayed with a batterer or why they returned to a batterer, over and over they say it was because they could not support themselves and their children financially, they had no skills for jobs, they could not get housing, transportation, medical care for their children. And how were they kept controlled? Through violence and threats of violence, both physical and verbal, so that they feared for their lives and the lives of their children and doubted their own abilities and self-worth. And why were they beaten? Because they were not good enough, were not "real women," were dykes, or because they stood up to him as no "real woman" would. And the male batterer, with societal backing, felt justified, often righteous, in his behavior—for his part in keeping women in their place.

Economics must be looked at first because many feminists consider it to be the root cause of sexism. Certainly the United Nations study released at the final conference of the International Decade on Women, held in Nairobi, Kenya, in 1985, supports that belief: of the world's population, women do 75% of the work, receive 10% of the pay and own 1% of the property. In the United States it is also supported by the opposition of the government to the idea of comparable worth and pay equity, as expressed by Ronald Reagan who referred to pay equity as "a joke." Obviously, it is considered a dangerous idea. Men profit not only from women's unpaid work in the home but from our underpaid work within horizontal female segregation such as clerical workers or upwardly mobile tokenism in the workplace where a few affirmative action promotions are expected to take care of all women's economic equality needs. Moreover, they profit from women's bodies through pornography, prostitution, and international female sexual slavery. And white men profit from both the labor of women and of men of color. Forced economic dependency puts women under male control and severely limits women's options for self-determination and self-sufficiency.

This truth is borne out by the fact that according to the National Commission on Working Women, on average, women of all races working year round earn only 64 cents to every one dollar a man makes. Also, the U.S. Census Bureau reports that only 9 percent of working women make over $25,000 a year. There is fierce opposition to women gaining employment in the nontraditional job market, that is, those jobs that traditionally employ less than 25 percent women. After a woman has gained one of these higher paying jobs, she is often faced with sexual harassment, lesbian baiting, and violence. It is clear that in the workplace there is an all-out effort to keep women in traditional roles so that the only jobs we are "qualified" for are the low-paid ones.

Actually, we have to look at economics not only as the root cause of sexism but also as the underlying, driving force that keeps all the oppressions in place. In the United States, our economic system is shaped like a pyramid, with a few people at the top, primarily white males, being supported by large numbers of unpaid or low-paid workers at the bottom. When we look at this pyramid, we begin to understand the major connection between sexism and racism because those groups at the bottom of the pyramid are women and people of color. We then begin to understand why there is such a fervent effort to keep those oppressive systems (racism and sexism and all the ways they are manifested) in place to maintain the unpaid and low-paid labor.

Susan DeMarco and Jim Hightower, writing for *Mother Jones,* report that *Forbes* magazine indicated that "the 400 richest families in America last year had an average net worth of $550 million each. These and less than a million other families—roughly one percent of our population—are at the prosperous tip of our society. . . . In 1976, the wealthiest 1 percent of America's families owned 19.2 percent of the nation's total wealth. (This sum of wealth counts all of America's cash, real estate, stocks, bonds, factories, art, personal property, and anything else of financial value.) By 1983, those at this 1 percent of our economy owned 34.3 percent of our wealth. . . . *Today the top 1 percent of Americans possesses more net wealth than the bottom 90 percent.*" (My italics.) (*May, 1988, pp. 32–33*)

In order for this top-heavy system of economic inequity to maintain itself, the 90 percent on the bottom must keep supplying cheap labor. A very complex, intricate system of institutionalized oppressions is necessary to maintain the status quo so that the vast majority will not demand its fair share of wealth and resources and bring the system down. Every institution—schools, banks, churches, government, courts, media, etc., as well as individuals must be enlisted in the campaign to maintain such a system of gross inequity.

What would happen if women gained the earning opportunities and power that men have? What would happen if these opportunities were distributed equitably, no matter what sex one was, no matter what race one was born into, and no matter where one lived? What if educational and training opportunities were equal? Would women spend most of our youth preparing for marriage? Would marriage be based on economic survival for women? What would happen to issues of power and control? Would women stay with our batterers? If a woman had economic independence in a society where women had equal opportunities, would she still be thought of as owned by her father or husband?

Economics is the great controller in both sexism and racism. If a person can't acquire food, shelter, and clothing and provide them for children, then that person can be forced to do many things in order to survive. The major tactic, worldwide, is to provide unrecompensed or inadequately recompensed labor for the benefit of those who control wealth. Hence, we see women performing unpaid labor in the home or filling low-paid jobs, and we see people of color in the lowest-paid jobs available.

The method is complex: limit educational and training opportunities for women and for people of color and then withhold adequate paying jobs with the excuse that people of color and women are incapable of filling them. Blame the economic victim and keep the victim's self-esteem low through invisibility and distortion within the media and education. Allow a few people of color and women to succeed among the profit-makers so that blaming those who don't "make it" can be intensified. Encourage those few who succeed in gaining power now to turn against those who remain behind rather than to use their resources to make change for all. Maintain the myth of scarcity—that there are not enough jobs, resources, etc., to go around—among the middle class so that they will not unite with laborers, immigrants, and the unemployed. The method keeps in place a system of control and profit by a few and a constant source of cheap labor to maintain it.

If anyone steps out of line, take her/his job away. Let homelessness and hunger do their work. The economic weapon works. And we end up saying, "I would do this or that—be openly who I am, speak out against injustice, work for civil rights, join a labor union, go to a political march, etc.—if I didn't have this job. I can't afford to lose it." We stay in an abusive situation because we see no other way to survive.

In the battered women's movement abusive relationships are said to be about power and control and the way out of them is through looking at the ways power and control work in our lives, developing support, improving self-esteem, and achieving control over our decisions and lives. We have yet to apply these methods successfully to our economic lives. Though requiring massive change, the way there also lies open for equality and wholeness. But the effort will require at least as much individual courage and risk and group support as it does for a battered woman to leave her batterer, and that requirement is very large indeed. Yet battered women find the courage to leave their batterers every day. They walk right into the unknown. To break away from economic domination and control will require a movement made up of individuals who possess this courage and ability to take risks.

Violence is the second means of keeping women in line, in a narrowly defined place and role. First there is the physical violence of battering, rape, and incest. Often when battered women come to shelters and talk about their lives, they tell stories of being not only physically beaten but also raped and their children subjected to incest. Work in the women's anti-violence movement during almost two decades has provided significant evidence that each of these acts, including rape and incest, is an attempt to seek power over and control of another person. In each case, the victim is viewed as an object and is used to meet the abuser's needs. The violence is used to wreak punishment and to demand compliance or obedience.

Violence against women is directly related to the condition of women in a society that refuses us equal pay, equal access to resources, and equal status with males. From this condition comes men's confirmation of their sense of ownership of women, power over women, and assumed right to control women for their own means. Men physically and emotionally abuse women because they *can*, because they live in a world that gives them permission. Male violence is fed by their sense of their *right* to dominate and control, and their sense of superiority over a group of people who, because of gender, they consider inferior to them.

It is not just the violence but the threat of violence that controls our lives. Because the burden of responsibility has been placed so often on the potential victim, as women we have curtailed our freedom in order to protect ourselves from violence. Because of the threat of rapists, we stay on alert, being careful not to walk in isolated places, being careful where we park our cars, adding incredible security measures to our homes—massive locks, lights, alarms, if we can afford them—and we avoid places where we will appear vulnerable or unprotected while the abuser walks with freedom. Fear, often now so commonplace that it is unacknowledged, shapes our lives, reducing our freedom.

As Bernice Reagan of the musical group Sweet Honey in the Rock said at the 1982 National Coalition Against Domestic Violence conference, women seem to carry a genetic memory that women were once burned as witches when we stepped out of line. To this day, mothers pass on to their daughters word of the dangers they face and teach them the ways they must limit their lives in order to survive.

Part of the way sexism stays in place is the societal promise of survival, false and unfulfilled as it is, that women will not suffer violence if we attach ourselves to a man to protect us. A woman without a man is told she is vulnerable to external violence and, worse, that there is something wrong with her. When the male abuser calls a woman a lesbian, he is not so much labeling her a woman who loves women as he is warning her that by resisting him, she is choosing to be outside society's protection from male institutions and therefore from wide-ranging, unspecified, ever-present violence. When she seeks assistance from woman friends or a battered women's shelter, he recognizes the power in woman bonding and fears loss of her servitude and loyalty: the potential loss of his control. The concern is not affectional/sexual identity: the concern is disloyalty and the threat is violence.

The threat of violence against women who step out of line or who are disloyal is made all the more powerful by the fact that women do not have to do anything—they may be paragons of virtue and subservience—to receive violence against our lives: the violence still comes. It comes because of the woman-hating that exists throughout society. Chance plays a larger part than virtue in keeping women safe. Hence, with violence always a threat to us, women can never feel completely secure and confident. Our sense of safety is always fragile and tenuous.

Many women say that verbal violence causes more harm than physical violence because it damages self-esteem so deeply. Women have not wanted to hear battered women say that the verbal abuse was as hurtful as the physical abuse: to acknowledge that truth would be tantamount to acknowledging that *virtually every woman is a battered woman*. It is difficult to keep strong against accusations of being a bitch, stupid, inferior, etc., etc. It is especially difficult when these individual assaults are backed up by a society that shows women in textbooks, advertising, TV programs, movies, etc., as debased, silly, inferior, and sexually objectified, and a society that gives tacit approval to pornography.

When we internalize these messages, we call the result "low self-esteem," a therapeutic individualized term. It seems to me we should use the more political expression: when we internalize these messages, we experience *internalized sexism,* and we experience it in common with all women living in a sexist world. The violence against us is supported by a society in which woman-hating is deeply imbedded.

In "Eyes on the Prize," a 1987 Public Television documentary about the Civil Rights Movement, an older white woman says about her youth in the South that it was difficult to be anything different from what was around her when there was no vision for another way to be. Our society presents images of women that say it is appropriate to commit violence against us. Violence is committed against women because we are seen as inferior in status and in worth. It has been the work of the women's movement to present a vision of another way to be.

Every time a woman gains the strength to resist and leave her abuser, we are given a model of the importance of stepping out of line, of moving toward freedom. And we all gain strength when she says to violence, "Never again!" Thousands of women in the last fifteen years have resisted their abusers to come to this country's 1100 battered women's shelters. There they have sat down with other women to share their stories, to discover that their stories again and again are the same, to develop an analysis that shows that violence is a statement about power and control, and to understand how sexism creates the climate for male violence. Those brave women are now a part of a movement that gives hope for another way to live in equality and peace.

Homophobia works effectively as a weapon of sexism because it is joined with a powerful arm, heterosexism. Heterosexism creates the climate for homophobia with its assumption that the world is and must be heterosexual and its display of power and privilege as the norm. Heterosexism is the systemic display of homophobia in the institutions of society. Heterosexism and homophobia work together to enforce compulsory heterosexuality and that bastion of patriarchal power, the nuclear family. The central focus of the right-wing attack against women's liberation is that women's equality, women's self-determination, women's control of our own bodies and lives will damage what they see as the crucial societal institution, the nuclear family. The attack has been led by fundamentalist ministers across the country. The two areas they have focused on most consistently are abortion and homosexuality, and their passion has led them to bomb women's clinics and to recommend deprogramming for homosexuals and establishing camps to quarantine people with AIDS. To resist marriage and/or heterosexuality is to risk severe punishment and loss.

It is not by chance that when children approach puberty and increased sexual awareness they begin to taunt each other by calling these names: "queer," "faggot," "pervert." It is at puberty that the full force of society's pressure to conform to heterosexuality and prepare for marriage is brought to bear. Children know what we have taught them, and we have given clear messages that those who deviate from standard expectations are to be made to get back in line. The best controlling tactic at puberty is to be treated as an outsider, to be ostracized at a time when it feels most vital to be accepted. Those who are different must be made to suffer loss. It is also at puberty that misogyny begins to be more apparent, and girls are pressured to conform to societal norms that do not permit them to realize their full potential. It is at this time that their academic achievements begin to decrease as they are coerced into compulsory heterosexuality and trained for dependency upon a man, that is, for economic survival.

There was a time when the two most condemning accusations against a woman meant to ostracize and disempower her were "whore" and "lesbian." The sexual revolution and changing attitudes about heterosexual behavior may have led to some lessening of the power of the word *whore*, though it still has strength as a threat to sexual property and prostitutes are stigmatized and abused. However, the word *lesbian* is still fully charged and carries with it the full threat of loss of power and privilege, the threat of being cut asunder, abandoned, and left outside society's protection.

To be a lesbian is to be *perceived* as someone who has stepped out of line, who has moved out of sexual/economic dependence on a male, who is woman-identified. A lesbian is perceived as someone who can live without a man, and who is therefore (however illogically) against men. A lesbian is perceived as being outside the acceptable, routinized order of things. She is seen as someone who has no societal institutions to protect her and who is not privileged to the protection of individual males. Many heterosexual women see her as someone who stands in contradiction to the sacrifices they have made to conform to compulsory heterosexuality. A lesbian is perceived as a threat to the nuclear family, to male dominance and control, to the very heart of sexism.

Gay men are perceived also as a threat to male dominance and control, and the homophobia expressed against them has the same roots in sexism as does homophobia against lesbians. Visible gay men are the objects of extreme hatred and fear by heterosexual men because their breaking ranks with male heterosexual solidarity is seen as a damaging rent in the very fabric of sexism. They are seen as betrayers, as traitors who must be punished and eliminated. In the beating and killing of gay men we see clear evidence of this hatred. When we see the fierce homophobia expressed toward gay men, we can begin to understand the ways sexism also affects males through imposing rigid, dehumanizing gender roles on them. The two circumstances in which it is legitimate for men to be openly physically affectionate with one another are in competitive sports and in the crisis of war. For many men, these two experiences are the highlights of their lives, and they think of them again and again with nostalgia. War and sports offer a cover of all-male safety and dominance to keep away the notion of affectionate openness being identified with homosexuality. When gay men break ranks with male roles through bonding and affection outside the arenas of war and sports, they are perceived as not being "real men," that is, as being identified with women, the weaker sex that must be dominated and that over the centuries has been the object of male hatred and abuse. Misogyny gets transferred to gay men with a vengeance and is increased by the fear that their sexual identity and behavior will bring down the entire system of male dominance and compulsory heterosexuality.

If lesbians are established as threats to the status quo, as outcasts who must be punished, homophobia can wield its power over all women through lesbian baiting. Lesbian baiting is an attempt to control women by labeling us as lesbians because our behavior is not acceptable, that is, when we are being independent, going our own way, living whole lives, fighting for our rights, demanding equal pay, saying no to violence, being self-assertive, bonding with and loving the company of women, assuming the right to our bodies, insisting upon our own authority, making changes that include us in society's decision-making; lesbian baiting occurs when women are called lesbians because we resist male dominance and control. And it has little or nothing to do with one's sexual identity.

To be named as lesbian threatens all women, not just lesbians, with great loss. And any woman who steps out of role risks being called a lesbian. To understand how this is a threat to all women, one must understand that any woman can be called a lesbian and there is no real way she can defend herself: there is no way to credential one's sexuality. ("The Children's Hour," a Lillian Hellman play, makes this point when a student asserts two teachers are lesbians and they have no way to disprove it.) She may be married or divorced, have children, dress in the most feminine manner, have sex with men, be celibate—but there are lesbians who do all those things. *Lesbians look like all women and all women look like lesbians*. There is no guaranteed method of identification, and as we all know, sexual identity can be kept hidden. (The same is true for men. There is no way to prove their sexual identity, though many go to extremes to prove heterosexuality.) Also, women are not necessarily born lesbian. Some seem to be, but others become lesbians later in life after having lived heterosexual lives. Lesbian baiting of heterosexual women would not work if there were a definitive way to identify lesbians (or heterosexuals).

We have yet to understand clearly how sexual identity develops. And this is disturbing to some people, especially those who are determined to discover how lesbian and gay identity is formed so that they will know where to start in eliminating it. (Isn't it odd that there is so little concern about discovering the causes of heterosexuality?) There are many theories: genetic makeup, hormones, socialization, environment, etc. But there is no conclusive evidence that indicates that heterosexuality comes from one process and homosexuality from another.

We do know, however, that sexual identity can be in flux, and we know that sexual identity means more than just the gender of people one is attracted to and has sex with. To be a lesbian has as many ramifications as for a woman to be heterosexual. It is more than sex, more than just the bedroom issue many would like to make it: it is a woman-centered life with all the social interconnections that entails. Some lesbians are in long-term relationships, some in short-term ones, some date, some are celibate, some are married to men, some remain as separate as possible from men, some have children by men, some by alternative insemination, some seem "feminine" by societal standards, some "masculine," some are doctors, lawyers and ministers, some laborers, housewives and writers: what all share in common is a sexual/affectional identity that focuses on women in its attractions and social relationships.

If lesbians are simply women with particular sexual identity who look and act like all women, then the major difference in living out a lesbian sexual identity as opposed to a heterosexual identity is that as lesbians we live in a homophobic world that threatens and imposes damaging loss on us for being *who we are*, for choosing to live whole lives. Homophobic people often assert that homosexuals have the choice of not being homosexual; that is, we don't have to act out our sexual identity. In that case, I want to hear heterosexuals talk about their willingness not to act out their sexual identity, including not just sexual activity but heterosexual social interconnections and heterosexual privilege. It is a question of wholeness. It is very difficult for one to be denied the life of a sexual being, whether expressed in sex or in physical affection, and to feel complete, whole. For our loving relationships with humans feed the life of the spirit and enable us to overcome our basic isolation and to be interconnected with humankind.

If, then, any woman can be named a lesbian and be threatened with terrible losses, what is it she fears? Are these fears real? Being vulnerable to a homophobic world can lead to these losses:

- *Employment.* The loss of job leads us right back to the economic connection to sexism. This fear of job loss exists for almost every lesbian except perhaps those who are self-employed or in a business that does not require societal approval. Consider how many businesses or organizations you know that will hire and protect people who are openly gay or lesbian.
- *Family.* Their approval, acceptance, love.
- *Children.* Many lesbians and gay men have children, but very, very few gain custody in court challenges, even if the other parent is a known abuser. Other children may be kept away from us as though gays and lesbians are abusers. There are written and unwritten laws prohibiting lesbians and gays from being foster parents or from adopting children. There is an irrational fear that children in contact with lesbians and gays will become homosexual through influence or that they will be sexually abused. Despite our knowing that 95 percent of those who sexually abuse children are heterosexual men, there are no policies keeping heterosexual men from teaching

or working with children, yet in almost every school system in America, visible gay men and lesbians are not hired through either written or unwritten law.

- *Heterosexual privilege and protection.* No institutions, other than those created by lesbians and gays—such as the Metropolitan Community Church, some counseling centers, political organizations such as the National Gay and Lesbian Task Force, the National Coalition of Black Lesbians and Gays, the Lambda Legal Defense and Education Fund, etc.—affirm homosexuality and offer protection. Affirmation and protection cannot be gained from the criminal justice system, mainline churches, educational institutions, the government.

- *Safety.* There is nowhere to turn for safety from physical and verbal attacks because the norm presently in this country is that it is acceptable to be overtly homophobic. Gay men are beaten on the streets; lesbians are kidnapped and "deprogrammed." The National Gay and Lesbian Task Force, in an extended study, has documented violence against lesbians and gay men and noted the inadequate response of the criminal justice system. One of the major differences between homophobia/heterosexism and racism and sexism is that because of the Civil Rights Movement and the women's movement racism and sexism are expressed more covertly (though with great harm); because there has not been a major, visible lesbian and gay movement, it is permissible to be overtly homophobic in any institution or public forum. Churches spew forth homophobia in the same way they did racism prior to the Civil Rights Movement. Few laws are in place to protect lesbians and gay men, and the criminal justice system is wracked with homophobia.

- *Mental health.* An overtly homophobic world in which there is full permission to treat lesbians and gay men with cruelty makes it difficult for lesbians and gay men to maintain a strong sense of well-being and self-esteem. Many lesbians and gay men are beaten, raped, killed, subjected to aversion therapy, or put in mental institutions. The impact of such hatred and negativity can lead one to depression and, in some cases, to suicide. The toll on the gay and lesbian community is devastating.

- *Community*. There is rejection by those who live in homophobic fear, those who are afraid of association with lesbians and gay men. For many in the gay and lesbian community, there is a loss of public acceptance, a loss of allies, a loss of place and belonging.
- *Credibility*. This fear is large for many people: the fear that they will no longer be respected, listened to, honored, believed. They fear they will be social outcasts.

The list goes on and on. But any one of these essential components of a full life is large enough to make one deeply fear its loss. A black woman once said to me in a workshop, "When I fought for Civil Rights, I always had my family and community to fall back on even when they didn't fully understand or accept what I was doing. I don't know if I could have borne losing them. And you people don't have either with you. It takes my breath away."

What does a woman have to do to get called a lesbian? Almost anything, sometimes nothing at all, but certainly anything that threatens the status quo, anything that steps out of role, anything that asserts the rights of women, anything that doesn't indicate submission and subordination. Assertiveness, standing up for oneself, asking for more pay, better working conditions, training for and accepting a non-traditional (you mean a man's?) job, enjoying the company of women, being financially independent, being in control of one's life, depending first and foremost upon oneself, thinking that one can do whatever needs to be done, but above all, working for the rights and equality of women.

In the backlash to the gains of the women's liberation movement, there has been an increased effort to keep definitions man-centered. Therefore, to work on behalf of women must mean to work against men. To love women must mean that one hates men. A very effective attack has been made against the word *feminist* to make it a derogatory word. In current backlash usage, *feminist* equals *man-hater* which equals *lesbian*. This formula is created in the hope that women will be frightened away from their work on behalf of women. Consequently, we now have women who believe in the rights of women and work for those rights while from fear deny that they are feminists, or refuse to use the word because it is so "abrasive."

So what does one do in an effort to keep from being called a lesbian? She steps back into line, into the role that is demanded of her, tries to behave in such a way that doesn't threaten the status of men, and if she works for women's rights, she begins modifying that work. When women's organizations begin doing significant social change work, they inevitably are lesbian-baited; that is, funders or institutions or community members tell us that they can't work with us because of our "man-hating attitudes" or the presence of lesbians. We are called too strident, told we are making enemies, not doing good.

The battered women's movement has seen this kind of attack: the pressure has been to provide services only, without analysis of the causes of violence against women and strategies for ending it. To provide only services without political analysis or direct action is to be in an approved "helping" role; to analyze the causes of violence against women is to begin the work toward changing an entire system of power and control. It is when we do the latter that we are threatened with the label of man-hater or lesbian. For my politics, if a women's social change organization has not been labeled lesbian or communist, it is probably not doing significant work; it is only "making nice."

Women in many of these organizations, out of fear of all the losses we are threatened with, begin to modify our work to make it more acceptable and less threatening to the male-dominated society which we originally set out to change. The work can no longer be radical (going to the root cause of the problem) but instead must be reforming, working only on the symptoms and not the cause. Real change for women becomes thwarted and stopped. The word *lesbian* is instilled with the power to halt our work and control our lives. And we give it its power with our fear.

In my view, homophobia has been one of the major causes of the failure of the women's liberation movement to make deep and lasting change. (The other major block has been racism.) We were fierce when we set out but when threatened with the loss of heterosexual privilege, we began putting on brakes. Our best-known nationally distributed women's magazine was reluctant to print articles about lesbians, began putting a man on the cover several times a year, and writing articles about women who succeeded in a man's world. We worried about our image, our being all right, our being "real women" despite our work. Instead of talking about the elimination of sexual gender roles, we stepped back and talked about "sex role stereotyping" as the issue. Change around the edges for middle class white women began to be talked about as successes. We accepted tokenism and integration, forgetting that equality for all women, for all people—and not just equality of white middle class women with white men—was the goal that we could never put behind us.

But despite backlash and retreats, change is growing from within. The women's liberation movement is beginning to gain strength again because there are women who are talking about liberation for all women. We are examining sexism, racism, homophobia, classism, anti-Semitism, ageism, ableism, and imperialism, and we see everything as connected. This change in point of view represents the third wave of the women's liberation movement, a new direction that does not get mass media coverage and recognition. It has been initiated by women of color and lesbians who were marginalized or rendered invisible by the white heterosexual leaders of earlier efforts. The first wave was the nineteenth and early twentieth century campaign for the vote; the second, beginning in the 1960s, focused on the Equal Rights Amendment and abortion rights. Consisting of predominantly white middle class women, both failed in recognizing issues of equality and empowerment for all women. The third wave of the movement, multi-racial and multi-issued, seeks the transformation of the world for us all. We know that we won't get there until everyone gets there; that we must move forward in a great strong line, hand in hand, not just a few at a time.

We know that the arguments about homophobia originating from mental health and Biblical/religious attitudes can be settled when we look at the sexism that permeates religious and psychiatric history. The women of the third wave of the women's liberation movement know that *without the existence of sexism there would be no homophobia.*

Finally, we know that as long as the word lesbian can strike fear in any woman's heart, then work on behalf of women can be stopped; the only successful work against sexism must include work against homophobia.

QUESTIONS

1. What are the explanations for homosexuality that Pharr examines? How does she use these explanations to con-

clude that sexuality is morally neutral? What does she mean by that claim?

2. What does Pharr identify as the system which hold patriarchal ideology in place? What are the three "weapons" of this system? How does Pharr define these "weapons"? How do they work to reinforce expectations about gender?

3. What is "compulsory heterosexuality"? How does Pharr use this concept in her claim that homophobia is primarily a reinforcer of gender expectations?

Re-scripting the Closet: Black Masculinity and the Down Low Subculture

Jami Harris

I continue to hope for a coalition of sexual minorities that will transcend the simple categories of identity, that will refuse the erasure of bisexuality, that will counter and dissipate the violence imposed by restrictive bodily norms.

—Judith Butler, *Gender Trouble*

The Down Low is a continuing controversy that vilifies participating Black men, both for their refusal to self-identify as "gay" or queer, and for their existence outside available categories or sexual identities. Equipped with all the scripts of masculinity, race and sexuality, wanting to be a straight Black "masculine" man who has sex with men is a complex-although precise and readable-desire, and yet not at all represented by the categories for sexual identity dominant culture prescribes. This community is perceived as being responsible for the spread of HIV/AIDS in the Black community, as well as harboring vast homophobic tendencies. Those within the DL community are also "traitors" to the gay/straight binary of sexuality. This paper explores the separate space created

Reprinted by permission of the author.

by the DL community in response to the rigidity of sexual identities, not accountable to the notions of race. Perceptions and portrayals of Black gay men as feminized, and therefore constituting a nonthreatening Black masculinity, have led these Black men to work to uphold constructions of an "authentic" Black masculinity as hyper-heterosexual while simultaneously challenging it by engaging secretly in same-sex sexual encounters (Collins 207). Although deceptive on a personal level, the DL lifestyle can read from the outside as politically or theoretically charged protest, a social protest. Labeling oneself as on the DL—a term popularized in the 1990s in the presumably heterosexual lyrics of performers like TLC and R. Kelly—has become a way for some black men to admit they like guys without resorting to words like gay, bisexual, or queer.

I contend that the Down Low community is a symptom of the rigid race and gender systems operating in dominant culture, as well as the perceived racially insensitivity if not overt racism within mainstream White gay culture. The Down Low subculture rejects the terms gay or bisexual not because of the perceived Black community's homophobia, but because they simply want to create their own identity outside of a racially insensitive classification. White hetero-masculine dominant culture wrote the script on masculinity and sexuality, leaving no room for fluid, new identities. These men also challenge this over-determination of "the closet" as a container of shame, pain, discomfort, and anxiety. The DL offers a counter-narrative of discretion as a tactic of survival (McCune 299). For DL men there is no "gay" essence to reveal, or a bisexual or straight one, for that matter. Unlike the traditional closet narrative, where men are in isolation, DL men tend to be relatively open about their sexuality, if only to each other, and often under the radar.

I start by asking the question: What is the Down Low phenomenon? Benoit Denizet-Lewis's article "Double Lives on the Down Low," states that the Down Low is an underground subculture largely made up of Black men who otherwise live straight lives (Denizet-Lewis 1). Keith Boykin, author of *Beyond the Down Low: Sex, Lies and Denial in Black America,* admits the Down Low is "a term (he) vaguely understood to mean men who have sex with men but do not identify as gay" (Boykin 6). Jeffery Q. McCune, Jr. author of "Out in the Club: The Down Low, Hip Hop, and the Architexture of Black Masculinity," states that "some black men who have sex with other men, who dis-identify with normative descriptors of sexuality, refer to themselves as 'men on the down low' " (McCune 298). According to these definitions, there are four basic traits for those on the DL: Black, male, in relationships with women, and secretly having sex with men (Boykin 14).

I find it very interesting, however, that this "phenomenon" of the Down Low emerged in the 1990's following the publication of several books written by Black men "outing" themselves. J. L. King's text, *On the Down Low: A Journey into the Lives of "Straight" Black Men Who Sleep With Men,* was one of the publications labeling this community. King describes his life on the Down Low as not being a gay man in the closet, but a Black man behind the closet. As a self-proclaimed veteran and voice of the DL lifestyle, King depicts an image of Black men who do not follow the rules on sexuality and identity. He tells a story filled with deceit, pain, cheating, and disease, as the construct for the DL identity. However, according to King, DL men are not necessarily gay. "The secret," he writes, "is that men who look like me, talk like me, and think like me are having sex with men but still love and want to be with their women. And they do not believe that they are gay" (King 9). King's definition seems to exclude men who do not date women, or worse believe that they possess women. In other words, men on the down low would have to be inherently bisexual. Painting a very definitive or narrow view of gay men, King states, "Open and out gay men are not confused about their sexuality. Some gay men are in the closet. But they are gay. They have a community that is aware of this fact and provides them with a comfortable environment in which to 'let their hair down' " (20). This also implies a notion of race and class into the mix. Working-class and poor MSMs, (men who have sex with men) of color have always had to be low-key about their sexual preference, since they have not had the same access to the safety nets that exist for white and middle-class men (Boykin 15). The mainstream media contends that men like himself, living on the DL, are causing great destruction to the Black community. Media opinion paints the DL community as a fraternity of closeted gay or bisexual Black men cheating on their wives or girlfriends. This "fraternity" is one that spreads both pain and disease throughout the Black community. The dominant popular culture narrative of the DL provides a set of fears about uncontrollable male bodies of color, and the volatile intersections of masculinity, race, and sexuality (Ward 415).

Given the stated above criteria, it seems that Black men in America are more apprehensive than any other group to openly admit their "alternative" sexuality, and have created a whole subculture based on closeting themselves around which society has created this phenomenon. This appears to be a result of dominant white hegemonic masculinity and representations of Black masculinity; being gay-identified is not an acceptable representation of a "real" Black man. However, the concept of a community of "heterosexual" men who secretly in engage in sex with other men to protect their unstable masculinity is nothing new. There have been plenty of white men throughout history that have exhibited similar behavior without an emerging phenomenon surrounding it. An ideal example is New Jersey governor James McGreevy. By announcing his affair with another man, this married governor provided an example of the White down low, if it can be called this. Other high profile examples such as Congressman Michael Huffington of California, Congressman Edward Schrock of Virginia, and actor Rock Hudson all help to prove this point. All of these men were in some fashion linked or married to women at the time their homosexual acts or practices were discovered and disclosed (Boykin 67–74). Homosexual behavior, like homophobia, is widespread in both the Black and White communities. White men do not live in a parallel universe where homosexuality is widely accepted. White men are on the down low just like Black men, and since we live in a country with far more White men than Black men, it stands to reason that there are far more White men on the Down Low than Black men. They, too, are secretly engaging in sexual relations with men while simultaneously carrying on heterosexual relationships. But if more White men are doing it than Black men, where is the public outcry about White men on the Down Low? Here, I plan to open up the discussion of "closeted" individuals from other racial and gendered backgrounds to explore the way society has packaged the Down Low as a "Black Thing," as a way to provide a simple and convenient mechanism to understand a complex issue.

A lack of discussion about White men on the DL has reinforced stereotypes about Black male sexuality as dangerous and predatory, as well as provided evidence that Blacks are more homophobic then Whites (Boykin 73). In addition, the combination of a concealed non-normative sexuality, a epidemic of a sexually transmitted disease (AIDS), and a population accused of misbehavior (Black men), plus a "subaltern genre of expressive culture" (Hip-Hop), and the existence of innocent victims (heterosexual women) have all the makings of moral panic (Ward 415). In addition to the racial components of the Down Low, the characterization of straight identified MSMs (Men who have Sex with Men) as closeted, exemplifies the dominant tendency to identify sexual acts as markers of true sexual self-hood (Ward 415). Michel Foucault, in *The History of Sexuality Volume 1*, explains that in the nineteenth century the homosexual act became an identity through the "habitual sin as a singular nature" (Foucault 43). Everything that comprises an individual and identity was now affected by his sexuality and sexual practice (43). However, "heterosexual" MSMs who are deemed closeted also glosses over the larger questions about the gendered and racialized construction of heterosexual and homosexual categories (Ward 415). To relegate men of DL to the closet, as one who is not true to himself, is problematic. Ward states, "According to the logic of the closet, same-sex sexual practices among heterosexuals signify sexual repression, or failure to be honest about who one is, and the sexual community or culture in which one belongs" (415). The need to identify DL men as closeted gay men implies that homophobia stems from an essential, ethno-racial culture of sexual repression (415). In other words, Black men inherently have an inability to come to terms with their own sexuality due to culturally or racially constructed homophobia. However, I contend that homophobia is a symptom of rigid gender structures that cite White hegemonic masculinity.

Hegemonic masculinity, by which all other masculinities are measured and evaluated, is defined as white, middle-class, and heterosexual (Kimmel 124). For hegemonic masculinity to exist, a point of deviance in race and sexuality must also exist-to be relegated as "other" and therefore uphold/support/define hegemony. In the case of race, the point of deviance is created by a "normalized" White heterosexuality that poses itself against a deviant Black heterosexuality to give its meaning (Collins 97). In the case of sexuality, the point of deviances is created by the same "normalized" White heterosexuality that depends on a deviant White homosexuality (97). This "normalized" White masculinity being installed in dominant culture as normal, natural, and ideal requires stigmatizing alternate races and sexualities as abnormal, dangerous, and sinful (Collins 97). Therefore, to uphold the construction of hegemonic White masculinity, Black masculinities, whether heterosexual or not, are posed as the deviant other. However, masculinity is constructed as a sort of hierarchy with those closest to hegemonic masculinity at the top, and all other succeeding below. "In this fashion, elite White men control the very definitions of masculinity, and they use these standards to evaluate their own masculine identities and those of all other men, including African American men" (186). In other words, White hegemonic masculinity not only controls dominant culture but also evaluates all other masculinities by how closely they represent dominant social norms.

Dominant culture has portrayed Black men on the one hand, as predatory and wild, as sex thirsty, violent animals lusting after White and Black women alike. On the other, Black men are portrayed as the harmless, bumbling "stepin fetchit" Black buddy. This depiction of Black masculinity as the Black buddy evolved to encompass the ever-growing representations of the ultimate "weak" or "sissified" Black man as the Black gay man (171). Constantly shown as the swishy, limp-wristed "Miss Thing," Black gay men have "operate(d) as further evidence that black men are 'weak', emasculated, and 'feminized' in relation to White men" (174). These representations uphold White hegemonic masculinity in that the sexual practices attributed to the Black "sissy" or Black gay man are deviant, and do not constitute a credible threat to White heterosexual men because the presence of Black gay sexuality constitutes a "feminized" and therefore nonthreatening Black masculinity (175).

"Historically and developmentally, masculinity has been defined as the flight from women, the repudiation from femininity" (Kimmel 126). As in Freud's psychoanalytic theory, during the oedipal stage of development the young boy must renounce his identification and emotional attachment with his mother and replace her with the father as the object of identification to secure his identity as a man (Kimmel 126). In this sense, hegemonic masculinity is benchmarked as defining "real" men as not being like women (Collins 188). "Real" men or paradigms of masculinity are constructed as in relation to not only race and sexuality but also as gender. However, "real" men not only have to display all the qualities that women seemingly lack (forceful, analytic, responsible, and willing to exert authority); they also require female validation as constant reminders of male superiority (189). In the case of African American men, this suggests that "real" men must couple with, control, and dominate "unnaturally" strong black women to shake the stigma of "weakness" (189). Therefore, in response to the representations of the weak or sissified Black man, Black popular culture "works to uphold constructions of an "authentic" Black masculinity as being hyper-heterosexual" (174). In other words, hegemonic masculinity's representation of what constitutes a "real" man leaves little room for Black men to deviate from hyper-heterosexuality, which leads to the emergence of the Down Low underground subculture's attempting to rescript masculinity.

In the Freudian model, the fear of the father's authority terrifies the young boy to renounce his desire for his mother and identify with his father (Kimmel 129). "This model links gender identity with sexual orientation: The little boy's identification with father (becoming masculine) allows him to now engage in sexual relations with women (he becomes heterosexual)" (129). As stated above, levels of masculinity rely on heterosexuality. Also, masculinity depends heavily on the acceptance of other men, of the approval of hegemonic masculinity. Homophobia is not entirely the fear of homosexuals, but also the fear of being perceived as a homosexual and therefore less masculine (131). Homophobia is a fear that hegemonic masculinity will unmask men, emasculate men, and reveal them as not "real" men (131). This in turn, creates a fear of humiliation, and shame of that fear. These implications of masculinity as homophobia, drives the vilification of Black men on the Down Low. This subculture is perceived as attempting to duplicate or enact masculinity through homophobia, and therefore remain closeted. The dominant discourse places these DL men in a place of fear and shame and therefore unable to "come out" of the closet for fear of emasculation.

In the narrative of the closet that has dominated the gay movement since the late 1960s, men are supposed to be full of self-loathing about their secret sexuality until they emerge into the public like fluttering butterflies or strutting peacocks. But DL offers a new-school remix of the old-school closet, an improvisation on the coming-out narrative that imagines a low-key way of being in the world. The standard idea of the coming-out process "holds that a person has experiences of same-sex desire and homosocial emotional bonding that eventually motivate her or him to come out and adopt a gay/lesbian identity" (Wilkerson

252). This model inherently depends on the person to eventually self identify as gay/lesbian/bisexual. In "Is There Something You Need to Tell Me," William S. Wilkerson argues that this picture of coming out "reinforces essentialist notions of identity in which experiences are taken as straightforward and unmediated sources of knowledge on which individuals can construct personal identities" (252). In other words, any individual who experiences same-sex desire and homosocial emotional bonding will eventually adopt a particular identity regardless of the effects on the individual by the social constructions of race, class, culture, gender, etc. Wilkerson contends that "coming out" is inherently essentialist, in that "it implies the revealing of an already present, but hidden, identity" (252).

Wilkerson then investigates Satya P. Mohanty's realist theory of identity, which views coming out as "the reinterpretation of homoerotic experiences, previously thought forbidden, as legitimate and positive" (252). Once the individual has come out, the "deviant" experiences and desires are no longer be viewed by the individual as deviant, but instead real and inherent. "The crucial point is that this change of values and self-understanding changes the character of the experiences, and so alters the very kind of experiences that motivated an individual to come out in the first place" (Wilkerson 252). In other words, these experiences would not only motivate the individual to come out, but also the process of coming out would change the way one views these experiences and accepts oneself in spite of prevalent homophobia.

This reading of realist theory of identity and experience claims that identity is constructed and discovered through experiences. However, these experiences are not meaningful in themselves, but are also both discovered and constructed (Wilkerson 252). "So the realist theory claims that both identity and experiences that serve as material for construction of identity are mediated by theoretical understandings of the world and one's place in it" (252). In other words, identity and experience construction and discovery depend on the individual's ability to navigate his/her understanding of dominant culture. However, an individual's lack of given or self-evident meanings in experience make individuals prone to error in understanding of said experiences and an "incorrect" identity. This theory promotes a deterministic viewpoint, in that with "correct" understanding of the world and one's place in it a specific identity will emerge. I object to such realist theories of experience because, as Wilkerson claims, "by claiming that there can be more and less accurate interpretations of experience, the realist theory faces a paradox when it comes to the structure of human experience" (253). The notion of coming out to a new sexual identity infers a reliance upon an individual to retrospectively know that they were this sexual identity all along. "If being gay is an accurate identity to infer from one's experiences, we would want to say that one had 'gay experiences' all along but didn't know it" (253). This requires a great deal of understanding and organization of one's own experiences to give a self-reflective idea on those experiences and attach an "accurate" identity to go along with it. Since one's interpretation of experience changes upon coming out and adopting a gay or lesbian identity, it seems difficult to infer that one's retroactive interpretation of experience applies to all experiences of one's life until that point (253).

This also implies that it is possible to be wrong about one's interpretation of experience and that there is a more "accurate" interpretation of experience (254). In other words, to come out as gay/lesbian is an accurate interpretation of homosocial experiences regardless of an individual person's self-identity. This means that someone else, namely, hegemonic culture at large, have the monopoly on identity. They are the ones doling out accurate identities to citizens regardless of a person's own interpretation of their experience and identity. "If one can be wrong about one's own sexuality, and another can be right about it, then it is at least possible that you (or I) could be wrong about your (my) sexuality, and for the majority of straight people. . . the possibility of being gay or lesbian or bisexual or transsexual is alarming" (255). Wilkerson describes experience as the awareness or "living through" of some event, needing no external aids in deciding the meaning of the experience, and therefore impossible to be inaccurate about that thing of which one is immediately aware (256). How is it possible that one could not be aware of one's own sexual and emotional desire and needs, when sex and desire are not things we easily pass over (256). I, along with Wilkerson, contend that "experience is contextual and dispersed, and is subject to reflection and reorganization by the experiencing subject" (258).

One's experience and subsequent identity should not rely on outside interpretation. One should posses autonomy when interpreting experience as well as reflecting upon it for the sake of self-identification. Reflective of hegemonic culture, it could be said that before coming out a "potentially gay person" had been "repressing or denying his or her desire" (261). This interpretation relies heavily on the idea that the subject has a "fully formed yet submerged" understanding of his/her experiences and is "awaiting recognition and expression" (261). To return to the discussion on the DL community, to interpret men on the DL as to be in denial about their inherent gay or bisexual identity is to say that these men have a fully formed understanding of their experiences, as neatly wrapped packages "awaiting recognition and expression." These men are closeted because they deny their own sexual desires. However, the Down Low lifestyle has created an entire subculture of Black men who oscillate sexual relations between male and female partners. However, it would be a mistake to call such man a closeted bisexual, since it would imply that underneath the veil has settled on a stable gender identity. This narrow understanding of coming out expresses a need to identify a person under limited constructions of the gay/straight binary. "Experiences are simply there with its meaning (a person always had the desire of a homosexual) or not there at all (the person did not have the desires)" (Wilkerson 264). In other words, an individual's experience must produce self-evidently meaningful or not meaningful at all. However, this self-evident meaningful discovery must be in line with dominant culture's ideals and interpretations. For example, same-sex sexual desires equates a homosexual or bisexual identity. As Wilkerson contends, that coming-out as gay/lesbian is a sort of transformation. "This new identity reflects a new and more accurate understanding of who one is in the world and how one can act in the world" (266). However, what if one refuses to come out into a gay/lesbian identity? But rather, one chooses to self-identify outside the bounds of dominant cultures scripts on identity, and therefore does not follow the trajectory of a coming-out at all.

Hegemonic dominant culture attempts to identify or locate DL men, to claim the sexual identities of these men, and therefore highlights the binaristic framework through which sexualities are viewed in mainstream dominant culture. DL men are assumed to be or identified as being "straight" or "gay," leaving out the category of bisexuality. To include the category of bisexuality "would blur the clean lines that link masculinity with male heterosexuality and effeminacy with male homosexuality" in dominant culture as well as "raise the issue of non-monogamous lifestyle choices and value systems that could supplant or compete with uncritically enforced norms of monogamy" (Phillips 12). It is very simple and convenient for dominant and mainstream culture to package these men up as closeted. However, these men do not self-identify generally as gay, so there is nothing to 'come out' to; there is no next step in understanding their experience (Denizet-Lewis 3). As Keith Boykin states, "By rejecting the homosexual label, they are not necessarily rejecting the sexual behavior associated with it. Black men often reject the term 'gay' to repudiate white social constructs of homosexuality but not to reject their own homosexual behavior" (Boykin 15). In other words, Black men on the Down Low have made a place for themselves outside of generally accepted sexual identities. This implies the possibility of sexual orientation or gender categories that have yet to be labeled or named (Phillips 12). For example, "some Black men who openly acknowledge that they have sex with other men have simply found other words to describe themselves, including the term 'same-gender-loving' " (Boykin 15). The identifiers of the mainstream gay community are insufficient in describing the sexual practices of DL men, in that these identifiers adhere to a white hegemonic ideal of sexuality. "Gay" as a identifying term invokes a host of negative connotations that these Black men are unwilling to live with. "Socially encoded scripts of identity are often formatted by phobic energies around race, sexuality, gender, and various other identificatory distinctions" (Muñoz 6). These men "simply want to create their own identities outside of what they perceive to be a racially insensitive white gay world" (Boykin 16). This new sexual identity is one that contains ethnic, gender, and sexually related elements in a new combination (Phillips 12). Rather then the closet or labels created by White hegemonic dominant culture, the DL identity is an identity in the making; one in of itself, not necessarily one of denial or shame, but one of pride, and community.

The result of an individual's reluctance to identify him/herself under the rigid gender and sexual systems available be makes for the vilification of said individual. Along the lines of Monique Wittig's assertion of universality, "you-will-be-straight-or-you-will-not-be," or in this case "you-will-be-gay-or-you-will-not-be" (Wittig 28). In *The Straight Mind and Other Essays*, Wittig discusses the need of the straight mind, or the discourse of modern theoretical systems and social science that function like primitive concepts in a conglomerate of all kinds of disciplines, theories, and current ideas, to "immediately universalize its production of concepts into general laws to which claim to hold true for all societies, all epochs, all individuals" (27). In other words, the straight mind cannot conceive constructed identities outside of this framework. Dominant culture does not allow for a space outside the straight/gay binary construct. The straight mind does, however, allow for a gay/lesbian identity, in that it is simply nothing but heterosexuality (28). For example, the butch/femme lesbian relationship, is in the eyes of dominant culture, adherent to the masculine/feminine gender binary and therefore mirroring heterosexuality. However, the opposition to the DL lifestyle is that these individuals refuse to adhere to the binary. DL men are described as masculine men who only engage in sexual relations with other DL masculine men. These men are in a sense gender outlaws, because they do not adhere to the normative, or to the norms that govern gender (Butler, *Gender* xxi).

On the other hand, Judith Butler, in *Gender Trouble,* states, "it is not possible to oppose the 'normative' forms of gender without at the same time subscribing to a certain normative view of how the gendered world ought to be" (xxii). In other words, these men are simultaneously opposing the normative forms of gender construction while employing some of the available tropes of masculinity. DL men attempt remain perceived as masculine and adhering to the hegemonic construction of masculinity all the while engaging in subversive acts (homosocial relations). I contend that the community of the DL is a performance of "normalized" gender. The DL is not an identity but a performance. This not a show or play that these men put on for the world, but a "lifestyle." As Butler describes, performativity is not a singular act, but a repetition and a ritual, which achieves its effects through its naturalization in the context of a body, understood, in part, as a culturally sustained temporal duration (Butler, *Gender* xv). In other words, men on the Down Low are performing their masculinity as constructed practices or actions that cite the hegemonic norm of masculinity. This view of gender as performative is used to show that what dominant culture takes to be essential, or given, in nature is in fact manufactured through a "sustained set of acts, posited through the gendered stylization of the body" (xv). Although, men on the DL intending to behave "naturally," or as "real" men, they are in fact performing their masculinity in adherence with to the strict gender roles in place by dominant culture. Also, these men are performing their "Blackness," to the benefit of the rigid racialized structure. There are racialized codes put into place to create a hierarchy of masculinity, as stated above. As a way to cite the White hegemonic masculinity, these men play their part. They perform their masculinity well, along with their "Blackness."

In McCune's article, cited above, he explores the black masculine performances in the club space. He describes this club space as a place for Black men on the DL and queers of color to perform their race, gender and sexuality. Using hip-hop as a catalyst, McCune shows how DL men negotiate their commitment to heteronormative understandings of self, while participating in homonormative social and sexual activities. While exploring The Gate, a queer Black dance club in Chicago, he notes that DL men perform "straight" masculine identity, while also engaging in homoerotic desire (McCune 300). The hip-hop music and fashions displayed in the club space are one way in which these individuals are able to display both their individuality and conformity (301). The space "circulates contradictory messages that supersede traditional boundaries of gender and sexuality, where men negotiate their relationship to and the relationship between masculine bravado and black queer culture" (302). In other words, these men perform their Black masculinity as "cool" and "thuggish" while activating sexual desires without fear of losing that "masculine" card.

The Gate is a gay domain once a week, described by McCune as the Friday night queer outlet for a large hip-hop queer mass (McCune 301). The club is broken up into two separate rooms, which offer the option of listening to house or hip-hop music. Given these very different modes of expression, it is clear that the house room and music are "fabulous," and the hip-hop room and music are deemed "cool" (301). As the author observes the house room, he notes the presence of "the voguers in high fashion from DKNY to Prada, traditional Kenneth Cole-wearing dancers, and the classic tight shirt-tight jeans models" (301). The overall look observed in the hip-hop room is more uniform, demonstrating people who are conscious of specific fashions trends traditionally associated with hip-hop music (301). The hip-hop culture displayed within this club illuminates the ways in which this one type of masculinity poses itself as *the cool* (McCune 308). "In this way, the hip-hop room and its patrons, through so-called performances of heterogender, position the hip-hop space as superior" (308). While inside the hip-hop room of the club, he hears a song "In Da Club" by Fifty Cent coming from the speaker. He notes a particular line in the song that "throws" him.

> *I'm that cat by the bar toasting to the good lifestyles*
> *You that faggot ass nigga trying to pull me back right?*

The lyrics are not what seem to shock McCune; it is that the whole room seems to erupt and shout out the whole line (307). He, as well as myself, find this moment contradictory, in that these queers of color re-articulate such a problematic rhetoric. Why would these DL men "seemingly draw pleasure from this chant of hate and homophobia?" (307). The queer subjects who yell out "faggot ass nigga" must feel that they are a part of a large Black masculine space, one who includes them in this performance of heterosexism (307). This hate speech exhibited by these sexually subversive men of color must posses an essence of "coolness." This coolness allows for these "real" men to contradict their own sexuality and race in a way that is pleasurable and masculine. Therefore, adhering to strict gender constructions, "real" men are both masculine and "cool."

Similarly, Benoit Denizet-Lewis describes a "cool" hip-hop DL scene he witnesses while interviewing DL men at places in Atlanta, Cleveland, Florida, New York and Boston. While surveying a crowded nightclub, he notes that it is almost entirely made up of DL "homo thugs," "Black guys dressed like gangsters and rappers (baggy jeans, do-rags, and FUBU jackets)" (Denizet-Lewis 2). Apparently these expressions are an announcement of "Blackness," masculinity, and a separation from white gay culture. One DL interviewee, when asked if he identifies as gay or bisexual replies, "I'm masculine, there's no way I'm gay. Gays are the faggots who dress, talk and act like girls. That's not me" (3). The DL dress code is one of Black masculinity, a constructed portrayal of a "real" man. Most DL men identify themselves not as gay or bisexual (or straight), but first and foremost Black. To them, a to many Blacks, that equates to being inherently masculine (1). A man on the DL must look "black enough," which seems to be code for looking masculine, cool, and "straight." In other words, it is more appealing and "cool" to identify as Black: seeing as coolness is a seemingly recent Black expression.

McCune reads this reliance on masculine "coolness" within the club space as an opportunity for these DL men can "de-queer" themselves (McCune 308). This is a strategy for DL men to disavow one brand of masculinity (that of gay men), while embracing another. "In this conceptualization, the 'others' who are outside of the traditionally masculine—those ascribed titles such as 'femmes,' 'bottoms,' or 'punks'—are marked as inferior, less than those who carry traditional masculine codes and behaviors" (308). This DL perspective suggests that it is less desirable to perform the non-dominant role during sex. This mimics hegemonic masculinity, in that "bottoms" are routinely described feminine one who that is figuratively and literally placed below the masculine "top," one that is above in the masculinity hierarchy. It seems as though DL men do not understand "bottoms" as a masculine position. DL men see the ways in which femininity is "always already devalued in patriarchal societies, and those associated with the feminine are also viewed as inferior" (308). Therefore, "femininity" is a less ideal performance of gender, marking the distinction between who is "properly" masculine and who is not (308). This understanding of gender is derived from the hegemonic notions which always use the feminine to describe "the gay," setting straight men apart from those who are identified as gay. Within the club space, DL men are able to affirm their allegiance to heterosexuality or heteronormativity through the devaluing of those who perform their "queerness," and "manliness," differently (309).

The "Blackness," "coolness," or even the masculinity attributed to DL men is a sort of drag. A sort of thuggish camp equipped with hip-hop gear and attitude. Judith Halberstam's article "F2M: the Making of Female Masculinity," illustrates the notion of masculinity as "dress." The DL's straight male "dress" is a costume that becomes equivalent to self: the heterosexuality he both wears and owns. "We all pass or we don't, we all wear our drag, and we all derive a different degree of pleasure–sexual or otherwise–from our costumes" (Halberstam, *F2M* 212). DL men are defiantly passing as well as enjoying their undercover performance. This notion of drag is not necessarily the putting on of a gender that belongs properly to some other group, "an act of expropriation or appropriation that assumes that gender is the rightful property of sex, that 'masculine' belongs to 'male' and 'feminine' belongs to 'female'" (Butler, "Imitation" 127). This act of expropriation is exhibited by individuals and impersonators such as "Drag Kings/Queens." However, Butler contends that there is no "proper" gender, "a gender proper to one sex rather than another" (127). Therefore all gender, as well as sexuality, is drag. "Drag constitutes the mundane way in which genders are appropriated, theatricalized, worn, and done; it implies that all gendering is a kind of impersonation and approximation" (127).

I contend that the DL subculture can be thought of as queer, and DL men as queer subjects. Although, not usually thought of as queer due to their lack of disclosure and seeming homophobia, queer can be expanded to include the Down Low lifestyle. As Judith Halberstam has argued in *In a Queer Time and Place: Transgender Bodies, Subcultural Lives*, "queer subjects might be redefined as those who live (deliberately, accidentally, or of necessity) during the hours when others sleep and in the spaces (physical, metaphysical, and economic) that others have abandoned" (Halberstam, *Queer Time* 10, Ward 417). This expands the boundaries of queerness to include subjects often not thought of as queer, and in a distant but similarly motivated move, other scholars, such as José Esteban Muñoz, have disidentified with mainstream or "homonormative" lesbian and gay politics and its focus on monogamy, domesticity, and prosperity. Queer is less about sexual practices than about a "way of life" that defies the rules of normative, respectable adult citizenship (Ward 417).

Within the DL community, Black men are able to inhabit a very fluid space. They are able to subvert performances of sexuality and gender within the club space— "men are able to be queer while also acting straight, or even straight while acting queer" (McCune 309). In other words, these men are able to re-enforce, resist, or subvert the dominant social order. They can identify or perform their queer desire as means of resistance or subversion and also participate in the rituals of patriarchy as a means of acceptance (McCune 309). By occupying this space, Black men are able to dis-identify with dominant hegemonic scripts concerning gender and sexuality. José Esteban Muñoz, in *Disidentifications: Queers of Color and the Performance of Politics,* defines disidentification as a mode of performance, a way of shuffling back and forth between reception and production (Muñoz 25). "Disidentification is a performative mode of tactical recognition that various minoritarian subjects employ in an effort to resist the oppressive and normalizing discourse of dominant ideology" (97). In other words, these Black men have created a network consisting of men of color, who recognize each other as DL, and they have this new concept or word to describe it that is not "gay," "straight," "bisexual," or "closeted." It is a way of projecting out an individual's likes and dislikes, a code of the way one experiences the world in relationship to desire and sexuality.

These men dis-identify with the dominant descriptors and performances of sexuality, their lives are often constructed as a black phenomenon of this contemporary moment, even though sexual politics have historically been a part of black male constructions of sexual identity and masculinity (McCune 299). As Butler states, "identity categories tend to be instruments of regulatory regimes, whether as the normalizing categories of oppressive structures or as the rallying points for liberatory contestation of that very oppression" (Butler, "Imitation" 121). While the identity categories from which DL men are fleeing are normalizing categories created by oppressive structures, they also promote the existence of the Down Low category. The way of life, or sexual culture of the DL is what violates social norms; dominant culture becomes the material of queer resistance (Ward 417).

In conclusion, the DL lifestyle provides an opportunity to examine the strict and rigid gender and sexual structures prescribed by dominant culture. However, the fact that deception and secrecy are associated with DL behavior is problematic. The truth of the matter is, individuals do have a tendency to hide what is socially unacceptable. In a Utopian society, choices about sex, gender, gender role identity, and sexual orientation would be free and unconstrained by social convention, social scripts, social pressure, or social opinion. In addition, disciplinary pressures created by the "isms"—racism, sexism, heterosexism/homophobia, classism, etc.—would not exist. It would become routine and unproblematic for individuals to disclose their preferred sex, gender, gender role identity, and sexual orientation to their prospective partners and society if one so chooses. However, until society has arrived at this utopia, the Down Low lifestyle is just the tip of the iceberg. Subversive identities, as well as undisclosed identities will continue to challenge dominant cultures limiting scripts and choices. In conclusion, the barriers that prevent us from this utopia should be what we vilify and focus on for change, not the Down Low lifestyle.

Works Cited

Boykin, Keith. *Beyond the Down Low: Sex, Lies and Denial in Black America*. New York: Carol & Graf Publishers, 2005.

Butler, Judith. "Imitation and Gender Insubordination." 1990 *The Judith Butler Reader*. Ed. Sara Salih. Massachusetts: Blackwell Publishing, 2004. 119–37.

—. *Gender Trouble: Feminism and the Subversion of Identity*. 1990. New York: Routledge Classics, 1999.

Collins, Patricia Hill. *Black Sexual Politics: African Americans, Gender, and the New Racism*. New York & London: Routledge, 2005.

Denizet-Lewis, Benoit. "Double Lives on the Down Low." *New York Times*. 2 Aug. 2003: 28 Retrieved September 30, 2008, from http://www.womenscollective.org/double_lives_on_the_down_lo w.pdf.

Foucault, Michel. *The Will to Knowledge: The History of Sexuality Volume 1*. Trans. Robert Hurley. London: Penguin Books, 1990.

Halberstam, Judith. F2M: the Making of Female Masculinity. *The Lesbian Postmodern*. Ed. Laura Doan. New York: Columbia University Publishing, 1994. 210–228.

—. *In a Queer Time and Place: Transgender Bodies, Subcultural Lives*. New York: New York University Press, 2005.

King, J. L. *On the Down Low: A Journey into the Lives of "Straight" Black Men Who Sleep with Men*. New York: Broadway Books, 2004.

Kimmel, Micheal. "Masculinity as Homophobia: Fear, Shame, and Silence in the Construction of Gender Identity." *Theorizing Masculinities*. Ed. Harry Brod and Micheal Kaufman. London: Sage Publishing, 1994. 119–141.

McCune, Jeffery Q. "Out in the Club: The Down Low, Hip-Hop, and the Architexture of Black Masculinity." *Text and Performance Quarterly* Vol. 28, No. 3. July 2008: 298–314.

Muñoz, José Esteban. *Disidentifications: Queers of Color and the Performance of Politics*. Minneapolis: University of Minnesota Press, 1999.

Phillips, Layli. "Deconstructing 'Down Low' Discourse: The Politics of Sexuality, Gender, Race, Aids, and Anxiety." *Journal of African American Studies*,Vol. 9, No. 2. Fall 2005: 3–15.

Ward, Jane. "Dude-Sex: White Masculinities and 'Authentic' Heterosexuality Among Dudes Who Have Sex With Dudes." *Sexualities* Vol. 11, No. 4. 2008: 414–434.

Wilkerson, William S. "Is There Something You Need to Tell Me: Coming Out and the Ambiguity of Experience." *Reclaiming Identity: Realist Theory and the Predicament of Postmodernism.* Ed. Paula M. L. Moya and Michael R. Hames-Garcia. Berkeley: University of California Press, 2000. 251–278.

Wittig, Monique. *The Straight Mind and Other Essays.* Boston: Beacon Press Books, 1992.

Excerpt from *White Weddings* (1999)

Chrys Ingraham

Turning wedding fantasies into reality comes with a hefty price tag. On average, American couples spend about nineteen thousand dollars to celebrate their nuptials, and in doing so, contribute to a thriving multibillion-dollar wedding industry. From elaborate reception halls to tiny satin-covered ring pillows, the wedding industry offers innumerable products and services to couples who want to create a "perfect" wedding day. Chrys Ingraham, drawing from her study on weddings in American culture, examines factors that keep the wedding industry flourishing even in economic downturns. She also analyzes how class and race shapes wedding rates and wedding patterns, lending multiple meanings to the phrase "white weddings." Ingraham is a professor of Sociology and Criminal Justice at Russell Sage

College and the author of two forthcoming studies from Routledge Press including Critical Heterosexuality: A Reader *(2003).*

Recently referred to by Wall Street analysts as "recession-proof," the wedding industry has reached such proportions that it can be more accurately described as a wedding-industrial complex. This structure reflects the close association among weddings, the

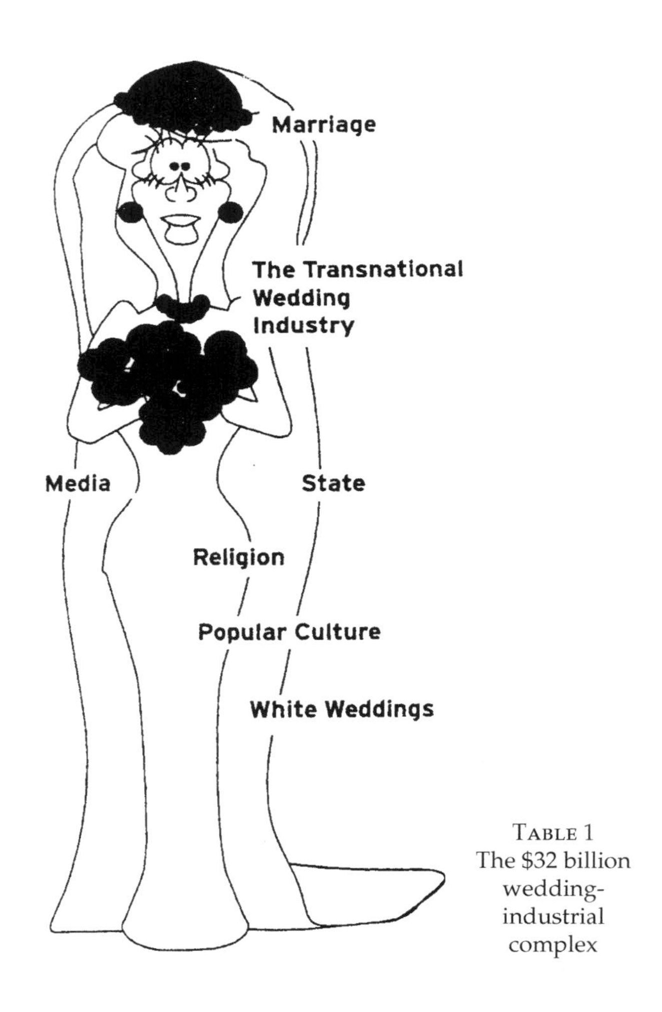

TABLE 1
The $32 billion wedding-industrial complex

transnational wedding industry, marriage, the state, religion, media, and popular culture. To understand the significance of white weddings, it is crucial to attain a sense of the operation of the wedding industry particularly in relation to the workings of the wedding-industrial complex. The scope of this selection is to provide an overview of the various components of this complex in order to make visible the historical and material foundation upon which the operation of the heterosexual imaginary depends.

The Transnational Wedding Industry

As of 1997, the *primary* wedding market in the United States represented total revenues of $32 billion. To put this in perspective, consider this: If these revenues were the product of one company, it would place in the top 25 *Fortune* 500 corporations. This multi-billion-dollar industry includes the sale of a diverse range of products, many of which are produced outside of the U.S.—wedding gowns, diamonds, honeymoon travel and apparel, and household equipment. Also included in the market are invitations, flowers, receptions, photos, gifts, home furnishings, wedding cakes, catering, alcohol, paper products, calligraphy, jewelry, party supplies, hair styling, makeup, manicures, music, books, and wedding accessories, e.g., ring pillows, silver, chauffeurs, and limousines (*Bride's* 1997; *Modern Bride* 1994; Fields and Fields 1997) (see Table 2)[1]. Although newlyweds make up only 2.6 percent of all American households, "they account for 75% of all the fine china, 29% of the tableware, and 21% of the jewelry and watches sold in this country every year" (Dogar 1997). Even insurers have entered the primary wedding market by offering coverage to cover the cost of any monies already spent on the wedding preparation "if wedding bells don't ring." Fireman's Fund Insurance Company offers "Weddingsurance" for wedding catastrophes such as flood or fire (but not for "change of heart") (Haggerty 1993). In fact, attach the words wedding or bridal to nearly any item and its price goes up. With June as the leading wedding month, followed by August and July, summer becomes a wedding marketer's dream.

According to industry estimates, the average wedding in the United States costs $19,104, with some regional variations. For instance, in the New York metro area the average wedding

Table 2
Bride's 1997 Millennium Report: Love & Money

Annual Revenues of $32 Billion Wedding Industry—1996	
Wedding apparel, invitations, flowers, reception, photos, gifts	$16.4 billion (51.3%)
Engagement/wedding rings	$3.3 billion (10.3%)
Honeymoon travel and apparel	$4.5 billion (14.1%)
Home furnishings, household equipment	$7.8 billion (24.3%)
	Total $32.0 Billion

increases to $29,454. In the Midwest, the cost drops to $16,195 and on the West Coast, $18,918 (*Bride's* 1997). Considered in relation to what Americans earn, the cost of the average wedding represents 51 percent of the mean earnings of a white family of four and 89 percent of the median earnings for black[2] families. The fact that 63.7 percent of Americans earn less than $25,000 per year (U.S. Bureau of the Census 1996) means the average cost of a wedding approximates a year's earnings for many Americans. It costs less to pay the average price for a year in college—$17,823 (College Board 1997)—and about the same to purchase a new Honda Accord or Ford Taurus (Wright 1999).

The Wedding Debt

The level of debt incurred by newlyweds has received some media attention but with little effect on wedding consumption patterns. One article in the *Boston Globe* in 1996 referred to the newlywed experience with the wedding industry as "wedding hell" (With 1996). The article described a fairly typical encounter with the wedding industry. Working against classic arguments such as "It's the happiest day of your life" and "It's a once-in-a-lifetime thing," the newlyweds in this article struggled to plan a wedding that would not exceed $5,000. What they found shocked them. After weeks of bartering with reception halls and caterers who were either unwilling to negotiate or were priced out of reach, the bride said, "I was exhausted. Planning a wedding is a full-time job, a second one for me—and not even as rewarding. My fiancé and I were feeling like the victims of highway robbers with sanctioned routines" (With 1996, 85:1). The final blow was attending a crowded bridal show where they had to "register" for numerous mailing lists and the bride was given a "silly sticker," which proclaimed her "a very important bride," and told to fill out fifty-eight coupons for special prizes. "These people must think *bride* is synonymous with *stupid,*" she thought. In the end, this couple decided not to get married yet and instead to put their $5,000 toward the purchase of a house, where, in the end, they could hold their own wedding and reception.

Another couple, having seen the corruption and greed of the wedding industry, decided to become consumer advocates. Denise and Alan Fields, authors of *Bridal Bargains* (1997) and *Bridal Gown Guide* (1998), have nearly single-handedly taken on the unregulated wedding industry. With statements such as "too many wedding businesses have the morals of an average slug" (1998a), the Fieldses have turned their negative experience in planning their own wedding into advocacy in the interests of newlyweds. In so doing, they have encountered the wrath of some wedding businesses attempting to preserve their questionable, and in some cases illegal, practices.

Who Are the Targets of the Wedding Industry?

Who marries, and who are the consumers of this enormous industry? On average, newlyweds are getting older. As of March 1997, the Census Bureau reported that the mean age for brides has risen to 25 and for grooms, 26.8 years. The age of first marriage has been rising steadily at a rate of one year every decade for first marriages. Social acceptance of couples living together prior to marriage, higher education, and career opportunities are contributing to these increases, which also change the marketing of weddings. Many young couples now own houses and many of the home furnishings they need before they marry. The effect is a shift in marketing strategy that opens up the wedding gift market to include everything from tools to lawnmowers to sports equipment.

The total number of marriages and remarriages in 1996 was 2,342,000, which represents 2 percent of the total U.S. age-fifteen-and-over population (*Bride's* 1996; U.S. Bureau of the Census 1996). This rate—of 8.8 per 1,000 persons—has remained relatively stable since 1990, when the number of marriages reached an all-time high of 2,448,000. Quite a considerable marketing niche!

Contributing to the health of the wedding industry, the remarriage market is large and complex and "includes some married people who want to reaffirm their vows in second ceremonies" (Dewitt 1992).[3] With the current divorce rate at 4.6 per 1,000 persons, about 46 percent of annual marriages are remarriages for at least one member of the couple. The average age for the divorced woman who remarries is 35, and the average for divorced men is 39. Even though remarriage weddings tend to be smaller, the wedding industry estimates they total up to 30 percent of their revenues, which shows that at least one sector in American society actually benefits from divorce. In fact, without remarriages, the wedding industry would be substantially smaller.

According to the wedding industry, today's newlyweds are also more likely to be dual-earner couples, with 83 percent of brides and 89 percent of grooms working; they earn a combined income currently twice that of the average household, at $65,076 (*Bride's* 1995/1996, Bridal Market Acquisition Report). Factoring in the age and financial standing of many of those remarrying, the probability of higher income increases, as does the focus of the wedding market on the consumption patterns of these newlyweds.

Fascinating, right? But there's something missing from this picture of the wedding market. In researching data on the wedding industry and its markets, one striking pattern emerges. Almost without exception, most state and industry analysts have overlooked the effects of race and class on consumption. For the most part, the data collected concerning wedding and marriage patterns focus primarily on middle-class whites. When recalculated to account for differences along racial, ethnic, and class lines, these figures change dramatically. For example, the average black couple spends an average of $10,000 on a wedding, significantly less than the average $19,104 mentioned in most research. The 88 percent marriage rate for Americans cited in wedding industry and census materials is primarily applicable to whites and is significantly lower for hispanics (68 percent) and even lower yet for blacks (46 percent). While blacks used to marry much younger, they now marry considerably later than the national average. Twenty-five percent of black women and less than 12 percent of black men have married by their early twenties, and more than 43.4 percent of blacks have never married, compared to 23.8 percent of whites. These numbers get even more dramatic when you break them down by sex (see Table 3).

What is significant about this data is the impact these patterns have on the wedding industry. Wedding marketers are aware that white middle-class women are more likely to consume wedding products than any other group, and so they target their marketing campaigns to white women.

TABLE 3
BLACK AND WHITE NEVER MARRIED RATES

Never Married	*Women*	*Men*
Black	40.3%	47.1%
White	20.2%	27.6%

Source: U.S. Dept of Commerce and the Census Bureau 1994.

The average combined income for marrieds from "other" groups is also significantly lower, given the disproportionate representation of blacks and Hispanics in lower income brackets. For instance, 33.1 percent of blacks have earnings below the national poverty threshold as compared with 14.5 percent of the entire U.S. population.[4] Even though blacks achieve parity with whites in elementary and secondary education, only 12.9 percent complete four or more years of college as compared with the national average of 22.2 percent (U.S. Bureau of the Census 1996). Given the relationship of education to earning potential, the combined earnings of black or Hispanic newlyweds are usually significantly lower than those of whites and are likely to remain lower throughout the course of the marriage (which is also shorter).

Why are there differences in marriage rates between whites, blacks, and hispanics? In attempting to answer this question, especially in relation to the high percentage of single mothers—blacks, 48 percent, hispanics, 25 percent, and whites, 14 percent—researchers have identified the problem of the "marriage penalty" (Besharov and Sullivan 1996; Steurle 1995). Marriages among the middle class generally increase the earning potential of individuals. Certainly, for middle- to upper-class white women, marriage means financial security. The rewards and benefits afforded these couples and their families—from health insurance to health club discounts—even though married persons incur a marriage tax penalty—are substantial.

However, among those earning minimum wage or living near or below the poverty line, marriage disqualifies many for the benefits they need to survive. The risk is that even a working husband's earnings may be "too much" for him to qualify for a host of programs including food stamps, school meals, and child care but not enough to lift the family out of poverty. As the 1997 census data indicate, an increasing number of couples are choosing to live together without "benefit" of marriage in order to avoid losing these programs, Social Security income, and some tax breaks. Ultimately, then, marriage only privileges those who already have the earnings to stay out of poverty. This means *marriage primarily benefits groups that are not disproportionately represented among the poor and that are able to secure and maintain goods and property.* Clearly, to blame the loss of "family values" as the "problem" with the poor is a myth! It is a myth that deceives the public, distorts the issues, and blames the victims.

The Future Market

Two factors of particular significance that may influence wedding marketers in the future have to do with new reports on "black consumption" patterns. In a study released in July 1998, economist Jeffrey Humphreys reported that black spending power is growing faster than the national average. The study forecasts that black consumers will "account for 8.2 percent of total buying power in 1999, compared with 7.4 percent in 1990" (Sewell 1998, C2). The other factor that may affect wedding marketers is the increase in the black population, which is also growing faster than the U.S. population as a whole, at 14 percent versus 9 percent. Humphreys credited these gains to economic expansion and educational progress made by blacks in recent years.

One of the key problems with Humphrey's study is history. These numbers reflect the gains made in education and economics in the past and do not show the effects of recent rollbacks in affirmative action, which are decreasing black enrollments in higher education. While gains have been made, black men still earn only 72 cents for every dollar white men make, and black women earn 85 cents for every dollar white women are paid. If these disparities continue, "white" weddings will persist as sites to exemplify and perpetuate racial hierarchies.

Wedding marketers are aware of these facts as well. They know that income patterns among whites promise greater return on their investment. Bridal magazines are notorious for overlooking women of color in their advertisements and marketing of weddings. The overriding effect of these patterns is that in terms of affordability and necessity, the wedding in American culture is primarily a ritual by, for, and about the white middle to upper classes. Truly, the *white* wedding.

The primary wedding market depends on numerous production and labor relations issues that underlie the consumption and accumulation involved in weddings. The central purpose of including them here is to make visible the historical and material conditions that set the conditions for the production of the white wedding. While gown marketing is probably the most insidious, other wedding products and services also warrant coverage. . . .

Primary Wedding Market

Background: White Wedding Gowns

Probably the most significant wedding purchase is the wedding gown. Industry analysts have noted that most brides would do without many things to plan a wedding and stay within budget, but they would not scrimp when it comes to the purchase of the wedding gown. With the national average expenditure at $823 for the gown and $199 for the veil, the bride's apparel becomes the centerpiece of the white wedding. Most of us have heard the various phrases associated with the bride and her gown, the symbolic significance attached to how she looks and how beautiful her gown is. In coverage of Barbra Streisand's wedding in *People* magazine, the bulk of the photos are of her in a white "shimmering crystal-beaded Donna Karan gown with a 15-foot diaphanous veil" (July 20, 1998). This reference, as well as those of many other celebrities, imitates the standard-bearers of fame, privilege, style, and perfection: Queen Victoria, Queen Elizabeth, Princess Grace, and Princess Diana.

Prior to Queen Victoria (1819–1901), white wedding gowns were not the norm. Brides wore brocades of golds and silvers, yellows and blues. Puritan women wore gray. But Victoria's wedding in February 1840 captured the imaginations of many when this powerful presider over the British empire, who many thought of as "plain," married a handsome man. She did so in an opulent ceremony where she wore a luxurious and beautiful (by nineteenth-century standards) *white* wedding gown. Following this grand event, many white Western middle-class brides imitated Victoria and adopted the white wedding gown. By the turn of the century, white had not only become the standard but had also become laden with symbolism—it stood for purity, virginity, innocence, and promise, as well as power and privilege. . . .

Notes

1. For an illuminating exposé of today's white weddings, see the excellent article "Something Old, Something New," in the March/April 1997 issue of *Might* magazine.

2. The language we use for identifying the race and ethnicity of people is frequently very awkward. To identify a group by color helps to perpetuate notions of race and racialization; to identify in terms of ethnicity erases the experience and effects of racism or of racial hierarchies. Much of the data presented here come from official sources. Almost without exception those sources use white, black, or hispanic as identifying categories. To be consistent with these sources I've use the racialized categories, though I am not comfortable with this option and generally believe we should rely on cultural signifers such as African, Latino, or Native American, for example. However, even this type of identification is problematic given that many of us do not belong exclusively to one category. As for hispanic, the debates over identification with the Spanish colonialists or with Latino history is a source of great debate. In this case, I've used hispanic instead of Latino primarily because of the earlier explanation. However, I have put it in lower case as a way to diminish its weight in relation to an imperialist history.

3. Not included in these figures but related to the wedding industry is the current boom in fiftieth wedding anniversary celebrations, which frequently include many of the same arrangements and expense. While later generations divorced more frequently, parents of baby boomers stayed married, and many of them are now celebrating this milestone in heterosexual culture.

   Additionally, the wedding industry has identified another lucrative niche in the lesbian and gay marriage market. As lesbians and gays await the final ruling by the Hawaiian Supreme Court on the legalization of gay marriage, a variety of businesses, especially the travel industry, are poised to serve this previously untapped market.

4. Black women are 5.5 times more likely to be receiving Aid to Families with Dependent Children than white women (20 percent versus 3.5 percent) (Besharov and Sullivan 1996).

QUESTIONS

1. What industries make up the "wedding-industrial complex"? How much does the average wedding cost? What racial, regional and class differences does Ingraham note in wedding expenditures?
2. Why do weddings cost as much as they do? Why are couples willing to spend as much as they do on their weddings?
3. How have marriage patterns shifted over time? What groups do wedding marketers target, and why? How have marketing tactics changed to accommodate shifting marriage patterns?
4. Ingraham states, "marriage primarily benefits groups not disproportionately represented among the poor." What does this mean? Why do marriage rates fluctuate across class and racial groups?
5. How do you feel about spending thousands of dollars on a wedding? How might couples reduce wedding expenditures? Consider the couple that used their $5,000 wedding budget as a downpayment for a home. How else might couples use their wedding budgets to enhance quality of life for either individual or social purposes?

I'M NOT FAT, I'M LATINA

Christy Haubegger

I recently read a newspaper article that reported that nearly 40 percent of Hispanic and African-American women are overweight. At least I'm in good company. Because according to even the most generous height and weight charts at the doctor's office, I'm a good 25 pounds overweight. And I'm still looking for the pantyhose chart that has me on it (according to Hanes, I don't exist).

But I'm happy to report that in the Latino community, my community, I fit right in.

Latinas in this country live in two worlds. People who don't know us may think we're fat. At home, we're called bien cuidadas (well cared for).

I love to go dancing at Cesar's Latin Palace here in the Mission District of San Francisco. At this hot all-night salsa club, it's the curvier bodies like mine that turn heads. I'm the one on the dance floor all night while some of my thinner friends spend more time waiting along the walls. Come to think of it, I wouldn't trade my body for any of theirs.

But I didn't always feel this way. I remember being in high school and noticing that none of the magazines showed models in bathing suits with bodies like mine. Handsome movie heroes were never hoping to find a chubby damsel in distress. The fact that I had plenty of attention from Latino boys wasn't enough. Real self-esteem cannot come from male attention alone.

Reprinted from *Essence*, December 1994, Essence Communications.

My turning point came a few years later. When I was in college, I made a trip to Mexico, and I brought back much more than sterling-silver bargains and colorful blankets.

I remember hiking through the awesome ruins of the Maya and the Aztecs, civilizations that created pyramids as large as the ones in Egypt. I loved walking through temple doorways whose clearance was only two inches above my head, and I realized that I must be a direct descendant of those ancient priestesses for whom those doorways had originally been built.

For the first time in my life, I was in a place where people like me were the beautiful ones. And I began to accept, and even like, the body that I have.

I know that medical experts say that Latinas are twice as likely as the rest of the population to be overweight. And yes, I know about the health problems that often accompany severe weight problems. But most of us are not in the danger zone, we're just bien cuidadas. Even the researchers who found that nearly 40 percent of us are overweight noted that there is a greater "cultural acceptance" of being overweight within Hispanic communities. But the article also commented on the cultural-acceptance factor as if it were something unfortunate, because it keeps Hispanic women from becoming healthier. I'm not so convinced that we're the ones with the problem.

If the medical experts were to try and get to the root of this so-called problem, they would probably find that it's part genetics, part enchiladas. Whether we're Cuban-American, Mexican-American, Puerto Rican or Dominican, food is a central part of Hispanic culture. While our food varies from fried plaintains to tamales, what doesn't change is its role in our lives. You feed people you care for, and so if you're well cared for, bien cuidada, you have been fed well.

I remember when I used to be envious of a Latina friend of mine who had always been on the skinny side. When I confided this to her a while ago, she laughed. It turns out that when she was growing up, she had always wanted to look more like me. She had trouble getting dates with Latinos in high school, the same boys that I dated. When she was little, the other kids in the neighborhood had even given her a cruel nickname: la seca, "the dry one." I'm glad I never had any of those problems.

Our community has always been accepting of us well-cared-for women. So why don't we feel beautiful? You only have to flip through a magazine or watch a movie to realize that beautiful for most of this country still means tall, blond and underfed. But now we know it's the magazines that are wrong. I, for one, am going to do what I can to make sure that mis hijas, my daughters, won't feel the way I did.

LEARNING FROM DRAG QUEENS

Verta Taylor and Leila J. Rupp

Drag queens can teach us a lot about sexual desire—especially our own.

In American society, people tend to think of males and females and heterosexuals and homosexuals as distinct and opposite categories. Drag performances challenge the biological basis of gender and the fixed nature of sexual identity. As a place where for an hour or two gay is normal and straight is other, drag shows use entertainment to educate straight people about gay, lesbian, bisexual, and transgendered lives.

Milla, one of the drag queens who performed at the 801 Cabaret, the Key West club we studied for our book *Drag Queens at the 801 Cabaret*, once proclaimed, with both exuberance and self-mockery, "We're going to be in classrooms all around the world! . . . No more George Washington, no more Albert Einstein, you'll be learning from us!" All the drag queens in the troupe laughed, but in fact, as we came to realize, they do teach their audience members complex lessons about the porous boundaries of gender and sexuality. Drag shows may be entertaining, and diverse people may flock to them to have a good time, but that does not belie the impact that a night of fun can have. The drag queens are, we think, more than entertainers. As Sushi, the house queen, insisted in a newspaper interview, "We're not just lip-synching up here, we're changing lives by showing people what we're all about." In the process of showing people what they are all about, they bring together diverse individuals, illustrating the official Key West philosophy that we are

Reprinted from *Contexts* 5, no.3 (2006), by permission of the American Sociological Association.

"One Human Family." How exactly do they do that? And do people take away the lessons they teach?

These were some of the questions we explored by studying the 801 Girls, a troupe of gay men who perform as drag queens every night of the year for mixed crowds of tourists and local residents, women and men, heterosexual, gay, lesbian, bisexual, and transgender people. The performers are economically marginal men who make barely enough to support themselves in a town where property is expensive and affordable housing is in short supply, as Barbara Ehrenreich conveyed so vividly in her depiction of Key West in *Nickel and Dimed: On (Not) Getting By in America*. We interviewed in all sorts of contexts and spent time with eight drag queens to find out why they do what they do and what their performances and interactions with audience members mean to them. We spent night after night at the shows, taping their banter and the songs they lipsynch and talking to audience members. And we recruited diverse people to come back the next day and talk to us about the shows in a focus-group setting. That is how we learned that there is more to drag shows than meets the eye.

Drag Shows

Drag shows have a long history as central institutions in gay communities and as places where, at least in tourist towns, straight people come in contact with gay life. From the drag balls in cities such as New York and Chicago in the 1920s to the famous Finocchio's in San Francisco in the 1940s and the popularity of RuPaul and Lady Chablis in the 1990s, men dressed in women's clothing have served as a visible segment of the gay community and have also enthralled straight audiences. The 801 Girls are no exception. On a one-by-four-mile island closer to Cuba than to Miami, populated by diverse communities—Cuban, Bahamian, gay and lesbian, hippie, and increasingly Central American and Eastern European—drag queens are central to the mix. They are everywhere: on stage, on the streets, at benefits. As the local paper put it, "You know you're from Key West when . . . your Mary Kay rep is a guy in drag."

The shows at the 801 Cabaret are an institution in Key West, described by visitors as "the best show in town." Every night at quarter after ten, four or five of the girls take to the sidewalk outside the bar, hand out flyers for the show, and banter with passersby. That is how they recruit an audience. Some tourists avert their eyes or cross the street, but most are intrigued, stop to chat, and many decide to come to the show. Upstairs over a gay bar, the cabaret has small tables up front where unsuspecting tourists serve as props for the girls, a bar in the center, and mostly standing-room-only space around the bar. Gay men congregate and cruise at the back, behind the bar.

A typical show consists of 15 to 20 numbers, some performed individually and some in groups. There is a lot of interaction with the audience, which sets the show apart from similar ones performed at gay bars across the country. But in terms of the repertoire of songs, the comedy, and the dialogue, what happens at the 801 is typical of a style of drag that emerged in conjunction with the gay and lesbian movement, a style of drag that goes beyond female impersonation.

For these drag queens, although they dress in women's clothing and can be as beautiful as biological women, there is no pretending. They announce from the start that they are gay men, they talk in men's voices, they make jokes about their large clitorises and "manginas" and complain that they are having "testical difficulties" when the music does not work. Some do not even shave their legs or underarms or tuck their genitals. Inga, a statuesque blond from Sweden, would be introduced as "Inga with a pinga," and Milla, often mistaken for African American, sometimes appeared with a dildo gripped in her crotch, calling attention to the real item hidden away. Sushi occasionally pulls down her dress and bra to reveal her male chest, provoking the same kind of wild audience response a real female stripper might, even though the sight of male nipples is nothing new in a tropical town where men do not need to wear shirts walking down the street. Sushi also performs "Crazy World" from *Victor/Victoria*, a song about a world "full of crazy contradictions." Behind a sheer white curtain, she strips down to nothing but keeps her genitals tucked between her legs as she backs off stage, revealing what transgender activists would call a "gender-queer" body.

For the final number of the weekend shows, R.V. Beaumont, who perfected drag while working at Disney World and learned to do Bette Midler numbers from watching Bette Midler impersonators, used to change out of drag on stage to the Charles

Aznevour ballad, "What Makes a Man a Man?," transforming himself from woman to man. And a regular feature of the Saturday night "Girlie Show" is Kylie, Sushi's best friend from high school, who does a mean California valley girl, stripping entirely to "Queen of the Night," leaving the audience with the contrast between her blond wig, makeup, high heels, and well-hung body. These are the ways they educate their audiences about the performativity of gender and the slipperiness of sexual desire.

"Troubling" Gender

The drag queens at the 801, at least some of them, have slipped back and forth between genders. Milla, who grew up in a working-class family in St. Petersburg, Florida, with an alcoholic and abusive father, "decided that I wanted to be a woman." She (the drag queens tend to use their drag names and female pronouns, although they also switch back and forth with some ease) got hormones from a counselor she was seeing for her adolescent drug problems by telling him that she would get them anyway from the drag queens on the street. She grew breasts and went out dressed as a woman and had "the men fall over, all over me, and with no clue, no clue." She loved it and seriously considered sex-reassignment surgery. But then "I started to love myself. I pulled away from that whole effeminate side . . . and I became a man." Milla continues to attract men and women of all sexual desires and pronounces herself "omnisexual."

Gugi, born to a Puerto Rican family in Chicago, also passed for a woman for a time. "What I've always wanted was to be a woman," Gugi said, although she added, "I don't know if it is because I wanted to be a woman or because I was attracted to men that I preferred to be a woman." She also took hormones for a time and grew breasts, but she stopped because "it wasn't the right time. . . . I did it to get away from my dad's death" and a painful breakup with a lover.

The one who is in charge of the shows and makes everything happen is Sushi, who never looks like a man even out of drag. Sushi, whose Japanese mother married an American G.I., describes herself as "some place in between" a woman and a man. She began to dress in drag in high school and for a time was a street prostitute in Los Angeles. At first, she thought that wanting to wear women's clothing meant that she wanted to be a woman, but then she came to realize that it just meant that she was a drag queen. "I know I'm a drag queen; I finally realized that I'm a gay man who puts on women's clothing and looks good." Yet she still worries that she is really a closeted transgendered person. One night we asked her the difference between being a drag queen and being transgendered and she replied, "A drag queen is someone like Kylie who has never ever thought about cutting her dick off."

What it means about the social basis of gender that men can look like beautiful women is not lost on audience members. A local straight woman described thinking of them as women during the show. A straight male tourist agreed, saying of Milla, "She was a woman." His wife agreed: "Uh-huh, she was a woman. It never even entered my mind. She was a beautiful woman." A young straight woman, at her first drag show, explained that she thought of them as both. "Back and forth, I think. Yeah, I was confused and went back about twelve times." A gay man, as if echoing what at least some of the girls might say about themselves, said, "I don't think of them as really any of it. I feel like they're their own thing. I feel like a drag queen is something completely different. . . . It's way more than being a woman and it's definitely not being a man."

As that last comment suggests, there is more going on here than just mimicking traditional female beauty. Even the girls who are the most beautiful in drag—Sushi, Milla, Inga, and Gugi—do not really look like women, because they are too tall or have muscled arms or men's waists and buttocks. They are beautiful as drag queens. And they perform alongside other girls who are old or overweight or do not shave their chests and who perform numbers that criticize traditional feminine ideals of beauty. Scabola Feces, whose very name belies any hint of impersonating beautiful women, performs "Wedding Bell Blues" in a ripped-up wedding dress, Coke-bottle glasses, and a mouthful of fake rotten buck teeth, and R.V. appears in hair curlers as a hooker or madam in such songs as "The Oldest Profession" and "When You're Good to Mama."

Their performances force audience members to think differently about what it means to be a man, what it means to be a woman. A local gay man described "older married couples" watching R.V. perform "What Makes a Man a Man?" "with their jaws hitting the floor. Especially when the eyelashes come off and the wig and the makeup disappears like that. . . . And they're like, I think they're still shocked when they leave that way like, 'Oh my god, I don't believe it.' They want to believe that they're women and it's hard for them to accept that they're not." This is what feminist scholars mean when they talk of "troubling" gender, causing people to think outside the binary of male/female. The 801 girls are very good teachers.

Arousing New Sexual Desires

The drag queens also have an impact by arousing sexual desires in audience members not congruent with their sexual identities. A central part of the show involves bringing audience members on stage to represent different sexual identity categories. The drag queens call for a straight man, a gay man, a straight woman, and a lesbian, sometimes a bisexual or transsexual. While this seems to affirm the boundaries of sexual desire, the intent of the drag queens is quite the opposite. First of all, they allow a great deal of latitude in who represents what categories, and audience members are creative, so that gay men might call out that they are lesbians and straight women might play lesbian for a night. And then, once on stage during the time that we studied the shows, the girls arranged the couples in positions simulating sex acts, the two women as the drag queens say "bumping pussy" and the gay man on his back with the straight man crouched over his pelvis. Each participant got a shot of liquor poured into his or her mouth with a lot of teasing about fellatio.

Usually the people on stage really get into the act. One night the straight woman seemed eager to have the lesbian touch her and said she was "willing to try pussy-licking." Another time one of our research assistants volunteered as the lesbian, and a woman there with her husband came up to her and said, "I'm totally straight, but that just turned me on" and kissed her on the mouth. A young straight woman described feeling sorry for a young straight man brought up on stage. "I thought for him it had to be confusing because the drag queen that was coming on to him was, to me, the prettiest, and I kept thinking, 'God, that's a guy, that's a guy.' . . . And he's probably thinking, 'God, she's hot.'

Forgetting that she's a he. And I think that when she got on top of him, he was probably embarrassed because he was turned on." Sometimes audience members take the initiative. One night a very thin young woman in skimpy clothes came onstage to dance with Desiray, a new member of the troupe who became a drag queen because he fell in love with the show as a tourist. The woman stripped down to a thong and eventually grabbed Desiray to mime having anal sex with her.

For the drag queens, a central part of the show is the arousal of straight men. They love to move through the crowd and touch and fondle them. One night a straight couple got in a fight because the man got an erection when Sushi grabbed his penis. A straight woman tourist, on the other hand, loved when the girls fondled her husband. "It's like here's this man touching my husband, it's like really cool. And he's standing there letting him." She found this the "sexiest" part of the show, "there was something crackling the most. . . . The line was crossed the most at that moment. . . . And I liked it." Her husband described his own response: "I'm sitting there and there's a little bit of me saying, 'This is sexually exciting' and there's another part of me saying, 'Wait a minute, don't do this. You're not supposed to be sexually excited, this is a man." At one show, a very macho young man there with his girlfriend took one look at Sushi and confided in us, "I could do her."

And it is not just straight men who experience sexual desires outside their identities. A lesbian described feeling very attracted to Milla: "She was so sexy," and a straight woman agreed, commenting that "I was very drawn to her sexually. I felt like kissing her. And I'm not gay at all." Yet she described being attracted because Milla "was a woman. She was a beautiful woman." Another straight woman "started falling in love with" Milla and announced, "I want to make love with her." When Sushi and Milla, or Sushi and Gugi, perform the lesbian duet "Take Me or Leave Me" from *Rent*, it has a powerful erotic impart on all sorts of audience members. More than once, during the shows, straight women started kissing their women friends. One night two Mormon women on vacation without their husbands started talking with us. By the end of the show, one confided that, if she were going to be with a woman, she would choose her friend.

As a result of these kinds of interactions and responses, many people at the shows conclude that the labels of "gay" and "straight," like "man" and "woman," just do not fit. For one gay man, "You leave them at the door." Said another, the drag queens are "challenging the whole idea of gender and so forth and they're breaking that down." A straight male tourist put it this way: "I think that one of the beauties of attending a show like this is that you do realize that you . . . shouldn't walk out and say, 'I only like men,' and you shouldn't say 'I only like women,' and it all kind of blends together a lot more so than maybe what we want to live in our normal daily lives." Because the drag shows have the potential to arouse powerful desires that people perceive as contrary to their sexual identities, they have a real impact on people's thinking about the boundaries of heterosexuality.

Drag Queens Creating Change

And this is just what the drag queens intend, as Milla's and Sushi's opening comments suggest. Kylie announces, "I intend to challenge people." Sushi explains that "I'm not just doing a number . . . I'm trying to make more of an experience, a learning thing. . . . And I have a platform now to teach the world . . . . Even less than five minutes of talking to somebody, just that little moment I share with somebody from New Zealand or Africa or your college professor or whoever, they go back to their hometown. They remember that five-minute conversation, they realize, 'I'm not gonna call this person a fag,' you know what I mean?" Says Milla, "We are attractive to everybody. We have taken gender and thrown it out of the way, and we've crossed a bridge here. And when we are all up there, there is no gay/straight or anything."

One of the remarkable things about the drag shows is the way they bring people together across all kinds of boundaries, not just differences in gender and sexual identities. Inga described the audiences as ranging "from the worst faggot to the butchiest lesbian to the happily married couple with the kids, the honeymoon people, the people who hate gays but maybe thought it was something interesting." A gay male tourist thought the shows had a "really big mass appeal to a cross section of everyone," and in fact we have met Mormons, brides out on the town the night before their weddings, transsexuals, grandmothers and grandfathers, female strippers, bikers, and everyone in between. Although the shows express and affirm pride in gay or lesbian or bisexual or transgender identities, they also emphasize what we all have in common.

Milla, putting a negative spin on it, confessed once, "What I love the most is that all these people come to our shows—professors, doctors, lawyers, rich people—and they're as fucked up as we are." Margo, a sixty-something New Yorker who also wrote a column for the local gay newspaper, introduced the classic gay anthem "I Am What I Am" in a more positive way: "The next song I'm going to do for you will explain to everyone who, what, and why we are. We are not taxi drivers or hotel clerks or refrigerator repair people. We are drag queens and we are proud of what we do. Whether you are gay or straight, lesbian, bisexual, trisexual, transgender, asexual, or whatever in between, be proud of who you are." Sushi, too, preaches a message of pride and love. One night she raised her glass to toast to gay love and then corrected herself, "Oh no, here's to love. To love, baby, all across the world." Another time, more vulgarly, she introduced her best friend Kylie and announced, "This is the person that . . . told me that I was special and that every single one of you is special no matter if you suck a cock or lick a pussy." Using words that typically describe same-sex sex acts to divide people into new categories, the drag queens bring together gay men and straight women, lesbians and straight men.

The audience takes in the lessons. A gay New Yorker put it this way, "The message really comes across that it doesn't matter who you are." Another gay man commented that, at the 801, "Everybody is equally fabulous." A local straight woman realtor who had seen the shows many times commented to us, "They bring a gay guy up, then a straight woman, and a straight man, and a lesbian. By the end, you just think, 'What's the difference?' "Summing up the hopes and dreams of the drag queens, a young gay man with theatrical ambitions explained that the show "signifies for me . . . that we have these differences but here we are all together within this small space. Communing, interacting, being entertained, having a good time and everything is going well . . . and I think the idea being to make some sort of, like, utopia or this is the way it could be. Once we all leave this bar, if we can all see four different people that are different and commune together, or at least respect each other, then when we leave this bar, wouldn't the world be a little bit better place?"

The drag queens do indeed work to make the world a better place. As one of the few ways that straight people encounter gay culture—where, in fact, straight people live for an hour or two in an environment where gay people are the majority—drag shows, especially in a tourist town like Key West, have the potential to bring people together and to create new gender and sexual possibilities. Precisely because drag shows are entertaining, they attract people who might never otherwise be exposed to gay politics. As one female audience member put it, they "take something difficult and make it light." Because the shows arouse visceral emotions, even sexual desires that fall outside people's usual sexual identities, they have the potential to make a real impact. Through a complex process of separating people into gender and sexual identity categories, then blurring and playing with those boundaries, and then bringing people all together again, the drag queens at the 801 succeed, as the comments of audience members attest, in "freeing people's minds," "removing their blinders," "opening their minds," sometimes even "changing their lives." The diverse individuals who flock to the 801 come away with an experience that makes it a little less possible to think in a simple way about gender and sexuality or to ignore the experiences of gay, lesbian, bisexual, and transgendered people in American society.

Recommended Resources

Patricia Gagné and Richard Tewskbury, eds. *Gendered Sexualities: Advances in Gender Research*, Volume 6 (JAI, 2002). A collection of articles that explore the intersection of gender and sexuality.

Esther Newton. *Mother Camp: Female Impersonators in American* (University of Chicago Press, 1972). The classic account of drag queens in the late 1960s, just before the emergence of the gay liberation movement.

Leila J. Rupp and Verta Taylor. *Drag Queens at the 801 Cabaret* (University of Chicago Press, 2003). A full analysis of the drag queens, their shows, and their impact on audiences.

Steven P. Schacht with Lisa Underwood, eds. *The Drag Queen Anthology* (Harrington Park Press, 2004). An interdisciplinary collection of articles about drag queens in different parts of the world.

Transgender Feminism: Queering the Woman Question

Susan Stryker

Many years ago, I paid a visit to my son's kindergarten room for parent-teacher night. Among the treats in store for us parents that evening was a chance to look at the *My Favorite Things* book that each child had prepared over the first few weeks of classes. Each page was blank except for a pre-printed line that said "My favorite color is (blank)," or "My favorite food is (blank)," or "My favorite story is (blank)"; students were supposed to fill in the blanks with their favorite things and draw an accompanying picture. My son had filled the blanks and empty spaces of his book with many such things as "green," "pizza" and "*Goodnight Moon*," but I was unprepared for his response to "My favorite animal is (blank)." His favorite animal was "yeast." I looked up at the teacher, who had been watching me in anticipation of this moment. "Yeast?" I said, and she, barely suppressing her glee, said, "Yeah. And when I asked why yeast was his favorite animal, he said, 'It just makes the category animal seem more interesting.'"

At the risk of suggesting that the category "woman" is somehow not interesting *enough* without a transgender supplement, which is certainly not my intent, I have to confess that there is a sense in which "woman," as a category of human personhood, is indeed, for me, *more* interesting when we include transgender

Reprinted from *Third Wave Feminism and Post Feminism, Second Edition*, by permission of Palgrave Publishers/Palgrave Macmillan.

phenomena within its rubric. The work required to encompass transgender within the bounds of womanhood takes women's studies, and queer feminist theorizing, in important and necessary directions. It takes us directly into the basic questions of the sex/gender distinction, and of the concept of a sex/gender system, that lie at the heart of Anglophone feminism. Once there, transgender phenomena ask us to follow basic feminist insights to their logical conclusion (biology is not destiny, and one is not born a woman, right?). And yet, transgender phenomena simultaneously threaten to refigure the basic conceptual and representational framework within which the category "woman" has been conventionally understood, deployed, embraced, and resisted.

Perhaps "gender," transgender tells us, is not related to "sex" in quite the same way that an apple is related to the reflection of a red fruit in the mirror; it is not a mimetic relationship. Perhaps "sex" is a category that, like citizenship, can be attained by the non-native residents of a particular location by following certain procedures. Perhaps gender has a more complex genealogy, at the level of individual psychobiography as well as collective sociohistorical process, than can be grasped or accounted for by the currently dominant binary sex/gender model of Eurocentric modernity. And perhaps what is to be learned by grappling with transgender concerns is relevant to a great many people, including nontransgendered women and men. Perhaps transgender discourses help us think in terms of embodied specificities, as *women's* studies has traditionally tried to do, while also giving us a way to think about gender as a system with multiple nodes and positions, as *gender* studies increasingly requires us to do. Perhaps transgender studies, which emerged in the academy at the intersection of feminism and queer theory over the course of the last decade or so, can be thought of as one productive way to "queer the woman question."

If we define "transgender phenomena" broadly as anything that disrupts or denaturalizes normative gender, and which calls our attention to the processes through which normativity is produced and atypicality achieves visibility, "transgender" becomes an incredibly useful analytical concept. What might "transgender feminism"—a feminism that focuses on marginalized gender expressions as well as normative ones—look like?

As an historian of the United States, my training encourages me to approach currently salient questions by looking at the past through new eyes. Questions that matter now, historians are taught to think, are always framed by enabling conditions that precede them. Thus, when I want to know what transgender feminism might be, I try to learn what it has already been. When I learned, for example, that the first publication of the post-WWII transgender movement, a short-lived early-1950s magazine called *Transvestia*, was produced by a group calling itself The Society for Equality in Dress, I not only saw that a group of male transvestites in Southern California had embraced the rhetoric of first-wave feminism and applied the concept of gender equality to the marginalized topic of cross-dressing; I also came to think differently about Amelia Bloomer and the antebellum clothing reform movement. To the extent that breaking out of the conventional constrictions of womanhood is both a feminist and a transgender practice, what we might conceivably call transgender feminism arguably has been around since the first half of the 19th century.

Looking back, it is increasingly obvious that transgender phenomena are not limited to individuals who have "transgendered" personal identities. Rather, they are signposts that point to many different kinds of bodies and subjects, and they can help us see how gender can function as part of a more extensive apparatus of social domination and control. Gender as a form of social control is not limited to the control of bodies defined as "women's bodies," or the control of female reproductive capacities. Because genders are categories through which we recognize the personhood of others (as well as ourselves), because they are categories without which we have great difficulty in recognizing personhood at all, gender also functions as a mechanism of control when some loss of gender status is threatened, or when claims of membership in a gender are denied. Why is it considered a heterosexist put-down to call some lesbians mannish? Why, if a working-class woman does certain kinds of physically demanding labor, or if a middle-class woman surpasses a certain level of professional accomplishment, is their feminine respectability called into question? Stripping away gender, and misattributing gender, are practices of social domination, regulation, and control that threaten social abjection; they operate by attaching transgender stigma to various unruly bodies and subject positions, not just to "transgendered" ones.

There is also, however, a lost history of feminist activism by self-identified transgender people waiting to be recovered. My own historical research into 20th-century transgender communities and identities teaches me that activists on transgender issues were involved in multi-issue political movements in the 1960s and 1970s, including radical feminism. The ascendancy of cultural feminism and lesbian separatism by the mid-1970s—both of which cast transgender practices, particularly transsexuality, as reactionary patriarchal anachronisms—largely erased knowledge of this early transgender activism from feminist consciousness. Janice Raymond, in her outrageously transphobic book *The Transsexual Empire,* went so far as to suggest that "the problem of transsexualism would best be served by morally mandating it out of existence." Even in this period, however, when identity politics effectively disconnected transgender feminism from the broader women's movement and before the queer cultural politics of the 1990s revitalized and expanded the transgender movement, it is possible to find startling historical episodes that compel us to reexamine what we think we know about the feminist history of the recent past. The Radical Queens drag collective in Philadelphia, for example, had a "sister house" relationship with a lesbian separatist commune during the early 1970s, and participated in mainstream feminist activism through involvement with the local chapter of N.O.W. In the later 1970s in Washington, D.C., secretive clubs for married heterosexual male cross-dressers began holding consciousness-raising sessions; they argued that to identify as feminine meant they were politically obligated to come out as feminists, speak out as transvestites, and work publicly for passage of the Equal Rights Amendment.

In addition to offering a revisionist history of feminist activism, transgender issues also engage many of the foundational questions in the social sciences and life sciences as they pertain to feminist inquiry. The biological body, which is typically assumed to be a single organically-unified natural object characterized by one and only one of two available sex statuses, is demonstrably no such thing. The so-called "sex of the body" is an interpretive fiction that narrates a complex amalgamation of gland secretions and reproductive organs, chromosomes and genes, morphological characteristics and physiognomic features. There are far more than two viable aggregations of sexed bodily being. At what cost, for what purposes, and through what means do we collapse this diversity of embodiment into the social categories "woman" and "man"? How does the psychical subject who forms in this material context become aware of itself, of its embodied situation, of its position in language, family, or society? How does it learn to answer to one or the other of the two personal pronouns "he" or "she," and to recognize "it" as a disavowed option that forecloses personhood? How do these processes vary from individual to individual, from place to place, and from time to time? These are questions of importance to feminism, usually relegated to the domains of biology and psychology, that transgender phenomena can help us think through. Transgender feminism gives us another axis, along with critical race studies or disability studies, to learn more about the ways in which bodily difference becomes the basis for socially constructed hierarchies, and helps us see in new ways how we are all inextricably situated, through the inescapable necessity of our own bodies, in terms of race, sex, gender, or ability.

When we look cross-culturally and trans-historically at societies, as anthropologists and sociologists tend to do, we readily see patterns of variations in the social organization of biological reproduction, labor, economic exchange, and kinship; we see a variety of culturally specific configurations of embodiment, identity, desire, social status, and social role. Which of these patterns do we call "gender," and which do we call "transgender"? The question makes sense only in reference to an unstated norm that allows us to distinguish between the two. To examine "transgender" cross-culturally and trans-historically is to articulate the masked assumptions that produce gender normativity in any given (time-bound and geographically constrained) context. To examine "transgender" is thus to risk decentering the privileged standpoint of white Eurocentric modernity. It is to denaturize and dereify the terms through which we ground our own genders, in order to confront the possibility of radically different ways of being in the world. This, too, is a feminist project.

A third set of concerns that make transgender feminism interesting for women's studies is the extent to which "transgender," for more than a decade now, has served as a laboratory and proving ground for the various postmodern and poststructuralist critical theories that have transformed humanities scholarship in general over the past half century, and which have played a role in structuring the generational debates about "second wave" and "third wave" feminism. This is a debate in which I take an explicitly partisan position, largely in response to the utterly inexcusable level of overt transphobia in second-wave feminisim.

An unfortunate consequence of the second-wave feminist turn to an untheorized female body as the ultimate ground for feminist practice (which has to be understood historically in the context of reactionary political pressures that fragmented all sorts of movements posing radical threats to the established order and required them to find new, often ontological, bases for political resistance) was that it steered feminist analysis in directions that ill equipped it to engage theoretically with the emerging material conditions of social life within advanced capitalism that collectively have come to be called, more or less usefully, "postmodernity." The overarching tendency of second-wave feminism to couch its political analyses within moral narratives that link "woman" with "natural," "natural" with "good," "good" with "true," and "true" with "right" has been predicated on an increasingly non-utilitarian modernist epistemology. Within the representational framework of Eurocentric modernity, which posits gender as the superstructural sign of the material referent of sex, transgender practices have been morally condemned as unnatural, bad, false, and wrong, in that they fundamentally misalign the proper relationship between sex and gender. The people who engage in such misrepresentations can be understood only as duped or duplicitous, fools or enemies to be pitied or scorned. The failure of second-wave feminism to do justice to transgender issues in the 1970s; 1980s, and afterward is rooted in its more fundamental theoretical failure to recognize the conceptual limits of modernist epistemology.

Transgender theorizing in third-wave feminism begins from a different—postmodern—epistemological standpoint which imagines new ways for sexed bodies to signify gender. Within the feminist third wave, and within humanities scholarship in general, transgender phenomena have come to constitute important evidence in recent arguments about essentialism and social construction, performativity and citationality, hybridity and fluidity, anti-foundationalist ontologies and non-referential epistemologies, the proliferation of perversities, the collapse of difference, the triumph of technology, the advent of posthumanism, and the end of the world as we know it. While it is easy to parody the specialized and sometimes alienating jargon of these debates, the issues at stake are quite large, involving as they do the actual as well as theoretical dismantling of power relations that sustain various privileges associated with normativity and injustices directed at minorities. Because these debates are irreducibly political, because they constitute an ideological landscape upon which material struggles are waged within the academy for research funds and promotions, for tenure and teaching loads, transgender phenomena have come to occupy a curiously strategic location in the working lives of humanities professionals, whether they like it or not. This brings me at last to the crux of my remarks.

For all the reasons I have suggested, transgender phenomena are *interesting* for feminism, women's studies, gender studies, sexuality studies, and so forth. But *interesting*, by itself, is not enough, when hard decisions about budgets and staffing have to be made in academic departments, priorities and commitments actualized through classroom allocations and affirmative action hiring goals. *Interesting* also has to be *important*, and transgender is rarely considered important. All too often transgender is thought to name only a largely irrelevant class of phenomena that occupy the marginal fringe of the hegemonic gender categories man and woman, or else it is seen as one of the later, minor accretions to the gay and lesbian movement, along with bisexual and intersexed. At best, transgender is considered a portent of a future that seems to await us, for good or ill. But it remains a canary in the cultural coal mine, not an analytical workhorse for pulling down the patriarchy and other associated social ills. As long as transgender is conceived as the fraction of a fraction of a fraction of a movement, as long as it is thought to represent only some inconsequential outliers in a bigger and more important set of data, there is very little reason to support transgender concerns at the institutional level. Transgender will always lose by the numbers. The transgender community is tiny. In (so-called) liberal democracies that measures political strength by the number of votes or the number of dollars, transgender doesn't count for much, or add up to a lot. But there is another way to think about the importance of transgender concerns at this moment in our history.

One measure of an issue's potential is not how many people directly identify with it, but rather, how many other issues it can be linked with in a productive fashion. How, in other words, can an issue be *articulated*, in the double sense of "articulation," meaning both "to bring into language," and "the act of flexibly conjoining." Articulating a transgender politics is part of the specialized work that I do as an activist transgender intellectual. How many issues can I link together through my experience of the category transgender?

To the extent I am perceived as a woman (which is most of the time), I experience the same misogyny as other women, and to the extent that I am perceived as a man (which happens every now and then), I experience the homophobia directed at gay men—both forms of oppression, in my experience, being rooted in a cultural devaluation of the feminine. My transgender status, to the extent that it is apparent to others, manifests itself through the appearance of my bodily surface and my shape, in much the same way that race is constructed, in part, through visuality and skin, and in much the same way that the beauty system operates by privileging certain modes of appearance. My transsexual body is different from most other bodies, and while this difference does not impair me, it has been medicalized, and I am sometimes disabled by the social oppression that takes aim at the specific form of my difference. Because I am formally classified as a person with a psychopathology known as Gender Identity Disorder, I am subject to the social stigma attached to mental illness, and I am more vulnerable to unwanted medical-psychiatric interventions. Because changing personal identification documents is an expensive and drawn-out affair, I have spent part of my life as an undocumented worker. Because identification documents such as drivers licenses and passports are coded with multiple levels of information, including previous names and "A.K.A.'s," my privacy, and perhaps my personal safety, are at risk every time I drive too fast or cross a border. When I travel I always have to ask myself—will some aspect of my appearance, some bit of data buried in the magnetic strip on some piece of plastic with my picture on it, create suspicion and result in my detention? In this era of terror and security, we are all surveiled, we are all profiled, but some of us have more to fear from the state than others. Staying home, however, does not make me safer. If I risk arrest by engaging in non-violent demonstrations, or violent political protest, the incarceration complex would not readily accommodate my needs; even though I am a post-operative male-to-female transsexual, I could wind up in a men's prison where I would be at extreme risk of rape and sexual assault. Because I am transgendered, I am more likely to experience discrimination in housing, employment, and access to health care, more likely to experience violence. These are not abstract issues: I have lost jobs, and not been offered jobs, because I am transgendered. I have had doctors walk out of exam rooms in disgust; I have had more trouble finding and retaining housing because I am transgendered; I have had my home burglarized and my property vandalized, and I have been assaulted, because I am transgendered.

Let me recapitulate what I can personally articulate through transgender: misogyny, homophobia, racism, looksism, disability, medical colonization, coercive psychiatrization, undocumented labor, border control, state surveillance, population profiling, the prison-industrial complex, employment discrimination, housing discrimination, lack of health care, denial of access to social services, and violent hate crimes. These issues are my issues, not because I think it's chic to be politically progressive. These issues are my issues, not because I feel guilty about being white, highly educated, or a citizen of the United States. These issues are my issues because my bodily being lives in the space where these issues intersect. I articulate these issues when my mouth speaks the words that my mind puts together from what my body knows. It is by winning the struggles over these issues that my body as it is lived for me survives—or by losing them, that it will die. If these issues are your issues as well, then transgender needs to be part of your intellectual and political agenda. It is one of your issues.

I conclude now with some thoughts on yet another aspect of transgender articulation, the one mentioned in my title, which is how transgender issues articulate, or join together, feminist and queer projects. "Trans-" is troublesome for both LGBT communities and feminism, but the kind of knowledge that emerges from this linkage is precisely the kind of knowledge that we desperately need in the larger social arena.

Trans is not a "sexual identity," and therefore fits awkwardly in the LGBT rubric. That is, "transgender" does not describe a sexual orientation (like homosexual, bisexual, heterosexual, or asexual), nor are transgender people typically attracted to other transgender people in the same way that lesbians are attracted to other lesbians, or gay men to other gay men. Transgender status is more like race or class, in that it cuts across the categories of sexual identity. Neither is transgender (at least currently, in

Eurocentric modernity) an identity term like "woman" or "man" that names a gender category within a social system. It is a way of being a man or a woman, or a way of marking resistance to those terms. Transgender analyses of gender oppression and hierarchy, unlike more normative feminist analyses, are not primarily concerned with the differential operations of power upon particular identity categories that create inequalities within gender systems, but rather on how the system itself produces a multitude of possible positions that it then works to center or to marginalize.

Transgender practices and identities are a form of gender trouble, in that they call attention to contradictions in how we tend to think about gender, sex, and sexuality. But the transgender knowledges that emerge from these troubling contradictions, I want to argue, can yoke together queer and feminist projects in a way that helps break the impasse of identity politics that has so crippled progressive movements in the United States. Since the early 1970s, progressive politics have fragmented along identity lines practically to the point of absurdity. While it undoubtedly has been vital over the past few decades of movement history to enunciate the particularities of all our manifold forms of bodily being in the world, it is equally important that we now find new ways of articulating our commonalities without falling into the equally dead-end logic of totalizing philosophies and programs.

Transgender studies offers us one critical methodology for thinking through the diverse particularities of our embodied lives, as well for thinking through the commonalities we share through our mutual enmeshment in more global systems. Reactionary political movements have been very effective in telling stories about shared values—family, religion, tradition. We who work at the intersection of queer and feminist movements, we who have a different vision of our collective future, need to become equally adept in telling stories that link us in ways that advance the cause of justice, and that hold forth the promise of happy endings for all our strivings. Bringing transgender issues into women's studies, and into feminist movement building, is one concrete way to be engaged in that important work.

While it is politically necessary to include transgender issues in feminist theorizing and organizing, it is not intellectually responsible, nor ethically defensible, to teach transgender studies in academic women's studies without being engaged in peer-to-peer conversations with various sorts of trans- and genderqueer people. Something crucial is lost when academically based feminists fail to support transgender inclusion in the academic workplace. Genderqueer youth who have come of age after the "queer '90s" are now passing through the higher education system, and they increasingly fail to recognize the applicability of prevailing modes of feminist discourse for their own lives and experiences. How we each live our bodies in the world is a vital source of knowledge for us all, and to teach trans studies without being in dialog with trans people is akin to teaching race studies only from a position of whiteness, or gender studies only from a position of masculinity. Why is transgender not a category targeted for affirmative action in hiring, and valued the same way that racial diversity is valued? It is past time for feminists who have imagined that transgender issues have not been part of their own concerns to take a long, hard look in the mirror. What in their own constructions of self, their own experiences of gender, prevents their recognition of transgender people as being somehow like themselves—as people engaged in parallel, intersecting, and overlapping struggles, who are not fundamentally Other?

Transgender phenomena now present queer figures on the horizon of feminist visibility. Their calls for attention are too often received, however, as an uncomfortable solicitation from an alien and unthinkable monstrosity best left somewhere outside the village gates. But justice, when we first feel its claims upon us, typically points us toward a future we can scarcely imagine. At the historical moment when racial slavery in the United States at long last became morally indefensible, and the nation plunged into civil war, what did the future of the nation look like? When greenhouse gas emissions finally become equally morally indefensible, what shape will a post-oil world take? Transgender issues make similar claims of justice upon us all, and promise equally unthinkable transformations. Recognizing the legitimacy of these claims will change the world, and feminism along with it, in ways we can now hardly fathom. It's about time.

X: A Fabulous Child's Story

Lois Gould

Once upon a time, a baby named X was born. This baby was named X so that nobody could tell whether it was a boy or a girl. Its parents could tell, of course, but they couldn't tell anybody else. They couldn't even tell Baby X, at first.

You see, it was all part of a very important Secret Scientific Xperiment, known officially as Project Baby X. The smartest scientists had set up this Xperiment at a cost of Xactly 23 billion dollars and 72 cents, which might seem like a lot for just one baby, even a very important Xperimental baby. But when you remember the prices of things like strained carrots and stuffed bunnies, and popcorn for the movies and booster shots for camp, let alone 28 shiny quarters from the tooth fairy, you begin to see how it adds up.

Also, long before Baby X was born, all those scientists had to be paid to work out the details of the Xperiment, and to write the *Official Instruction Manual* for Baby X's parents and, most important of all, to find the right set of parents to bring up Baby X. These parents had to be selected very carefully. Thousands of volunteers had to take thousands of tests and answer thousands of tricky questions. Almost everybody failed because, it turned out, almost everybody really wanted either a baby boy or a baby girl, and not Baby X at all. Also, almost everybody was afraid that a Baby X would be a lot more trouble than a boy or a girl. (They were probably right, the scientists admitted, but Baby X needed parents who wouldn't *mind* the Xtra trouble.)

Reprinted by permission of *Ms. Magazine*, December 1978.

There were families with grandparents named Milton and Agatha, who didn't see why the baby couldn't be named Milton or Agatha instead of X, even if it *was* an X. There were families with aunts who insisted on knitting tiny dresses and uncles who insisted on sending tiny baseball mitts. Worst of all, there were families that already had other children who couldn't be trusted to keep the secret. Certainly not if they knew the secret was worth 23 billion dollars and 72 cents—and all you had to do was take one little peek at Baby X in the bathtub to know if it was a boy or a girl.

But, finally, the scientists found the Joneses, who really wanted to raise an X more than any other kind of baby—no matter how much trouble it would be. Ms. and Mr. Jones had to promise they would take equal turns caring for X, and feeding it, and singing it lullabies. And they had to promise never to hire any baby-sitters. The government scientists knew perfectly well that a baby-sitter would probably peek at X in the bathtub, too.

The day the Joneses brought their baby home, lots of friends and relatives came over to see it. None of them knew about the secret Xperiment, though. So the first thing they asked was what kind of a baby X was. When the Joneses smiled and said, "It's an X!" nobody knew what to say. They couldn't say, "Look at her cute little dimples!" And they couldn't say, "Look at his husky little biceps!" And they couldn't even say just plain "kitchy-coo." In fact, they all thought the Joneses were playing some kind of rude joke.

But, of course, the Joneses were not joking. "It's an X" was absolutely all they would say. And that made the friends and relatives very angry. The relatives all felt embarrassed about having an X in the family. "People will think there's something wrong with it!" some of them whispered. "There *is* something wrong with it!" others whispered back.

"Nonsense!" the Joneses told them all cheerfully. "What could possibly be wrong with this perfectly adorable X?"

Nobody could answer that, except Baby X, who had just finished its bottle. Baby X's answer was a loud, satisfied burp.

Clearly, nothing at all was wrong. Nevertheless, none of the relatives felt comfortable about buying a present for a Baby X. The cousins who sent the baby a tiny football helmet would not come and visit any more. And the neighbors who sent a pink-flowered romper suit pulled their shades down when the Joneses passed their house.

The *Official Instruction Manual* had warned the new parents that this would happen, so they didn't fret about it. Besides, they were too busy with Baby X and the hundreds of different Xercises for treating it properly.

Ms. and Mr. Jones had to be Xtra careful about how they played with little X. They knew that if they kept bouncing it up in the air and saying how *strong* and *active* it was, they'd be treating it more like a boy than an X. But if all they did was cuddle it and kiss it and tell it how *sweet* and *dainty* it was, they'd be treating it more like a girl than an X.

On page 1,654 of the *Official Instruction Manual*, the scientists prescribed: "plenty of bouncing and plenty of cuddling, *both*. X ought to be strong and sweet and active. Forget about *dainty* altogether."

Meanwhile, the Joneses were worrying about other problems. Toys, for instance. And clothes. On his first shopping trip, Mr. Jones told the store clerk, "I need some clothes and toys for my new baby." The clerk smiled and said, "Well, now, is it a boy or a girl?" "It's an X," Mr. Jones said, smiling back. But the clerk got all red in the face and said huffily, "In *that* case, I'm afraid I can't help you, sir." So Mr. Jones wandered helplessly up and down the aisles trying to find what X needed. But everything in the store was piled up in sections marked "Boys" or "Girls." There were "Boys' Pajamas" and "Girls' Underwear" and "Boys' Fire Engines" and "Girls' Housekeeping Sets." Mr. Jones went home without buying anything for X. That night he and Ms. Jones consulted page 2,326 of the *Official Instruction Manual*. "Buy plenty of everything!" it said firmly.

So they bought plenty of sturdy blue pajamas in the Boys' Department and cheerful flowered underwear in the Girls' Department. And they bought all kinds of toys. A boy doll that made pee-pee and cried, "Pa-pa." And a girl doll that talked in three languages and said, "I am the Pres-i-dent of Gener-al Mo-tors." They also bought a storybook about a brave princess who rescued a handsome prince from his ivory tower, and another one about a sister and brother who grew up to be a baseball star and a ballet star, and you had to guess which was which.

The head scientists of Project Baby X checked all their purchases and told them to keep up the good work. They also reminded the Joneses to see page 4,629 of the *Manual*, where it said, "Never make Baby X feel *embarrassed* or *ashamed* about what it wants to play with. And if X gets dirty climbing rocks, never say 'Nice little Xes don't get dirty climbing rocks.'"

Likewise, it said, "If X falls down and cries, never say 'Brave little Xes don't cry.' Because, of course, nice little Xes *do* get dirty, and brave little Xes *do* cry. No matter how dirty X gets, or how hard it cries, don't worry. It's all part of the Xperiment."

Whenever the Joneses pushed Baby X's stroller in the park, smiling strangers would come over and coo: "Is that a boy or a girl?" The Joneses would smile back and say, "It's an X." The strangers would stop smiling then, and often snarl something nasty—as if the Joneses had snarled at *them*.

By the time X grew big enough to play with other children, the Joneses' troubles had grown bigger, too. Once a little girl grabbed X's shovel in the sandbox, and zonked X on the head with it. "Now, now, Tracy," the little girl's mother began to scold, "little girls mustn't hit little—" and she turned to ask X, "Are you a little boy or a little girl, dear?"

Mr. Jones, who was sitting near the sandbox, held his breath and crossed his fingers.

X smiled politely at the lady, even though X's head had never been zonked so hard in its life. "I'm a little X," X replied.

"You're a what?" the lady exclaimed angrily. "You're a little b-r-a-t, you mean!"

"But little girls mustn't hit little Xes, either!" said X, retrieving the shovel with another polite smile. "What good does hitting do, anyway?"

X's father, who was still holding his breath, finally let it out, uncrossed his fingers, and grinned back at X.

And at their next secret Project Baby X meeting, the scientists grinned, too. Baby X was doing fine.

But then it was time for X to start school. The Joneses were really worried about this, because school was even more full of rules for boys and girls, and there were no rules for Xes. The teacher would tell boys to form one line, and girls to form another line. There would be boys' games and girls' games, and boys' secrets and girls' secrets. The school library would have a list of recommended books for girls, and a different list of recommended books for boys. There would even be a bathroom marked BOYS and another one marked GIRLS. Pretty soon boys and girls would hardly talk to each other. What would happen to poor little X?

The Joneses spent weeks consulting their *Instruction Manual* (there were 249 1/2 pages of advice under "First Day of School"), and attending urgent special conferences with the smart scientists of Project Baby X.

The scientists had to make sure that X's mother had taught X how to throw and catch a ball properly, and that X's father had been sure to teach X what to serve at a doll's tea party. X had to know how to shoot marbles and how to jump rope and, most of all, what to say when the Other Children asked whether X was a Boy or a Girl.

Finally, X was ready. The Joneses helped X button on a nice new pair of red-and-white checked overalls, and sharpened six pencils for X's nice new pencilbox, and marked X's name clearly on all the books in its nice new bookbag. X brushed its teeth and combed its hair, which just about covered its ears, and remembered to put a napkin in its lunchbox.

The Joneses had asked X's teacher if the class could line up alphabetically, instead of forming separate lines for boys and girls. And they had asked if X could use the principal's bathroom, because it wasn't marked anything except BATHROOM. X's teacher promised to take care of all those problems. But nobody could help X with the biggest problem of all—Other Children.

Nobody in X's class had ever known an X before. What would they think? How would X make friends?

You couldn't tell what X was by studying its clothes—overalls don't even button right-to-left, like girls' clothes, or left-to-right, like boys' clothes. And you couldn't guess whether X had a girl's short haircut or a boy's long haircut. And it was very hard to tell by the games X liked to play. Either X played ball very well for a girl or played house very well for a boy.

Some of the children tried to find out by asking X tricky questions, like "Who's your favorite sports star?" That was easy. X had two favorite sports stars: a girl jockey named Robyn Smith and a boy archery champion named Robin Hood. Then they asked, "What's your favorite TV program?" And that was even easier. X's favorite TV program was "Lassie," which stars a girl dog played by a boy dog.

When X said that its favorite toy was a doll, everyone decided that X must be a girl. But then X said that the doll was really a robot, and that X had computerized it, and that it was programmed to bake fudge brownies and then clean up the kitchen. After X told them that, the other children gave up guessing what X was. All they knew was they'd sure like to see X's doll.

After school, X wanted to play with the other children. "How about shooting some baskets in the gym?" X asked the girls. But all they did was make faces and giggle behind X's back.

"How about weaving some baskets in the arts and crafts room?" X asked the boys. But they all made faces and giggled behind X's back, too.

That night, Ms. and Mr. Jones asked X how things had gone at school. X told them sadly that the lessons were okay, but otherwise school was a horrible place for an X. It seemed as if the Other Children would never want an X for a friend.

Once more, the Joneses reached for the *Instruction Manual*. Under "Other Children," they found the following message: "What did you Xpect? *Other Children* have to obey all the silly boy-girl rules, because their parents taught them to. Lucky X—you don't have to stick to the rules at all! All you have to do is be yourself. P.S. We're not saying it'll be easy."

X liked being itself. But X cried a lot that night, partly because it felt afraid. So X's father held X tight, and cuddled it, and couldn't help crying a little, too. And X's mother cheered them both up by reading an Xciting story about an enchanted prince called Sleeping Handsome, who woke up when Princess Charming kissed him.

The next morning, they all felt much better, and little X went back to school with a brave smile and a clean pair of red-and-white checked overalls.

There was a seven-letter-word spelling bee in class that day. And a seven-lap boys' relay race in the gym. And a seven-layer-cake baking contest in the girls' kitchen corner. X won the spelling bee. X also won the relay race. And X almost won the baking contest, except it forgot to light the oven. Which only proves that nobody's perfect.

One of the Other Children noticed something else, too. He said: "Winning or losing doesn't seem to count to X. X seems to have fun being good at boys' skills *and* girls' skills."

"Come to think of it," said another one of the Other Children, "maybe X is having twice as much fun as we are!"

So after school that day, the girl who beat X at the baking contest gave X a big slice of her prizewinning cake. And the boy X beat in the relay race asked X to race him home.

From then on, some really funny things began to happen. Susie, who sat next to X in class, suddenly refused to wear pink dresses to school any more. She insisted on wearing red-and-white checked overalls—just like X's. Overalls, she told her parents, were much better for climbing monkey bars.

Then Jim, the class football nut, started wheeling his little sister's doll carriage around the football field. He'd put on his entire football uniform, except for the helmet. Then he'd put the helmet *in* the carriage, lovingly tucked under an old set of shoulder pads. Then he'd start jogging around the field, pushing the carriage and singing "Rockabye Baby" to his football helmet. He told his family that X did the same thing, so it must be okay. After all, X was now the team's star quarterback.

Susie's parents were horrified by her behavior, and Jim's parents were worried sick about him. But the worst came when the twins, Joe and Peggy, decided to share everything with each other. Peggy used Joe's hockey skates, and his microscope, and took half his newspaper route. Joe used Peggy's needlepoint kit, and her cookbooks, and took two of her three baby-sitting jobs. Peggy started running the lawn mower, and Joe started running the vacuum cleaner.

Their parents weren't one bit pleased with Peggy's wonderful biology experiments, or with Joe's terrific needlepoint pillows. They didn't care that Peggy mowed the lawn better, and that Joe vacuumed the carpet better. In fact, they were furious. It's all that little X's fault, they agreed. Just because X doesn't know what it is, or what it's supposed to be, it wants to get everybody *else* mixed up, too!

Peggy and Joe were forbidden to play with X any more. So was Susie, and then Jim, and then *all* the Other Children. But it was too late; the Other Children stayed mixed up and happy and free, and refused to go back to the way they'd been before X.

Finally, Joe and Peggy's parents decided to call an emergency meeting of the school's Parents' Association, to discuss "The X Problem." They sent a report to the principal stating that X was a "disruptive influence." They demanded immediate action. The Joneses, they said, should be *forced* to tell whether X was a boy or a girl. And then X should be *forced* to behave like whichever it was. If the Joneses refused to tell, the Parents' Association said, then X must take an Xamination. The school psychiatrist must Xamine it physically and mentally, and issue a full report. If X's test showed it was a boy, it would have to obey all the boys' rules. If it proved to be a girl, X would have to obey all the girls' rules.

And if X turned out to be some kind of mixed-up misfit, then X should be Xpelled from the school. Immediately!

The principal was very upset. Disruptive influence? Mixed-up misfit? But X was an Xcellent student. All the teachers said it was a delight to have X in their classes. X was president of the student council. X had won first prize in the talent show, and second prize in the art show, and honorable mention in the science fair, and six athletic events on field day, including the potato race.

Nevertheless, insisted the Parents' Association, X is a Problem Child. X is the Biggest Problem Child we have ever seen!

So the principal reluctantly notified X's parents that numerous complaints about X's behavior had come to the school's attention. And that after the psychiatrist's Xamination, the school would decide what to do about X.

The Joneses reported this at once to the scientists, who referred them to page 85,759 of the *Instruction Manual.* "Sooner or later," it said, "X will have to be Xamined by a psychiatrist. This may be the only way any of us will know for sure whether X is mixed up—or whether everyone else is."

The night before X was to be Xamined, the Joneses tried not to let X see how worried they were. "What if—?" Mr. Jones would say. And Ms. Jones would reply, "No use worrying." Then a few minutes later, Ms. Jones would say, "What if—?" and Mr. Jones would reply, "No use worrying."

X just smiled at them both, and hugged them hard and didn't say much of anything. X was thinking, What if—? And then X thought: No use worrying.

At Xactly 9 o'clock the next day, X reported to the school psychiatrist's office. The principal, along with a committee from the Parents' Association, X's teacher, X's classmates, and Ms. and Mr. Jones, waited in the hall outside. Nobody knew the details of the tests X was to be given, but everybody knew they'd be *very* hard, and that they'd reveal Xactly what everyone wanted to know about X, but were afraid to ask.

It was terribly quiet in the hall. Almost spooky. Once in a while, they would hear a strange noise inside the room. There were buzzes. And a beep or two. And several bells. An occasional light would flash under the door. The Joneses thought it was a white light, but the principal thought it was blue. Two or three children swore it was either yellow or green. And the Parents' Committee missed it completely.

Through it all, you could hear the psychiatrist's low voice, asking hundreds of questions, and X's higher voice, answering hundreds of answers.

The whole thing took so long that everyone knew it must be the most complete Xamination anyone had ever had to take. Poor X, the Joneses thought. Serves X right, the Parents' Committee thought. I wouldn't like to be in X's overalls right now, the children thought.

At last, the door opened. Everyone crowded around to hear the results. X didn't look any different; in fact, X was smiling. But the psychiatrist looked terrible. He looked as if he was crying! "What happened?" everyone began shouting. Had X done something disgraceful? "I wouldn't be a bit surprised!" muttered Peggy and Joe's parents. "Did X flunk the *whole* test?" cried Susie's parents. "Or just the most important part?" yelled Jim's parents. "Oh, dear," sighed Mr. Jones.

"Oh, dear," sighed Ms. Jones.

"Sssh," ssshed the principal. "The psychiatrist is trying to speak."

Wiping his eyes and clearing his throat, the psychiatrist began, in a hoarse whisper. "In my opinion," he whispered—you could tell he must be very upset—"in my opinion, young X here—"

"Yes? Yes?" shouted a parent impatiently.

"Sssh!" ssshed the principal.

"Young *Sssh* here, I mean young X," said the doctor, frowning, "is just about—"

"Just about *what*? Let's have it!" shouted another parent. ". . . just about the *least* mixed-up child I've ever Xamined!" said the psychiatrist.

"Yay for X!" yelled one of the children. And then the others began yelling, too. Clapping and cheering and jumping up and down.

"SSSH!" SSShed the principal, but nobody did.

The Parents' Committee was angry and bewildered. How *could* X have passed the whole Xamination? Didn't X have an *identity* problem? Wasn't X mixed up at *all*? Wasn't X *any* kind of a misfit? How could it *not* be, when it didn't even *know* what it was? And why was the psychiatrist crying?

Actually, he had stopped crying and was smiling politely through his tears. "Don't you see?" he said. "I'm crying because it's wonderful! X has absolutely no identity problem! X isn't one bit mixed-up! As for being a misfit—ridiculous! X knows perfectly well what it is! Don't you, X?" The doctor winked. X winked back.

"But what *is* X?" shrieked Peggy and Joe's parents. "*We* still want to know what it is!"

"Ah, yes," said the doctor, winking again. "Well, don't worry. You'll all know one of these days. And you won't need me to tell you."

"What? What does he mean?" some of the parents grumbled suspiciously.

Susie and Peggy and Joe all answered at once. "He means that by the time X's sex matters, it won't be a secret any more!"

With that, the doctor began to push through the crowd toward X's parents. "How do you do," he said, somewhat stiffly. And then he reached out to hug them both. "If I ever have an X of my own," he whispered, "I sure hope you'll lend me your instruction manual."

Needless to say, the Joneses were very happy. The Project Baby X scientists were rather pleased, too. So were Susie, Jim, Peggy, Joe, and all the Other Children. The Parents' Association wasn't, but they had promised to accept the psychiatrist's report, and not make any more trouble. They even invited Ms. and Mr. Jones to become honorary members, which they did.

Later that day, all X's friends put on their red-and-white checked overalls and went over to see X. They found X in the back yard, playing with a very tiny baby that none of them had ever seen before. The baby was wearing very tiny red-and-white checked overalls.

"How do you like our new baby?" X asked the Other Children proudly.

"It's got cute dimples," said Jim.

"It's got husky biceps, too," said Susie.

"What kind of baby is it?" asked Joe and Peggy.

X frowned at them. "Can't you tell?" Then X broke into a big, mischievous grin. *"It's a Y!"* [1972]